READINGS IN THE
WESTERN HUMANITIES

READINGS IN THE WESTERN HUMANITIES

VOLUME II

Third Edition

Edited by

ROY T. MATTHEWS
F. DEWITT PLATT

Michigan State University

MAYFIELD PUBLISHING COMPANY

Mountain View, California

London • Toronto

Library of Congress Cataloging-in-Publication Data

Readings in the Western humanities.—3rd ed. / edited by Roy T. Matthews,
    F. DeWitt Platt.
       p.   cm.
    Designed to accompany Matthews and Platt's textbook, Western
humanities, 3rd ed.
    ISBN 1-55934-577-2 (v. 1).—ISBN 1-55934-578-0 (v. 2)
    1. Civilization, Western—History—Sources.   I. Matthews, Roy T.
II. Platt, F. DeWitt.   III. Matthews, Roy T.   Western humanities.
CB245.R39   1997   96-52519
909'. 09812—dc21   CIP

Manufactured in the United States of America

10   9   8   7   6   5   4   3   2

Mayfield Publishing Company
1280 Villa Street
Mountain View, CA 94041

Sponsoring editor, Holly J. Allen; production editor, Julianna Scott Fein; manuscript editor, Darlene Bledsoe; design manager, Susan Breitbard; text and cover designer, Susan Breitbard; manufacturing manager, Randy Hurst; cover art, *L'Arlesienne*, by Vincent Van Gogh, The Metropolitan Museum of Art, Bequest of Samuel A. Lewisohn, 1951. (51.112.3) Photograph © 1979 The Metropolitan Museum of Art. The text was set in 9/11 Palatino by Archetype Book Composition and printed on acid-free 45# Amherst Matte by Malloy Lithographing, Inc.

Acknowledgments and copyrights continue at the back of the book on pages 317–319, which constitute an extension of the copyright page.

For Dixie Leigh

"Many women have done excellently, but you surpassed them all."
— *Book of Proverbs 31:29*
FDP

—∞—

For Randy and Elizabeth

We taught them the past, and they have brought us happiness.
Now, they show us the future by making the world a better place.
RTM

PREFACE

—m—

We are pleased to present the third edition of *Readings in the Western Humanities,* an anthology of literary and philosophic writings. This is the first edition of this work for which we have had sole responsibility, although we have been associated with it since its inception. The anthology began as a complementary resource for our textbook *The Western Humanities* (and so it remains today); but concurrent time constraints—seeing our book through press and teaching courses at Michigan State University—kept us from assuming the initial editorship. Members of the editorial staff at Mayfield Publishing Company—Julie Wildhaber, Kate Engelberg, and C. Lansing Hays—stepped into the breach and, working from a tentative Table of Contents drawn up by us, as well as from suggestions by a number of experienced humanities faculty, produced the first edition of the anthology. This proved to be a useful collection, which was adopted at many colleges and universities around the country.

. . .

The selections in this anthology reflect the educational ideal expressed first by the nineteenth-century poet and critic Matthew Arnold and adopted by us in *The Western Humanities*—that to be truly educated, students need to be exposed to "the best that has been thought and said." We think that this ideal can be an effective bulwark against the twin dangers of the late twentieth century: a cyberspace culture divorced from history and a mass culture catering to the lowest common denominator. We have assembled this anthology with the hope that it will give students an understanding of the West's literary and philosophical heritage and thus empower them to greater heights by expanding their horizons.

Starting in about 3000 B.C. and ranging over five thousand years, Western philosophy and literature have left a vast, diverse, and complex record. To keep this anthology to a manageable length, we adopted two principles of selection: Include works that have significantly influenced Western culture, and offer as many diverse and representative voices as possible. The readings are presented in chronological order, arranged into twenty-one chapters, just as is *The Western Humanities,* and divided into two volumes. Volume I covers ancient Mesopotamia through the Renaissance; Volume II, the Renaissance through the twentieth century.

. . .

As in the anthology's Volume I, we have maintained in Volume II most of the time-honored works that appeared in the first edition and are also discussed in *The Western Humanities,* such as passages from Erasmus's *The Praise of Folly,* Montaigne's *Essays,* Milton's *Paradise Lost,* Descartes's *Discourse on Method,* Pope's *An Essay on Man,* Wordsworth's "Tintern Abbey" (complete), Austen's *Pride and Prejudice,* Shelley's *Frankenstein, Narrative of the Life of Frederick Douglass,* Brontë's *Jane Eyre,* Freud's *Civilization and Its*

Discontents, Woolf's *To the Lighthouse,* Sartre's *The Humanism of Existentialism,* Beauvoir's *The Second Sex,* and Kundera's *The Unbearable Lightness of Being.*

Again, as in Volume I, we changed a few selections in Volume II to make them more representative, such as replacing a single scene from Shakespeare's *Hamlet* with the full text of the play and including synopses of scenes. We augmented the excerpt from Locke's *Treatise of Civil Government* to make his argument clearer; added the last chapter of Voltaire's *Candide* to show the famous moral ("[W]e must go and work in the garden."); replaced the readings from Thoreau and King with selections from "Civil Disobedience" and "Letter from a Birmingham Jail," respectively, because Thoreau's work strongly influenced King's life and thought. We also expanded the selection from Nietzsche's *The Gay Science* to include the description of "the last man," a savage indictment of the modern world; and replaced Baldwin's "My Dungeon Shook," although a moving essay, with the more powerful "Stranger in the Village."

Perhaps the most drastic changes in the entire anthology are the additions and deletions we made in Volume II. We added selections from Sister Juana Inés de la Cruz's poetry in which she called for equal education for women in seventeenth-century Mexico; Diderot's *Encyclopédie,* the most representative work of the Enlightenment; and the thinker Hegel's *Reason in History,* a philosophy of history that influenced Marx and Engels, among many others. We introduced Marx and Engels's *The Communist Manifesto,* the bible of Marxism; Huysmans's *Against Nature,* the most representative novel of the Decadent movement; and Lessing's *Martha Quest,* one of the best modern novels about a young woman's coming-of-age. We also added Solzhenitsyn's *One Day in the Life of Ivan Denisovich,* the novel that exposed the existence of Soviet labor camps to the world; Kenzaburo Oë's *A Personal Matter,* a novel reflecting the impact of Western culture on Japanese society; and Foucault's *Discipline and Punish,* a treatise on the prison, based on structural analysis, a post-modernist type of thinking. Finally, we included Fukuyama's *The Last Man and the End of History,* a work of political theory that builds on Hegel's philosophy and Nietzsche's concept of the "last man."

To accommodate the new selections, we then deleted from Volume II the excerpts from Queen Elizabeth's writings, Marlowe's *Doctor Faustus,* Donne's poetry, Swift's *A Modest Proposal,* Hume's *A Treatise of Human Nature,* Tennyson's poetry, Twain's *The Adventures of Huckleberry Finn,* Wilde's *The Picture of Dorian Gray,* Yeats's poetry, Auden's poetry, Camus's *The Myth of Sisyphus,* and Rich's poetry.

. . .

We want to thank the faculty around the country who adopted earlier editions of this anthology, because that demand has warranted the publication of this edition. We especially want to thank the humanities teachers who acted as readers and gave us helpful advice in making these selections: Camille Weiss, West Virginia University; Bertha Wise, Oklahoma City Community College; and Martha Durant Kirchmer, Grand Valley State University. We also express our appreciation to Holly Allen, our sponsoring editor, who made this project possible, and to Darlene Bledsoe, the copyeditor, whose eagle-eyed concern has saved us from many mistakes. Special thanks must go to Julianna Scott Fein for shepherding the manuscript through the various production stages. To our former humanities students at Michigan State University who served as guinea pigs for most of the anthology's selections, we offer our gratitude; their informed responses helped hone the way we interpret literature and philosophy. If our headnotes are clear and apposite, then part of the praise must be shared with those students.

CONTENTS

"

THE EARLY RENAISSANCE
Return to Classical Roots
1400–1494

LEON BATTISTA ALBERTI

Selection from *On Painting*

Alberti's *On Painting* helped ensure the triumph of the new Renaissance style over older medieval art. Published in Latin (1435) and Italian (1436) just as the Renaissance was picking up steam, this was the first modern treatise on the theory of painting. It became the era's authoritative guide for painters, both within and outside Florence, including Fra Angelico (about 1400–1455), Piero della Francesca (1420–1492), and perhaps Leonardo da Vinci (1452–1519). From 1600 until 1800, Alberti's treatise was invoked as an authority for painting practices approved by Europe's art academies. Today's historians still find this work invaluable, for it prepared the way for the art, the artist, and the patron of the Renaissance.

Alberti wrote his treatise "as a painter speaking to painters." The work is divided into three "books," or parts. Book I presents a mathematical method for creating perspective—the illusion of depth on a flat surface. Some perspectival ideas had long been used in Italy, but he was the first to codify them into an accessible work. Book II deals with painterly matters, such as color, drawing, and grace and beauty in poses and movements. Book III sets forth a type of humanist painting that uses Greco-Roman themes and depicts the soul's condition through bodily gestures and facial expressions.

Leon Battista Alberti (1404–1472) was the "universal man," the beau ideal of the age, and his achievements rivaled those of the later Leonardo da Vinci. Besides painting, Alberti also mastered music, mathematics, engineering, architecture, sculpture, poetry, drama, and civil and canon law and wrote books on most of these fields. A friend of Cosimo de' Medici (1389–1464), the merchant-banker who dominated Florence, Alberti was active in Cosimo's Platonic Academy, the club of artists and thinkers who studied Plato (see *Phaedo* and *The Republic*). Alberti's spirit had such force that his friends called him the complete genius, hence the authority attributed to his works.

Reading the Selection

This selection from Book II of *On Painting* shows Alberti as a Renaissance humanist, making the case for a radical new role for the age's painters. These painters are characterized by intellect, with the ascendancy of mind over hand visible in their art. Humanism is the theme: "[P]ainting contributes to the most honorable delights of the soul." This argument echoes the familiar rationale of humanists that studying and practicing grammar, rhetoric, logic, arithmetic, geometry, music, and astronomy—the seven liberal arts—are good exercises for the soul. What is radical in Alberti's claim is the ranking of painting with the liberal arts. In fact, in the Middle Ages, painting ranked low, on a par with crafts (shoemaking, weaving, and such). The favorable reception of this treatise encouraged the rise of independent artists, as evidenced around 1500 in the careers of Michelangelo, Leonardo da Vinci, and Raphael.

Alberti also argued that painting should be part of the core curriculum of the schools. To prove his case, he used examples from antiquity showing that the best families required that painting be taught to their sons and daughters. By 1513, Alberti's hope was realized in the well-rounded backgrounds of the idealized lady and gentleman of Castiglione's highly influential *The Book of the Courtier.*

Finally, Alberti was a pioneer in his claim for the sovereign power of painting: "Who can doubt that painting is the master art?" A generation later Leonardo gave voice to the identical claim.

—⁓—

Book II

Because this [process of] learning may perhaps appear a fatiguing thing to young people, I ought to prove here that painting is not unworthy of consuming all our time and study.

Painting contains a divine force which not only makes absent men present, as friendship is said to do, but moreover makes the dead seem almost alive. Even after many centuries they are recognized with great pleasure and with great admiration for the painter. Plutarch says that Cassander, one of the captains of Alexander, trembled through all his body because he saw a portrait of his King. Agesilaos, the Lacedaemonian, never permitted anyone to paint him or to represent him in sculpture; his own form so displeased him that he avoided being known by those who would come after him. Thus the face of a man who is already dead certainly lives a long life through painting. Some think that painting shaped the gods who were adored by the nations. It certainly was their greatest gift to mortals, for painting is most useful to that piety which joins us to the gods and keeps our souls full of religion. They say that Phidias made in Aulis a god Jove so beautiful that it considerably strengthened the religion then current.

The extent to which painting contributes to the most honourable delights of the soul and to the dignified beauty of things can be clearly seen not only from other things but especially from this: you can conceive of almost nothing so precious which is not made far richer and much more beautiful by association with painting. Ivory, gems and similar expensive things become more precious when worked by the hand of the painter. Gold worked by the art of painting outweighs an equal amount of unworked gold. If figures were made by the hand of Phidias or Praxiteles from lead itself—the lowest of metals—they would be valued more highly than silver. The painter, Zeuxis, began to give away his things because, as he said, they could not be bought. He did not think it possible to come to a just price which would be satisfactory to the painter, for in painting animals he set himself up almost as a god.

Therefore, painting contains within itself this virtue that any master painter who sees his works adored will feel himself considered another god. Who can doubt that painting is the master art or at least not a small ornament of things? The architect, if I am not mistaken, takes from the painter architraves, bases, capitals, columns, façades and other similar things. All the smiths, sculptors, shops and guilds are governed by the rules and art of the painter. It is scarcely possible to find any superior art which is not concerned with painting, so that whatever beauty is found can be said to be born of painting. *But also this, a dignified painting is held in high honour by many so that among all artists some smiths are named, only this is not the rule among smiths.* For this reason, I say among my friends that Narcissus who was changed into a flower, according to the poets, was the inventor of painting. Since painting is already the flower of every art, the story of Narcissus is most to the point. What else can you call painting but a similar embracing with art of what is presented on the surface of the water in the fountain?

Quintilian said that the ancient painters used to circumscribe shadows cast by the sun, and from this our art has grown. There are those who say that a certain Philocles, an Egyptian, and a Cleantes were among the first inventors of this art. The Egyptians affirm that painting was in use among them a good 6000 years before it was carried into Greece. They say that painting was brought to us from Greece after the victory of Marcellus over Sicily. But we are not interested in knowing who was the inventor of the art or the first painter, since we are not telling stories like Pliny. We are, however, building anew an art of painting about which nothing, as I see it, has been written in this age. They say that Euphranor of Isthmus wrote something about measure and about colours, that Antigonos and Xenocrates exchanged something in their letters about painting, and that Apelles wrote to Pelleus about painting. Diogenes Laertius recounts that Demetrius made commentaries on painting. Since all the other arts were recommended in letters by our great men, and since painting was not neglected by our Latin writers, I believe that our ancient Tuscan [ancestors] were already most expert masters in painting.

Christianity

Trismegistus, an ancient writer, judged that painting and sculpture were born at the same time as religion, *for thus he answered Aesclepius: mankind portrays the gods in his own image from his memories of nature and his own origins.* Who can here deny that in all things public and private, profane and religious, painting has taken all the most honourable parts to itself so that nothing has ever been so esteemed by mortals?

The incredible prices of painted pictures have been recorded. Aristides the Theban sold a single picture for one hundred talents. They say that Rhodes was not burned by King Demetrius for fear that a painting of Protogenes' should perish. It could be said that the city of Rhodes was ransomed from the enemy by a single painting. Pliny collected many other such things in which you can see that good painters have always been greatly honoured by all. The most noble citizens, philosophers and quite a few kings not only enjoyed painted things but also painted with their own hands. Lucius Manilius, Roman citizen, and Fabius, a most noble man, were painters. Turpilius, a Roman knight, painted at Verona. Sitedius, praetor and proconsul, acquired renown as a painter. Pacuvius, tragic poet and nephew of the poet Ennius, painted Hercules in the Roman forum. Socrates, Plato, Metrodorus, Pyrrho were connoisseurs of painting. The emperors Nero, Valentinian, and Alexander Severus were most devoted to painting. It would be too long, however, to recount here how many princes and kings were pleased by painting. Nor does it seem necessary to me to recount all the throng of ancient painters. Their number is seen in the fact that 360 statues, part on horseback and part in chariots, were completed in four hundred days for Demetrius Phalerius, son of Phanostratus. In a land in which there was such a great number of sculptors, can you believe that painters were lacking? I am certain that both these arts are related and nurtured by the same genius, painting with sculpture. But I always give higher rank to the genius of the painter because he works with more difficult things.

Classical

However, let us return to our work. Certainly the number of sculptors and painters was great in those times when princes and plebeians, learned and unlearned enjoyed painting, and when painted panels and portraits, considered the choicest booty from the provinces, were set up in the theatres. Finally L. Paulus Aemilius and not a few other Roman citizens taught their sons painting along with the fine arts and the art of living piously and well.

This excellent custom was frequently observed among the Greeks who, because they wished their sons to be well educated, taught them painting along with geometry and music. It was also an honour among women to know how to paint. Martia, daughter of Varro, is praised by the writers because she knew how to paint. Painting had such reputation and honour among the Greeks that laws and edicts were passed forbidding slaves to learn painting. It was certainly well that they did this, for the art of painting has always been most worthy of liberal minds and noble souls.

As for me, I certainly consider a great appreciation of painting to be the best indication of a most perfect mind, even though it happens that this art is pleasing to the uneducated as well as to the educated. It occurs rarely in any other art that what delights the experienced also moves the inexperienced. In the same way you will find that many greatly desire to be well versed in painting. Nature herself seems to delight in painting, for in the cut faces of marble she often paints centaurs and faces of bearded and curly headed kings. It is said, moreover, that in a gem from Pyrrhus all nine Muses, each with her symbol, are to be found clearly painted by nature. Add to this that in no other art does it happen that both the experienced and the inexperienced of every age apply themselves so voluntarily to the learning and exercising of it. Allow me to speak of myself here. Whenever I turn to painting for my recreation, which I frequently do when I am tired of more pressing affairs, I apply myself to it with so much pleasure that I am surprised that three or four hours have passed. Thus this art gives pleasure and praise to whoever is skilled in it; riches and perpetual fame to one who is master of it. Since these things are so, since painting is the best and most ancient ornament of things, worthy of free men, pleasing to learned and unlearned, I greatly encourage our studious youth to exert themselves as much as possible in painting.

Therefore, I recommend that he who is devoted to painting should learn this art. The first great care of one who seeks to obtain eminence in painting is to acquire the fame and renown of the ancients. It is useful to remember that avarice is always the enemy of virtue. Rarely can anyone given to acquisition of wealth acquire renown. I have seen many in the first flower of learning suddenly sink to money-making. As a result they acquire neither riches nor praise. However, if they had increased their talent with study, they would have easily soared into great renown. Then they would have acquired much riches and pleasure. . . .

GIOVANNI PICO DELLA MIRANDOLA
Selections from *On the Dignity of Man*

The Latin oration *On the Dignity of Man* is a tour de force by Pico (1463–1494), a son of the noble house of Mirandola (Italy). Written when Pico was twenty-four, the oration is a mixture of Aristotelean, Hebraic, Arabic, Persian, and Aramaic notions held together by Neo-Platonism—a blend of Plato's ideas and Christian beliefs. Its central Neo-Platonic motif is that love is the divine glue unifying the universe. Christian in structure, this heady synthesis of ideas breaks free of its frame to become a nonsectarian philosophy.

Pico's oration embodies the Renaissance spirit. In its appeal to wide-ranging sources, it expresses Renaissance zeal for the Classic texts of Greece and Rome as well as hitherto ignored ancient sources. Its theme is the Renaissance belief that the findings of reason and the truths of the Bible share a basic unity that is reflected in the history of thought. Most of all, its view that human nature has no limits is the prototype of the Renaissance idea of unlimited possibility. Today this idea, with its corollary of free expression, is a defining trait of Western culture.

The oration was composed to introduce a debate Pico scheduled for Rome in 1487. In this debate, Pico proposed to defend nine hundred theses gleaned from his vast readings; he even offered to pay his potential opponents' travel expenses. The debate, however, did not take place because Pope Innocent VIII forbade it. The pope also appointed a commission to examine the debate topics, with the result that seven theses were condemned as heretical, and six more were suspect. Threatened by church officials, Pico subsequently settled in Florence, where he was caught up in the anti-Renaissance crusade of the monk Savonarola. Pico's plan to wander as an evangelist was cut short in 1494, when he suddenly died at age thirty-one.

Reading the Selections

The first selection from the oration *On the Dignity of Man* begins with a greeting—"Most venerable fathers"—thus establishing that the work was meant to be recited orally, ostensibly before a group of clergy. The major insights to be gained from this selection are Pico's concept of human nature and his style of reasoning.

Pico's concept of human nature is his major contribution to Western thought. For him, human nature is not fixed, and the will is perfectly free. In a burst of lyricism he claimed that human beings are shape-shifting creatures who may be vegetative, bestial, rational, divine, or even co-equal with God: When humanity's quest ends, "We shall . . . not be ourselves, but He himself who made us." Brushing aside medieval ideas, Pico expresses the radiant faith of Renaissance humanism, that human beings are not flawed by original sin but are capable of becoming godlike.

Pico's style of reasoning reflects the Renaissance trend of treating old problems in new ways. To deal with the question of human nature, he takes the Platonic concept of the Great Chain of Being, which maintains that creation is a linked cord reaching step-by-step from the simplest life to God, and gives it a modern twist. Ancient thinkers had used the Great Chain of Being to argue that human potential is limited, since the place of human beings in the chain is fixed, and that change would destroy the whole creation. In contrast, Pico claimed that human beings may make of themselves anything they please, because as hybrids of the whole creation, they exist both outside and above the Great Chain of Being.

—m—

Most venerable fathers, I have read in the records of the Arabians that Abdul the Saracen, on being asked what thing on, so to speak, the world's stage, he viewed as most greatly worthy of wonder, answered that he viewed nothing more wonderful than man. And Mercury's, "a great wonder, Asclepius, is man!" agrees with that opinion. On thinking over the reason for these sayings, I was not satisfied by the many assertions made by many men concerning the outstandingness of human nature: that man is the messenger between creatures, familiar with the upper and king of the lower; by the sharpsightedness of the senses, by the hunting-power of reason, and by the light of intelligence, the interpreter of nature; the part in between the standstill of eternity and the flow of time, and, as the Persians say, the bond tying the world together, nay, the nuptial bond; and, according to David, "a little lower than the angels." These reasons are great but not the chief ones, that is, they are not reasons for a lawful claim to the highest wonder as to a prerogative. Why should we not wonder more at the angels themselves and at the very blessed heavenly choirs?

Finally, it seemed to me that I understood why man is the animal that is most happy, and is therefore worthy of all wonder; and lastly, what the state is that is allotted to man in the succession of things, and that is capable of arousing envy not only in the brutes but also in the stars and even in minds beyond the world. It is wonderful and beyond belief. For this is the reason why man is rightly said and thought to be a great marvel and the animal really worthy of wonder. Now hear what it is, fathers; and with kindly ears and for the sake of your humanity, give me your close attention:

Now the highest Father, God the master-builder, had, by the laws of his secret wisdom, fabricated this house, this world which we see, a very superb temple of divinity. He had adorned the super-celestial region with minds. He had animated the celestial globes with eternal souls; he had filled with a diverse throng of animals the cast-off and residual parts of the lower world. But, with the work finished, the Artisan desired that there be someone to reckon up the reason of such a big work, to love its beauty, and to wonder at its greatness. Accordingly, now that all things had been completed, as Moses and Timaeus testify, He lastly considered creating man. But there was nothing in the archetypes from which He could mold a new sprout, nor anything in His storehouses which He could bestow as a heritage upon a new son, nor was there an empty judiciary seat where this contemplator of the universe could sit. Everything was filled up; all things had been laid out in the highest, the lowest, and the middle orders. But it did not belong to the paternal power to have failed in the final parturition, as though exhausted by child-bearing; it did not belong to wisdom, in a case of necessity, to have been tossed back and forth through want of a plan; it did not belong to the loving-kindness which was going to praise divine liberality in others to be forced to condemn itself. Finally, the best of workmen decided that that to which nothing of its very own could be given should be, in composite fashion, whatsoever had belonged individually to each and every thing. Therefore He took up man, a work of indeterminate form; and, placing him at the midpoint of the world, He spoke to him as follows:

"We have given to thee, Adam, no fixed seat, no form of thy very own, no gift peculiarly thine, that thou mayest feel as thine own, have as thine own, possess as thine own the seat, the form, the gifts which thou thyself shalt desire. A limited nature in other creatures is confined within the laws written down by Us. In conformity with thy free judgment, in whose hand We have placed thee, thou art confined by no bounds; and thou wilt fix limits of nature for thyself. I have placed thee at the center of the world, that from there thou mayest more conveniently look around and see whatsoever is in the world. Neither heavenly nor earthly, neither mortal nor immortal have We made thee. Thou, like a judge appointed for being honorable, art the molder and maker of thyself; thou mayest sculpt thyself into whatever shape thou dost prefer. Thou canst grow downward into the lower natures which are brutes. Thou canst again grow upward from thy soul's reason into the higher natures which are divine."

O great liberality of God the Father! O great and wonderful happiness of man. It is given him to have that which he chooses and to be that which he wills. As soon as brutes are born, they bring with them, "from their dam's bag," as Lucilius says, what they are going to possess. Highest spirits have been, either from the beginning or soon after, that which they are going to be throughout everlasting eternity. At man's birth the Father placed in him every sort of seed and sprouts of every kind of life. The seeds that each man cultivates will grow and bear their fruit in him. If he cultivates vegetable seeds, he will become a plant. If the seeds of sensation, he will grow into brute. If rational, he will come out a heavenly animal. If intellectual, he will be an angel, and a son of God. And if he is not contented with the lot of any creature but takes himself up into the center of his own unity, then, made one spirit with God and settled in the solitary darkness of the Father, who is above all things, he will stand ahead of all things. Who does not wonder at this chameleon which we are? Or who at all feels more wonder at anything else whatsoever? It was not unfittingly that Asclepius the Athenian said that man was symbolized by Prometheus in the secret rites, by reason of our nature sloughing its skin and transforming itself; hence metamorphoses were popular among the Jews and the Pythagoreans. For the more secret Hebrew theology at one time reshapes holy Enoch into an angel of divinity, whom they call *malach hashechina*, and at other times reshapes other men into other divinities. According to the Pythagoreans, wicked men are deformed into brutes and, if you believe Empedocles, into plants too. And copying them, Maumeth [Mohammed] often had it on his lips that he who draws back from divine law becomes a brute. And his saying so was reasonable: for it is not the rind which makes the plant, but a dull and non-sentient nature; not the hide which makes a beast of burden, but a brutal and sensual soul; not the spherical body which makes the heavens, but right reason; and not a separateness from the body but a spiritual intelligence which makes an angel. For example, if you see a man given over to his belly and crawling upon the ground, it is a bush not a man that you see. If you see anyone blinded by the illusions of his empty and Calypso-like imagination, seized by the desire of scratching, and delivered over to the senses, it is a brute not a man that you see. If you come upon a philosopher winnowing out all things by right reason, he is a heavenly not an earthly animal. If you come upon a pure contemplator, ignorant of the body, banished to the innermost places of the mind, he is not an earthly, not a heavenly animal; he more superbly is a divinity clothed with human flesh.

Who is there that does not wonder at man? And it is not unreasonable that in the mosaic and Christian holy writ man is sometimes denoted by the name "all flesh" and at other times by that of "every creature"; and man fashions, fabricates, transforms himself into the shape of all flesh, into the character of every creature. Accordingly, where Evantes the Persian tells of the Chaldaean theology, he writes that man is not any inborn image of himself, but many images coming in from the outside: hence that say-ing of the Chaldaeans: *enosh hu shinuy vekamah tevaoth baal chayim,* that is, man is an animal of diverse, multiform, and destructible nature.

But why all this? In order for us to understand that, after having been born in this state so that we may be what we will to be, then, since we are held in honor, we ought to take particular care that no one may say against us that we do not know that we are made similar to brutes and mind-less beasts of burden. But rather, as Asaph the prophet says: "Ye are all gods, and sons of the most high," unless by abusing the very indulgent liberality of the Father, we make the free choice, which he gave to us, harmful to our-selves instead of helpful toward salvation. Let a certain holy ambition invade the mind, so that we may not be con-tent with mean things but may aspire to the highest things and strive with all our forces to attain them: for if we will to, we can. Let us spurn earthly things; let us struggle to-ward the heavenly. Let us put in last place whatever is of the world; and let us fly beyond the chambers of the world to the chamber nearest the most lofty divinity. There, as the sacred mysteries reveal, the seraphim, cherubim, and thrones occupy the first places. Ignorant of how to yield to them and unable to endure the second places, let us com-pete with the angels in dignity and glory. When we have willed it, we shall be not at all below them. . . .

—⚏—

. . . Not only the Mosaic or Christian mysteries but also the theology of the ancients show the advantages for us and the dignity of these liberal arts about which I have come here to dispute. For what else is meant by the degrees of initiation that are customary in the secret rites of the Greeks? First, to those who had been purified by moral and dialectic arts, which we have called, as it were, purga-tive, befell the reception of the mysteries. And what else can this reception be but the interpretation of more hidden nature by means of philosophy? Then lastly, to those who had been thus prepared, came that ἐποπτεία, that is, a vi-sion of divine things by means of the light of theology. Who does not seek to be initiated into such rites? Who does not set all human things at a lower value and, con-temning the goods of fortune and neglecting the body, does not desire, while still continuing on earth, to become the drinking-companion of the gods; and, drunken with the nectar of eternity, to bestow the gift of immortality upon the mortal animal? Who does not wish to have breathed into him the Socratic frenzies sung by Plato in the *Phaedrus,* that by the oarlike movement of wings and feet he may quickly escape from here, that is, from this world where he is laid down as in an evil place, and be carried in speediest flight to the heavenly Jerusalem. We shall be pos-sessed, fathers, we shall be possessed by these Socratic frenzies, which will so place us outside of our minds that they will place our mind and ourselves in God. We shall be possessed by them if we have first done what is in us to do. For if through morality the forces of the passions will have been so stretched to the [proper] measure, through due proportions, that they sound together in fixed concord, and if through dialectic, reason will have moved, keeping time in her forward march, then, aroused by the frenzy of the muses, we shall drink in the heavenly harmony of our ears. Then Bacchus the leader of the muses, in his own mysteries, that is, in the visible signs of nature, will show the invisible things of God to us as we philosophize, and will make us drunk with the abundance of the house of God. In this house, if we are faithful like Moses, holiest theology will approach, and will inspire us with a twofold frenzy. We, raised up into the loftiest watchtower of theol-ogy, from which, measuring with indivisible eternity the things that are, will be, and shall have been, and looking at their primeval beauty, shall be prophets of Phoebus, his winged lovers, and finally, aroused with ineffable charity as with fire, placed outside of ourselves like burning Seraphim, filled with divinity, we shall now not be our-selves, but He himself who made us.

12

THE HIGH RENAISSANCE AND EARLY MANNERISM

1494–1564

NICCOLÒ MACHIAVELLI

Selections from *The Prince*

The Prince is a short and strikingly honest handbook on how to win power and keep it. Based on Niccolò Machiavelli's (1469–1527) personal experiences as diplomat and government employee (in the service of his beloved Florence), the book has become the foundation of modern political theory. In his other works, in particular his histories of Italy and Florence, Machiavelli drew upon his Classical education and personal experiences to develop this message: Learn from the past what works and what does not. But nowhere else does Machiavelli express his thesis so boldly and succinctly as in *The Prince:* "The end justifies any means."

    The Prince's harsh and amoral attitude toward politics sparked controversies when first published. Many of Machiavelli's contemporaries, who were witnessing the end of the medieval Age of Faith and experiencing the dawn of a more secular time, were sharply divided over the meaning of his writings. Especially damaging to the book's reputation was its persistent low opinion of human nature. Succeeding generations have debated his analysis of human behavior and his consequent rationale for a strong government. In modern secular society, many readers have come to accept Machiavelli's view that political power, driven by personal or group interests, must be understood in utilitarian and practical terms.

    The Prince, a treatise on the art of successful governing, is composed of three parts. The first part, comprising eleven chapters, categorizes and describes the various types of existing governments. The second part, which consists of fourteen chapters, offers advice and examples on winning and maintaining political power. In these fourteen chapters, Machiavelli instructs the ruler on how to raise and organize armies, how to keep subjects loyal, and how to avoid the pitfalls of overconfidence and flattery. Throughout *The Prince,* the author compares and contrasts key traits that make a ruler a success or a failure. He also addresses the issue of fortune—what is now called opportunity—and emphasizes how often it affects a ruler. In the third part—the concluding chapter—Machiavelli calls upon "the prince" to unite the Italians against foreign oppressors and drive them from Italy.

Reading the Selections

Chapters XV, XVI, and XVII appear in the second part of *The Prince*, in which Machiavelli discusses the most effective way for a ruler to govern his subjects. He points out that his discussion is rooted in practical politics, rather than based on imaginary regimes created by writers—a reference to the idealized commonwealths of Plato and medieval Christian authors. In Chapter XV, Machiavelli lists traits for which rulers are praised or blamed—such as being called stubborn or flexible, religious or skeptical—and notes that no ruler could continuously practice the best of these without damaging his ability to govern. Thus, in a crisis the ruler should not shrink from being blamed for vices if they are needed to safeguard the state, though most of the time, the prince should pretend to be what he is not in order to keep his subjects' loyalty.

In Chapter XVI, Machiavelli focuses on the traits of generosity and miserliness and shows, through ancient and current examples, the consequences for rulers who practiced one or the other of them. He concludes, given his dark view of human nature, that a ruler is better to be miserly than generous. In Chapter XVII, Machiavelli raises perhaps the most controversial question in the treatise: Is it better for the ruler to be loved or feared? Ideally, the ruler should be both loved and feared, but as this is nearly impossible, then the ruler should be feared. Machiavelli, realizing that fear has its limits, ends on a cautionary note: The "wise prince" must avoid being hated by his subjects, for hatred is the soil out of which rebellions grow.

Chapter XV
The Things for Which Men, and Especially Princes, Are Praised or Blamed

It now remains for us to see how a prince should govern his conduct towards his subjects or his friends. I know that this has often been written about before, and so I hope it will not be thought presumptuous for me to do so, as, especially in discussing this subject, I draw up an original set of rules. But since my intention is to say something that will prove of practical use to the inquirer, I have thought it proper to represent things as they are in real truth, rather than as they are imagined. Many have dreamed up republics and principalities which have never in truth been known to exist; the gulf between how one should live and how one does live is so wide that a man who neglects what is actually done for what should be done learns the way to self-destruction rather than self-preservation. The fact is that a man who wants to act virtuously in every way necessarily comes to grief among so many who are not virtuous. Therefore if a prince wants to maintain his rule he must learn how not to be virtuous, and to make use of this or not according to need.

So leaving aside imaginary things, and referring only to those which truly exist, I say that whenever men are discussed (and especially princes, who are more exposed to view), they are noted for various qualities which earn them either praise or condemnation. Some, for example, are held to be generous, and others miserly (I use the Tuscan word rather than the word avaricious: we call a man who is mean with what he possesses, miserly, and a man who wants to plunder others, avaricious). Some are held to be benefactors, others are called grasping; some cruel, some compassionate; one man faithless, another faithful; one man effeminate and cowardly, another fierce and courageous; one man courteous, another proud; one man lascivious, another pure; one guileless, another crafty; one stubborn, another flexible; one grave, another frivolous; one religious, another sceptical; and so forth. I know everyone will agree that it would be most laudable if a prince possessed all the qualities deemed to be good among those I have enumerated. But, human nature being what it is, princes cannot possess those qualities, or rather they cannot always exhibit them. So a prince should be so prudent that he knows how to escape the evil reputation attached to those vices which could lose him his state, and how to avoid those vices which are not so dangerous, if he possibly can; but, if he cannot, he need not worry so much about the latter. And then, he must not flinch from being blamed for vices which are necessary for safeguarding the state. This is because, taking everything into account, he will find that some of the things that appear to be virtues will, if he practises them, ruin him, and some of the things that appear to be wicked will bring him security and prosperity.

Chapter XVI
Generosity and Parsimony

So, starting with the first of the qualities I enumerated above, I say it would be splendid if one had a reputation for generosity; nonetheless if your actions are influenced by the desire for such a reputation you will come to grief. This is because if your generosity is good and sincere it may pass unnoticed and it will not save you from being reproached for its opposite. If you want to acquire a reputation for generosity, therefore, you have to be ostentatiously lavish; and a prince acting in that fashion will soon squander all his resources, only to be forced in the end, if he wants to maintain his reputation, to lay excessive burdens on the people, to impose extortionate taxes, and to do everything else he can to raise money. This will start to make his subjects hate him, and, since he will have impoverished himself, he will be generally despised. As a result, because of this generosity of his, having injured many and rewarded few, he will be vulnerable to the first minor setback, and the first real danger he encounters will bring him to grief. When he realizes this and tries to retrace his path he will immediately be reputed a miser.

So as a prince cannot practise the virtue of generosity in such a way that he is noted for it, except to his cost, he should if he is prudent not mind being called a miser. In time he will be recognized as being essentially a generous man, seeing that because of his parsimony his existing revenues are enough for him, he can defend himself against an aggressor, and he can embark on enterprises without burdening the people. So he proves himself generous to all those from whom he takes nothing, and they are innumerable, and miserly towards all those to whom he gives nothing, and they are few. In our own times great things have been accomplished only by those who have been held miserly, and the others have met disaster. Pope Julius II made use of a reputation for generosity to win the papacy, but subsequently he made no effort to maintain this reputation, because he wanted to be able to finance his wars. The present king of France has been able to wage so many wars without taxing his subjects excessively only because his long-standing parsimony enabled him to meet the additional expenses involved. Were the present king of Spain renowned for his generosity he would not have started and successfully concluded so many enterprises.

So if a prince does not have to rob his subjects, if he can defend himself, if he is not plunged into poverty and shame, if he is not forced to become rapacious, he ought not to worry about being called a miser. Miserliness is one of those vices which sustain his rule. Someone may object: Caesar came to power by virtue of his generosity, and many others, because they practised and were known for their generosity, have risen to the very highest positions. My answer to this is as follows. Either you are already a prince, or you are on the way to becoming one. In the first case, your generosity will be to your cost; in the second, it is certainly necessary to have a reputation for generosity. Caesar was one of those who wanted to establish his own rule over Rome; but if, after he had established it, he had remained alive and not moderated his expenditure he would have fallen from power.

Again, someone may retort: there have been many princes who have won great successes with their armies, and who have had the reputation of being extremely generous. My reply to this is: the prince gives away what is his own or his subjects', or else what belongs to others. In the first case he should be frugal; in the second, he should indulge his generosity to the full. The prince who campaigns with his armies, who lives by pillaging, sacking, and extortion, disposes of what belongs to aliens; and he must be open-handed, otherwise the soldiers would refuse to follow him. And you can be more liberal with what does not belong to you or your subjects, as Caesar, Cyrus, and Alexander were. Giving away what belongs to strangers in no way affects your standing at home; rather it increases it. You hurt yourself only when you give away what is your own. There is nothing so self-defeating as generosity: in the act of practising it, you lose the ability to do so, and you become either poor and despised or, seeking to escape poverty, rapacious and hated. A prince should try to avoid, above all else, being despised and hated; and generosity results in your being both. Therefore it is wiser to incur the reputation of being a miser, which invites ignominy but not hatred, than to be forced by seeking a name for generosity to incur a reputation for rapacity, which brings you hatred as well as ignominy.

—ᴍ—

Chapter XVII
Cruelty and Compassion; and Whether It Is Better to Be Loved Than Feared, or the Reverse

Taking others of the qualities I enumerated above, I say that a prince should want to have a reputation for compassion rather than for cruelty: nonetheless, he should be careful that he does not make bad use of compassion. Cesare Borgia was accounted cruel; nevertheless, this cruelty of his reformed the Romagna, brought it unity, and restored order and obedience. On reflection, it will be seen that there was more compassion in Cesare than in the Florentine people, who, to escape being called cruel, allowed Pistoia to be devastated.* So a prince should not worry if he incurs reproach for his cruelty so long as he keeps his subjects united and loyal. By making an example or two he will prove more compassionate than those who, being too compassionate, allow disorders which lead to murder and rapine. These nearly always harm the whole community, whereas executions ordered by a prince only affect individuals. A new prince, of all rulers, finds it impossible to avoid a reputation for cruelty, because of the abundant dangers inherent in a newly won state. Vergil, through the mouth of Dido, says:

> *Res dura, et regni novitas me talia cogunt*
> *Moliri, et late fines custode tueri.*†

Nonetheless, a prince should be slow to take action, and should watch that he does not come to be afraid of his own shadow; his behaviour should be tempered by humanity and prudence so that over-confidence does not make him rash or excessive distrust make him unbearable.

From this arises the following question: whether it is better to be loved than feared, or the reverse. The answer is that one would like to be both the one and the other; but because it is difficult to combine them, it is far better to be feared than loved if you cannot be both. One can make this generalization about men: they are ungrateful, fickle, liars, and deceivers, they shun danger and are greedy for profit; while you treat them well, they are yours. They would shed their blood for you, risk their property, their lives, their children, so long, as I said above, as danger is remote; but when you are in danger they turn against you. Any prince who has come to depend entirely on promises and has taken no other precautions ensures his own ruin; friendship which is bought with money and not with greatness and nobility of mind is paid for, but it does not last and it yields nothing. Men worry less about doing an injury to one who makes himself loved than to one who makes himself feared. The bond of love is one which men, wretched creatures that they are, break when it is to their advantage to do so; but fear is strengthened by a dread of punishment which is always effective.

The prince should nonetheless make himself feared in such a way that, if he is not loved, at least he escapes being hated. For fear is quite compatible with an absence of hatred; and the prince can always avoid hatred if he abstains from the property of his subjects and citizens and from their women. If, even so, it proves necessary to execute someone, this should be done only when there is proper justification and manifest reason for it. But above all a prince should abstain from the property of others; because men sooner forget the death of their father than the loss of their patrimony. It is always possible to find pretexts for confiscating someone's property; and a prince who starts to live by rapine always finds pretexts for seizing what belongs to others. On the other hand, pretexts for executing someone are harder to find and they are less easily sustained.

However, when a prince is campaigning with his soldiers and is in command of a large army then he need not worry about having a reputation for cruelty; because, without such a reputation, he can never keep his army united and disciplined. Among the admirable achievements of Hannibal is included this: that although he led a huge army, made up of countless different races, on foreign campaigns, there was never any dissension, either among the troops themselves or against their leader, whether things were going well or badly. For this, his inhuman cruelty was wholly responsible. It was this, along with his countless other qualities, which made him feared and respected by his soldiers. If it had not been for his cruelty, his other qualities would not have been enough. The historians, having given little thought to this, on the one hand admire what Hannibal achieved, and on the other condemn what made his achievements possible.

That his other qualities would not have been enough by themselves can be proved by looking at Scipio, a man unique in his own time and through all recorded history. His armies mutinied against him in Spain, and the only reason for this was his excessive leniency, which allowed his soldiers more licence than was good for military discipline. Fabius Maximus reproached him for this in the Senate and called him a corrupter of the Roman legions. Again, when the Locri were plundered by one of Scipio's officers, he neither gave them satisfaction nor punished his officer's insubordination; and this was all because of his having too lenient a nature. By way of excuse for him some senators argued that many men were better at not making mistakes themselves than at correcting them in others. But in time Scipio's lenient nature would have spoilt his fame and glory had he continued to indulge it during his command; when he lived under orders from the Senate, however, this fatal characteristic of his was not only concealed but even brought him glory.

So, on this question of being loved or feared, I conclude that since some men love as they please but fear when the prince pleases, a wise prince should rely on what he controls, not on what he cannot control. He should only endeavour, as I said, to escape being hated.

---

*Pistoia was a subject-city of Florence, which forcibly restored order there when conflict broke out between two rival factions in 1501–2. Machiavelli was concerned with this business at first hand.

†'Harsh necessity, and the newness of my kingdom, force me to do such things and to guard my frontiers everywhere.' *Aeneid* i, 563.

BALDASSARE CASTIGLIONE
Selections from *The Book of the Courtier*

The Book of the Courtier (*courtier* being a "gentleman") belongs to the genre of etiquette books that flourished in Renaissance Europe as a religious-based culture gave way to a more humanistic world. Books of this type were much in evidence, in response to this period's ideal that secular life in the upper levels of society should be marked by reserved grace, especially between the sexes. Court life, whether in the royal or aristocratic domain, already had well-established rules of behavior derived from the medieval chivalric code; however, courts were still dominated by a male ethos, manifested in rough speech, crude manners, and general lack of refinement between men and women. Whereas most Renaissance etiquette books were meant to correct crude behavior and speech, *The Courtier* took a broader view by offering an idealized vision of court life in which courteous ladies became the arbiters of society. Published in 1528 and translated into most Western languages by 1600, this work became the bible of politeness for Europe's upper classes, and its rules were formalized into strict expectations. This Renaissance book is the source from which modern notions of "lady" and "gentleman" descend.

The Courtier's author, Baldassare Castiglione (1478–1529), was himself a polished courtier, growing up among the Italian nobility and studying the Classics at the University of Milan. Later, he was attached to various northern Italian ducal courts (Milan, Urbino, and Mantua), for whose rulers he performed military and diplomatic missions. While serving as the Duke of Mantua's ambassador to Rome, he was brought by his duties into the cultivated court of the Medici pope, Leo X. A later pope, Clement VII, made Castiglione the papal representative to Spain, a post he held until he died.

The Courtier, Castiglione's only publication, was his life's work. He was moved to write it during his eleven years at the ducal court of Urbino, which was the center of an accomplished circle of artists, writers, and intellectuals presided over by the old duke and his young wife, Elisabetta. This Urbino circle, with its witty talk, integrity, and grace, came to embody Castiglione's social ideal. When he wrote *The Courtier*, he tried to capture the conversational tone of this circle by making the work a dialogue, divided into four books, set during an evening in the ducal palace. In his book, as in life, Duchess Elisabetta is the playful leader of the group.

Reading the Selections

These selections from *The Book of the Courtier* are excerpts from Books I and III, dealing respectively with the qualities that define a courtier and a lady. Not based on real life, these attributes are ideals meant as a guide for correct deportment and had been gleaned from Castiglione's readings in medieval and Classical literature. Of the ideal courtier, the participants agree that he should be both a soldier trained in the bearing of arms and a scholar skilled in the liberal arts and social graces; however, they are of two minds as to which role should dominate.

No such dispute divides Castiglione's participants over the ideal lady: All concur that she should be the consummate hostess—charming, witty, graceful, physically attractive, and utterly feminine. An innovative aspect of this idealized model is the insistence that a lady be educated in the liberal arts in the same way as a gentleman. This idea swept away the barrier that, since the Middle Ages had excluded women from higher learning. However, women remained barred from universities until the nineteenth century.

Book I

. . .

'But to come to specific details, I judge that the first and true profession of the courtier must be that of arms; and this above everything else I wish him to pursue vigorously. Let him also stand out from the rest as enterprising, bold, and loyal to whomever he serves. And he will win a good reputation by demonstrating these qualities whenever and wherever possible, since failure to do so always incurs the gravest censure. Just as once a woman's reputation for purity has been sullied it can never be restored, so once the reputation of a gentleman-at-arms has been stained through cowardice or some other reproachful behaviour, even if only once, it always remains defiled in the eyes of the world and covered with ignominy. The more our courtier excels in this art, therefore, the more praise he will deserve, although I do not think he needs to have the professional knowledge of such things and the other qualities appropriate to a military commander. However, since the subject of what constitutes a great captain takes us into very deep waters, we shall be content, as we said, for the courtier to show complete loyalty and an undaunted spirit, and for these to be always in evidence. For men demonstrate their courage far more often in little things than in great. Very often in the face of appalling danger but where there are numerous witnesses one will find those who, though ready to drop dead with fear, driven on by shame or the presence of others, will press forward, with their eyes closed, and do their duty; and only God knows how. But in things of trifling importance, when they believe they can avoid danger without its being noticed, they are only too willing to play for safety. As for those who, even when they are sure they are not being observed or seen or recognized by anyone, are full of ardour and avoid doing anything, no matter how trivial, for which they would incur reproach, they possess the temper and quality we are looking for in our courtier. All the same, we do not wish the courtier to make a show of being so fierce that he is always blustering and bragging, declaring that he is married to his cuirass, and glowering with the haughty looks that we know only too well in Berto. To these may very fairly be said what a worthy lady once remarked jokingly, in polite company, to a certain man (I don't want just now to mention him by name) whom she had honoured by asking him to dance and who not only refused but would not listen to music or take part in the many other entertainments offered, protesting all the while that such frivolities were not his business. And when at length the lady asked what his business was, he answered with a scowl: "Fighting . . ."

' "Well then," the lady retorted, "I should think that since you aren't at war at the moment and you are not engaged in fighting, it would be a good thing if you were to have yourself well greased and stowed away in a cupboard with all your fighting equipment, so that you avoid getting rustier than you are already."

'And of course everyone burst out laughing at the way she showed her contempt for his stupid presumption.

'Therefore,' Count Lodovico went on, 'the man we are seeking should be fierce, rough and always to the fore, in the presence of the enemy; but anywhere else he should be kind, modest, reticent and anxious above all to avoid ostentation or the kind of outrageous self-glorification by which a man always arouses loathing and disgust among those who have to listen to him. . . .

'I should like our courtier to be a more than average scholar, at least in those studies which we call the humanities; and he should have a knowledge of Greek as well as Latin, because of the many different things that are so beautifully written in that language. He should be very well acquainted with the poets, and no less with the orators and historians, and also skilled at writing both verse and prose, especially in our own language; for in addition to the satisfaction this will give him personally, it will enable him to provide constant entertainment for the ladies, who are usually very fond of such things. But if because of his other activities or through lack of study he fails to achieve a commendable standard in his writing, then he should take pains to suppress his work, to avoid ridicule, and he should show it only to a friend he can trust. And the exercise of writing will be profitable for him at least to the extent that it will teach him how to judge the work of others. For it is very unusual for someone who is not a practised writer, however erudite he may be, to understand completely the demanding work done by writers, or appreciate their stylistic accomplishments and triumphs and those subtle details characteristic of the writers of the ancient world. Moreover, these studies will make our courtier well informed and eloquent and (as Aristippus said to the tyrant) self-confident and assured no matter whom he is talking to. However, I should like our courtier to keep one precept firmly in mind: namely, that in what I have just discussed and in everything else he should always be diffident and reserved rather than forward, and he should be on his guard against assuming that he knows what he does not know. For we are instinctively all too greedy for praise, and there is no sound or song that comes sweeter to our ears; praise, like Sirens' voices, is the kind of music that causes shipwreck to the man who does not stop his ears to its deceptive harmony. Recognizing this danger, some of the philosophers of the ancient world wrote books giving advice on how a man can tell the difference between a true friend and a flatterer. Even so, we may well ask what use is this, seeing that there are so many who realize perfectly well that they are listening to flattery, and yet love the flatterer and detest the one who tells them the truth. Indeed, very often, deciding that the one who praises them is not being fulsome enough, they lend him a hand themselves and say such things that even the most outrageous flatterer feels ashamed. Let us leave these blind fools to their errors and decide that our courtier should possess such good judgement that he will not be told that black is white or presume anything of himself unless he is certain that it is true, and especially in regard to those flaws which, if you remember, when he was suggesting his game for the evening Cesare recalled we had often used to demonstrate the particular folly of this person or another. To make no mistake at all, the courtier should, on the contrary, when he knows the praises he receives are deserved, not assent to them too openly nor let them pass without some protest. Rather he should tend to disclaim them modestly, always giving the impression that arms are, as indeed they should be, his chief profession, and that all his other fine accomplishments serve merely as adornments; and this should especially be his attitude when he is in the company of soldiers, lest he behave like those who in the world of scholarship want to be taken for warriors and among warriors want to seem men of letters. In this way, as we have said, he will avoid affectation, and even his modest achievements will appear great.'

At this point, Pietro Bembo interrupted: 'I cannot see, my dear Count, why you wish this courtier, who is so literate and so well endowed with other worthy qualities, to regard everything as serving to adorn the profession of arms, and not arms and the rest as serving to adorn the profession of letters, which, taken by themselves, are as superior in dignity to arms as is the soul to the body, since letters are a function of the soul, just as arms are of the body.'

Then the Count answered: 'On the contrary, the profession of arms pertains both to the soul and to the body. But I should not want you to be the judge of this, Pietro, because by one of the parties concerned it would be assumed that you were prejudiced. And as this is a controversy that the wisest men have already thrashed out, there is no call to re-open it. As it is, I consider that it has been settled in favour of arms; and since I may form our courtier as I wish, I want him to be of the same opinion. If you think the contrary, wait until you hear of a contest in which the man who defends the cause of arms is allowed to use them, just as those who defend the cause of letters make use of letters in their defence; for if each one uses his own weapons, you will see that the men of letters will lose.'

'Ah,' said Pietro Bembo, 'you were only too ready earlier on to damn the French for their scant appreciation of letters, and you mentioned the glory that they bring to men and the way they make a man immortal. And now you seem to have changed your mind. Do you not remember that:

> *Giunto Alessandro alla famosa tomba*
> *del fero Achille, sospirando disse:*
> *O fortunato, che sì chiara tromba*
> *trovasti, e chi di te sì alto scrisse!**

*The first quatrain of a sonnet by Petrarch, literally: 'When Alexander reached the famous tomb of fierce Achilles, he sighed and said: O happy man, who found so illustrious a trumpet, and one to write of you so nobly!'

And if Alexander was envious of Achilles not because of what he had done himself but because of the way he was blessed by fortune in having his deeds celebrated by Homer, we must conclude that he put a higher value on the writings of Homer than on the arms of Achilles. What other judge do you want, or what other verdict on the relative worth of arms and letters than the one delivered by one of the greatest commanders that has ever lived?'

The Count replied: 'I blame the French for believing that letters are harmful to the profession of arms, and I maintain myself that it is more fitting for a warrior to be educated than for anyone else; and I would have these two accomplishments, the one helping the other, as is most fitting, joined together in our courtier. I do not think that this means I have changed my opinion. But, as I said, I do not wish to argue which of them is more praiseworthy. Let it be enough that men of letters hardly ever choose to praise other than great men and glorious deeds, which deserve praise both on their own account and because, in addition, they provide writers with a truly noble theme. And this subject-matter embellishes what is written and, no doubt, is the reason why such writings endure, for otherwise, if they dealt not with noble deeds but with vain and trivial subjects, they would surely be read and appreciated less. And if Alexander was envious of Achilles because he was praised by Homer, it still does not necessarily follow that he thought more of letters than of arms; and if he had thought that he was as inferior to Achilles as a soldier as he believed that all those who would write about him were inferior to Homer as writers, he would, I am sure, have far preferred brave exploits on his own part to brave talk from others. Therefore I believe that when he said what he did, Alexander was tacitly praising himself, and expressing a desire for what he thought he lacked, namely supreme ability as a writer, rather than for what he took for granted he already had, namely prowess as a warrior, in which he was far from acknowledging Achilles as his superior. So when he called Achilles fortunate he meant that if so far his own fame did not rival that of Achilles (which had been made bright and illustrious through so inspired a poem) this was not because his valour and merits were less notable or less deserving of the highest praise but because of the way fortune had granted Achilles a born genius to be his herald and to trumpet his deeds to the world. Moreover, perhaps Alexander wanted to encourage some gifted person to write about him, showing that his pleasure in this would be as great as his love and respect for the sacred monuments of literature. And now we have said enough about this subject.'

'Indeed, far too much,' remarked signor Lodovico, 'for I don't think that one could discover anywhere in the world a vessel big enough to hold all the things you want to put into our courtier.' . . .

—〰—

Book III

. . .

Thus just as it is very fitting that a man should display a certain robust and sturdy manliness, so it is well for a woman to have a certain soft and delicate tenderness, with an air of feminine sweetness in her every movement, which, in her going and staying and whatsoever she does, always makes her appear a woman, without any resemblance to a man. If this precept be added to the rules that these gentlemen have taught the courtier, then I think that she ought to be able to make use of many of them, and adorn herself with the finest accomplishments, as signor Gaspare says. For I consider that many virtues of the mind are as necessary to a woman as to a man; as it is to be of good family; to shun affectation: to be naturally graceful; to be well mannered, clever and prudent; to be neither proud, envious or evil-tongued, nor vain, contentious or clumsy; to know how to gain and keep the favour of her mistress and of everyone else; to perform well and gracefully the sports suitable for women. It also seems to me that good looks are more important to her than to the courtier, for much is lacking to a woman who lacks beauty. She must also be more circumspect and at greater pains to avoid giving an excuse for someone to speak ill of her; she should not only be beyond reproach but also beyond even suspicion, for a woman lacks a man's resources when it comes to defending herself. And now, seeing that Count Lodovico has explained in great detail what should be the principal occupation of a courtier, namely, to his mind, the profession of arms, it seems right for me to say what I consider ought to be that of the lady at Court. And when I have done this, then I shall believe that most of my task has been carried out.

'Leaving aside, therefore, those virtues of the mind which she must have in common with the courtier, such as prudence, magnanimity, continence and many others besides, and also the qualities that are common to all kinds of women, such as goodness and discretion, the ability to take good care, if she is married, of her husband's belongings and house and children, and the virtues belonging to a good mother, I say that the lady who is at Court should properly have, before all else, a certain pleasing affability whereby she will know how to entertain graciously every kind of man with charming and honest conversation, suited to the time and the place and the rank of the person with whom she is talking. And her serene and modest behaviour, and the candour that ought to inform all her actions, should be accompanied by a quick and vivacious spirit by which she shows her freedom from boorishness; but with such a virtuous manner that she makes herself thought no less chaste, prudent and benign than she is pleasing, witty and discreet. Thus she must observe a cer-

tain difficult mean, composed as it were of contrasting qualities, and take care not to stray beyond certain fixed limits. . . .

'Now since signor Gaspare also asks what are the many things a lady at Court should know about, how she ought to converse, and whether her virtues should be such as to contribute to her conversation, I declare that I want her to understand what these gentlemen have said the courtier himself ought to know; and as for the activities we have said are unbecoming to her, I want her at least to have the understanding that people can have of things they do not practise themselves; and this so that she may know how to value and praise the gentlemen concerned in all fairness, according to their merits. And, to repeat in just a few words something of what has already been said, I want this lady to be knowledgeable about literature and painting, to know how to dance and play games, adding a discreet modesty and the ability to give a good impression of herself to the other principles that have been taught the courtier. And so when she is talking or laughing, playing or jesting, no matter what, she will always be most graceful, and she will converse in a suitable manner with whomever she happens to meet, making use of agreeable witticisms and jokes. And although continence, magnanimity, temperance, fortitude of spirit, prudence and the other virtues may not appear to be relevant in her social encounters with others, I want her to be adorned with these as well, not so much for the sake of good company, though they play a part in this too, as to make her truly virtuous, and so that her virtues, shining through everything she does, make her worthy of honour.'

'I am quite surprised,' said signor Gaspare with a laugh, 'that since you endow women with letters, continence, magnanimity and temperance, you do not want them to govern cities as well, and to make laws and lead armies, while the men stay at home to cook and spin.'

The Magnifico replied, also laughing: 'Perhaps that would not be so bad, either.'

Then he added: 'Do you not know that Plato, who was certainly no great friend of women, put them in charge of the city and gave all the military duties to the men? Don't you think that we might find many women just as capable of governing cities and armies as men? But I have not imposed these duties on them, since I am fashioning a Court lady and not a queen. I'm fully aware that you would like by implication to repeat the slander that signor Ottaviano made against women yesterday, namely, that they are most imperfect creatures, incapable of any virtuous act, worth very little and quite without dignity compared with men. But truly both you and he would be very much in error if you really thought this.' . . .

13

THE RELIGIOUS REFORMATIONS, NORTHERN HUMANISM, THE NORTHERN RENAISSANCE, AND LATE MANNERISM

1500–1603

DESIDERIUS ERASMUS

Selection from *The Praise of Folly*

Between 1470 and the onset of the Protestant Reformation in the 1520s, the Renaissance spread from Italy north across the Alps where it fused with existing Christian thought to create northern humanism. As in Italy, humanists in the north looked to the Greco-Roman past for inspiration, thereby reviving widespread interest in Classicism. Unlike in Italy, however, scholars in northern Europe were Christians first and humanists second; they used Classical learning to shed light on perceived religious problems, namely corruption in the clergy, the church's emphasis on ritual to the neglect of moral order, and the general breakdown in spiritual life. In this way, the northern humanists pointed the way to the Protestant Reformation and helped shape Mannerism, the dominant cultural style between 1520 and 1600.

The most influential voice of northern humanism was the Dutch scholar Desiderius Erasmus (about 1466–1536), who was called by his colleagues the Prince of Humanists. Though educated in traditional Classical studies, he planned a career in the church, joining a monastery and also becoming a priest. But his love of learning and his distaste for monastic life combined to lead him to literature. His writings, beginning with the *Adagia* (1500), a collection of his commentaries on quotations from Classical authors, quickly made him a well-known scholar. He traveled across Europe as the guest of princes, kings, and church leaders, and his gentle manner brought a calm to the period's religious debates. But as the Protestant revolt divided Europe, Erasmus's plea for tolerance was swept away by both sides. Still, Erasmus's treatises, letters, and especially his Greek edition of the New Testament (based on the then latest sources) ensured his position as leader of northern humanism.

15

Reading the Selection

Erasmus is best remembered for *The Praise of Folly* (1516), a biting satire on human vanity that still rings true today. Written during one of his visits to England and dedicated to his friend and fellow humanist Sir Thomas More (see *Utopia*), it held up to ridicule his period's leaders (such as scholars, lawyers, monks, and cardinals) and exposed their hypocrisy and worldly appetites. Though Erasmus thought his book had little lasting merit, deeming it an intellectual joke tossed off to amuse his friends, *The Praise of Folly* nonetheless echoed the thoughts of many contemporaries, and subsequent generations have enjoyed its wicked satire. Today, it is the one work by Erasmus most likely to be known to educated readers.

Erasmus, in *The Praise of Folly*, uses the literary device of personification, employed earlier by Boethius (see *The Consolation of Philosophy*) and Christine de Pizan (see *The Book of the City of Ladies*). He speaks through Dame Folly, a "goddess" who delights in her foolish followers. As this section opens, Dame Folly speaks, identifying herself, her parents, and her attendants: self-love, flattery, forgetfulness, pleasure, and sensuality. Ironically, she says human life would be unbearable without her (folly), for if people were always sensible, then everyone would be miserable.

Dame Folly then surveys the human comedy, laying out the foolish things in which each profession excels. Beneath the satire against the church, Erasmus's Christian humanism shines forth; for example, the work claims that points of theology and monkish pride have become more important than "mending a poor man's shoes"—a metaphor for the church's neglect of the needy.

—⁂—

[Folly is speaking.] In the same realm are those who are authors of books. All of them are highly indebted to me, especially those who blacken their pages with sheer triviality. For those who write learnedly to be criticized by a few scholars, not even ruling out a Persius or a Laelius as a judge, seem to be more pitiable than happy to me, simply because they are continuously torturing themselves. They add, they alter, they cross something out, they reinsert it, they recopy their work, they rearrange it, they show it to friends, and they keep it for nine years; yet they still are not satisfied with it. At such a price, they buy an empty reward, namely praise—and the praise of only a handful, at that. They buy this at the great expense of long hours, no sleep, so much sweat, and so many vexations. Add also the loss of health, the deterioration of their physical appearance, the possibility of blindness or partial loss of their sight, poverty, malice, premature old age, an early death, and if you can think of more, add them to this list. The scholar feels that he has been compensated for such ills when he wins the sanction of one or two other weak-eyed scholars. But my author is crazy in a far happier way for he, without any hesitation, rapidly writes down anything that comes to mind, his pen, or even his dreams. There is little or no waste of paper, since he knows that if the trifles are trivial enough the majority of the readers, that is, the fools and ignoramuses, will approve of them. What is the difference if one should ignore two or three scholars, even though he may have read them? Or what weight will the censure of a few scholars carry, so long as the multitudes give it acclaim?

Actually, the wiser writers are those who put out the work of someone else as their own. By a few alterations they transfer someone else's glory to themselves, disregarding the other person's long labor and comforting themselves with the thought that even though they might be publicly convicted of plagiarism, meanwhile they shall have enjoyed the fruits and glory of authorship. It is worth one's while to observe how pleased authors are with their own works when they are popular and pointed out in a crowd—as celebrities! Their work is on display in bookstores, with three cryptic words in large type on the title page, something like a magician's spell. Ye gods! After all, what are they but words? Few people will ever hear of them, compared to the total world population, and far fewer will admire them, since people's tastes vary so, even among the common people. And why is it that the very names of the authors are often false, or stolen from the books of the ancients? One calls himself Telemachus, another Stelenus or Laertes, still another Polycrates, and another Thrasymachus. As a result, nowadays it does not matter whether you dedicate your book to a chameleon or a gourd, or simply to alpha or beta, as the philosophers do.

The most touching event is when they compliment each other and turn around in an exchange of letters, verses, and superfluities. They are fools praising fools and dunces praising dunces. The first, in the opinion of the second, is an Alcaeus, and the second, in the opinion of the first, is a Callimachus. One holds another in higher esteem than Cicero, the other finds the one more learned than Plato. Or sometimes they will choose a competitor and increase their reputation by rivaling themselves with him. As a result the public is split with opposing viewpoints, until finally, when the dispute is over, each reigns as victor and has a triumphal parade. Wise men deride this as being absolute nonsense, which is just what it is. Who will deny it? Meanwhile, our authors are leading a luxurious life because of my excellence, and they would not exchange their accomplishments for even those of Scipius. And while the scholars most certainly derive a great deal of pleasure from laughing at them, relishing to the utmost the madnesses of others, they themselves owe me a great deal, which they cannot deny without being most ungrateful men.

Among men of the learned professions, a most self-satisfied group of men, the lawyers may hold themselves in the highest esteem. For while they laboriously roll up the stone of Sisyphus by the force of weaving six hundred laws together at the same time, by the stacking of commentary upon commentary and opinion upon opinion regardless of how far removed from the purpose, they contrive to make their profession seem to be most difficult of all. What is actually tedious they consider brilliant. Let us include with them the logicians and sophists, a breed of men more loquacious than the famed brass kettles of Dodona. Any one of them can outtalk any twenty women. They would be happier, though, if they were just talkative and not quarrelsome as well. In fact, they are so quarrelsome that they will argue and fight over a lock of a goat's wool, absurdly losing sight of the truth in the furor of their dispute. Their egotistical love keeps them happy, and manned with but three syllogisms, they will unflinchingly argue on any subject with any man. Their mere obstinacy affords them victory, even though you place Stentor against them.

Next in line are the scientists, revered for their beards and the fur on their gowns. They feel that they are the only men with any wisdom, and all other men float about as shadows. How senilely they daydream, while they construct their countless worlds and shoot the distance to the sun, the moon, the stars, and spheres, as with a thumb and line. They postulate causes for lightning, winds, eclipses, and other inexplicable things, never hesitating for a moment, as if they had exclusive knowledge about the secrets of nature, designer of elements, or as if they visited us directly from the council of the gods. Yet all this time nature is heartily laughing at them and their conjectures. It is a sufficient argument just proving that they have good intelligence for nothing. They can never explain why they always disagree with each other on every subject. In summation, knowing nothing in general they profess to know everything in particular. They are ignorant even to themselves, and at times they do not see the ditch or stone lying across their path, because many of them are day-dreamers and are absent-minded. Yet they proclaim that they perceive ideas, universals, forms without matter, primary substances, quiddities, entities, and things so tenuous that I'm afraid that Lynceus could not see them himself. The common people are especially disdained when they bring out their triangles, quadrangles, circles, and mathematical figures of the like. They place one on top of the other and arrange them into a maze. Then they deploy some letters precisely, as if in a battle formation, and finally they reverse them. And all of this is done only to confuse those who are ignorant of the field. These scientists do not like those who predict the future from the stars, and promise even more fantastic miracles. And these fortunate men find people who believe them.

Perhaps it would be better to pass silently over the theologians. Dealing with them, since they are hot-tempered, is like crossing Lake Camarina or eating poisonous beans.

They may attack me with six hundred arguments and force me to retract what I hold; for if I refuse, they will immediately declare me a heretic. By this blitz action they show a desire to terrify anyone to whom they are ill-disposed. No other people are so adverse to acknowledge my favors to them, yet the divines are bound to me by extraordinary obligations. These theologians are happy in their self-love, and as if they were presently inhabiting a third heaven, they look down on all men as though they were animals that crawled along the ground, coming near to pity them. They are protected by a wall of scholastic definitions, arguments, corollaries, and implicit and explicit propositions. They have so many hideouts that not even the net of Vulcan would be able to catch them; for they back down from their distinctions, by which they also cut through the knots of an argument, as if with a double-blade ax from Tenedos; and they come forth with newly invented terms and monstrous-sounding words. Furthermore, they explain the most mysterious matters to suit themselves, for instance, the method by which the world was set in order and began, through what channels original sin has come down to us through generations, by what means, in what measure, and how long the Omnipotent Christ was in the Virgin's womb, and how accidents subsist in the Eucharist without their substance.

But those have been beaten to death down through the ages. Here are some questions that are worthy of great (and some call them) illuminated theologians, questions that will really make them think, if they should ever encounter them. Did divine generation take place at a particular time? Are there several sonships in Christ? Whether this is a possible proposition: Does God the Father hate the Son? Could God the Father have taken upon Himself the likeness of a woman, a devil, an ass, a gourd, or a piece of flint? Then how would that gourd have preached, performed miracles, or been crucified? Also, what would Peter have consecrated, if he had administered the Eucharist, while Christ's body hung on the cross? Another thought: could Christ have been said to be a man at that very moment? Will we be forbidden to eat and drink after the resurrection? (Now, while there is time, they are providing against hunger and thirst!) These intricate subtleties are infinite, and there are others that are even more subtle, concerning instances of time, notions, relations, accidents, quiddities, and entities, which no one can perceive unless, like Lynceus, he can see in the blackest darkness things that aren't there.

We must insert those maxims, rather contradictions, that, compared to the Stoic paradoxes, appear to be the most common simplicity. For instance: it is a lesser crime to cut the throats of a thousand men than to sew a stitch on a poor man's shoe on the sabbath; it is better to want the earth to perish, body, boots, and breeches (as the saying goes), than to tell a single lie, however inconsequential. The methods that our scholastics follow only render more subtle the subtlest of subtleties; for you will more easily escape from a labyrinth than from the snares of the Realists, Nominalists, Thomists, Albertists, Occamists, and Scotists. I have not named them all, only a few of the major ones. But there is so much learning and difficulty in all of these sects that I should think the apostles themselves must have the need of some help from some other's spirit if they were to try to argue these topics with our new generation of theologians....

Those who are the closest to these in happiness are generally called "the religious" or "monks," both of which are deceiving names, since for the most part they stay as far away from religion as possible and frequent every sort of place. I cannot, however, see how any life could be more gloomy than the life of these monks if I did not assist them in many ways. Though most people detest these men so much that accidentally meeting one is considered to be bad luck, the monks themselves believe that they are magnificent creatures. One of the chief beliefs is that to be illit-

erate is to be of a high state of sanctity, and so they make sure that they are not able to read. Another is that when braying out their gospels in church they are making themselves very pleasing and satisfying to God, when in fact they are uttering these psalms as a matter of repetition rather than from their hearts. Indeed, some of these men make a good living through their uncleanliness and beggary by bellowing their petitions for food from door to door; there is not an inn, an announcement board, or a ship into which they are not accessible, here having a great advantage over other common beggars. According to them, though, they are setting an apostolic example for us by their filthiness, their ignorance, their bawdiness, and their insolence....

SIR THOMAS MORE

Selection from *Utopia*

Sir Thomas More's *Utopia* (1516) is the first work of utopian literature in modern times. It is also the source of this genre's name, *utopia* (from Greek, "not-place") being a pun on *eutopia* (from Greek, "well-place," or "place [where all is] well"). Written in Latin, it was printed both abroad and in England and soon became the talk of Europe. Since Thomas More (1478–1535) wrote, more than one hundred books have appeared on this idea.

The idea of a perfect place grew as Western history unfolded. It was first glimpsed by the immortal Utnapishtim, the Babylonian Noah, in *The Epic of Gilgamesh* (about 2500 B.C.). In the *Odyssey*, Homer named it the Elysian Fields. Another version was the Isles of the Blessed, as described by Horace. In Christianity it became paradise, called by St. Augustine (see *Confessions*) the Heavenly City. For the next thousand years, the celestial paradise (in contrast to the Earthly City) held sway in Europe. The Renaissance and the rise of secularism opened the way for More's earthly utopia.

More's *Utopia,* inspired by Plato's *The Republic,* was in tune with Christian humanism (1500–1550), the literary movement (see Erasmus's *The Praise of Folly*) that used both Classical texts and the Bible as guides. To effect his goal—a critique of Europe—More presented an ideal society in the New World. This disguise was necessary, for rash opinions could and did lead to prison or death in this age. More, a Catholic, was eventually beheaded for his beliefs, at the command of Henry VIII, the founder of the Protestant sect called Anglicanism.

The inhabitants of More's Utopia are portrayed as having solved the problems plaguing Europe at the time. Utopia was a welfare state run on communistic lines, with no private property and no money. There was universal free education, six hours' labor daily, uniforms for citizens, free medical treatment, communal meals (with musical and reading accompaniment) in civic restaurants. Tolerance was granted to all religions. The penal code was simple, and parties to legal suits were expected to plead their own cases, as no lawyers were allowed. The law was harsh in sexual matters; adultery could result in slavery, repeated offenses in death. Divorce, however, was allowed by mutual consent. Gold was not to be used as currency but for useful objects such as chamberpots. Common storehouses of grains were maintained as reserves against famine. Completing More's dreamworld was a Utopian alphabet and language.

When first published, this work was so convincing that some readers, unable to decode More's intellectual puzzles (such as his made-up Greek names), downgraded its literary value, thinking it merely a translation of a travel book to the New World.

Scholars now disagree over the meaning of More's playful work. One group labels it a Catholic allegory whose purpose was to shame Christians into behaving better than the Utopians. Another group claims More as a Marxist before Marx, and the book as a political tract whose goal was to make Utopia's communism a model for Europe.

Reading the Selection

In this selection from Book II, Raphael Hythlodaeus (from Greek, "speaker of nonsense") describes Utopia's perfect society. In its communist system, all citizens worked to eat, except for thinkers and elected officials. The economy was run by syphogrants, controllers in charge of thirty households. In terms of war, the Utopians were peaceable, choosing violence only when all other methods failed.

—m—

Book II

Their Economy and Occupations

All the Utopians, men and women alike, work at agriculture, and no one is inexperienced in it. They are trained in it from childhood, partly by school instruction and partly by practice. School children are often taken into the nearby fields as though for play, where they not only see men and women working, but get exercise by working themselves.

Besides sharing in the farm work, every person has some particular trade of his own, such as the manufacture of wool or linen, masonry, metal work, or carpentry. There is no other craft which is practiced by any considerable number of them. People wear the same sort of clothes throughout the island, except for the distinctions which mark the difference between the married and the unmarried. The fashion of clothing never changes. Their clothing looks well, does not hinder their movements, and is suitable both for summer and winter. Every household makes its own clothing, but each man and woman also learns one of the other trades I have mentioned. The women, being the weaker, practice the lighter crafts, such as working with wool or linen. The heavier crafts are left to the men. Generally the same trade passes down from father to son, often by natural inclination. But if anyone's interests lie elsewhere, he is adopted into a family practicing the trade he prefers. When anyone makes such a change, both his father and the magistrates see to it that he is transferred to a responsible and upright house-holder. After a man has learned one trade, if he desires to acquire another, it is managed in the same manner. When he has learned both, he follows whichever he likes better, unless the public has special need for the other.

The chief and almost the only business of the syphogrants is to see that no one sits around in idleness, and that everyone works hard at his trade. But no one has to wear himself out with endless toil from morning till night, as if he were a beast of burden. Such a life, though it is the common life of workmen in all other countries, is no better than a slave's. The Utopians work six hours out of the twenty-four. They work three hours before dinner. After dinner they rest two hours, and then go to work for another three hours. Then they have supper and at eight o'clock, counting from noon, they go to bed and sleep eight hours.

The other hours of the day, those that are not used for work, sleep, and meals, are left to their individual choice, on the understanding that they shall not waste them idly and wantonly. They use their free time busily on any pursuit that pleases them. Many of them fill these intervals with reading. They have the custom of giving public lectures daily before daybreak, which none are obliged to attend except such as are selected for pursuit of learning. Yet a great many from all ranks, both men and women, go to hear lectures of one sort or another, according to their interests. If anyone whose mind does not delight in intellectual pursuits prefers to spend his free time at his trade, as many do, this is not forbidden, but commended as beneficial to the commonwealth. After supper they spend an hour in some recreation, in summer gardening, in winter diverting themselves in their dining halls with music or talk. They know nothing about gambling with dice or other such foolish and ruinous games. They play two games not unlike our chess. One is a battle of numbers, in which one number plunders another. The other is a game in which the vices battle against the virtues. In this game the co-operation of the vices against the virtues and their opposition to each other is shown up very cleverly, as well as the special oppositions between particular virtues and vices, and the methods by which the vices openly assault or secretly undermine the virtues, and how the virtues break the strength of the vices and by what means finally one side or the other wins the victory.

To understand their way of life fully we must look at one point more carefully. They allot only six hours to labor, and you might think that a scarcity of essential goods would result. Actually their working hours are sufficient to provide not only an abundance, but even a superabundance of all the necessities and conveniences of life. You will easily understand this if you consider how large a part of the population in other countries is idle. In the first place, the women (and they are half the whole population) usually do no work, or if they do, their husbands lie snoring. Secondly, there is the multitude of priests and so-called religious men, as numerous as they are idle. Add to these all the rich men, especially great landlords, who are commonly called wellborn and noble. Add their henchmen, the whole flock of swaggering bullies. Reckon in with these the strong and lusty beggars, who go about feigning some disease to excuse their laziness. You will find that the actual number of workers who supply the needs of mankind is much smaller than you would think. And now consider how few of these workers are employed in really necessary work. Because we measure values by money, we have to carry on many superfluous trades to support luxury and wantonness. If the multitude of our workers produced only what men need for good living, there would be such an abundance of goods that prices would go down and workmen could not subsist. You can easily imagine how little time would be enough to produce the goods that man's needs and convenience demand (and his pleasure too if it were true and natural pleasure), if only the workers in useless trades were placed in worthwhile occupations and all the idlers who languish in sloth but eat twice as much as laborers were put to work on useful tasks.

The truth of this supposition is very apparent in Utopia. Out of all the men and women whose age or health permit them to work, scarcely five hundred are exempted in each city and its surrounding area. Among these are the syphogrants, who are excused from labor by law. Yet they do not excuse themselves from it, because they incite others to work more easily by setting them an example. The Utopians grant the same exemption to some who apply themselves exclusively to learning, but only at the recommendation of the priests and in accordance with a secret vote of the syphogrants. If one of these persons disappoints their hopes, he is made a workman again. On the other hand it sometimes happens that a worker devotes his free time so zealously to learning and progresses so far through his diligence, that he is excused from his trade and is transferred to the class of the learned men. From this class are chosen ambassadors, priests, tranibors, and the prince himself (of old called the Barzanes, but later the Ademus). Since the rest of the entire population is neither idle nor engaged in useless occupations, it is easy to understand how they produce so much in so short a work day. . . .

Their Warfare

They hate and detest war as a thing manifestly brutal, and yet practiced by man more constantly than by any kind of beast. Contrary to almost all other peoples they consider nothing so inglorious as the glory won in war. Nevertheless both the men and the women of Utopia regularly practice military exercises on certain days, so that they will be prepared when the need arises. They go to war cautiously and reluctantly, only to protect their own territory or that of their friends if an enemy has invaded it, or to free some wretched people from tyrannous oppression and servitude. They help their friends not only in defense, but also to avenge injuries. They do this only if they are consulted in the whole affair, if the facts are proved, and if the stolen plunder is not returned. Then they think they should wage war against the aggressor. They decide on this policy when booty is taken from their friends by force or when the merchants of one country are oppressed in another country by unjust laws or by twisting good laws. This they think is a greater evil than direct attack.

This was the sole cause of the war which the Utopians waged against the Alaopolitans for the sake of the Nephelogetes some time before our arrival, when a wrong seemed to have been done under pretext of right to Neph-

elogete merchants resident among the Alaopolitans. Whether or not an injustice was done, it was avenged by a terrible war, the strength of each side being augmented by the resources and the hatred of their neighbors. Some prosperous nations were ruined and others were greatly shaken. In the end after a series of misfortunes, the Alaopolitans, who had been a very thriving people compared to the Nephelogetes, were conquered and reduced to bondage by the Nephelogetes. Vigorously as the Utopians stood by their friends in the matter of reparations, they sought none for themselves.

If the Utopians themselves are cheated in this way, they carry their anger only to the point of cutting off trade with that country, provided no bodily injury is done. Not that they care less for their own citizens than for their neighbors, but they think it worse for their neighbors' property to be seized than their own. Their neighbors' merchants suffer a great injury because they lose their own property, but the Utopians think little of their loss, for only common goods have been lost. Besides whatever is exported must be in superfluous abundance at home, or it would not be shipped out. So they think it cruel to avenge a relatively unimportant loss by killing many men, whose death would only affect the lives and livelihood of others. But if any Utopian citizens are unjustly hurt or killed, whether by private or public policy, they send envoys demanding that the guilty persons be handed over to them. If that is refused, they declare war. If the guilty men are given up, their punishment is death or bondage.

The Utopians are troubled and ashamed when they gain a bloody victory, like merchants who have paid too high a price for what they have bought. If they overwhelm the enemy by skill and cunning, they exult and celebrate a public triumph, and erect a memorial for a victory efficiently won. When they win a victory by the strength of understanding (as only men can), they pride themselves on acting bravely and manfully. Bears, lions, boars, wolves, dogs, and other wild beasts fight with their bodies, and many of them surpass us in strength and ferocity as much as we surpass them in understanding and reason. 10

The Utopians have this one aim in war, to accomplish what they would gladly have achieved without war if just terms had been granted in time. Or if that cannot be done, they aim to exact so severe a revenge from those that have injured them that they will be afraid to do it again. Their policies are directed to these ends, which they strive toward in such a way as to avoid danger rather than to attain glory and fame.

As soon as war is declared, they at once arrange to have many small notices, which are marked with their official seal, set up by stealth in the most conspicuous places in the enemy's country. In these proclamations they promise great rewards to any one who will kill the enemy's king, and smaller rewards (but still very great) for killing those whom they regard as most responsible after the king for plotting aggression against them. They double the reward for anyone who brings in the proscribed man alive. Also they offer like rewards, as well as exemption from punishment, to any of the proscribed men who turn against their countrymen. As a result the proscribed men soon suspect everyone, distrust each other, and become distracted by their danger. It has often turned out that many of them, and even princes, have been betrayed by those whom they most trusted. The Utopians realize that rewards will spur men on to any sort of crime, and consequently they promise incredible gifts. Mindful of the danger which the assassins run, they see to it that the compensation is proportionate to the risk, and promise an immense amount of gold and also rich estates safely placed in neighboring countries. They keep these promises most faithfully. Though this manner of waging war by bidding for and buying enemies may seem like the cruel villainy of an ignoble mind, it is considered by the Utopians as a wise and praiseworthy policy, since it enables them to wage great wars without any battle at all. They even think themselves humane and merciful, because by the death of a few bad men they spare the lives of many innocent men who would otherwise die in battle, some fighting on their own side, some on the enemy's. Indeed they pity the mass of enemy soldiers no less than their own, for they know that they do not fight willingly, but are driven to it by the madness of their rulers.

If this method does not succeed, they sow the seeds of discord among the enemy by inciting the king's brother or some member of the nobility to plot for the crown. If these internal factions languish, then they arouse the neighboring people against the enemy and induce them to revive some old claims, such as kings never lack.

When they promise their resources to help in a war, they furnish money abundantly, but citizens very sparingly. They hold their own men most dear and of such account that they will not willingly exchange one of the citizens for an enemy's king. Since they keep their gold and silver for this single purpose, they spend it without reluctance, the more so as they will live no less well if they spend it all. Besides the wealth which they have at home, they have also boundless treasure abroad, many neighboring nations being in their debt, as I have said. So they hire mercenary soldiers from all sides, especially from the Zapoletes.

These people live five hundred miles from Utopia toward the east. They are a rude, fierce, wild people, who delight in the forests and mountains among which they are brought up. They are sturdy, well able to endure heat, cold, and hard work. They are unacquainted with luxuries or with agriculture, and are indifferent about housing and clothing. Their only productive occupation is taking care of cattle. For the most part they live by hunting and theft. It is as if they were born for war, and they watch carefully for any chance to engage in it. When they find such a chance they eagerly embrace it, great numbers of them going out and offering themselves at a low price to any one seeking soldiers. They know only one art for earning a living, the art of taking away life. They fight for their employers fiercely and with incorruptible fidelity. But they will not bind themselves to serve for any set time. They stipulate that they may fight next day for the enemy, if higher pay is offered, and come back on the day after that for still higher pay. There is seldom a war in which a considerable number of them are not fighting on both sides. So it commonly happens that men who are related to one another by blood and have served together in intimacy in the same campaigns are enlisted on opposite sides. Forgetful of their relationship and their friendship, they kill one another for no other reason than that they have been hired for a paltry wage by different kings. They think so much of money that they will change sides readily for an increase of only a penny a day. Thus they grow greedier and greedier for money, but money is of no use to them, for what they acquire with their blood, they soon waste profligately on contemptible pleasures.

This nation serves the Utopians against all people whatsoever, for they give higher pay than any others. Just as the Utopians seek out the best possible men to use at home, by the same principle they seek the worst men to misuse in war. When need requires, they induce the Zapoletes with promises of rich rewards to face hazards from which most of them never return. The Utopians pay the rewards in good faith to those who escape death, to incite them to similar deeds of daring later. And the Utopians have no concern over how many are killed, thinking they would deserve the thanks of the human race if they could purge the world of the whole of that disgusting and vicious people. . . .

FRANÇOIS RABELAIS

Selection from *The Histories of Gargantua and Pantagruel*

Rabelais's *The Histories of Gargantua and Pantagruel* marks a fresh departure in Western letters. These robust satires, the first literary works to treat bodily functions and copulation graphically and without apology, gave the world the adjective *Rabelaisian*, meaning earthiness of speech. Because of their crudeness, the works became an underground classic—enjoyed in private but very little imitated. Only today, with the rise of freer public discourse, has Rabelais's legacy come into its own, as, for example, in the writings of Joyce (see *Ulysses*) and Ginsberg (see "A Supermarket in California").

Another reason these works represent a milestone in Western letters is that they signal the coming of the Renaissance to France. Lasting from 1515 until 1604, the French Renaissance was inspired by writers' and artists' "discovery" of Italy; literature and art clearly were altered by closer contact with ancient culture and Classical forms. The Classic ideal—the dominance of order over diversity, reason over passion—became a guiding force in French culture. François Rabelais (ca. 1494–1553) was a leader of this rebirth, though his sprawling books did not chime with Classicism's orderly ideal. More to the point, his works reflected this period's transitional nature. On one side he mocked the dying Middle Ages, with its tedious theological study; on the other side he praised the dawning Renaissance, with its love of Classical lore. In his works he was also friendly to Protestantism, stressing simple piety just as its reformers did.

The Histories of Gargantua and Pantagruel is actually five books dealing with a legendary family of giants. *Gargantua* (1534), the second written, is now known as Book I, opening the series with the bawdy tale of Gargantua, focusing on his childhood and training for kingship. *Pantagruel* (1532), the first written, tells of Gargantua's giant son, Pantagruel, and is known as Book II. Basically a satire on scholastic education (see Aquinas's *Summa Theologica*), it also ridicules many timely topics—courtroom delays, lying lawyers, and pseudointellectuals. The other three books (the last published posthumously) contain further adventures of Pantagruel.

Rabelais's career mirrored this stormy age. Entered in a monastery as a youth, he abandoned the cloister and theology to study medicine. He later served as physician in a number of posts, mainly in France. To the disgust of critics, he spent his last years as a parish priest, delegating the duties but keeping the income. Because of his books, he was hounded by the authorities, but friends in church and state always came to his rescue.

Reading the Selection

This selection contains probably the most famous passage from Book I on *Gargantua*. It features Gargantua's friend, the rascally Friar John ("the monk") and his "ideal" Abbey of Thélème, where "monks" and "nuns" were to live in accordance with the abbey's unchristian rule: "Do what you will." This abbey, with its pleasure-driven inmates, satirizes the faults that the Protestant reformers claimed against sixteenth-century monks. Beneath the broad satire, the story seems to reinforce humanist morals: The best way to regulate one's life is "by the promptings of reason and good sense," and free people have a "natural spur and instinct" to seek virtue and avoid vice.

This passage also shows Rabelais's passion for words. For example, in the inscription over the Great Gate of Thélème, the words tumble down like a waterfall, offering an exaggerated list of those to be denied entry as well as those to be welcomed to the abbey.

Book I

How Gargantua Had the Abbey of Thélème Built for the Monk

There only remained the monk to be provided for, and Gargantua wanted to make him abbot of Seuilly, but he refused the post. He next proposed to give him the abbey of Bourgueil or of Saint-Florant, whichever would suit him better, or both, if he fancied them. But the monk answered categorically that he wanted neither charge nor government of monks.

'For how should I be able to govern others,' he said, 'when I don't know how to govern myself? If it seems to you that I have done you, and may in the future do you welcome service, give me leave to found an abbey after my own devices.'

This request pleased Gargantua, and he offered him all his land of Thélème, beside the River Loire, to within six miles of the great forest of Port-Huault. The monk then requested Gargantua to institute his religious order in an exactly contrary way to all others.

'First of all, then,' said Gargantua, 'you mustn't build walls round it. For all other abbeys have lofty walls (murs).'

'Yes,' said the monk, 'and not without reason. Where there's a *mur* before and a *mur* behind, there are plenty of murmurs, envy, and mutual conspiracy.'

Moreover, seeing that in certain monasteries in this world it is the custom that if any woman enters—I speak of chaste and honest women—they wash the place where she trod, it was ordained that if any monk or nun happened to enter here, the spot where he or she had stood should be scrupulously washed likewise. And because in the religious foundations of this world everything is encompassed, limited, and regulated by hours, it was decreed that there should be no clock or dial at all, but that affairs should be conducted according to chance and opportunity. For Gargantua said that the greatest waste of time he knew was the counting of hours—what good does it do?—and the greatest nonsense in the world was to regulate one's life by the sound of a bell, instead of by the promptings of reason and good sense. Item, because at that time they put no women into religious houses unless they were one-eyed, lame, hunchbacked, ugly, malformed, lunatic, half-witted, bewitched, and blemished, or men that were not sickly, low-born, stupid, or a burden on their family. . . .

'By the way,' said the monk, 'if a woman is neither fair nor good, what can you do with her?'

'Make her a nun,' said Gargantua.

'Yes,' said the monk, 'and a sempstress of shirts.'

It was decreed that here no women should be admitted unless they were beautiful, well-built, and sweet-natured, nor any men who were not handsome, well-built, and of pleasant nature also.

Item, because men never entered nunneries except secretly and by stealth, it was decreed that here there should be no women when there were no men, and no men when there were no women.

Item, because both men and women, once accepted into a monastic order, after their novitiate year, were compelled and bound to remain for ever, so long as they lived, it was decreed that both men and women, once accepted, could depart from there whenever they pleased, without let or hindrance.

Item, because ordinarily monks and nuns made three vows, that is of chastity, poverty, and obedience, it was decreed that there anyone could be regularly married, could become rich, and could live at liberty.

With regard to the lawful age of entry, women were to be received at from ten to fifteen, and men at from twelve to eighteen. . . .

. . .

THE INSCRIPTION SET ABOVE THE GREAT GATE OF THÉLÈME

Enter not here, vile hypocrites and bigots,
Pious old apes, and puffed-up snivellers,
Wry-necked creatures sawnier than the Goths,
Or Ostrogoths, precursors of Gog and Magog,
Woe-begone scoundrels, mock-godly sandal-wearers,
Beggars in blankets, flagellating canters,
Hooted at, pot-bellied, stirrers up of troubles,
Get along elsewhere to sell your dirty swindles.
    Your hideous deceits
    Would fill my fields and streets
    With villainy
    And with their falsity
    Would untune my song's notes,
    Your hideous deceits.
Enter not here, lawyers insatiable,
Ushers, lawyers' clerks, devourers of the people,

Holders of office, scribes, and pharisees,
Ancient judges who tie up good citizens
Like stray dogs with cord on their necks,
Your reward is earned now, and it is the gibbet.
So go and bray there. Here is done no violence,
Such as in your courts sets men fighting lawsuits.
    Lawsuits and wrangling
    Set us not jangling;
    We come here for pleasure.
    But may your leisure
    Be filled up with tangling
    Lawsuits and wrangling.
Enter not here, miserly usurers,
Gluttons and lechers, everlasting gatherers,
Tricksters and swindlers, mean pettifoggers,
Hunchbacked and snub-nosed, who in your lockers
Never have enough of gold coin and silver.
However much you pocket you're never satisfied.
You pile up still more, you mean-featured dastards,
May cruel death for this spoil your faces.
    Most hideous of faces,
    Take them and their grimaces,
    Shave them elsewhere, for here
    They're out of place, I fear.
    Shift them to other places,
    Most hideous of faces.
Enter not here, you rambling mastiff curs,
Morning nor evening, jealous, old and spiteful,
Nor you either, seditious mutineers,
Spirits, goblins, and fond husbands' familiars,
Greeks or Latins, more to be feared than wolves,
Nor you with your sores, gnawed to the bone by pox,
Take your ulcers elsewhere and show them to others,
Scabby from head to toe and brimful of dishonour,
    Grace, honour, praise, and light
    Are here our sole delight;
    Of them we make our song,
    Our limbs are sound and strong.
    This blessing fills us quite,
    Grace, honour, praise, and light.
Enter in here, and you shall be most welcome,
And having come, stay noble gentlemen!
Here is the place where income comes in well,
And having come affords good entertainment
For great and small, though thousands of them come.
Be then my cronies, my especial favourites,
Merry and nimble, jolly, gay, and sprightly,
And, in a word, the best of good companions.
    All worthy gentlemen,
    Keen witted and serene,
    From every coarseness free,
    Here find civility,
    Among your hosts will reign,
    All worthy gentlemen.
Enter in here, you who preach with vigour
Christ's Holy Gospel, never mind who scoffs,
Here you will find a refuge and a tower
Against the foeman's error, the picked arguments,
Which falsely seek to spread about their poison.
Enter, here let us found a faith profound,

And then let us confound by speech and writing,
All that are the foemen of the Holy Writ.
   Our Holy Writ and Word
   For ever shall be heard   80
   In this most holy spot.
   Each wears it on his heart,
   Each wears it as a sword,
   Our Holy Writ and Word.
Enter in here, you ladies of high lineage,
Here be frank and fearless, enter gaily in,
Flowers of all beauty, with heaven in your faces,
Upright in bearing, modest in behaviour,
Here you will find the dwelling-place of honour.
That noble gentleman who of this place was donor,   90
And gives rewards, has destined it for you.
He has provided gold sufficient for its upkeep.
   Gold freely given,
   A man's freely shriven,
   In exchange for awards.
   For it brings rewards
   To all mortal men,
   Gold freely given.

. . .

The Rules According to Which the Thélèmites Lived

All their life was regulated not by laws, statutes, or rules,   1
but according to their free will and pleasure. They rose
from bed when they pleased, and drank, ate, worked, and
slept when the fancy seized them. Nobody woke them; nobody compelled them either to eat or to drink, or to do
anything else whatever. So it was that Gargantua had established it. In their rules there was only one clause:

Do what you will

because people who are free, well-born, well-bred, and
easy in honest company have a natural spur and instinct
which drives them to virtuous deeds and deflects them
from vice; and this they called honour. When these same
men are depressed and enslaved by vile constraint and
subjection, they use this noble quality which once impelled them freely towards virtue, to throw off and break
this yoke of slavery. For we always strive after things forbidden and covet what is denied us.

Making use of this liberty, they most laudably rivalled
one another in all of them doing what they saw pleased one.
If some man or woman said, 'Let us drink,' they all drank; if
he or she said, 'Let us play,' they all played; if it was 'Let us
go and amuse ourselves in the fields,' everyone went there.
If it were for hawking or hunting, the ladies, mounted on
fine mares, with their grand palfreys following, each carried
on their daintily gloved wrists a sparrow-hawk, a lanneret,
or a merlin, the men carrying the other birds.

So nobly were they instructed that there was not a
man or woman among them who could not read, write,
sing, play musical instruments, speak five or six languages, and compose in them both verse and prose. Never
were seen such worthy knights, so valiant, so nimble both
on foot and horse; knights more vigorous, more agile,
handier with all weapons than they were. Never were seen
ladies so good-looking, so dainty, less tiresome, more
skilled with the fingers and the needle, and in every free
and honest womanly pursuit than they were.

For that reason, when the time came that anyone in
that abbey, either at his parents' request or for any other
reason, wished to leave it, he took with him one of the
ladies, the one who had accepted him as her admirer, and
they were married to one another; and if at Thélème they
had lived in devotion and friendship, they lived in still
greater devotion and friendship when they were married.
Indeed, they loved one another to the end of their days as
much as they had done on their wedding day.

—ɯ—

MICHEL DE MONTAIGNE

Selection from *Essays*

The essay is ancient in form but the name is modern, coined by the French writer Montaigne in his *Es-*
says (from the French, *essai*, "attempt"), the first series published in 1580. Montaigne's personal essays
were "attempts" at self-definition, to discover a sane and kindly way of living. With quiet authority,
yet treating all truths as opinions, these essays impress his readers, then and now. His works made
the essay the West's most versatile literary form.

   In form, Montaigne's essays are rambling and long (most run to several thousand words) and
cover diverse topics (Smells, The Affection of Fathers for their Children, and The Length of Life). They
are learned, yet jargon free; serious, yet marked by dry wit; and based on personal experience, while
making points applicable to all. Widely read, Montaigne packed his pages with ideas from Plato (see
Phaedo and *The Republic*), Plutarch, Cicero (see *On the Republic*), St. Augustine (see *Confessions*), and his

MICHEL DE MONTAIGNE | Selection from *Essays*   **25**

own contemporaries, without always giving them credit. The result was a style linking pagan and Christian antiquity with the modern era.

Montaigne's constant subject is himself. Michel Eyquem de Montaigne (1533–1592) lived a divided life. He was a highly public figure (as counselor to the *Parlement* [law court] of Bordeaux, 1561–1570, and mayor of Bordeaux, 1581–1585), and he was a quiet philosopher, devoting himself to reading and writing. He worked on the *Essays* from 1572 until his death. With few references to career and family, the essays paint a "self-portrait" of his body, mind, and character. Driven by self-awareness—unique in this period but common today—he offers a running commentary on his kidney stones, eating habits, and vanity. He claimed he was "various and wavering," and the essays demonstrate these qualities in frequent digressions and shifting points of view.

What ultimately gives unity to the *Essays* is Montaigne's growing skepticism. He was repulsed by the fanatical wars between Protestants and Catholics that engulfed France and Europe at this time. In private siding with Catholic tradition, he nevertheless, in his essays, attached little weight to Christian ethics. Nor did he find in the ancient philosophies a moral code able to control humanity. He concluded that humans were vain and doomed to doubts—a view often voiced in the Age of Mannerism (1520–1600), a period marked by anti-Renaissance norms and the belief in human depravity.

Reading the Selection

"Of Cannibals" is part of Chapter XXXI of Book I of the *Essays*. It reflected Montaigne's knowledge of the New World, which was gleaned from the works of historians, including those who detailed the horrors of the conquest, or heard from American Indians themselves in France. Montaigne learned of the "cannibals" from Antarctic France (Brazil) in a work (1557) by Durand de Villegaignon, a French noble.

As horizons opened in the New World, old certainties gave way to doubts about European values. Montaigne, brought face-to-face with New World "cannibals," reacted with unusual (for his time) insight: "each man calls barbarism whatever is not his own practice"—one of the West's first instances of cultural relativism.

Montaigne's cultural relativism has been termed "primitivism," meaning respect for barbarous peoples and admiration for much of their culture based on an understanding of their motives. It resembles the "noble savage" belief of Rousseau (see *Confessions*), except that Montaigne accepted that savages can be as cruel as Europeans.

―⁓―

Book I

Chapter XXXI. Of Cannibals

When King Pyrrhus passed over into Italy, after he had reconnoitered the formation of the army that the Romans were sending to meet him, he said: "I do not know what barbarians these are" (for so the Greeks called all foreign nations), "but the formation of this army that I see is not at all barbarous." The Greeks said as much of the army that Flaminius brought into the country, and so did Philip, seeing from a knoll the order and distribution of the Roman camp, in his kingdom, under Publius Sulpicius Galba. Thus we should beware of clinging to vulgar opinions, and judge things by reason's way, not by popular say.

I had with me for a long time a man who had lived for ten or twelve years in that other world which has been discovered in our century, in the place where Villegaignon landed, and which he called Antarctic France. This discovery of a boundless country seems worthy of consideration.

I don't know if I can guarantee that some other such discovery will not be made in the future, so many personages greater than ourselves having been mistaken about this one. I am afraid we have eyes bigger than our stomachs, and more curiosity than capacity. We embrace everything, but we clasp only wind.

Plato brings in Solon, telling how he had learned from the priests of the city of Saïs in Egypt that in days of old, before the Flood, there was a great island named Atlantis, right at the mouth of the Strait of Gibraltar, which contained more land than Africa and Asia put together, and that the kings of that country, who not only possessed that island but had stretched out so far on the mainland that they held the breadth of Africa as far as Egypt, and the length of Europe as far as Tuscany, undertook to step over into Asia and subjugate all the nations that border on the Mediterranean, as far as the Black Sea; and for this purpose crossed the Spains, Gaul, Italy, as far as Greece, where the Athenians checked them; but that some time after, both the Athenians and themselves and their island were swallowed up by the Flood.

It is quite likely that that extreme devastation of waters made amazing changes in the habitations of the earth, as people maintain that the sea cut off Sicily from Italy—

'Tis said an earthquake once asunder tore
These lands with dreadful havoc, which before
Formed but one land, one coast

VIRGIL

—Cyprus from Syria, the island of Euboea from the mainland of Boeotia; and elsewhere joined lands that were divided, filling the channels between them with sand and mud:

A sterile marsh, long fit for rowing, now
Feeds neighbor towns, and feels the heavy plow.

HORACE

But there is no great likelihood that that island was the new world which we have just discovered; for it almost touched Spain, and it would be an incredible result of a flood to have forced it away as far as it is, more than twelve hundred leagues; besides, the travels of the moderns have already almost revealed that it is not an island, but a mainland connected with the East Indies on one side, and elsewhere with the lands under the two poles; or, if it is separated from them, it is by so narrow a strait and interval that it does not deserve to be called an island on that account.

It seems that there are movements, some natural, others feverish, in these great bodies, just as in our own. When I consider the inroads that my river, the Dordogne, is making in my lifetime into the right bank in its descent, and that in twenty years it has gained so much ground and stolen away the foundations of several buildings, I clearly see that this is an extraordinary disturbance; for if it had always gone at this rate, or was to do so in the future, the face of the world would be turned topsy-turvy. But rivers are subject to changes: now they overflow in one direction, now in another, now they keep to their course. I am not speaking of the sudden inundations whose causes are manifest. In Médoc, along the seashore, my brother, the sieur d'Arsac, can see an estate of his buried under the sands that the sea spews forth; the tops of some buildings are still visible; his farms and domains have changed into very thin pasturage. The inhabitants say that for some time the sea has been pushing toward them so hard that they have lost four leagues of land. These sands are its harbingers; and we see great dunes of moving sand that march half a league ahead of it and keep conquering land.

The other testimony of antiquity with which some would connect this discovery is in Aristotle, at least if that little book *Of Unheard-of Wonders* is by him. He there relates that certain Carthaginians, after setting out upon the Atlantic Ocean from the Strait of Gibraltar and sailing a long time, at last discovered a great fertile island, all clothed in woods and watered by great deep rivers, far remote from any mainland; and that they, and others since, attracted by the goodness and fertility of the soil, went there with their wives and children, and began to settle there. The lords of Carthage, seeing that their country was gradually becoming depopulated, expressly forbade anyone to go there any more, on pain of death, and drove out these new inhabitants, fearing, it is said, that in course of time they might come to multiply so greatly as to supplant their former masters and ruin their state. This story of Aristotle does not fit our new lands any better than the other.

This man I had was a simple, crude fellow—a character fit to bear true witness; for clever people observe more things and more curiously, but they interpret them; and to lend weight and conviction to their interpretation, they cannot help altering history a little. They never show you things as they are, but bend and disguise them according to the way they have seen them; and to give credence to their judgment and attract you to it, they are prone to add something to their matter, to stretch it out and amplify it. We need a man either very honest, or so simple that he has not the stuff to build up false inventions and give them plausibility; and wedded to no theory. Such was my man; and besides this, he at various times brought sailors and merchants, whom he had known on that trip, to see me. So I content myself with his information, without inquiring what the cosmographers say about it.

We ought to have topographers who would give us an exact account of the places where they have been. But because they have over us the advantage of having seen Palestine, they want to enjoy the privilege of telling us news about all the rest of the world. I would like everyone to write what he knows, and as much as he knows, not only in this, but in all other subjects; for a man may have some special knowledge and experience of the nature of a river or a fountain, who in other matters knows only what everybody knows. However, to circulate this little scrap of knowledge, he will undertake to write the whole of physics. From this vice spring many great abuses.

Now, to return to my subject, I think there is nothing barbarous and savage in that nation, from what I have been told, except that each man calls barbarism whatever is not his own practice; for indeed it seems we have no other test of truth and reason than the example and pattern of the opinions and customs of the country we live in. *There* is always the perfect religion, the perfect government, the perfect and accomplished manners in all things. Those people are wild, just as we call wild the fruits that Nature has produced by herself and in her normal course; whereas really it is those that we have changed artificially and led astray from the common order, that we should rather call wild. The former retain alive and vigorous their genuine, their most useful and natural, virtues and properties, which we have debased in the latter in adapting them to gratify our corrupted taste. And yet for all that, the savor and delicacy of some uncultivated fruits of those countries is quite as excellent, even to our taste, as that of our own. It is not reasonable that art should win the place of honor over our great and powerful mother Nature. We have so overloaded the beauty and richness of her works by our inventions that we have quite smothered her. Yet wherever her purity shines forth, she wonderfully puts to shame our vain and frivolous attempts:

> *Ivy comes readier without our care;*
> *In lonely caves the arbutus grows more fair;*
> *No art with artless bird song can compare.*
>
> PROPERTIUS

All our efforts cannot even succeed in reproducing the nest of the tiniest little bird, its contexture, its beauty and convenience; or even the web of the puny spider. All things, says Plato, are produced by nature, by fortune, or by art; the greatest and most beautiful by one or the other of the first two, the least and most imperfect by the last.

These nations, then, seem to me barbarous in this sense, that they have been fashioned very little by the human mind, and are still very close to their original naturalness. The laws of nature still rule them, very little corrupted by ours; and they are in such a state of purity that I am sometimes vexed that they were unknown earlier, in the days when there were men able to judge them better than we. I am sorry that Lycurgus and Plato did not know of them; for it seems to me that what we actually see in these nations surpasses not only all the pictures in which poets have idealized the golden age and all their inventions in imagining a happy state of man, but also the conceptions and the very desire of philosophy. They could not imagine a naturalness so pure and simple as we see by experience; nor could they believe that our society could be maintained with so little artifice and human solder. This is a nation, I should say to Plato, in which there is no sort of traffic, no knowledge of letters, no science of numbers, no name for magistrate or for political superiority, no custom of servitude, no riches or poverty, no contracts, no successions, no partitions, no occupations but leisure ones, no care for any but common kinship, no clothes, no agriculture, no metal, no use of wine or wheat. The very words that signify lying, treachery, dissimulation, avarice, envy, belittling, pardon—unheard of. How far from this perfection would he find the republic that he imagined: *Men fresh sprung from the gods* [Seneca].

These manners nature first ordained.
VIRGIL

For the rest, they live in a country with a very pleasant and temperate climate, so that according to my witnesses it is rare to see a sick man there; and they have assured me that they never saw one palsied, bleary-eyed, toothless, or bent with age. They are settled along the sea and shut in on the land side by great high mountains, with a stretch about a hundred leagues wide in between. They have a great abundance of fish and flesh which bear no resemblance to ours, and they eat them with no other artifice than cooking. The first man who rode a horse there, though he had had dealings with them on several other trips, so horrified them in this posture that they shot him dead with arrows before they could recognize him.

Their buildings are very long, with a capacity of two or three hundred souls; they are covered with the bark of great trees, the strips reaching to the ground at one end and supporting and leaning on one another at the top, in the manner of some of our barns, whose covering hangs down to the ground and acts as a side. They have wood so hard that they cut with it and make of it their swords and grills to cook their food. Their beds are of a cotton weave, hung from the roof like those in our ships, each man having his own; for the wives sleep apart from their husbands.

They get up with the sun, and eat immediately upon rising, to last them through the day; for they take no other meal than that one. Like some other Eastern peoples, of whom Suidas tells us, who drank apart from meals, they do not drink then; but they drink several times a day, and to capacity. Their drink is made of some root, and is of the color of our claret wines. They drink it only lukewarm. This beverage keeps only two or three days; it has a slightly sharp taste, is not at all heady, is good for the stomach, and has a laxative effect upon those who are not used to it; it is a very pleasant drink for anyone who is accustomed to it. In place of bread they use a certain white substance like preserved coriander. I have tried it; it tastes sweet and a little flat.

The whole day is spent in dancing. The younger men go to hunt animals with bows. Some of the women busy themselves meanwhile with warming their drink, which is their chief duty. Some one of the old men, in the morning before they begin to eat, preaches to the whole barnful in common, walking from one end to the other, and repeating one single sentence several times until he has completed the circuit (for the buildings are fully a hundred paces long). He recommends to them only two things: valor against the enemy and love for their wives. And they never fail to point out this obligation, as their refrain, that it is their wives who keep their drink warm and seasoned.

There may be seen in several places, including my own house, specimens of their beds, of their ropes, of their wooden swords and the bracelets with which they cover their wrists in combats, and of the big canes, open at one end, by whose sound they keep time in their dances. They are close shaven all over, and shave themselves much more cleanly than we, with nothing but a wooden or stone razor. They believe that souls are immortal, and that those who have deserved well of the gods are lodged in that part of heaven where the sun rises, and the damned in the west.

They have some sort of priests and prophets, but they rarely appear before the people, having their home in the mountains. On their arrival there is a great feast and solemn assembly of several villages—each barn, as I have described it, makes up a village, and they are about one French league from each other. The prophet speaks to them in public, exhorting them to virtue and their duty; but their whole ethical science contains only these two articles: resoluteness in war and affection for their wives. He prophesies to them things to come and the results they are to expect from their undertakings, and urges them to war or holds them back from it; but this is on the condition that when he fails to prophesy correctly, and if things turn out otherwise than he has predicted, he is cut into a thousand pieces if they catch him, and condemned as a false prophet. For this reason, the prophet who has once been mistaken is never seen again.

Divination is a gift of God; that is why its abuse should be punished as imposture. Among the Scythians, when the soothsayers failed to hit the mark, they were laid, chained hand and foot, on carts full of heather and drawn by oxen, on which they were burned. Those who handle matters subject to the control of human capacity are excusable if they do the best they can. But these others, who come and trick us with assurances of an extraordinary faculty that is beyond our ken, should they not be punished for not making good their promise, and for the temerity of their imposture?

They have their wars with the nations beyond the mountains, further inland, to which they go quite naked, with no other arms than bows or wooden swords ending in a sharp point, in the manner of the tongues of our boar spears. It is astonishing what firmness they show in their combats, which never end but in slaughter and bloodshed; for as to routs and terror, they know nothing of either.

Each man brings back as his trophy the head of the enemy he has killed, and sets it up at the entrance to his dwelling. After they have treated their prisoners well for a long time with all the hospitality they can think of, each man who has a prisoner calls a great assembly of his acquaintances. He ties a rope to one of the prisoner's arms, by the end of which he holds him, a few steps away, for fear of being hurt, and gives his dearest friend the other arm to hold in the same way; and these two, in the presence of the whole assembly, kill him with their swords. This done, they roast him and eat him in common and send some pieces to their absent friends. This is not, as people think, for nourishment, as of old the Scythians used to do; it is to betoken an extreme revenge. And the proof of this came when they saw the Portuguese, who had joined forces with their adversaries, inflict a different kind of death on them when they took them prisoner, which was to bury them up to the waist, shoot the rest of their body full of arrows, and afterward hang them. They thought that these people from the other world, being men who had sown the knowledge of many vices among their neighbors and were much greater masters than themselves in every sort of wickedness, did not adopt this sort of vengeance without some reason, and that it must be more painful than their own; so they began to give up their old method and to follow this one.

I am not sorry that we notice the barbarous horror of such acts, but I am heartily sorry that, judging their faults rightly, we should be so blind to our own. I think there is more barbarity in eating a man alive than in eating him dead; and in tearing by tortures and the rack a body still full of feeling, in roasting a man bit by bit, in having him bitten and mangled by dogs and swine (as we have not only read but seen within fresh memory, not among ancient enemies, but among neighbors and fellow citizens, and what is worse, on the pretext of piety and religion), than in roasting and eating him after he is dead.

Indeed, Chrysippus and Zeno, heads of the Stoic sect, thought there was nothing wrong in using our carcasses for any purpose in case of need, and getting nourishment from them; just as our ancestors, when besieged by Caesar in the city of Alésia, resolved to relieve their famine by eating old men, women, and other people useless for fighting.

The Gascons once, 'tis said, their life renewed
By eating of such food.
                                                              JUVENAL

And physicians do not fear to use human flesh in all sorts of ways for our health, applying it either inwardly or outwardly. But there never was any opinion so disordered as to excuse treachery, disloyalty, tyranny, and cruelty, which are our ordinary vices.

So we may well call these people barbarians, in respect to the rules of reason, but not in respect to ourselves, who surpass them in every kind of barbarity.

Their warfare is wholly noble and generous, and as excusable and beautiful as this human disease can be; its only basis among them is their rivalry in valor. They are not fighting for the conquest of new lands, for they still enjoy that natural abundance that provides them without toil and trouble with all necessary things in such profusion that they have no wish to enlarge their boundaries. They are still in that happy state of desiring only as much as their natural needs demand; anything beyond that is superfluous to them.

They generally call those of the same age, brothers; those who are younger, children; and the old men are fathers to all the others. These leave to their heirs in common the full possession of their property, without division or any other title at all than just the one that Nature gives to her creatures in bringing them into the world.

If their neighbors cross the mountains to attack them and win a victory, the gain of the victor is glory, and the advantage of having proved the master in valor and virtue; for apart from this they have no use for the goods of the vanquished, and they return to their own country, where they lack neither anything necessary nor that great thing, the knowledge of how to enjoy their condition happily and be content with it. These men of ours do the same in their turn. They demand of their prisoners no other ransom than that they confess and acknowledge their defeat. But there is not one in a whole century who does not choose to die rather than to relax a single bit, by word or look, from the grandeur of an invincible courage; not one who would not rather be killed and eaten than so much as ask not to be. They treat them very freely, so that life may be all the dearer to them, and usually entertain them with threats of their coming death, of the torments they will have to suffer, the preparations that are being made for that purpose, the cutting up of their limbs, and the feast that will be made at their expense. All this is done for the sole purpose of extorting from their lips some weak or base word, or making them want to flee, so as to gain the advantage of having terrified them and broken down their firmness. For indeed, if you take it the right way, it is in this point alone that true victory lies:

It is no victory
Unless the vanquished foe admits your mastery.
                                                              CLAUDIAN

The Hungarians, very bellicose fighters, did not in olden times pursue their advantage beyond putting the enemy at their mercy. For having wrung a confession from him to this effect, they let him go unharmed and unransomed, except, at most, for exacting his promise never again to take up arms against them.

We win enough advantages over our enemies that are borrowed advantages, not really our own. It is the quality of a porter, not of valor, to have sturdier arms and legs; agility is a dead and corporeal quality; it is a stroke of luck to make our enemy stumble, or dazzle his eyes by the sunlight; it is a trick of art and technique, which may be found in a worthless coward, to be an able fencer. The worth and value of a man is in his heart and his will; there lies his real honor. Valor is the strength, not of legs and arms, but of heart and soul; it consists not in the worth of our horse or our weapons, but in our own. He who falls obstinate in his courage, *if he has fallen, he fights on his knees* [Seneca]. He who relaxes none of his assurance, no matter how great the danger of imminent death; who, giving up his soul, still looks firmly and scornfully at his enemy—he is beaten not by us, but by fortune; he is killed, not conquered.

The most valiant are sometimes the most unfortunate. Thus there are triumphant defeats that rival victories. Nor did those four sister victories, the fairest that the sun ever set eyes on—Salamis, Plataea, Mycale, and Sicily—ever dare match all their combined glory against the glory of the annihilation of King Leonidas and his men at the pass of Thermopylae.

Who ever hastened with more glorious and ambitious desire to win a battle than Captain Ischolas to lose one? Who ever secured his safety more ingeniously and painstakingly than he did his destruction? He was charged to defend a certain pass in the Peloponnesus against the Arcadians. Finding himself wholly incapable of doing this, in view of the nature of the place and the inequality of the forces, he made up his mind that all who confronted the enemy would necessarily have to remain on the field. On the other hand, deeming it unworthy both of his own virtue and magnanimity and of the Lacedaemonian name to fail in his charge, he took a middle course between these two extremes, in this way. The youngest and fittest of his band he preserved for the defense and service of their country, and sent them home; and with those whose loss was less important, he determined to hold this pass, and by their death to make the enemy buy their entry as dearly as he could. And so it turned out. For he was presently surrounded on all sides by the Arcadians, and after slaughtering a large number of them, he and his men were all put to the sword. Is there a trophy dedicated to victors that would not be more due to these vanquished? The role of true victory is in fighting, not in coming off safely; and the honor of valor consists in combating, not in beating.

To return to our story. These prisoners are so far from giving in, in spite of all that is done to them, that on the contrary, during the two or three months that they are kept, they wear a gay expression; they urge their captors to hurry and put them to the test; they defy them, insult 30

them, reproach them with their cowardice and the number of battles they have lost to the prisoners' own people.

I have a song composed by a prisoner which contains this challenge, that they should all come boldly and gather to dine off him, for they will be eating at the same time their own fathers and grandfathers, who have served to feed and nourish his body. "These muscles," he says, "this flesh and these veins are your own, poor fools that you are. You do not recognize that the substance of your ancestors' limbs is still contained in them. Savor them well; you will find in them the taste of your own flesh." An idea that certainly does not smack of barbarity. Those that paint these people dying, and who show the execution, portray the prisoner spitting in the face of his slayers and scowling at them. Indeed, to the last gasp they never stop braving and defying their enemies by word and look. Truly here are real savages by our standards; for either they must be thoroughly so, or we must be; there is an amazing distance between their character and ours.

The men there have several wives, and the higher their reputation for valor the more wives they have. It is a remarkably beautiful thing about their marriages that the same jealousy our wives have to keep us from the affection and kindness of other women, theirs have to win this for them. Being more concerned for their husbands' honor than for anything else, they strive and scheme to have as many companions as they can, since that is a sign of their husbands' valor.

Our wives will cry "Miracle!" but it is no miracle. It is a properly matrimonial virtue, but one of the highest order. In the Bible, Leah, Rachel, Sarah, and Jacob's wives gave their beautiful handmaids to their husbands; and Livia seconded the appetites of Augustus, to her own disadvantage; and Stratonice, the wife of King Deiotarus, not only lent her husband for his use a very beautiful young chambermaid in her service, but carefully brought up her children, and backed them up to succeed to their father's estates.

And lest it be thought that all this is done through a simple and servile bondage to usage and through the pressure of the authority of their ancient customs, without reasoning or judgment, and because their minds are so stupid that they cannot take any other course, I must cite some examples of their capacity. Besides the warlike song I have just quoted, I have another, a love song, which begins in this vein: "Adder, stay; stay, adder, that from the pattern of your coloring my sister may draw the fashion and the workmanship of a rich girdle that I may give to my love; so may your beauty and your pattern be forever preferred to all other serpents." This first couplet is the refrain of the song. Now I am familiar enough with poetry to be a judge of this: not only is there nothing barbarous in this fancy, but it is altogether Anacreontic. Their language, moreover, is a soft language, with an agreeable sound, somewhat like Greek in its endings.

Three of these men, ignorant of the price they will pay 35 some day, in loss of repose and happiness, for gaining knowledge of the corruptions of this side of the ocean; ignorant also of the fact that of this intercourse will come their ruin (which I suppose is already well advanced: poor wretches, to let themselves be tricked by the desire for new things, and to have left the serenity of their own sky to come and see ours!)—three of these men were at Rouen, at the time the late King Charles IX was there. The king talked to them for a long time; they were shown our ways, our splendor, the aspect of a fine city. After that, someone asked their opinion, and wanted to know what they had found most amazing. They mentioned three things, of which I have forgotten the third, and I am very sorry for it; but I still remember two of them. They said that in the first place they thought it very strange that so many grown men, bearded, strong, and armed, who were around the king (it is likely that they were talking about the Swiss of his guard) should submit to obey a child, and that one of them was not chosen to command instead. Second (they have a way in their language of speaking of men as halves of one another), they had noticed that there were among us men full and gorged with all sorts of good things, and that their other halves were beggars at their doors, emaci-

ated with hunger and poverty; and they thought it strange that these needy halves could endure such an injustice, and did not take the others by the throat, or set fire to their houses.

I had a very long talk with one of them; but I had an interpreter who followed my meaning so badly, and who was so hindered by his stupidity in taking in my ideas, that I could get hardly any satisfaction from the man. When I asked him what profit he gained from his superior position among his people (for he was a captain, and our sailors called him king), he told me that it was to march foremost in war. How many men followed him? He pointed to a piece of ground, to signify as many as such a space could hold; it might have been four or five thousand men. Did all his authority expire with the war? He said that this much remained, that when he visited the villages dependent on him, they made paths for him through the underbrush by which he might pass quite comfortably.

All this is not too bad—but what's the use? They don't wear breeches.

MIGUEL DE CERVANTES

Selection from *Don Quixote*

Cervantes's *Don Quixote*, arguably the greatest work in the Spanish language, has been one of the world's best-selling books since it appeared in the early seventeenth century. Over the centuries, this work has entertained millions with its satirical adventures of the dim-witted Don Quixote and his coarse side-kick, Sancho Panza. These unlikely heroes have been embraced by the world as lovable characters and have often been celebrated in other mediums (art, music, and films).

Don Quixote is essentially a satire on chivalry, the courtly code of the Middle Ages practiced by knights and ladies, especially in literature (see Chrètien de Troyes's *Arthurian Romances*). Chivalry was on the wane from 1400 onward, but chivalrous romances and love ballads retained their appeal in Spain throughout the 1500s. Spain's mania for the ballads and stories of chivalry led Cervantes to write this satire. More than half in love with the object of his satire, he in fact composed a book more romantically adventurous than the material he parodied.

In form, *Don Quixote* is one of the earliest novels. This should come as no surprise, since the novel form was more advanced in Spain than in the rest of Europe. This work, like early novels elsewhere (see Fielding's *The History of Tom Jones*), has a rambling structure, covering about one thousand pages. Its plot is rather planless, consisting of a string of episodes enlivened with flashes of wit and happy phrases.

Carried along on Cervantes's river of words are the ridiculous heroes, the knight Don Quixote and the son of the soil Sancho Panza. Don Quixote is a hopeless romantic whose exploits come to nothing. He is forever either the butt of the jokes of others (for instance, when he is tricked by the priest disguised as a damsel in distress) or the victim of his own madness (for example, when he mistakes an ugly serving girl for Dulcinea, the beautiful lady of his dreams). In contrast, Sancho Panza is the soul of common sense who doggedly tries to save his master from misadventures. Together, they stand for Spain's divided soul: Quixote symbolizes the self-absorbed aristocratic spirit consumed by honor and titles; Panza, the enduring peasant eternally exploited by the nobility.

These characters also embody the novel's theme—the tension between dreams and reality. To live in dreams is to build castles in the air, like Don Quixote. But life without dreams leads to despair, like Sancho Panza. As Panza rides with Quixote through filthy ditches and over rampaging pigs, he comes to love and admire the don's saintly nature, even though he considers him mad. Thus the moral is, Follow one's dreams, even though they come to naught.

For years Miguel de Cervantes (1547–1615) led a swashbuckling life as a soldier, being wounded, captured, enslaved, and ransomed. After 1580 he tried to support his family through writing and often wound up in prison. His fortune was made when Part I of *Don Quixote* was published in 1605; Part II followed in 1615.

Reading the Selection

This selection, Chapter VIII of Part I, contains the best-known episode in *Don Quixote:* Quixote attacks forty windmills, mistaking them for giants. Deaf to Panza's pleas, Quixote winds up utterly defeated. This episode is the source of the English saying "to tilt at windmills," meaning to fight with phantom enemies.

The second part of this selection deals with a Basque knight. It shows Cervantes resorting to an old literary device; he pretends that his "history" is actually a translation from an Arabic work.

Part I

Chapter VIII. Of the valorous Don Quixote's success in the dreadful and never before imagined Adventure of the Windmills, with other events worthy of happy record.

At that moment they caught sight of some thirty or forty windmills, which stand on that plain, and as soon as Don Quixote saw them he said to his squire: 'Fortune is guiding our affairs better than we could have wished. Look over there, friend Sancho Panza, where more than thirty monstrous giants appear. I intend to do battle with them and take all their lives. With their spoils we will begin to get rich, for this is a fair war, and it is a great service to God to wipe such a wicked brood from the face of the earth.'

'What giants?' asked Sancho Panza.

'Those you see there,' replied his master, 'with their long arms. Some giants have them about six miles long.'

'Take care, your worship,' said Sancho; 'those things over there are not giants but windmills, and what seem to be their arms are the sails, which are whirled round in the wind and make the millstone turn.'

'It is quite clear,' replied Don Quixote, 'that you are not experienced in this matter of adventures. They are giants, and if you are afraid, go away and say your prayers, whilst I advance and engage them in fierce and unequal battle.'

As he spoke, he dug his spurs into his steed Rocinante, paying no attention to his squire's shouted warning that beyond all doubt they were windmills and no giants he was advancing to attack. But he went on, so positive that they were giants that he neither listened to Sancho's cries nor noticed what they were, even when he got near them. Instead he went on shouting in a loud voice: 'Do not fly, cowards, vile creatures, for it is one knight alone who assails you.'

At that moment a slight wind arose, and the great sails began to move. At the sight of which Don Quixote shouted: 'Though you wield more arms than the giant Briareus, you shall pay for it!' Saying this, he commended himself with all his soul to his Lady Dulcinea, beseeching her aid in his great peril. Then, covering himself with his shield and putting his lance in the rest, he urged Rocinante forward at a full gallop and attacked the nearest windmill, thrusting his lance into the sail. But the wind turned it with such violence that it shivered his weapon in pieces, dragging the horse and his rider with it, and sent the knight rolling badly injured across the plain. Sancho Panza rushed to his assistance as fast as his ass could trot, but when he came up he found that the knight could not stir. Such a shock had Rocinante given him in their fall.

'O my goodness!' cried Sancho. 'Didn't I tell your worship to look what you were doing, for they were only windmills? Nobody could mistake them, unless he had windmills on the brain.'

'Silence, friend Sancho,' replied Don Quixote. 'Matters of war are more subject than most to continual change. What is more, I think—and that is the truth—that the same sage Friston who robbed me of my room and my books has turned those giants into windmills, to cheat me of the glory of conquering them. Such is the enmity he bears me; but in the very end his black arts shall avail him little against the goodness of my sword.'

'God send it as He will,' replied Sancho Panza, helping the knight to get up and remount Rocinante, whose shoulders were half dislocated.

As they discussed this last adventure they followed the road to the pass of Lapice where, Don Quixote said, they could not fail to find many and various adventures, as many travellers passed that way. He was much concerned, however, at the loss of his lance, and, speaking of it to his squire, remarked: 'I remember reading that a certain Spanish knight called Diego Perez de Vargas, having broken his sword in battle, tore a great bough or limb from an oak, and performed such deeds with it that day, and pounded so many Moors, that he earned the surname of the Pounder, and thus he and his descendants from that day onwards have been called Vargas y Machuca. I mention this because I propose to tear down just such a limb from the first oak we meet, as big and as good as his; and I intend to do such deeds with it that you may consider yourself most fortunate to have won the right to see them. For you will witness things which will scarcely be credited.'

'With God's help,' replied Sancho, 'and I believe it all as your worship says. But sit a bit more upright, sir, for you seem to be riding lop-sided. It must be from the bruises you got when you fell.'

'That is the truth,' replied Don Quixote. 'And if I do not complain of the pain, it is because a knight errant is not allowed to complain of any wounds, even though his entrails may be dropping out through them.'

'If that's so, I have nothing more to say,' said Sancho, 'but God knows I should be glad if your worship would complain if anything hurt you. I must say, for my part, that I have to cry out at the slightest twinge, unless this business of not complaining extends to knights errants' squires as well.'

Don Quixote could not help smiling at his squire's simplicity, and told him that he could certainly complain how and when he pleased, whether he had any cause or no, for up to that time he had never read anything to the contrary in the law of chivalry.

Sancho reminded him that it was time for dinner, but his master replied that he had need of none, but that his squire might eat whenever he pleased. With this permission Sancho settled himself as comfortably as he could on his ass and, taking out what he had put into the saddle-bags, jogged very leisurely along behind his master, eating all the while; and from time to time he raised the bottle with such relish that the best-fed publican in Malaga might have envied him. Now, as he went along like this, taking repeated gulps, he entirely forgot the promise his master had made him, and reckoned that going in search of adventures, however dangerous, was more like pleasure than hard work.

They passed that night under some trees, from one of which our knight tore down a dead branch to serve him as some sort of lance, and stuck into it the iron head of the one that had been broken. And all night Don Quixote did not sleep but thought about his Lady Dulcinea, to conform to what he had read in his books about knights errant spending many sleepless nights in woodland and desert dwelling on the memory of their ladies. Not so Sancho Panza; for, as his stomach was full, and not of chicory water, he slept right through till morning. And, if his master had not called him, neither the sunbeams, which struck him full on the face, nor the song of the birds, who in great number and very joyfully greeted the dawn of the new day, would have been enough to wake him. As he got up he made a trial of his bottle, and found it rather limper than the night before; whereat his heart sank, for he did not think they were taking the right road to remedy this defect very quickly. Don Quixote wanted no breakfast for,

as we have said, he was determined to subsist on savoury memories. Then they turned back on to the road they had been on before, towards the pass of Lapice, which they sighted about three in the afternoon.

'Here,' exclaimed Don Quixote on seeing it, 'here, brother Sancho Panza, we can steep our arms to the elbows in what they call adventures. But take note that though you see me in the greatest danger in the world, you must not put your hand to your sword to defend me, unless you know that my assailants are rabble and common folk; in which case you may come to my aid. But should they be knights, on no account will it be legal or permissible, by the laws of chivalry, for you to assist me until you are yourself knighted.'

'You may be sure, sir,' replied Sancho, 'that I shall obey your worship perfectly there. Especially as I am very peaceable by nature and all against shoving myself into brawls and quarrels. But as to defending myself, sir, I shan't take much notice of those rules, because divine law and human law allow everyone to defend himself against anyone who tries to harm him.'

'I never said otherwise,' replied Don Quixote, 'but in the matter of aiding me against knights, you must restrain your natural impulses.'

'I promise you I will,' replied Sancho, 'and I will observe this rule as strictly as the Sabbath.'

In the middle of this conversation two monks of the order of St. Benedict appeared on the road, mounted on what looked like dromedaries; for the two mules they were riding were quite as big. They were wearing riding-masks against the dust and carrying sunshades. And behind them came a coach, with four or five horsemen escorting it, and two muleteers on foot.

In the coach, as it afterwards turned out, was a Basque lady travelling to Seville to join her husband, who was going out to take up a very important post in the Indies. The monks were not of her company, but merely journeying on the same road.

Now no sooner did Don Quixote see them in the distance than he said to his squire: 'Either I am much mistaken, or this will prove the most famous adventure ever seen. For those dark shapes looming over there must, beyond all doubt, be enchanters bearing off in that coach some princess they have stolen; and it is my duty to redress this wrong with all my might.'

'This will be a worse job than the windmills,' said Sancho. 'Look, sir, those are Benedictine monks, and the coach must belong to some travellers. Listen to me, sir. Be careful what you do, and don't let the Devil deceive you.'

'I have told you,' replied Don Quixote, 'that you know very little of this subject of adventures. What I say is true, and now you will see it.'

So saying, he rode forward and took up his position in the middle of the road along which the monks were coming; and when they got so near that he thought they could hear him, he called out in a loud voice: 'Monstrous and diabolical crew! Release immediately the noble princesses whom you are forcibly carrying off in that coach, or prepare to receive instant death as the just punishment for your misdeeds.'

The monks reined in their mules, and stopped in astonishment at Don Quixote's appearance and at his speech.

'Sir Knight,' they replied, 'we are neither monstrous nor diabolical, but two monks of St Benedict travelling about our business, nor do we know whether there are any princesses being carried off in that coach or not.'

'No fair speeches for me, for I know you, perfidious scoundrels!' cried Don Quixote. Then, without waiting for their reply, he spurred Rocinante and, with his lance lowered, charged at the foremost monk with such vigour and fury that, if he had not slid from his mule, he would have been thrown to the ground and badly hurt, if not killed outright. The second monk, on seeing his companion so treated, struck his heels into his stout mule's flanks and set her galloping over the plain fleeter than the wind itself. When Sancho Panza saw the monk on the ground, he got down lightly from his ass, ran up and started to strip him of his clothes. Upon this, two servants of the monks arrived and asked him why he was stripping their master. Sancho replied that the clothes fell rightly to his share as spoils of the battle which his master, Don Quixote, had won. The lads, who did not get the joke nor understand this talk of spoils and battles, saw that Don Quixote had gone off and was talking with the ladies in the coach, and so fell upon Sancho and knocked him down. And, pulling every hair from his beard, they kicked him mercilessly, and left him stretched on the ground, breathless and stunned. Then, without a moment's hesitation, the monk remounted his mule, trembling, terrified and as white as a sheet; and as soon as he was up he spurred after his comrade, who was waiting for him some distance off, watching to see the upshot of this sudden attack. But without caring to wait for the end of the adventure, they went on their way, crossing themselves more often than if they had had the Devil himself at their backs.

Don Quixote, as we have said, was talking with the lady in the coach: 'Your fair ladyship may now dispose of yourself as you desire, for now the pride of your ravishers lies in the dust, overthrown by this strong arm of mine. And lest you be racked with doubt as to the name of your deliverer, know that I am Don Quixote de la Mancha, knight errant, adventurer and captive to the peerless and beautiful lady, Dulcinea del Toboso. And in requital of the benefit you have received from me, I would ask no more of you than to go to El Toboso and present yourself on my behalf before that lady, telling her what I have done for your deliverance.'

All that Don Quixote said was overheard by one of the squires accompanying the coach, a Basque. And when he saw that the knight would not let them pass, but was talking of their turning back at once to El Toboso, he went up to Don Quixote and, grasping his lance, addressed him in bad Castilian and worse Basque.

'Get along, you ill-gotten knight. By God who made me, if you do not leave coach I kill you, sure as I be Basque.'

Don Quixote understood him very well, and replied with great calm: 'If you were a knight, as you are not, I should have punished your rash insolence by now, you slavish creature.'

'I not gentleman? I swear you liar, as I am a Christian. You throw down lance and draw sword, and you will see you are carrying the water to the cat. Basque on land, gentleman at sea. A gentleman, by the devil, and you lie if you say otherwise!'

'"Now you shall see," said Agrages,' quoted Don Quixote, and threw his lance down on the ground. Then, drawing his sword and grasping his shield, he rushed at his antagonist, determined to take his life. When the Basque saw him coming he would have liked to get down from his mule, as it was a poor sort of hired beast and not to be trusted, but there was nothing for it but to draw his sword. He was, however, lucky enough to be near the coach, from which he was able to snatch a cushion to serve as a shield; whereupon they immediately fell to, as if they had been two mortal enemies. The rest of the party tried to pacify them, but could not; for the Basque swore in his uncouth language that if they did not let him finish the battle, he would himself kill his mistress and all who hindered him.

The lady in the coach, amazed and terrified at the sight, made the coachman drive off a little way, and sat watching the deadly struggle from a distance. In the course of the fight the Basque dealt Don Quixote a mighty blow on one shoulder, thrusting above his shield, and had our knight been without defence he would have been cleft to the waist. When Don Quixote felt the weight of that tremendous stroke he cried out aloud: 'O lady of my soul, Dulcinea, flower of beauty, come to the aid of this your knight, who for the sake of your great goodness is now in this dire peril!'

To speak, to raise his sword, to cover himself with his shield and attack the Basque: all this was the work of a moment. For he had resolved to risk everything upon a single stroke. The Basque, seeing him come on, judged Don Quixote's courage by his daring, and decided to do the same as he. So he covered himself well with his cushion and waited, unable to turn his mule in either direction, for the beast was now dead weary, and not being made for such games, could not budge a step.

Don Quixote, as we have said, rushed at the wary Basque with sword aloft, determined to cleave him to the waist; and the Basque watched, with his sword also raised and well guarded by his cushion; while all the by-standers trembled in terrified suspense, hanging upon the issue of the dreadful blows with which they threatened one another. And the lady of the coach and her waiting-women offered a thousand vows and prayers to all the images and places of devotion in Spain, that God might deliver their squire and them from the great peril they were in.

But the unfortunate thing is that the author of this history left the battle in suspense at this critical point, with the excuse that he could find no more records of Don Quixote's exploits than those related here. It is true that the second author of this work would not believe that such a curious history could have been consigned to oblivion, or that the learned of La Mancha could have been so incurious as not to have in their archives or in their registries some documents relating to this famous knight. So, strong in this opinion, he did not despair of finding the conclusion of this delightful story and, by the favour of Heaven, found it, as shall be told in our second part.

WILLIAM SHAKESPEARE

Hamlet

Excepting the Bible, Shakespeare's *Hamlet* is perhaps the West's most famous literary work. Hardly a day passes without this play being acted, either on a commercial stage or in a school or college; and many versions of the play, on film and on tape, ensure its universal visibility. Hamlet's role is usually defined as the most difficult in the theater, and many actors, and a few actresses, often choose to play Hamlet as a crown to their careers. It is so well known that the world uses the term *Hamletlike* to describe people unable to make up their minds.

The hectic world in which *Hamlet* appeared gave no forecast of the play's future greatness. First staged in 1600, the play was one of a series that William Shakespeare (1564–1616) was turning out for the nearly insatiable demands of the commercial stage. He was fresh to London in 1590 from a middle-class youth in Stratford-upon-Avon. When Shakespeare retired to gentlemanly leisure in Stratford in 1610, he had written thirty-seven dramas—almost two plays a year.

The London audiences did not want masterpieces; instead, they craved violence, ghosts, and murders galore. They wanted revenge tragedies, the most popular dramatic form in the Age of Elizabeth (1558–1603), England's golden age. This taste for blood is not surprising, for Elizabethan England made national heroes of pirate patriots like Francis Drake and accepted as normal that Protestants and Catholics should burn heretics alive. It was for this violence-filled age that Shakespeare wrote *Hamlet*, based on a bloody revenge tale that had already inspired one play during the 1580s.

Reading the Selection

Shakespeare's *Hamlet* is set at the royal Danish court. Its revenge theme is activated by the murder of old King Hamlet. Prince Hamlet, depressed by his father's death, is plunged into a court seething with intrigue, carousing, ghosts, and spies. There are also wandering actors, an oath sworn on swords, a secret letter, a deadly duel, and a hasty funeral. Lest these devices be insufficiently entertaining, Hamlet himself veers from madman to scholar to prince to swordsman before he gets his revenge. At the end, the stage is littered with corpses and the major characters are all dead.

What rescues *Hamlet* from mere melodrama and pushes it into the stratosphere of great art are Shakespeare's majestic language and complete mastery of psychology. The theater, reborn in medieval productions like *Everyman*, with its simple morals and even simpler psychology, now came to maturity in Shakespeare's hands.

Dramatis Personae

CLAUDIUS *King of Denmark*

HAMLET *Son to the late, and nephew to the present king*

POLONIUS *Lord Chamberlain*

HORATIO *Friend to Hamlet*

LAERTES *Son to Polonius*

VOLTIMAND
CORNELIUS
ROSENCRANTZ } *Courtiers*
GUILDENSTERN
OSRIC
A GENTLEMAN

A PRIEST

MARCELLUS } *Officers*
BERNARDO

FRANCISCO *A soldier*

REYNALDO *Servant to Polonius*

PLAYERS

TWO CLOWNS *Grave-diggers*

FORTINBRAS *Prince of Norway*

A CAPTAIN

ENGLISH AMBASSADORS

GERTRUDE *Queen of Denmark, and mother to Hamlet*

OPHELIA *Daughter to Polonius*

LORDS, LADIES, OFFICERS, SOLDIERS, SAILORS, MESSENGERS, *and* OTHER ATTENDANTS

GHOST *of Hamlet's father*

SCENE—DENMARK

Act I

Scene I—Elsinore. A platform before the castle

The two opening scenes put the spectator in full possession of the situation of affairs in Denmark. The death and character of the late king, his reappearance to denote some unknown evil, the threats of war, and the consequent need for strong men are emphasized in the first; the second adds the personal relations of HAMLET *with the royal house, and depicts his state of mind at the beginning of the action.*

HORATIO is carefully differentiated from MARCELLUS, BERNARDO, and FRANCISCO: they are unlettered soldiers; he is a scholar, and, as such, has his touches both of imagination and scepticism.

The scene opens amid nervous suspense; there is a tradition that it was written in a charnel-house. "'Tis bitter cold," and silent, and the watcher is "sick at heart." On two previous nights the GHOST *has appeared, to* BERNARDO *and* MARCELLUS. *BERNARDO's agitation shows itself in the way he challenges the guard, instead of waiting to be challenged.*

FRANCISCO *at his post. Enter to him* BERNARDO

BER.   Who's there?   1
FRAN.   Nay, answer me: stand, and unfold yourself.
BER.   Long live the king!
FRAN.   Bernardo?
BER.   He.
FRAN.   You come most carefully upon your hour.
BER.   'Tis now struck twelve; get thee to bed, Francisco.
FRAN.   For this relief much thanks: 'tis bitter cold,
And I am sick at heart.
BER.   Have you had quiet guard?   10
FRAN.   Not a mouse stirring.
BER.   Well, good night.
If you do meet Horatio and Marcellus,
The rivals of my watch, bid them make haste.
FRAN.   I think I hear them. Stand, ho! Who's there?

Enter HORATIO *and* MARCELLUS

HOR.   Friends to this ground.
MAR.   And liegemen to the Dane.
FRAN.   Give you good night.
MAR.   O, farewell, honest soldier:
Who hath relieved you?   20
FRAN.   Bernardo has my place.
Give you good night.   [*Exit.*
MAR.   Holla! Bernardo!
BER.   Say,
What, is Horatio there?
HOR.   A piece of him.
BER.   Welcome, Horatio: welcome, good Marcellus.
HOR.   What, has this thing appear'd again tonight?
BER.   I have seen nothing.
MAR.   Horatio says 'tis but our fantasy,   30
And will not let belief take hold of him
Touching this dreaded sight, twice seen of us:
Therefore I have entreated him along

With us to watch the minutes of this night;
That if again this apparition come,
He may approve our eyes and speak to it.
HOR.   Tush, tush, 't will not appear.
BER.   Sit down awhile;
And let us once again assail your ears,
That are so fortified against our story
What we have two nights seen.   40
HOR.   Well, sit we down,
And let us hear Bernardo speak of this.
BER.   Last night of all,
When yond same star that's westward from the pole
Had made his course to illume that part of heaven
Where now it burns, Marcellus and myself,
The bell then beating one,—

Enter GHOST

MAR.   Peace, break thee off; look, where it comes again!
BER.   In the same figure, like the king that's dead. 50
MAR.   Thou art a scholar; speak to it, Horatio.
BER.   Looks it not like the king? mark it, Horatio.
HOR.   Most like: it harrows me with fear and wonder.
BER.   It would be spoke to.
MAR.   Question it, Horatio.
HOR.   What art thou that usurp'st this time of night,
Together with that fair and warlike form
In which the majesty of buried Denmark
Did sometimes march? by heaven I charge thee, speak!
MAR.   It is offended.   60
BER.   See, it stalks away!
HOR.   Stay! speak, speak! I charge thee, speak!
                                    [*Exit Ghost.*
MAR.   'Tis gone, and will not answer.
BER.   How now, Horatio! you tremble and look pale:
Is not this something more than fantasy?
What think you on 't?
HOR.   Before my God, I might not this believe
Without the sensible and true avouch
Of mine own eyes.
MAR.   Is it not like the king?   70
HOR.   As thou art to thyself:
Such was the very armour he had on
When he the ambitious Norway combated;
So frown'd he once, when, in an angry parle,
He smote the sledded pole-axe on the ice.
'Tis strange.
MAR.   Thus twice before, and jump at this dead hour,
With martial stalk hath he gone by our watch.
HOR.   In what particular thought to work I know not;
But in the gross and scope of my opinion,   80
This bodes some strange eruption to our state.
MAR.   Good now, sit down, and tell me, he that knows,
Why this same strict and most observant watch
So nightly toils the subject of the land,
And why such daily cast of brazen cannon,

And foreign mart for implements of war;
Why such impress of shipwrights, whose sore task
Does not divide the Sunday from the week;
What might be toward, that this sweaty haste
Doth make the night joint-labourer with the day: 90
Who is 't that can inform me?
HOR.   That can I;
At least, the whisper goes so. Our last king,
Whose image even but now appear'd to us,
Was, as you know, by Fortinbras of Norway,
Thereto prick'd on by a most emulate pride,
Dared to the combat; in which our valiant Hamlet—
For so this side of our known world esteem'd him—
Did slay this Fortinbras; who, by a seal'd compact,
Well ratified by law and heraldry, 100
Did forfeit, with his life, all those his lands
Which he stood seized of, to the conqueror:
Against the which, a moiety competent
Was gaged by our king; which had return'd
To the inheritance of Fortinbras,
Had he been vanquisher; as, by the same covenant,
And carriage of the article design'd,
His fell to Hamlet. Now, sir, young Fortinbras,
Of unapproved mettle hot and full,
Hath in the skirts of Norway here and there 110
Shark'd up a list of lawless resolutes,
For food and diet, to some enterprise
That hath a stomach in 't; which is no other—
As it doth well appear unto our state—
But to recover of us, by strong hand
And terms compulsatory, those foresaid lands
So by his father lost: and this, I take it,
Is the main motive of our preparations,
The source of this our watch and the chief head
Of this post-haste and romage in the land. 120
BER.   I think it be no other but e'en so:
Well may it sort that this portentous figure
Comes armed through our watch; so like the king
That was and is the question of these wars.
HOR.   A mote it is to trouble the mind's eye.
In the most high and palmy state of Rome,
A little ere the mightiest Julius fell,
The graves stood tenantless and the sheeted dead
Did squeak and gibber in the Roman streets:
As stars with trains of fire and dews of blood, 130
Disasters in the sun; and the moist star
Upon whose influence Neptune's empire stands
Was sick almost to doomsday with eclipse:
And even the like precurse of fierce events,
As harbingers preceding still the fates
And prologue to the omen coming on,
Have heaven and earth together demonstrated
Unto our climatures and countrymen.—
But soft, behold! lo, where it comes again!

Re-enter GHOST

I'll cross it, though it blast me. Stay, illusion! 140
If thou hast any sound, or use of voice   [*It spreads its arms.*
Speak to me:
If there be any good thing to be done,

That may to thee do ease and grace to me,
Speak to me:
If thou art privy to thy country's fate,
Which, happily, foreknowing may avoid,
O, speak!
Or if thou hast uphoarded in thy life
Extorted treasure in the womb of earth, 150
For which, they say, you spirits oft walk in death,
                              [*The cock crows.*
Speak of it: stay, and speak! Stop it, Marcellus.
MAR.   Shall I strike at it with my partisan?
HOR.   Do, if it will not stand.
BER.   'Tis here!
HOR.   'Tis here!
MAR.   'Tis gone!   [*Exit Ghost.*
We do it wrong, being so majestical,
To offer it the show of violence;
For it is, as the air, invulnerable, 160
And our vain blows malicious mockery.
BER.   It was about to speak, when the cock crew.
HOR.   And then it started like a guilty thing
Upon a fearful summons. I have heard,
The cock, that is the trumpet to the morn,
Doth with his lofty and shrill-sounding throat
Awake the god of day; and, at his warning,
Whether in sea or fire, in earth or air,
The extravagant and erring spirit hies
To his confine: and of the truth herein 170
This present object made probation.
MAR.   It faded on the crowing of the cock.
Some say that ever 'gainst that season comes
Wherein our Saviour's birth is celebrated,
The bird of dawning singeth all night long:
And then, they say, no spirit dare stir abroad;
The nights are wholesome; then no planets strike,
No fairy takes, nor witch hath power to charm,
So hallow'd and so gracious is the time.
HOR.   So have I heard and do in part believe it. 180
But, look, the morn, in russet mantle clad,
Walks o'er the dew of yon high eastward hill:
Break we our watch up; and by my advice,
Let us impart what we have seen to-night
Unto young Hamlet; for, upon my life,
This spirit, dumb to us, will speak to him.
Do you consent we shall acquaint him with it,
As needful in our loves, fitting our duty?
MAR.   Let's do 't, I pray; and I this morning know
Where we shall find him most conveniently. [*Exeunt.* 190

Scene II—A room of state in the castle

HAMLET's *brief dialogue with the* KING *and* QUEEN *and his subsequent soliloquy sufficiently acquaint us with his mood. He has no idea of his uncle's crime, though he detests his character; but his moral sense has received a severe shock from his mother's marriage. The whole world appears to him, in consequence, under the dominion of evil; he would gladly be quit of it. But that cannot be, and, moreover, he cannot do anything, nor even utter his feelings. He must take refuge in irony and sarcasm, or, when possible, in silence.*
    CLAUDIUS *is a hypocrite, but his hypocrisy is that of a statesman; he plays his part with a dignity and a keen insight into what is*

needful for the welfare of the state, which explains how the council
came to choose him king.

The scene opens with a bridal procession. It is the custom of the
stage for HAMLET *to come on last, slowly and reluctantly, and clad*
in black, among the glittering draperies of the court.

Enter CLAUDIUS, *King of Denmark,* GERTRUDE *the Queen,*
HAMLET, POLONIUS, LAERTES *and his sister* OPHELIA,
LORDS ATTENDANT

KING.   Though yet of Hamlet our dear brother's death   1
The memory be green, and that it us befitted
To bear our hearts in grief and our whole kingdom
To be contracted in one brow of woe,
Yet so far hath discretion fought with nature
That we with wisest sorrow think on him,
Together with remembrance of ourselves.
Therefore our sometime sister, now our queen,
The imperial jointress to this warlike state,
Have we, as 't were with a defeated joy,—   10
With an auspicious and a dropping eye,
With mirth in funeral and with dirge in marriage,
In equal scale weighing delight and dole,—
Taken to wife: nor have we herein barr'd
Your better wisdoms, which have freely gone
With this affair along. For all, our thanks.
Now follows, that you know, young Fortinbras,
Holding a weak supposal of our worth,
Or thinking by our late dear brother's death
Our state to be disjoint and out of frame,   20
Colleagued with the dream of his advantage,
He hath not fail'd to pester us with message,
Importing the surrender of those lands
Lost by his father, with all bonds of law,
To our most valiant brother. So much for him.
Now for ourself and for this time of meeting:
Thus much the business is: we have here writ
To Norway, uncle of young Fortinbras,—
Who, impotent and bed-rid, scarcely hears
Of this his nephew's purpose,—to suppress   30
His further gait herein; in that the levies,
The lists and full proportions, are all made
Out of his subject: and we here dispatch
You, good Cornelius, and you, Voltimand,
For bearers of this greeting to old Norway;
Giving to you no further personal power
To business with the king, more than the scope
Of these delated articles allow.
Farewell, and let your haste commend your duty.
COR. }
VOL. }   In that and all things will we show our duty.   40
KING.   We doubt it nothing: heartily farewell.
                        [*Exeunt Voltimand and Cornelius.*
And now, Laertes, what's the news with you?
You told us of some suit; what is 't, Laertes?
You cannot speak of reason to the Dane,
And lose your voice: what wouldst thou beg, Laertes,
That shall not be my offer, not thy asking?
The head is not more native to the heart,
The hand more instrumental to the mouth,
Than is the throne of Denmark to thy father.

What wouldst though have, Laertes?   50
LAER.   My dread lord,
Your leave and favour to return to France;
From whence though willingly I came to Denmark,
To show my duty in your coronation,
Yet now, I must confess, that duty done,
My thoughts and wishes bend again toward France
And bow them to your gracious leave and pardon.
KING.   Have you your father's leave? What says
    Polonius?
POL.   He hath, my lord, wrung from me my slow leave
By laboursome petition, and at last   60
Upon his will I seal'd my hard consent:
I do beseech you, give him leave to go.
KING.   Take thy fair hour, Laertes; time be thine,
And thy best graces spend it at thy will!
But now, my cousin Hamlet, and my son,—
HAM.   [*Aside*] A little more than kin, and less than kind.
KING.   How is it that the clouds still hang on you?
HAM.   Not so, my lord; I am too much i' the sun.
QUEEN.   Good Hamlet, cast thy nighted colour off,
And let thine eye look like a friend on Denmark.   70
Do not for ever with they vailed lids
Seek for thy noble father in the dust:
Thou know'st 'tis common; all that lives must die,
Passing through nature to eternity.
HAM.   Ay, madam, it is common.
QUEEN.   If it be,
Why seems it so particular with thee?
HAM.   Seems, madam! nay, it is; I know not "seems."
'Tis not alone my inky cloak, good mother,
Nor customary suits of solemn black,   80
Nor windy suspiration of forced breath,
No, nor the fruitful river in the eye,
Nor the dejected 'haviour of the visage,
Together with all forms, moods, shows of grief,
That can denote me truly: these indeed seem,
For they are actions that a man might play:
But I have that within which passeth show;
These but the trappings and the suits of woe.
KING.   'Tis sweet and commendable in your nature,
    Hamlet,
To give these mourning duties to your father: 90
But, you must know, your father lost a father;
That father lost, lost his, and the survivor bound
In filial obligation for some term
To do obsequious sorrow: but to persever
In obstinate condolement is a course
Of impious stubbornness; 'tis unmanly grief;
It shows a will most incorrect to heaven,
A heart unfortified, a mind impatient,
An understanding simple and unschool'd:
For what we know must be and is as common   100
As any the most vulgar thing to sense,
Why should we in our peevish opposition
Take it to heart? Fie! 'tis a fault to heaven,
A fault against the dead, a fault to nature,
To reason most absurd; whose common theme
Is death of fathers, and who still hath cried,
From the first corse till he that died to-day,

"This must be so." We pray you, throw to earth
This unprevailing woe, and think of us
As of a father: for let the world take note,　　　　　110
You are the most immediate to our throne;
And with no less nobility of love
Than that which dearest father bears his son,
Do I impart toward you. For your intent
In going back to school in Wittenberg,
It is most retrograde to our desire:
And we beseech you, bend you to remain
Here, in the cheer and comfort of our eye,
Our chiefest courtier, cousin, and our son.
QUEEN.　Let not thy mother lose her prayers, Hamlet:　120
I pray thee, stay with us; go not to Wittenberg.
HAM.　I shall in all my best obey you, madam.
KING.　Why, 'tis a loving and a fair reply:
Be as ourself in Denmark. Madam, come;
This gentle and unforced accord of Hamlet
Sits smiling to my heart: in grace whereof,
No jocund health that Denmark drinks to-day,
But the great cannon to the clouds shall tell,
And the king's rouse the heavens shall bruit again,
Re-speaking earthly thunder. Come away.　　　130
　　　　　　　　[*Exeunt all but Hamlet.*
HAM.　O, that this too too solid flesh would melt,
Thaw and resolve itself into a dew!
Or that the Everlasting had not fix'd
His canon 'gainst self-slaughter! O God! God!
How weary, stale, flat and unprofitable,
Seem to me all the uses of this world!
Fie on 't! ah fie! 'tis an unweeded garden,
That grows to seed; things rank and gross in nature
Possess it merely. That it should come to this!
But two months dead: nay, not so much, not two:　140
So excellent a king; that was, to this,
Hyperion to a satyr; so loving to my mother
That he might not beteem the winds of heaven
Visit her face too roughly. Heaven and earth!
Must I remember? why, she would hang on him,
As if increase of appetite had grown
By what it fed on: and yet, within a month—
Let me not think on 't—Frailty, thy name is woman!—
A little month, or ere those shoes were old
With which she follow'd my poor father's body,　150
Like Niobe, all tears:—why she, even she—
O God! a beast, that wants discourse of reason,
Would have mourn'd longer—married with my uncle,
My father's brother, but no more like my father
Than I to Hercules: within a month:
Ere yet the salt of most unrighteous tears
Had left the flushing in her galled eyes,
She married. O, most wicked speed, to post
With such dexterity to incestuous sheets!
It is not nor it cannot come to good:　　　　160
But break, my heart; for I must hold my tongue.

Enter HORATIO, MARCELLUS, *and* BERNARDO

HOR.　Hail to your lordship!
HAM.　　　　　　I am glad to see you well:

Horatio,—or I do forget myself.
HOR.　The same, my lord, and your poor servant ever.
HAM.　Sir, my good friend; I'll change that name with
　　you:
And what make you from Wittenberg, Horatio?
Marcellus?
MAR.　My good lord—
HAM.　I am very glad to see you. Good even, sir.　　170
But what, in faith, make you from Wittenberg?
HOR.　A truant disposition, good my lord.
HAM.　I would not hear your enemy say so,
Nor shall you do mine ear that violence,
To make it truster of your own report
Against yourself: I know you are no truant.
But what is your affair in Elsinore?
We'll teach you to drink deep ere you depart.
HOR.　My lord, I came to see your father's funeral.
HAM.　I pray thee, do not mock me, fellow-student;　180
I think it was to see my mother's wedding.
HOR.　Indeed, my lord, it follow'd hard upon.
HAM.　Thrift, thrift, Horatio! the funeral baked meats
Did coldly furnish forth the marriage tables.
Would I had met my dearest foe in heaven
Or ever I had seen that day, Horatio!
My father—methinks I see my father.
HOR.　Where, my lord?
HAM.　　　　　　　In my mind's eye, Horatio.
HOR.　I saw him—once; he was a goodly king.　　　190
HAM.　He was a man, take him for all in all,
I shall not look upon his like again.
HOR.　My lord, I think I saw him yesternight.
HAM.　Saw? who?
HOR.　My lord, the king your father.
HAM.　　　　　　　　　　　The king my father!
HOR.　Season your admiration for a while
With an attent ear, till I may deliver,
Upon the witness of these gentlemen,
This marvel to you.　　　　　　　　　　200
HAM.　　　　　For God's love, let me hear.
HOR.　Two nights together had these gentlemen,
Marcellus and Bernardo, on their watch,
In the dead waste and middle of the night,
Been thus encounter'd. A figure like your father,
Armed at point exactly, cap-a-pe,
Appears before them, and with solemn march
Goes slow and stately by them: thrice he walk'd
By their oppress'd and fear-surprised eyes,
Within his truncheon's length; whilst they, distill'd　210
Almost to jelly with the act of fear,
Stand dumb and speak not to him. This to me
In dreadful secrecy impart they did;
And I with them the third night kept the watch:
Where, as they had deliver'd, both in time,
Form of the thing, each word made true and good,
The apparition comes: I knew your father;
These hands are not more like.
HAM.　　　　　　　　　But where was this?
MAR.　My lord, upon the platform where we watch'd.　220
HAM.　Did you not speak to it?
HOR.　　　　　　　My lord, I did;

But answer made it none: yet once methought
It lifted up its head and did address
Itself to motion, like as it would speak;
But even then the morning cock crew loud,
And at the sound it shrunk in haste away,
And vanish'd from our sight.

HAM.   'Tis very strange.
HOR.   As I do live, my honour'd lord, 'tis true;   230
And we did think it writ down in our duty
To let you know of it.
HAM.   Indeed, indeed, sirs, but this troubles me.
Hold you the watch to-night?
MAR.⎫
BER.⎭   We do, my lord.
HAM.   Arm'd, say you?
MAR.⎫
BER.⎭   Arm'd, my lord.
HAM.   From top to toe?
MAR.⎫
BER.⎭   My lord, from head to foot.
HAM.   Then saw you not his face?   240
HOR.   Oh, yes, my lord; he wore his beaver up.
HAM.   What, look'd he frowningly?
HOR.   A countenance more in sorrow than in anger.
HAM.   Pale or red?
HOR.   Nay, very pale.
HAM.   And fix'd his eyes upon you?
HOR.   Most constantly.
HAM.   I would I had been there.
HOR.   It would have much amazed you.
HAM.   Very like, very like. Stay'd it long?   250
HOR.   While one with moderate haste might tell a
    hundred.
MAR.⎫
BER.⎭   Longer, longer.
HOR.   Not when I saw 't.
HAM.   His beard was grizzled,—no?
HOR.   It was, as I have seen it in his life,
A sable silver'd.
HAM.   I will watch to-night;
Perchance 't will walk again.
HOR.   I warrant it will.
HAM.   If it assume my noble father's person,   260
I'll speak to it, though hell itself should gape
And bid me hold my peace. I pray you all,
If you have hitherto conceal'd this sight,
Let it be tenable in your silence still;
And whatsoever else shall hap to-night,
Give it an understanding, but no tongue:
I will requite your loves. So, fare you well:
Upon the platform, 'twixt eleven and twelve,
I'll visit you.
ALL.   Our duty to your honour.   270
HAM.   Your loves, as mine to you: farewell.
                        [*Exeunt all but Hamlet.*
My father's spirit in arms! all is not well;
I doubt some foul play: would the night were come!
Till then sit still, my soul: foul deeds will rise,
Though all the earth o'erwhelm them, to men's eyes.
                                        [*Exit.*

Scene III—A room in Polonius' house

The principal elements in the situation of things at Elsinore have been put before us in the first two scenes: the need for a man of action, and the supernatural suggestion of some hidden evil in Scene I, the position and nature of HAMLET *in Scene II. The present scene completes the picture by showing the contrast to* HAMLET *afforded by the family of* POLONIUS, *who may be taken as typical of the court at Elsinore. All are carefully drawn on a lower scale than his, shallow where he is subtle, commonplace where he is original. None the less, the portrait of the gentle maiden,* OPHELIA, *is touched so as to win our sympathies. She is no mate for* HAMLET; *yet in her own sphere she is a beautiful and lovable character.* POLONIUS *is a politician without being a statesman,* LAERTES *an apt representative of gilded youth as it existed at the court of Elizabeth. Both have low ideals: the father is consumed with the conceit of his own intellect and experience, which have shown him only the lower side of humanity; the son is "Italianate," degraded in tone by his life in a foreign city. Both are incredulous, not only of the purity and honor of* HAMLET, *but of that of* OPHELIA *herself.*

Enter LAERTES *and* OPHELIA

LAER.   My necessaries are embark'd: farewell: 1
And, sister, as the winds give benefit
And convoy is assistant, do not sleep,
But let me hear from you.
OPH.   Do you doubt that?
LAER.   For Hamlet and the trifling of his favour,
Hold it a fashion and a toy in blood,
A violet in the youth of primy nature,
Forward, not permanent, sweet, not lasting,
The perfume and suppliance of a minute;   10
No more.
OPH.   No more but so?
LAER.   Think it no more:
For nature, crescent, does not grow alone
In thews and bulk, but, as this temple waxes,
The inward service of the mind and soul
Grows wide withal. Perhaps he loves you now,
And now no soil nor cautel doth besmirch
The virtue of his will: but you must fear,
His greatness weigh'd, his will is not his own;   20
For he himself is subject to his birth:
He may not, as unvalued persons do,
Carve for himself; for on his choice depends
The safety and health of this whole state;
And therefore must his choice be circumscribed
Unto the voice and yielding of that body
Whereof he is the head. Then if he says he loves you,
It fits your wisdom so far to believe it
As he in his particular act and place
May give his saying deed; which is no further   30
Than the main voice of Denmark goes withal.
Then weigh what loss your honour may sustain,
If with too credent ear you list his songs,
Or lose your heart, or your chaste treasure open
To his unmaster'd importunity.
Fear it, Ophelia, fear it, my dear sister,
And keep you in the rear of your affection,
Out of the shot and danger of desire.
The chariest maid is prodigal enough,

If she unmask her beauty to the moon: 40
Virtue itself 'scapes not calumnious strokes:
The canker galls the infants of the spring,
Too oft before their buttons be disclosed,
And in the morn and liquid dew of youth
Contagious blastments are most imminent.
Be wary then; best safety lies in fear:
Youth to itself rebels, though none else near.
OPH.   I shall the effect of this good lesson keep,
As watchman to my heart. But, good my brother,
Do not, as some ungracious pastors do, 50
Show me the steep and thorny way to heaven;
Whiles, like a puff'd and reckless libertine,
Himself the primrose path of dalliance treads,
And recks not his own rede.
LAER.   O, fear me not.
I stay too long: but here my father comes.

Enter POLONIUS

A double blessing is a double grace;
Occasion smiles upon a second leave.
POL.   Yet here, Laertes! aboard, aboard, for shame!
The wind sits in the shoulder of your sail, 60
And you are stay'd for. There; my blessing with thee!
And these few precepts in thy memory
See thou character. Give thy thoughts no tongue,
Nor any unproportion'd thought his act.
Be thou familiar, but by no means vulgar.
Those friends thou hast, and their adoption tried,
Grapple them to thy soul with hoops of steel;
But do not dull thy palm with entertainment
Of each new-hatch'd, unfledged comrade. Beware
Of entrance to a quarrel, but being in, 70
Bear 't that the opposed may beware of thee.
Give every man thy ear, but few thy voice;
Take each man's censure, but reserve thy judgement.
Costly thy habit as thy purse can buy,
But not express'd in fancy; rich, not gaudy;
For the apparel oft proclaims the man,
And they in France of the best rank and station
Are of a most select and generous choice in that.
Neither a borrower nor a lender be;
For loan oft loses both itself and friend, 80
And borrowing dulls the edge of husbandry.
This above all: to thine own self be true,
And it must follow, as the night the day,
Thou canst not then be false to any man.
Farewell: my blessing season this in thee!
LAER.   Most humbly do I take my leave, my lord.
POL.   The time invites you; go; your servants tend.
LAER.   Farewell, Ophelia; and remember well
What I have said to you.
OPH.   'Tis in my memory lock'd, 90
And you yourself shall keep the key of it.
LAER.   Farewell.   [*Exit.*
POL.   What is 't, Ophelia, he hath said to you?
OPH.   So please you, something touching the Lord
    Hamlet.
POL.   Marry, well bethought:
'Tis told me, he hath very oft of late

Given private time to you; and you yourself
Have of your audience been most free and bounteous:
If it be so, as so 'tis put on me,
And that in way of caution, I must tell you, 100
You do not understand yourself so clearly
As it behoves my daughter and your honour.
What is between you? give me up the truth.
OPH.   He hath, my lord, of late made many tenders
Of his affection to me.
POL.   Affection! pooh! you speak like a green girl,
Unsifted in such perilous circumstance.
Do you believe his tenders, as you call them?
OPH.   I do not know, my lord, what I should think.
POL.   Marry, I'll teach you: think yourself a baby; 110
That you have ta'en these tenders for true pay,
Which are not sterling. Tender yourself more dearly;
Or—not to crack the wind of the poor phrase,
Running it thus—you'll tender me a fool.
OPH.   My lord, he hath importuned me with love
In honourable fashion.
POL.   Ay, fashion you may call it; go to, go to.
OPH.   And hath given countenance to his speech, my
    lord,
With almost all the holy vows of heaven.
POL.   Ay, springes to catch woodcocks. I do know, 120
When the blood burns, how prodigal the soul
Lends the tongue vows: these blazes, daughter,
Giving more light than heat, extinct in both,
Even in their promise, as it is a-making,
You must not take for fire. From this time
Be somewhat scanter of your maiden presence;
Set your entreatments at a higher rate
Than a command to parley. For Lord Hamlet,
Believe so much in him, that he is young,
And with a larger tether may he walk 130
Than may be given you: in few, Ophelia,
Do not believe his vows; for they are brokers,
Not of that dye which their investments show,
But mere implorators of unholy suits,
Breathing like sanctified and pious bonds,
The better to beguile. This is for all:
I would not, in plain terms, from this time forth,
Have you so slander any moment leisure,
As to give words or talk with the Lord Hamlet.
Look to 't, I charge you: come your ways. 140
OPH.   I shall obey my lord.   [*Exeunt.*

Scene IV—The platform

*The elements of the tragedy are now before the mind of the spectator;
the revelation of the* GHOST *is the spark that sets them in motion.
With this the first act, or prologue to the main action, naturally
ends.* HAMLET'*s problem is presented to him; the question is,
"What will he make of it?" This must be decided in the course of the
play by the laws of his character and circumstances. His first impulse is to believe and to revenge; yet, even so early as this, the
hastily conceived design of simulating madness is a foretaste of
what is to follow.*

*Scenes IV and V are dramatically continuous; they are only
separated scenically by the need for a slight change of locality.*

Enter HAMLET, HORATIO, *and* MARCELLUS

HAM.   The air bites shrewdly; it is very cold.   1
HOR.   It is a nipping and an eager air.
HAM.   What hour now?
HOR.   I think it lacks of twelve.
MAR.   No, it is struck.
HOR.   Indeed? I heard it not: then it draws near the
   season
Wherein the spirit held his wont to walk.
         [*A flourish of trumpets, and ordnance shot off, within.*
What does this mean, my lord?
HAM.   The king doth wake to-night and takes his rouse,
Keeps wassail, and the swaggering up-spring reels;   10
And, as he drains his draughts of Rhenish down,
The kettle-drum and trumpet thus bray out
The triumph of his pledge.
HOR.   Is it a custom?
HAM.   Ay, marry, is 't:
But to my mind, though I am native here
And to the manner born, it is a custom
More honour'd in the breach than the observance.
This heavy-headed revel east and west
Makes us traduced and tax'd of other nations: 20
They clepe us drunkards, and with swinish phrase
Soil our addition; and indeed it takes
From our achievements, though perform'd at height
The pith and marrow of our attribute.
So, oft it chances in particular men,
That for some vicious mole of nature in them,
As, in their birth—wherein they are not guilty,
Since nature cannot choose his origin—
By the o'ergrowth of some complexion,
Oft breaking down the pales and forts of reason,   30
Or by some habit that too much o'er-leavens
The form of plausive manners, that these men,
Carrying, I say, the stamp of one defect,
Being nature's livery, or fortune's star,—
Their virtues else—be they as pure as grace,
As infinite as man may undergo—
Shall in the general censure take corruption
From that particular fault: the dram of eale
Doth all the noble substance of a doubt
To his own scandal.   40
HOR.   Look, my lord, it comes!

Enter GHOST

HAM.   Angels and ministers of grace defend us!
Be thou a spirit of health or goblin damn'd,
Bring with thee airs from heaven or blasts from hell,
Be thy intents wicked or charitable,
Thou comest in such a questionable shape
That I will speak to thee: I'll call thee Hamlet,
King, father, royal Dane: O, answer me!
Let me not burst in ignorance; but tell
Why thy canonized bones, hearsed in death,   50
Have burst their cerements; why the sepulchre,
Wherein we saw thee quietly inurn'd,
Hath oped his ponderous and marble jaws,
To cast thee up again. What may this mean,

That thou, dead corse, again in complete steel
Revisit'st thus the glimpses of the moon,
Making night hideous; and we fools of nature
So horridly to shake our disposition
With thoughts beyond the reaches of our souls?
Say, why is this? wherefore? what should we do?   60
         [*Ghost beckons Hamlet.*
HOR.   It beckons you to go away with it,
As if it some impartment did desire
To you alone.
MAR.   Look, with what courteous action
It waves you to a more removed ground:
But do not go with it.
HOR.   No, by no means.
HAM.   It will not speak; then I will follow it.
HOR.   Do not, my lord.
HAM.   Why, what should be the fear?   70
I do not set my life at a pin's fee;
And for my soul, what can it do to that,
Being a thing immortal as itself?
It waves me forth again: I'll follow it.
HOR.   What if it tempt you toward the flood, my lord,
Or to the dreadful summit of the cliff
That beetles o'er his base into the sea,
And there assume some other horrible form,
Which might deprive your sovereignty of reason
And draw you into madness? think of it: 80
The very place puts toys of desperation,
Without more motive, into every brain
That looks so many fathoms to the sea
And hears it roar beneath.
HAM.   It waves me still.
Go on; I'll follow thee.
MAR.   You shall not go, my lord.
HAM.   Hold off your hands.
HOR.   Be ruled; you shall not go.
HAM.   My fate cries out,   90
And makes each petty artery in this body
As hardy as the Nemean lion's nerve.
Still am I call'd. Unhand me, gentlemen.
By heaven, I'll make a ghost of him that lets me!
I say, away! Go on; I'll follow thee.
         [*Exeunt Ghost and Hamlet.*
HOR.   He waxes desperate with imagination.
MAR.   Let's follow; 'tis not fit thus to obey him.
HOR.   Have after. To what issue will this come?
MAR.   Something is rotten in the state of Denmark.
HOR.   Heaven will direct it.   100
MAR.   Nay, let's follow him. [*Exeunt.*

Scene V—Another part of the platform

(*See synopsis for Act I, Scene IV.*)

Enter GHOST *and* HAMLET

HAM.   Where wilt thou lead me? speak; I'll go no further.   1
GHOST.   Mark me.
HAM.   I will.
GHOST.   My hour is almost come,

When I to sulphurous and tormenting flames
Must render up myself.
HAM.   Alas, poor ghost!
GHOST.   Pity me not, but lend thy serious hearing
To what I shall unfold.
HAM.   Speak; I am bound to hear.
GHOST.   So art thou to revenge, when thou shalt hear.   10
HAM.   What?
GHOST.   I am thy father's spirit,
Doom'd for a certain term to walk the night,
And for the day confined to fast in fires
Till the foul crimes done in my days of nature
Are burnt and purged away. But that I am forbid
To tell the secrets of my prison-house,
I could a tale unfold whose lightest word
Would harrow up thy soul, freeze thy young blood,   20
Make thy two eyes, like stars, start from their spheres,
Thy knotted and combined locks to part
And each particular hair to stand an end,
Like quills upon the fretful porpentine:
But this eternal blazon must not be
To ears of flesh and blood. List, list, O, list!
If thou didst ever thy dear father love—
HAM.   O God!
GHOST.   Revenge his foul and most unnatural murder.
HAM.   Murder!   30
GHOST.   Murder most foul, as in the best it is;
But this most foul, strange and unnatural.
HAM.   Haste me to know 't, that I, with wings as swift
As meditation or the thoughts of love,
May sweep to my revenge.
GHOST.   I find thee apt;
And duller shouldst thou be than the fat weed
That roots itself in ease on Lethe wharf,
Wouldst thou not stir in this. Now, Hamlet, hear:
'Tis given out that, sleeping in my orchard,   40
A serpent stung me; so the whole ear of Denmark
Is by a forged process of my death
Rankly abused: but know, thou noble youth,
The serpent that did sting thy father's life
Now wears his crown.
HAM.   O my prophetic soul!
My uncle!
GHOST.   Ay, that incestuous, that adulterate beast,
With witchcraft of his wit, with traitorous gifts,—
O wicked wits and gifts, that have the power   50
So to seduce!—won to his shameful lust
The will of my most seeming-virtuous queen:
O Hamlet, what a falling-off was there!
From me, whose love was of that dignity
That it went hand in hand even with the vow
I made to her in marriage, and to decline
Upon a wretch whose natural gifts were poor
To those of mine!
But virtue, as it never will be moved,
Though lewdness court it in a shape of heaven,   60
So lust, though to a radiant angel link'd,
Will sate itself in a celestial bed,
And prey on garbage.
But, soft! methinks I scent the morning air;
Brief let me be. Sleeping within my orchard,

My custom always of the afternoon,
Upon my secure hour thy uncle stole,
With juice of cursed Hebona in a vial,
And in the porches of my ears did pour
The leperous distilment; whose effect   70
Holds such an enmity with blood of man
That swift as quicksilver it courses through
The natural gates and alleys of the body,
And with a sudden vigour it doth posset
And curd, like eager droppings into milk,
The thin and wholesome blood: so did it mine;
And a most instant tetter bark'd about,
Most lazar-like, with vile and loathsome crust,
All my smooth body.
Thus was I, sleeping, by a brother's hand   80
Of life, of crown, of queen, at once dispatch'd:
Cut off even in the blossoms of my sin,
Unhousel'd, disappointed, unaneled,
No reckoning made, but sent to my account
With all my imperfections on my head:
O, horrible! O, horrible! most horrible!
If thou hast nature in thee, bear it not;
Let not the royal bed of Denmark be
A couch for luxury and damned incest.
But, howsoever thou pursuest this act,   90
Taint not thy mind, nor let thy soul contrive
Against thy mother aught: leave her to heaven
And to those thorns that in her bosom lodge,
To prick and sting her. Fare thee well at once!
The glow-worm shows the matin to be near,
And 'gins to pale his uneffectual fire:
Adieu, adieu! Hamlet, remember me.   [Exit.
HAM.   O all you host of heaven! O earth! what else?
And shall I couple hell? O, fie! Hold, hold, my heart;
And you, my sinews, grow not instant old,   100
But bear me stiffly up. Remember thee!
Ay, thou poor ghost, while memory holds a seat
In this distracted globe. Remember thee!
Yea, from the table of my memory
I'll wipe away all trivial fond records,
All saws of books, all forms, all pressures past,
That youth and observation copied there;
And thy commandment all alone shall live
Within the book and volume of my brain,
Unmix'd with baser matter: yes, by heaven!   110
O most pernicious woman!
O villain, villain, smiling, damned villain!
My tables,—meet it is I set it down,
That one may smile, and smile, and be a villain;
At least I'm sure it may be so in Denmark: [Writing.
So, uncle, there you are. Now to my word;
It is "Adieu, adieu! remember me."
I have sworn 't.
HOR. ⎫
MAR. ⎬   [Within] My lord, my lord,—
MAR.   [Within] Lord Hamlet,—   120
HOR.   [Within] Heaven secure him!
HAM.   So be it!
HOR.   [Within] Hillo, ho, ho, my lord!
HAM.   Hillo, ho, ho, boy! come, bird, come.

Enter HORATIO *and* MARCELLUS

MAR.   How is 't, my noble lord?

HOR.   What news, my lord?

HAM.   O, wonderful!

HOR.   Good my lord, tell it.

HAM.   No; you'll reveal it.

HOR.   Not I, my lord, by heaven.   130

MAR.   Nor I, my lord.

HAM.   How say you, then; would heart of man once
      think it?

But you'll be secret?

HOR. ⎫
MAR. ⎭   Ay, by heaven, my lord.

HAM.   There's ne'er a villain dwelling in all Denmark

But he's an arrant knave.

HOR.   There needs no ghost, my lord, come from the
      grave

To tell us this.

HAM.   Why, right; you are i' the right;

And so, without more circumstance at all,   140

I hold it fit that we shake hands and part:

You, as your business and desire shall point you;

For every man has business and desire,

Such as it is; and for mine own poor part,

Look you, I'll go pray.

HOR.   These are but wild and whirling words, my lord.

HAM.   I'm sorry they offend you, heartily;

Yes, 'faith, heartily.

HOR.   There's no offence, my lord.

HAM.   Yes, by Saint Patrick, but there is, Horatio,   150

And much offence too. Touching this vision here,

It is an honest ghost, that let me tell you:

For your desire to know what is between us,

O'ermaster 't as you may. And now, good friends,

As you are friends, scholars and soldiers,

Give me one poor request.

HOR.   What is 't, my lord? we will.

HAM.   Never make known what you have seen to-night.

HOR. ⎫
MAR. ⎭ My lord, we will not.

HAM.   Nay, but swear 't.   160

HOR.   In faith,

My lord, not I.

MAR.   Nor I, my lord, in faith.

HAM.   Upon my sword.

MAR.   We have sworn, my lord, already.

HAM.   Indeed, upon my sword, indeed.

GHOST.   [*Beneath*] Swear.

HAM.   Ah, ha, boy! say'st thou so? art thou there,
      true-penny?

Come on—you hear this fellow in the cellarage—

Consent to swear.   170

HOR.   Propose the oath, my lord.

HAM.   Never to speak of this that you have seen,

Swear by my sword.

GHOST.   [*Beneath*] Swear.

HAM.   Hic et ubique? then we'll shift our ground.

Come hither, gentlemen,

And lay your hands again upon my sword:

Never to speak of this that you have heard,

Swear by my sword.

GHOST.   [*Beneath*] Swear.   180

HAM.   Well said, old mole! canst work i' the earth so fast?

A worthy pioneer! Once more remove, good friends.

HOR.   O day and night, but this is wondrous strange!

HAM.   And therefore as a stranger give it welcome.

There are more things in heaven and earth, Horatio,

Than are dreamt of in our philosophy.

But come;

Here, as before, never, so help you mercy,

How strange or odd soe'er I bear myself,

As I perchance hereafter shall think meet   190

To put an antic disposition on,

That you, at such times seeing me, never shall,

With arms encumber'd thus, or this head-shake,

Or by pronouncing of some doubtful phrase,

As "Well, well, we know," or "We could, an if we would,"

Or "If we list to speak," or "There be, an if they might,"

Or such ambiguous giving out, to note

That you know aught of me: this not to do,

So grace and mercy at your most need help you,

Swear.   200

GHOST.   [*Beneath*] Swear.

HAM.   Rest, rest, perturbed spirit! [*They swear.*]

      So, gentlemen,

With all my love I do commend me to you:

And what so poor a man as Hamlet is

May do, to express his love and friending to you,

God willing, shall not lack. Let us go in together;

And still your fingers on your lips, I pray.

The time is out of joint: O cursed spite,

That ever I was born to set it right!

Nay, come, let's go together.   [*Exeunt.*   210

Act II

Scene I—A room in Polonius' house

Act I has been a sort of prologue; it contains the possibilities of which the remaining acts show the tragic development. As usual with Shakespeare, there is a crisis or turning-point at about the middle of the play, in the scene where HAMLET *has a definite opportunity of killing the* KING *and misses it (Act III, Scene III). Up to that point we are concerned with the cause of the tragedy, the action and reaction of the* GHOST's *injunction and* HAMLET's *character upon each other, the puttings off, the assumed madness. After that follows the effect; the successive fatal consequences due to that one cause are unrolled before us.*

The first part of Scene I is important chiefly as showing us at once that a considerable interval has elapsed. LAERTES *has had time to reach Paris and make friends there. It leads up to the more important questions, What has become of* HAMLET *during the interval? Is* CLAUDIUS *dead yet?*

Enter POLONIUS *and* REYNALDO

POL.   Give him this money and these notes, Reynaldo.   1
REY.   I will, my lord.
POL.   You shall do marvellous wisely, good Reynaldo,
Before you visit him, to make inquire
Of his behaviour.
REY.   My lord, I did intend it.
POL.   Marry, well said; very well said. Look you, sir,
Inquire me first what Danskers are in Paris;
And how, and who, what means, and where they keep,
What company, at what expense; and finding   10
By this encompassment and drift of question
That they do know my son, come you more nearer
Than your particular demands will touch it.
Take you, as 't were, some distant knowledge of him;
As thus, "I know his father and his friends,
And in part him": do you mark this, Reynaldo?
REY.   Ay, very well, my lord.
POL.   "And in part him; but" you may say "not well:
But, if 't be he I mean, he's very wild;
Addicted so and so": and there put on him   20
What forgeries you please: marry, none so rank
As may dishonour him; take heed of that;
But, sir, such wanton, wild and usual slips
As are companions noted and most known
To youth and liberty.
REY.   As gaming, my lord.
POL.   Ay, or drinking, fencing, swearing, quarrelling,
Drabbing: you may go so far.
REY.   My lord, that would dishonour him.
POL.   'Faith, no; as you may season it in the charge.   30
You must not put another scandal on him,
That he is open to incontinency;
That's not my meaning: but breathe his faults so quaintly
That they may seem the taints of liberty,
The flash and outbreak of a fiery mind,
A savageness in unreclaimed blood,
Of general assault.
REY.   But, my good lord,—
POL.   Wherefore should you do this?
REY.   Ay, my lord,   40
I would know that.
POL.   Marry, sir, here's my drift;
And, I believe, it is a fetch of warrant:
You laying these slight sullies on my son,
As 't were a thing a little soil'd i' the working,
Mark you,
Your party in converse, him you would sound,
Having ever seen in the prenominate crimes
The youth you breathe of guilty, be assured
He closes with you in this consequence;   50
"Good sir," or so, or "friend," or "gentleman,"
According to the phrase or the addition
Of man and country.

REY.   Very good, my lord.
POL.   And then, sir, does he this—he does—
What was I about to say? By the mass, I was about to say
something: where did I leave?
REY.   At "closes in the consequence," at "friend or so,"
and "gentleman."
POL.   At "closes in the consequence," ay, marry;   60
He closes thus: "I know the gentleman;
I saw him yesterday, or t' other day,
Or then, or then; with such, or such; and, as you say,
There was a' gaming; there o'ertook in 's rouse;
There falling out at tennis": or perchance,
"I saw him enter such a house of sale,"
Videlicet, a brothel, or so forth.
See you now;
Your bait of falsehood takes this carp of truth:
And thus do we of wisdom and of reach,   70
With windlasses and with assays of bias,
By indirections find directions out:
So by my former lecture and advice,
Shall you my son. You have me, have you not?
REY.   My lord, I have.
POL.   God be wi' you; fare you well.
REY.   Good my lord!
POL.   Observe his inclination in yourself.
REY.   I shall, my lord.
POL.   And let him ply his music.   80
REY.   Well, my lord.
POL.   Farewell!   [*Exit Reynaldo.*

Enter OPHELIA

How now, Ophelia! what's the matter?
OPH.   O, my lord, my lord, I have been so affrighted!
POL.   With what, i' the name of God?
OPH.   My lord, as I was sewing in my closet,
Lord Hamlet, with his doublet all unbraced;
No hat upon his head; his stockings foul'd,
Ungarter'd, and down-gyved to his ancle;
Pale as his shirt; his knees knocking each other;   90
And with a look so piteous in purport
As if he had been loosed out of hell
To speak of horrors,—he comes before me.
POL.   Mad for thy love?
OPH.   My lord, I do not know;
But truly, I do fear it.
POL.   What said he?
OPH.   He took me by the wrist and held me hard;
Then goes he to the length of all his arm;
And, with his other hand thus o'er his brow,   100
He falls to such perusal of my face
As he would draw it. Long stay'd he so;
At last, a little shaking of mine arm
And thrice his head thus waving up and down,
He raised a sigh so piteous and profound
As it did seem to shatter all his bulk
And end his being: that done, he lets me go:
And, with his head over his shoulder turn'd,
He seem'd to find his way without his eyes;
For out o' doors he went without their helps,   110
And, to the last, bended their light on me.

POL.   Come, go with me: I will go seek the king.
This is the very ecstasy of love,
Whose violent property fordoes itself
And leads the will to desperate undertakings
As oft as any passion under heaven
That does afflict our natures. I am sorry.
What, have you given him any hard words of late?
OPH.   No, my good lord, but, as you did command,
I did repel his letters and denied   120
His access to me.
POL.   That hath made him mad.
I am sorry that with better heed and judgement
I had not quoted him: I fear'd he did but trifle.
And meant to wreck thee; but, beshrew my jealousy!
By heaven, it is as proper to our age
To cast beyond ourselves in our opinions
As it is common for the younger sort
To lack discretion. Come, go we to the king:
This must be known; which, being kept close, might move   130
More grief to hide than hate to utter love.   [*Exeunt.*

Scene II—A room in the castle

*This long scene contains two main dramatic motives. In the latter
part of it, from the entry of the* PLAYERS, *we get the gradual approach to that crisis of the action that is brought about by the play
scene. The rest gives us, so to speak, a summary of the mental condition of* HAMLET *and of his attitude to the court during the months
of delay. The points to notice are (1) the assumption of madness,
which deceives* GERTRUDE, OPHELIA, POLONIUS, ROSEN-
CRANTZ, *and* GUILDENSTERN, *though the* KING, *who has a better key to* HAMLET'*s behavior than any of these, is not without his
suspicions; (2) the delight which* HAMLET *takes in the opportunity
thus afforded him of venting irony upon his enemies, and especially
upon* POLONIUS; (3) *his invariable tendency to pass from the consideration of his own position into general satire and invective upon
society. It is to be observed that* HAMLET *is not always acting the
madman; he does so, for instance, with* ROSENCRANTZ *and*
GUILDENSTERN *only when he begins to suspect their good faith.
And further, the pretence is easy for him. It requires only a slight exaggeration of his natural self. His thoughts and feelings, especially
under conditions of nervous excitement, are always on a plane
hardly intelligible to ordinary men. To appear mad he has only to
relax the control that he normally exerts.*

Enter KING, QUEEN, ROSENCRANTZ, GUILDENSTERN, *and*
ATTENDANTS

KING.   Welcome, dear Rosencrantz and Guildenstern!   1
Moreover that we much did long to see you,
The need we have to use you did provoke
Our hasty sending. Something have you heard
Of Hamlet's transformation; so call it,
Since nor the exterior nor the inward man
Resembles that it was. What it should be,
More than his father's death, that thus hath put him
So much from the understanding of himself,
I cannot dream of: I entreat you both,   10
That, being of so young days brought up with him,
And since so neighbour'd to his youth and humour,
That you vouchsafe your rest here in our court
Some little time: so by your companies

To draw him on to pleasures, and to gather,
So much as from occasion you may glean,
Whether aught, to us unknown, afflicts him thus,
That, open'd, lies within our remedy.
QUEEN.   Good gentlemen, he hath much talk'd of you;
And sure I am two men there are not living   20
To whom he more adheres. If it will please you
To show us so much gentry and good will
As to expend your time with us awhile,
For the supply and profit of our hope,
Your visitation shall receive such thanks
As fits a king's remembrance.
ROS.   Both your majesties
Might, by the sovereign power you have of us,
Put your dread pleasures more into command
Than to entreaty.   30
GUIL.   But we both obey,
And here give up ourselves, in the full bent
To lay our service freely at your feet,
To be commanded.
KING.   Thanks, Rosencrantz and gentle Guildenstern.
QUEEN.   Thanks, Guildenstern and gentle Rosencrantz:
And I beseech you instantly to visit
My too much changed son. Go, some of you,
And bring these gentlemen where Hamlet is.
GUIL.   Heavens make our presence and our practices   40
Pleasant and helpful to him!
QUEEN.   Ay, amen!
    [*Exeunt Rosencrantz, Guildenstern, and some Attendants.*

Enter POLONIUS

POL.   The ambassadors from Norway, my good lord,
Are joyfully return'd.
KING.   Thou still hast been the father of good news.
POL.   Have I, my lord? I assure my good liege,
I hold my duty, as I hold my soul,
Both to my God and to my gracious king:
And I do think, or else this brain of mine
Hunts not the trail of policy so sure   50
As it hath used to do, that I have found
The very cause of Hamlet's lunacy.
KING.   O, speak of that; that do I long to hear.
POL.   Give first admittance to the ambassadors;
My news shall be the fruit to that great feast.
KING.   Thyself do grace to them, and bring them in.
                                        [*Exit Polonius.*
He tells me, my dear Gertrude, he hath found
The head and source of all your son's distemper.
QUEEN.   I doubt it is no other but the main;
His father's death, and our o'erhasty marriage.   60
KING.   Well, we shall sift him.

Re-enter POLONIUS, *with* VOLTIMAND *and* CORNELIUS
                              Welcome, my good friends!
Say, Voltimand, what from our brother Norway?
VOLT.   Most fair return of greetings and desires.
Upon our first, he sent out to suppress
His nephew's levies; which to him appear'd
To be a preparation 'gainst the Polack;

But, better look'd into, he truly found
It was against your highness: whereat grieved,
That so his sickness, age and impotence   70
Was falsely borne in hand, sends out arrests
On Fortinbras; which he, in brief, obeys;
Receives rebuke from Norway, and in fine
Makes vow before his uncle never more
To give the assay of arms against your majesty.
Whereon old Norway, overcome with joy,
Gives him three thousand crowns in annual fee,
And his commission to employ those soldiers,
So levied as before, against the Polack:
With an entreaty, herein further shown,   [*Giving a paper.* 80
That it might please you to give quiet pass
Through your dominions for this enterprise,
On such regards of safety and allowance
As therein are set down.
KING.   It likes us well;
And at our more consider'd time we'll read,
Answer, and think upon this business.
Meantime we thank you for your well-took labour:
Go to your rest; at night we'll feast together:
Most welcome home!   [*Exeunt Voltimand and Cornelius.* 90
POL.   This business is well ended.
My liege, and madam, to expostulate
What majesty should be, what duty is,
Why day is day, night night, and time is time,
Were nothing but to waste night, day and time.
Therefore, since brevity is the soul of wit,
And tediousness the limbs and outward flourishes,
I will be brief: your noble son is mad:
Mad call I it; for, to define true madness,
What is 't but to be nothing else but mad?   100
But let that go.
QUEEN.   More matter, with less art.
POL.   Madam, I swear I use no art at all.
That he is mad, 'tis true: 'tis true 'tis pity;
And pity 'tis 'tis true: a foolish figure;
But farewell it, for I will use no art.
Mad let us grant him, then: and now remains
That we find out the cause of this effect,
Or rather say, the cause of this defect,
For this effect defective comes by cause: 110
Thus it remains, and the remainder thus.
Perpend.
I have a daughter—have while she is mine—
Who, in her duty and obedience, mark,
Hath given me this: now gather, and surmise.   [*Reads.*
"To the celestial and my soul's idol, the most beautified
Ophelia,"—
That's an ill phrase, a vile phrase; "beautified" is a vile
phrase: but you shall hear. Thus: [*Reads.*
"In her excellent white bosom, these, &c."   120
QUEEN.   Came this from Hamlet to her?
POL.   Good madam, stay awhile; I will be faithful. [*Reads.*
      "Doubt thou the stars are fire;
          Doubt that the sun doth move;
      Doubt truth to be a liar;
          But never doubt I love.
"O dear Ophelia, I am ill at these numbers; I have not art

to reckon my groans: but that I love thee best, O most best,
believe it. Adieu.
      "Thine evermore, most dear lady, whilst this   130
              machine is to him, HAMLET."
This, in obedience, hath my daughter shown me,
And more above, hath his solicitings,
As they fell out by time, by means and place,
All given to mine ear.
KING.   But how hath she
Received his love?
POL.   What do you think of me?
KING.   As of a man faithful and honourable.
POL.   I would fain prove so. But what might you think,   140
When I had seen this hot love on the wing—
As I perceived it, I must tell you that,
Before my daughter told me—what might you,
Or my dear majesty your queen here, think,
If I had play'd the desk or table-book,
Or given my heart a winking, mute and dumb,
Or look'd upon this love with idle sight;
What might you think? No, I went round to work,
And my young mistress thus I did bespeak:
"Lord Hamlet is a prince, out of thy star;   150
This must not be": and then I prescripts gave her,
That she should lock herself from his resort,
Admit no messengers, receive no tokens.
Which done, she took the fruits of my advice;
And he, repulsed—a short tale to make—
Fell into a sadness, then into a fast,
Thence to a watch, thence into a weakness,
Thence to a lightness, and, by this declension,
Into the madness wherein now he raves,
And all we mourn for.   160
KING.   Do you think 'tis this?
QUEEN.   It may be, very likely.
POL.   Hath there been such a time—I'd fain know that—
That I have positively said "'Tis so,"
When it proved otherwise?
KING.   Not that I know.
POL.   [*Pointing to his head and shoulder*] Take this from
      this, if this be otherwise:
If circumstances lead me, I will find
Where truth is hid, though it were hid indeed
Within the centre.   170
KING.   How may we try it further?
POL.   You know, sometimes he walks four hours together
Here in the lobby.
QUEEN.   So he does indeed.
POL.   At such a time I'll loose my daughter to him:
Be you and I behind an arras then;
Mark the encounter: if he love her not
And be not from his reason fall'n thereon,
Let me be no assistant for a state,
But keep a farm and carters.   180
KING.   We will try it.
QUEEN.   But, look, where sadly the poor wretch comes
      reading.
POL.   Away, I do beseech you, both away:
I'll board him presently.
                  [*Exeunt King, Queen, and Attendants.*

Enter HAMLET, *reading*

O, give me leave:
How does my good Lord Hamlet?
HAM.   Well, God-a-mercy.
POL.   Do you know me, my lord?
HAM.   Excellent well; you are a fishmonger.
POL.   Not I, my lord.   190
HAM.   Then I would you were so honest a man.
POL.   Honest, my lord!
HAM.   Ay, sir; to be honest, as this world goes, is to be
one man picked out of ten thousand.
POL.   That's very true, my lord.
HAM.   For if the sun breed maggots in a dead dog, being
a god kissing carrion,—Have you a daughter?
POL.   I have, my lord.
HAM.   Let her not walk i' the sun: conception is a bless-
ing: but not as your daughter may conceive. Friend,   200
look to 't.
POL.   [*Aside*] How say you by that? Still harping on my
daughter: yet he knew me not at first; he said I was a fishmonger: he is far gone, far gone: and truly in my youth I
suffered much extremity for love; very near this. I'll speak
to him again. What do you read, my lord?
HAM.   Words, words, words.
POL.   What is the matter, my lord?
HAM.   Between who?
POL.   I mean, the matter that you read, my lord.   210
HAM.   Slanders, sir: for the satirical rogue says here that
old men have grey beards, that their faces are wrinkled,
their eyes purging thick amber and plum-tree gum and
that they have a plentiful lack of wit, together with most
weak hams: all which, sir, though I most powerfully and
potently believe, yet I hold it not honesty to have it thus
set down, for yourself, sir, should be old as I am, if like a
crab you could go backward.
POL.   [*Aside*] Though this be madness, yet there is
method in 't. Will you walk out of the air, my lord?   220
HAM.   Into my grave.
POL.   Indeed, that is out o' the air. [*Aside*] How pregnant
sometimes his replies are! a happiness that often madness
hits on, which reason and sanity could not so prosper-
ously be delivered of. I will leave him, and suddenly
contrive the means of meeting between him and my
daughter.—My honourable lord, I will most humbly take
my leave of you.
HAM.   You cannot, sir, take from me any thing that I will
more willingly part withal: except my life, except my life, 230
except my life.
POL.   Fare you well, my lord.
HAM.   These tedious old fools!

Enter ROSENCRANTZ *and* GUILDENSTERN

POL.   You go to seek the Lord Hamlet; there he is.
ROS.   [*To* POLONIUS] God save you, sir!   [*Exit Polonius.*
GUIL.   My honoured lord!
ROS.   My most dear lord!
HAM.   My excellent good friends! How dost thou,
Guildenstern? Ah, Rosencrantz! Good lads, how do ye
both?   240

ROS.   As the indifferent children of the earth.
GUIL.   Happy, in that we are not over-happy;
On fortune's cap we are not the very button.
HAM.   Nor the soles of her shoe?
ROS.   Neither, my lord.
HAM.   Then you live about her waist, or in the middle of
her favours? What's the news?
ROS.   None, my lord, but that the world's grown honest.
HAM.   Then is doomsday near: but your news is not true.
Let me question more in particular: what have you, my   250
good friends, deserved at the hands of fortune, that she
sends you to prison hither?
GUIL.   Prison, my lord!
HAM.   Denmark's a prison.
ROS.   Then is the world one.
HAM.   A goodly one; in which there are many confines,
wards and dungeons, Denmark being one o' the worst.
ROS.   We think not so, my lord.
HAM.   Why, then, 'tis none to you; for there is nothing ei-
ther good or bad, but thinking makes it so: to me it is a   260
prison.
ROS.   Why then, your ambition makes it one; 'tis too nar-
row for your mind.
HAM.   O God, I could be bounded in a nutshell and
count myself a king of infinite space, were it not that I
have bad dreams.
GUIL.   Which dreams indeed are ambition, for the very
substance of the ambitious is merely the shadow of a
dream.
HAM.   A dream itself is but a shadow.   270
ROS.   Truly, and I hold ambition of so airy and light a
quality that it is but a shadow's shadow.
HAM.   Then are our beggars bodies, and our monarchs
and outstretched heroes the beggars' shadows. Shall we to
the court? for, by my fay, I cannot reason.
ROS. ⎱
GUIL. ⎰ We'll wait upon you.
HAM.   No such matter: I will not sort you with the rest of
my servants, for, to speak to you like an honest man, I am
most dreadfully attended. But, in the beaten way of
friendship, what make you at Elsinore?   280
ROS.   To visit you, my lord; no other occasion.
HAM.   Beggar that I am, I am even poor in thanks; but I
thank you: and sure, dear friends, my thanks are too dear
a halfpenny. Were you not sent for? Is it your own inclin-
ing? Is it a free visitation? Come, deal justly with me:
come, come; nay, speak.
GUIL.   What should we say, my lord?
HAM.   Why, any thing, but to the purpose. You were sent
for; and there is a kind of confession in your looks which
your modesties have not craft enough to colour: I know   290
the good king and queen have sent for you.
ROS.   To what end, my lord?
HAM.   That you must teach me. But let me conjure you,
by the rights of our fellowship, by the consonancy of our
youth, by the obligation of our ever-preserved love, and
by what more dear a better proposer could charge you
withal, be even and direct with me, whether you were
sent for, or no?
ROS.   [*Aside to* GUIL.] What say you?

HAM.   [*Aside*] Nay, then, I have an eye of you.—If you   300
love me, hold not off.

GUIL.   My lord, we were sent for.

HAM.   I will tell you why; so shall my anticipation prevent your discovery, and your secrecy to the king and
queen moult no feather. I have of late—but wherefore I
know not—lost all my mirth, forgone all custom of exercises; and indeed it goes so heavily with my disposition
that this goodly frame, the earth, seems to me a sterile
promontory, this most excellent canopy, the air, look you,
this brave o'erhanging firmament, this majestical roof fret-   310
ted with golden fire, why, it appears no other thing to me
than a foul and pestilent congregation of vapours. What a
piece of work is a man! how noble in reason! how infinite
in faculty! in form and moving how express and admirable! in action how like an angel! in apprehension how
like a god! the beauty of the world! the paragon of animals! And yet, to me, what is this quintessence of dust?
man delights not me: no, nor woman neither, though by
your smiling you seem to say so.

ROS.   My lord, there was no such stuff in my thoughts.   320

HAM.   Why did you laugh then, when I said "man delights not me"?

ROS.   To think, my lord, if you delight not in man, what
lenten entertainment the players shall receive from you:
we coted them on the way; and hither are they coming, to
offer you service.

HAM.   He that plays the king shall be welcome; His
majesty shall have tribute of me; the adventurous knight
shall use his foil and target; the lover shall not sigh gratis;
the humorous man shall end his part in peace; the clown   330
shall make those laugh whose lungs are tickle o' the sere;
and the lady shall say her mind freely, or the blank verse
shall halt for 't. What players are they?

ROS.   Even those you were wont to take delight in, the
tragedians of the city.

HAM.   How chances it they travel? their residence, both
in reputation and profit, was better both ways.

ROS.   I think their inhibition comes by the means of the
late innovation.

HAM.   Do they hold the same estimation they did when I   340
was in the city? are they so followed?

ROS.   No, indeed, are they not.

HAM.   How comes it? do they grow rusty?

ROS.   Nay, their endeavour keeps in the wonted pace:
but there is, sir, an aery of children, little eyases, that cry
out on the top of question, and are most tyrannically
clapped for 't: these are now the fashion, and so berattle
the common stages—so they call them—that many wearing rapiers are afraid of goose-quills and dare scarce come
thither.   350

HAM.   What, are they children? who maintains 'em? how
are they escoted? Will they pursue the quality no longer
than they can sing? will they not say afterwards, if they
should grow themselves to common players—as it is
most like, if their means are no better—their writers do
them wrong, to make them exclaim against their own
succession?

ROS.   'Faith, there has been much to do on both sides;
and the nation holds it no sin to tarre them to controversy:

there was, for a while, no money bid for argument, unless   360
the poet and the player went to cuffs in the question.

HAM.   Is 't possible?

GUIL.   O, there has been much throwing about of brains.

HAM.   Do the boys carry it away?

ROS.   Ay, that they do, my lord; Hercules and his load too.

HAM.   It is not very strange; for mine uncle is king of
Denmark, and those that would make mows at him while
my father lived, give twenty, forty, fifty, an hundred
ducats a-piece for his picture in little. 'Sblood, there is
something in this more than natural, if philosophy could   370
find it out.   [*Flourish of trumpets within.*

GUIL.   There are the players.

HAM.   Gentlemen, you are welcome to Elsinore. Your
hands, come then: the appurtenance of welcome is fashion
and ceremony: let me comply with you in this garb, lest
my extent to the players, which, I tell you, must show
fairly outward, should more appear like entertainment
than yours. You are welcome: but my uncle-father and
aunt-mother are deceived.

GUIL.   In what, my dear lord?   380

HAM.   I am but mad north-north-west: when the wind is
southerly I know a hawk from a handsaw.

Re-enter POLONIUS

POL.   Well be with you, gentlemen!

HAM.   Hark you, Guildenstern; and you too: at each ear
a hearer: that great baby you see there is not yet out of his
swaddling-clouts.

ROS.   Happily he's the second time come to them; for
they say an old man is twice a child.

HAM.   I will prophesy he comes to tell me of the players;
mark it. You say right, sir: o' Monday morning; 'twas so   390
indeed.

POL.   My lord, I have news to tell you.

HAM.   My lord, I have news to tell you. When Roscius
was an actor in Rome,

POL.   The actors are come hither, my lord.

HAM.   Buz, buz!

POL.   Upon mine honour,—

HAM.   Then came each actor on his ass,—

POL.   The best actors in the world, either for tragedy,
comedy, history, pastoral, pastoral-comical, historical-   400
pastoral, tragical-historical, tragical-comical-historical-
pastoral, scene individable, or poem unlimited: Seneca
cannot be too heavy, nor Plautus too light. For the law of
writ and the liberty, these are the only men.

HAM.   O Jephthah, judge of Israel, what a treasure hadst
thou!

POL.   What a treasure had he, my lord?

HAM.   Why,
          "One fair daughter, and no more,
           The which he loved passing well."   410

POL.   [*Aside*] Still on my daughter.

HAM.   Am I not i' the right, old Jephthah?

POL.   If you call me Jephthah, my lord, I have a daughter
that I love passing well.

HAM.   Nay, that follows not.

POL.   What follows, then, my lord?

HAM.   Why,

"As by lot, God wot,"

and then, you know,

"It came to pass, as most like it was,"— 420

the first row of the pious chanson will show you more; for
look, where my abridgement comes.

Enter four or five PLAYERS

You are welcome, masters; welcome, all. I am glad to see
thee well. Welcome, good friends. O, my old friend! thy
face is valanced since I saw thee last: comest thou to beard
me in Denmark? What, my young lady and mistress! By 'r
lady, your ladyship is nearer to heaven than when I saw
you last, by the altitude of a chopine. Pray God, your
voice, like a piece of uncurrent gold, be not cracked within
the ring. Masters, you are all welcome. We'll e'en to 't like 430
French falconers, fly at any thing we see: we'll have a
speech straight: come, give us a taste of your quality;
come, a passionate speech.

FIRST PLAYER.   What speech, my lord?

HAM.   I heard thee speak me a speech once, but it was
never acted; or, if it was, not above once; for the play, I remember, pleased not the million; 'twas caviare to the general: but it was—as I received it, and others, whose
judgements in such matters cried in the top of mine—an
excellent play, well digested in the scenes, set down with 440
as much modesty as cunning. I remember, one said there
were no sallets in the lines to make the matter savoury, nor
no matter in the phrase that might indict the author of affectation; but called it an honest method, as wholesome as
sweet, and by very much more handsome than fine. One
speech in it I chiefly loved: 'twas Aeneas' tale to Dido; and
thereabout of it especially, where he speaks of Priam's
slaughter: if it live in your memory, begin at this line: let
me see, let me see—

"The rugged Pyrrhus, like the Hyrcanian beast," 450

—it is not so:—it begins with Pyrrhus:—

"The rugged Pyrrhus, he whose sable arms,
Black as his purpose, did the night resemble
When he lay couched in the ominous horse,
Hath now this dread and black complexion smear'd
With heraldry more dismal; head to foot
Now is he total gules; horridly trick'd
With blood of fathers, mothers, daughters, sons,
Baked and impasted with the parching streets,
That lend a tyrannous and damned light 460
To their lord's murder: roasted in wrath and fire,
And thus o'er-sized with coagulate gore,
With eyes like carbuncles, the hellish Pyrrhus
Old grandsire Priam seeks."

So, proceed you.

POL.   'Fore God, my lord, well spoken, with good accent
and good discretion.

FIRST PLAYER.   "Anon he finds him
Striking too short at Greeks; his antique sword,
Rebellious to his arm, lies where it falls, 470
Repugnant to command: unequal match'd,
Pyrrhus at Priam drives; in rage strikes wide;
But with the whiff and wind of his fell sword
The unnerved father falls. Then senseless Ilium,
Seeming to feel this blow, with flaming top
Stoops to his base, and with a hideous crash

Takes prisoner Pyrrhus' ear: for, lo! his sword
Which was declining on the milky head
Of reverend Priam, seem'd i' the air to stick:
So, as a painted tyrant, Pyrrhus stood, 480
And like a neutral to his will and matter,
Did nothing.
But, as we often see, against some storm,
A silence in the heavens, the rack stand still,
The bold winds speechless and the orb below
As hush as death, anon the dreadful thunder
Doth rend the region, so, after Pyrrhus' pause,
Aroused vengeance sets him new a-work:
And never did the Cyclops' hammers fall
On Mars's armour forged for proof eterne 490
With less remorse than Pyrrhus' bleeding sword
Now falls on Priam.
Out, out, thou strumpet, Fortune! All you gods,
In general synod, take away her power:
Break all the spokes and fellies from her wheel,
And bowl the round nave down the hill of heaven,
As low as to the fiends!"

POL.   This is too long.

HAM.   It shall to the barber's, with your beard. Prithee,
say on: he's for a jig or a tale of bawdry, or he sleeps: say 500
on: come to Hecuba.

FIRST PLAYER.   "But who, O, who had seen the mobled
queen—"

HAM.   "The mobled queen?"

POL.   That's good; "mobled queen" is good.

FIRST PLAYER.   "Run barefoot up and down, threatening
the flames
With bisson rheum; a clout upon that head
Where late the diadem stood, and for a robe,
About her lank and all o'er-teemed loins,
A blanket, in the alarm of fear caught up;
Who this had seen, with tongue in venom steep'd, 510
'Gainst Fortune's state would treason have
pronounced:
But if the gods themselves did see her then
When she saw Pyrrhus make malicious sport
In mincing with his sword her husband's limbs,
The instant burst of clamour that she made,
Unless things mortal move them not at all,
Would have made milch the burning eyes of
heaven,
And passion in the gods."

POL.   Look, whether he has not turned his colour and
has tears in 's eyes. Pray you, no more. 520

HAM.   'Tis well; I'll have thee speak out the rest soon.
Good my lord, will you see the players well bestowed? Do
you hear, let them be well used; for they are the abstract
and brief chronicles of the time: after your death you were
better have a bad epitaph than their ill report while you
live.

POL.   My lord, I will use them according to their desert.

HAM.   God's bodykins, man, much better: use every man
after his desert, and who should 'scape whipping? Use
them after your own honour and dignity: the less they de- 530
serve, the more merit is in your bounty. Take them in.

POL.   Come, sirs.

HAM.   Follow him, friends; we'll hear a play to-morrow.

[*Exit Polonius with all the Players but the First.*] Dost thou hear me, old friend; can you play the Murder of Gonzago?

FIRST PLAYER.   Ay, my lord.

HAM.   We'll ha 't to-morrow night. You could, for a need, study a speech of some dozen or sixteen lines, which I would set down and insert in 't, could you not?

FIRST PLAYER.   Ay, my lord.   540

HAM.   Very well. Follow that lord; and look you mock him not. [*Exit First Player.*] My good friends, I'll leave you till night: you are welcome to Elsinore.

ROS.   Good my lord!

HAM.   Ay, so, God be wi' ye; [*Exeunt Rosencrantz and Guildenstern.*] Now I am alone.

O, what a rogue and peasant slave am I!
Is it not monstrous that this player here,
But in a fiction, in a dream of passion,
Could force his soul so to his own conceit   550
That from her working all his visage wann'd,
Tears in his eyes, distraction in 's aspect,
A broken voice, and his whole function suiting
With forms to his conceit? and all for nothing!
For Hecuba!
What's Hecuba to him, or he to Hecuba,
That he should weep for her? What would he do,
Had he the motive and the cue for passion
That I have? He would drown the stage with tears
And cleave the general ear with horrid speech,   560
Make mad the guilty and appal the free,
Confound the ignorant, and amaze indeed
The very faculties of eyes and ears.
Yet I,
A dull and muddy-mettled rascal, peak,
Like John-a-dreams, unpregnant of my cause,
And can say nothing; no, not for a king,
Upon whose property and most dear life
A damn'd defeat was made. Am I a coward?

Who calls me villain? breaks my pate across?   570
Plucks off my beard, and blows it in my face?
Tweaks me by the nose? gives me the lie i' the throat,
As deep as to the lungs? who does me this?
Ha!
'Swounds, I should take it: for it cannot be
But I am pigeon-liver'd and lack gall
To make oppression bitter, or ere this
I should have fatted all the region kites
With this slave's offal: bloody, bawdy villain!
Remorseless, treacherous, lecherous, kindless villain!   580
O, vengeance!
Why, what an ass am I! This is most brave,
That I, the son of a dear father murder'd,
Prompted to my revenge by heaven and hell,
Must, like a whore, unpack my heart with words,
And fall a-cursing, like a very drab,
A scullion!
Fie upon 't! foh! About, my brain! I have heard
That guilty creatures sitting at a play
Have by the very cunning of the scene   590
Been struck so to the soul that presently
They have proclaim'd their malefactions;
For murder, though it have no tongue, will speak
With most miraculous organ. I'll have these players
Play something like the murder of my father
Before mine uncle: I'll observe his looks;
I'll tent him to the quick: if he but blench,
I know my course. The spirit that I have seen
May be the devil: and the devil hath power
To assume a pleasing shape; yea, and perhaps   600
Out of my weakness and my melancholy,
As he is very potent with such spirits,
Abuses me to damn me: I'll have grounds
More relative than this: the play's the thing
Wherein I'll catch the conscience of the king.   [*Exit.*

Act III

Scene I—A room in the castle

This short scene sums up the precise situation of affairs at the moment when the crisis is coming on. There are three points to be noticed:

HAMLET *has resolved to make the play the solution of all his doubts; if that test shows the* KING *guilty, he shall die. Even as he forms this determination, his heart fails him. He turns to an alternative which has dimly presented itself before (Act I, Scene II, Line 131), and deliberately considers the desirability of suicide. But such a way out of the difficulty is too simple, too easy for his over-speculative nature. He sees the future filled with countless possibilities, which puzzle his will, and this enterprise also loses the name of action.*

HAMLET *has long known that no help is to be had from* OPHELIA. *Yet when she appears before him, his old tenderness revives. He speaks gently to her, and then—discovers that she is deceiving him, acting as a decoy for* POLONIUS. *This obliges him to play the madman again, and his paradoxes express a feeling of revulsion from the poor foolish girl. His mother's sin has already made him lose faith in womanhood, and now he sees* OPHELIA, *too, spotted with all the vileness of her sex. He assails her with reproaches so inappropriate to herself that she can only take them as the sign of a shattered mind.*

With POLONIUS *and the like* HAMLET*'s acting is successful; but the* KING *is shrewder. His suspicions are awakened, and he at once plots to get his nephew out of the way.* HAMLET *has, therefore, gone too far on the path of delay, and though he does not know it, the opportunities of revenge are fast slipping away from him.*

Enter KING, QUEEN, POLONIUS, OPHELIA, ROSENCRANTZ, *and* GUILDENSTERN

KING.   And can you, by no drift of circumstance,   1
Get from him why he puts on this confusion,

Grating so harshly all his days of quiet
With turbulent and dangerous lunacy?
ROS.   He does confess he feels himself distracted;
But from what cause he will by no means speak.
GUIL.   Nor do we find him forward to be sounded,
But, with a crafty madness, keeps aloof,
When we would bring him on to some confession
Of his true state.   10
QUEEN.   Did he receive you well?
ROS.   Most like a gentleman.
GUIL.   But with much forcing of his disposition.
ROS.   Niggard of question; but, of our demands,
Most free in his reply.
QUEEN.   Did you assay him
To any pastime?
ROS.   Madam, it so fell out, that certain players
We o'er-raught on the way: of these we told him;
And there did seem in him a kind of joy   20
To hear of it: they are about the court,
And, as I think, they have already order
This night to play before him.
POL.   'Tis most true:
And he beseech'd me to entreat your majesties
To hear and see the matter.
KING.   With all my heart; and it doth much content me
To hear him so inclined.
Good gentlemen, give him a further edge,
And drive his purpose on to these delights.   30
ROS.   We shall, my lord.
                    [*Exeunt Rosencrantz and Guildenstern.*
KING.   Sweet Gertrude, leave us too;
For we have closely sent for Hamlet hither,
That he, as 't were by accident, may here
Affront Ophelia:
Her father and myself, lawful espials,
Will so bestow ourselves that, seeing, unseen,
We may of their encounter frankly judge,
And gather by him, as he is behaved,
If 't be the affliction of his love or no   40
That thus he suffers for.
QUEEN.   I shall obey you;
And for your part, Ophelia, I do wish
That your good beauties be the happy cause
Of Hamlet's wildness: so shall I hope your virtues
Will bring him to his wonted way again,
To both your honours.
OPH.   Madam, I wish it may.   [*Exit Queen.*
POL.   Ophelia, walk you here. Gracious, so please you,
We will bestow ourselves. [*To* OPHELIA] Read on this book;   50
That show of such an exercise may colour
Your loneliness. We are oft to blame in this,—
'Tis too much proved—that with devotion's visage
And pious action we do sugar o'er
The devil himself.
KING.   [*Aside*] O, 'tis too true!
How smart a lash that speech doth give my conscience!
The harlot's cheek, beautied with plastering art,
Is not more ugly to the thing that helps it
Than is my deed to my most painted word: 60
O heavy burthen!

POL.   I hear him coming: let's withdraw, my lord.
                    [*Exeunt King and Polonius.*

Enter HAMLET

HAM.   To be, or not to be: that is the question:
Whether 'tis nobler in the mind to suffer
The slings and arrows of outrageous fortune,
Or to take arms against a sea of troubles,
And by opposing end them? To die: to sleep;
No more; and by a sleep to say we end
The heart-ache and the thousand natural shocks
That flesh is heir to, 'tis a consummation   70
Devoutly to be wish'd. To die, to sleep;
To sleep: perchance to dream: ay, there's the rub;
For in that sleep of death what dreams may come
When we have shuffled off this mortal coil,
Must give us pause: there's the respect
That makes calamity of so long life;
For who would bear the whips and scorns of time,
The oppressor's wrong, the proud man's contumely,
The pangs of despised love, the law's delay,
The insolence of office and the spurns   80
That patient merit of the unworthy takes,
When he himself might his quietus make
With a bare bodkin? who would fardels bear,
To grunt and sweat under a weary life,
But that the dread of something after death,
The undiscover'd country from whose bourn
No traveller returns, puzzles the will
And makes us rather bear those ills we have
Than fly to others that we know not of?
Thus conscience does make cowards of us all;   90
And thus the native hue of resolution
Is sicklied o'er with the pale cast of thought,
And enterprises of great pitch and moment
With this regard their currents turn awry,
And lose the name of action.—Soft you now!
The fair Ophelia! Nymph, in thy orisons
Be all my sins remember'd.
OPH.   Good my lord,
How does your honour for this many a day?
HAM.   I humbly thank you; well, well, well.   100
OPH.   My lord, I have remembrances of yours,
That I have longed long to re-deliver;
I pray you, now receive them.
HAM.   No, not I;
I never gave you aught.
OPH.   My honour'd lord, you know right well
   you did;
And, with them, words of so sweet breath composed
As made the things more rich: their perfume lost,
Take these again; for to the noble mind
Rich gifts wax poor when givers prove unkind.   110
There, my lord.
HAM.   Ha, ha! are you honest?
OPH.   My lord?
HAM.   Are you fair?
OPH.   What means your lordship?
HAM.   That if you be honest and fair, your honesty
should admit no discourse to your beauty.

OPH.   Could beauty, my lord, have better commerce than with honesty?

HAM.   Ay, truly; for the power of beauty will sooner transform honesty from what it is to a bawd than the force of honesty can translate beauty into his likeness: this was sometime a paradox, but now the time gives it proof. I did love you once.   120

OPH.   Indeed, my lord, you made me believe so.

HAM.   You should not have believed me; for virtue cannot so inoculate our old stock but we shall relish of it: I loved you not.

OPH.   I was the more deceived.

HAM.   Get thee to a nunnery: why wouldst thou be a breeder of sinners? I am myself indifferent honest; but yet I could accuse me of such things that it were better my mother had not borne me: I am very proud, revengeful, ambitious, with more offences at my beck than I have thoughts to put them in, imagination to give them shape, or time to act them in. What should such fellows as I do crawling between earth and heaven? We are arrant knaves, all; believe none of us. Go thy ways to a nunnery. Where's your father?   130

OPH.   At home, my lord.   140

HAM.   Let the doors be shut upon him, that he may play the fool no where but in 's own house. Farewell.

OPH.   O, help him, you sweet heavens!

HAM.   If thou dost marry, I'll give thee this plague for thy dowry: be thou as chaste as ice, as pure as snow, thou shalt not escape calumny. Get thee to a nunnery, go: farewell. Or, if thou wilt needs marry, marry a fool; for wise men know well enough what monsters you make of them. To a nunnery, go, and quickly too. Farewell.

OPH.   O heavenly powers, restore him!   150

HAM.   I have heard of your paintings too, well enough; God has given you one face, and you make yourselves another: you jig, you amble, and you lisp, and nick-name God's creatures, and make your wantonness your ignorance. Go to, I'll no more on 't; it hath made me mad. I say, we will have no more marriages: those that are married already, all but one, shall live; the rest shall keep as they are. To a nunnery, go.   [*Exit.*

OPH.   O, what a noble mind is here o'erthrown!
The courtier's, soldier's, scholar's, eye, tongue, sword;   160
The expectancy and rose of the fair state,
The glass of fashion and the mould of form,
The observed of all observers, quite, quite down!
And I, of ladies most deject and wretched,
That suck'd the honey of his music vows,
Now see that noble and most sovereign reason.
Like sweet bells jangled, out of tune and harsh;
That unmatch'd form and feature of blown youth
Blasted with ecstasy: O, woe is me,
To have seen what I have seen, see what I see!   170

Re-enter KING *and* POLONIUS

KING.   Love! his affections do not that way tend;
Nor what he spake, though it lack'd form a little,
Was not like madness. There's something in his soul,
O'er which his melancholy sits on brood;
And I do doubt the hatch and the disclose
Will be some danger: which for to prevent,
I have in quick determination
Thus set it down: he shall with speed to England,
For the demand of our neglected tribute:
Haply the seas and countries different   180
With variable objects shall expel
This something-settled matter in his heart,
Whereon his brains still beating puts him thus
From fashion of himself. What think you on 't?

POL.   It shall do well: but yet do I believe
The origin and commencement of his grief
Sprung from neglected love. How now, Ophelia!
You need not tell us what Lord Hamlet said;
We heard it all. My lord, do as you please;
But, if you hold it fit, after the play   190
Let his queen mother all alone entreat him
To show his grief: let her be round with him;
And I'll be placed, so please you, in the ear
Of all their conference. If she find him not,
To England send him, or confine him where
Your wisdom best shall think.

KING.   It shall be so:
Madness in great ones must not unwatch'd go.   [*Exeunt.*

Scene II—A hall in the castle

This important scene finally convinces HAMLET *of the* KING's *guilt; it closes with a resolution to "do bitter business."* HAMLET *is throughout in a state of extreme nervous tension; at the success of his plot he breaks into the wildest excitement. Hence the nonsense he talks to* OPHELIA, *and his riotous fooling with the* COURTIERS. *The episodes with the* PLAYERS *and* HORATIO *serve partly as a quiet opening to the turbulent emotions of the play scene, partly to show that* HAMLET's *action is fundamentally sane and rational. It is characteristic of him to be able to interest himself at such a critical moment in the niceties of the actor's art.*

Enter HAMLET *and* PLAYERS

HAM.   Speak the speech, I pray you, as I pronounced it   1
to you, trippingly on the tongue: but if you mouth it, as many of your players do, I had as lief the town-crier spoke my lines. Nor do not saw the air too much with your hand, thus, but use all gently; for in the very torrent, tempest, and, as I may say, the whirlwind of passion, you must acquire and beget a temperance that may give it smoothness. O, it offends me to the soul to hear a robustious periwig-pated fellow tear a passion to tatters, to very rags, to split the ears of the groundlings, who for the most part are capable of nothing but inexplicable dumb-shows and noise: I   10
would have such a fellow whipped for o'erdoing Termagant; it out-herods Herod: pray you, avoid it.

FIRST PLAYER.   I warrant your honour.

HAM.   Be not too tame neither, but let your own discretion be your tutor: suit the action to the word, the word to the action; with this special observance, that you o'erstep not the modesty of nature: for any thing so overdone is from the purpose of playing, whose end, both at the first and now, was and is, to hold, as 't were, the mirror up to nature; to show virtue her own feature, scorn her own   20
image, and the very age and body of the time his form and

pressure. Now this overdone, or come tardy off, though it make the unskilful laugh, cannot but make the judicious grieve; the censure of the which one must in your allowance o'erweigh a whole theatre of others. O, there be players that I have seen play, and heard others praise, and that highly, not to speak it profanely, that, neither having the accent of Christians nor the gait of Christian, pagan, nor man, have so strutted and bellowed that I have thought some of nature's journeymen had made men and not made them well, they imitated humanity so abominably.   30

FIRST PLAYER.   I hope we have reformed that indifferently with us, sir.

HAM.   O, reform it altogether. And let those that play your clowns speak no more than is set down for them; for there be of them that will themselves laugh, to set on some quantity of barren spectators to laugh too; though, in the mean time, some necessary question of the play be then to   40
be considered: that's villainous, and shows a most pitiful ambition in the fool that uses it. Go, make you ready.

                                                  [*Exeunt Players.*

Enter POLONIUS, ROSENCRANTZ, *and* GUILDENSTERN

How now, my lord: will the king hear this piece of work?

POL.   And the queen too, and that presently.

HAM.   Bid the players make haste. [*Exit Polonius.*] Will you two help to hasten them?

ROS. ⎱
GUIL. ⎰ We will, my lord.

                    [*Exeunt Rosencrantz and Guildenstern.*

HAM.   What ho! Horatio!

Enter HORATIO

HOR.   Here, sweet lord, at your service.

HAM.   Horatio, thou art e'en as just a man   50
As e'er my conversation coped withal.

HOR.   O, my dear lord,—

HAM.   Nay, do not think I flatter;
For what advancement may I hope from thee
That no revenue hast but thy good spirits,
To feed and clothe thee? Why should the poor be flatter'd?
No, let the candied tongue lick absurd pomp,
And crook the pregnant hinges of the knee
Where thrift may follow fawning. Dost thou hear?
Since my dear soul was mistress of her choice   60
And could of men distinguish, her election
Hath seal'd thee for herself; for thou hast been
As one, in suffering all, that suffers nothing,
A man that fortune's buffets and rewards
Hast ta'en with equal thanks: and blest are those
Whose blood and judgement are so well commingled,
That they are not a pipe for fortune's finger
To sound what stop she please. Give me that man
That is not passion's slave, and I will wear him
In my heart's core, ay, in my heart of heart,   70
As I do thee.—Something too much of this.—
There is a play to-night before the king;
One scene of it comes near the circumstance
Which I have told thee of my father's death:
I prithee, when thou seest that act afoot,

Even with the very comment of thy soul
Observe mine uncle: if his occulted guilt
Do not itself unkennel in one speech,
It is a damned ghost that we have seen,
And my imaginations are as foul   80
As Vulcan's stithy. Give him heedful note;
For I mine eyes will rivet to his face,
And after we will both our judgements join
In censure of his seeming.

HOR.   Well, my lord:
If he steal aught the whilst this play is playing,
And 'scape detecting, I will pay the theft.

HAM.   They are coming to the play; I must be idle:
Get you a place.

Danish march. A flourish. Enter KING, QUEEN, POLONIUS, OPHELIA, ROSENCRANTZ, GUILDENSTERN *and others*

KING.   How fares our cousin Hamlet?   90

HAM.   Excellent, i' faith; of the chameleon's dish: I eat the air, promise-crammed: you cannot feed capons so.

KING.   I have nothing with this answer, Hamlet; these words are not mine.

HAM.   No, nor mine now. [*To* POLONIUS] My lord, you played once i' the university, you say?

POL.   That I did, my lord; and was accounted a good actor.

HAM.   What did you enact?

POL.   I did enact Julius Caesar: I was killed i' the Capitol;   100
Brutus killed me.

HAM.   It was a brute part of him to kill so capital a calf there. Be the players ready?

ROS.   Ay, my lord; they stay upon your patience.

QUEEN.   Come hither, my dear Hamlet, sit by me.

HAM.   No, good mother, here's metal more attractive.

                    [*Lying down at Ophelia's feet.*

POL.   [*To the* KING] O, ho! do you mark that?

OPH.   You are merry, my lord.

HAM.   Who, I?

OPH.   Ay, my lord.   110

HAM.   O God, your only jig-maker. What should a man do but be merry? for, look you, how cheerfully my mother looks, and my father died within these two hours.

OPH.   Nay, 'tis twice two months, my lord.

HAM.   So long? Nay then, let the devil wear black, for I'll have a suit of sables. O heavens! die two months ago, and not forgotten yet? Then there's hope a great man's memory may outlive his life half a year: but, by 'r, lady, he must build churches, then; or else shall he suffer not thinking on, with the hobby-horse, whose epitaph is "For, O, for, O,   120
the hobby-horse is forgot."

Hautboys play. The dumb-show enters

Enter a KING *and a* QUEEN *very lovingly; the* QUEEN *embracing him, and he her. She kneels, and makes show of protestation unto him. He takes her up, and declines his head upon her neck: lays him down upon a bank of flowers: she, seeing him asleep, leaves him. Anon comes in a fellow, takes off his crown, kisses it, and pours poison in the* KING's *ears, and exit. The* QUEEN *returns; finds the* KING *dead, and makes passionate action. The*

POISONER, *with some two or three* MUTES, *comes in again, seeming to lament with her. The dead body is carried away. The* POISONER *wooes the* QUEEN *with gifts: she seems loath and unwilling awhile, but in the end accepts his love.* [*Exeunt.*

OPH.   What means this, my lord?
HAM.   Marry, this is miching mallecho; it means mischief.
OPH.   Belike this show imports the argument of the play.

Enter PROLOGUE

HAM.   We shall know by this fellow: the players cannot keep counsel; they'll tell all.
PRO.   For us, and for our tragedy,
Here, stooping to your clemency,
We beg your hearing patiently.   [*Exit.*
HAM.   Is this a prologue, or the posy of a ring?   130
OPH.   'Tis brief, my lord.
HAM.   As woman's love.

Enter two PLAYERS, KING *and* QUEEN

P. KING.   Full thirty times hath Phoebus' cart gone round
Neptune's salt-wash and Tellus' orbed ground,
And thirty dozen moons with borrow'd sheen
About the world have times twelve thirties been
Since love our hearts and Hymen did our hands
Unite commutual in most sacred bands.
P. QUEEN.   So many journeys may the sun and moon
Make us again count o'er ere love be done!   140
But, woe is me, you are so sick of late,
So far from cheer and from your former state,
That I distrust you. Yet, though I distrust,
Discomfort you, my lord, it nothing must:
For women's fear and love holds quantity;
In neither aught, or in extremity.
Now, what my love is, proof hath made you know;
And as my love is sized, my fear is so:
Where love is great, the littlest doubts are fear;
Where little fears grow great, great love grows there.   150
P. KING.   'Faith, I must leave thee, love, and shortly too;
My operant powers their functions leave to do:
And thou shalt live in this fair world behind,
Honour'd, beloved; and haply one as kind
For husband shalt thou—
P. QUEEN.   O, confound the rest!
Such love must needs be treason in my breast:
In second husband let me be accurst!
None wed the second but who kill'd the first.
HAM.   [*Aside*] Wormwood, wormwood.   160
P. QUEEN.   The instances that second marriage move
Are base respects of thrift, but none of love:
A second time I kill my husband dead,
When second husband kisses me in bed.
P. KING.   I do believe you think what now you speak;
But what we do determine oft we break.
Purpose is but the slave to memory,
Of violent birth, but poor validity:
Which now, like fruit unripe, sticks on the tree;
But fall, unshaken, when they mellow be.   170
Most necessary 'tis that we forget
To pay ourselves what to ourselves is debt:

What to ourselves in passion we propose,
The passion ending, doth the purpose lose.
The violence of either grief or joy
Their own enactures with themselves destroy:
Where joy most revels, grief doth most lament;
Grief joys, joy grieves, on slender accident.
This world is not for aye, nor 'tis not strange
That even our loves should with our fortunes change;   180
For 'tis a question left us yet to prove,
Whether love lead fortune, or else fortune love.
The great man down, you mark his favourite flies;
The poor advanced makes friends of enemies.
And hitherto doth love on fortune tend;
For who not needs shall never lack a friend,
And who in want a hollow friend doth try,
Directly seasons him his enemy.
But, orderly to end where I begun,
Our wills and fates do so contrary run   190
That our devices still are overthrown;
Our thoughts are ours, their ends none of our own:
So think thou wilt no second husband wed;
But die thy thoughts when thy first lord is dead.
P. QUEEN.   Nor earth to me give food, nor heaven light!
Sport and repose lock from me day and night!
To desperation turn my trust and hope!
An anchor's cheer in prison be my scope!
Each opposite that blanks the face of joy
Meet what I would have well and it destroy!   200
Both here and hence pursue me lasting strife,
If, once a widow, ever I be wife!
HAM.   If she should break it now!
P. KING.   'Tis deeply sworn. Sweet, leave me here awhile;
My spirits grow dull, and fain I would beguile
The tedious day with sleep.   [*Sleeps.*
P. QUEEN.   Sleep rock thy brain;
And never come mischance between us twain!   [*Exit.*

HAM.   Madam, how like you this play?
QUEEN.   The lady doth protest too much, methinks.   210
HAM.   O, but she'll keep her word.
KING.   Have you heard the argument? Is there no offence in 't?
HAM.   No, no, they do but jest, poison in jest; no offence i' the world.
KING.   What do you call the play?
HAM.   The Mouse-trap. Marry, how? Tropically. This play is the image of a murder done in Vienna: Gonzago is the duke's name; his wife, Baptista: you shall see anon; 'tis a knavish piece of work: but what o' that? your majesty   220
and we that have free souls, it touches us not: let the galled jade wince, our withers are unwrung.

Enter LUCIANUS

This is one Lucianus, nephew to the king.
OPH.   You are as good as a chorus, my lord.
HAM.   I could interpret between you and your love, if I could see the puppets dallying.
OPH.   You are keen, my lord, you are keen.
HAM.   It would cost you a groaning to take off my edge.

OPH.   Still better, and worse.

HAM.   So you mistake your husbands. Begin, murderer; pox, leave thy damnable faces, and begin. Come: "the croaking raven doth bellow for revenge." 230

LUC.   Thoughts black, hands apt, drugs fit, and time agreeing;

Confederate season, else no creature seeing;
Thou mixture rank, of midnight weeds collected,
With Hecate's ban thrice blasted, thrice infected,
Thy natural magic and dire property,
On wholesome life usurp immediately.

                  [Pours poison into the sleeper's ears.

HAM.   He poisons him i' the garden for 's estate. His name's Gonzago: the story is extant, and writ in choice 240 Italian: you shall see anon how the murderer gets the love of Gonzago's wife.

OPH.   The king rises.

HAM.   What, frighted with false fire!

QUEEN.   How fares my lord?

POL.   Give o'er the play.

KING.   Give me some light: away!

ALL.   Lights, lights, lights!

                  [Exeunt all but Hamlet and Horatio.

HAM.   Why, let the stricken deer go weep,
    The hart ungalled play;   250
    For some must watch, while some must sleep:
    So runs the world away.

Would not this, sir, and a forest of feathers—if the rest of my fortunes turn Turk with me—with two Provincial roses on my razed shoes, get me a fellowship in a cry of players, sir?

HOR.   Half a share.

HAM.   A whole one, I.
    For thou dost know, O Damon dear,
      This realm dismantled was   260
    Of Jove himself; and now reigns here
      A very, very—pajock.

HOR.   You might have rhymed.

HAM.   O good Horatio, I'll take the ghost's word for a thousand pound. Didst perceive?

HOR.   Very well, my lord.

HAM.   Upon the talk of the poisoning?

HOR.   I did very well note him.

HAM.   Ah, ha! Come, some music! come, the recorders!
    For if the king like not the comedy,   270
    Why then, belike, he likes it not, perdy.

Come, some music!

Re-enter ROSENCRANTZ *and* GUILDENSTERN

GUIL.   Good my lord, vouchsafe me a word with you.

HAM.   Sir, a whole history.

GUIL.   The king, sir,—

HAM.   Ay, sir, what of him?

GUIL.   Is in his retirement marvellous distempered.

HAM.   With drink, sir?

GUIL.   No, my lord, rather with choler.

HAM.   Your wisdom should show itself more richer to 280 signify this to his doctor; for, for me to put him to his purgation would perhaps plunge him into far more choler.

GUIL.   Good my lord, put your discourse into some frame, and start not so wildly from my affair.

HAM.   I am tame, sir: pronounce.

GUIL.   The queen, your mother, in most great affliction of spirit, hath sent me to you.

HAM.   You are welcome.

GUIL.   Nay, good my lord, this courtesy is not of the right breed. If it shall please you to make me a wholesome an- 290 swer, I will do your mother's commandment: if not, your pardon and my return shall be the end of my business.

HAM.   Sir, I cannot.

GUIL.   What, my lord?

HAM.   Make you a wholesome answer; my wit's diseased: but, sir, such answer as I can make, you shall command; or, rather, as you say, my mother: therefore no more, but to the matter: my mother, you say,—

ROS.   Then thus she says; your behaviour hath struck her into amazement and admiration. 300

HAM.   O wonderful son, that can so astonish a mother! But is there no sequel at the heels of this mother's admiration? Impart.

ROS.   She desires to speak with you in her closet, ere you go to bed.

HAM.   We shall obey, were she ten times our mother. Have you any further trade with us?

ROS.   My lord, you once did love me.

HAM.   So I do still, by these pickers and stealers.

ROS.   Good my lord, what is your cause of distemper? 310 you do, surely, bar the door upon your own liberty, if you deny your griefs to your friend.

HAM.   Sir, I lack advancement.

ROS.   How can that be, when you have the voice of the king himself for your succession in Denmark?

HAM.   Ay, sir, but "While the grass grows,"—the proverb is something musty.

Re-enter PLAYERS *with recorders*

O, the recorders! let me see one. To withdraw with you:— why do you go about to recover the wind of me, as if you would drive me into a toil? 320

GUIL.   O, my lord, if my duty be too bold, my love is too unmannerly.

HAM.   I do not well understand that. Will you play upon this pipe?

GUIL.   My lord, I cannot.

HAM.   I pray you.

GUIL.   Believe me, I cannot.

HAM.   I do beseech you.

GUIL.   I know no touch of it, my lord.

HAM.   'Tis as easy ay lying: govern these ventages with 330 your fingers and thumb, give it breath with your mouth, and it will discourse most eloquent music. Look you, these are the stops.

GUIL.   But these cannot I command to any utterance of harmony; I have not the skill.

HAM.   Why, look you now, how unworthy a thing you make of me! You would play upon me; you would seem to know my stops; you would pluck out the heart of my mystery; you would sound me from my lowest note to the top of my compass: and there is much music, excellent 340 voice, in this little organ; yet cannot you make it speak.

'Sblood, do you think I am easier to be played on than a
pipe? Call me what instrument you will, though you can
fret me, yet you cannot play upon me.

Enter POLONIUS

God bless you, sir!
POL.   My lord, the queen would speak with you, and
presently.
HAM.   Do you see yonder cloud that's almost in shape of
a camel?
POL.   By the mass, and 'tis like a camel, indeed.   350
HAM.   Methinks it is like a weasel.
POL.   It is backed like a weasel.
HAM.   Or like a whale?
POL.   Very like a whale.
HAM.   Then I will come to my mother by and by. They
fool me to the top of my bent. I will come by and by.
POL.   I will say so.
HAM.   By and by is easily said.   [*Exit Polonius.*]
Leave me, friends.   [*Exeunt all but Hamlet.*
'Tis now the very witching time of night,   360
When churchyards yawn and hell itself breathes out
Contagion to this world: now could I drink hot blood,
And do such bitter business as the day
Would quake to look on. Soft! now to my mother.
O heart, lose not thy nature; let not ever
The soul of Nero enter this firm bosom:
Let me be cruel, not unnatural:
I will speak daggers to her, but use none;
My tongue and soul in this be hypocrites;
How in my words soever she be shent,   370
To give them seals never, my soul, consent!   [*Exit.*

Scene III—A room in the castle

HAMLET *has his opportunity to translate resolution into action
and misses it. Critics have objected to what they regard as the cold-
blooded cruelty of his reasons for not killing the* KING *while he is
praying. But they do not observe that these are not reasons, only excuses.* HAMLET *would kill the* KING *if he could, but he has delayed
so long that he cannot now commit himself to the definite immediate
act. But the hour is slipping from him.* CLAUDIUS, *in spite of his
momentary weakness of contrition, is determined to get rid, in one
way or another, of this dangerous prince.*

Enter KING, ROSENCRANTZ, *and* GUILDENSTERN

KING.   I like him not, nor stands it safe with us   1
To let his madness range. Therefore prepare you;
I your commission will forthwith dispatch,
And he to England shall along with you:
The terms of our estate may not endure
Hazard so near us as doth hourly grow
Out of his lunacies.
GUIL.   We will ourselves provide:
Most holy and religious fear it is
To keep those many many bodies safe
That live and feed upon your majesty.   10
ROS.   The single and peculiar life is bound,
With all the strength and armour of the mind,

To keep itself from noyance; but much more
That spirit upon whose weal depend and rest
The lives of many. The cease of majesty
Dies not alone; but, like a gulf, doth draw
What's near it with it: it is a massy wheel,
Fix'd on the summit of the highest mount,
To whose huge spokes ten thousand lesser things   20
Are mortised and adjoin'd; which, when it falls,
Each small annexment, petty consequence,
Attends the boisterous ruin. Never alone
Did the king sigh, but with a general groan.
KING.   Arm you, I pray you, to this speedy voyage;
For we will fetters put upon this fear,
Which now goes too free-footed.
ROS.⎫
GUIL.⎭   We will haste us.
          [*Exeunt Rosencrantz and Guildenstern.*

Enter POLONIUS

POL.   My lord, he's going to his mother's closet:
Behind the arras I'll convey myself,   30
To hear the process; I'll warrant she'll tax him home:
And, as you said, and wisely was it said,
'Tis meet that some more audience than a mother,
Since nature makes them partial, should o'erhear
The speech, of vantage. Fare you well, my liege:
I'll call upon you ere you go to bed,
And tell you what I know.
KING.   Thanks, dear my lord.
          [*Exit Polonius.*

O, my offence is rank, it smells to heaven;
It hath the primal eldest curse upon 't,   40
A brother's murder. Pray can I not,
Though inclination be as sharp as will:
My stronger guilt defeats my strong intent;
And, like a man to double business bound,
I stand in pause where I shall first begin,
And both neglect. What if this cursed hand
Were thicker than itself with brother's blood,
Is there not rain enough in the sweet heavens
To wash it white as snow? Whereto serves mercy
But to confront the visage of offence?   50
And what's in prayer but this two-fold force,
To be forestalled ere we come to fall,
Or pardon'd being down? Then I'll look up;
My fault is past. But, O, what form of prayer
Can serve my turn? "Forgive me my foul murder"?
That cannot be; since I am still possess'd
Of those effects for which I did the murder,
My crown, mine own ambition and my queen.
May one be pardon'd and retain the offence?
In the corrupted currents of this world   60
Offence's gilded hand may shove by justice,
And oft 'tis seen the wicked prize itself
Buys out the law: but 'tis not so above;
There is no shuffling, there the action lies
In his true nature; and we ourselves compell'd,
Even to the teeth and forehead of our faults,
To give in evidence. What then? what rests?
Try what repentance can: what can it not?

Yet what can it when one can not repent?
O wretched state! O bosom black as death!   70
O limed soul, that, struggling to be free,
Art more engaged! Help, angels! Make assay!
Bow, stubborn knees; and, heart with strings of steel,
Be soft as sinews of the new-born babe!
All may be well.   [*Retires and kneels.*

Enter HAMLET

HAM.   Now might I do it pat, now he is praying;
And now I'll do 't. And so he goes to heaven:
And so am I revenged. That would be scann'd:
A villain kills my father; and for that,
I, his sole son, do this same villain send   80
To heaven.
O, this is hire and salary, not revenge.
He took my father grossly, full of bread;
With all his crimes broad blown, as flush as May;
And how his audit stands who knows save heaven?
But in our circumstance and course of thought,
'Tis heavy with him: and am I then revenged,
To take him in the purging of his soul,
When he is fit and season'd for his passage?
No!   90
Up, sword; and know thou a more horrid hent:
When he is drunk asleep, or in his rage,
Or in the incestuous pleasure of his bed;
At gaming, swearing, or about some act
That has no relish of salvation in 't;
Then trip him, that his heels may kick at heaven,
And that his soul may be as damn'd and black
As hell, whereto it goes. My mother stays:
This physic but prolongs thy sickly days.   [*Exit.*
KING.   [*Rising*] My words fly up, my thoughts remain
    below: 100
Words without thoughts never to heaven go.   [*Exit.*

Scene IV—The Queen's closet

There has been much critical controversy on the question of GERTRUDE'*s guilt or innocence in the matter of her husband's murder. The natural inference from this scene (especially Line 30), and from the* GHOST'*s story in Act I, Scene V, is that she knew nothing of it. She was guilty of a sinful love for* CLAUDIUS, *but was not an accomplice in his greater crime.* HAMLET, *indeed, assumes throughout that the stain of murder as well as of adultery is upon her, but he is naturally inclined to take the blackest view.*

In any case, it is his mother's faithlessness in love that HAMLET *resents most bitterly, and with this chiefly he upbraids her. At first he is successful: the stings of remorse begin to make themselves felt. Then comes the* GHOST, *and she is convinced that* HAMLET *is mad. From that moment she is overcome with fear, and his words pass over her unheeded. For the rest of the play her heart is cleft in twain; she vacillates to the end between good and evil, between her son and her lover.*

Enter QUEEN *and* POLONIUS

POL.   He will come straight. Look you lay home to him: 1
Tell him his pranks have been too broad to bear with,
And that your grace hath screen'd and stood between
Much heat and him. I'll silence me even here.
Pray you, be round with him.
HAM.   [*Within*] Mother, mother, mother!
QUEEN.   I'll warrant you,
Fear me not: withdraw, I hear him coming.
                      [*Polonius hides behind the arras.*

Enter HAMLET

HAM.   Now, mother, what's the matter?
QUEEN.   Hamlet, thou hast thy father much offended.   10
HAM.   Mother, you have my father much offended.
QUEEN.   Come, come, you answer with an idle tongue.
HAM.   Go, go, you question with a wicked tongue.
QUEEN.   Why, how now, Hamlet!
HAM.   What's the matter now?
QUEEN.   Have you forgot me?
HAM.   No, by the rood, not so:
You are the queen, your husband's brother's wife;
And—would it were not so!—you are my mother.
QUEEN.   Nay, then, I'll set those to you that can speak.   20
HAM.   Come, come, and sit you down; you shall not
    budge;
You go not till I set you up a glass
Where you may see the inmost part of you.
QUEEN.   What wilt thou do? thou wilt not murder me?
Help, help, ho!
POL.   [*Behind*] What, ho! help, help, help!
HAM.   [*Drawing*] How now! a rat? Dead, for a ducat,
    dead!   [*Makes a pass through the arras.*
POL.   [*Behind*] O, I am slain!   [*Falls and dies.*
QUEEN.   O me, what hast thou done?
HAM.   Nay, I know not: 30
Is it the king?
QUEEN.   O, what a rash and bloody deed is this!
HAM.   A bloody deed! almost as bad, good mother,
As kill a king, and marry with his brother.
QUEEN.   As kill a king!
HAM.   Ay, lady, 't was my word.
          [*Lifts up the arras and discovers Polonius.*
Thou wretched, rash, intruding fool, farewell!
I took thee for thy better: take thy fortune;
Thou find'st to be too busy is some danger.
Leave wringing of your hands: peace! sit you down,   40
And let me wring your heart; for so I shall,
If it be made of penetrable stuff,
If damned custom have not brass'd it so
That it be proof and bulwark against sense.
QUEEN.   What have I done, that thou darest wag thy
    tongue
In noise so rude against me?
HAM.   Such an act
That blurs the grace and blush of modesty,
Calls virtue hypocrite, takes off the rose
From the fair forehead of an innocent love   50
And sets a blister there, makes marriage-vows
As false as dicers' oaths: O, such a deed
As from the body of contraction plucks
The very soul, and sweet religion makes

A rhapsody of words: heaven's face doth glow;
Yea, this solidity and compound mass,
With tristful visage, as against the doom,
Is thought-sick at the act.
QUEEN.   Ay me, what act,
That roars so loud, and thunders in the index?   60
HAM.   Look here, upon this picture, and on this,
The counterfeit presentment of two brothers.
See, what a grace was seated on this brow;
Hyperion's curls; the front of Jove himself;
An eye like Mars, to threaten and command;
A station like the herald Mercury
New-lighted on a heaven-kissing hill;
A combination and a form indeed,
Where every god did seem to set his seal,
To give the world assurance of a man: 70
This was your husband. Look you now, what follows:
Here is your husband; like a mildew'd ear,
Blasting his wholesome brother. Have you eyes?
Could you on this fair mountain leave to feed,
And batten on this moor? Ha! have you eyes?
You cannot call it love; for at your age
The hey-day in the blood is tame, it's humble,
And waits upon the judgement: and what judgement
Would step from this to this? Sense, sure, you have,
Else could you not have motion; but sure, that sense   80
Is apoplex'd; for madness would not err,
Nor sense to ecstasy was ne'er so thrall'd
But it reserved some quantity of choice,
To serve in such a difference. What devil was 't
That thus hath cozen'd you at hoodman blind?
Eyes without feeling, feeling without sight,
Ears without hands or eyes, smelling sans all,
Or but a sickly part of one true sense
Could not so mope.
O shame! where is thy blush? Rebellious hell,   90
If thou canst mutine in a matron's bones,
To flaming youth let virtue be as wax,
And melt in her own fire: proclaim no shame
When the compulsive ardour gives the charge,
Since frost itself as actively doth burn
And reason panders will.
QUEEN.   O Hamlet, speak no more:
Thou turn'st mine eyes into my very soul;
And there I see such black and grained spots
As will not leave their tinct. O, speak to me no more;   100
These words, like daggers, enter in mine ears;
No more, sweet Hamlet!
HAM.   A murderer and a villain;
A slave that is not twentieth part the tithe
Of your precedent lord; a vice of kings,
A cutpurse of the empire and the rule,
That from a shelf the precious diadem stole,
And put it in his pocket!
QUEEN.   No more!
HAM.   A king of shreds and patches,—   110

Enter GHOST

Save me, and hover o'er me with your wings,
You heavenly guards! What would your gracious figure?

QUEEN.   Alas, he's mad!
HAM.   Do you not come your tardy son to chide,
That, lapsed in time and passion, lets go by
The important acting of your dread command?
O, say!
GHOST.   Do not forget: this visitation
Is but to whet thy almost blunted purpose.
But, look, amazement on thy mother sits: 120
O, step between her and her fighting soul.
Conceit in weakest bodies strongest works:
Speak to her, Hamlet.
HAM.   How is it with you, lady?
QUEEN.   Alas, how is 't with you,
That you do bend your eye on vacancy
And with the incorporal air do hold discourse?
Forth at your eyes your spirits wildly peep;
And, as the sleeping soldiers in the alarm,
Your bedded hair, like life in excrements,   130
Start up, and stand an end. O gentle son,
Upon the heat and flame of thy distemper
Sprinkle cool patience. Whereon do you look?
HAM.   On him, on him! Look you, how pale he glares!
His form and cause conjoin'd, preaching to stones,
Would make them capable. Do not look upon me;
Lest with this piteous action you convert
My stern effects: then what I have to do
Will want true colour; tears perchance for blood.
QUEEN.   To whom do you speak this?   140
HAM.   Do you see nothing there?
QUEEN.   Nothing at all; yet all that is I see.
HAM.   Nor did you nothing hear?
QUEEN.   No, nothing but ourselves.
HAM.   Why, look you there! look, how it steals away!
My father, in his habit as he lived!
Look, where he goes, even now, out at the portal!
                                        [*Exit Ghost.*

QUEEN.   This is the very coinage of your brain:
This bodiless creation ecstasy
Is very cunning in.   150
HAM.   Ecstasy!
My pulse, as yours, doth temperately keep time,
And makes as healthful music: it is not madness
That I have utter'd: bring me to the test,
And I the matter will re-word; which madness
Would gambol from. Mother, for love of grace,
Lay not that flattering unction to your soul,
That not your trespass, but my madness speaks:
It will but skin and film the ulcerous place,
Whiles rank corruption, mining all within,   160
Infects unseen. Confess yourself to heaven;
Repent what's past; avoid what is to come;
And do not spread the compost on the weeds,
To make them ranker. Forgive me this my virtue;
For in the fatness of these pursy times
Virtue itself of vice must pardon beg,
Yea, curb and woo for leave to do him good.
QUEEN.   O Hamlet, thou hast cleft my heart in twain.
HAM.   O, throw away the worser part of it,
And live the purer with the other half.   170
Good night: but go not to mine uncle's bed;

Assume a virtue, if you have it not.
That monster, custom, who all sense doth eat,
Of habits devil, is angel yet in this,
That to the use of actions fair and good
He likewise gives a frock or livery,
That aptly is put on. Refrain to-night,
And that shall lend a kind of easiness
To the next abstinence: the next more easy;
For use almost can change the stamp of nature,   180
And either . . . the devil, or throw him out
With wondrous potency. Once more, good night:
And when you are desirous to be bless'd,
I'll blessing beg of you. For this same lord,
                              [*Pointing to Polonius.*
I do repent: but heaven hath pleased it so,
To punish me with this and this with me,
That I must be their scourge and minister.
I will bestow him, and will answer well
The death I gave him. So, again, good night.
I must be cruel, only to be kind: 190
Thus bad begins and worse remains behind.
One word more, good lady.
QUEEN.   What shall I do?
HAM.   Not this, by no means, that I bid you do:
Let the bloat king tempt you again to bed;
Pinch wanton on your cheek; call you his mouse;
And let him, for a pair of reechy kisses,
Or paddling in your neck with his damn'd fingers,
Make you to ravel all this matter out,
That I essentially am not in madness,   200
But mad in craft. 'T were good you let him know;

For who, that's but a queen, fair, sober, wise,
Would from a paddock, from a bat, a gib,
Such dear concernings hide? who would do so?
No, in despite of sense and secrecy,
Unpeg the basket on the house's top,
Let the birds fly, and, like the famous ape,
To try conclusions, in the basket creep,
And break your own neck down.
QUEEN.   Be thou assured, if words be made of breath,   210
And breath of life, I have no life to breathe
What thou hast said to me.
HAM.   I must to England; you know that?
QUEEN.   Alack,
I had forgot: 'tis so concluded on.
HAM.   There's letters seal'd: and my two schoolfellows,
Whom I will trust as I will adders fang'd,
They bear the mandate; they must sweep my way,
And marshal me to knavery. Let it work;
For 'tis the sport to have the enginer   220
Hoist with his own petar: and 't shall go hard
But I will delve one yard below their mines,
And blow them at the moon: O, 'tis most sweet,
When in one line two crafts directly meet.
This man shall set me packing:
I'll lug the guts into the neighbour room.
Mother, good night. Indeed this counsellor
Is now most still, most secret and most grave,
Who was in life a foolish prating knave.
Come, sir, to draw toward an end with you.   230
Good night, mother.
                 [*Exeunt severally; Hamlet dragging in Polonius.*

Act IV

Scene I—A room in the castle

*This scene is practically continuous with Act III, Scene IV. As soon
as* HAMLET *has left his mother's closet,* CLAUDIUS *enters, to learn
the result of the interview. He finds the* QUEEN *overwhelmed and
hardly able to speak—the combined effect of her son's reproaches
and of her grief at his insanity.*

Enter KING, QUEEN, ROSENCRANTZ, *and* GUILDENSTERN

KING.   There's matter in these sighs, these profound
        heaves: 1
You must translate: 'tis fit we understand them.
Where is your son?
QUEEN.   Bestow this place on us a little while.
                    [*Exeunt Rosencrantz and Guildenstern.*
Ah, mine own lord, what have I seen to-night!
KING.   What, Gertrude? How does Hamlet?
QUEEN.   Mad as the sea and wind, when both contend
Which is the mightier: in his lawless fit,
Behind the arras hearing something stir,
Whips out his rapier, cries, "A rat, a rat!"   10

And, in this brainish apprehension, kills
The unseen good old man.
KING.   O heavy deed!
It had been so with us, had we been there:
His liberty is full of threats to all;
To you yourself, to us, to every one.
Alas, how shall this bloody deed be answer'd?
It will be laid to us, whose providence
Should have kept short, restrain'd and out of haunt,
This mad young man: but so much was our love,   20
We would not understand what was most fit;
But, like the owner of a foul disease,
To keep it from divulging, let it feed
Even on the pith of life. Where is he gone?
QUEEN.   To draw apart the body he hath kill'd:
O'er whom his very madness, like some ore
Among a mineral of metals base,
Shows itself pure; he weeps for what is done.
KING.   O Gertrude, come away!
The sun no sooner shall the mountains touch,   30
But we will ship him hence: and this vile deed

We must, with all our majesty and skill,
Both countenance and excuse. Ho, Guildenstern!

Re-enter ROSENCRANTZ *and* GUILDENSTERN

Friends both, go join you with some further aid:
Hamlet in madness hath Polonius slain,
And from his mother's closet hath he dragg'd him:
Go seek him out; speak fair, and bring the body
Into the chapel. I pray you, haste in this.
                    [*Exeunt Rosencrantz and Guildenstern.*
Come, Gertrude, we'll call up our wisest friends;
And let them know, both what we mean to do,   40
And what's untimely done . . .
Whose whisper o'er the world's diameter,
As level as the cannon to his blank,
Transports his poison'd shot, may miss our name,
And hit the woundless air. O, come away!
My soul is full of discord and dismay.   [*Exeunt.*

Scene II—Another room in the castle

In this scene and the following, HAMLET *continues his assumption of madness. He is not at all unwilling to be sent to England; it will compel him to further delay; and he promises himself an intellectual treat in checkmating any design that his companions may have against him.*

Enter HAMLET

HAM.   Safely stowed.   1
ROS. ⎫
GUIL. ⎭ [*Within*] Hamlet! Lord Hamlet!
HAM.   But soft, what noise? who calls on Hamlet?
O, here they come.

Enter ROSENCRANTZ *and* GUILDENSTERN

ROS.   What have you done, my lord, with the dead body?
HAM.   Compounded it with dust, whereto 'tis kin.
ROS.   Tell us where 'tis, that we may take it thence
And bear it to the chapel.
HAM.   Do not believe it.
ROS.   Believe what?   10
HAM.   That I can keep your counsel and not mine own.
Besides, to be demanded of a sponge! what replication
should be made by the son of a king?
ROS.   Take you me for a sponge, my lord?
HAM.   Ay, sir, that soaks up the king's countenance, his
rewards, his authorities. But such officers do the king best
service in the end: he keeps them, like an ape, in the cor-
ner of his jaw; first mouthed, to be last swallowed: when
he needs what you have gleaned, it is but squeezing you,
and, sponge, you shall be dry again.   20
ROS.   I understand you not, my lord.
HAM.   I am glad of it: a knavish speech sleeps in a foolish
ear.
ROS.   My lord, you must tell us where the body is, and
go with us to the king.
HAM.   The body is with the king, but the king is not with
the body. The king is a thing—
GUIL.   A thing, my lord!

HAM.   Of nothing: bring me to him. Hide fox, and all
after.   [*Exeunt.*   30

Scene III—Another room in the castle

(See synopsis for Act IV, Scene II.)

Enter KING, *attended*

KING.   I have sent to seek him, and to find the body.   1
How dangerous is it that this man goes loose!
Yet must not we put the strong law on him:
He's loved of the distracted multitude,
Who like not in their judgement, but their eyes;
And where 'tis so, the offender's scourge is weigh'd,
But never the offence. To bear all smooth and even,
This sudden sending him away must seem
Deliberate pause: diseases desperate grown
By desperate appliance are relieved,   10
Or not at all.

Enter ROSENCRANTZ

How now! what hath befall'n?
ROS.   Where the dead body is bestow'd, my lord,
We cannot get from him.
KING.   But where is he?
ROS.   Without, my lord; guarded, to know your pleasure.
KING.   Bring him before us.
ROS.   Ho, Guildenstern! bring in my lord.

Enter HAMLET *and* GUILDENSTERN

KING.   Now, Hamlet, where's Polonius?
HAM.   At supper.   20
KING.   At supper! where?
HAM.   Not where he eats, but where he is eaten: a certain
convocation of politic worms are e'en at him. Your worm
is your only emperor for diet: we fat all creatures else to
fat us, and we fat ourselves for maggots: your fat king and
your lean beggar is but variable service, two dishes, but to
one table: that's the end.
KING.   Alas, alas!
HAM.   A man may fish with the worm that hath eat of a
king, and eat of the fish that hath fed of that worm.   30
KING.   What dost thou mean by this?
HAM.   Nothing but to show you how a king may go a
progress through the guts of a beggar.
KING.   Where is Polonius?
HAM.   In heaven; send thither to see: if your messenger
find him not there, seek him i' the other place yourself.
But indeed, if you find him not within this month, you
shall nose him as you go up the stairs into the lobby.
KING.   Go seek him there.   [*To some Attendants.*
HAM.   He will stay till you come.   [*Exeunt Attendants.*   40

KING.   Hamlet, this deed, for thine especial safety,—
Which we do tender, as we dearly grieve
For that which thou hast done,—must send thee hence
With fiery quickness: therefore prepare thyself;
The bark is ready, and the wind at help,

The associates tend, and every thing is bent
For England.
HAM.　　　For England!
KING.　　　　Ay, Hamlet.
HAM.　　　　　　　Good.　　　　　　50
KING.　So is it, if thou knew'st our purposes.
HAM.　I see a cherub that sees them. But, come; for England! Farewell, dear mother.
KING.　Thy loving father, Hamlet.
HAM.　My mother: father and mother is man and wife; man and wife is one flesh; and so, my mother. Come, for England!　　　　　　[*Exit.*
KING.　Follow him at foot; tempt him with speed aboard;
Delay it not; I'll have him hence to-night:
Away! for every thing is seal'd and done　　60
That else leans on the affair: pray you, make haste.
　　　　[*Exeunt Rosencrantz and Guildenstern.*
And, England, if my love thou hold'st at aught—
As my great power thereof may give thee sense,
Since yet thy cicatrice looks raw and red
After the Danish sword, and thy free awe
Pays homage to us—thou mayst not coldly set
Our sovereign process; which imports at full,
By letters congruing to that effect,
The present death of Hamlet. Do it, England;
For like the hectic in my blood he rages,　　70
And thou must cure me: till I know 'tis done,
Howe'er my haps, my joys were ne'er begun.　[*Exit.*

Scene IV—A plain in Denmark

The present act works out the results of HAMLET's *failure until they bring about the catastrophe of Act V. There are two main threads of incident: (1) there is the failure of the plot against* HAMLET's *life, which leads to his return to Denmark, and drives* CLAUDIUS *to new devices; and (2)* HAMLET's *unkindness to* OPHELIA, *together with the death of* POLONIUS, *makes her insane.* LAERTES *returns, burning for revenge, and readily becomes the* KING's *accomplice.*

The stress laid upon the fortunes of OPHELIA *in the latter part of the play has its dramatic purpose. It impresses us with the fact that* HAMLET's *ineffectiveness has its tragic results outside his own life; and at the same time the pathos of the situation makes us feel pity rather than anger toward him, since his deep affection for* OPHELIA *is manifest throughout. And it is essential to the effect of tragedy that the sympathies of the spectator should be at the end with the hero.*

The scene with the CAPTAIN *serves as a transition to the new act; at the same time it strikes the note of contrast between* HAMLET *and* FORTINBRAS, *the strong, practical man. The perception of this contrast is characteristically put in* HAMLET's *own mouth.*

Enter FORTINBRAS, *a* CAPTAIN, *and* SOLDIERS, *marching*

FORT.　Go, captain, from me greet the Danish king;　1
Tell him that, by his license, Fortinbras
Craves the conveyance of a promised march
Over his kingdom. You know the rendezvous.
If that his majesty would aught with us,
We shall express our duty in his eye;
And let him know so.
CAP.　　　　　　I will do 't, my lord.
FORT.　Go softly on.　　[*Exeunt Fortinbras and Soldiers.*

Enter HAMLET, ROSENCRANTZ, GUILDENSTERN, *and others*

HAM.　Good sir, whose powers are these?　　10
CAP.　They are of Norway, sir.
HAM.　How purposed, sir, I pray you?
CAP.　Against some part of Poland.
HAM.　Who commands them, sir?
CAP.　The nephew to old Norway, Fortinbras.
HAM.　Goes it against the main of Poland, sir,
Or for some frontier?
CAP.　Truly to speak, and with no addition,
We go to gain a little patch of ground
That hath in it no profit but the name.　　20
To pay five ducats, five, I would not farm it:
Nor will it yield to Norway or the Pole
A ranker rate, should it be sold in fee.
HAM.　Why, then the Polack never will defend it.
CAP.　Yes, it is already garrison'd.
HAM.　Two thousand souls and twenty thousand ducats
Will not debate the question of this straw:
This is the imposthume of much wealth and peace,
That inward breaks, and shows no cause without
Why the man dies. I humbly thank you, sir.　　30
CAP.　God be wi' you, sir.　　　　　　[*Exit.*
ROS.　　　　　　Will 't please you go, my lord?
HAM.　I'll be with you straight. Go a little before.
　　　　　　[*Exeunt all except Hamlet.*
How all occasions do inform against me,
And spur my dull revenge! What is a man,
If his chief good and market of his time
Be but to sleep and feed? a beast, no more.
Sure, he that made us with such large discourse,
Looking before and after, gave us not
That capability and god-like reason　　40
To fust in us unused. Now, whether it be
Bestial oblivion, or some craven scruple
Of thinking too precisely on the event,
A thought which, quarter'd, hath but one part wisdom
And ever three parts coward, I do not know
Why yet I live to say "This thing's to do";
Sith I have cause and will and strength and means
To do 't. Examples gross as earth exhort me:
Witness this army of such mass and charge
Led by a delicate and tender prince,　　50
Whose spirit with divine ambition puff'd
Makes mouths at the invisible event,
Exposing what is mortal and unsure
To all that fortune, death and danger dare,
Even for an egg-shell. Rightly to be great
Is not to stir without great argument,
But greatly to find quarrel in a straw
When honour's at the stake. How stand I then,
That have a father kill'd, a mother stain'd,
Excitements of my reason and my blood,　　60
And let all sleep? while, to my shame, I see
The imminent death of twenty thousand men,
That, for a fantasy and trick of fame,

Go to their graves like beds, fight for a plot
Whereon the numbers cannot try the cause,
Which is not tomb enough and continent
To hide the slain? O, from this time forth,
My thoughts be bloody, or be nothing worth!   [*Exit.*

Scene V—Elsinore. A room in the castle

*The interest of Scenes V and VII lies partly in the ingenuity with
which the* KING *turns* LAERTES *to his purposes, partly in the
pathos of* OPHELIA*'s madness and death.* LAERTES *is a youth of
high spirit and true emotions, but his French training has left him
without high principle, and he is weak enough to be easily led. The
genuine insanity of* OPHELIA *is a pendant to that assumed by*
HAMLET; *the immediate cause is her father's death, yet the loss of
her lover must also have affected her deeply. The character of the
songs she sings—they are not given in full in this edition—is not
inconsistent with perfect purity; all who have had experience with
mad patients can confirm this; and therefore it gives no support to
the curious theory, held by no less a critic than Goethe, that she had
been* HAMLET*'s mistress.*

Enter QUEEN, HORATIO, *and a* GENTLEMAN

QUEEN.   I will not speak with her.   1
GENT.   She is importunate, indeed distract:
Her mood will needs be pitied.
QUEEN.   What would she have?
GENT.   She speaks much of her father; says she hears
There's tricks i' the world; and hems, and beats her heart;
Spurns enviously at straws; speaks things in doubt,
That carry but half sense: her speech is nothing,
Yet the unshaped use of it doth move
The hearers to collection; they aim at it,   10
And botch the words up fit to their own thoughts;
Which, as her winks, and nods, and gestures yield them,
Indeed would make one think there might be thought,
Though nothing sure, yet much unhappily.
HOR.   'T were good she were spoken with; for she may
        strew
Dangerous conjectures in ill-breeding minds.
QUEEN.   Let her come in.   [*Exit Horatio.*
To my sick soul, as sin's true nature is,
Each toy seems prologue to some great amiss:
So full of artless jealousy is guilt,   20
It spills itself in fearing to be spilt.

Re-enter HORATIO, *with* OPHELIA

OPH.   Where is the beauteous majesty of Denmark?
QUEEN.   How now, Ophelia!
OPH.   [*Sings*] How should I your true love know
                From another one?
                    By his cockle hat and staff,
                        And his sandal shoon.
QUEEN.   Alas, sweet lady, what imports this song?
OPH.   Say you? nay, pray you, mark.
[*Sings*]   He is dead and gone, lady,   30
            He is dead and gone;
                At his head a grass-green turf,
                    At his heels a stone.

QUEEN.   Nay, but, Ophelia,—
OPH.   Pray you, mark.
[*Sings*] White his shroud as the mountain snow,—

Enter KING

QUEEN.   Alas, look here, my lord.
OPH.   [*Sings*] Larded with sweet flowers;
                Which bewept to the grave did go
                    With true-love showers.   40
KING.   How do you, pretty lady?
OPH.   Well, God 'ild you! They say the owl was a baker's
daughter. Lord, we know what we are, but know not what
we may be. God be at your table!
KING.   Conceit upon her father.
OPH.   Pray you, let's have no words of this; but when
they ask you what it means, say you this:
[*Sings*]   To-morrow is Saint Valentine's day,
            All in the morning betime,
                And I a maid at your window,   50
                    To be your Valentine.
KING.   How long hath she been thus?
OPH.   I hope all will be well. We must be patient: but I
cannot choose but weep, to think they should lay him i'
the cold ground. My brother shall know of it: and so I
thank you for your good counsel. Come, my coach! Good
night, ladies; good night, sweet ladies; good night, good
night.   [*Exit.*
KING.   Follow her close; give her good watch, I pray you.
                        [*Exit Horatio.*
O, this is the poison of deep grief; it springs   60
All from her father's death. O Gertrude, Gertrude,
When sorrows come, they come not single spies,
But in battalions. First, her father slain:
Next, your son gone; and he most violent author
Of his own just remove: the people muddied,
Thick and unwholesome in their thoughts and whispers,
For good Polonius' death; and we have done but greenly,
In hugger-mugger to inter him: poor Ophelia
Divided from herself and her fair judgement,
Without the which we are pictures, or mere beasts: 70
Last, and as much containing as all these,
Her brother is in secret come from France:
Feeds on his wonder, keeps himself in clouds,
And wants not buzzers to infect his ear
With pestilent speeches of his father's death;
Wherein necessity, of matter beggar'd,
Will nothing stick our person to arraign
In ear and ear. O my dear Gertrude, this,
Like to a murdering-piece, in many places
Gives me superfluous death.   [*A noise within.*   80
QUEEN.   Alack, what noise is this?
KING.   Where are my Switzers? Let them guard the door.

Enter another GENTLEMAN

What is the matter?
GENT.   Save yourself, my lord:
The ocean, overpeering of his list,
Eats not the flats with more impetuous haste
Than young Laertes, in a riotous head,
O'erbears your officers. The rabble call him lord;

And, as the world were now but to begin,
Antiquity forgot, custom not known,   90
The ratifiers and props of every word,
They cry "Choose we: Laertes shall be king":
Caps, hands and tongues, applaud it to the clouds:
"Laertes shall be king, Laertes king!"
QUEEN.   How cheerfully on the false trail they cry!
O, this is counter, you false Danish dogs!
KING.   The doors are broke.   [*Noise within.*

Enter LAERTES, *armed; Danes following*

LAER.   Where is this king? Sirs, stand you all without.
DANES.   No, let's come in.
LAER.   I pray you, give me leave.   100
DANES.   We will, we will.
                              [*They retire without the door.*
LAER.   I thank you: keep the door. O thou vile king,
Give me my father!
QUEEN.   Calmly, good Laertes.
LAER.   That drop of blood that's calm proclaims me
    bastard,
Cries cuckold to my father, brands the harlot
Even here, between the chaste unsmirched brows
Of my true mother.
KING.   What is the cause, Laertes,
That thy rebellion looks so giant-like?   110
Let him go, Gertrude; do not fear our person:
There's such divinity doth hedge a king,
That treason can but peep to what it would,
Acts little of his will. Tell me, Laertes,
Why thou art thus incensed. Let him go, Gertrude.
Speak, man.
LAER.   Where is my father?
KING.   Dead.
QUEEN.   But not by him.
KING.   Let him demand his fill.   120
LAER.   How came he dead? I'll not be juggled with:
To hell, allegiance! vows, to the blackest devil!
Conscience and grace, to the profoundest pit!
I dare damnation. To this point I stand,
That both the worlds I give to negligence,
Let come what comes; only I'll be revenged
Most thoroughly for my father.
KING.   Who shall stay you?
LAER.   My will, not all the world:
And for my means, I'll husband them so well,   130
They shall go far with little.
KING.   Good Laertes,
If you desire to know the certainty
Of your dear father's death, is 't writ in your revenge,
That, swoopstake, you will draw both friend and foe,
Winner and loser?
LAER.   None but his enemies.
KING.   Will you know them then?
LAER.   To his good friends thus wide I'll ope my arms;
And like the kind life-rendering pelican,   140
Repast them with my blood.
KING.   Why, now you speak
Like a good child and a true gentleman.
That I am guiltless of your father's death,

And am most sensibly in grief for it,
It shall as level to your judgement pierce
As day does to your eye.
DANES.   [*Within*] Let her come in.
LAER.   How now! what noise is that?

Re-enter OPHELIA

O heat, dry up my brains! tears seven times salt,   150
Burn out the sense and virtue of mine eye!
By heaven, thy madness shall be paid with weight,
Till our scale turn the beam. O rose of May!
Dear maid, kind sister, sweet Ophelia!
O heavens! is 't possible, a young maid's wits
Should be as mortal as an old man's life?
Nature is fine in love, and where 'tis fine,
It sends some precious instance of itself
After the thing it loves.
OPH.   [*Sings*]
    They bore him barefaced on the bier;   160
    Hey non nonny, nonny, hey nonny;
    And in his grave rain'd many a tear:—
Fare you well, my dove!
LAER.   Hadst thou thy wits, and didst persuade revenge,
It could not move thus.
OPH.   [*Sings*] You must sing a-down a-down,
    An you call him a-down-a.
O, how the wheel becomes it! It is the false steward, that
stole his master's daughter.
LAER.   This nothing's more than matter.   170
OPH.   There's rosemary, that's for remembrance; pray,
love, remember: and there is pansies, that's for thoughts.
LAER.   A document in madness, thoughts and remem-
brance fitted.
OPH.   There's fennel for you, and columbines: there's rue
for you; and here's some for me: we may call it herb-grace
o' Sundays: O, you must wear your rue with a difference.
There's a daisy: I would give you some violets, but they
withered all when my father died: they say he made a
good end,—   180
[*Sings*] For bonny sweet Robin is all my joy.
LAER.   Thought and affliction, passion, hell itself,
She turns to favour and to prettiness.
OPH.   [*Sings*] And will he not come again?
    And will he not come again?
        No, no, he is dead:
        Go to thy death-bed:
    He never will come again.

    His beard was as white as snow,
    All flaxen was his poll: 190
        He is gone, he is gone,
        And we cast away moan:
    God ha' mercy on his soul!
And of all Christian souls, I pray God. God be wi' ye.
                                          [*Exit.*

LAER.   Do you see this, O God?
KING.   Laertes, I must commune with your grief,
Or you deny me right. Go but apart,
Make choice of whom your wisest friends you will,
And they shall hear and judge 'twixt you and me:
If by direct or by collateral hand   200

They find us touch'd, we will our kingdom give,
Our crown, our life, and all that we call ours,
To you in satisfaction; but if not,
Be you content to lend your patience to us,
And we shall jointly labour with your soul
To give it due content.
LAER.   Let this be so;
His means of death, his obscure burial—
No trophy, sword, nor hatchment o'er his bones,
No noble rite nor formal ostentation—   210
Cry to be heard, as 't were from heaven to earth,
That I must call 't in question.
KING.   So you shall;
And where the offence is let the great axe fall.
I pray you, go with me.   [*Exeunt.*

Scene VI—Another room in the castle

This scene serves to keep the fortunes of HAMLET *in our mind during the period of his absence. It is simultaneous with Scenes V and VII, the action of which is practically continuous, and in a modern play it would probably be made to take place in a corner of the same hall, while the* KING *and* LAERTES *whisper apart.*

Enter HORATIO *and a* SERVANT

HOR.   What are they that would speak with me?   1
SERV.   Sea-faring men, sir: they say they have letters for you.
HOR.   Let them come in.   [*Exit Servant.*
I do not know from what part of the world
I should be greeted, if not from lord Hamlet.

Enter SAILORS

FIRST SAILOR.   God bless you, sir.
HOR.   Let him bless thee too.
FIRST SAILOR.   He shall, sir, an 't please him. There's a letter for you, sir; it comes from the ambassador that was   10
bound for England; if your name be Horatio, as I am let to know it is.
HOR.   [*Reads*] "Horatio, when thou shalt have overlooked this, give these fellows some means to the king: they have letters for him. Ere we were two days old at sea, a pirate of very warlike appointment gave us chase. Finding ourselves too slow of sail, we put on a compelled valour, and in the grapple I boarded them: on the instant they   20
got clear of our ship; so I alone became their prisoner. They have dealt with me like thieves of mercy: but they knew what they did; I am to do a good turn for them. Let the king have the letters I have sent; and repair thou to me with as much speed as thou wouldst fly death. I have words to speak in thine ear will make thee dumb; yet are they much too light for the bore of the matter. These good fellows will bring thee where I am. Rosencrantz and Guildenstern hold their course for England: of them I have much to tell thee. Farewell.
            "He that thou knowest thine, HAMLET."
Come, I will make you way for these your letters;   30
And do 't the speedier, that you may direct me
To him from whom you brought them.   [*Exeunt.*

Scene VII—Another room in the castle

The LAERTES *motive and the* OPHELIA *motive of Scene V are continued here.* LAERTES *proves an easy tool for the* KING's *ingenious villainy. His naturally impetuous temper, made degenerate by such a life in France as is suggested in Act III, Scene I, snatches at even an ignoble chance of revenge.*

Enter KING *and* LAERTES

KING.   Now must your conscience my acquittance seal,   1
And you must put me in your heart for friend,
Sith you have heard, and with a knowing ear,
That he which hath your noble father slain
Pursued my life.
LAER.   It well appears: but tell me
Why you proceeded not against these feats,
So crimeful and so capital in nature,
As by your safety, wisdom, all things else,
You mainly were stirr'd up.   10
KING.   O, for two special reasons;
Which may to you, perhaps, seem much unsinew'd,
But yet to me they are strong. The queen his mother
Lives almost by his looks; and for myself—
My virtue or my plague, be it either which—
She's so conjunctive to my life and soul,
That, as the star moves not but in his sphere,
I could not but by her. The other motive,
Why to a public count I might not go,
Is the great love the general gender bear him;   20
Who, dipping all his faults in their affection,
Would, like the spring that turneth wood to stone,
Convert his gyves to graces; so that my arrows,
Too slightly timber'd for so loud a wind,
Would have reverted to my bow again,
And not where I had aim'd them.
LAER.   And so have I a noble father lost;
A sister driven into desperate terms,
Whose worth, if praises may go back again,
Stood challenger on mount of all the age   30
For her perfections: but my revenge will come.
KING.   Break not your sleeps for that: you must not think
That we are made of stuff so flat and dull
That we can let our beard be shook with danger
And think it pastime. You shortly shall hear more:
I loved your father, and we love ourself;
And that, I hope, will teach you to imagine—

Enter a MESSENGER

How now! what news?
MESS.   Letters, my lord, from Hamlet:
This to your majesty; this to the queen.   40
KING.   From Hamlet! who brought them?
MESS.   Sailors, my lord, they say; I saw them not:
They were given me by Claudio; he received them
Of him that brought them.
KING.   Laertes, you shall hear them.
Leave us.   [*Exit Messenger.*
[*Reads*] "High and mighty, You shall know I am set naked
on your kingdom. To-morrow shall I beg leave to see
your kingly eyes: when I shall, first asking your pardon

thereunto, recount the occasion of my sudden and more   50
strange return.
                                            "HAMLET."
What should this mean? Are all the rest come back?
Or is it some abuse, and no such thing?
LAER.   Know you the hand?
KING.   'Tis Hamlet's character. "Naked!"
And in a postscript here, he says, "alone."
Can you advise me?
LAER.   I'm lost in it, my lord. But let him come;
It warms the very sickness in my heart,   60
That I shall live and tell him to his teeth,
"Thus didest thou."
KING.   If it be so, Laertes—
As how should it be so? how otherwise?—
Will you be ruled by me?
LAER.   Ay, my lord;
So you will not o'errule me to a peace.
KING.   To thine own peace. If he be now return'd,
As checking at his voyage, and that he means
No more to undertake it, I will work him   70
To an exploit, now ripe in my device,
Under the which he shall not choose but fall:
And for his death no wind of blame shall breathe,
But even his mother shall uncharge the practice
And call it accident.
LAER.   My lord, I will be ruled;
The rather, if you could devise it so
That I might be the organ.
KING.   It falls right.
You have been talk'd of since your travel much,   80
And that in Hamlet's hearing, for a quality
Wherein, they say, you shine: your sum of parts
Did not together pluck such envy from him
As did that one, and that, in my regard,
Of the unworthiest siege.
LAER.   What part is that, my lord?
KING.   A very riband in the cap of youth,
Yet needful too; for youth no less becomes
The light and careless livery that it wears
Than settled age his sables and his weeds,   90
Importing health and graveness. Two months since,
Here was a gentleman of Normandy:—
I've seen myself, and served against, the French,
And they can well on horseback: but this gallant
Had witchcraft in 't; he grew onto his seat;
And to such wondrous doing brought his horse,
As had he been incorpsed and demi-natured
With the brave beast: so far he topp'd my thought,
That I, in forgery of shapes and tricks,
Come short of what he did.   100
LAER.   A Norman, was 't?
KING.   A Norman.
LAER.   Upon my life, Lamond.
KING.   The very same.
LAER.   I know him well: he is the brooch indeed
And gem of all the nation.
KING.   He made confession of you,
And gave you such a masterly report
For art and exercise in your defence

And for your rapier most especial,   110
That he cried out, 't would be a sight indeed,
If one could match you: the scrimers of their nation,
He swore, had neither motion, guard, nor eye
If you opposed them. Sir, this report of his
Did Hamlet so envenom with his envy
That he could nothing do but wish and beg
Your sudden coming o'er, to play with him.
Now, out of this,—
LAER.   What out of this, my lord?
KING.   Laertes, was your father dear to you?   120
Or are you like the painting of a sorrow,
A face without a heart?
LAER.   Why ask you this?
KING.   Not that I think you did not love your father;
But that I know love is begun by time;
And that I see, in passages of proof,
Time qualifies the spark and fire of it.
There lives within the very flame of love
A kind of wick or snuff that will abate it;
And nothing is at a like goodness still;   130
For goodness, growing to a plurisy,
Dies in his own too much: that we would do,
We should do when we would; for this "would" changes
And hath abatements and delays as many
As there are tongues, are hands, are accidents;
And then this "should" is like a spendthrift sigh,
That hurts by easing. But, to the quick o' the ulcer:—
Hamlet comes back: what would you undertake,
To show yourself your father's son in deed
More than in words?   140
LAER.   To cut his throat i' the church.
KING.   No place, indeed, should murder sanctuarize;
Revenge should have no bounds. But, good Laertes,
Will you do this, keep close within your chamber.
Hamlet return'd shall know you are come home:
We'll put on those shall praise your excellence
And set a double varnish on the fame
The Frenchman gave you, bring you in fine together
And wager on your heads: he, being remiss,
Most generous and free from all contriving,   150
Will not peruse the foils; so that, with ease,
Or with a little shuffling, you may choose
A sword unbated, and in a pass of practice
Requite him for your father.
LAER.   I will do 't:
And, for that purpose, I'll anoint my sword.
I bought an unction of a mountebank,
So mortal that, but dip a knife in it,
Where it draws blood no cataplasm so rare,
Collected from all simples that have virtue   160
Under the moon, can save the thing from death
That is but scratch'd withal: I'll touch my point
With this contagion, that, if I gall him slightly,
It may be death.
KING.   Let's further think of this;
Weigh what convenience both of time and means
May fit us to our shape: if this should fail,
And that our drift look through our bad performance,
'T were better not assay'd: therefore this project

Should have a back or second, that might hold,
If this should blast in proof. Soft! let me see:
We'll make a solemn wager on your cunnings:
I ha 't:
When in your motion you are hot and dry—
As make your bouts more violent to that end—
And that he calls for drink, I'll have prepared him
A chalice for the nonce, whereon but sipping,
If he by chance escape your venom'd stuck,
Our purpose may hold there.

Enter QUEEN

                How now, sweet queen!   180
QUEEN.   One woe doth tread upon another's heel,
So fast they follow: your sister's drown'd, Laertes.
LAER.   Drown'd! O, where?
QUEEN.   There is a willow grows aslant a brook,
That shows his hoar leaves in the glassy stream;
There with fantastic garlands did she come
Of crow-flowers, nettles, daisies, and long purples
That liberal shepherds give a grosser name,
But our cold maids do dead men's fingers call them:
There, on the pendent boughs her coronet weeds   190
Clambering to hang, an envious sliver broke;

170

When down her weedy trophies and herself
Fell in the weeping brook. Her clothes spread wide;
And, mermaid-like, awhile they bore her up:
Which time she chanted snatches of old tunes;
As one incapable of her own distress,
Or like a creature native and indued
Unto that element: but long it could not be
Till that her garments, heavy with their drink,
Pull'd the poor wretch from her melodious lay   200
To muddy death.
LAER.   Alas, then, she is drown'd?
QUEEN.   Drown'd, drown'd.
LAER.   Too much of water hast thou, poor Ophelia,
And therefore I forbid my tears: but yet
It is our trick; nature her custom holds,
Let shame say what it will: when these are gone,
The woman will be out. Adieu, my lord:
I have a speech of fire, that fain would blaze,
But that this folly douts it.   [*Exit.* 210
KING.   Let's follow, Gertrude:
How much I had to do to calm his rage!
Now fear I this will give it start again;
Therefore let's follow.   [*Exeunt.*

—⁂—

Act V

Scene I—A churchyard

This scene does not advance the action much, for HAMLET'*s quarrel with* LAERTES *has very little to do with their subsequent encounter; it only serves to bring into contrast the opposing characters of the two men. But we want a moment or two of relief before the breathless rush with which the play closes, and this the grim humor of the grave-diggers and* HAMLET'*s moralizing afford. The solemnity of* OPHELIA'*s burial helps us to realize the pathos of her fate, and therein the tragedy of* HAMLET'*s failure.*

    The dialogue between the CLOWNS *affords an example of Shakespeare's unrivaled power of insight into the mental habits and modes of reasoning of uneducated people.*

Enter two CLOWNS, *with spades, &c.*

FIRST CLO.   Is she to be buried in Christian burial that wilfully seeks her own salvation?   1
SEC. CLO.   I tell thee she is: and therefore make her grave straight: the crowner hath sat on her, and finds it Christian burial.
FIRST CLO.   How can that be, unless she drowned herself in her own defence?
SEC. CLO.   Why, 'tis found so.
FIRST CLO.   It must be "se offendendo"; it cannot be else. For here lies the point: if I drown myself wittingly, it argues an act: and an act hath three branches; it is, to act, to do, and to perform: argal, she drowned herself wittingly.   10
SEC. CLO.   Nay, but hear you, goodman delver,—
FIRST CLO.   Give me leave. Here lies the water; good:

here stands the man; good: if the man go to this water, and drown himself, it is, will he, nill he, he goes,—mark you that; but if the water come to him and drown him, he drowns not himself: argal, he that is not guilty of his own death shortens not his own life.   20
SEC. CLO.   But is this law?
FIRST CLO.   Ay, marry, is 't; crowner's quest law.
SEC. CLO.   Will you ha' the truth on 't? If this had not been a gentlewoman, she should have been buried out o' Christian burial.
FIRST CLO.   Why, there thou say'st: and the more pity that great folk should have countenance in this world to drown or hang themselves, more than their even Christian. Come, my spade. There is no ancient gentlemen but gardeners, ditchers, and grave-makers: they hold up   30
Adam's profession.
SEC. CLO.   Was he a gentleman?
FIRST CLO.   'A was the first that ever bore arms.
SEC. CLO.   Why, he had none.
FIRST CLO.   What, art a heathen? How dost thou understand the Scripture? The Scripture says "Adam digged": could he dig without arms? I'll put another question to thee: if thou answerest me not to the purpose, confess thyself—
SEC. CLO.   Go to.   40
FIRST CLO.   What is he that builds stronger than either the mason, the shipwright, or the carpenter?
SEC. CLO.   The gallows-maker; for that frame outlives a thousand tenants.

FIRST CLO.   I like thy wit well, in good faith: the gallows does well; but how does it well? it does well to those who do ill: now thou dost ill to say the gallows is built stronger than the church: argal, the gallows may do well to thee. To 't again, come.

SEC. CLO.   "Who builds stronger than a mason, a ship-wright, or a carpenter?"   50

FIRST CLO.   Ay, tell me that, and unyoke.

SEC. CLO.   Marry, now I can tell.

FIRST CLO.   To 't.

SEC. CLO.   Mass, I cannot tell.

Enter HAMLET *and* HORATIO, *at a distance*

FIRST CLO.   Cudgel thy brains no more about it, for your dull ass will not mend his pace with beating; and, when you are asked this question next, say "a grave-maker": the houses that he makes last till doomsday. Go, get thee to Yaughan: fetch me a stoup of liquor.   [*Exit Sec. Clown.* 60
[*He digs, and sings.*

In youth, when I did love, did love,
    Methought it was very sweet,
To contract, O, the time, for, ah, my behove,
    O, methought, there was nothing meet.

HAM.   Has this fellow no feeling of his business, that he sings at grave-making?

HOR.   Custom hath made it in him a property of easiness.

HAM.   'Tis e'en so: the hand of little employment hath the daintier sense.

FIRST CLO.   [*Sings*]

But age, with his stealing steps   70
    Hath claw'd me in his clutch,
And hath shipped me intil the land,
    As if I had never been such.

[*Throws up a skull.*

HAM.   That skull had a tongue in it, and could sing once: how the knave jowls it to the ground, as if it were Cain's jawbone, that did the first murder! It might be the pate of a politician, which this ass now o'er-reaches; one that would circumvent God, might it not?

HOR.   It might, my lord.

HAM.   Or of a courtier: which could say "Good morrow,   80 sweet lord! How dost thou, good lord?" This might be my lord such-a-one, that praised my lord such-a-one's horse, when he meant to beg it; might it not?

HOR.   Ay, my lord.

HAM.   Why, e'en so: and now my Lady Worm's; chap-less, and knocked about the mazzard with a sexton's spade: here's fine revolution, an we had the trick to see 't. Did these bones cost no more the breeding, but to play at loggats with 'em? mine ache to think on 't.

FIRST CLO.   [*Sings*]

A pick-axe, and a spade, a spade,   90
    For and a shrouding sheet:
O, a pit of clay for to be made
    For such a guest is meet.

[*Throws up another skull.*

HAM.   There's another: why may not that be the skull of a lawyer? Where be his quiddities now, his quillets, his cases, his tenures, and his tricks? why does he suffer this rude knave now to knock him about the sconce with a dirty shovel, and will not tell him of his action of battery? Hum! This fellow might be in 's time a great buyer of land, with his statutes, his recognizances, his fines, his double   100 vouchers, his recoveries: is this the fine of his fines, and the recovery of his recoveries, to have his fine pate full of fine dirt? will his vouchers vouch him no more of his pur-chases, and double ones too, than the length and breadth of a pair of indentures? The very conveyances of his lands will hardly lie in this box; and must the inheritor himself have no more, ha?

HOR.   Not a jot more, my lord.

HAM.   Is not parchment made of sheep-skins?

HOR.   Ay, my lord, and of calf-skins too.   110

HAM.   They are sheep and calves which seek out assur-ance in that. I will speak to this fellow. Whose grave's this, sirrah?

FIRST CLO.   Mine, sir.
[*Sings*]   O, a pit of clay for to be made
            For such a guest is meet.

HAM.   I think it be thine, indeed; for thou liest in 't.

FIRST CLO.   You lie out on 't, sir, and therefore it is not yours: for my part, I do not lie in 't, and yet it is mine.

HAM.   Thou dost lie in 't, to be in 't and say it is thine: 120 'tis for the dead, not for the quick; therefore thou liest.

FIRST CLO.   'Tis a quick lie, sir; 't will away again, from me to you.

HAM.   What man dost thou dig it for?

FIRST CLO.   For no man, sir.

HAM.   What woman, then?

FIRST CLO.   For none, neither.

HAM.   Who is to be buried in 't?

FIRST CLO.   One that was a woman, sir; but, rest her soul, she's dead.   130

HAM.   How absolute the knave is! we must speak by the card, or equivocation will undo us. By the Lord, Horatio, these three years I have taken note of it; the age is grown so picked that the toe of the peasant comes so near the heel of the courtier, he galls his kibe. How long hast thou been a grave-maker?

FIRST CLO.   Of all the days i' the year, I came to 't that day that our last king Hamlet overcame Fortinbras.

HAM.   How long is that since?

FIRST CLO.   Cannot you tell that? every fool can tell that: 140 it was the very day that young Hamlet was born; he that is mad, and sent into England.

HAM.   Ay, marry, why was he sent into England?

FIRST CLO.   Why, because he was mad: he shall recover his wits there; or, if he do not, it's no great matter there.

HAM.   Why?

FIRST CLO.   'T will not be seen in him there; there the men are as mad as he.

HAM.   How came he mad?

FIRST CLO.   Very strangely, they say.   150

HAM.   How strangely?

FIRST CLO.   Faith, e'en with losing his wits.

HAM.   Upon what ground?

FIRST CLO.   Why, here in Denmark: I have been sexton here, man and boy, thirty years.

HAM.   How long will a man lie i' the earth ere he rot?

FIRST CLO.   I' faith, if he be not rotten before he die, he

will last you some eight year or nine year: a tanner will
last you nine year.

HAM.   Why he more than another?   160

FIRST CLO.   Why, sir, his hide is so tanned with his trade,
that he will keep out water a great while; and your water
is a sore decayer of your dead body. Here's a skull now;
this skull has lain in the earth three and twenty years.

HAM.   Whose was it?

FIRST CLO.   A mad fellow's it was: whose do you think
it was?

HAM.   Nay, I know not.

FIRST CLO.   A pestilence on him for a mad rogue! a'
poured a flagon of Rhenish on my head once. This same   170
skull, sir, was Yorick's skull, the king's jester.

HAM.   This?

FIRST CLO.   E'en that.

HAM.   Let me see.   [Takes the skull.]
Alas, poor Yorick! I knew him, Horatio: a fellow of infinite
jest, of most excellent fancy: he hath borne me on his back
a thousand times; and now, how abhorred in my imagination it is! my gorge rises at it. Here hung those lips that I
have kissed I know not how oft. Where be your gibes
now? your gambols? your songs? your flashes of merri-   180
ment, that were wont to set the table on a roar? Not one
now, to mock your own grinning? quite chap-fallen? Now
get you to my lady's chamber, and tell her, let her paint an
inch thick, to this favour she must come; make her laugh
at that. Prithee, Horatio, tell me one thing.

HOR.   What's that, my lord?

HAM.   Dost thou think Alexander looked o' this fashion
i' the earth?

HOR.   E'en so.

HAM.   And smelt so? pah!   [Puts down the skull.   190

HOR.   E'en so, my lord.

HAM.   To what base uses we may return, Horatio! Why
may not imagination trace the noble dust of Alexander, till
he find it stopping a bung-hole?

HOR.   'T were to consider too curiously, to consider so.

HAM.   No, faith, not a jot; but to follow him thither with
modesty enough, and likelihood to lead it: as thus:
Alexander died, Alexander was buried, Alexander return-
eth into dust; the dust is earth; of earth we make loam;
and why of that loam, whereto he was converted, might   200
they not stop a beer-barrel?

  Imperious Caesar, dead and turn'd to clay,
  Might stop a hole to keep the wind away:
   O, that that earth, which kept the world in awe,
   Should patch a wall to expel the winter's flaw!
But soft! but soft! aside: here comes the king,

Enter PRIESTS, *&c. in procession; the Corpse of* OPHELIA,
LAERTES *and* MOURNERS *following;* KING, QUEEN, *their
trains, &c.*

The queen, the courtiers: who is this they follow?
And with such maimed rites? This doth betoken
The corse they follow did with desperate hand
Fordo it own life: 't was of some estate.   210
Couch we awhile, and mark.   [Retiring with Horatio.

LAER.   What ceremony else?

HAM.   That is Laertes,
A very noble youth: mark.

LAER.   What ceremony else?

FIRST PRIEST.   Her obsequies have been as far enlarged
As we have warranty: her death was doubtful;
And, but that great command o'ersways the order,
She should in ground unsanctified have lodged
Till the last trumpet; for charitable prayers,   220
Shards, flints and pebbles should be thrown on her:
Yet here she is allow'd her virgin crants,
Her maiden strewments and the bringing home
Of bell and burial.

LAER.   Must there no more be done?

FIRST PRIEST.   No more be done:
We should profane the service of the dead
To sing a requiem and such rest to her
As to peace-parted souls.

LAER.   Lay her i' the earth: 230
And from her fair and unpolluted flesh
May violets spring! I tell thee, churlish priest,
A ministering angel shall my sister be,
When thou liest howling.

HAM.   What, the fair Ophelia!

QUEEN.   Sweets to the sweet: farewell!
                                   [Scattering flowers.
I hoped thou shouldst have been my Hamlet's wife;
I thought thy bride-bed to have deck'd, sweet maid,
And not have strew'd thy grave.

LAER.   O, treble woe   240
Fall ten times treble on that cursed head,
Whose wicked deed thy most ingenious sense
Deprived thee of! Hold off the earth awhile,
Till I have caught her once more in mine arms:
                                   [Leaps into the grave.
Now pile your dust upon the quick and dead,
Till of this flat a mountain you have made,
To o'ertop old Pelion, or the skyish head
Of blue Olympus.

HAM.   [Advancing] What is he whose grief
Bears such an emphasis? whose phrase of sorrow   250
Conjures the wandering stars, and makes them stand
Like wonder-wounded heroes? This is I,
Hamlet the Dane.   [Leaps into the grave.

LAER.   The devil take thy soul!
                                   [Grappling with him.

HAM.   Thou pray'st not well.
I prithee, take thy fingers from my throat;
For, though I am not splenitive and rash,
Yet have I something in me dangerous,
Which let thy wiseness fear: hold off thy hand.

KING.   Pluck them asunder.   260

QUEEN.   Hamlet, Hamlet!

ALL.   Gentlemen,—

HOR.   Good my lord, be quiet.
  [The ATTENDANTS part them, and they come out of the grave.

HAM.   Why, I will fight with him upon this theme
Until my eyelids will no longer wag.

QUEEN.   O my son, what theme?

HAM.   I loved Ophelia: forty thousand brothers

Could not, with all their quantity of love,
Make up my sum. What wilt thou do for her?
KING.   O, he is mad, Laertes.   270
QUEEN.   For love of God, forbear him.
HAM.   'Swounds, show me what thou 'lt do:
Woo 't weep? woo 't fight? woo 't fast? woo 't tear thyself?
Woo 't drink up eisel? eat a crocodile?
I'll do 't. Dost thou come here to whine?
To outface me with leaping in her grave?
Be buried quick with her, and so will I:
And, if thou prate of mountains, let them throw
Millions of acres on us, till our ground,
Singeing his pate against the burning zone,   280
Make Ossa like a wart! Nay, an thou 'lt mouth,
I'll rant as well as thou.
QUEEN.   This is mere madness:
And thus awhile the fit will work on him;
Anon, as patient as the female dove,
When that her golden couplets are disclosed,
His silence will sit drooping.
HAM.   Hear you, sir;
What is the reason that you use me thus?
I loved you ever: but it is no matter;   290
Let Hercules himself do what he may,
The cat will mew and dog will have his day.   [*Exit.*
KING.   I pray you, good Horatio, wait upon him.
                               [*Exit Horatio.*
[*To* LAERTES] Strengthen your patience in our last
   night's speech;
We'll put the matter to the present push.
Good Gertrude, set some watch over your son.
This grave shall have a living monument:
An hour of quiet shortly shall we see;
Till then, in patience our proceeding be.   [*Exeunt.*

Scene II—A hall in the castle

It is necessary first that HAMLET*'s reappearance should be explained. This is done by his narrative to* HORATIO. *Then follows the brief scene with* OSRIC, *which declares* HAMLET*'s character to be fundamentally unchanged; and then comes the end.* HAMLET*'s revenge is accomplished at last, not deliberately, but by a sudden impulse, and at what a cost!* CLAUDIUS *died justly, but—over and beyond* OPHELIA—*the blood that is shed is at* HAMLET*'s door. "The rest is silence," and the entry of* FORTINBRAS *and* HAMLET*'s dying submission symbolize the triumph of another order of mind.*

Enter HAMLET *and* HORATIO

HAM.   So much for this, sir: now shall you see the other: 1
You do remember all the circumstance?
HOR.   Remember it, my lord!
HAM.   Sir, in my heart there was a kind of fighting,
That would not let me sleep: methought I lay
Worse than the mutines in the bilboes. Rashly,
And praised be rashness for it, let us know,
Our indiscretion sometimes serves us well,
When our deep plots do pall: and that should teach us
There's a divinity that shapes our ends,   10
Rough-hew them how we will,—

HOR.   That is most certain.
HAM.   Up from my cabin,
My sea-gown scarf'd about me, in the dark
Groped I to find out them; had my desire,
Finger'd their packet, and in fine withdrew
To mine own room again; making so bold,
My fears forgetting manners, to unseal
Their grand commission; where I found, Horatio,—
O royal knavery!—an exact command,   20
Larded with many several sorts of reasons
Importing Denmark's health and England's too,
With, ho! such bugs and goblins in my life,
That, on the supervise, no leisure bated,
No, not to stay the grinding of the axe,
My head should be struck off.
HOR.   Is 't possible?
HAM.   Here's the commission: read it at more leisure.
But wilt thou hear me how I did proceed?
HOR.   I beseech you.   30
HAM.   Being thus be-netted round with villanies,—
Ere I could make a prologue to my brains,
They had begun the play—I sat me down,
Devised a new commission, wrote it fair:
I once did hold it, as our statists do,
A baseness to write fair and labour'd much
How to forget that learning, but, sir, now
It did me yeoman's service: wilt thou know
The effect of what I wrote?
HOR.   Ay, good my lord.   40
HAM.   An earnest conjuration from the king,
As England was his faithful tributary,
As love between them like the palm might flourish,
As peace should still her wheaten garland wear
And stand a comma 'tween their amities,
And many such-like "As"es of great charge,
That, on the view and knowing of these contents,
Without debatement further, more or less,
He should the bearers put to sudden death,
Not shriving-time allow'd.   50
HOR.   How was this seal'd?
HAM.   Why, even in that was heaven ordinant.
I had my father's signet in my purse,
Which was the model of that Danish seal;
Folded the writ up in form of the other,
Subscribed it, gave 't the impression, placed it safely,
The changeling never known. Now, the next day
Was our sea-fight; and what to this was sequent
Thou know'st already.
HOR.   So Guildenstern and Rosencrantz go to 't.   60
HAM.   Why, man, they did make love to this
   employment;
They are not near my conscience; their defeat
Does by their own insinuation grow:
'Tis dangerous when the baser nature comes
Between the pass and fell incensed points
Of mighty opposites.
HOR.   Why, what a king is this!
HAM.   Does it not, think'st thee, stand me now upon—
He that hath kill'd my king and whored my mother,

Popp'd in between the election and my hopes,   70
Thrown out his angle for my proper life,
And with such cozenage—is 't not perfect conscience,
To quit him with this arm? and is 't not to be damn'd,
To let this canker of our nature come
In further evil?
HOR.   It must be shortly known to him from England
What is the issue of the business there.
HAM.   It will be short: the interim is mine;
And a man's life's no more than to say "One."
But I am very sorry, good Horatio,   80
That to Laertes I forgot myself;
For, by the image of my cause, I see
The portraiture of his: I'll court his favours:
But, sure, the bravery of his grief did put me
Into a towering passion.
HOR.   Peace! who comes here?

Enter OSRIC

OSR.   Your lordship is right welcome back to Denmark.
HAM.   I humbly thank you, sir. Dost know this water-fly?
HOR.   No, my good lord.
HAM.   Thy state is the more gracious; for 'tis a vice to   90
know him. He hath much land, and fertile: let a beast be
lord of beasts, and his crib shall stand at the king's mess:
'tis a chough; but, as I say, spacious in the possession
of dirt.
OSR.   Sweet lord, if your lordship were at leisure, I
should impart a thing to you from his majesty.
HAM.   I will receive it, sir, with all diligence of spirit. Put
your bonnet to his right use; 'tis for the head.
OSR.   I thank your lordship, it is very hot.
HAM.   No, believe me, 'tis very cold; the wind is   100
northerly.
OSR.   It is indifferent cold, my lord, indeed.
HAM.   But yet methinks it is very sultry and hot for my
complexion.
OSR.   Exceedingly, my lord; it is very sultry,—as 't
were,—I cannot tell how. But, my lord, his majesty bade
me signify to you that he has laid a great wager on your
head: sir, this is the matter,—
HAM.   I beseech you, remember—
                    [*Hamlet moves him to put on his hat.*
OSR.   Nay, good my lord; for mine ease, in good faith. Sir,   110
here is newly come to court Laertes; believe me, an absolute gentleman, full of most excellent differences, of
very soft society and great showing: indeed, to speak feelingly of him, he is the card or calendar of gentry, for you
shall find in him the continent of what part a gentleman
would see.
HAM.   Sir, his definement suffers no perdition in you;
though, I know, to divide him inventorially would dizzy
the arithmetic of memory, and yet but yaw neither, in respect of his quick sail. But, in the verity of extolment, I   120
take him to be a soul of great article; and his infusion of
such dearth and rareness, as, to make true diction of him,
his semblable is his mirror; and who else would trace him,
his umbrage, nothing more.
OSR.   Your lordship speaks most infallibly of him.

HAM.   The concernancy, sir? why do we wrap the gentle-
man in our more rawer breath?
OSR.   Sir?
HOR.   Is 't not possible to understand in another tongue?
You will do 't, sir, really.   130
HAM.   What imports the nomination of this gentleman?
OSR.   Of Laertes?
HOR.   His purse is empty already; all 's golden words are
spent.
HAM.   Of him, sir.
OSR.   I know you are not ignorant—
HAM.   I would you did, sir; yet, in faith, if you did, it
would not much approve me. Well, sir?
OSR.   You are not ignorant of what excellence Laertes is—
HAM.   I dare not confess that, lest I should compare with   140
him in excellence; but, to know a man well, were to know
himself.
OSR.   I mean, sir, for his weapon; but in the imputation
laid on him by them, in his meed he's unfellowed.
HAM.   What's his weapon?
OSR.   Rapier and dagger.
HAM.   That's two of his weapons: but, well.
OSR.   The king, sir, hath wagered with him six Barbary
horses: against the which he has imponed, as I take it, six
French rapiers and poniards, with their assigns, as girdle,   150
hangers, and so: three of the carriages, in faith, are very
dear to fancy, very responsible to the hilts, most delicate
carriages, and of very liberal conceit.
HAM.   What call you the carriages?
HOR.   I knew you must be edified by the margent ere
you had done.
OSR.   The carriages, sir, are the hangers.
HAM.   The phrase would be more german to the matter,
if we could carry cannon by our sides: I would it might be
hangers till then. But, on: six Barbary horses against six   160
French swords, their assigns, and three liberal-conceited
carriages; that's the French bet against the Danish. Why is
this "imponed," as you call it?
OSR.   The king, sir, hath laid, that in a dozen passes between yourself and him, he shall not exceed you three hits:
he hath laid on twelve for nine; and it would come to immediate trial, if your lordship would vouchsafe the answer.
HAM.   How if I answer "no"?
OSR.   I mean, my lord, the opposition of your person   170
in trial.
HAM.   Sir, I will walk here in the hall: if it please his
majesty, 'tis the breathing time of day with me; let the foils
be brought, the gentleman willing, and the king hold his
purpose, I will win for him an I can; if not, I will gain
nothing but my shame and the odd hits.
OSR.   Shall I re-deliver you e'en so?
HAM.   To this effect, sir; after what flourish your na-
ture will.
OSR.   I commend my duty to your lordship.   180
HAM.   Yours, yours. [*Exit Osric.*] He does well to com-
mend it himself; there are no tongues else for 's turn.
HOR.   This lapwing runs away with the shell on his head.
HAM.   He did comply with his dug, before he sucked it.
Thus has he—and many more of the same breed that I

know the drossy age dotes on—only got the tune of the time and outward habit of encounter; a kind of yesty collection, which carries them through and through the most fond and winnowed opinions; and do but blow them to their trial, the bubbles are out.   190

Enter a LORD

LORD.   My lord, his majesty commended him to you by young Osric, who brings back to him, that you attend him in the hall; he sends to know if your pleasure hold to play with Laertes, or that you will take longer time.
HAM.   I am constant to my purposes; they follow the king's pleasure: if his fitness speaks, mine is ready; now or whensoever, provided I be so able as now.
LORD.   The king and queen and all are coming down.
HAM.   In happy time.
LORD.   The queen desires you to use some gentle enter-   200
tainment to Laertes before you fall to play.
HAM.   She well instructs me.   [*Exit Lord.*
HOR.   You will lose this wager, my lord.
HAM.   I do not think so; since he went into France, I have been in continual practice; I shall win at the odds. But thou wouldst not think how ill all 's here about my heart: but it is no matter.
HOR.   Nay, good my lord,—
HAM.   It is but foolery; but it is such a kind of gain-giving, as would perhaps trouble a woman.   210
HOR.   If your mind dislike any thing, obey it: I will forestal their repair hither, and say you are not fit.
HAM.   Not a whit, we defy augury: there's a special providence in the fall of a sparrow. If it be now, 'tis not to come; if it be not to come, it will be now; if it be not now, yet it will come: the readiness is all: since no man knows aught of what he leaves, what is 't to leave betimes?

Enter KING, QUEEN, LAERTES, LORDS, OSRIC, *and*
ATTENDANTS *with foils, &c.*

KING.   Come, Hamlet, come, and take this hand
from me.   [*The King puts Laertes' hand into Hamlet's.*
HAM.   Give me your pardon, sir: I've done you wrong;   220
But pardon 't, as you are a gentleman.
This presence knows,
And you must needs have heard, how I am punish'd
With sore distraction. What I have done,
That might your nature, honour and exception
Roughly awake, I here proclaim was madness.
Was 't Hamlet wrong'd Laertes? Never Hamlet:
If Hamlet from himself be ta'en away,
And when he's not himself does wrong Laertes,
Then Hamlet does it not, Hamlet denies it.   230
Who does it, then? His madness: if 't be so,
Hamlet is of the faction that is wrong'd;
His madness is poor Hamlet's enemy.
Sir, in this audience,
Let my disclaiming from a purposed evil
Free me so far in your most generous thoughts,
That I have shot mine arrow o'er the house,

And hurt my brother.
LAER.   I am satisfied in nature,
Whose motive, in this case, should stir me most   240
To my revenge: but in my terms of honour
I stand aloof; and will no reconcilement,
Till by some elder masters, of known honour,
I have a voice and precedent of peace,
To keep my name ungored. But till that time,
I do receive your offer'd love like love,
 And will not wrong it.
HAM.   I embrace it freely;
And will this brother's wager frankly play.
Give us the foils. Come on.   250
LAER.   Come, one for me.
HAM.   I'll be your foil, Laertes: in mine ignorance
Your skill shall, like a star i' the darkest night,
Stick fiery off indeed.
LAER.   You mock me, sir.
HAM.   No, by this hand.
KING.   Give them the foils, young Osric. Cousin Hamlet,
You know the wager?
HAM.   Very well, my lord;
Your grace hath laid the odds o' the weaker side.   260
KING.   I do not fear it; I have seen you both:
But since he is better'd, we have therefore odds.
LAER.   This is too heavy, let me see another.
HAM.   This likes me well. These foils have all a length?
                          [*They prepare to play.*

OSR.   Ay, my good lord.
KING.   Set me the stoups of wine upon that table.
If Hamlet give the first or second hit,
Or quit in answer of the third exchange,
Let all the battlements their ordnance fire;
The king shall drink to Hamlet's better breath;   270
And in the cup an union shall he throw,
Richer than that which four successive kings
In Denmark's crown have worn. Give me the cups;
And let the kettle to the trumpet speak,
The trumpet to the cannoneer without,
The cannons to the heavens, the heavens to earth,
"Now the king drinks to Hamlet." Come, begin:
And you, the judges, bear a wary eye.
HAM.   Come on, sir.
LAER.   Come, my lord.   [*They play.*   280
HAM.   One.
LAER.   No.
HAM.   Judgment.
OSR.   A hit, a very palpable hit.
LAER.   Well; again.
KING.   Stay; give me drink. Hamlet, this pearl is thine;
Here's to thy health.
                  [*Trumpets sound, and cannon shot off within.*
                      Give him the cup.
HAM.   I'll play this bout first; set it by awhile.
Come. [*They play.*] Another hit; what say you?   290
LAER.   A touch, a touch, I do confess.

14

THE BAROQUE AGE
Glamour and Grandiosity
1600–1715

MOLIÈRE

Selection from *The Misanthrope*

Following the fall of Rome, comic theater simply vanished for about one thousand years. During the Renaissance, theaters reappeared and again echoed with laughter. Comedy reemerged first in Italy (Machiavelli's *Mandragola,* 1520) and next in England (Shakespeare's comedies, 1590–1610) and Spain (Lope de Vega's comedies of intrigue, 1590–1635). Only after 1650 was comedy revived in France, by Molière, whom many claim as the greatest comic dramatist of the modern world.

Before Molière, French comedy was largely devoted to formula farces, often of Italian origin, which had improbable plots and stock characters who voiced predictable thoughts. Molière's genius enabled him to transform this low comedy into a great art. Most memorably, he sprinkled his comedy with provocative themes, such as religious hypocrisy and social climbing, so that it rivaled tragedy—the West's premiere literary form since ancient Greece. Europe grew to love his thoughtful comedy, so that many consider it the standard for comic drama in the world today.

Molière's plays crackle with buffoonery, pratfalls, and sight gags, but for the most part, his comedy is about character and human weakness. Taking the stock figures of farce, some as old as Menander (see *The Woman of Samos*), Molière breathed new life into them to create a gallery of modern social types. He delighted in the missteps of a social climber (*The Bourgeois Gentleman,* 1670) or the antics of a penny-pincher (*The Miser,* 1668), and his "heroes" were never saved in the end. Compassionate but no social reformer, he was offended by hypocrisy, self-deception, and vanity. His moral distaste sprang not from religious scruples but from rationalism, for he thought that humans had better natures than their actions revealed.

Molière (Jean Baptiste Poquelin, 1622–1673) came to Paris with a theater troupe in 1658, after twelve years in the provinces. He soon established himself as a brilliant actor and a writer with a biting wit. In the 1660s he wrote two plays whose reception threatened his career: *Tartuffe* (1664), a satire on religious hypocrisy, and *Don Juan* (1665), a sympathetic portrait of the legendary lover. These controversial plays aroused a host of enemies, causing *Tartuffe* to be withdrawn (though a revised version

74

appeared in 1669) and *Don Juan* to have only a limited run. These enemies would have driven Molière from the scene, too, had it not been for the unwavering patronage of King Louis XIV. It was in this context that Molière wrote *The Misanthrope* (1666), his masterpiece.

Reading the Selection

The Misanthrope (Greek, "hater of mankind") is Molière's ironic portrait of Alceste, who deludes himself while trying to be honest with everyone else. The comic foil is Philinte, Alceste's opposite, who accepts that flattery and self-censorship are small prices to pay for social peace. The plot revolves around Alceste's doomed passion for the fickle Célimène. The play ends on a dark note as Alceste is "betrayed on all sides" by Célimène and Philinte.

This selection, Act I of the five-act play, reveals the basic natures of Alceste and Philinte. Alceste is a misanthrope: "All men are . . . detestable"; Philinte is devoted to a golden mean: "Good sense views all extremes with detestation,/And bids us to be noble in moderation." Scholars believe that the Alceste–Philinte tension is a psychodrama reflecting an ongoing battle within Molière himself. Indeed, part of the play's popularity probably stems from the fact that there's a bit of misanthropy in the best of humankind.

—⁓—

Act I

Scene I

PHILINTE, ALCESTE

PHILINTE
Now, what's got into you?   1

ALCESTE (*seated*)
Kindly leave me alone.

PHILINTE
Come, come, what is it? This lugubrious tone . . .

ALCESTE
Leave me, I said; you spoil my solitude.

PHILINTE
Oh, listen to me, now, and don't be rude.

ALCESTE
I choose to be rude, Sir, and to be hard of hearing.

PHILINTE
These ugly moods of yours are not endearing;
Friends though we are, I really must insist . . .

ALCESTE (*abruptly rising*)
Friends? Friends, you say? Well, cross me off your list.
I've been your friend till now, as you well know;   10
But after what I saw a moment ago
I tell you flatly that our ways must part.
I wish no place in a dishonest heart.

PHILINTE
Why, what have I done, Alceste? Is this quite just?

ALCESTE
My God, you ought to die of self-disgust.
I call your conduct inexcusable, Sir,
And every man of honor will concur.
I see you almost hug a man to death,
Exclaim for joy until you're out of breath,
And supplement these loving demonstrations   20
With endless offers, vows, and protestations;
Then when I ask you "Who was that?", I find
That you can barely bring his name to mind!
Once the man's back is turned, you cease to love him,
And speak with absolute indifference of him!
By God, I say it's base and scandalous
To falsify the heart's affections thus;
If I caught myself behaving in such a way,
I'd hang myself for shame, without delay.

PHILINTE
It hardly seems a hanging matter to me;   30
I hope that you will take it graciously
If I extend myself a slight reprieve,
And live a little longer, by your leave.

ALCESTE
How dare you joke about a crime so grave?

PHILINTE
What crime? How else are people to behave?

ALCESTE

I'd have them be sincere, and never part
With any word that isn't from the heart.

PHILINTE

When someone greets us with a show of pleasure,
It's but polite to give him equal measure,
Return his love the best that we know how,   40
And trade him offer for offer, vow for vow.

ALCESTE

No, no, this formula you'd have me follow,
However fashionable, is false and hollow,
And I despise the frenzied operations
Of all these barterers of protestations,
These lavishers of meaningless embraces,
These utterers of obliging commonplaces,
Who court and flatter everyone on earth
And praise the fool no less than the man of worth.
Should you rejoice that someone fondles you,   50
Offers his love and service, swears to be true,
And fills your ears with praises of your name,
When to the first damned fop he'll say the same?
No, no: no self-respecting heart would dream
Of prizing so promiscuous an esteem;
However high the praise, there's nothing worse
Than sharing honors with the universe.
Esteem is founded on comparison:
To honor all men is to honor none.
Since you embrace this indiscriminate vice,   60
Your friendship comes at far too cheap a price;
I spurn the easy tribute of a heart
Which will not set the worthy man apart:
I choose, Sir, to be chosen; and in fine,
The friend of mankind is no friend of mine.

PHILINTE

But in polite society, custom decrees
That we show certain outward courtesies. . . .

ALCESTE

Ah, no! we should condemn with all our force
Such false and artificial intercourse.
Let men behave like men; let them display   70
Their inmost hearts in everything they say;
Let the heart speak, and let our sentiments
Not mask themselves in silly compliments.

PHILINTE

In certain cases it would be uncouth
And most absurd to speak the naked truth;
With all respect for your exalted notions,
It's often best to veil one's true emotions.
Wouldn't the social fabric come undone
If we were wholly frank with everyone?
Suppose you met with someone you couldn't bear;   80
Would you inform him of it then and there?

ALCESTE

Yes.

PHILINTE

Then you'd tell old Emilie it's pathetic
The way she daubs her features with cosmetic
And plays the gay coquette at sixty-four?

ALCESTE

I would.

PHILINTE

And you'd call Dorilas a bore,
And tell him every ear at court is lame
From hearing him brag about his noble name?

ALCESTE

Precisely.   90

PHILINTE

Ah, you're joking.

ALCESTE

Au contraire:
In this regard there's none I'd choose to spare.
All are corrupt; there's nothing to be seen
In court or town but aggravates my spleen.
I fall into deep gloom and melancholy
When I survey the scene of human folly,
Finding on every hand base flattery,
Injustice, fraud, self-interest, treachery. . . .
Ah, it's too much; mankind has grown so base,   100
I mean to break with the whole human race.

PHILINTE

This philosophic rage is a bit extreme;
You've no idea how comical you seem;
Indeed, we're like those brothers in the play
Called *School for Husbands,* one of whom was prey . . .

ALCESTE

Enough, now! None of your stupid similes.

PHILINTE

Then let's have no more tirades, if you please.
The world won't change, whatever you say or do;
And since plain speaking means so much to you,
I'll tell you plainly that by being frank   110
You've earned the reputation of a crank,
And that you're thought ridiculous when you rage
And rant against the manners of the age.

ALCESTE

So much the better; just what I wish to hear.
No news could be more grateful to my ear.

All men are so detestable in my eyes,
I should be sorry if they thought me wise.

PHILINTE

Your hatred's very sweeping, is it not?

ALCESTE

Quite right: I hate the whole degraded lot.

PHILINTE

Must all poor human creatures be embraced,   120
Without distinction, by your vast distaste?
Even in these bad times, there are surely a few . . .

ALCESTE

No, I include all men in one dim view:
Some men I hate for being rogues; the others
I hate because they treat the rogues like brothers,
And, lacking a virtuous scorn for what is vile,
Receive the villain with a complaisant smile.
Notice how tolerant people choose to be
Toward that bold rascal who's at law with me.
His social polish can't conceal his nature;   130
One sees at once that he's a treacherous creature;
No one could possibly be taken in
By those soft speeches and that sugary grin.
The whole world knows the shady means by which
The low-brow's grown so powerful and rich,
And risen to a rank so bright and high
That virtue can but blush, and merit sigh.
Whenever his name comes up in conversation,
None will defend his wretched reputation;
Call him knave, liar, scoundrel, and all the rest,   140
Each head will nod, and no one will protest.
And yet his smirk is seen in every house,
He's greeted everywhere with smiles and bows,
And when there's any honor that can be got
By pulling strings, he'll get it, like as not.
My God! It chills my heart to see the ways
Men come to terms with evil nowadays;
Sometimes, I swear, I'm moved to flee and find
Some desert land unfouled by humankind.

PHILINTE

Come, let's forget the follies of the times   150
And pardon mankind for its petty crimes;
Let's have an end of rantings and of railings,
And show some leniency toward human failings.
This world requires a pliant rectitude;
Too stern a virtue makes one stiff and rude;
Good sense views all extremes with detestation,
And bids us to be noble in moderation.
The rigid virtues of the ancient days
Are not for us; they jar with all our ways
And ask of us too lofty a perfection.   160
Wise men accept their times without objection,
And there's no greater folly, if you ask me,
Than trying to reform society.

misanthrope

Like you, I see each day a hundred and one
Unhandsome deeds that might be better done,
But still, for all the faults that meet my view,
I'm never known to storm and rave like you.
I take men as they are, or let them be,
And teach my soul to bear their frailty;
And whether in court or town, whatever the scene,   170
My phlegm's as philosophic as your spleen.

ALCESTE

This phlegm which you so eloquently commend,
Does nothing ever rile it up, my friend?
Suppose some man you trust should treacherously
Conspire to rob you of your property,
And do his best to wreck your reputation?
Wouldn't you feel a certain indignation?

PHILINTE

Why, no. These faults of which you so complain
Are part of human nature, I maintain,
And it's no more a matter for disgust   180
That men are knavish, selfish and unjust,
Than that the vulture dines upon the dead,
And wolves are furious, and apes ill-bred.

ALCESTE

Shall I see myself betrayed, robbed, torn to bits,
And not . . . Oh, let's be still and rest our wits.
Enough of reasoning, now. I've had my fill.

PHILINTE

Indeed, you would do well, Sir, to be still.
Rage less at your opponent, and give some thought
To how you'll win this lawsuit that he's brought.

ALCESTE

I assure you I'll do nothing of the sort.   190

PHILINTE

Then who will plead your case before the court?

ALCESTE *optimist*

Reason and right and justice will plead for me.

PHILINTE

Oh, Lord. What judges do you plan to see?

ALCESTE

Why, none. The justice of my cause is clear.

PHILINTE

Of course, man; but there's politics to fear. . . .

ALCESTE

No, I refuse to lift a hand. That's flat.
I'm either right, or wrong.

PHILINTE

                    Don't count on that.

ALCESTE

No, I'll do nothing.

PHILINTE

                    Your enemy's influence   200
Is great, you know . . .

ALCESTE

                    That makes no difference.

PHILINTE

It will; you'll see.

ALCESTE

                    Must honor bow to guile?
If so, I shall be proud to lose the trial.

PHILINTE

Oh, really . . .

ALCESTE

                    I'll discover by this case
Whether or not men are sufficiently base
And impudent and villainous and perverse
To do me wrong before the universe.   210

PHILINTE

What a man!

ALCESTE

                    Oh, I could wish, whatever the cost,
Just for the beauty of it, that my trial were lost.

PHILINTE

If people heard you talking so, Alceste,
They'd split their sides. You name would be a jest.

ALCESTE

So much the worse for jesters.

PHILINTE

                    May I enquire
Whether this rectitude you so admire,
And these hard virtues you're enamored of
Are qualities of the lady whom you love?
It much surprises me that you, who seem   220
To view mankind with furious disesteem,
Have yet found something to enchant your eyes
Amidst a species which you so despise.
And what is more amazing, I'm afraid,

Is the most curious choice your heart has made.
The honest Eliante is fond of you,
Arsinoé, the prude, admires you too;
And yet your spirit's been perversely led
To choose the flighty Célimène instead,   230
Whose brittle malice and coquettish ways
So typify the manners of our days.
How is it that the traits you most abhor
Are bearable in this lady you adore?
Are you so blind with love that you can't find them?
Or do you contrive, in her case, not to mind them?

ALCESTE

My love for that young widow's not the kind
That can't perceive defects; no, I'm not blind.
I see her faults, despite my ardent love,
And all I see I fervently reprove.
And yet I'm weak; for all her falsity,
That woman knows the art of pleasing me,   240
And though I never cease complaining of her,
I swear I cannot manage not to love her.
Her charm outweighs her faults; I can but aim
To cleanse her spirit in my love's pure flame.

PHILINTE

That's no small task; I wish you all success.
You think then that she loves you?

ALCESTE

                                        Heavens, yes!
I wouldn't love her did she not love me.   250

PHILINTE

Well, if her taste for you is plain to see,
Why do these rivals cause you such despair?

ALCESTE

True love, Sir, is possessive, and cannot bear
To share with all the world. I'm here today
To tell her she must send that mob away.

PHILINTE

If I were you, and had your choice to make,
Eliante, her cousin, would be the one I'd take;
That honest heart, which cares for you alone,
Would harmonize far better with your own.

ALCESTE

True, true: each day my reason tells me so;   260
But reason doesn't rule in love, you know.

PHILINTE

I fear some bitter sorrow is in store;
This love . . .

Scene II

ORONTE, ALCESTE, PHILINTE

ORONTE (*to* ALCESTE)

        The servants told me at the door   1
That Eliante and Célimène were out,
But when I heard, dear Sir, that you were about,
I came to say, without exaggeration,
That I hold you in the vastest admiration,
And that it's always been my dearest desire
To be the friend of one I so admire.
I hope to see my love of merit requited,
And you and me in friendship's bond united.
I'm sure you won't refuse—if I may be frank—   10
A friend of my devotedness—and rank.

(*During this speech of* ORONTE's, ALCESTE *is abstracted, and seems unaware that he is being spoken to. He only breaks off his reverie when* ORONTE *says:*)

It was for you, if you please, that my words were
    intended.

ALCESTE

For me, Sir?

ORONTE

        Yes, for you. You're not offended?

ALCESTE

By no means. But this much surprises me. . . .
The honor comes most unexpectedly. . . .

ORONTE

My high regard should not astonish you;
The whole world feels the same. It is your due.

ALCESTE

Sir . . .

ORONTE

        Why, in all the State there isn't one   20
Can match your merits; they shine, Sir, like the sun.

ALCESTE

Sir . . .

ORONTE

        You are higher in my estimation
Than all that's most illustrious in the nation.

ALCESTE

Sir . . .

ORONTE

        If I lie, may heaven strike me dead!
To show you that I mean what I have said,
Permit me, Sir, to embrace you most sincerely,

And swear that I will prize our friendship dearly.
Give me your hand. And now, Sir, if you choose,   30
We'll make our vows.

ALCESTE

        Sir . . .

ORONTE

        What! You refuse?

ALCESTE

Sir, it's a very great honor you extend:
But friendship is a sacred thing, my friend;
It would be profanation to bestow
The name of friend on one you hardly know.
All parts are better played when well-rehearsed;
Let's put off friendship, and get acquainted first.
We may discover it would be unwise   40
To try to make our natures harmonize.

ORONTE

By heaven! You're sagacious to the core;
This speech has made me admire you even more.
Let time, then, bring us closer day by day;
Meanwhile, I shall be yours in every way.
If, for example, there should be anything
You wish at court, I'll mention it to the King.
I have his ear, of course; it's quite well known
That I am much in favor with the throne.
In short, I am your servant. And now, dear friend,   50
Since you have such fine judgment, I intend
To please you, if I can, with a small sonnet
I wrote not long ago. Please comment on it,
And tell me whether I ought to publish it.

ALCESTE

You must excuse me, Sir; I'm hardly fit
To judge such matters.

ORONTE

        Why not?

ALCESTE

        I am, I fear,
Inclined to be unfashionably sincere.

ORONTE

Just what I ask; I'd take no satisfaction   60
In anything but your sincere reaction.
I beg you not to dream of being kind.

ALCESTE

Since you desire it, Sir, I'll speak my mind.

ORONTE

Sonnet. It's a sonnet. . . . *Hope* . . . The poem's addressed
To a lady who wakened hopes within my breast.

Hope . . . this is not the pompous sort of thing,
Just modest little verses, with a tender ring.

ALCESTE

Well, we shall see.

ORONTE

     Hope . . . I'm anxious to hear
Whether the style seems properly smooth and clear,   70
And whether the choice of words is good or bad.

ALCESTE

We'll see, we'll see.

ORONTE

     Perhaps I ought to add
That it took me only a quarter-hour to write it.

ALCESTE

The time's irrelevant, Sir: kindly recite it.

ORONTE (*reading*)

 Hope comforts us awhile, t'is true,
 Lulling our cares with careless laughter,
 And yet such joy is full of rue,
 My Phyllis, if nothing follows after.

PHILINTE

I'm charmed by this already; the style's delightful.   80

ALCESTE (*sotto voce, to* PHILINTE)

How can you say that? Why, the thing is frightful.

ORONTE

 Your fair face smiled on me awhile,
 But was it kindness so to enchant me?
 'Twould have been fairer not to smile,
 If hope was all you meant to grant me.

PHILINTE

What a clever thought! How handsomely you phrase it!

ALCESTE (*sotto voce, to* PHILINTE)

You know the thing is trash. How dare you praise it?

ORONTE

 If it's to be my passion's fate
 Thus everlasting to wait,
 Then death will come to set me free: 90
 For death is fairer than the fair;
 Phyllis, to hope is to despair
 When one must hope eternally.

PHILINTE

The close is exquisite—full of feeling and grace.

ALCESTE (*sotto voce, aside*)

Oh, blast the close; you'd better close your face
Before you send your lying soul to hell.

PHILINTE

I can't remember a poem I've liked so well.

ALCESTE (*sotto voce, aside*)

Good Lord!

ORONTE (*to* PHILINTE)

     I fear you're flattering me a bit.

PHILINTE

Oh, no!   100

ALCESTE (*sotto voce, aside*)

    What else d'you call it, you hypocrite?

ORONTE (*to* ALCESTE)

But you, Sir, keep your promise now: don't shrink
From telling me sincerely what you think.

ALCESTE

Sir, these are delicate matters; we all desire
To be told that we've the true poetic fire.
But once, to one whose name I shall not mention,
I said, regarding some verse of his invention,
That gentlemen should rigorously control
That itch to write which often afflicts the soul;
That one should curb the heady inclination   110
To publicize one's little avocation;
And that in showing off one's works of art
One often plays a very clownish part.

ORONTE

Are you suggesting in a devious way
That I ought not . . .

ALCESTE

      Oh, that I do not say.
Further, I told him that no fault is worse
Than that of writing frigid, lifeless verse,
And that the merest whisper of such a shame
Suffices to destroy a man's good name.   120

ORONTE

D'you mean to say my sonnet's dull and trite?

ALCESTE

I don't say that. But I went on to cite
Numerous cases of once-respected men
Who came to grief by taking up the pen.

ORONTE

And am I like them? Do I write so poorly?

ALCESTE

I don't say that. But I told this person, "Surely
You're under no necessity to compose;
Why you should wish to publish, heaven knows.
There's no excuse for printing tedious rot
Unless one writes for bread, as you do not.   130
Resist temptation, then, I beg of you;
Conceal your pastimes from the public view;
And don't give up, on any provocation,
Your present high and courtly reputation,
To purchase at a greedy printer's shop
The name of silly author and scribbling fop."
These were the points I tried to make him see.

ORONTE

I sense that they are also aimed at me;
But now—about my sonnet—I'd like to be told . . .

ALCESTE

Frankly, that sonnet should be pigeonholed.   140
You've chosen the worst models to imitate.
The style's unnatural. Let me illustrate:

> For example, *Your fair face smiled on me awhile,*
> Followed by, *'Twould have been fairer not to smile!*
> Or this: *such joy is full of rue;*
> Or this: *For death is fairer than the fair;*
> Or, *Phyllis, to hope is to despair*
>   *When one must hope eternally!*

This artificial style, that's all the fashion,
Has neither taste, nor honesty, nor passion;   150
It's nothing but a sort of wordy play,
And nature never spoke in such a way.
What, in this shallow age, is not debased?
Our fathers, though less refined, had better taste;
I'd barter all that men admire today
For one old love-song I shall try to say:

> *If the King had given me for my own*
> *Paris, his citadel,*
> *And I for that must leave alone*
> *Her whom I love so well,*   160
> *I'd say then to the Crown,*
> *Take back your glittering town;*
> *My darling is more fair, I swear,*
> *My darling is more fair.*

The rhyme's not rich, the style is rough and old,
But don't you see that it's the purest gold
Beside the tinsel nonsense now preferred,
And that there's passion in its every word?

> *If the King had given me for my own*
> *Paris, his citadel,*   170
> *And I for that must leave alone*
> *Her whom I love so well,*
> *I'd say then to the Crown,*
> *Take back your glittering town;*
> *My darling is more fair, I swear,*
> *My darling is more fair.*

There speaks a loving heart. (*To* PHILINTE) You're
   laughing, eh?
Laugh on, my precious wit. Whatever you say,
I hold that song's worth all the bibelots
That people hail today with ah's and oh's.   180

ORONTE

And I maintain my sonnet's very good.

ALCESTE

It's not at all surprising that you should.
You have your reasons; permit me to have mine
For thinking that you cannot write a line.

ORONTE

Others have praised my sonnet to the skies.

ALCESTE

I lack their art of telling pleasant lies.

ORONTE

You seem to think you've got no end of wit.

ALCESTE

To praise your verse, I'd need still more of it.

ORONTE

I'm not in need of your approval, Sir.

ALCESTE

That's good; you couldn't have it if you were.   190

ORONTE

Come now, I'll lend you the subject of my sonnet;
I'd like to see you try to improve upon it.

ALCESTE

I might, by chance, write something just as shoddy;
But then I wouldn't show it to everybody.

ORONTE

You're most opinionated and conceited.

ALCESTE

Go find your flatterers, and be better treated.

ORONTE

Look here, my little fellow, pray watch your tone.

ALCESTE

My great big fellow, you'd better watch your own.

PHILINTE (*stepping between them*)

Oh, please, please, gentlemen! This will never do.

ORONTE

The fault is mine, and I leave the field to you.   200
I am your servant, Sir, in every way.

ALCESTE

And I, Sir, am your most abject valet.

Scene III

PHILINTE, ALCESTE

PHILINTE

Well, as you see, sincerity in excess   1
Can get you into a very pretty mess;
Oronte was hungry for appreciation. . . .

ALCESTE

Don't speak to me.

PHILINTE

What?

ALCESTE

No more conversation.

PHILINTE

Really, now . . .

ALCESTE

Leave me alone.

PHILINTE

If I . . .

ALCESTE

Out of my sight!   10

PHILINTE

But what . . .

ALCESTE

I won't listen.

PHILINTE

But . . .

ALCESTE

Silence!

PHILINTE

Now, is it polite . . .

ALCESTE

By heaven, I've had enough. Don't follow me.

PHILINTE

Ah, you're just joking. I'll keep you company.

JOHN MILTON

Selection from *Paradise Lost*

Milton's *Paradise Lost* reflected the craze for epic that swept Europe in the 1600s. It towers above this period's other epics, which are largely unread today. Often called the Protestant epic, it was intended by Milton (who belonged to the Calvinist faith) as a response to Dante's *Divine Comedy*. While not the greatest poem in English (as some admirers claim)—its religious theme is out of tune with the pervasive secularism of the modern world—it most certainly is the most ambitious poem in the English language.

Milton's ambition is evident both in his poem's great length—more than 10,000 lines divided into twelve books, or chapters—and in its grand theme—original sin, or the belief that all humans, male and female, are born evil. This Christian belief has few supporters today, being replaced by the secular belief of socially created "evil"; but when Milton wrote, original sin was a defining feature of Western culture. Milton thus tackled one of his period's basic beliefs in an effort to "justify the ways of God to men."

Milton's three major sources are the epics of Homer (see *Iliad, Odyssey*) and Vergil (see *Aeneid*) and the Book of Genesis (see *The Revised Standard Version of the Holy Bible*). From Homer and Vergil come the full epic apparatus of invocations, digressions, similes, long speeches, history, folklore, perilous journeys, battles, and scenes in the underworld. The range is colossal, the sweep majestic, and the tone lofty. From Genesis comes the plot: the creation of Adam and Eve, their first sin, and expulsion from the Garden of Eden, or paradise. Milton's artistic purpose was to transform the Genesis story, along with related theological problems, into epic poetry.

Paradise Lost reflects the era of its birth, Restoration England (1661–1688), when the Stuarts once again ruled and the Puritan experiment was over. Milton now had leisure to write, since from 1639 to 1659 he had lived for politics; first he was a propagandist for the Puritan cause and then an official in the Protectorate, Oliver Cromwell's dictatorship. Milton, though blind, composed this epic between 1660 and 1665, publishing it in 1665. The descriptions of Satan, "his horrid crew," and the construction of hell may be interpreted as political allegory—Satan has been associated with both Charles I and Cromwell. The story, the loss of paradise, may express Milton's despair over the failure of the Protectorate, which had been regarded by its leaders as biblical doctrine in political and social practice, a kind of substitute for Eden before the fall.

Reading the Selection

This selection contains about one-fourth of Book I of *Paradise Lost*. "The Argument" gives a general overview and a summary of Book I. The poem is in blank verse, the verse form used by Shakespeare (see *Hamlet*), but not heretofore adopted by poets. Milton's example blazed a path for later poets, such as Wordsworth (see "Tintern Abbey").

The opening lines announce Milton's theme: "man's first disobedience, and [its] fruit . . . death . . . and all our woe." As Homer invoked Calliope, the muse of epic poetry, so Milton prays that the Holy Ghost, the third member of the Christian Trinity, will act as a "Heavenly Muse." This passage also introduces Milton's glamorous anti-hero, Satan, the Prince of Darkness and fallen angel, who takes pleasure in his evil work: "[E]ver to do ill our sole delight." Pious readers of Milton have often complained that Satan steals the show with his fascinating villainy, as shown here in verbal exchanges with his second-in-command, Beelzebub.

—⁓—

Book I

The Argument

This first book proposes, first in brief, the whole subject, man's disobedience, and the loss thereupon of Paradise, wherein he was placed: then touches the prime cause of his fall, the serpent, or rather Satan in the serpent; who, revolting from God, and drawing to his side many legions of angels, was, by the command of God, driven out of Heaven with all his crew, into the great deep. Which action passed over, the poem hastes into the midst of things; presenting Satan, with his angels, now fallen into Hell—described here not in the center (for heaven and earth may be supposed as yet not made, certainly not yet accursed), but in a place of utter darkness, fitliest called Chaos. Here Satan with his angels lying on the burning lake, thunderstruck and astonished, after a certain space recovers, as from confusion; calls up him who, next in order and dignity, lay by him; they confer of their miserable fall. Satan awakens all his legions, who lay till then in the same manner confounded. They rise: their numbers; array of battle; their chief leaders named, according to the idols known afterwards in Canaan and the countries adjoining. To these Satan directs his speech; comforts them with hope yet of regaining Heaven; but tells them, lastly, of a new world and new kind of creature to be created, according to an an-

cient prophecy or report in Heaven; for that angels were long before this visible creation was the opinion of many ancient fathers. To find out the truth of this prophecy, and what to determine thereon, he refers to a full council. What his associates thence attempt. Pandemonium, the palace of Satan, rises, suddenly built out of the deep: the infernal peers there sit in council.

Of man's first disobedience, and the fruit   1
Of that forbidden tree whose mortal taste
Brought death into the world, and all our woe,
With loss of Eden, till one greater Man
Restore us, and regain the blissful seat,
Sing, Heavenly Muse, that on the secret top
Of Oreb, or of Sinai, didst inspire
That shepherd who first taught the chosen seed
In the beginning how the heavens and earth
Rose out of Chaos: or, if Sion hill   10
Delight thee more, and Siloa's brook that flowed
Fast by the oracle of God, I thence
Invoke thy aid to my adventurous song,
That with no middle flight intends to soar
Above th' Aonian mount, while it pursues
Things unattempted yet in prose or rhyme.
And chiefly thou, O Spirit, that dost prefer

Before all temples th' upright heart and pure,
Instruct me, for thou know'st; thou from the first
Wast present, and, with mighty wings outspread,   20
Dovelike sat'st brooding on the vast abyss,
And mad'st it pregnant: what in me is dark
Illumine; what is low, raise and support;
That to the height of this great argument
I may assert Eternal Providence,
And justify the ways of God to men.

　　Say first (for Heaven hides nothing from thy view,
Nor the deep tract of Hell), say first what cause
Moved our grandparents, in that happy state,
Favored of Heaven so highly, to fall off   30
From their Creator, and transgress his will
For one restraint, lords of the world besides?
Who first seduced them to that foul revolt?

　　Th' infernal serpent; he it was, whose guile,
Stirred up with envy and revenge, deceived
The mother of mankind, what time his pride
Had cast him out from Heaven, with all his host
Of rebel angels, by whose aid aspiring
To set himself in glory above his peers,
He trusted to have equaled the Most High,   40
If he opposed; and with ambitious aim
Against the throne and monarchy of God
Raised impious war in Heaven and battle proud,
With vain attempt. Him the Almighty Power
Hurled headlong flaming from th' ethereal sky
With hideous ruin and combustion down
To bottomless perdition, there to dwell
In adamantine chains and penal fire,
Who durst defy th' Omnipotent to arms.

　　Nine times the space that measures day and night   50
To mortal men, he with his horrid crew
Lay vanquished, rolling in the fiery gulf
Confounded though immortal. But his doom
Reserved him to more wrath; for now the thought
Both of lost happiness and lasting pain
Torments him; round he throws his baleful eyes,
That witnessed huge affliction and dismay,
Mixed with obdurate pride and steadfast hate.
At once, as far as angels ken, he views
The dismal situation waste and wild: 60
A dungeon horrible, on all sides round
As one great furnace flamed; yet from those flames
No light, but rather darkness visible
Served only to discover sights of woe,
Regions of sorrow, doleful shades, where peace
And rest can never dwell, hope never comes
That comes to all, but torture without end
Still urges, and a fiery deluge, fed
With ever-burning sulphur unconsumed:
Such place Eternal Justice had prepared   70
For those rebellious; here their prison ordained
In utter darkness and their portion set
As far removed from God and light of Heaven
As from the center thrice to th' utmost pole.
O how unlike the place from whence they fell!
There the companions of his fall, o'erwhelmed
With floods and whirlwinds of tempestuous fire,

He soon discerns; and, weltering by his side,
One next himself in power, and next in crime,
Long after known in Palestine, and named   80
Beëlzebub. To whom th' arch-enemy,
And thence in Heaven called Satan, with bold words
Breaking the horrid silence thus began:

　　"If thou beëst he—but O how fallen! how changed
From him who in the happy realms of light
Clothed with transcendent brightness didst outshine
Myriads, though bright! if he whom mutual league,
United thoughts and counsels, equal hope
And hazard in the glorious enterprise,
Joined with me once, now misery hath joined   90
In equal ruin; into what pit thou seest
From what height fallen, so much the stronger proved
He with his thunder: and till then who knew
The force of those dire arms? Yet not for those,
Nor what the potent Victor in his rage
Can else inflict, do I repent or change,
Though changed in outward luster, that fixed mind
And high disdain, from sense of injured merit,
That with the Mightiest raised me to contend,
And to the fierce contention brought along   100
Innumerable force of spirits armed,
That durst dislike his reign, and me preferring,
His utmost power with adverse power opposed
In dubious battle on the plains of Heaven,
And shook his throne. What though the field be lost?
All is not lost: the unconquerable will,
And study of revenge, immortal hate,
And courage never to submit or yield:
And what is else not to be overcome?
That glory never shall his wrath or might   110
Extort from me. To bow and sue for grace
With suppliant knee, and deify his power
Who from the terror of this arm so late
Doubted his empire—that were low indeed;
That were an ignominy and shame beneath
This downfall; since, by fate, the strength of gods
And this empyreal substance cannot fail;
Since, through experience of this great event,
In arms not worse, in foresight much advanced,
We may with more successful hope resolve   120
To wage by force or guile eternal war,
Irreconcilable to our grand Foe,
Who now triùmphs, and in th' excess of joy
Sole reigning holds the tyranny of Heaven."

　　So spake th' apostate angel, though in pain,
Vaunting aloud, but racked with deep despair;
And him thus answered soon his bold compeer:

　　"O prince, O chief of many thronèd powers,
That led th' embattled seraphim to war
Under thy conduct, and in dreadful deeds   130
Fearless, endangered Heaven's perpetual King,
And put to proof his high supremacy,
Whether upheld by strength, or chance, or fate!
Too well I see and rue the dire event
That with sad overthrow and foul defeat
Hath lost us Heaven, and all this mighty host
In horrible destruction laid thus low,

As far as gods and heavenly essences
Can perish: for the mind and spirit remains
Invincible, and vigor soon returns,   140
Though all our glory extinct, and happy state
Here swallowed up in endless misery.
But what if he our Conqueror (whom I now
Of force believe almighty, since no less
Than such could have o'erpowered such force as ours)
Have left us this our spirit and strength entire,
Strongly to suffer and support our pains,
That we may so suffice his vengeful ire,
Or do him mightier service as his thralls
By right of war, whate'er his business be,   150
Here in the heart of Hell to work in fire,
Or do his errands in the gloomy deep?
What can it then avail though yet we feel
Strength undiminished, or eternal being
To undergo eternal punishment?"
    Whereto with speedy words th' arch-fiend replied:
"Fallen cherub, to be weak is miserable,
Doing or suffering: but of this be sure,
To do aught good never will be our task,
But ever to do ill our sole delight,   160
As being the contrary to his high will
Whom we resist. If then his providence
Out of our evil seek to bring forth good,
Our labor must be to pervert that end,

And out of good still to find means of evil;
Which ofttimes may succeed, so as perhaps
Shall grieve him, if I fail not, and disturb
His inmost counsels from their destined aim.
But see! the angry Victor hath recalled
His ministers of vengeance and pursuit   170
Back to the gates of Heaven; the sulphurous hail,
Shot after us in storm, o'erblown hath laid
The fiery surge that from the precipice
Of Heaven received us falling; and the thunder,
Winged with red lightning and impetuous rage,
Perhaps hath spent his shafts, and ceases now
To bellow through the vast and boundless deep.
Let us not slip th' occasion, whether scorn
Or satiate fury yield it from our Foe.
Seest thou yon dreary plain, forlorn and wild,   180
The seat of desolation, void of light,
Save what the glimmering of these livid flames
Casts pale and dreadful? Thither let us tend
From off the tossing of these fiery waves;
There rest, if any rest can harbor there;
And reassembling our afflicted powers,
Consult how we may henceforth most offend
Our enemy, our own loss how repair,
How overcome this dire calamity,
What reinforcement we may gain from hope,   190
If not, what resolution from despair.". . .

APHRA BEHN

"The Willing Mistress"

Aphra Behn (1640–1689) was England's first professional woman of letters. She was not financially successful, though, for the literary world was still ruled by rich patrons. Ignored by would-be patrons, she was forced into debtors' prison for a time. Undaunted, she pressed on and left a distinguished literary legacy. She blamed her failure partly on being marginal in a male domain. In one play, for example, she railed against men who abused her for being a *woman* writer, and she claimed instead that wit had no gender. Of Behn, Virginia Woolf (see *To the Lighthouse*) wrote in 1915: "All [English] women together ought to let flowers fall upon the tomb of Aphra Behn, for it was she who earned them the right to speak their minds."

Of obscure origins, Behn is thought to have spent two years in the then English colony of Surinam (modern Suriname) before settling in London. To some degree, this encounter with the world beyond Europe freed her of Eurocentrism, giving her a unique outlook for the time. She drew on this colonial world for *Oroonoko* (1688), a short story set in Surinam and focused on the doomed love of a black slave-prince and a slave woman. In this story she expressed, through the slave heroes, her fantasy of a golden age of social and sexual frankness—a type of primitivism similar to that of Montaigne (see "Of Cannibals"). Works like *Oroonoko* prepared the way for the next century's long romantic novels (see Fielding's *The History of Tom Jones*), often with non-European settings.

Behn also won renown as a comic dramatist. In form, her plays (almost twenty in number) belong to Restoration comedy, the comedy genre that flourished after the restoration of the monarchy (the later Stuart dynasty) in 1661; it featured sexual and marital intrigue. Her works, such as *The Rover* (1677) and *The City Heiress* (1682), have been described as quite "as obscene and successful as" other plays of this period. One of her few serious dramas, *The Widow Ranter* (1690), was about colonial rebellion. It was the first English play set in the American colonies and may have reflected a visit to Virginia.

Behn also composed poetry and it, like her plays, chimed with the ruling artistic code in Restoration England. She wrote mainly love lyrics that catered to her audience's need to see themselves as members of an elegant and stylish society. The voice with which her poems spoke was some unnamed lady of fashion, and the situations generally involved sexual intrigue with a gentleman of fashion and often bordered on the licentious. Rather than breaking new ground, Behn's works typify this era's fashionable love lyrics.

Reading the Selection

"The Willing Mistress" (1672), with its theme of a woman happily joining in her own seduction, is unusual only in that it was composed by a woman. Otherwise, it is typical of Restoration love verses in which male poets repeatedly portrayed women as willing partners. She sets this seduction in a kind of Classical golden age where there is no realistic context to spoil the amorous play. This setting is indicated by the lover's name, Amyntas, a familiar name from pastoral poetry—a Classical genre that idealized rural life and enjoyed a revival in the seventeenth century. The poem's sensual language is highly suggestive of sexual dalliance—"kiss" (used three times), "gently" (used twice), "yielding," "willing," "wanton," and "easy." In form, the poem is an octave, a stanza of eight lines; the octave itself is a doubling of the quatrain, a four-line stanza, which is the commonest stanza form in European poetry. This poem first appeared under Behn's name in the *Covent Garden Drolery*, and it was also included as a song lyric in her comic play *The Dutch Lover* (1673).

—◆—

Sings

Amyntas led me to a Grove,   1
  Where all the Trees did shade us;
The Sun it self, tho it had strove,
  Yet could not have betray'd us.
The place secure from human Eyes,
  No other fear allows,
But when the Winds that gently rise
  Do kiss the yielding Boughs.

Down there we sat upon the Moss,
  And did begin to play
A thousand wanton Tricks, to pass   10
  The Heat of all the Day.

A many Kisses he did give,
  And I return'd the same:
Which made me willing to receive
  That which I dare not name.

His charming Eyes no aid requir'd,
  To tell their amorous Tale;
On her that was already fir'd,
  'Twas easy to prevail.   20
He did but kiss and clasp me round,
  Whilst they his thoughts exprest,
And laid me gently on the Ground;
  Oh! who can guess the rest?

JEAN RACINE

Selection from *Phaedra*

Racine's *Phaedra* (1677) is considered by some to be the most famous tragedy in the French language. Written at the height of Racine's powers, when his plays were moving from triumph to triumph on the stage, this tragedy is thought to be his masterpiece. The role of Phaedra is the goal of all French actresses, as that of Hamlet is for English actors.

Racine's century was the age of the Baroque; but, specifically in France, it was the age of King Louis XIV, whose official court style was Classicism. The king used his rich patronage, the most lavish toward writers in all history, to make this period the zenith of French literature. Racine, though a recipient of Louis XIV's patronage, did not write simply to please the king, for Classicism had been the dominant thread in French culture since being imported from Italy in about 1500. Of all Racine's works, *Phaedra* most embodies the ideals of this style, which favored dignity, order, and good form.

The source for Racine's tragedy was the legend told by the ancient Greek dramatist Euripides: Phaedra, wife of Theseus, King of Athens, became sexually obsessed with Hippolytus, son of Theseus from an earlier marriage. Learning that Hippolytus had cold feelings toward women, Phaedra hanged herself, but had her revenge by leaving a note accusing him of attempted rape. Theseus then banished his innocent son, who was later killed while driving a chariot beside the sea. Racine altered this story, making Phaedra poison herself after hearing of Hippolytus's death. Racine also made Phaedra's love for her stepson incestuous, as would have been the case under seventeenth-century French law.

In retelling the tragedy of Phaedra, Racine was hemmed in by the strict rules of Classicism, which permitted no deviation in verse form (a twelve-syllable line), number of acts (five), plot (simple), amount of scenery (minimal and unchanging), prohibition of certain topics (no criticism of French society), and ending (never happy). With little room to innovate or use his imagination, Racine turned his talents to depict human character and emotions. He rivaled the romantics in the emotionalism of Phaedra's love; and Hippolytus, contrary to the legend, lusts after another woman. So successful were *Phaedra* and Racine's other plays that French Classicism dominated European theater for the next century.

The plays of Jean Racine (1639–1699) reflected his tragic sense of life, probably acquired during his youth in Jansenist circles, the sect of French Catholics who shared Calvin's beliefs about predestination and original sin. Though a mainstream Catholic, Racine treated sin and destiny along Jansenist lines in his plays.

Reading the Selection

Act II, Scene V, of *Phaedra* sets the scene for the unfolding of the tragedy. Phaedra first cautiously, then in an uncontrollable burst of passion, tells Hippolytus of her "insane" love for him. At this point, King Theseus is thought to be dead and thus the throne is vacant. Hippolytus is slow to recognize the meaning of her words, but then Phaedra admits, "'Twas no mistake." Having made this shameful admission, she asks him to kill her or she will take her own life. Phaedra's fate is now sealed. In later scenes, Theseus returns alive, and events move inexorably to their tragic end. Hippolytus, banished because of Phaedra's lies, is dragged to his death by frightened horses; Phaedra, finally confessing her guilt, commits suicide.

―⁓―

Act II

Scene V

PHAEDRA, HIPPOLYTUS, OENONE

PHAEDRA (*to* OENONE, *at stage rear*)

He's here. Blood rushes to my heart: I'm weak,   1
And can't recall the words I meant to speak.

OENONE

Think of your son, whose one hope rests with you.

PHAEDRA

My lord, they say you leave us. Before you do,
I've come to join your sorrows and my tears,
And tell you also of a mother's fears.
My son now lacks a father; and he will learn
Ere long that death has claimed me in my turn.
A thousand foes already seek to end
His hopes, which you, you only, can defend.   10
Yet I've a guilty fear that I have made
Your ears indifferent to his cries for aid.
I tremble lest you visit on my son
Your righteous wrath at what his mother's done.

HIPPOLYTUS

So base a thought I could not entertain.

PHAEDRA

Were you to hate me, I could not complain,
My lord. You've seen me bent on hurting you,
Though what was in my heart you never knew.
I sought your enmity. I would not stand
Your dwelling with me in the selfsame land.   20
I vilified you, and did not feel free
Till oceans separated you and me.
I went so far, indeed, as to proclaim
That none should, in my hearing, speak your name.
Yet if the crime prescribes the culprit's fate,
If I must hate you to have earned your hate,
Never did woman more deserve, my lord,
Your pity, or less deserve to be abhorred.

HIPPOLYTUS

It's common, Madam, that a mother spites
The stepson who might claim her children's rights.   30
I know that in a second marriage-bed
Anxiety and mistrust are often bred.
Another woman would have wished me ill
As you have, and perhaps been harsher still.

PHAEDRA

Ah, Prince! The Gods, by whom I swear it, saw
Fit to except me from that general law.
By what a different care am I beset!

HIPPOLYTUS

My lady, don't give way to anguish yet.
Your husband still may see the light of day;
Heaven may hear us, and guide his sail this way.   40
Neptune protects him, and that deity
Will never fail to heed my father's plea.

PHAEDRA

No one goes twice among the dead; and since
Theseus has seen those gloomy regions, Prince,
No god will bring him back, hope though you may,
Nor greedy Acheron yield up his prey.
But no! He is not dead; he breathes in you.
My husband still seems present to my view.
I see him, speak with him. . . . Ah, my lord, I feel
Crazed with a passion which I can't conceal.   50

HIPPOLYTUS

In your strong love, what wondrous power lies!
Theseus, though dead, appears before your eyes.
For love of him your soul is still on fire.

PHAEDRA

Yes, Prince, I burn for him with starved desire,
Though not as he was seen among the shades,
The fickle worshiper of a thousand maids,
Intent on cuckolding the King of Hell;
But constant, proud, a little shy as well,
Young, charming, irresistible, much as we
Depict our Gods, or as you look to me.   60
He had your eyes, your voice, your virile grace,
It was your noble blush that tinged his face
When, crossing on the waves, he came to Crete
And made the hearts of Minos' daughters beat.
Where were you then? Why no Hippolytus
Among the flower of Greece he chose for us?
Why were you yet too young to join that band
Of heroes whom he brought to Minos' land?
You would have slain the Cretan monster then,
Despite the endless windings of his den.   70
My sister would have armed you with a skein
Of thread, to lead you from that dark domain.
But no: I'd first have thought of that design,
Inspired by love; the plan would have been mine.
It's I who would have helped you solve the maze,
My Prince, and taught you all its twisting ways.
What I'd have done to save that charming head!
My love would not have trusted to a thread.
No, Phaedra would have wished to share with you
Your perils, would have wished to lead you through   80
The Labyrinth, and thence have side by side
Returned with you; or else, with you, have died.

HIPPOLYTUS

Gods! What are you saying, Madam? Is Theseus not
Your husband, and my sire? Have you forgot?

PHAEDRA

You think that I forgot those things? For shame,
My lord. Have I no care for my good name?

HIPPOLYTUS

Forgive me, Madam. I blush to have misread
The innocent intent of what you said.
I'm too abashed to face you; I shall take
My leave. . . .   90

PHAEDRA

       Ah, cruel Prince, 'twas no mistake.
You understood; my words were all too plain.
Behold then Phaedra as she is, insane
With love for you. Don't think that I'm content
To be so, that I think it innocent,
Or that by weak compliance I have fed
The baneful love that clouds my heart and head.
Poor victim that I am of Heaven's curse,
I loathe myself; you could not hate me worse.
The Gods could tell how in this breast of mine   100
They lit the flame that's tortured all my line,
Those cruel Gods for whom it is but play
To lead a feeble woman's heart astray.

You too could bear me out; remember, do,
How I not only shunned but banished you.
I wanted to be odious in your sight;
To balk my love, I sought to earn your spite.
But what was gained by all of that distress?
You hated me the more; I loved no less,
And what you suffered made you still more dear.   110
I pined, I withered, scorched by many a tear.
That what I say is true, your eyes could see
If for a moment they could look at me.
What have I said? Do you suppose I came
To tell, of my free will, this tale of shame?
No, anxious for a son I dared not fail,
I came to beg you not to hate him. Frail
Indeed the heart is that's consumed by love!
Alas, it's only you I've spoken of.
Avenge yourself, now; punish my foul desire.   120
Come, rid the world, like your heroic sire,
Of one more monster; do as he'd have done.
Shall Theseus' widow dare to love his son?
No, such a monster is too vile to spare.
Here is my heart. Your blade must pierce me there.
In haste to expiate its wicked lust,
My heart already leaps to meet your thrust.
Strike, then. Or if your hatred and disdain
Refuse me such a blow, so sweet a pain,
If you'll not stain your hand with my abhorred   130
And tainted blood, lend me at least your sword.
Give it to me! . . .

15

THE BAROQUE AGE II
Revolutions in Scientific and Political Thought
1600–1715

FRANCIS BACON

Selection from *Essays*

Sir Francis Bacon (1561–1626), the son of a high-ranking official under England's Queen Elizabeth I, seemed destined for a career as a courtier. He did indeed spend much of his life serving Elizabeth and her successor, James I, but he also found time to write extensively about the implications of the Scientific Revolution, which during the 1600s, was destroying the medieval world picture and establishing the scientific method as the basic way to understand the natural world. Inspired by the Renaissance, and in revolt against Aristotle and scholastic logic, Bacon proposed an inductive method of discovering truth; founded upon empirical observation, he proposed analysis of observed data resulting in hypotheses and verification of hypotheses through continued observation and experiment. The purpose of the Baconian method was to enable humanity to gain mastery over nature for humanity's own benefit.

Although Bacon had no laboratory and made no discoveries, he became the period's most persuasive champion of the "new learning." With his encouragement, science became a movement as he gave it a sense of direction, wrote endlessly about its usefulness, and predicted that it would improve life. Both his enthusiasm for a better tomorrow built on the scientific method and his abiding faith in the capacity of humans to advance themselves inspired later generations to believe that they could make the world better. The zenith of Bacon's influence was in the eighteenth-century Enlightenment when Voltaire (see *Candide*), the age's leading thinker, called him "the Secretary of Nature."

Bacon's scientific works included *The Advancement of Learning* and the *New Organon,* or "New Method," (1620). He also wrote a history of King Henry VII of England, legal works, and treatises on religious matters. Probably his most lasting impact was on English letters, as he made the essay genre a standard prose form. Borrowed from Montaigne (see *Essays*), the essay, in Bacon's hands, became a short composition: Terse, moralistic, and aloof in style, it seldom exceeded a few hundred words.

Despite outstanding achievements as a writer, he ended his political career in scandal. Made Lord Chancellor, the highest position a commoner could hold in the English government under James I, Bacon quickly fell from power. Charged with receiving bribes, to which he confessed, he died five years later in disgrace, his political reputation ruined.

Reading the Selection

Much like Montaigne's, Bacon's essays embrace a miscellany of subjects, reflecting his restless intellect. Many appeal to the highest ideals, such as love, friendship, and truth; others are incisive, sometimes cynical, observations on greed and riches, or on ambition and the struggle for power. As a rule, he omits his own experiences and instead distills what he has witnessed into political guidelines, advice, and aphorisms (pithy sayings).

"Of Studies," taken from Bacon's first group of *Essays* (1597), offers sound advice about learning, then and now. He claims that all knowledge is useful and defines three goals of study: studying for private pleasure, for public discourse, and for practical application. He recommends three paths to learning: reading, discussing, and writing. He also thinks that studying many different subjects, such as history, mathematics, poetry, and natural philosophy (science), makes humans more versatile.

—⁓—

Of Studies

Studies serve for delight, for ornament, and for ability. Their chief use for delight is in privateness and retiring; for ornament, is in discourse; and for ability, is in the judgment and disposition of business. For expert men can execute, and perhaps judge of particulars, one by one; but the general counsels, and the plots and marshaling of affairs, come best from those that are learned. To spend too much time in studies is sloth; to use them too much for ornament is affectation; to make judgment wholly by their rules is the humor of a scholar. They perfect nature, and are perfected by experience; for natural abilities are like natural plants, that need pruning by study; and studies themselves do give forth directions too much at large, except they be bounded in by experience. Crafty men condemn studies, simple men admire them, and wise men use them, for they teach not their own use; but that is a wisdom without them, and above them, won by observation. Read not to contradict and confute, nor to believe and take for granted, nor to find talk and discourse, but to weigh and consider. Some books are to be tasted, others to be swallowed, and some few to be chewed and digested; that is, some books are to be read only in parts; others to be read, but not curiously; and some few to be read wholly, and with diligence and attention. Some books also may be read by deputy and extracts made of them by others, but that would be only in the less important arguments and the meaner sort of books; else distilled books are like common distilled waters, flashy things. Reading maketh a full man, conference a ready man, and writing an exact man. And therefore, if a man write little, he had need have a great memory; if he confer little, he had need have a present wit; and if he read little, he had need have much cunning, to seem to know that he doth not. Histories make men wise; poets, witty; the mathematics, subtle; natural philosophy, deep; moral, grave; logic and rhetoric, able to contend. *Abeunt studia in mores.** Nay, there is no stond [obstacle] or impediment in the wit but may be wrought out by fit studies, like as diseases of the body may have appropriate exercises. Bowling is good for the stone and reins [kidneys], shooting for the lungs and breast, gentle walking for the stomach, riding for the head, and the like. So if a man's wit be wandering, let him study the mathematics; for in demonstrations, if his wit be called away never so little, he must begin again. If his wit be not apt to distinguish or find differences, let him study the schoolmen, for they are *cumini sectores*. If he be not apt to beat over matters and to call up one thing to prove and illustrate another, let him study the lawyer's cases. So every defect of the mind may have a special receipt.

* "Studies culminate in manners." (Ovid)

RENÉ DESCARTES

Selections from *Discourse on Method*

The French thinker and mathematician René Descartes (1596–1650) is one of the intellectual founders of the modern world. He lived during the age of the Scientific Revolution, 1550–1700, when the earth-centered model of the universe was slowly giving way to the sun-centered model, when medieval modes of reasoning were being replaced by mathematics and induction. He made important contributions to the new science, such as helping to establish the final form of the law of inertia and developing analytic geometry; however, it is for his rational (deductive) method that he is best remembered today.

Descartes's reasoning method first appeared in an introductory essay called *Discourse of the Method of Rightly Conducting the Reason and Seeking Truth in the Field of Science* (1637), which was attached to a treatise setting forth his discoveries in optics, meteorology, and geometry. The treatise is seldom read today, but the *Discourse on Method* (the essay's short title) has become a classic text of modern thought. Proposing a rational, deductive approach to all problems, Descartes's method had a double-edged effect: helping to end the reign of Aristotle and scholastic logic, while ensuring that deduction would play a major role in the new science. Cartesian deduction, with its mathematical emphasis, and Baconian (see "Of Studies") induction, with its stress on experimentation, became the twin pillars of modern science. And Cartesian skepticism, as shown in the *Discourse,* became the starting point of modern philosophy.

Ironically, Descartes, the advocate of rationalism, became a philosopher because of a mystical experience. After completing his schooling in 1612 at the Jesuit school at La Flèche, France, he spent the next nine years in travel and military service. Even though he profited from La Flèche, he was disillusioned by traditional studies with their crumbling worldview. Especially troubling was that in the sciences, no new absolute criterion of truth seemed available to replace the old. While on military duty in 1619, he had a series of dreams, which according to his later accounts, pointed the way to certainty in the sciences, using mathematics. After 1621, he devoted the remainder of his life to study and writing, in fulfillment of this mystical mission.

Reading the Selections

These two excerpts from Descartes's *Discourse on Method* contain the heart of the argument justifying his method. Part II lays out his four-step method, of which step one is the most famous. Step one declares that he will accept as true only those ideas that register on his reason as clear, distinct, and free from internal contradiction—his standard of certainty in philosophy, which he thought would give results equivalent to those reached in science using geometry. These are the remaining steps of his method: Divide each problem into manageable parts; solve each part in an orderly fashion, moving from the simplest to the most complex; and finally, check the results.

Part IV shows Descartes doubting everything as a necessary stage to clear the slate of philosophic confusion and to define the truths that can "clearly and distinctly" be affirmed without question. At the end of this process, he is left with the undeniable idea, "I think, therefore I am," meaning that he can doubt everything, except that *he himself is doubting.* From this first principle of self-awareness, Descartes deduces the existence of the physical world and, finally, God.

—⁓—

Part II

... Thus it is by custom ·and example that we are persuaded, much more than by any certain knowledge; at the same time, a majority of votes is worthless as a proof, in regard to truths that are even a little difficult of discovery; for it is much more likely that one man should have hit upon them for himself than that a whole nation should. Accordingly I could choose nobody whose opinions I thought preferable to other men's; and I was as it were forced to become my own guide.

But, like a man walking alone in the dark, I resolved to go so slowly, and use so much circumspection in all matters, as to be secured against falling, even if I made very little progress. In fact, I would not begin rejecting out of hand any of the opinions that might have previously crept into my belief without being introduced by reason, until I had first taken enough time to plan the work I was undertaking, and to look for the true method of attaining knowledge of everything that my mind could grasp.

The subjects I had studied a little when I was younger included, among the branches of philosophy, logic, and in mathematics, geometrical analysis and algebra. These three arts or sciences, it appeared, ought to make some contribution towards my design. But on examination I found that so far as logic is concerned, syllogisms and most of the other techniques serve for explaining to others what one knows; or even, like the art of Lully, for talking without judgment about matters one is ignorant of; rather than for learning anything. And although logic comprises many correct and excellent rules, there are mixed up with these so many others that are harmful or superfluous, that sorting them out is almost as difficult as extracting a Diana or Minerva from a block of rough marble. As for the analysis of the ancients, and the algebra of our time, besides their covering only a highly abstract and apparently useless range of subjects, the former is always so restricted to the consideration of figures, that it cannot exercise the understanding without greatly wearying the imagination; and in the latter, there is such a complete slavery to certain

rules and symbols that there results a confused and obscure art that embarrasses the mind, instead of a science that develops it. That was why I thought I must seek for some other method, which would comprise the advantages of these three and be exempt from their defects. And as a multitude of laws often gives occasion for vices, so that a State is much better ruled when it has only a very few laws which are very strictly observed; in the same way, instead of the great number of rules that make up logic, I thought the following four would be enough, provided that I made a firm and constant resolution not to fail even once in the observance of them.

The first was never to accept anything as true if I had not evident knowledge of its being so; that is, carefully to avoid precipitancy and prejudice, and to embrace in my judgment only what presented itself to my mind so clearly and distinctly that I had no occasion to doubt it.

The second, to divide each problem I examined into as many parts as was feasible, and as was requisite for its better solution.

The third, to direct my thoughts in an orderly way; beginning with the simplest objects, those most apt to be known, and ascending little by little, in steps as it were, to the knowledge of the most complex; and establishing an order in thought even when the objects had no natural priority one to another. · · ·

And the last, to make throughout such complete enumerations and such general surveys that I might be sure of leaving nothing out.

Those long chains of perfectly simple and easy reasonings by means of which geometers are accustomed to carry out their most difficult demonstrations had led me to fancy that everything that can fall under human knowledge forms a similar sequence; and that so long as we avoid accepting as true what is not so, and always preserve the right order for deduction of one thing from another, there can be nothing too remote to be reached in the end, or too well hidden to be discovered. ...

—⁓—

Part IV

... I had noticed long before, as I said just now, that in conduct one sometimes has to follow opinions that one knows to be most uncertain just as if they were indubitable; but since my present aim was to give myself up to the pursuit of truth alone, I thought I must do the very opposite, and reject as if absolutely false anything as to which I could imagine the least doubt, in order to see if I should not be left at the end believing something that was absolutely indubitable. So, because our senses sometimes deceive us, I chose to suppose that nothing was such as they lead us to

imagine. Because there are men who make mistakes in reasoning even as regards the simplest points of geometry and perpetrate fallacies, and seeing that I was as liable to error as anyone else, I rejected as false all the arguments I had so far taken for demonstrations. Finally, considering that the very same experiences (*pensées*) as we have in waking life may occur also while we sleep, without there being at that time any truth in them, I decided to feign that everything that had entered my mind hitherto was no more true than the illusions of dreams. But immediately upon this I noticed that while I was trying to think every-thing false, it must needs be that I, who was thinking this (*qui le pensais*), was something. And observing that this truth 'I am thinking (*je pense*), therefore I exist' was so solid and secure that the most extravagant suppositions of the sceptics could not overthrow it, I judged that I need not scruple to accept it as the first principle of philosophy that I was seeking. . . .

THOMAS HOBBES

Selection from *Leviathan*

The English philosopher Thomas Hobbes (1588–1679) was probably the most radical thinker to be spawned by the Scientific Revolution of the 1600s. He was a scandalous figure to his contemporaries, for he was thought to be an atheist, and possibly was, though he denied it. Well-placed friends, in-cluding King Charles II, who forgave Hobbes's religious doubts and welcomed his defense of monar-chy, intervened to save him from prison or burning at the stake. Hobbes developed a philosophy of mechanistic materialism that was characterized by lack of free will and identification of mind as a "motion in the head." It owed its method to the geometric reasoning of Descartes (see *Discourse on Method*), its empiricism to Bacon ("Of Studies"), and its atomistic structure of nature to the ancient Atomists (see Epicurus's *Letter to Menoeceus*) and their modern followers, such as Galileo Galilei (1564–1642). Galileo, whom Hobbes met in Italy, especially impressed him with the idea that human matter is in constant motion, guided by natural laws—the notion that Hobbes later made the guiding principle in *Leviathan*, his pioneering work in modern political theory. It is for his political writings that he is known today, his scientific works having passed into oblivion.

Hobbes's *Leviathan* (1651), in which he advocated absolute monarchy, reflected his disgust at the English Civil War, 1642–1647, which resulted in the abolition of England's kingship and the set-ting up of a republic. Having sat out the war in France, where he sought sanctuary, 1640–1651, he be-came convinced that only an absolute king could restore social order and maintain national unity. He found the word *Leviathan* in the Book of Job (chapter 41), where God used it as a term for a sea mon-ster "king" who rules "over all the children of pride"—an image of divine power. In Hobbes's book, "Leviathan" refers to an all-encompassing state, or commonwealth, that absorbs and directs all human actions.

Hobbes's method in *Leviathan* was to try to found a science of politics based on the idea that the world is a machine of matter, moving according to law. Like Descartes, he wanted to establish an undeniable truth from which to deduce the rest of his philosophy. He located his truth in his gloomy view of human nature: Left to their own devices, human beings would fight with each other all the time. This is his notion of the "war of every man against every man" that he thought existed in a "state of nature," that is, in periods when rule by law had broken down or else had never been established. It is to escape this anarchy that humanity gives up all its rights and its claims to self-government to a powerful state—Leviathan—that will protect them from themselves.

Reading the Selection

"Of Man," taken from Chapter XIII of Part I of *Leviathan*, sets forth Hobbes's theory of human nature as imagined in the state of nature. It is not that human beings are naturally evil, for there are no laws at first to prescribe what is good and bad; rather, it is that humans are by nature more selfish than so-cial. They are created equal—"Nature hath made men . . . equal in the faculties of body and mind"—but they are driven by their passions, or desires, and all want the same things: "gain," "safety," and "reputation." Since "there is no power able to overawe them all," the result is a "time of war, where every man is enemy to every man." Thus, given free rein in the state of nature, humans create a form of life that is "solitary, poor, nasty, brutish, and short."

Part I

Chapter XIII
Of the Natural Condition of Mankind, as Concerning Their Felicity and Misery

Nature hath made men so equal in the faculties of body and mind as that though there be found one man sometimes manifestly stronger in body, or of quicker mind than another, yet when all is reckoned together, the difference between man and man is not so considerable as that one man can thereupon claim to himself any benefit to which another may not pretend as well as he. For as to the strength of body, the weakest has strength enough to kill the strongest, either by secret machination, or by confederacy with others that are in the same danger with himself.

And as to the faculties of the mind, setting aside the arts grounded upon words, and especially that skill of proceeding upon general and infallible rules, called science, which very few have, and but in few things as being not a native faculty, born with us, nor attained, as prudence, while we look after somewhat else, I find yet a greater equality amongst men than that of strength. For prudence is but experience; which equal time equally bestows on all men, in those things they equally apply themselves unto. That which may perhaps make such equality incredible is but a vain conceit of one's own wisdom, which almost all men think they have in a greater degree than the vulgar; that is, than all men but themselves and a few others, whom by fame or for concurring with themselves they approve. For such is the nature of men, that howsoever they may acknowledge many others to be more witty or more eloquent or more learned, yet they will hardly believe there be many so wise as themselves. For they see their own wit at hand, and other men's at a distance. But this proveth rather that men are in that point equal, than unequal. For there is not ordinarily a greater sign of the equal distribution of anything than that every man is contented with his share.

From this equality of ability ariseth equality of hope in the attaining of our ends. And therefore if any two men desire the same thing, which nevertheless they cannot both enjoy, they become enemies; and in the way to their end (which is principally their own conservation, and sometimes their delectation only), endeavor to destroy or subdue one another. And from hence it comes to pass, that where an invader hath no more to fear than another man's single power, if one plant, sow, build or possess a convenient seat, others may probably be expected to come prepared with forces united to dispossess and deprive him, not only of the fruit of his labor, but also of his life or liberty. And the invader again is in the like danger of another.

And from this difference of one another, there is no way for any man to secure himself so reasonable as anticipation; that is, by force or wiles to master the persons of all men he can, so long till he see no other power great enough to endanger him; and this is no more than his own

conservation requireth, and is generally allowed. Also because there be some, that taking pleasure in contemplating their own power in the acts of conquest, which they pursue farther than their security requires; if others, that otherwise would be glad to be at ease within modest bounds, should not by invasion increase their power, they would not be able, long time, by standing only on their defense, to subsist. And by consequence, such augmentation of dominion over men, being necessary to a man's conservation, it ought to be allowed him.

Again, men have no pleasure, but on the contrary a great deal of grief, in keeping company, where there is no power able to overawe them all. For every man looketh that his companion should value him at the same rate he sets upon himself; and upon all signs of contempt or undervaluing, naturally endeavors, as far as he dares (which amongst them that have no common power to keep them in quiet, is far enough to make them destroy each other), to extort a greater value from his contemners, by damage; and from others, by the example.

So that in the nature of man, we find three principal causes of quarrel. First, competition; secondly, diffidence; thirdly, glory.

The first maketh men invade for gain; the second, for safety; and the third, for reputation. The first use violence, to make themselves masters of other men's persons, wives, children, and cattle; the second, to defend them; the third, for trifles, as a word, a smile, a different opinion, and any other sign of undervalue, either direct in their persons, or by reflection in their kindred, their friends, their nation, their profession, or their name.

Hereby it is manifest, that during the time men live without a common power to keep them all in awe, they are in that condition which is called war; and such a war as is of every man, against every man. For war consisteth not in battle only or the act of fighting; but in a tract of time, wherein the will to contend by battle is sufficiently known; and therefore the notion of time is to be considered in the nature of war, as it is in the nature of weather. For as the nature of foul weather lieth not in a shower or two of rain, but in an inclination thereto of many days together; so the nature of war consisteth not in actual fighting, but in the known disposition thereto during all the time there is no assurance of the contrary. All other time is peace.

Whatsoever therefore is consequent to a time of war, where every man is enemy to every man, the same is consequent to the time wherein men live without other security than what their own strength and their own invention shall furnish them withal. In such condition there is no place for industry, because the fruit thereof is uncertain; and consequently no culture of the earth; no navigation, nor use of the commodities that may be imported by sea; no commodious building; no instruments of moving and removing such things as require much force; no knowledge of the face of the earth; no account of time; no arts; no letters; no society; and, which is worst of all, continual fear, and danger of violent death; and the life of man, solitary, poor, nasty, brutish, and short.

It may seem strange to some man that has not well weighed these things, that nature should thus dissociate and render men apt to invade and destroy one another; and he may therefore, not trusting to this inference made from the passions, desire perhaps to have the same confirmed by experience. Let him therefore consider with himself; when taking a journey, he arms himself, and seeks to go well accompanied; when going to sleep, he locks his doors; when even in his house he locks his chests; and then when he knows there be laws and public officers, armed, to revenge all injuries shall be done him; what opinion he has of his fellow-subjects, when he rides armed; of his fellow-citizens, when he locks his doors; and of his children and servants, when he locks his chests. Does he not there as much accuse mankind by his actions as I do by my words? But neither of us accuse man's nature in it. The desires and other passions of man are in themselves no sin. No more are the actions that proceed from those passions, till they know a law that forbids them; which till laws be made they cannot know; nor can any law be made till they have agreed upon the person that shall make it.

It may peradventure be thought there was never such a time nor condition of war as this; and I believe it was never generally so over all the world; but there are many places where they live so now. For the savage people in many places of America, except the government of small families, the concord whereof dependeth on natural lust, have no government at all, and live at this day in that brutish manner, as I said before. Howsoever, it may be perceived what manner of life there would be, where there were no common power to fear, by the manner of life which men that have formerly lived under a peaceful government used to degenerate into in a civil war.

But though there had never been any time wherein particular men were in a condition of war one against another, yet in all times, kings and persons of sovereign authority, because of their independency, are in continual jealousies, and in the state and posture of gladiators; having their weapons pointing, and their eyes fixed on one another; that is, their forts, garrisons, and guns, upon the frontiers of their kingdoms; and continual spies upon their neighbors; which is a posture of war. But because they uphold thereby the industry of their subjects, there does not follow from it that misery which accompanies the liberty of particular men.

To this war of every man against every man, this also is consequent, that nothing can be unjust. The notions of right and wrong, justice and injustice, have there no place. Where there is no common power, there is no law; where no law, no injustice. Force and fraud are in war the two cardinal virtues. Justice and injustice are none of the faculties neither of the body nor mind. If they were, they might be in a man that were alone in the world, as well as his senses and passions. They are qualities that relate to men in society, not in solitude. It is consequent also to the same condition that there be no propriety, no dominion, no "mine" and "thine" distinct; but only that to be every man's that he can get; and for so long as he can keep it. And thus much for the ill condition which every man by mere nature is actually placed in; though with a possibility to come out of it, consisting partly in the passions, partly in his reason.

The passions that incline men to peace are fear of death, desire of such things as are necessary to commodious living, and a hope by their industry to obtain them. And reason suggesteth convenient articles of peace, upon which men may be drawn to agreement. These articles are they which otherwise are called the laws of nature. . . .

JOHN LOCKE

Selections from the *Second Treatise of Civil Government*

No other modern thinker has influenced Western political thought as much as the English philosopher John Locke (1632–1704). He lived during an age of political upheaval called the Glorious (or Bloodless) Revolution (1688), in which the Tories and the Whigs, England's first two political parties, joined together to rid their country of the tyrannical James II and welcomed as their new co-rulers his daughter, Mary, and her Dutch husband, William (William III and Mary II). Locke witnessed these events from the Netherlands, where he had fled in 1683 because he foresaw the accession of the absolutist and Catholic-leaning James II. When the entourage of William sailed to England in 1689 to claim the throne, Locke was on the ship that carried the future Queen Mary.

Locke's political theory is set forth in *Two Treatises of Government* (1690), which were published in the shadow of England's change in its ruling dynasty. The *First Treatise*, directed against Sir Robert Filmer's *Patriarcha* (1680), is an attack on the theory of absolute monarchy as based on the father's role in the family. In the more famous *Second Treatise of Civil Government*, Locke explains his own views in opposition to Filmer and (indirectly) Hobbes. Advocating the right to revolution and calling for government by consent of the governed, the *Second Treatise* seems to be simply a justification for the Glorious Revolution. But Locke had been working on both treatises since the 1680s, so they represent his mature political views.

Although Hobbes is never mentioned by name in the *Second Treatise*, it is clear that *Leviathan* was very much on Locke's mind when he wrote this little work. In contrast to Hobbes's centralized government with its claim to absolute power, Locke proposed a weak centralized government, its powers limited by a set of clearly defined personal rights: life, liberty, and most especially, property. Locke also took a more optimistic view of human nature than Hobbes, seeing human beings as basically rational and capable of both controlling their passions on an individual level and ruling themselves in society. In the long run, Locke's *Second Treatise* laid the foundations for liberalism—a political theory that advocated natural rights and representative government.

The son of a lawyer, Locke graduated from Oxford, where he was disillusioned with its outdated curriculum. He practiced medicine off and on during his life, tutored the sons of the wealthy, and served as private secretary for several prominent nobles. He held high government positions under William and Mary until his death.

Reading the Selections

The selection from Chapter IX of Locke's *Second Treatise* shows Locke giving a point-by-point refutation of Hobbes's political theory. Like Hobbes, Locke sees life as violent in the state of nature, but unlike Hobbes, he attributes this violence to the lack of an "established, settled, known law," "an indifferent judge," and an independent executive (the germ of "the separation of powers" idea). These three things, while lacking in the state of nature, are acquired by humans when they enter into a social contract, thus enabling natural rights to be enjoyed in civil society.

The selection from Chapter XIX lays out Locke's argument in support of the right to revolution, pointing out that the innate conservatism of human beings will prevent its abuse.

—⚏—

Chapter IX
Of the Ends of Political Society and Government

If man in the state of Nature be so free as has been said, if he be absolute lord of his own person and possessions, equal to the greatest and subject to nobody, why will he part with his freedom, this empire, and subject himself to the dominion and control of any other power? To which it is obvious to answer, that though in the state of Nature he hath such a right, yet the enjoyment of it is very uncertain and constantly exposed to the invasion of others; for all being kings as much as he, every man his equal, and the greater part no strict observers of equity and justice, the enjoyment of the property he has in this state is very unsafe, very insecure. This makes him willing to quit this condition which, however free, is full of fears and continual dangers; and it is not without reason that he seeks out and is willing to join in society with others who are already united, or have a mind to unite for the mutual preservation of their lives, liberties and estates, which I call by the general name—property.

The great and chief end, therefore, of men uniting into commonwealths, and putting themselves under government, is the preservation of their property; to which in the state of Nature there are many things wanting.

Firstly, there wants an established, settled, known law, received and allowed by common consent to be the standard of right and wrong, and the common measure to decide all controversies between them. For though the law of Nature be plain and intelligible to all rational creatures, yet men, being biased by their interest, as well as ignorant for want of study of it, are not apt to allow of it as a law binding to them in the application of it to their particular cases.

Secondly, in the state of Nature there wants a known and indifferent judge, with authority to determine all differences according to the established law. For every one in that state being both judge and executioner of the law of Nature, men being partial to themselves, passion and revenge is very apt to carry them too far, and with too much heat in their own cases, as well as negligence and unconcernedness, make them too remiss in other men's.

Thirdly, in the state of Nature there often wants power to back and support the sentence when right, and to give it due execution. They who by any injustice offended will seldom fail where they are able by force to make good their injustice. Such resistance many times makes the punishment dangerous, and frequently destructive to those who attempt it.

Thus mankind, notwithstanding all the privileges of the state of Nature, being but in an ill condition while they remain in it are quickly driven into society. Hence it comes to pass, that we seldom find any number of men live any time together in this state. The inconveniences that they are therein exposed to by the irregular and uncertain exercise of the power every man has of punishing the transgressions of others, make them take sanctuary under the established laws of government, and therein seek the preservation of their property. It is this makes them so willingly give up every one his single power of punishing to be exercised by such alone as shall be appointed to it amongst them, and by such rules as the community, or those authorised by them to that purpose, shall agree on. And in this we have the original right and rise of both the legislative and executive power as well as of the governments and societies themselves.

For in the state of Nature to omit the liberty he has of innocent delights, a man has two powers. The first is to do whatsoever he thinks fit for the preservation of himself and others within the permission of the law of Nature; by which law, common to them all, he and all the rest of mankind are one community, make up one society distinct from all other creatures, and were it not for the corruption and viciousness of degenerate men, there would be no need of any other, no necessity that men should separate from this great and natural community, and associate into lesser combinations. The other power a man has in the state of Nature is the power to punish the crimes committed against that law. Both these he gives up when he joins in a private, if I may so call it, or particular political society, and incorporates into any commonwealth separate from the rest of mankind.

The first power—viz., of doing whatsoever he thought fit for the preservation of himself and the rest of mankind, he gives up to be regulated by laws made by the society, so far forth as the preservation of himself and the rest of that society shall require; which laws of the society in many things confine the liberty he had by the law of Nature.

Secondly, the power of punishing he wholly gives up, and engages his natural force, which he might before employ in the execution of the law of Nature, by his own single authority, as he thought fit, to assist the executive power of the society as the law thereof shall require. For being now in a new state, wherein he is to enjoy many conveniences from the labour, assistance, and society of others in the same community, as well as protection from its whole strength, he is to part also with as much of his natural liberty, in providing for himself, as the good, prosperity, and safety of the society shall require, which is not only necessary but just, since the other members of the society do the like.

But though men when they enter into society give up [10] the equality, liberty, and executive power they had in the state of Nature in the hands of the society, to be so far disposed of by the legislative as the good of the society shall require, yet it being only with an intention in every one the better to preserve himself, his liberty and property (for no rational creature can be supposed to change his condition with an intention to be worse), the power of the society or legislative constituted by them can never be supposed to extend farther than the common good, but is obliged to secure every one's property by providing against those three defects above mentioned that made the state of Nature so unsafe and uneasy. And so, whoever has the legislative or supreme power of any commonwealth, is bound to govern by established standing laws, promulgated and known to the people, and not by extemporary decrees, by indifferent and upright judges, who are to decide controversies by those laws; and to employ the force of the community at home only in the execution of such laws, or abroad to prevent or redress foreign injuries and secure the community from inroads and invasion. And all this to be directed to no other end but the peace, safety, and public good of the people. . . .

—⚬—

Chapter XIX
Of the Dissolution of Governments

. . . He that will, with any clearness, speak of the dissolution [1] of government, ought in the first place to distinguish between the dissolution of the society and the dissolution of the government. That which makes the community, and brings men out of the loose state of Nature into one political society, is the agreement which everyone has with the rest to incorporate and act as one body, and so be one distinct commonwealth. The usual, and almost only way whereby this union is dissolved, is the inroad of foreign force making a conquest upon them. For in that case (not being able to maintain and support themselves as one entire and independent body) the union belonging to that body, which consisted therein, must necessarily cease, and so every one return to the state he was in before, with a liberty to shift for himself and provide for his own safety, as he thinks fit, in some other society. Whenever the society is

dissolved, it is certain the government of that society cannot remain. Thus conquerors' swords often cut up governments by the roots, and mangle societies to pieces, separating the subdued or scattered multitude from the protection of and dependence on that society which ought to have preserved them from violence. The world is too well instructed in, and too forward to allow of this way of dissolving of governments, to need any more to be said of it; and there wants not much argument to prove that where the society is dissolved, the government cannot remain; that being as impossible as for the frame of a house to subsist when the materials of it are scattered and displaced by a whirlwind, or jumbled into a confused heap by an earthquake.

Besides this overturning from without, governments are dissolved from within:

First. When the legislative is altered, civil society being a state of peace amongst those who are of it, from whom the state of war is excluded by the umpirage which they have provided in their legislative for the ending of all differences that may arise amongst any of them; it is in their legislative that the members of a commonwealth are united and combined together into one coherent living body. This is the soul that gives form, life, and unity to the commonwealth; from hence the several members have their mutual influence, sympathy, and connection; and therefore when the legislative is broken, or dissolved, dissolution and death follows. For the essence and union of the society consisting in having one will, the legislative, when once established by the majority, has the declaring and, as it were, keeping of that will. The constitution of the legislative is the first and fundamental act of society, whereby provision is made for the continuation of their union under the direction of persons and bonds of laws, made by persons authorized thereunto, by the consent and appointment of the people, without which no one man, or number of men, amongst them can have authority of making laws that shall be binding to the rest. When any one, or more, shall take upon them to make laws whom the people have not appointed so to do, they make laws without authority, which the people are not therefore bound to obey; by which means they come again to be out of subjection, and may constitute to themselves a new legislative, as they think best, being in full liberty to resist the force of those who, without authority, would impose anything upon them. Every one is at the disposure of his own will, when those who had, by the delegation of the society, the declaring of the public will, are excluded from it, and others usurp the place, who have no such authority or delegation.

This being usually brought about by such in the commonwealth, who misuse the power they have, it is hard to consider it aright, and know at whose door to lay it, without knowing the form of government in which it happens. Let us suppose, then, the legislative placed in the concurrence of three distinct persons: First, a single hereditary person having the constant, supreme, executive power, and with it power of convoking and dissolving the other two within certain periods of time. Secondly, an assembly of hereditary nobility. Thirdly, an assembly of representatives chosen, *pro tempore,* by the people. Such a form of government supposed, it is evident—

First, that when such a single person or prince sets up [5] his own arbitrary will in place of the laws which are the will of the society declared by the legislative, then the legislative is changed. For that being, in effect, the legislative whose rules and laws are put in execution, and required to be obeyed when other laws are set up, and other rules pretended and enforced than what the legislative, constituted by the society, have enacted, it is plain that the legislative is changed. Whoever introduces new laws, not being thereunto authorized, by the fundamental appointment of the society, or subverts the old, disowns and overturns the power by which they were made, and so sets up a new legislative.

Secondly, when the prince hinders the legislative from assembling in its due time, or from acting freely, pursuant to those ends for which it was constituted, the legislative is altered. For it is not a certain number of men—no, nor their meeting, unless they have also freedom of debating and leisure of perfecting what is for the good of the society wherein the legislative consists; when these are taken away, or altered, so as to deprive the society of the due exercise of their power, the legislative is truly altered. For it is not names that constitute governments, but the use and exercise of those powers that were intended to accompany them; so that he who takes away the freedom, or hinders the acting of the legislative in its due seasons, in effect takes away the legislative, and puts an end to the government.

Thirdly, when, by the arbitrary power of the prince, the electors or ways of election are altered without the consent and contrary to the common interest of the people, there also the legislative is altered. For if others than those whom the society hath authorized thereunto do choose, or in another way than what the society hath prescribed, those chosen are not the legislative appointed by the people.

Fourthly, the delivery also of the people into the subjection of a foreign power, either by the prince or by the legislative, is certainly a change of the legislative, and so a dissolution of the government. For the end why people entered into society being to be preserved one entire, free, independent society, to be governed by its own laws, this is lost whenever they are given up into the power of another.

Why, in such a constitution as this, the dissolution of the government in these cases is to be imputed to the prince is evident, because he, having the force, treasure, and offices of the State to employ, and often persuading himself or being flattered by others, that, as supreme magistrate, he is incapable of control; he alone is in a condition to make great advances towards such changes under pretense of lawful authority, and has it in his hands to terrify or suppress opposers as factious, seditious, and enemies to the government; whereas no other part of the legislative, or people, is capable by themselves to attempt any alteration of the legislative without open and visible rebellion, apt enough to be taken notice of, which, when it prevails, produces effects very little different from foreign conquest. Besides, the prince, in such a form of government, having the power of dissolving the other parts of the legislative, and thereby rendering them private persons, they can never, in opposition to him, or without his concurrence, alter the legislative by a law, his consent being necessary to give any of their decrees that sanction. But yet so far as the other parts of the legislative any way contribute to any attempt upon the government, and do either promote, or not, what lies in them, hinder such designs, they are guilty, and partake in this, which is certainly the greatest crime men can be guilty of one towards another.

There is one way more whereby such a government [10] may be dissolved, and that is: When he who has the supreme executive power neglects and abandons that charge, so that the laws already made can no longer be put in execution; this is demonstratively to reduce all to anarchy, and so effectually to dissolve the government. For laws not being made for themselves, but to be, by their execution, the bonds of the society to keep every part of the body politic in its due place and function. When that totally ceases, the government visibly ceases, and the people become a confused multitude without order or connection. Where there is no longer the administration of justice for the securing of men's rights, nor any remaining power within the community to direct the force, or provide for the necessities of the public, there certainly is no government left. Where the laws cannot be executed it is all one as if there were no laws, and a government without laws is, I suppose, a mystery in politics inconceivable to human capacity, and inconsistent with human society.

In these, and the like cases, when the government is dissolved, the people are at liberty to provide for themselves by erecting a new legislative differing from the other by the change of persons, or form, or both, as they shall find it most for their safety and good. For the society can never, by the fault of another, lose the native and original right it has to preserve itself, which can only be done by a settled legislative and a fair and impartial execution of the laws made by it. But the state of mankind is not so miserable that they are not capable of using this remedy till it be too late to look for any. To tell people they may provide for themselves by erecting a new legislative, when, by oppression, artifice, or being delivered over to a foreign power, their old one is gone, is only to tell them they may expect relief when it is too late, and the evil is past cure. This is, in effect, no more than to bid them first be slaves, and then to take care of their liberty, and, when their chains are on, tell them they may act like free men. This, if barely so, is rather mockery than relief, and men can never be secure from tyranny if there be no means to escape it till they are perfectly under it; and, therefore, it is that they have not only a right to get out of it, but to prevent it.

There is, therefore, secondly, another way whereby governments are dissolved, and that is, when the legislative, or the prince, either of them act contrary to their trust.

First: the legislative acts against the trust reposed in them when they endeavor to invade the property of the subject, and to make themselves, or any part of the community, masters or arbitrary disposers of the lives, liberties, or fortunes of the people.

The reasons why men enter into society is the preservation of their property; and the end while they choose and authorize a legislative is that there may be laws made, and rules set, as guards and fences to the properties of all the society, to limit the power, and moderate the dominion of every part and member of the society. For since it can never be supposed to be the will of the society that the legislative should have a power to destroy that which everyone designs to secure by entering into society, and for which the people submitted themselves to legislators of their own making; whenever the legislators endeavor to take away and destroy the property of the people, or to reduce them to slavery under arbitrary power, they put themselves into a state of war with the people, who are thereupon absolved from any further obedience, and are left to the common refuge which God hath provided for all men against force and violence. Whensoever, therefore, the legislative shall transgress this fundamental rule of society, and either by ambition, fear, folly, or corruption, endeavor to grasp themselves, or put into the hands of any other, an absolute power over the lives, liberties, and estates of the people; by this breach of trust they forfeit the power the people had put into their hands for quite contrary ends, and it devolves to the people, who have a right to resume their original liberty, and by the establishment of a new legislative (such as they shall think fit), provide for their own safety and security, which is the end for which they are in society. What I have said here concerning the legislative in general holds true also concerning the supreme executor, who having a double trust put in him, both to have a part in the legislative and the supreme execution of the law, acts against both; when he goes about to set up his own arbitrary will as the law of the society. He acts also contrary to his trust when he employs the force, treasure, and offices of the society to corrupt the representatives, and gain them to his purposes, when he openly pre-engages the electors, and prescribes, to their choice, such whom he has, by solicitation, threats, promises, or otherwise, won to his designs, and employs them to bring in such who have promised beforehand what to vote and what to enact. Thus to regulate candidates and electors, and new model the ways of election, what is it but to cut up the government by the roots, and poison the very fountain of public security? For the people having reserved to themselves the choice of their representatives as the fence to their properties, could do it for no other end but that they might always be freely chosen, and so chosen, freely act and advise as the necessity of the commonwealth and the public good should, upon examination and mature debate, be judged to require. This, those who give their votes before they hear the debate, and have weighed the reasons on all sides, are not capable of doing. To prepare such an assembly as this, and endeavor to set up the declared abettors of his own will, for the true representatives of the people, and the law-makers of the society, is certainly as great a breach of trust, and as perfect a declaration of a design to subvert the government, as is possible to be met with. To which, if one shall add rewards and punishments visibly employed to the same end, and all the arts of perverted law made use of to take off and destroy all that stand in the way of such a design, and will not comply and consent to betray the liberties of their country, it will be past doubt what is doing. What power they ought to have in the society who thus employ it contrary to the trust went along with it in its first institution, is easy to determine; and one cannot but see that he who has once attempted any such thing as this cannot any longer be trusted.

To this, perhaps, it will be said that the people being ignorant and always discontented, to lay the foundation of government in the unsteady opinion and uncertain humor of the people is to expose it to certain ruin; and no government will be able long to subsist if the people may set up a new legislative whenever they take offense at the old one. To this I answer, quite the contrary. People are not so easily got out of their old forms as some are apt to suggest. They are hardly to be prevailed with to amend the acknowledged faults in the frame they have been accustomed to. And if there be any original defects, or adventitious ones introduced by time or corruption, it is not an easy thing to get them changed, even when all the world sees there is an opportunity for it. This slowness and aversion in the people to quit their old constitutions has in the many revolutions that have been seen in this kingdom, in this and former ages, still kept us to, or after some interval of fruitless attempts, still brought us back again to our old legislative of king, lords and commons; and whatever provocations have made the crown be taken from some of our princes' heads, they never carried the people so far as to place it in another line.

But it will be said this hypothesis lays a ferment for frequent rebellion. To which I answer:

First: no more than any other hypothesis. For when the people are made miserable, and find themselves exposed to the ill usage of arbitrary power, cry up their governors as much as you will for sons of Jupiter, let them be sacred and divine, descended or authorized from Heaven; give them out for whom or what you please, the same will happen. The people generally ill treated, and contrary to right, will be ready upon any occasion to ease themselves of a burden that sits heavy upon them. They will wish and seek for the opportunity, which in the change, weakness, and accidents of human affairs, seldom delays long to offer itself. He must have lived but a little while in the world, who has not seen examples of this in his time; and he must have read very little who cannot produce examples of it in all sorts of governments in the world.

Secondly: I answer, such revolutions happen not upon every little mismanagement in public affairs. Great mistakes in the ruling part, many wrong and inconvenient laws, and all the slips of human frailty will be borne by the people without mutiny or murmur. But if a long train of abuses, prevarications, and artifices, all tending the same way, make the design visible to the people, and they cannot but feel what they lie under, and see whither they are going, it is not to be wondered that they should then rouse themselves, and endeavor to put the rule into such hands which may secure to them the ends for which government was at first erected, and without which, ancient names and specious forms are so far from being better, that they are much worse than the state of Nature or pure anarchy; the inconveniences being all as great and as near, but the remedy farther off and more difficult.

Thirdly: I answer, that this power in the people of providing for their safety anew by a new legislative when their legislators have acted contrary to their trust by invading their property, is the best fence against rebellion, and the probablest means to hinder it. For rebellion being an opposition, not to persons, but authority, which is founded only in the constitutions and laws of the government; those, whoever they be, who, by force, break through, and, by force, justify their violation of them, are truly and properly rebels. For when men, by entering into society and civil government, have excluded force, and introduced laws for the preservation of property, peace, and unity amongst themselves, those who set up force again in opposition to the laws, do *rebellare*—that is, bring back again the state of war, and are properly rebels, which they who are in power, by the pretense they have to authority, the temptation of force they have in their hands, and the flattery of those about them being likeliest to do, the properest way to prevent the evil is to show them the danger and injustice of it who are under the greatest temptation to run into it. . . .

But if they who say it lays a foundation for rebellion mean that it may occasion civil wars or intestine broils to tell the people they are absolved from obedience when illegal attempts are made upon their liberties or properties, and may oppose the unlawful violence of those who were their magistrates when they invade their properties, contrary to the trust put in them, and that, therefore, this doctrine is not to be allowed, being so destructive to the peace of the world; they may as well say, upon the same ground, that honest men may not oppose robbers or pirates, because this may occasion disorder or bloodshed. If any mischief come in such cases, it is not to be charged upon him who defends his own right, but on him that invades his neighbor's. If the innocent honest man must quietly quit all he has for peace sake to him who will lay violent hands upon it, I desire it may be considered what a kind of peace there will be in the world which consists only in violence and rapine, and which is to be maintained only for the benefit of robbers and oppressors. Who would not think it an admirable peace betwixt the mighty and the mean, when the lamb, without resistance, yielded his throat to be torn by the imperious wolf? Polyphemus's den gives us a perfect pattern of such a peace. Such a government wherein Ulysses and his companions had nothing to do but quietly to suffer themselves to be devoured. And no doubt Ulysses, who was a prudent man, preached up passive obedience, and exhorted them to a quiet submission by representing to them of what concernment peace was to mankind, and by showing the inconveniences might happen if they should offer to resist Polyphemus, who had now the power over them.

The end of government is the good of mankind; and which is best for mankind, that the people should be always exposed to the boundless will of tyranny, or that the rulers should be sometimes liable to be opposed when they grow exorbitant in the use of their power, and employ it for the destruction, and not the preservation, of the properties of their people? . . .

Here it is like the common question will be made, Who shall be judge whether the prince or legislative act contrary to their trust? This, perhaps, ill-affected and factious men may spread amongst the people, when the prince only makes use of his due prerogative. To this I reply, The people shall be judge; for who shall be judge whether his trustee or deputy acts well and according to the trust reposed in him, but he who deputes him and must, by having deputed him, have still a power to discard him when he fails in his trust? If this be reasonable in particular cases of private men, why should it be otherwise in that of the greatest moment, where the welfare of millions is concerned and also where the evil, if not prevented, is greater, and the redress very difficult, dear, and dangerous?

But, farther, this question, Who shall be judge? cannot mean that there is no judge at all. For where there is no judicature on earth to decide controversies amongst men, God in heaven is judge. He alone, it is true, is judge of the right. But every man is judge for himself, as in all other cases so in this, whether another hath put himself into a state of war with him, and whether he should appeal to the supreme Judge, as Jephtha did.

If a controversy arise betwixt a prince and some of the people in a matter where the law is silent or doubtful, and the thing be of great consequence, I should think the proper umpire in such a case should be the body of the people. For in cases where the prince hath a trust reposed in him, and is dispensed from the common, ordinary rules of the law, there, if any men find themselves aggrieved, and think the prince acts contrary to, or beyond that trust, who so proper to judge as the body of the people (who at first lodged that trust in him) how far they meant it should extend? But if the prince, or whoever they be in the administration, decline that way of determination, the appeal then lies nowhere but to Heaven. Force between either persons who have no known superior on earth, or which permits no appeal to a judge on earth, being properly a state of war, wherein the appeal lies only to Heaven; and in that state the injured party must judge for himself when he will think fit to make use of that appeal and put himself upon it.

To conclude. The power that every individual gave the society when he entered into it can never revert to the individuals again, as long as the society lasts, but will always remain in the community; because without this there can be no community—no commonwealth, which is contrary to the original agreement; so also when the society hath placed the legislative in any assembly of men, to continue in them and their successors, with direction and authority for providing such successors, the legislative can never revert to the people whilst that government lasts; because, having provided a legislative with power to continue for ever, they have given up their political power to the legislative, and cannot resume it. But if they have set limits to the duration of their legislative, and made this supreme power in any person or assembly only temporary; or else, when, by the miscarriages of those in authority, it is forfeited; upon the forfeiture of their rulers, or at the determination of the time set, it reverts to the society, and the people have a right to act as supreme, and continue the legislative in themselves or place it in a new form, or new hands, as they think good.

25

SISTER JUANA INÉS DE LA CRUZ

Poems

The writer Sister (Sor) Juana Inés de la Cruz (1651–1695) has long been admired and studied in the Spanish-speaking world. Only in this century, prompted by feminist scholars, has the English-speaking world become acquainted with this remarkable woman. Her adult years began in the worldly climate of Mexico's viceregal court presided over by the Spanish governor and ended in the cloistered atmosphere of a nunnery (1667–1695). Her literary legacy reflects this divided existence: secular and religious poetry, lyric verses, court poems, secular plays, liturgical plays, and a theological treatise. These works establish her as one of the great literary figures of the colonial period in the Americas.

Sister Juana has been called the "quintessence of the Baroque" and the "bridge to the Enlightenment," and both are true. Her writings, in terms of genres, subjects, and complexity, express the Baroque style of contemporary Spanish authors; and in certain poems she enriches the already elaborate Baroque by drawing on local dialects and native languages of Mexico. At the same time, she anticipates the Enlightenment by urging the right of women to be educated and to think for themselves. She made this claim in *Respuesta a Sor Filotea (The Reply to Sister Filotea)* (1691), an autobiographical letter addressed to the bishop of Puebla, her ecclesiastical superior. Ironically, having made this plea, she submitted to male religious authority and lapsed into silence. She died of the plague in 1695, not knowing that three centuries later scholars would hail her as "the first feminist of the New World."

That Sister Juana succeeded in religiously conformist and tradition-bound Mexico is a tribute to her genius and strong will. To even be received at court, she had to overcome obstacles such as illegitimacy, financial hardship, lack of formal education, and rural upbringing. Here, education was the key. In her life story she claimed to be self-taught in the classics, except for twenty Latin lessons. Celebrated as a child prodigy, she caught the eye of the viceroy's wife, who made her a maid-in-waiting. For five years she remained in this capacity, joining in the court's ceremonial and social life while pursuing scholarly interests. Her abrupt decision to become a nun probably reflected her lack of suitable prospects for marriage. Without family or dowry, she ultimately was dependent on her wits and charm to survive.

Reading the Selections

Sister Juana's sonnet "She refutes the praises dedicated to her portrait" expresses the Baroque sensibility, which sees death in the midst of life. Baroque-era clerics preached this message, and England's metaphysical poets made it a major theme in their verses. This sonnet is chilling, as the poet deflects an unnamed person's admiration of her portrait by pointing out that painting is "a highly colored hoax" and all humans are mortal.

The second poem, addressed to a male audience, reflects Sister Juana's exasperation with *macho* culture. In the poem she describes the sexual double bind that court ladies suffer: If they refuse men's overtures, they are called heartless; if they yield, they are whores. Either way, women can't win. Sister Juana's vision for escaping from this trap is to educate women in order to make them virtuous ("make them what you'd like to see")—an idea espoused a century later by Mary Wollstonecraft (see Chapter 16).

She refutes the praises dedicated to her portrait

This that you see, a highly colored hoax   1
Which demonstrates the excellence of art,
Upon the senses plays its crafty jokes
With faulty syllogisms on its part.

This, with which flattery tries to evade
The unrelenting horrors of the years
And, conquering the sallies time has made,
To triumph over age and all its cares,

Is just a vain device of apprehension,
Is just a fragile flower in the wind,   10
Is just a vain defense against our lot,
Is a foolish and impossible intention,
Is labor lost, and, to the thoughtful mind,
Is but a corpse, is dust, is shade, is nought.

In which she condemns the inconsistency of men, who blame women for what they themselves have caused

Stupid men, fond of abusing   1
All women, without any shame,
Not seeing you're the ones to blame
For the very faults that you're accusing:

If, with a single-minded will,
You seek her well-deserved disdain,
Why do you want her to remain
Good, while inciting her to ill?

You strive to conquer her resistance,
Then with a solemn treachery   10
Attribute to her lechery
What was only done through your persistence.

Your mad position seems to fit
That of a child who draws a spook
And, when he dares to take a look,
Finds that he's afraid of it.

Showing presumptuous indiscretion,
You want to find her you're pursuing
To be Thais while you are wooing
And Lucretia when she's in possession.   20

What quirky humor could be more queer
Than his who, from all reason banned,
Smudges a mirror with his hand,
Then whines because it isn't clear?

If favor or disdain we tell,
You give us the same reception, madly—
Complaining when we treat you badly,
And sneering when we treat you well.

No female reputation's sure:
The most cautious woman in the town   30
Is an ingrate if she turns you down;
If she gives in to you she's a whore.

In stupidity you're all the same,
Each one an inconsistent fool;
You blame one girl for being cruel,
While the yielding one you also blame.

Your expectation is truly curious,
Of the woman who would seek your love;
The one who's ungrateful you reprove,
And the one who's available makes you furious.   40

But whatever the rage, whatever the plaints
That your capricious minds may fashion,
Lucky is one who feels no passion;
Just go somewhere else with your complaints.

Your amorous blandishments give wing
To a lady's libertine inclination,
But having seduced her in sinful fashion,
You want her to be a most virtuous thing.

In the errant passion two may loll in,
Whose fault would you describe as baser: 50

Hers who falls because you chase her,
Or his who chases because he's fallen?

Or who the greater guilt does win,
Whatever shameful pact is made:
She who sins because she's paid,
Or he who pays so he may sin?

But why do you pretend to be
Surprised at your sins, when you've displayed them?
Wish women to be what you have made them,
Or make them what you'd like to see.   60

Stop your own solicitations,
And then you may possess the right
To accuse a girl of being light
When she comes to you with unchaste persuasions.

Your arrogance fights on every level,
I note, with strong and well-aimed batteries,
For with ceaseless promises and flatteries
You unite the world, the flesh, the devil.

16

THE AGE OF REASON
1700–1789

ALEXANDER POPE

Selections from *An Essay on Man*

The poet and essayist Alexander Pope (1688–1744) lived during one of the great eras in English letters, the Augustan Age (ca. 1660–1760). This period's authors drew inspiration from the first Augustan Age—that is, the reign of Emperor Augustus (27 B.C.–A.D. 14)—when many fine writers flourished, notably Vergil, Horace, and Ovid. Imitating the style of the Roman heritage, Pope and the rest of these latter-day Augustans transformed their period into a time of harmony, decorum ("good taste"), and proportion. The Augustan ideal was correctness, and writers were under some moral and aesthetic obligation to instruct as well as to please. From the vantage of European letters, the Augustan Age was part of the Neoclassical movement then sweeping across the West, whose writers (see Racine's *Phaedra*) believed that the Classical authors had set the literary standards for all time.

Early in his career, Alexander Pope, ever sensitive to the spirit of Classicism, developed a European-wide reputation and made himself financially secure with his translation of Homer's *Iliad* and *Odyssey*. He cemented his high literary position with his later works, such as poems, satires, epistles (letters in verse), and collected prose letters. Nowhere was his devotion to Classicism so evident as in his poetry, where he wrote in heroic couplets—a verse form nearly always in iambic pentameter rhymed in pairs, aa, bb, cc, dd, etc., with ten syllables in each line. This form began perhaps with Chaucer (see *The Canterbury Tales*) but was perfected by the Augustan poets.

Pope's life was beset with misfortune. A Roman Catholic at a time when Protestantism, under King William and Queen Mary, reached new heights of popularity, he as a youth was barred from England's best educational institutions, its public (meaning "private") schools. Thus he was tutored by several Catholic priests, studied at two private schools, and after age thirteen, taught himself at home. Pope was never physically strong, being subject to a tubercular infection that left him small in stature and with curvature of the spine. He also was forced to endure his critics' bitter attacks on his writings, though he gave as good as he got, as for example in *The Dunciad,* a satire against the bad poets ("dunces") of his period. Nonetheless, he persevered to become a dominant voice of the Augustan Age.

Reading the Selections

Pope considered *An Essay on Man* one of his most important works. To thwart his critics and gain the best possible reception for this long work, he published two poems that his enemies attacked while he then anonymously issued the *Essay on Man,* which was highly praised. Typically, the *Essay* is composed in heroic couplets.

Addressed to Pope's patron, Henry St. John Bolingbroke ("St. John," line 1), the *Essay* comprises four epistles on the favorite topic of Neoclassical writers, man and his activities: "The proper study of mankind is man." Epistle 1 deals with man in the cosmos; Epistle 2 analyzes man as an individual; Epistle 3 examines man in society; and Epistle 4 explores the theme of happiness, concluding that personal and social happiness are the same.

Pope's basic conservatism, though not in a negative sense, is shown in the following excerpts from the *Essay.* In Epistle 1 he advocates the seemingly fatalistic principle that "Whatever is, is right," but in Epistle 2 he encourages the study of man and his environment, with the end goal of fitting into the moral order.

—⁂—

To Henry St. John, Lord Bolingbroke

Epistle 1. Of the Nature and State of Man with Respect to the Universe

Awake, my St. John! leave all meaner things   1
To low ambition, and the pride of kings.
Let us (since life can little more supply
Than just to look about us and to die)
Expatiate free o'er all this scene of man;
A mightly maze! but not without a plan;
A wild, where weeds and flowers promiscuous shoot,
Or garden, tempting with forbidden fruit.
Together let us beat this ample field,
Try what the open, what the covert yield;   10
The latent tracts, the giddy heights, explore
Of all who blindly creep, or sightless soar;
Eye Nature's walks, shoot folly as it flies,
And catch the manners living as they rise;
Laugh where we must, be candid where we can;
But vindicate the ways of God to man.

1. Say first, of God above, or man below,
What can we reason, but from what we know?
Of man, what see we but his station here,
From which to reason, or to which refer?   20
Through worlds unnumbered though the God be known,
'Tis ours to trace him only in our own.
He, who through vast immensity can pierce,
See worlds on worlds compose one universe,
Observe how system into system runs,
What other planets circle other suns,
What varied being peoples every star,
May tell why Heaven has made us as we are.
But of this frame the bearings, and the ties,
The strong connections, nice dependencies,   30
Gradations just, has thy pervading soul
Looked through? or can a part contain the whole?
Is the great chain, that draws all to agree,
And drawn supports, upheld by God, or thee?

2. Presumptuous man! the reason wouldst thou find,
Why formed so weak, so little, and so blind?
First, if thou canst, the harder reason guess,
Why formed no weaker, blinder, and no less!
Ask of thy mother earth, why oaks are made
Taller or stronger than the weeds they shade?   40
Or ask of yonder argent fields above,
Why Jove's satellites are less than Jove?
Of systems possible, if 'tis confessed
That Wisdom Infinite must form the best,
Where all must full or not coherent be,
And all that rises, rise in due degree;
Then, in the scale of reasoning life, 'tis plain,
There must be, somewhere, such a rank as man:
And all the question (wrangle e'er so long)
Is only this, if God has placed him wrong?   50
Respecting man, whatever wrong we call,
May, must be right, as relative to all.
In human works, though labored on with pain,
A thousand movements scarce one purpose gain;
In God's, one single can its end produce;
Yet serves to second too some other use.
So man, who here seems principal alone,
Perhaps acts second to some sphere unknown,
Touches some wheel, or verges to some goal;
'Tis but a part we see, and not a whole.   60
When the proud steed shall know why man restrains
His fiery course, or drives him o'er the plains;
When the dull ox, why now he breaks the clod,
Is now a victim, and now Egypt's god:
Then shall man's pride and dullness comprehend
His actions', passions', being's use and end;
Why doing, suffering, checked, impelled; and why
This hour a slave, the next a deity.
Then say not man's imperfect, Heaven in fault;
Say rather, man's as perfect as he ought;   70
His knowledge measured to his state and place,
His time a moment, and a point his space.

If to be perfect in a certain sphere,
What matter, soon or late, or here or there?
The blest today is as completely so,
As who began a thousand years ago.

   3. Heaven from all creatures hides the book of Fate,
All but the page prescribed, their present state:
From brutes what men, from men what spirits know:
Or who could suffer being here below?   *80*
The lamb thy riot dooms to bleed today,
Had he thy reason, would he skip and play?
Pleased to the last, he crops the flowery food,
And licks the hand just raised to shed his blood.
O blindness to the future! kindly given,
That each may fill the circle marked by Heaven:
Who sees with equal eye, as God of all,
A hero perish, or a sparrow fall,
Atoms or systems into ruin hurled,
And know a bubble burst, and now a world.   *90*
   Hope humbly then; with trembling pinions soar;
Wait the great teacher Death, and God adore!
What future bliss, he gives not thee to know,
But gives that hope to be thy blessing now.
Hope springs eternal in the human breast:
Man never is, but always to be blest:
The soul, uneasy and confined from home,
Rests and expatiates in a life to come.
   Lo! the poor Indian, whose untutored mind
Sees God in clouds, or hears him in the wind;   *100*
His soul proud Science never taught to stray
Far as the solar walk, or milky way;
Yet simple Nature to his hope has given,
Behind the cloud-topped hill, an humbler heaven;
Some safer world in depth of woods embraced,
Some happier island in the watery waste,
Where slaves once more their native land behold,
No fiends torment, no Christians thirst for gold!
To be, contents his natural desire,
He asks no angel's wing, no seraph's fire;   *110*
But thinks, admitted to that equal sky,
His faithful dog shall bear him company.

   4. Go, wiser thou! and, in thy scale of sense,
Weigh thy opinion against Providence;
Call imperfection what thou fancy'st such,
Say, here he gives too little, there too much;
Destroy all creatures for thy sport or gust,
Yet cry, if man's unhappy, God's unjust;
If man alone engross not Heaven's high care,
Alone made perfect here, immortal there: *120*
Snatch from his hand the balance and the rod,
Rejudge his justice, be the God of God!
In pride, in reasoning pride, our error lies;
All quit their sphere, and rush into the skies.
Pride still is aiming at the blest abodes,
Men would be angels, angels would be gods.
Aspiring to be gods, if angels fell,
Aspiring to be angels, men rebel:
And who but wishes to invert the laws
Of order, sins against the Eternal Cause.   *130*

   5. Ask for what end the heavenly bodies shine,
Earth for whose use? Pride answers, "'Tis for mine:
For me kind Nature wakes her genial power,
Suckles each herb, and spreads out every flower;
Annual for me, the grape, the rose renew
The juice nectareous, and the balmy dew;
For me, the mine a thousand treasures brings;
For me, health gushes from a thousand springs;
Seas roll to waft me, suns to light me rise;
My footstool earth, my canopy the skies."   *140*
   But errs not Nature from this gracious end,
From burning suns when livid deaths descend,
When earthquakes swallow, or when tempests sweep
Towns to one grave, whole nations to the deep?
"No," 'tis replied, "the first Almighty Cause
Acts not by partial, but by general laws;
The exceptions few; some change since all began,
And what created perfect?"—Why then man?
If the great end be human happiness,
Then Nature deviates; and can man do less?   *150*
As much that end a constant course requires
Of showers and sunshine, as of man's desires;
As much eternal springs and cloudless skies,
As men forever temperate, calm, and wise.
If plagues or earthquakes break not Heaven's design,
Why then a Borgia, or a Catiline?
Who knows but he whose hand the lightning forms,
Who heaves old ocean, and who wings the storms,
Pours fierce ambition in a Caesar's mind,
Or turns young Ammon loose to scourge mankind?   *160*
From pride, from pride, our very reasoning springs;
Account for moral, as for natural things:
Why charge we Heaven in those, in these acquit?
In both, to reason right is to submit.
   Better for us, perhaps, it might appear,
Were there all harmony, all virtue here;
That never air or ocean felt the wind;
That never passion discomposed the mind:
But ALL subsists by elemental strife;
And passions are the elements of life.   *170*
The general ORDER, since the whole began,
Is kept in Nature, and is kept in man.

   6. What would this man? Now upward will he soar,
And little less than angel, would be more;
Now looking downwards, just as grieved appears
To want the strength of bulls, the fur of bears.
Made for his use all creatures if he call,
Say what their use, had he the powers of all?
Nature to these, without profusion, kind,
The proper organs, proper powers assigned;   *180*
Each seeming want compénsated of course,
Here with degrees of swiftness, there of force;
All in exact proportion to the state;
Nothing to add, and nothing to abate.
Each beast, each insect, happy in its own;
Is Heaven unkind to man, and man alone?
Shall he alone, whom rational we call,
Be pleased with nothing, if not blessed with all?
   The bliss of man (could pride that blessing find)

Is not to act or think beyond mankind; 190
No powers of body or of soul to share,
But what his nature and his state can bear.
Why has not man a microscopic eye?
For this plain reason, man is not a fly.
Say what the use, were finer optics given,
To inspect a mite, not comprehend the heaven?
Or touch, if tremblingly alive all o'er,
To smart and agonize at every pore?
Or quick effluvia darting through the brain,
Die of a rose in aromatic pain? 200
If nature thundered in his opening ears,
And stunned him with the music of the spheres,
How would he wish that Heaven had left him still
The whispering zephyr, and the purling rill?
Who finds not Providence all good and wise,
Alike in what it gives, and what denies?

   7. Far as creation's ample range extends,
The scale of sensual, mental powers ascends:
Mark how it mounts, to man's imperial race,
From the green myriads in the peopled grass: 210
What modes of sight betwixt each wide extreme,
The mole's dim curtain, and the lynx's beam:
Of smell, the headlong lioness between,
And hound sagacious on the tainted green:
Of hearing, from the life that fills the flood,
To that which warbles through the vernal wood:
The spider's touch, how exquisitely fine!
Feels at each thread, and lives along the line:
In the nice bee, what sense so subtly true
From poisonous herbs extracts the healing dew: 220
How instinct varies in the groveling swine,
Compared, half-reasoning elephant, with thine!
'Twixt that, and reason, what a nice barrier,
Forever separate, yet forever near!
Remembrance and reflection how allied;
What thin partitions sense from thought divide;
And middle natures, how they long to join,
Yet never pass the insuperable line!
Without this just gradation, could they be
Subjected, these to those, or all to thee? 230
The powers of all subdued by thee alone,
Is not thy reason all these powers in one?

   8. See, through this air, this ocean, and this earth,
All matter quick, and bursting into birth.
Above, how high progressive life may go!
Around, how wide! how deep extend below!
Vast Chain of Being! which from God began,
Natures ethereal, human, angel, man,
Beast, bird, fish, insect, what no eye can see,
No glass can reach! from Infinite to thee, 240
From thee to nothing.—On superior powers
Were we to press, inferior might on ours:
Or in the full creation leave a void,
Where, one step broken, the great scale's destroyed:
From Nature's chain whatever link you strike,
Tenth or ten thousandth, breaks the chain alike.
   And, if each system in gradation roll

Alike essential to the amazing Whole,
The least confusion but in one, not all
That system only, but the Whole must fall. 250
Let earth unbalanced from her orbit fly,
Planets and suns run lawless through the sky,
Let ruling angels from their spheres be hurled,
Being on being wrecked, and world on world,
Heaven's whole foundations to their center nod,
And Nature tremble to the throne of God:
All this dread ORDER break—for whom? for thee?
Vile worm!—oh, madness, pride, impiety!

   9. What if the foot, ordained the dust to tread,
Or hand, to toil, aspired to be the head? 260
What if the head, the eye, or ear repined
To serve mere engines to the ruling Mind?
Just as absurd, to mourn the tasks or pains,
The great directing MIND of ALL ordains.
   All are but parts of one stupendous whole,
Whose body Nature is, and God the soul;
That, changed through all, and yet in all the same,
Great in the earth, as in the ethereal frame,
Warms in the sun, refreshes in the breeze,
Glows in the stars, and blossoms in the trees, 270
Lives through all life, extends through all extent,
Spreads undivided, operates unspent,
Breathes in our soul, informs our mortal part,
As full, as perfect, in a hair as heart;
As full, as perfect, in vile man that mourns,
As the rapt seraph that adores and burns;
To him no high, no low, no great, no small;
He fills, he bounds, connects, and equals all.

   10. Cease then, nor ORDER imperfection name:
Our proper bliss depends on what we blame. 280
Know thy own point: this kind, this due degree
Of blindness, weakness, Heaven bestows on thee.
Submit—In this, or any other sphere,
Secure to be as blest as thou canst bear:
Safe in the hand of one disposing Power,
Or in the natal, or the mortal hour.
All Nature is but art, unknown to thee;
All chance, direction, which thou canst not see;
All discord, harmony not understood;
All partial evil, universal good: 290
And, spite of pride, in erring reason's spite,
One truth is clear: Whatever IS, is RIGHT.

Epistle 2. Of the Nature and State of Man with Respect to Himself, as an Individual

   1. Know then thyself, presume not God to scan; 1
The proper study of mankind is Man.
Placed on this isthmus of a middle state,
A being darkly wise, and rudely great:
With too much knowledge for the skeptic side,
With too much weakness for the Stoic's pride,
He hangs between; in doubt to act, or rest,
In doubt to deem himself a god, or beast;

In doubt his mind or body to prefer,
Born but to die, and reasoning but to err;
Alike in ignorance, his reason such,
Whether he thinks too little, or too much:
Chaos of thought and passion, all confused;
Still by himself abused, or disabused;

10 Created half to rise, and half to fall;
Great lord of all things, yet a prey to all;
Sole judge of truth, in endless error hurled:
The glory, jest, and riddle of the world!

. . .

HENRY FIELDING

Selection from *The History of Tom Jones*

Henry Fielding (1707–1754) did not invent the modern novel—that honor belongs to Cervantes (see *Don Quixote*). Fielding's works, however, were so far advanced in form over their predecessors, such as Defoe's *Robinson Crusoe* (1719) and Richardson's *Pamela* (1740), that he must count as one of its founders. His most innovative work, *The History of Tom Jones, a Foundling,* has been called the finest English novel.

Fielding's works were noted for their realism, the hallmark of novels ever since. Modern in spirit, he abhorred the medieval past, the "centuries of monkish dullness when the whole world seems to have been asleep." In his never dull novels, he used real-life characters rather than universal types, and he chose historically accurate settings instead of scenes dictated by literary custom. He enhanced his plots' vividness by rooting them in minutely observed time. Rounding out the realism, Fielding narrated his novels in a unique voice that convinced many readers they must be true. Innovations like these helped rid literature of aristocratic heroes and heroines, the West's dominant mode since *The Epic of Gilgamesh,* and allowed the novel to focus on ordinary men and women.

Fielding's novels also reflected the growing power of England's Protestant middle class, who made literature into a marketplace. Only fairly well-off readers, however, could afford to own his novels; *Tom Jones* (1749), for example, cost eighteen shillings, enough money to feed a family for a week. Though an aristocrat, Fielding knew his audience well, having already won success with his plays. In his novels he gave this public what they wanted: high-spirited entertainments that were basically moralistic and religious in tone.

Tom Jones is an eight hundred–page novel of the comic and bawdy exploits of its robust hero. It concerns Jones, a foundling who loses and then regains the respect of those he loves and at the same time uncovers his true identity. Its moral core is Christian—reflected in hatred of liars and hypocrites—but blended with tolerance for sexual sins. Jones, for instance, who is hotblooded, suffers penalties for his indiscretions, but virtue wins in the end. In form, this many-layered novel has characters popping in and out to create surprises as they reappear. This plotting reflects Fielding's dramatic instinct, honed by his years in the theater.

Reading the Selection

Book 9, Chapter 3, of *Tom Jones* describes the events at the Upton village inn. Located exactly halfway through the novel—there are eighteen books total—this episode marks a turning point in Jones's career. Jones, after rescuing Mrs. Waters (whose identity will not be revealed until the last book) from attempted rape by Northerton, takes her to safety. A battle takes place, of which the end result is to keep Jones's friend Partridge from seeing Mrs. Waters, whom he could identify (wrongly) as Jones's mother. Thus this scene serves to prolong the plot and set up a later (false) recognition scene, when Jones will be identified as Mrs. Waters's abandoned son.

Book 9, Chapter 5, thickens the plot with its hint of incest, as love heats up between Jones and Mrs. Waters. As pointed out above, Partridge (wrongly) thinks that Mrs. Waters is Jones's mother and will make this claim in the last book, before it is disproved. Chapter 5, with its dining/seduction scene, shows also the worldly, teasing, and learned tone of the narrator. This episode was memorably captured on film in Stanley Kubrick's *Tom Jones.*

Book IX

Chapter III
The Arrival of Mr Jones, with his Lady,
at the Inn; with a very full Description
of the Battle of Upton

Tho' the reader, we doubt not, is very eager to know who this lady was, and how she fell into the hands of Mr Northerton; we must beg him to suspend his curiosity for a short time, as we are obliged, for some very good reasons, which hereafter perhaps he may guess, to delay his satisfaction a little longer.

Mr Jones and his fair companion no sooner entered the town, than they went directly to that inn which, in their eyes, presented the fairest appearance to the street. Here Jones, having ordered a servant to shew a room above stairs, was ascending, when the dishevelled fair hastily following, was laid hold on by the master of the house, who cried, 'Hey day, where is that beggar wench going? Stay below stairs, I desire you;' but Jones at that instant thundered from above, 'Let the lady come up,' in so authoritative a voice, that the good man instantly withdrew his hands, and the lady made the best of her way to the chamber.

Here Jones wished her joy of her safe arrival, and then departed, in order, as he promised, to send the landlady up with some cloaths. The poor woman thanked him heartily for all his kindness, and said, she hoped she should see him again soon, to thank him a thousand times more. During this short conversation, she covered her white bosom as well as she could possibly with her arms: for Jones could not avoid stealing a sly peep or two, tho' he took all imaginable care to avoid giving any offence.

Our travellers had happened to take up their residence at a house of exceedingly good repute, whither Irish ladies of strict virtue, and many northern lasses of the same predicament, were accustomed to resort in their way to Bath. The landlady therefore would by no means have admitted any conversation of a disreputable kind to pass under her roof. Indeed so foul and contagious are all such proceedings, that they contaminate the very innocent scenes where they are committed, and give the name of a bad house, or of a house of ill repute, to all those where they are suffered to be carried on.

Not that I would intimate, that such strict chastity as was preserved in the temple of Vesta can possibly be maintained at a public inn. My good landlady did not hope for such a blessing, nor would any of the ladies I have spoken of, or indeed any others of the most rigid note, have expected or insisted on any such thing. But to exclude all vulgar concubinage, and to drive all whores in rags from within the walls, is within the power of everyone. This my landlady very strictly adhered to, and this her virtuous guests, who did not travel in rags, would very reasonably have expected of her.

Now it required no very blameable degree of suspicion, to imagine that Mr Jones and his ragged companion had certain purposes in their intention, which, tho' tolerated in some Christian countries, connived at in others, and practised in all; are however as expressly forbidden as murder, or any other horrid vice, by that religion which is universally believed in those countries. The landlady therefore had no sooner received an intimation of the entrance of the abovesaid persons, than she began to meditate the most expeditious means for their expulsion. In order to do this, she had provided herself with a long and deadly instrument, with which, in times of peace, the chambermaid was wont to demolish the labours of the industrious spider. In vulgar phrase, she had taken up the broomstick, and was just about to sally from the kitchen, when Jones accosted her with a demand of a gown, and other vestments, to cover the half-naked woman above stairs.

Nothing can be more provoking to the human temper, nor more dangerous to that cardinal virtue, patience, than solicitations of extraordinary offices of kindness, on behalf of those very persons with whom we are highly incensed. For this reason Shakespear hath artfully introduced his Desdemona soliciting favours for Cassio of her husband, as the means of enflaming not only his jealousy, but his rage, to the highest pitch of madness; and we find the unfortunate Moor less able to command his passion on this occasion, than even when he beheld his valued present to his wife in the hands of his supposed rival. In fact, we regard these efforts as insults on our understanding, and to such the pride of man is very difficultly brought to submit.

My landlady, though a very good-tempered woman, had, I suppose, some of this pride in her composition; for Jones had scarce ended his request, when she fell upon him with a certain weapon, which, tho' it be neither long, nor sharp, nor hard, nor indeed threatens from its appearance with either death or wound, hath been however held in great dread and abhorrence by many wise men; nay, by many brave ones; insomuch that some who have dared to look into the mouth of a loaded cannon, have not dared to look into a mouth where this weapon was brandished; and rather than run the hazard of its execution, have contented themselves with making a most pitiful and sneaking figure in the eyes of all their acquaintance.

To confess the truth, I am afraid Mr Jones was one of these; for tho' he was attacked and violently belaboured with the aforesaid weapon, he could not be provoked to make any resistance; but in a most cowardly manner applied, with many entreaties, to his antagonist to desist from pursuing her blows: in plain English, he only begged her with the utmost earnestness to hear him; but before he could obtain his request, my landlord himself entered into the fray, and embraced that side of the cause which seemed to stand very little in need of assistance.

There are a sort of heroes who are supposed to be determined in their chusing or avoiding a conflict, by the character and behaviour of the person whom they are to engage. These are said to know their man, and Jones, I believe, knew his woman; for tho' he had been so submissive to her, he was no sooner attacked by her husband, than he demonstrated an immediate spirit of resentment, and enjoined him silence under a very severe penalty; no less than that, I think, of being converted into fuel for his own fire.

The husband, with great indignation, but with a mixture of pity, answered, 'You must pray first to be made able; I believe I am a better man than yourself; ay, every way, that I am;' and presently proceeded to discharge half a dozen whores at the lady above stairs, the last of which had scarce issued from his lips, when a swinging blow from the cudgel that Jones carried in his hand assaulted him over the shoulders.

It is a question whether the landlord or the landlady was the most expeditious in returning this blow. My landlord, whose hands were empty, fell to with his fist, and the good wife, uplifting her broom, and aiming at the head of Jones, had probably put an immediate end to the fray, and to Jones likewise, had not the descent of this broom been prevented,—not by the miraculous intervention of any heathen deity, but by a very natural, tho' fortunate accident; *viz.* by the arrival of Partridge; who entered the house at that instant (for fear had caused him to run every step from the hill) and who, seeing the danger which threatened his master, or companion, (which you chuse to call him) prevented so sad a catastrophe, by catching hold of the landlady's arm, as it was brandished aloft in the air.

The landlady soon perceived the impediment which prevented her blow; and being unable to rescue her arm from the hands of Partridge, she let fall the broom; and then leaving Jones to the discipline of her husband, she fell with the utmost fury on that poor fellow, who had already given some intimation of himself, by crying, 'Zounds! do you intend to kill my friend?'

Partridge, though not much addicted to battle, would not however stand still when his friend was attacked; nor was he much displeased with that part of the combat which fell to his share: he therefore returned my landlady's blows as soon as he received them; and now the fight was obstinately maintained on all parts, and it seemed doubtful to which side Fortune would incline, when the naked lady, who had listened at the top of the stairs to the dialogue which preceded the engagement, descended suddenly from above, and without weighing the unfair inequality of two to one, fell upon the poor woman who was boxing with Partridge; nor did that great champion desist, but rather redoubled his fury, when he found fresh succours were arrived to his assistance.

Victory must now have fallen to the side of the travellers (for the bravest troops must yield to numbers) had not Susan the chambermaid come luckily to support her mistress. This Susan was as two-handed a wench (according to the phrase) as any in the country, and would, I believe, have beat the famed Thalestris herself, or any of her subject Amazons; for her form was robust and manlike, and every way made for such encounters. As her hands

and arms were formed to give blows with great mischief to an enemy, so was her face as well contrived to receive blows without any great injury to herself: her nose being already flat to her face; her lips were so large, that no swelling could be perceived in them, and moreover they were so hard, that a fist could hardly make any impression on them. Lastly, her cheekbones stood out, as if nature had intended them for two bastions to defend her eyes in those encounters for which she seemed so well calculated, and to which she was most wonderfully well inclined.

This fair creature entering the field of battle, immediately filed to that wing where her mistress maintained so unequal a fight with one of either sex. Here she presently challenged Partridge to single combat. He accepted the challenge, and a most desperate fight began between them.

Now the dogs of war being let loose, began to lick their bloody lips; now Victory with golden wings hung hovering in the air. Now Fortune taking her scales from her shelf, began to weight the fates of Tom Jones, his female companion, and Partridge, against the landlord, his wife, and maid; all which hung in exact balance before her; when a good-natured accident put suddenly an end to the bloody fray, with which half of the combatants had already sufficiently feasted. This accident was the arrival of a coach and four; upon which my landlord and landlady immediately desisted from fighting, and at their entreaty obtained the same favour of their antagonists; but Susan was not so kind to Partridge; for that Amazonian fair having overthrown and bestrid her enemy, was now cuffing him lustily with both her hands, without any regard to his request of a cessation of arms, or to those loud exclamations of murder which he roared forth.

No sooner, however, had Jones quitted the landlord, than he flew to the rescue of his defeated companion, from whom he with much difficulty drew off the enraged chambermaid; but Partridge was not immediately sensible of his deliverance; for he still lay flat on the floor, guarding his face with his hands, nor did he cease roaring till Jones had forced him to look up, and to perceive that the battle was at an end.

The landlord who had no visible hurt, and the landlady hiding her well scratched face with her handkerchief, ran both hastily to the door to attend the coach, from which a young lady and her maid now alighted. These the landlady presently ushered into that room, where Mr Jones had at first deposited his fair prize, as it was the best apartment in the house. Hither they were obliged to pass through the field of battle, which they did with the utmost haste, covering their faces with their handkerchiefs, as desirous to avoid the notice of anyone. Indeed their caution was quite unnecessary: for the poor unfortunate Helen, the fatal cause of all the bloodshed, was entirely taken up in endeavouring to conceal her own face, and Jones was no less occupied in rescuing Partridge from the fury of Susan; which being happily effected, the poor fellow immediately departed to the pump to wash his face, and to stop that bloody torrent which Susan had plentifully set a flowing from his nostrils.

. . .

Chapter V
An Apology for all Heroes who have good Stomachs, with a Description of a Battle of the amorous Kind

Heroes, notwithstanding the high ideas, which by the means of flatterers they may entertain of themselves, or the world may conceive of them, have certainly more of mortal than divine about them. However elevated their minds may be, their bodies at least (which is much the major part of most) are liable to the worst infirmities, and subject to the vilest offices of human nature. Among these latter the act of eating, which hath by several wise men been considered as extremely mean and derogatory from the philosophic dignity, must be in some measure performed by the greatest prince, heroe, or philosopher upon earth; nay, sometimes nature hath been so frolicksome as to exact of these dignified characters, a much more exorbitant share of this office, than she hath obliged those of the lowest order to perform.

To say the truth, as no known inhabitant of this globe is really more than man, so none need be ashamed of submitting to what the necessities of man demand; but when those great personages I have just mentioned, condescend to aim at confining such low offices to themselves; as when by hoarding or destroying, they seem desirous to prevent any others from eating, they then surely become very low and despicable.

Now after this short preface, we think it no disparagement to our heroe to mention the immoderate ardour with which he laid about him at this season. Indeed it may be doubted, whether Ulysses, who by the way seems to have had the best stomach of all the heroes in that eating poem of the Odyssey, ever made a better meal. Three pounds at least of that flesh which formerly had contributed to the composition of an ox, was now honoured with becoming part of the individual Mr Jones.

This particular we thought ourselves obliged to mention, as it may account for our heroe's temporary neglect of his fair companion; who eat but very little, and was indeed employed in considerations of a very different nature, which passed unobserved by Jones, till he had entirely satisfied that appetite which a fast of twenty-four hours had procured him; but his dinner was no sooner ended, than his attention to other matters revived; with these matters therefore we shall now proceed to acquaint the reader.

Mr Jones, of whose personal accomplishments we have hitherto said very little, was in reality, one of the handsomest young fellows in the world. His face, besides being the picture of health, had in it the most apparent marks of sweetness and good-nature. These qualities were indeed so characteristical in his countenance, that while the spirit and sensibility in his eyes, tho' they must have been perceived by an accurate observer, might have escaped the notice of the less discerning, so strongly was this good-nature painted in his look, that it was remarked by almost everyone who saw him.

It was, perhaps, as much owing to this, as to a very fine complection, that his face had a delicacy in it almost inexpressible, and which might have given him an air rather too effeminate, had it not been joined to a most masculine person and mien; which latter had as much in them of the Hercules, as the former had of the Adonis. He was besides active, genteel, gay, and good-humoured, and had a flow of animal spirits, which enlivened every conversation where he was present.

When the reader hath duly reflected on these many charms which all centered in our heroe, and considers at the same time the fresh obligations which Mrs Waters had to him, it will be a mark of more prudery than candour to entertain a bad opinion of her, because she conceived a very good opinion of him.

But whatever censures may be passed upon her, it is my business to relate matters of fact with veracity. Mrs Waters had, in truth, not only a good opinion of our heroe, but a very great affection for him. To speak out boldly at once, she was in love, according to the present universally received sense of that phrase, by which love is applied indiscriminately to the desirable objects of all our passions, appetites, and senses, and is understood to be that preference which we give to one kind of food rather than to another.

But tho' the love to these several objects may possibly be one and the same in all cases, its operations however must be allowed to be different; for how much soever we may be in love with an excellent surloin of beef, or bottle of Burgundy; with a damask rose, or Cremona fiddle; yet do we never smile, nor ogle, nor dress, nor flatter, nor endeavour by any other arts or tricks to gain the affection of the said beef, &c. Sigh indeed we sometimes may; but it is generally in the absence, not in the presence of the beloved object. For otherwise we might possibly complain of their ingratitude and deafness, with the same reason as Pasiphae doth of her bull, whom she endeavoured to engage by all the coquetry practised with good success in the drawing-room, on the much more sensible, as well as tender, hearts of the fine gentlemen there.

The contrary happens, in that love which operates between persons of the same species, but of different sexes. Here we are no sooner in love, than it becomes our principal care to engage the affection of the object beloved. For what other purpose indeed are our youth instructed in all the arts of rendering themselves agreeable? If it was not with a view to this love, I question whether any of those trades which deal in setting off and adorning the human person would procure a livelihood. Nay, those great polishers of our manners, who are by some thought to teach what principally distinguishes us from the brute creation, even dancing-masters themselves, might possibly find no place in society. In short, all the graces which young ladies and young gentlemen too learn from others; and the many improvements which, by the help of a looking-glass, they add of their own, are in reality those very *spicula & faces amoris*, so often mentioned by Ovid; or, as they are sometimes called in our own language, *the whole artillery of love*.

Now Mrs Waters and our heroe had no sooner sat down together, than the former began to play this artillery upon the latter. But here, as we are about to attempt a description hitherto unessayed either in prose or verse, we think proper to invoke the assistance of certain aerial beings, who will, we doubt not, come kindly to our aid on this occasion.

'Say then, you Graces, you that inhabit the heavenly mansions of Seraphina's countenance; for you are truly divine, are always in her presence, and well know all the arts of charming; say, what were the weapons now used to captivate the heart of Mr Jones.'

'First, from two lovely blue eyes, whose bright orbs flashed lightning at their discharge, flew forth two pointed ogles. But happily for our heroe, hit only a vast piece of beef which he was then conveying into his plate, and harmless spent their force. The fair warrior perceived their miscarriage, and immediately from her fair bosom drew forth a deadly sigh. A sigh, which none could have heard unmoved, and which was sufficient at once to have swept off a dozen beaus; so soft, so sweet, so tender, that the insinuating air must have found its subtle way to the heart of our heroe, had it not luckily been driven from his ears by the coarse bubbling of some bottled ale, which at that time he was pouring forth. Many other weapons did she assay; but the God of Eating (if there be any such deity; for I do not confidently assert it) preserved his votary; or perhaps it may not be *dignus vindice nodus,* and the present security of Jones may be accounted for by natural means: for as love frequently preserves from the attacks of hunger, so may hunger possibly, in some cases, defend us against love.

'The fair one, enraged at her frequent disappointments, determined on a short cessation of arms. Which interval she employed in making ready every engine of amorous warfare for the renewing of the attack, when dinner should be over.

'No sooner then was the cloth removed, than she again began her operations. First, having planted her right

eye sideways against Mr Jones, she shot from its corner a most penetrating glance; which, tho' great part of its force was spent before it reached our heroe, did not vent itself absolutely without effect. This the fair one perceiving, hastily withdrew her eyes, and leveled them downwards as if she was concerned for what she had done: tho' by this means she designed only to draw him from his guard, and indeed to open his eyes, through which she intended to surprize his heart. And now, gently lifting up those two bright orbs which had already begun to make an impression on poor Jones, she discharged a volley of small charms at once from her whole countenance in a smile. Not a smile of mirth, nor of joy; but a smile of affection, which most ladies have always ready at their command, and which serves them to show at once their good-humour, their pretty dimples, and their white teeth.

'This smile our heroe received full in his eyes, and was immediately staggered with its force. He then began to see the designs of the enemy, and indeed to feel their success. A parley now was set on foot between the parties; during which the artful fair so slily and imperceptibly carried on her attack, that she had almost subdued the heart of our heroe, before she again repaired to acts of hostility. To confess the truth, I am afraid Mr Jones maintained a kind of Dutch defence, and treacherously delivered up the garrison, without duly weighing his allegiance to the fair Sophia. In short, no sooner had the amorous parley ended, and the lady had unmasked the royal battery, by carelessly letting her handkerchief drop from her neck, than the heart of Mr Jones was entirely taken, and the fair conqueror enjoyed the usual fruits of her victory.'

Here the Graces think proper to end their description, and here we think proper to end the chapter.

VOLTAIRE

Selections from *Candide*

Voltaire's *Candide* was the most popular novel of the Age of Reason. It is a delightful, sometimes bawdy tale that satirizes the follies of the Western world of the time. Presumably because of fear that the sharp satire might give offense in certain quarters, Voltaire is nowhere identified as the book's author. Instead, its title page says simply, "Translated from the German by Dr. Ralph"—a disguise that fooled no one, as readers recognized Voltaire's biting wit and deft touch. After two hundred years, *Candide* survives as one of the best-loved fictional works in the world.

That Voltaire's novel survives is surprising, since it is a satire on topical events, and such satires are thought to grow stale as quickly as today's newspaper. What saves it from the dustbin of history is its glowing style—lighthearted, worldly, and sly—and the fact that most modern Westerners see the world much as Voltaire did. Who today does not share Voltaire's hatred of slavery, war, snobbery, religious persecution, and crooked clergy, or his skepticism about divine kings and utopian societies? Of course, not all of the satire works today, as in the anti-Semitic jokes and the portrayal of women as fickle. Still, the novel charms most readers as it pays homage to humanity's unsinkable spirit.

Candide (1759) is the story of the education of its naive hero, Candide, as he moves from West-phalia, a province in Prussia, across much of the Western world, including South America. What drives Candide's odyssey is the hope of marrying the lovely Cunégonde, a Westphalian baroness who keeps slipping from his grasp. Despite Candide's love for Cunégonde, the novel is not a love story, since their troubles are treated as comedy. Instead, it is a novel of ideas whose characters, except for Candide, show little or no growth and simply express Voltaire's point of view.

The novel is subtitled *Optimism*, and it was facile optimism that aroused Voltaire's anger. Facile optimism, derived from the German thinker Leibniz, denies that evil exists and insists that the world is basically good. In the novel, Leibniz is represented by Pangloss (from Greek, "all tongue"), who, faced with constant trials, offers this advice: "This is the best of all possible worlds." Pangloss's oppo-site is Martin, a facile pessimist who thinks all happens for the worst. In the end, Candide rejects both rival philosophies, opting instead for pragmatism: "We must cultivate our gardens."

Voltaire (1694–1778) (born François Marie Arouet) dominated his age unlike any writer before or since. A universal genius, he wrote tragedies, poems, essays, novels, histories, dictionaries, letters, memoirs, philosophical treatises, and a work popularizing science. Very little of this vast work is widely read today, except for *Candide*. Voltaire's spirit survives in the term *Voltarean*, meaning a skeptic yet one who tolerates all religious points of view.

Reading the Selections

Included here are Chapters I through VI and Chapter XXX, the conclusion to the novel. The opening chapters cover Candide's travel from Westphalia, his homeland, to Lisbon, Portugal, where he barely survives an *auto-da-fé*—an "act of faith" in which heretics are persecuted. As calamities rain down on Candide, faithful Pangloss offers his optimistic bromides. Pangloss's litany quickly becomes absurd, though not to Candide.

After Chapter VI, Candide and Pangloss are rescued and join Candide's long-lost love, Cuné-gonde, and others in a series of adventures that take them from Portugal to South America and back to Europe. In the last chapter, Voltaire reunites the main characters on Candide's farm in Turkey, where they continue to debate the meaning of life. A Turkish neighbor, satisfied with his simple farm life, advises them to work in order to eliminate the evils of boredom, vice, and poverty. Taking the Turkish farmer's advice to heart, Candide concludes that one must "work in the garden"—that is, tend to what has to be done in order to survive and make sense of the human comedy.

—⁂—

Chapter I
How Candide was brought up in a beautiful country house, and how he was driven away

There lived in Westphalia, at the country seat of Baron Thunder-ten-tronckh, a young lad blessed by nature with the most agreeable manners. You could read his character in his face. He combined sound judgment with unaffected simplicity; and that, I suppose, was why he was called Candide. The old family servants suspected that he was the son of the Baron's sister by a worthy gentleman of that neighbourhood, whom the young lady would never agree to marry because he could only claim seventy-one quar-terings, the rest of his family tree having suffered from the ravages of time.

The Baron was one of the most influential noblemen in Westphalia, for his house had a door and several win-dows and his hall was actually draped with tapestry. Every dog in the courtyard was pressed into service when he went hunting, and his grooms acted as whips. The vil-lage curate was his private chaplain. They all called him Your Lordship, and laughed at his jokes.

The Baroness, whose weight of about twenty-five stone made her a person of great importance, entertained with a dignity which won her still more respect. Her daughter, Cunégonde, was a buxom girl of seventeen with a fresh, rosy complexion; altogether seductive. The Baron's son was in every way worthy of his father. His tutor, Pangloss, was the recognised authority in the house-hold on all matters of learning, and young Candide lis-tened to his teaching with that unhesitating faith which marked his age and character.

Pangloss taught metaphysico-theologo-cosmolo-nig-ology. He proved incontestably that there is no effect without a cause, and that in this best of all possible worlds, his lordship's country seat was the most beautiful of mansions and her ladyship the best of all possible ladyships.

'It is proved,' he used to say, 'that things cannot be ⁵ other than they are, for since everything was made for a purpose, it follows that everything is made for the best purpose. Observe: our noses were made to carry spectacles, so we have spectacles. Legs were clearly intended for breeches, and we wear them. Stones were meant for carving and for building houses, and that is why my lord has a most beautiful house; for the greatest baron in Westphalia ought to have the noblest residence. And since pigs were made to be eaten, we eat pork all the year round. It follows that those who maintain that all is right talk nonsense; they ought to say that all is for the best.'

Candide listened attentively, and with implicit belief; for he found Lady Cunégonde extremely beautiful, though he never had the courage to tell her so. He decided that the height of good fortune was to have been born Baron Thunder-ten-tronckh and after that to be Lady Cunégonde. The next was to see her every day, and failing that to listen to his master Pangloss, the greatest philosopher in Westphalia, and consequently the greatest in all the world.

One day Cunégonde was walking near the house in a little coppice, called 'the park', when she saw Dr. Pangloss behind some bushes giving a lesson in experimental physics to her mother's waiting-woman, a pretty little brunette who seemed eminently teachable. Since Lady Cunégonde took a great interest in science, she watched the experiments being repeated with breathless fascination. She saw clearly the Doctor's 'sufficient reason', and took note of cause and effect. Then, in a disturbed and thoughtful state of mind, she returned home filled with a desire for learning, and fancied that she could reason equally well with young Candide and he with her.

On her way home she met Candide, and blushed. Candide blushed too. Her voice was choked with emotion as she greeted him, and Candide spoke to her without knowing what he said. The following day, as they were leaving the dinner table, Cunégonde and Candide happened to meet behind a screen. Cunégonde dropped her handkerchief, and Candide picked it up. She quite innocently took his hand, he as innocently kissed hers with singular grace and ardour. Their lips met, their eyes flashed, their knees trembled, and their hands would not keep still. Baron Thunder-ten-tronckh, happening to pass the screen at that moment, noticed both cause and effect, and drove Candide from the house with powerful kicks on the backside. Cunégonde fainted, and on recovering her senses was boxed on the ears by the Baroness. Thus consternation reigned in the most beautiful and delightful of all possible mansions.

Chapter II
What happened to Candide amongst the Bulgars

After being turned out of this earthly paradise, Candide ¹ wandered off without thinking which way he was going. As he plodded along he wept, glancing sometimes towards heaven, but more often in the direction of the most beautiful of houses, which contained the loveliest of barons' daughters. He lay down for the night in the furrow of a ploughed field with snow falling in thick flakes; and, to make matters worse, he had nothing to eat. Next day, perished with cold and hunger, and without a penny in his pocket, he dragged his weary limbs to a neighboring town called Waldberghoff-trarbk-dikdorff, where he stopped at an inn and cast a pathetic glance towards the door.

Two men in blue noticed him.

'There's a well-made young fellow, chum,' said one to the other, 'and just the height we want.'

They went up to Candide and politely asked him to dine with them.

'Gentlemen,' said Candide modestly, 'I deeply appre- ⁵ ciate the honour, but I haven't enough money to pay my share.'

'People of your appearance and merit, Sir, never pay anything,' said one of the men in blue; 'aren't you five feet five inches tall?'

'Yes, gentlemen, that is my height,' said Candide, with a bow.

'Very well, Sir, sit down; we'll pay your share, and what's more we shall not allow a man like you to go short of money. That's what men are for, to help each other.'

'You are quite right,' said Candide; 'for that is what Mr. Pangloss used to tell me. I am convinced by your courteous behaviour that all is for the best.'

His new companions then asked him to accept a few ¹⁰ shillings. Candide took them gratefully and wanted to give a receipt; but his offer was brushed aside, and they all sat down to table.

'Are you not a devoted admirer . . . ?' began one of the men in blue.

'Indeed I am,' said Candide earnestly, 'I am a devoted admirer of Lady Cunégonde.'

'No doubt,' replied the man; 'but what we want to know is whether you are a devoted admirer of the King of the Bulgars.'

'Good Heavens, no!' said Candide; 'I've never seen him.'

'Oh, but he is the most amiable of kings and we must ¹⁵ drink his health.'

'By all means, gentlemen,' replied Candide, and emptied his glass.

'That's enough,' they cried. 'You are now his support and defender, and a Bulgar hero into the bargain. Your fortune is made. Go where glory waits you.'

And with that they clapped him into irons and hauled him off to the barracks. There he was taught 'right turn', 'left turn', and 'quick march', 'slope arms' and 'order arms', how to aim and how to fire, and was given thirty strokes of the 'cat'. Next day his performance on parade was a little better, and he was given only twenty strokes. The following day he received a mere ten and was thought a prodigy by his comrades.

The bewildered Candide was still rather in the dark about his heroism. One fine spring morning he took it into his head to decamp and walked straight off, thinking it a privilege common to man and beast to use his legs when he wanted. But he had not gone six miles before he was caught, bound, and thrown into a dungeon by four other six-foot heroes. At the court martial he was graciously permitted to choose between being flogged thirty-six times by the whole regiment or having twelve bullets in his brain. It was useless to declare his belief in Free Will and say he wanted neither; he had to make his choice. So, exercising that divine gift called Liberty, he decided to run the gauntlet thirty-six times, and survived two floggings. The regiment being two thousand strong, he received four thousand strokes, which exposed every nerve and muscle from the nape of his neck to his backside. The course had been set for the third heat, but Candide could endure no more and begged them to do him the kindness of beheading him instead. The favour was granted, his eyes were bandaged, and he was made to kneel down. The King of the Bulgars passed by at that moment and asked what crime the culprit had committed. Since the King was a man of great insight, he recognised from what he was told about Candide that here was a young philosopher utterly ignorant of the way of the world, and granted him a pardon, an exercise of mercy which will be praised in every newspaper and in every age. Candide was cured in three weeks by a worthy surgeon with ointments originally prescribed by Dioscorides; and he had just enough skin on his feet to walk, when the King of the Bulgars joined battle with the King of the Abars.

Chapter III
How Candide escaped from the Bulgars, and what happened to him afterwards

Those who have never seen two well-trained armies drawn up for battle, can have no idea of the beauty and brilliance of the display. Bugles, fifes, oboes, drums, and salvoes of artillery produced such a harmony as Hell itself could not rival. The opening barrage destroyed about six thousand men on each side. Rifle-fire which followed rid this best of worlds of about nine or ten thousand villains who infested its surface. Finally, the bayonet provided 'sufficient reason' for the death of several thousand more. The total casualties amounted to about thirty thousand. Candide trembled like a philosopher, and hid himself as best he could during this heroic butchery.

When all was over and the rival kings were celebrating their victory with Te Deums in their respective camps, Candide decided to find somewhere else to pursue his reasoning into cause and effect. He picked his way over piles of dead and dying, and reached a neighbouring village on the Abar side of the border. It was now no more than a smoking ruin, for the Bulgars had burned it to the ground in accordance with the terms of international law. Old men, crippled with wounds, watched helplessly the death-throes of their butchered women-folk, who still clasped their children to their bloodstained breasts. Girls who had satisfied the appetites of several heroes lay disembowelled in their last agonies. Others, whose bodies were badly scorched, begged to be put out of their misery.

Whichever way he looked, the ground was strewn with the legs, arms, and brains of dead villagers.

Candide made off as quickly as he could to another village. This was in Bulgar territory, and had been treated in the same way by Abar heroes. Candide walked through the ruins over heaps of writhing bodies and at last left the theatre of war behind him. He had some food in his knapsack, and his thoughts still ran upon Lady Cunégonde. His provisions were exhausted by the time he reached Holland, but as he had heard that everyone in that country was rich and all were Christians, he had no doubt that he would be treated as kindly as he had been at Castle Thunder-ten-tronckh before Lady Cunégonde's amorous glances caused his banishment.

He appealed for alms from several important-looking people, who all told him that if he persisted in begging he would be sent to a reformatory to be taught how to earn his daily bread.

At last he approached a man who had just been addressing a big audience for a whole hour on the subject of charity. The orator peered at him, and said:

'What is your business here? Do you support the Good Old Cause?'

'There is no effect without a cause,' replied Candide modestly. 'All things are necessarily connected and arranged for the best. It was my fate to be driven from Lady Cunégonde's presence and made to run the gauntlet, and now I have to beg my bread until I can earn it. Things could not have happened otherwise.'

'Do you believe that the Pope is Antichrist, my friend?' said the minister.

'I have never heard anyone say so,' replied Candide; 'but whether he is or he isn't I want some food.'

'You don't deserve to eat,' said the other. 'Be off with you, you villain, you wretch! Don't come near me again or you'll suffer for it.'

The minister's wife looked out the window at that moment, and seeing a man who was not sure that the Pope was Antichrist, emptied over his head a pot full of . . . , which shows to what lengths ladies are driven by religious zeal.

A man who had never been christened, a worthy Anabaptist called James, had seen the cruel and humiliating treatment of his brother man, a creature without wings but with two legs and a soul; he brought him home and washed him, gave him some bread and beer and a couple of florins, and even offered to apprentice him to his business of manufacturing those Persian silks that are made in Holland. Candide almost fell at his feet.

'My tutor, Pangloss, was quite right,' he exclaimed, 'when he told me that all is for the best in this world of ours, for your generosity moves me much more than the harshness of that gentleman in the black gown and his wife.'

While taking a walk the next day, Candide met a beggar covered with sores. His eyes were lifeless, the end of his nose had rotted away, his mouth was all askew and his teeth were black. His voice was sepulchral, and a violent cough tormented him, at every bout of which he spat out a tooth.

Chapter IV
How Candide met his old tutor, Dr. Pangloss, and what came of it

Candide was moved more by compassion than by horror at the sight of this ghastly scarecrow, and gave him the two florins he had received from James, the honest Anabaptist. The apparition looked at him intently and, with tears starting to his eyes, fell on the young man's neck. Candide drew back in terror.

'Does this mean,' said one wretch to the other, 'that you don't recognize your dear Pangloss any more?'

'Pangloss!' cried Candide. 'Can this be my beloved master in such a shocking state! What misfortune has befallen you? What has driven you from the most lovely of mansions? What has happened to Lady Cunégonde, that pearl among women, the masterpiece of nature?'

'My breath fails me,' murmured Pangloss.

At this Candide quickly led him to the Anabaptist's stable, where he made him eat some bread, and as soon as he had revived, said to him:

'You mentioned Cunégonde?'

'She is dead,' replied the other.

At these words Candide fainted, but his friend restored him to his senses with a little sour vinegar which happened to be in the stable. Candide opened his eyes.

'Cunégonde is dead!' said he. 'Oh, what has become of the best of worlds? . . . But what did she die of? No doubt it was grief at seeing me sent flying from her father's lovely mansion at the point of a jack-boot?'

'No,' said Pangloss. 'She was disembowelled by Bulgar soldiers after being ravished as much as a poor woman could bear. When my lord tried to defend her, they broke his head. Her ladyship was cut into small pieces, and my poor pupil treated in precisely the same way as his sister. As for the house, not one stone was left standing on another; not a barn was left, not a sheep, not a duck, not a tree. But we have been amply avenged, for the Abars did just the same in a neighbouring estate which belonged to a Bulgar nobleman.'

At this tale Candide fainted once more. When he recovered his senses, he first said all that was called for, and then enquired into cause and effect, and into the 'sufficient reason' that had reduced Pangloss to such a pitiable state.

'I fear it is love,' said his companion; 'love, the comforter of humanity, the preserver of the universe, the soul of all living beings; tender love!'

'I know what this love is,' said Candide, with a shake of his head, 'this sovereign of hearts and quintessence of our souls: my entire reward has been a kiss and twenty kicks on the backside. But how could such a beautiful cause produce so hideous an effect upon you?'

'My dear Candide,' replied Pangloss, 'you remember Pacquette, that pretty girl who used to wait on our noble lady. In her arms I tasted the delights of Paradise, and they produced these hellish torments by which you see me devoured. She was infected, and now perhaps she is dead. Paquette was given this present by a learned Franciscan, who had traced it back to its source. He had had it from an old countess, who had had it from a cavalry officer, who was indebted for it to a marchioness. She took it from her page, and he had received it from a Jesuit who, while still a novice, had had it in direct line from one of the companions of Christopher Columbus. As for me, I shall not give it to anyone, for I am a dying man.'

'What a strange genealogy, Pangloss!' exclaimed Candide. 'Isn't the devil at the root of it?'

'Certainly not,' replied the great man. 'It is indispensable in this best of worlds. It is a necessary ingredient. For if Columbus, when visiting the West Indies, had not caught this disease, which poisons the source of generation, which frequently even hinders generation, and is clearly opposed to the great end of Nature, we should have neither chocolate nor cochineal. We see, too, that to this very day the disease, like religious controversy, is peculiar to us Europeans. The Turks, the Indians, the Persians, the Chinese, the Siamese, the Japanese as yet have no knowledge of it; but there is a 'sufficient reason' for their experiencing it in turn in the course of a few centuries. Meanwhile, it has made remarkable progress amongst us, and most of all in these huge armies of honest, well-trained mercenaries, who decide the destinies of nations. It can safely be said that when thirty thousand men are ranged against an army of equal numbers, there will be about twenty thousand infected with pox on each side.'

'I could listen to you for ever,' said Candide; 'but you must be cured.'

'How can I be cured?' said Pangloss. 'I haven't a penny, my dear friend, and there is not a doctor in all this wide world who will bleed you or purge you without a fee.'

This last remark decided Candide. He hurried to James, the charitable Anabaptist, and, falling at his feet, painted so moving a picture of the state to which his friend had been reduced that the good man did not hesitate to take Dr. Pangloss in and had him cured at his own expense. During treatment, Pangloss lost only an eye and an ear. He still wrote well and had a perfect command of arithmetic, so the Anabaptist appointed him his accountant. Two months later he was obliged to go to Lisbon on business and set sail in his own ship, taking the two philosophers with him. On the voyage Pangloss explained to him how all was designed for the best. James did not share this view.

'Men,' he said, 'must have somewhat altered the course of nature; for they were not born wolves, yet they have become wolves. God did not give them twenty-four-pounders or bayonets, yet they have made themselves bayonets and guns to destroy each other. In the same category I place not only bankruptcies, but the law which carries off the bankrupts' effects, so as to defraud their creditors.'

'More examples of the indispensable!' remarked the one-eyed doctor. 'Private misfortunes contribute to the general good, so that the more private misfortunes there are, the more we find that all is well.'

While he was pursuing his argument the sky became overcast, the winds blew from the four corners of the earth, and the ship was caught in a most terrible storm in sight of the port of Lisbon.

Chapter V
Describing tempest, shipwreck, and earthquake, and what happened to Dr. Pangloss, Candide, and James, the Anabaptist

Half the passengers were at the last gasp of nervous and physical exhaustion from the pitching and tossing of the vessel, and were so weak that they had no strength left to realise their danger. The other half uttered cries of alarm and said their prayers, for the sails were torn, the masts were broken, and the ship was splitting. Work as they might, all were sixes and sevens, for there was no one to take command. The Anabaptist gave what help he could in directing the ship's course, and was on the poop when a madly excited sailor struck him a violent blow, which laid him at full length on the deck. The force of his blow upset the sailor's own balance, and he fell head first overboard; but, in falling, he was caught on a piece of the broken mast and hung dangling over the ship's side. The worthy James ran to his assistance and helped him to climb on board again. The efforts he made were so strenuous, however, that he was pitched into the sea in full view of the sailor, who left him to perish without taking the slightest notice. Candide was in time to see his benefactor reappear above the surface for one moment before being swallowed up for ever. He wanted to throw himself into the sea after the Anabaptist, but the great philosopher, Pangloss, stopped him by proving that Lisbon harbour was made on purpose for this Anabaptist to drown there. Whilst he was proving this from first principles, the ship split in two and all perished except Pangloss, Candide, and the brutal sailor who had been the means of drowning the honest Anabaptist. The villain swam successfully to shore; and Pangloss and Candide, clinging to a plank, were washed up after him.

When they had recovered a little of their strength, they set off towards Lisbon, hoping they had just enough money in their pockets to avoid starvation after escaping the storm.

Scarcely had they reached the town, and were still mourning their benefactor's death, when they felt the earth tremble beneath them. The sea boiled up in the harbour and broke the ships which lay at anchor. Whirlwinds of flame and ashes covered the streets and squares. Houses came crashing down. Roofs toppled on to their foundations, and the foundations crumbled. Thirty thousand men, women and children were crushed to death under the ruins.

The sailor chuckled:

'There'll be something worth picking up here,' he remarked with an oath.

'What can be the "sufficient reason" for this phenomenon?' said Pangloss.

'The Day of Judgment has come,' cried Candide.

The sailor rushed straight into the midst of the debris and risked his life searching for money. Having found some, he ran off with it to get drunk; and after sleeping off the effects of the wine, he bought the favours of the first girl of easy virtue he met amongst the ruined houses with the dead and dying all around. Pangloss pulled him by the sleeve and said:

'This will never do, my friend; you are not obeying the universal rule of Reason; you have misjudged the occasion.'

'Bloody hell,' replied the other. 'I am a sailor and was born in Batavia. I have had to trample on the crucifix four times in various trips I've been to Japan. I'm not the man for your Universal Reason!'

Candide had been wounded by splinters of flying masonry and lay helpless in the road, covered with rubble.

'For Heaven's sake,' he cried to Pangloss, 'fetch me some wine and oil! I am dying.'

'This earthquake is nothing new,' replied Pangloss; 'the town of Lima in America experienced the same shocks last year. The same causes produce the same effects. There is certainly a vein of sulphur running under the earth from Lima to Lisbon.'

'Nothing is more likely,' said Candide; 'but oil and wine, for pity's sake!'

'Likely!' exclaimed the philosopher. 'I maintain it's proved!'

Candide lost consciousness, and Pangloss brought him a little water from a fountain close by.

The following day, while creeping amongst the ruins, they found something to eat and recruited their strength. They then set to work with the rest to relieve those inhabitants who had escaped death. Some of the citizens whom they had helped gave them as good a dinner as could be managed after such a disaster. The meal was certainly a sad affair, and the guests wept as they ate; but Pangloss consoled them with the assurance that things could not be otherwise:

'For all this,' said he, 'is a manifestation of the rightness of things, since if there is a volcano at Lisbon it could not be anywhere else. For it is impossible for things not to be where they are, because everything is for the best.'

A little man in black, an officer of the Inquisition, who was sitting beside Pangloss, turned to him and politely said:

'It appears, Sir, that you do not believe in original sin; for if all is for the best, there can be no such thing as the fall of Man and eternal punishment.'

'I most humbly beg your Excellency's pardon,' replied Pangloss, still more politely, 'but I must point out that the fall of Man and eternal punishment enter, of Necessity, into the scheme of the best of all possible worlds.'

'Then you don't believe in Free Will, Sir?' said the officer.

'Your Excellency must excuse me,' said Pangloss; 'Free Will is consistent with Absolute Necessity, for it was ordained that we should be free. For the Will that is Determined . . .'

Pangloss was in the middle of his sentence when the officer nodded to his henchman, who was pouring him out a glass of port wine.

Chapter VI
How a magnificent auto-da-fé was staged to prevent further earthquakes, and how Candide was flogged

The University of Coimbra had pronounced that the sight [1] of a few people ceremoniously burned alive before a slow fire was an infallible prescription for preventing earthquakes; so when the earthquake had subsided after destroying three-quarters of Lisbon, the authorities of that country could find no surer means of avoiding total ruin than by giving the people a magnificent auto-da-fé.

They therefore seized a Basque, convicted of marrying his godmother, and two Portuguese Jews who had refused to eat bacon with their chicken; and after dinner Dr. Pangloss and his pupil, Candide, were arrested as well, one for speaking and the other for listening with an air of approval. Pangloss and Candide were led off separately and closeted in exceedingly cool rooms, where they suffered no inconvenience from the sun, and were brought out a week later to be dressed in sacrificial cassocks and paper mitres. The decorations on Candide's mitre and cassock were penitential in character, inverted flames and devils without tails or claws; but Pangloss's devils had tails and claws, and his flames were upright. They were then marched in procession, clothed in these robes, to hear a moving sermon followed by beautiful music in counterpoint. Candide was flogged in time with the anthem; the Basque and the two men who refused to eat bacon were burnt; and Pangloss was hanged, though that was not the usual practice on those occasions. The same day another earthquake occurred and caused tremendous havoc.

The terrified Candide stood weltering in blood and trembling with fear and confusion.

'If this is the best of all possible worlds,' he said to himself, 'what can the rest be like? Had it only been a matter of flogging, I should not have questioned it, for I have had that before from the Bulgars. But when it comes to my dear Pangloss being hanged—the greatest of philosophers—I must know the reason why. And was it part of the scheme of things that my dear Anabaptist (the best of men!) should be drowned in sight of land? And Lady Cunégonde, that pearl amongst women! Was it really necessary for her to be disembowelled?'

He had been preached at, flogged, absolved, and [5] blessed, and was about to stagger away, when an old woman accosted him and said:

'Pull yourself together, young man, and follow me.'

. . .

Chapter XXX
Conclusion

At the bottom of his heart, Candide had no wish to marry [1] Cunégonde, but the Baron's intransigence determined him to go through with the match; and besides, Cunégonde was pressing him so strongly that he could not retract. He consulted Pangloss, Martin, and the faithful Cacambo. Pangloss compiled a beautiful memorandum in which he proved that the Baron had no rights over his sister, and that in accordance with Imperial law she could give Candide her left hand in marriage. Martin recommended throwing the Baron into the sea, while Cacambo decided that he must be given back to the Levantine captain and replaced in the galleys, after which he should be sent to Rome to the Father General by the very first ship. Cacambo's advice seemed the most sensible, and was approved by the old woman, but nothing was said to Cunégonde about the plan. It was carried out at little cost, and they enjoyed the double pleasure of overreaching a Jesuit and punishing the pride of a German baron.

It would be natural to suppose that, after so many disasters, Candide should lead the most pleasing life imaginable, married at last to his mistress, and living with the philosophical Pangloss, the philosophical Martin, the prudent Cacambo, and the old woman, especially as he had brought away so many diamonds from the country once occupied by the Incas. But he had been so badly cheated by the Jews, that he had nothing left beyond his little farm. His wife daily grew uglier, and became more and more cantankerous and insufferable. The old woman was now quite infirm, and had developed an even worse temper than Cunégonde's. Cacambo, whose job was to work in the garden and sell vegetables in Constantinople, was quite worn out with toil, and cursed his lot. Pangloss was vexed to think that he was not the master spirit in some German university. As for Martin, he was firmly persuaded that a man is badly off wherever he is, so he suffered in patience. Candide, Martin, and Pangloss sometimes discussed metaphysics and morals. From the windows of the farmhouse boats were often seen passing, crowded with Turkish statesmen, military governors, and judges, bound for exile in Lemnos, Mytilene, or Erzerum, and other judges, governors, and statesmen were seen coming to take the place of the banished, only to be banished in their turn. Heads, too, were to be seen, decently impaled for display at the Sublime Porte. Sights such as these made the philosophers renew their disputations; and when there was no discussion, the boredom was so intolerable that the old woman was provoked one day to remark:

'I should like to know which is the worst, to be ravished a hundred times by negro pirates, to have one buttock cut off, to run the gauntlet of a Bulgar regiment, to be whipped and hanged at an auto-da-fé, to be dissected, to row in the galleys—in fact, to experience all the miseries through which we have passed—or just to stay here with nothing to do?'

'That's a difficult question,' said Candide.

The old woman's speech produced fresh reflections. [5] Martin's conclusion was that man was born to suffer from the restlessness of anxiety or from the lethargy of boredom. Candide did not agree, but he admitted nothing. Pangloss allowed that his sufferings had been uniformly horrible; but as he had once maintained that everything would turn out right in some marvellous way, he still maintained it would, however little he believed it.

One day an incident occurred which confirmed Martin in his detestable views, and at the same time embarrassed

Pangloss and made Candide more dubious than ever. It was the arrival of Pacquette and Brother Giroflée at the little farm in the utmost distress. They had soon got through their three thousand piastres, and had parted company only to be reconciled and to quarrel once again. They had been in prison and had escaped, and Brother Giroflée had at last turned Turk. Pacquette had continued to practise her profession but without a shadow of profit to herself.

'I knew quite well,' said Martin to Candide, 'that your presents would soon be spent and would leave them much worse off than before. You've squandered millions of piastres, you and Cacambo between you, and you are no happier than Brother Giroflée and Pacquette.'

'My dear child,' cried Pangloss to Pacquette, 'so Heaven has brought you back to us at last! Do you realise that you cost me an eye, an ear, and the end of my nose? What a state you are in! What a world this is!'

This fresh adventure drove them back to their discussions with redoubled ardour.

There lived in the neighbourhood a famous dervish, who was reputed to be the greatest philosopher in Turkey. They went to consult him, and chose Pangloss as their spokesman.

'Master,' said he, 'we have come to ask a favour. Will you kindly tell us why such a strange animal as man was ever made?'

'What has that got to do with you?' said the dervish. 'Is it your business?'

'But surely, reverend father,' said Candide, 'there is a great deal of evil in the world.'

'And what if there is?' said the dervish. 'When His Highness sends a ship to Egypt, do you suppose he worries whether the ship's mice are comfortable or not?'

'What ought to be done, then?' said Pangloss.

'Keep your mouth shut!' said the dervish.

'I had been looking forward,' said Pangloss, 'to a little discussion with you about cause and effect, the best of all possible worlds, the origin of evil, the nature of the soul, and pre-established harmony.'

At these words the dervish got up and slammed the door in their faces.

During this conversation, news had spread that two cabinet ministers and a judge had been strangled at Constantinople, and that several of their friends had been impaled. This catastrophe kept people talking for several hours. On their way back to the little farm, Pangloss, Candide, and Martin noticed an old man of patriarchal appearance sitting at his door under an arbour of orange-trees enjoying the fresh air. Pangloss, who liked gossip as much as argument, asked the old fellow the name of the judge who had been strangled.

'I have no idea,' he replied. 'I could not tell you the name of any judge or any minister. I am utterly ignorant of what you have been talking about. I suppose it's true that those who enter politics sometimes come to a miserable end, and deserve it; but I never bother myself about what happens in Constantinople. I send my garden stuff to be sold there, and that's enough for me.'

With these words, he invited the strangers into his house, where his two sons and daughters offered them several kinds of sherbet which they had made themselves, as well as drinks flavoured with candied lemon peel, oranges, lemons, citrons, pineapples, and pistachios, and pure Mocha coffee unmixed with the bad coffee you get from Batavia and the West Indies. After this refreshment the worthy Mussulman's two daughters perfumed the beards of the three visitors.

'You must have a magnificent estate,' said Candide to the Turk.

'Only twenty acres,' replied the Turk; 'my children help me to farm it, and we find that the work banishes those three great evils, boredom, vice, and poverty.'

As he walked back to the farm, Candide reflected on what the Turk had said. 'That old fellow,' said he, turning to Pangloss and Martin, 'seemed to me to have done much better for himself than those six kings we had the honour of supping with.'

'High estate,' said Pangloss, 'is always dangerous, as every philosopher knows. For Eglon, King of Moab, was assassinated by Ehud, and Absalom was hanged by his hair and stabbed with three spears; King Nadab, the son of Jeroboam, was killed by Baasha; King Elah by Zimri; Joram by Jehu; Athaliah by Jehoiada; and King Jehoiakim, King Jehoiachin, and King Zedekiah all became slaves. You know the miserable fate of Croesus, Astyages, Darius, Dionysius of Syracuse, Pyrrhus, Perseus, Hannibal, Jugurtha, Ariovistus, Caesar, Pompey, Nero, Otho, Vitellius, Domitian, Richard II of England, Edward II, Henry VI, Richard III, Mary Queen of Scots, Charles I, the three Henrys of France, and the Emperor Henry IV? You know . . . ?'

'I also know,' said Candide, 'that we must go and work in the garden.'

'You are quite right,' said Pangloss. 'When man was placed in the Garden of Eden, he was put there "to dress it and to keep it", to work, in fact; which proves that man was not born to an easy life.'

'We must work without arguing,' said Martin; 'that is the only way to make life bearable.'

The entire household agreed to this admirable plan, and each began to exercise his talents. Small as the estate was, it bore heavy crops. There was no denying that Cunégonde was decidedly ugly, but she soon made excellent pastry. Pacquette was clever at embroidery, and the old woman took care of the linen. No one refused to work, not even Brother Giroflée, who was a good carpenter, and thus became an honest man. From time to time Pangloss would say to Candide:

'There is a chain of events in this best of all possible worlds; for if you had not been turned out of a beautiful mansion at the point of a jackboot for the love of Lady Cunégonde, and if you had not been involved in the Inquisition, and had not wandered over America on foot, and had not struck the Baron with your sword, and lost all those sheep you brought from Eldorado, you would not be here eating candied fruit and pistachio nuts.'

'That's true enough,' said Candide; 'but we must go and work in the garden.'

JEAN-JACQUES ROUSSEAU
Selection from *Confessions*

Voltaire (see *Candide*) dominated the Age of Reason, but from today's vantage point, he takes second place to the Swiss thinker Rousseau, whose literary works significantly reshaped the West. Rousseau's works were often greeted with cries for his exile or arrest, but most of his causes are now familiar parts of the modern landscape. For example, he is often credited with the "discovery" of childhood; for in *Émile* (1761) he was one of the first to urge school reform based on graded stages of child development. In *The New Heloise* (1762) he pioneered the idea that marriages should be based on love and not simply be arranged, and in *The Social Contract* (1762) he established the principles of modern direct democracy. His spirit foreshadowed the Romantic cultural movement, notably in *The Reveries of the Solitary Walker* (1792), a veritable anthology of what later became Romantic clichés about God in Nature. Finally, he was a Marxist before Marx, calling property the root of social inequality (*The Second Discourse*, 1755).

Jean-Jacques Rousseau (1712–1778) seemed to have his finger on the pulse of Western culture, perhaps because he was guided by his inner voice. That voice, contradictory and passionate, may still be heard speaking from the pages of his autobiography, *Confessions* (1781). Like almost everything Rousseau touched, the autobiography left a revolution in its wake. Other writers had taken themselves as subjects, most notably Augustine (see *Confessions*) and Montaigne (see *Essays*), but no one before Rousseau had written with such uncensored frankness. Rousseau's work pointed the way for modern confessional writing in both autobiography and fiction; it inspired writers to search their childhoods for patterns that shaped their maturity (see Wordsworth's "Tintern Abbey").

Reading the Selection

This selection from the *Confessions* covers Rousseau's life from birth to seven years of age. It is memorable for establishing Rousseau's unique voice. The voice is obsessive, as shown by seventeen instances of "I," "my," or "myself" in the first seven sentences; self-pitying, as in the story of his birth that "cost my mother her life"; and emotional in both language ("cry," "groan," "romantic") and behavior (his exaggerated love of novels). The voice is also self-dramatizing, convinced that the world is listening, as when he imagines the Last Judgment with "numberless . . . men gather[ed] round me, [to] hear my confessions."

Rousseau presents himself as a "judge-penitent"; that is, he confesses to a moral weakness and then turns around and judges himself better than others for having exposed his own failing. In effect, he aims at moral power by revealing his sins. This pattern is in the Last Judgment fantasy, when he admits to "depravities" and then says that no witness to his recital can say, "'I was a better man than he.'" This behavior, an outgrowth of his Calvinist faith, is the central motif of the *Confessions*. It leads him to reveal sexual hang-ups, religious vacillation, and a decision to place his five offspring in an orphanage as soon as each was born. The "judge-penitent" motif is confirmed at the end when he warns that anyone who doubts his honor, "even if he has not read my writings . . . deserves to be stifled."

Rousseau was a superb prose stylist who was fond of pithy sayings, or aphorisms, that when taken out of context could lead to misunderstandings. Two aphorisms appear here: "I felt before I thought" and "I had grasped nothing; I had sensed everything."

—⁊⁊⁊—

Book I
1712–1719

I have resolved on an enterprise which has no precedent, and which, once complete, will have no imitator. My purpose is to display to my kind a portrait in every way true to nature, and the man I shall portray will be myself.

Simply myself. I know my own heart and understand my fellow man. But I am made unlike any one I have ever met; I will even venture to say that I am like no one in the whole world. I may be no better, but at least I am different. Whether Nature did well or ill in breaking the mould in which she formed me, is a question which can only be resolved after the reading of my book.

Let the last trump sound when it will, I shall come forward with this work in my hand, to present myself before my Sovereign Judge, and proclaim aloud: 'Here is what I have done, and if by chance I have used some immaterial embellishment it has been only to fill a void due to a defect of memory. I may have taken for fact what was no more than probability, but I have never put down as true what I knew to be false. I have displayed myself as I was, as vile and despicable when my behaviour was such, as good, generous, and noble when I was so. I have bared my secret soul as Thou thyself hast seen it, Eternal Being! So let the numberless legion of my fellow men gather round me, and hear my confessions. Let them groan at my depravities, and blush for my misdeeds. But let each one of them reveal his heart at the foot of Thy throne with equal sincerity, and may any man who dares, say "I was a better man than he."'

I was born at Geneva in 1712, the son of Isaac Rousseau, a citizen of that town, and Susanne Bernard, his wife. My father's inheritance, being a fifteenth part only of a very small property which had been divided among as many children, was almost nothing, and he relied for his living entirely on his trade of watchmaker, at which he was very highly skilled. My mother was the daughter of a minister of religion and rather better-off. She had besides both intelligence and beauty, and my father had not found it easy to win her. Their love had begun almost with their birth; at eight or nine they would walk together every evening along La Treille, and at ten they were inseparable. Sympathy and mental affinity strengthened in them a feeling first formed by habit. Both, being affectionate and sensitive by nature, were only waiting for the moment when they would find similar qualities in another; or rather the moment was waiting for them, and both threw their affections at the first heart that opened to receive them. Fate, by appearing to oppose their passion, only strengthened it. Unable to obtain his mistress, the young lover ate out his heart with grief, and she counselled him to travel and forget her. He travelled in vain, and returned more in love than ever, to find her he loved still faithful and fond. After such a proof, it was inevitable that they should love one another for all their lives. They swore to do so, and Heaven smiled on their vows.

Gabriel Bernard, one of my mother's brothers, fell in love with one of my father's sisters, and she refused to marry him unless her brother could marry my mother at the same time. Love overcame all obstacles, and the two pairs were wedded on the same day. So it was that my uncle married my aunt, and their children became my double first cousins. Within a year both couples had a child, but at the end of that time each of them was forced to separate.

My uncle Bernard, who was an engineer, went to serve in the Empire and Hungary under Prince Eugène, and distinguished himself at the siege and battle of Belgrade. My father, after the birth of my only brother, left for Constantinople, where he had been called to become watchmaker to the Sultan's Seraglio. While he was away my mother's beauty, wit, and talents brought her admirers, one of the most pressing of whom was M. de la Closure, the French Resident in the city. His feelings must have been very strong, for thirty years later I have seen him moved when merely speaking to me about her. But my mother had more than her virtue with which to defend herself; she deeply loved my father, and urged him to come back. He threw up everything to do so, and I was the unhappy fruit of his return. For ten months later I was born, a poor and sickly child, and cost my mother her life. So my birth was the first of my misfortunes.

I never knew how my father stood up to his loss, but I know that he never got over it. He seemed to see her again in me, but could never forget that I had robbed him of her; he never kissed me that I did not know by his sighs and his convulsive embrace that there was a bitter grief mingled with his affection, a grief which nevertheless intensified his feeling for me. When he said to me, 'Jean-Jacques, let us talk of your mother,' I would reply: 'Very well, father, but we are sure to cry.' 'Ah,' he would say with a groan; 'Give her back to me, console me for her, fill the void she has left in my heart! Should I love you so if you were not more to me than a son?' Forty years after he lost her he died in the arms of a second wife, but with his first wife's name on his lips, and her picture imprinted upon his heart.

Such were my parents. And of all the gifts with which Heaven endowed them, they left me but one, a sensitive heart. It had been the making of their happiness, but for me it has been the cause of all the misfortunes in my life.

I was almost born dead, and they had little hope of saving me. I brought with me the seed of a disorder which has grown stronger with the years, and now gives me only occasional intervals of relief in which to suffer more painfully in some other way. But one of my father's sisters, a nice sensible woman, bestowed such care on me that I survived; and now, as I write this, she is still alive at the age of eighty, nursing a husband rather younger than herself but ruined by drink. My dear aunt, I pardon you for causing me to live, and I deeply regret that I cannot repay you in the evening of your days all the care and affection you lavished on me at the dawn of mine. My nurse Jacqueline is still alive too, and healthy and strong. Indeed the fingers that opened my eyes at birth may well close them at my death.

I felt before I thought: which is the common lot of man, though more pronounced in my case than in another's. I know nothing of myself till I was five or six. I do not know how I learnt to read. I only remember my first books and their effect upon me; it is from my earliest reading that I date the unbroken consciousness of my own existence. My mother had possessed some novels, and my father and I began to read them after our supper. At first it was only to give me some practice in reading. But soon my interest in this entertaining literature became so strong that we read by turns continuously, and spent whole nights so engaged. For we could never leave off till the end of the book. Sometimes my father would say with shame as we heard the morning larks: 'Come, let us go to bed. I am more a child than you are.'

In a short time I acquired by this dangerous method, not only an extreme facility in reading and expressing myself, but a singular insight for my age into the passions. I had no idea of the facts, but I was already familiar with every feeling. I had grasped nothing; I had sensed everything. These confused emotions which I experienced one after another, did not warp my reasoning powers in any way, for as yet I had none. But they shaped them after a special pattern, giving me the strangest and most romantic notions about human life, which neither experience nor reflection has ever succeeded in curing me of.

DENIS DIDEROT

Selections from *Encyclopédie*

In France, the *Encyclopédie,* issued between 1751 and 1772, expressed the ideals and vision of the Enlightenment—the eighteenth-century movement that was devoted to a critical reexamination of accepted doctrines and institutions from the point of view of rationalism (as defined by Francis Bacon, René Descartes, and John Locke) and Newtonian science. In twenty-eight volumes, of which seventeen were text and eleven plates and illustrations, this vast work was perhaps the most ambitious publishing venture of its day. Embracing the Enlightenment ideal that knowledge is useful, the *Encyclopédie* covered practical knowledge (explaining the arts, crafts, and technology, and most especially, how things are manufactured, traded, and used) and philosophical knowledge (describing existing institutions and beliefs and critiquing their underlying rationales). This project engaged the talents of more than 160 writers, who, while not always in agreement, were deeply committed to freeing their age from the ignorance and prejudices of the past. These *philosophes,* as the encyclopedists were also known, shared a vision that reason and science, when applied to human affairs, would have a progressive effect on individuals and society. Applicable to all races and classes, this vision called for a universal standard of moral behavior, assuring a sense of dignity to everyone based on a uniform code of civil rights.

The *Encyclopédie*'s editor was Denis Diderot (1713–1784), who performed heroically under fire. Sharing chores with Diderot was the eloquent and scientific-minded Jean le Rond d'Alembert (1717–1783), who took charge of the essays on mathematics and physics. Nevertheless, Diderot was the project's guiding spirit. For more than twenty years, he fought and outmaneuvered the French censors, confronted printed attacks by Catholic leaders, most notably the Jesuits, and still kept the presses running, by means of subterfuge when they were officially shut by the state. At the same time he was managing the project's financial affairs, meeting deadlines, writing many of the essays himself, and most difficult of all, soothing the egos of his famous contributors, such as Voltaire (who wrote over forty essays), Rousseau, and Montesquieu. Besides editing the *Encyclopédie,* Diderot also wrote plays, novels, and critical essays on art, the latter helping to establish the field of art history. He was later befriended by Russia's Catherine the Great (r. 1762–1796), at whose court he spent one of his last years.

Reading the Selections

"Encyclopedia" and "Intolerance" were written by Diderot, and both reflect his faith in the moral value of learning. In "Encyclopedia," he first explains the Greek origins of the word "encyclopedia" and then defines an encyclopedia's purpose: to collect and preserve all knowledge to the end that future generations will be "more virtuous and happier." He next expresses the hope that posterity will honor the encyclopedists for their efforts to improve human life. He then pleads for full examination of "all things," "without exception and without regard for anyone's feelings," so that the arts and sciences will be widely understood and thus benefit all people, rather than the current few.

The second selection concerns intolerance, which Diderot defines as "a violent emotion inciting people to hate and persecute individuals with erroneous notions." His hatred of intolerance is based on the *philosophes'* view that centuries of privilege and arrogance enjoyed by the church and its leaders have resulted in the institutionalization of intolerance. Perhaps to avoid the wrath of the censors, Diderot sets aside the question of religion's truth or falsity, what he calls ecclesiastical intolerance. Instead, he focuses on secular intolerance, in both its passive form—the breaking of social ties—and its violent form—persecution by all sorts of means. Calling for tolerance, he invokes the words of St. Paul, the church fathers, and Jesus Christ. He asks that the intolerant open their eyes to the cruelty resulting from their feelings, and he calls for the tolerant to join in destroying the "atrocious system" of bigotry that is an "injustice in the eyes of God and man." Diderot's impassioned request for tolerance is as relevant today as it was when he wrote this essay.

ENCYCLOPEDIA, f. n. (*Philosophy*). This word means the *interrelation of all knowledge*; it is made up of the Greek prefix *en,* in, and the noun *kyklos,* circle, and *paideia,* instruction, science, knowledge. In truth, the aim of an *encyclopedia* is to collect all the knowledge scattered over the face of the earth, to present its general outlines and structure to the men with whom we live, and to transmit this to those who will come after us, so that the work of past centuries may be useful to the following centuries, that our children, by becoming more educated, may at the same time become more virtuous and happier, and that we may not die without having deserved well of the human race.

. . .

We have seen that our *Encyclopedia* could only have been the endeavor of a philosophical century; that this age has dawned, and that fame, while raising to immortality the names of those who will perfect man's knowledge in the future, will perhaps not disdain to remember our own names. We have been heartened by the ever so consoling and agreeable idea that people may speak to one another about us, too, when we shall no longer be alive; we have been encouraged by hearing from the mouths of a few of our contemporaries a certain voluptuous murmur that suggests what may be said of us by those happy and educated men in whose interests we have sacrificed ourselves, whom we esteem and whom we love, even though they have not yet been born. We have felt within ourselves the development of those seeds of emulation which have moved us to renounce the better part of ourselves to accomplish our task, and which have ravished away into the void the few moments of our existence of which we are genuinely proud. Indeed, man reveals himself to his contemporaries and is seen by them for what he is: a peculiar mixture of sublime attributes and shameful weaknesses. But our weaknesses follow our mortal remains into the tomb and disappear with them; the same earth covers them both, and there remains only the total result of our attributes immortalized in the monuments we raise to ourselves or in the memorials that we owe to public respect and gratitude—honors which a proper awareness of our own deserts enables us to enjoy in anticipation, an enjoyment that is as pure, as great, and as real as any other pleasure and in which there is nothing imaginary except, perhaps, the titles on which we base our pretensions. Our own claims are deposited in the pages of this work, and posterity will judge them.

I have said that it could only belong to a philosophical age to attempt an *encyclopedia;* and I have said this because such a work constantly demands more intellectual daring than is commonly found in ages of pusillanimous taste. All things must be examined, debated, investigated without exception and without regard for anyone's feelings. . . . We must ride roughshod over all these ancient puerilities, overturn the barriers that reason never erected, give back to the arts and sciences the liberty that is so precious to them. . . . We have for quite some time needed a reasoning age when men would no longer seek the rules in classical authors but in nature, when men would be conscious of what is false and true about so many arbitrary treatises on aesthetics: and I take the term *treatise on aesthetics* in its most general meaning, that of a system of given rules to which it is claimed that one must conform in any genre whatsoever in order to succeed.

. . .

INTOLERANCE, f. n. (*Ethics.*). It is generally understood that intolerance is a violent emotion inciting people to hate and persecute individuals with erroneous notions. For the sake of clarity let us first distinguish between ecclesiastic and secular forms of *intolerance.*

Ecclesiastic *intolerance* consists in regarding as false all other religions except one's own and in demonstrating or shouting this true religion from the rooftops without being stopped by any form of terror, sense of decency, or even the risk of death. This article will not be concerned with the particular heroism that created so many martyrs in the long history of the Church.

Secular *intolerance* consists in breaking off all relations with those people who have a different conception and way of worshiping God and in persecuting them by all sorts of violent means.

A few extracts from Holy Scripture, the Fathers of the Church, and various ecclesiastic councils will be sufficient to show that the *intolerant* person, according to the second definition, is an evil man, a bad Christian, a dangerous individual, a bad politician, and a bad citizen.

Before we begin to quote from some of these most respectable authorities, we must give credit to our Catholic theologians because several of them have endorsed the following opinions without any reservations. 5

Tertullian said (*Apolog. ad Scapul*): *Humani juris et naturalis potestatis est unicuique quod putaverit, colere; nec alii obest aut prodest alterius religio. Sed nec religionis est cogere religionem quae sponte suscipi debeat, non vi; cum et hostiae ab animo lubenti expostulentur.*[1]

This is what the weak and persecuted Christians pointed out to the idolaters who forced them to kneel at their altars.

It is impious to expose religion to the odious charges of being tyrannical, severe, unjust, and unsociable, even with the intent of bringing back to the fold those people who have unfortunately strayed.

The mind can only consent to what seems true, the heart can only love what appears good. Force will make a hypocrite out of a weak man, but a martyr out of a courageous one. Whether weak or courageous, he will feel the injustice of persecution and become indignant.

Education, persuasion, and prayer are the only legitimate means of spreading religious faith. 10

Any method that produces hatred, indignation, and contempt is impious.

Any method that arouses the passions and supports selfish interests is impious.

Any method that weakens the natural bonds of the family and alienates fathers from their children, brothers from brothers, and sisters from sisters is impious.

Any method that would tend to stir up men, to arm nations, and to soak the earth with blood is impious.

It is impious to want to impose laws upon man's conscience: this is a universal rule of conduct. People must be enlightened and not constrained. 15

Men who are sincerely mistaken are to be pitied, never to be punished.

Neither sincere nor dishonest men should be tormented: they should be abandoned to the judgment of God.

If you break off all bonds of friendship with an individual who is considered impious, then you will also break off all ties with those people who are considered miserly, immodest, ambitious, irascible, and vicious. You will soon advise your friends to break off relations with these people, and three or four *intolerant* individuals will be sufficient to destroy an entire society.

If you can pull out a hair from the head of a person who thinks differently than we do, then his head is also at your disposal, because there are no limits set for injustice. Either profit or fanaticism, the moment or the circumstance will decide whether the greater or the lesser evil will be allowed.

If a prince who is an unbeliever were to ask the missionaries of an *intolerant* religion how they treat those who do not believe in their faith, they would have to acknowledge an odious thing, lie, or remain shamefully silent. 20

What did Christ recommend to his disciples when he sent them among the Gentiles? Was it to kill or to die? Was it to persecute or to suffer?

Saint Paul wrote to the Thessalonians: *If someone should come among you proclaiming another Christ or another Holy Ghost and preaching another Gospel, you will suffer his presence.*—Intolerant people! Is it in this fashion that you treat those who have nothing to propose, nothing to announce, and nothing to preach?

Furthermore, he wrote: *Do not look on any man as an enemy because he does not share our views; only warn him as a brother. Intolerant people!* Is this the way you act?

If your opinions entitle you to hate me, why will not my opinions also entitle me to hate you?

If you cry out that the truth is on your side, I will cry out as loudly that I have the truth on my side, but I will add: it does not matter who is mistaken, provided that there is peace among us. If I am blind, must you strike a blind person in the face? 25

If an *intolerant* person were to explain clearly what he is, which corner of the earth would not be closed to him? And where is the sensible man who would dare to approach the country where this *intolerant* person lives?

You can read in Origen, in Minutius Felix, and in the Fathers of the Church during the first three centuries the following comments: *Religion persuades, and does not command. Man must have a free choice in the form of his worship; the persecutor causes his God to be hated; the persecutor slanders his own religion.* Tell me if it was ignorance or deception that created these maxims?

In an *intolerant* state the prince would only be a torturer in the pay of the priest. The prince is the universal father of his subjects; and his apostolate is to make them all happy.

If one had to proclaim a law in order to treat people in a severe manner, there would not be any tyrants.

On some occasions we are as strongly persuaded by error as by truth. This fact can only be contested by those individuals who were never sincerely mistaken. 30

If your truth ostracizes me, then my error that I take for the truth will likewise ostracize you.

Stop being violent, or stop reproaching pagans and Muslims for their violence.

Is it the spirit of God that moves you to hate your brother and preach hatred to your neighbor?

[1]"It is a fundamental human right and a law of nature that any and every man should worhip in accordance with his own views, for the beliefs of one are of no value to another. Morever, it is not consistent with the essence of religious belief to force itself on anyone, for it should be received of one's own free will: even sacrificial victims are demanded in a pleasant manner."

Christ said: *My kingdom is not of this world.* And you, his disciple, you want to tyrannize the world!

He said: *I am gentle and lowly in heart.* Are you gentle and lowly in heart?

He said: *Blessed are the meek, the peacemakers, and the merciful.* Examine your conscience and see if you deserve this blessing; are you meek, peacemakers, and merciful?

He said: *I am the lamb who was led to the slaughter without complaining.* And you are quite ready to take the butcher's knife and cut the throat of the one for whom the blood of the lamb was shed.

He said: *When they persecute you, flee.* And you chase those who will let you speak and who do not ask for anything more than to live peacefully by your side.

He said: *You would like me to send down the wrath of heaven upon your enemies; you do not know what spirit moves you.* And I repeat for you His very words: *intolerant* people, you do not know what spirit moves you.

Listen to Saint John: *My children, love one another.*

Saint Athanasius: *If they persecute you, this alone is clear proof that they are neither pious nor do they fear God. It is the very nature of piety not to constrain but to persuade, in imitation of our Lord who allowed everyone the freedom to follow him. As for the devil, since he does not possess the truth, he comes with hatchets and axes.*

Saint John Chrysostom: *Jesus Christ asked his disciples if they also want to go away in peace, for this must be the attitude of the person who does not do violence to anyone.*

Salvien: *These men are deluded, but they do not know it. In our company they are mistaken, but with their own kind they are not mistaken. They consider themselves such good Catholics that they call us heretics. What they are in our eyes, we are in theirs. They are misguided but have good intentions. What will be their fate? Only the Great Judge knows. Until the final judgment He tolerates them.*

Saint Augustine: *Let those people abuse you, who know not how difficult it is to find the truth and not be deceived. Let those people abuse you, who know not how extraordinary and painful it is to master the fantasms of the flesh. Let those people abuse you, who know not that it is necessary to moan and sigh to understand something from God. Let those people abuse you, who have not fallen into error.*

Saint Hilary: *You use constraint in a cause where only reason is necessary; you employ force where only understanding is necessary.*

The Constitutions of the Holy Pope Clement I: *The Lord left to men the use of their free will, not punishing them with a temporal death but summoning them into the other world to account for their actions.*

The Fathers of a council of Toledo: *Do no violence of any kind to people in order to lead them back to the faith, for God is merciful or severe to whomever He chooses.*

We could fill volumes with these frequently forgotten quotations from the Christians of our day.

Saint Martin repented his entire life for having communicated with the persecutors of heretics.

All wise men have disapproved the violence committed against the Samaritans by Emperor Justinian.

Writers who have advised penal laws against disbelief have been detested.

Recently the apologist of the Revocation of the Edict of Nantes was considered a bloody creature with whom it was advisable not to share the same roof.

Which is the true voice of humanity, the persecutor who strikes or the persecuted who moans?

If an unbelieving prince has an undeniable right to demand obedience from his subject, does not an infidel subject have an undeniable right to demand the protection of his prince? It is a reciprocal obligation.

If the prince says that the infidel subject does not deserve to live, is it not to be feared that the subject might say that the infidel prince does not deserve to rule? *Intolerant people*, men of blood, see the consequences of your principles and shudder. Men of good will, whatever your beliefs, it is for you that I have collected these thoughts, and I beg you to meditate upon them. If you do so, then you will renounce an atrocious system that is not proper for an honest mind and a kind heart.

Effect your own salvation. Pray for mine, and believe that everything that you allow yourself beyond this is an abominable injustice in the eyes of God and man.

(Diderot)

MARY WOLLSTONECRAFT

Selection from *A Vindication of the Rights of Woman*

A Vindication of the Rights of Woman (1792) is a key text of feminism. Its author, Mary Wollstonecraft, was not the first feminist, for this cause began with Christine de Pizan (see *The Book of the City of Ladies*) in the 1400s, when it was called the "Woman Question." Wollstonecraft, however, gave feminism its modern focus (see Beauvoir's *The Second Sex*) as she made women's rights part of the struggle for human rights in general.

Human rights was the defining issue of the Enlightenment, but no thinker before Wollstonecraft, including Voltaire (see *Candide*), Rousseau (see *Confessions*), and Jefferson (see *The Declaration of Independence*), even considered applying the concept of rights to women. In her treatise she forever changed the character of the debate on rights by arguing that men and women alike shared in the rights bestowed by nature. For her, the rights of liberty and equality applied to both men and women, and if fraternity made all men brothers, then men must accept that they had sisters as well.

Wollstonecraft stood in Rousseau's shadow, but she rejected his argument that the "duties" of women are "to please, to be useful to [men], to make [men] love and esteem them, to educate [men] when young, and take care of [men] when grown up, to advise, to console [men], and to render [men's] lives easy and agreeable." While admitting that Rousseau accurately reflected existing society, she found his view morally wrong. She argued that women, as rational creatures, should be treated like men; that is, educated for virtue. Society's goal should be the full, free expression of both sexes.

The feminism of Mary Wollstonecraft (1759–1797) sprang from her marginal status. Born into genteel poverty in England, she made her way in the world only with great difficulty. A failed career in teaching taught her the pain of being female and poor, without respect or independence. With her intellectual gifts, she was drawn into progressive circles where Enlightenment ideas flourished. When revolution broke out in France, she traveled to Paris, where she shared with French militants their hopes for a new society free of oppression. Back in London, she joined the radicals grouped around William Godwin (1756–1836), an ex-minister and novelist. When she was made pregnant by Godwin, they secretly married, fearing to offend radical friends by the disclosure of their wedding. She died in childbirth in 1797, giving life to the child later known as Mary Wollstonecraft Shelley, the author of *Frankenstein*.

Reading the Selection

This selection—the treatise's introduction—offers a summary of Wollstonecraft's views. Like Rousseau, she accepts that men are physically stronger than women; unlike Rousseau, however, she maintains that men use this fact as a pretext to impose a greater inequality than nature allows, thus keeping women in "perpetual childhood."

According to her, men keep women in their place by treating them as "alluring mistresses," or sex objects. To this end, men have created a vocabulary in praise of feminine virtues, such as "soft phrases . . . [and] delicacy of sentiments." These, rather than being words of praise, are in reality words of subjection to man's demands, from a love of power. She condemns women for going along with men, in thinking themselves the "weaker vessels." She thinks that women should cease to be men's toys and make their own moral choices. Only then, when women can freely choose between reason and the passions, just as men do, will they become "affectionate wives and rational mothers"—the goal of this early feminist tract.

---※---

Introduction

After considering the historic page, and viewing the living world with anxious solicitude, the most melancholy emotions of sorrowful indignation have depressed my spirits, and I have sighed when obliged to confess, that either nature has made a great difference between man and man, or that the civilization which has hitherto taken place in the world has been very partial. I have turned over various books written on the subject of education, and patiently observed the conduct of parents and the management of schools; but what has been the result?—a profound conviction that the neglected education of my fellow-creatures is the grand source of the misery I deplore; and that women, in particular, are rendered weak and wretched by a variety of concurring causes, originating from one hasty conclusion. The conduct and manners of women, in fact, evidently prove that their minds are not in a healthy state; for, like flowers which are planted in too rich a soil, strength and usefulness are sacrificed to beauty; and the flaunting leaves, after having pleased a fastidious eye, fade, disregarded on the stalk, long before the season when they ought to have arrived at maturity.—One cause of this barren blooming I attribute to a false system of education, gathered from the books written on this subject by men who, considering females rather as women than human creatures, have been more anxious to make them alluring mistresses than affectionate wives and rational mothers; and the understanding of the sex has been so bubbled by this specious homage, that the civilized women of the present century, with a few exceptions, are only anxious to inspire love, when they ought to cherish a nobler ambition, and by their abilities and virtues exact respect.

In a treatise, therefore, on female rights and manners, the works which have been particularly written for their improvement must not be overlooked; especially when it is asserted, in direct terms, that the minds of women are enfeebled by false refinement; that the books of instruction, written by men of genius, have had the same tendency as more frivolous productions; and that, in the true style of Mahometanism, they are treated as a kind of subordinate beings, and not as a part of the human species, when improveable reason is allowed to be the dignified distinction which raises men above the brute creation, and puts a natural sceptre in a feeble hand.

Yet, because I am a woman, I would not lead my readers to suppose that I mean violently to agitate the contested question respecting the equality or inferiority of the sex; but as the subject lies in my way, and I cannot pass it over without subjecting the main tendency of my reasoning to misconstruction, I shall stop a moment to deliver, in a few words, my opinion.—In the government of the physical world it is observable that the female in point of strength is, in general, inferior to the male. This is the law of nature; and it does not appear to be suspended or abrogated in favour of women. A degree of physical superiority cannot, therefore, be denied—and it is a noble prerogative! But not content with this natural pre-eminence, men endeavour to sink us still lower, merely to render us alluring objects for a moment; and women, intoxicated by the adoration which men, under the influence of their senses, pay them, do not seek to obtain a durable interest in their hearts, or to become the friends of the fellow creatures who find amusement in their society.

I am aware of an obvious inference:—from every quarter have I heard exclamations against masculine women; but where are they to be found? If by this appellation men mean to inveigh against their ardour in hunting, shooting, and gaming, I shall most cordially join in the cry; but if it be against the imitation of manly virtues, or, more properly speaking, the attainment of those talents and virtues, the exercise of which ennobles the human character, and which raise females in the scale of animal being, when they are comprehensively termed mankind;—all those who view them with a philosophic eye must, I should think, wish with me, that they may every day grow more and more masculine.

This discussion naturally divides the subject. I shall first consider women in the grand light of human creatures, who, in common with men, are placed on this earth to unfold their faculties; and afterwards I shall more particularly point out their peculiar designation.

I wish also to steer clear of an error which many respectable writers have fallen into; for the instruction which has hitherto been addressed to women, has rather been applicable to *ladies*, if the little indirect advice, that is scattered through Sandford and Merton, be excepted; but, addressing my sex in a firmer tone, I pay particular attention to those in the middle class, because they appear to be in the most natural state. Perhaps the seeds of false-

refinement, immorality, and vanity, have ever been shed by the great. Weak, artificial beings, raised above the common wants and affections of their race, in a premature unnatural manner, undermine the very foundation of virtue, and spread corruption through the whole mass of society! As a class of mankind they have the strongest claim to pity; the education of the rich tends to render them vain and helpless, and the unfolding mind is not strengthened by the practice of those duties which dignify the human character.—They only live to amuse themselves, and by the same law which in nature invariably produces certain effects, they soon only afford barren amusement.

But as I propose taking a separate view of the different ranks of society, and of the moral character of women, in each, this hint is, for the present, sufficient; and I have only alluded to the subject, because it appears to me to be the very essence of an introduction to give a cursory account of the contents of the work it introduces.

My own sex, I hope, will excuse me, if I treat them like rational creatures, instead of flattering their *fascinating* graces, and viewing them as if they were in a state of perpetual childhood, unable to stand alone. I earnestly wish to point out in what true dignity and human happiness consists—I wish to persuade women to endeavour to acquire strength, both of mind and body, and to convince them that the soft phrases, susceptibility of heart, delicacy of sentiment, and refinement of taste, are almost synonymous with epithets of weakness, and that those beings who are only the objects of pity and that kind of love, which has been termed its sister, will soon become objects of contempt.

Dismissing then those pretty feminine phrases, which the men condescendingly use to soften our slavish dependence, and despising that weak elegancy of mind, exquisite sensibility, and sweet docility of manners, supposed to be the sexual characteristics of the weaker vessel, I wish to shew that elegance is inferior to virtue, that the first object of laudable ambition is to obtain a character as a human being, regardless of the distinction of sex; and that secondary views should be brought to this simple touchstone.

This is a rough sketch of my plan; and should I express my conviction with the energetic emotions that I feel whenever I think of the subject, the dictates of experience and reflection will be felt by some of my readers. Animated by this important object, I shall disdain to cull my phrases or polish my style;—I aim at being useful, and sincerity will render me unaffected; for, wishing rather to persuade by the force of my arguments, than dazzle by the elegance of my language, I shall not waste my time in rounding periods, or in fabricating the turgid bombast of artificial feelings, which, coming from the head, never reach the heart.—I shall be employed about things, not words!—and, anxious to render my sex more respectable members of society, I shall try to avoid that flowery diction which has slided from essays into novels, and from novels into familiar letters and conversation.

These pretty superlatives, dropping glibly from the tongue, vitiate the taste, and create a kind of sickly delicacy that turns away from simple unadorned truth, and a deluge of false sentiments and overstretched feelings, stifling the natural emotions of the heart, render the domestic pleasures insipid, that ought to sweeten the exercise of those severe duties, which educate a rational and immortal being for a nobler field of action.

The education of women has, of late, been more attended to than formerly; yet they are still reckoned a frivolous sex, and ridiculed or pitied by the writers who endeavour by satire or instruction to improve them. It is acknowledged that they spend many of the first years of their lives in acquiring a smattering of accomplishments; meanwhile strength of body and mind are sacrificed to libertine notions of beauty, to the desire of establishing themselves,—the only way women can rise in the world,—by marriage. And this desire making mere animals of them, when they marry they act as such children may be expected to act:—they dress; they paint, and nickname God's creatures.—Surely these weak beings are only fit for a seraglio!—Can they be expected to govern a family with judgment, or take care of the poor babes whom they bring into the world?

If then it can be fairly deduced from the present conduct of the sex, from the prevalent fondness for pleasure which takes place of ambition and those nobler passions that open and enlarge the soul; that the instruction which women have hitherto received has only tended, with the constitution of civil society, to render them insignificant objects of desire—mere propagators of fools!—if it can be proved that in aiming to accomplish them, without cultivating their understandings, they are taken out of their sphere of duties, and made ridiculous and useless when the short-lived bloom of beauty is over, I presume that *rational* men will excuse me for endeavouring to persuade them to become more masculine and respectable.

Indeed the word masculine is only a bugbear: there is little reason to fear that women will acquire too much courage or fortitude; for their apparent inferiority with respect to bodily strength, must render them, in some degree, dependent on men in the various relations of life, but why should it be increased by prejudices that give a sex to virtue, and confound simple truths with sensual reveries?

Women are, in fact, so much degraded by mistaken notions of female excellence, that I do not mean to add a paradox when I assert, that this artificial weakness produces a propensity to tyrannize, and gives birth to cunning, the natural opponent of strength, which leads them to play off those contemptible infantine airs that undermine esteem even whilst they excite desire. Let men become more chaste and modest, and if women do not grow wiser in the same ratio, it will be clear that they have weaker understandings. It seems scarcely necessary to say, that I now speak of the sex in general. Many individuals have more sense than their male relatives; and, as nothing preponderates where there is a constant struggle for an equilibrium, without it has naturally more gravity, some women govern their husbands without degrading themselves, because intellect will always govern.

REVOLUTION, REACTION, AND CULTURAL RESPONSE

1760–1830

THOMAS JEFFERSON

Selection from *The Declaration of Independence*

The American writer and statesman Thomas Jefferson (1743–1826) personified the liberal and rational ideals of the Age of Reason. In *The Declaration of Independence,* the document that severed ties between the American colonies and Britain, and which Jefferson chiefly wrote, he translated this age's values into ringing phrases still echoed around the world. In his distinguished career, he worked to bring to fruition this era's vision. He held many public offices, both appointive and elective, including member of the Virginia House of Burgesses, delegate to the Continental Congress, ambassador to France, secretary of state, vice president, and president.

Jefferson, a plantation owner, was born into the gentry of colonial Virginia, which assured him a comfortable life, the best available education, and opportunities for leadership when war with Britain came. In college, he studied the classics, Shakespeare, Milton, and above all three figures whose knowledge of science, human nature, and politics greatly influenced his thinking: Newton, Bacon (see *Essays*), and Locke (see *Second Treatise*). A member of the third generation of Enlightenment thinkers, Jefferson developed a philosophy geared to the improvement of life for individuals and society; it was inspired by faith in education and natural law theory. In the debates leading up to the American Revolution, he was guided by this philosophy and made a name for himself as an outspoken defender of free speech, free thought, and liberty of religious conscience. Thus it was perhaps inevitable that in Philadelphia in 1776, as the delegates to the Continental Congress inched their way toward making a break with the British crown, they should appoint a committee to draw up a declaration of independence, and the committee would select Jefferson to draft the document.

Reading the Selection

The Declaration of Independence contains four sections. The first section echoed in plain and firm terms what Jefferson called "the harmonizing sentiments of the day." These ideas were part of a set of beliefs shared by the members of the Continental Congress; they could be traced back to Locke and had found recent voice in the colonists' writings leveled against the British. The second part is a specific bill of twenty-seven accusations against King George III's policies toward the American colonies. In the third section, the delegates maintain that they have, in vain, petitioned the British government many times to redress their grievances. In the fourth part, they conclude that the Congress has no alternative but to declare the colonies "free and independent," calling on the "Protection of divine Providence" as they pledge their lives, fortunes, and honor to each other in support of the declaration.

Jefferson, who spent the better part of a month drafting and polishing the document, later asserted that it was intended to be "an expression of the American mind." He drew on longstanding principles: equal rights for all citizens as based on the laws of nature, popular sovereignty, and limited, constitutional government. He chose his words with great care. In particular, the phrase "life, liberty and the pursuit of happiness," which, unlike Locke's wording ("life, liberty and property"), expressed Jefferson's own Enlightenment philosophy: that society has more noble goals than the protection of citizens' wordly possessions.

—⁓—

When in the course of human events, it becomes necessary for one people to dissolve the political bands which have connected them with another, and to assume among the powers of the earth, the separate and equal station to which the Law of Nature and of Nature's God entitle them, a decent respect to the opinions of mankind requires that they should declare the causes which impel them to the separation.

We hold these truths to be self-evident, that all men are created equal, that they are endowed by their Creator with certain unalienable rights, that among these are life, liberty and the pursuit of happiness. That to secure these rights, governments are instituted among men, deriving their just powers from the consent of the governed. That whenever any form of government becomes destructive of these ends, it is the right of the people to alter or to abolish it, and to institute new government, laying its foundation on such principles and organizing its powers in such form,

as to them shall seem most likely to effect their safety and happiness. Prudence, indeed, will dictate that governments long established should not be changed for light and transient causes; and accordingly all experience hath shown, that mankind are more disposed to suffer, while evils are sufferable, than to right themselves by abolishing the forms to which they are accustomed. But when a long train of abuses and usurpations, pursuing invariably the same object, evinces a design to reduce them under absolute despotism, it is their right, it is their duty, to throw off such government, and to provide new guards for their future security. Such has been the patient sufferance of these Colonies; and such is now the necessity which constrains them to alter their former systems of government. This history of the present King of Great Britain is a history of repeated injuries and usurpations, all having in direct object the establishment of an absolute tyranny over these States. . . .

trying to define Laws of Nature in Science

—⁓—

Declaration of the Rights of Man and Citizen

Like the American *Declaration of Independence*, which it resembles in its call for an end to tyranny and the establishment of a new political order, the French *Declaration of the Rights of Man and Citizen* reflected the ideals of the Age of Reason. These included the natural rights theory of Locke (see the *Second Treatise of Civil Government*) and the constitutional principles of the English political settlement of 1688. But this French document was firmly rooted in French history, for it meant to wipe out centuries of feudal privilege founded on tradition, blood, and wealth. At the same time, it assured French citizens of their natural and inalienable rights of liberty, property, security, and resistance to oppression, denied under the old regime.

In contrast to the American document, which appeared at the start of a revolution to justify future events, the French document was drafted after the French Revolution began and became one of a number of important pieces of legislation approved by the National Assembly in the summer of 1789. By the time the National Assembly passed the *Declaration of the Rights of Man and Citizen* on August 27, 1789, the revolution was in full swing. The Bastille, the symbolic prison of royal tyranny, had fallen on July 14; on August 3, the French aristocrats representing their Estate in the Assembly had risen, noble by noble, to renounce their feudal rights. When the declaration of August 27 was passed, the way was cleared to deal with suffrage, taxes, the Catholic church, and the drafting of a constitution setting up a limited monarchy.

Reading the Selection

The founding document of the French Revolution has stood the test of time, outlasting the Reign of Terror (1793–1794), the Napoleonic emperorship, later revolutions, constitutional crises, and five re-publics. After a brief preamble in which the past is blamed for the ills of the present and a rationale is presented justifying the presentation of these natural and civil rights, there follows a list of seventeen "rights of man and citizen."

The concepts of rights and law are joined together in many ways in the document. Law is re-ferred to in nine of the seventeen articles. The committee that drafted the declaration felt that since French law had been abused so often under the old regime, it must now specify how the law was to protect citizens from arbitrary arrests, unfair trials, and *ex post facto* legislation. Law, as explained by the thinker Rousseau, expressed the general will that was embodied in representative government. Thus citizens became eligible for public office according to their talents and not, as with past practice, because of their class position. This is a revolutionary aspect of this revolutionary document, for it transforms people from subjects to be acted on into citizens who are self-governing.

The declaration proclaimed that all citizens would be taxed, a correction of an abuse from the old regime in which the rich were exempt from paying taxes. A "public force," or army, was still deemed necessary; however, it was not to be operated by the privileged few—once more, a reference to the past when army officers were uniformly of the nobility. Finally, the declaration asserted that the free circulation of ideas was a "precious" right—a provision meant to remove the censorship that had muzzled society in the past.

―――※―――

The representatives of the French people, organized in Na-tional Assembly, considering that ignorance, forgetfulness, or contempt of the rights of man are the sole causes of pub-lic misfortunes and of the corruption of governments, have resolved to set forth in a solemn declaration the nat-ural, inalienable, and sacred rights of man, in order that such declaration, continually before all members of the so-cial body, may be a perpetual reminder of their rights and duties; in order that the acts of the legislative power and those of the executive power may constantly be compared with the aim of every political institution and may accord-ingly be more respected; in order that the demands of the citizens, founded henceforth upon simple and incon-testable principles, may always be directed towards the maintenance of the Constitution and the welfare of all.

Accordingly, the National Assembly recognizes and proclaims, in the presence and under the auspices of the Supreme Being, the following rights of man and citizen.

1. Men are born and remain free and equal in rights; social distinctions may be based only upon general use-fulness.

2. The aim of every political association is the pres-ervation of the natural and inalienable rights of man; these rights are liberty, property, security, and resistance to op-pression.

3. The source of all sovereignty resides essentially in the nation; no group, no individual may exercise authority not emanating expressly therefrom.

4. Liberty consists of the power to do whatever is not injurious to others; thus the enjoyment of the natural rights of every man has for its limits only those that assure other members of society the enjoyment of those same rights; such limits may be determined only by law.

5. The law has the right to forbid only actions which are injurious to society. Whatever is not forbidden by law may not be prevented, and no one may be constrained to do what it does not prescribe.

6. Law is the expression of the general will; all citi-zens have the right to concur personally, or through their representatives, in its formation; it must be the same for all, whether it protects or punishes. All citizens, being equal before it, are equally admissible to all public offices, positions, and employments, according to their capacity, and without other distinction than that of virtues and talents.

7. No man may be accused, arrested, or detained ex-cept in the cases determined by law, and according to the forms prescribed thereby. Whoever solicit, expedite, or ex-ecute arbitrary orders, or have them executed, must be punished; but every citizen summoned or apprehended in pursuance of the law must obey immediately; he renders himself culpable by resistance.

8. The law is to establish only penalties that are absolutely and obviously necessary; and no one may be punished except by virtue of a law established and pro-mulgated prior to the offence and legally applied.

9. Since every man is presumed innocent until declared guilty, if arrest be deemed indispensable, all unnecessary severity for securing the person of the accused must be severely repressed by law.

10. No one is to be disquieted because of his opinions, even religious, provided their manifestation does not disturb the public order established by law.

11. Free communication of ideas and opinions is one of the most precious of the rights of man. Consequently, every citizen may speak, write, and print freely, subject to responsibility for the abuse of such liberty in the cases determined by law.

12. The guarantee of the rights of man and citizen necessitates a public force; such a force, therefore, is instituted for the advantage of all and not for the particular benefit of those to whom it is entrusted.

13. For the maintenance of the public force and for

the expenses of administration a common tax is indispensable; it must be assessed equally on all citizens in proportion to their means.

14. Citizens have the right to ascertain, by themselves or through their representatives, the necessity of the public tax, to consent to it freely, to supervise its use, and to determine its quota, assessment, payment, and duration.

15. Society has the right to require of every public agent an accounting of his administration.

16. Every society in which the guarantee of rights is not assured or the separation of powers not determined has no constitution at all.

17. Since property is a sacred and inviolable right, no one may be deprived thereof unless a legally established public necessity obviously requires it, and upon condition of a just and previous indemnity.

15

WILLIAM WORDSWORTH

"Lines Composed a Few Miles Above Tintern Abbey"

Wordsworth's poem, "Lines Composed a Few Miles Above Tintern Abbey," represents a turning point in English letters. Before it appeared, poetry was dominated by the Neoclassical style (1660–1798), which was characterized by correctness in language and moral sentiments supportive of the existing social order. Neoclassical poets revered the Classical authors, especially the Romans, using their literary genres as models and sources of rules (see Pope's *An Essay on Man*). With the appearance of Wordsworth's poem (1798), poetry fell under the sway of the Romantic style, which was marked by rejection of the ideals and rules of Classicism and Neoclassicism. Romantic poets advocated the free, subjective expression of passion and personal feelings.

"Tintern Abbey" was one of the poems in *Lyrical Ballads* by William Wordsworth (1770–1850) and Samuel Taylor Coleridge (1772–1834). The poems in this collection were revolutionary in form, replacing what the two poets termed the artificial style of the Neoclassicists with a more natural verse. For Coleridge, this meant ballad forms; for Wordsworth, simple lyrics voiced in the common language of the "middle and lower classes." This desire to reproduce customary speech, a reflection of the age's democratic revolutions, became henceforth a prominent motif in Western letters, even after the formal end of the Romantic period in 1848 (see Hurston's "How It Feels to Be Colored Me").

Wordsworth may have been a rebel in aesthetics, but he was a conservative in his social and political views, except for a brief flirtation with liberal ideas at the dawn of the French Revolution. From *Lyrical Ballads* onward, he used his poetry to express fears of the emerging modern world, such as teeming cities, mass democracy, and lack of community. He made the unspoiled countryside his symbol for the disappearing world of village England, under siege by the Industrial Revolution. For him, rural equaled good, urban equaled evil. His love for rural values was, at bottom, an attempt to revive the structures and symbols of the Middle Ages.

Reading the Selection

"Tintern Abbey" reflects Wordsworth's lifelong (religious) love affair with nature, which he conceives in pantheistic terms. Indeed, it is a classic expression of pantheism (Greek, "all gods"), the doctrine that identifies God with the forces and workings of nature. To this end, he describes nature in terms usually reserved for God, such as finding peace of mind in nature and calling the natural world "The anchor of my purest thoughts, the nurse, / The guide, the guardian of my heart, and soul / Of all my moral being."

The poem is a conversation, albeit one-sided, in which the poet speaks directly to his sister Dorothy ("My dear, dear Sister!"). Its conversational tone is established by the blank verse—a Renaissance verse form often used by Romantic poets—and the informal speech. Its theme is the cult of nature, about which, Wordsworth explains to Dorothy, his feelings have changed since he, "like a roe [deer]," roamed this spot five years before. Sadder but wiser, he now finds himself less exalted in mood, "but hearing . . . / The still, sad music of humanity." He tries to describe his younger self but finally gives up: "I cannot paint / What then I was." He, however, recognizes in his sister his old feelings ("in thy voice I catch / The language of my former heart"), hence his lecture on nature's moral power. Sharing nature in the company of a loved one, as seen in "Tintern Abbey," became a familiar theme in later Romantic poetry and art.

Five years have past; five summers, with the length 1
Of five long winters! and again I hear
These waters, rolling from their mountain-springs
With a soft inland murmur.—Once again
Do I behold these steep and lofty cliffs,
That on a wild secluded scene impress
Thoughts of more deep seclusion; and connect
The landscape with the quiet of the sky.
The day is come when I again repose
Here, under this dark sycamore, and view 10
These plots of cottage-ground, these orchard-tufts,
Which at this season, with their unripe fruits,
Are clad in one green hue, and lose themselves
'Mid groves and copses. Once again I see
These hedge-rows, hardly hedge-rows, little lines
Of sportive wood run wild: these pastoral farms,
Green to the very door; and wreaths of smoke
Sent up, in silence, from among the trees!
With some uncertain notice, as might seem
Of vagrant dwellers in the houseless woods, 20
Or of some Hermit's cave, where by his fire
The Hermit sits alone.

　　　　　　These beauteous forms,
Through a long absence, have not been to me
As is a landscape to a blind man's eye:
But oft, in lonely rooms, and 'mid the din
Of towns and cities, I have owed to them
In hours of weariness, sensations sweet,
Felt in the blood, and felt along the heart;
And passing even into my purer mind, 30
With tranquil restoration:—feelings too
Of unremembered pleasure: such, perhaps,
As have no slight or trivial influence
On that best portion of a good man's life,
His little, nameless, unremembered, acts
Of kindness and of love. Nor less, I trust,
To them I may have owed another gift,
Of aspect more sublime; that blessed mood,
In which the burthen of the mystery,
In which the heavy and the weary weight 40

Of all this unintelligible world,
Is lightened:—that serene and blessed mood,
In which the affections gently lead us on,—
Until, the breath of this corporeal frame
And even the motion of our human blood
Almost suspended, we are laid asleep
In body, and become a living soul:
While with an eye made quiet by the power
Of harmony, and the deep power of joy,
We see into the life of things. 50

　　　　　　If this
Be but a vain belief, yet, oh! how oft—
In darkness and amid the many shapes
Of joyless daylight; when the fretful stir
Unprofitable, and the fever of the world,
Have hung upon the beatings of my heart—
How oft, in spirit, have I turned to thee,
O sylvan Wye! thou wanderer thro' the woods,
How often has my spirit turned to thee!

　　　　And now, with gleams of half-extinguished thought, 60
With many recognitions dim and faint,
And somewhat of a sad perplexity,
The picture of the mind revives again:
While here I stand, not only with the sense
Of present pleasure, but with pleasing thoughts
That in this moment there is life and food
For future years. And so I dare to hope,
Though changed, no doubt, from what I was when first
I came among these hills; when like a roe
I bounded o'er the mountains, by the sides 70
Of the deep rivers, and the lonely streams,
Wherever nature led: more like a man
Flying from something that he dreads, than one
Who sought the thing he loved. For nature then
(The coarser pleasures of my boyish days,
And their glad animal movements all gone by)
To me was all in all.—I cannot paint
What then I was. The sounding cataract
Haunted me like a passion: the tall rock,

The mountain, and the deep and gloomy wood,   80
Their colours and their forms, were then to me
An appetite; a feeling and a love,
That had no need of a remoter charm,
By thought supplied, nor any interest
Unborrowed from the eye.—That time is past,
And all its aching joys are now no more,
And all its dizzy raptures. Not for this
Faint I, nor mourn nor murmur; other gifts
Have followed; for such loss, I would believe,
Abundant recompense. For I have learned   90
To look on nature, not as in the hour
Of thoughtless youth; but hearing oftentimes
The still, sad music of humanity,
Nor harsh nor grating, though of ample power
To chasten and subdue. And I have felt
A presence that disturbs me with the joy
Of elevated thoughts; a sense sublime
Of something far more deeply interfused,
Whose dwelling is the light of setting suns,
And the round ocean and the living air,   100
And the blue sky, and in the mind of man:
A motion and a spirit, that impels
All thinking things, all objects of all thought,
And rolls through all things. Therefore am I still
A lover of the meadows and the woods,
And mountains; and of all that we behold
From this green earth; of all the mighty world
Of eye, and ear,—both what they half create,
And what perceive; well pleased to recognise
In nature and the language of the sense,   110
The anchor of my purest thoughts, the nurse,
The guide, the guardian of my heart, and soul
Of all my moral being.

         Nor perchance,
If I were not thus taught, should I the more
Suffer my genial spirits to decay:
For thou art with me here upon the banks
Of this fair river; thou my dearest Friend,
My dear, dear Friend; and in thy voice I catch
The language of my former heart, and read   120

My former pleasures in the shooting lights
Of thy wild eyes. Oh! yet a little while
May I behold in thee what I was once,
My dear, dear Sister! and this prayer I make,
Knowing that Nature never did betray
The heart that loved her; 'tis her privilege,
Through all the years of this our life, to lead
From joy to joy: for she can so inform
The mind that is within us, so impress
With quietness and beauty, and so feed   130
With lofty thoughts, that neither evil tongues,
Rash judgments, nor the sneers of selfish men,
Nor greetings where no kindness is, nor all
The dreary intercourse of daily life,
Shall e'er prevail against us, or disturb
Our cheerful faith, that all which we behold
Is full of blessings. Therefore let the moon
Shine on thee in thy solitary walk;
And let the misty mountain-winds be free
To blow against thee: and, in after years,   140
When these wild ecstasies shall be matured
Into a sober pleasure; when thy mind
Shall be a mansion for all lovely forms,
Thy memory be as a dwelling-place
For all sweet sounds and harmonies; oh! then,
If solitude, or fear, or pain, or grief,
Should be thy portion, with what healing thoughts
Of tender joy wilt thou remember me,
And these my exhortations! Nor, perchance—
If I should be where I no more can hear   150
Thy voice, nor catch from thy wild eyes these gleams
Of past existence—wilt thou then forget
That on the banks of this delightful stream
We stood together; and that I, so long
A worshipper of Nature, hither came
Unwearied in that service; rather say
With warmer love—oh! with far deeper zeal
Of holier love. Nor wilt thou then forget,
That after many wanderings, many years
Of absence, these steep woods and lofty cliffs,   160
And this green pastoral landscape, were to me
More dear, both for themselves and for thy sake!

JOHANN WOLFGANG VON GOETHE

Selection from *Faust*, Part I

Goethe is generally acknowledged as Germany's greatest author, and *Faust* is considered his master-piece. A play in verse, *Faust* is the most popular drama in Germany, where hardly a day passes without its being performed on some stage. Outside Germany, it is better known as a work to be read. This play's appeal is in its portrait of Faust as archetypal rebel, ready to trade his soul for forbidden knowl-edge. Some read a more sinister meaning into its appeal, making the Faustian quest a metaphor for what they perceive to be the West's drive for world dominion and mastery of nature.

Goethe's play merits comparison with Marlowe's *Dr. Faustus*, since both were based on the same legend. Where Marlowe's ending is morally ambiguous—Is his Faust a noble martyr who played God or a sinner meant to warn others?—Goethe's Faust, despite his mistakes, is ultimately saved by God. Notwithstanding the clarity of its ending, Goethe introduced a new dimension of ambiguity into this work: *Why* God rescues the wayward hero is not made clear.

Goethe recognized the moral uncertainty of his approach. Unable to finish the play, he first presented it to the world with the hero Faust left alive and in despair. Subtitled Part I, this portion of *Faust* was issued in 1808. For the rest of Goethe's life he wrestled with Part II, finishing it before he died in 1832.

Despite the unresolved ending, Part I is Goethe's finest work. Faust is presented in this era's Romantic language, which rejected historic religion but believed there was a mystery at the core of life. Thus Faust is revealed as obsessed with human ignorance ("ignorance is our fate, / And this I hate"). Disappointed in science, he calls up the devil Mephistopheles to learn "what the universe engirds." Faust, joined by Mephistopheles, then goes through a series of adventures in quest of life's elusive meaning. At the end of Part I, Faust's quest, rather than bringing knowledge, has brought despair; he prays, "Would I had never been born."

In Part II Goethe further muddles the play's moral. It ends with Faust ironically yielding his soul to Mephistopheles, thinking he is doing it for the good of humanity. Faust's motive is pure, but his act rests on an illusion: Mephistopheles has tricked him into a meaningless death. And yet, by saving Faust from hell, Goethe seems to say that to God, dreams count more than deeds.

The middle-class Johann Wolfgang von Goethe (1749–1832) was one of the West's last universal men. Besides being a dramatist, he was also an essayist, author of lyric verse, novelist, lawyer, and scientist, writing on botany, anatomy, and the theory of color. No ivory-tower intellectual, he was for many years a bureaucrat in Weimar, capital of the petty duchy of Saxe-Weimar-Eisenach.

Reading the Selection

This selection contains most of *Faust*'s first scene. Introduced here are the two scholars, Wagner and Faust, who symbolize rival paths to truth, sense or sensibility, Enlightenment or Romanticism. Wagner is sense, dedicated to reason and determined to make "books my drink and meat." Faust, bored with Wagner ("this lickspittle of learning"), is sensibility, so devoted to feeling that he is paradoxically prepared to commit suicide to calm his soul. During the rest of Part I, Faust's commitment to Romantic feeling brings destruction in its wake. Perhaps because of destruction's link with feeling, Goethe later condemned Romanticism as "unhealthy."

---〜〜---

The Tragedy

Night, Faust's Study (i)

In a high-vaulted, narrow, gothic chamber, FAUST *is discovered restless at his desk.*

FAUST.   Philosophy have I digested,   1
The whole of Law and Medicine,
From each its secrets I have wrested,
Theology, alas, thrown in.
Poor fool, with all this sweated lore,
I stand no wiser than I was before.
Master and Doctor are my titles;
For ten years now, without repose,
I've held my erudite recitals
And led my pupils by the nose.   10
And round we go, on crooked ways or straight,

And well I know that ignorance is our fate,
And this I hate.
I have, I grant, outdistanced all the others,
Doctors, pedants, clergy and lay-brothers;
All plague of doubts and scruples I can quell,
And have no fear of devil or of hell,
And in return am destitute of pleasure,
Knowing that knowledge tricks us beyond measure,
That man's conversion is beyond my reach,   20
Knowing the emptiness of what I teach.
Meanwhile I live in penury,
No worldly honour falls to me.
No dog would linger on like this,
And so I turn to the abyss
Of necromancy, try if art
Can voice or power of spirits start,
To do me service and reveal

The things of Nature's secret seal,
And save me from the weary dance   30
Of holding forth in ignorance.
Then shall I see, with vision clear,
How secret elements cohere,
And what the universe engirds,
And give up huckstering with words.
    O silver majesty of night,
Moon, look no more upon my plight,
You whom my eyes at midnight oft
Have gazed upon, when slow and soft
You crossed my papers and my books   40
With friendly, melancholy looks.
Would that my soul could tranquil stray
On many a moonlit mountain way,
By cavernous haunts with ghostly shadows,
Or thread the silver of the meadows,
Released from learning's smoky stew
To lave me in the moonlit dew.
    But, ah, this prison has my soul,
Damnable, bricked-in, cabined hole,
Where even the heaven's dear light must pass   50
Saddened through the painted glass.
Hemmed in with stacks of books am I,
Where works the worm with dusty mange,
While to the vaulted roof on high
The smoky ranks of papers range;
Retorts and jars my crib encumber,
And crowded instruments and, worse,
Loads of hereditary lumber—
And this, ay this, is called my universe.
    And shall I wonder why my heart   60
Is lamed and frightened in my breast,
Why all the springs of life that start
Are strangely smothered and oppressed?
Instead of all that life can hold
Of Nature's free, god-given breath,
I take to me the smoke and mould
Of skeletons and dust and death.
Up and away! A distant land
Awaits me in this secret book
From Nostradamus' very hand,   70
Nor for a better guide I look.
Now shall I read the starry pole,
In Nature's wisdom shall I seek
And know, with rising power of soul,
How spirit doth to spirit speak.
No dusty logic can divine
The meaning of a sacred sign.
Mysterious spirits, hovering near,
Answer me, if now ye hear!

(He opens the book and lights upon the Sign of the Macrocosm.)

Ah, strangely comes an onset of delight,   80
Invading all my senses as I gaze:
Young, sacred bliss-of-life springs at the sight,
And fires my blood in all its branching ways.
Was it a god who made this mystic scroll,
To touch my spirit's tumult with its healing,
And fill my wretched heart with joyous feeling,

And bring the secret world before my soul,
The hidden drive of Nature's force revealing?
Myself a god?—With lightened vision's leap
I read the riddle of the symbols, hear   90
The looms of Nature's might, that never sleep,
And know at last things spoken of the seer:
'Tis not the spirit world is sealed;
Thy heart is dead, thy senses' curtain drawn.
But, scholar, bathe, rejoicing, healed,
Thy earthly breast in streams of roseate dawn.'

(He studies the sign.)

Lo, single things inwoven, made to blend,
To work in oneness with the whole, and live
Members one of another, while ascend
Celestial powers, who ever take and give   100
Vessels of gold on heaven's living stair,
Their pinions fragrant with the bliss they bear,
Pervading all, that heaven and earth agree,
Transfixing all the world with harmony.
    O endless pageant!—But a pageant still,
A show, that mocks my touch or grasp or will!
Where are the nipples, Nature's springs, ah where
The living source that feeds the universe?
You flow, you give to drink, mysterious nurse,
And yet my soul is withered in despair.   110

(Disconsolately he turns the pages until his glance rests on the sign of the Spirit of Earth.)

A curious change affects me in this sign:
You, kindred Sprite of Earth, come strangely nearer;
My spirits rise, my powers are stronger, clearer,
As from the glow of a refreshing wine.
I gather heart to risk the world's encounter,
To bear my human fate as fate's surmounter,
To front the storm, in joy or grief not palter,
Even in the gnash of shipwreck never falter.
    The clouds close in above me
And hidden is the moon;   120
The lamp dies down.
A vapour grows—red quiverings
Dart round my head—there creeps
A shuddering from the vaulted roof
And seizes me!
I know, dread spirit of my call, 'tis you.
Stand forth, disclosed!
Ah, how my heart is harrowed through!
In tumult of feeling
My mind is riven, my senses reeling.   130
To you I yield, nor care if I am lost.
This thing must be, though life should be the cost.

(He seizes the book and pronounces the secret sign of the SPIRIT. A reddish flame shoots up and the SPIRIT appears in the flame.)

SPIRIT. Who calls on me?
FAUST *(turning away)*. O fearful form!
SPIRIT.   At length
You have compelled me here. Your strength
Has wrestled long about my sphere,
And now—

FAUST.   I tremble: come not near.

SPIRIT.   With bated breath you laboured to behold me,   140
To hear my voice, to see me face to face.
You prayed with might, with depth that has controlled me,
And here am I!—What horror now can chase
The colour from your lips, my superman?
Where the soul's cry? The courage that began
To shape a world, and bear and foster it?
The heart that glowed, with lofty ardour lit,
To claim ethereal spirits as your peers?
Are you that Faust whose challenge smote my ears,
Who beat his way to me, proclaimed his hour,   150
And trembles now in presence of my power,
Writhes from the breath of it, a frightened worm?

FAUST.   And shall I, thing of flame, flinch at the sequel?
My name is Faust, in everything your equal.

SPIRIT.   In flood of life, in action's storm
I ply on my wave
With weaving motion
Birth and the grave,
A boundless ocean,
Ceaselessly giving   160
Weft of living,
Forms unending,
Glowing and blending.
So work I on the whirring loom of time,
The life that clothes the deity sublime.

FAUST.   Swift Spirit, you whose projects have no end,
How near akin our natures seem to be!

SPIRIT.   You match the spirit that you comprehend,
Not me. (*He vanishes.*)

FAUST.   (*filled with dismay*). Not you!   170
Whom then?
I, made in God's own image,
And not with you compare! (*A knock.*)
Damnation, that will be my Servitor!
My richest hope is in confusion hurled:
He spoils my vision of the spirit world,
This lickspittle of learning at my door.

(WAGNER *in dressing-gown and night-cap, carrying a lamp.*
FAUST *turns reluctantly.*)

WAGNER.   Beg pardon, but I heard you, Sir, declaiming—
Some tragedy, I'll warrant, from the Greek?—
That's just the learned art at which I'm aiming,   180
For people are impressed when scholars speak.
Indeed, I've heard the stage can be a teacher,
So that the actor can inspire the preacher.

FAUST.   Past question, if the parson is a mummer—
A thing you may discover, now and then.

WAGNER.   But, Sir, if learning ties us, winter, summer,
With holiday so rare, that we see men

As through a glass, remote and ill-defined,
How shall our counsel serve to lead mankind?

FAUST.   If feeling fails you, vain will be your course,   190
And idle what you plan unless your art
Springs from the soul with elemental force
To hold its sway in every listening heart.
Well, well, keep at it: ply the shears and paste,
Concoct from feasts of other men your hashes,
And should the thing be wanting fire or taste,
Blow into flame your little heap of ashes:
You'll find some apes and children who'll admire,
If admiration is your chief desire;
But what is uttered from the heart alone   200
Will win the hearts of others to your own.

WAGNER.   Yet by his style a speaker stands to win;
That I know well, and that I'm backward in.

FAUST.   Trust honesty, to win success,
Be not a noisy jingling fool.
Good sense, Sir, and rightmindedness
Have little need to speak by rule.
And if your mind on urgent truth is set,
Need you go hunting for an epithet?
Nay, these your polished speeches that you make,   210
Serving mankind your snipped-out pie-frill papers,
They nourish us no more than winds that shake
The withered leaves, or shred the autumnal vapours.

WAGNER.   Ah me, Sir, long indeed is art;
Our life is very short, however,
And often, in my studious endeavour
A fearful dread assails my head and heart.
How hard it is to master ways and means
By which a man may reach the fountain-head!
And, ere he's half-way there, fate intervenes: 220
Before he knows it, the poor devil's dead.

FAUST.   Is parchment, then, your well of living water,
Where whosoever drinks shall be made whole?
Look not to stem your craving in that quarter:
The spring is vain that flows not from the soul.

WAGNER.   The pleasure, by your leave, is great, to cast
The mind into the spirit of the past,
And scan the former notions of the wise,
And see what marvellous heights we've reached at last.

FAUST.   Most nobly have we, up to the starry skies!   230
My friend, for us the alluring times of old
Are like a book that's sealed-up sevenfold.
And what you call the Spirit of the Ages
Is but the spirit of your learned sages,
Whose mirror is a pitiful affair,
Shunned by mankind after a single stare,
A mouldy dustbin, or a lumber attic,
Or at the most a blood-and-thunder play
Stuffed full of wit sententious and pragmatic,
Fit for the sawdust puppetry to say.   240

WAGNER.   And yet the world, the human heart and
    mind—
To understand these things must be our aim.

FAUST.   To understand—and how is that defined?
Who dares to give that child its proper name?
The few of understanding, vision rare,
Who veiled not from the herd their hearts, but tried,
Poor generous fools, to lay their feelings bare,
Them have men always burnt and crucified.
Excuse me, friend, it grows deeps into night,
And now is time to think about adjourning.   250

WAGNER.   I could have stayed up longer with delight,
To join in discourse with your lofty learning.
But, Sir, to-morrow comes our Easter Day,
When I shall ask more questions, if I may.
I've learnt a deal, made books my drink and meat,
But cannot rest till knowledge is complete. *(Exit.)*

FAUST.   How strange, that he who cleaves to shallow
    things
Can keep his hopes alive on empty terms,
And dig with greed for precious plunderings,
And find his happiness unearthing worms!   260
   How dared this voice to raise its human bleat
Where waits the spirit world in immanent power?
And yet the man, so barren and effete,
Deserves my thanks in this most perilous hour.
He snatched me from a desperate despite
Fit to unhinge my reason, or to slay.
The apparition towered to such a height
My soul was dwarfed within me, in dismay.
   I, God's own image, who have seemed, forsooth,
Near to the mirror of eternal truth,   270
Compassed the power to shed the mortal clay
And revel in the self's celestial day,
I, who presumed in puissance to out-soar
The cherubim, to flow in Nature's veins,
With god-like joy in my creative pains,
I rode too high, and deep must I deplore:
One thunder-word has robbed me of my reins.
   I dare not, Spirit, count me in your sphere:
For, though I had the power to call you here,
No force have I that binds you or retains.   280
And in that moment dread and wondrous,
When I, so puny, grew so great,
You thrust me with a verdict thund'rous
Back to uncertain mortal fate.
Who is my guide? What shall I shun?
Or what imperious urge obey?
Alas, not only woes, but actions done,
Walk by us still, to hedge us on our way.
   The spirit's splendour, in the soul unfurled,
Is ever stifled with a stranger stuff.   290
High values, matched with good things of this world,
Mocking recede, and seem an airy bluff.
Our nobler veins, the true, life-giving springs,
Are choked with all the dust of earthy things.
   What though imaginate spread her wings

In early hope towards the things eternal,
Shrunk is her spacious realm in the diurnal
Defeat that loss and disappointment brings.
Full soon in deepest hearts care finds a nest,
And builds her bed of pain, in secret still,   300
There rocks herself, disturbing joy and rest,
And ever takes new shapes to work her will,
With fluttering fears for home or wife or child,
A thought of poison, flood or perils wild;
For man must quail at bridges never crossed,
Lamenting even things he never lost.
   Shall I then rank with gods? Too well I feel
My kinship with the worm, who bores the soil,
Who feeds on dust until the wanderer's heel
Gives sepulture to all his care and toil.   310
   Is it not dust, that fills my hundred shelves,
And walls me in like any pedant hack?
Fellow of moth that flits and worm that delves,
I drag my life through learned bric-a-brac.
And shall I here discover what I lack,
And learn, by reading countless volumes through,
That mortals mostly live on misery's rack,
That happiness is known to just a few?
You hollow skull, what has your grin to say,
But that a mortal brain, with trouble tossed,   320
Sought once, like mine, the sweetness of the day,
And strove for truth, and in the gloam was lost.
You instruments, you mock me to my face,
With wheel and gimbal, cylinder and cog;
You were my key to unlock the secret place:
The wards are cunning, but the levers clog.
For Nature keeps her veil inviolate,
Mysterious still in open light of day,
And where the spirit cannot penetrate
Your screws and irons will never make a way.   330
Here stands the gear that I have never touched,
My father's stuff, bequeathed to be my prison,
With scrolls of vellum, blackened and besmutched,
Where still the desk-lamp's dismal smoke has risen.
Better have spent what little was my own,
Than sweat for petty gains by midnight oil.
The things that men inherit come alone
To true possession by the spirit's toil.
What can't be used is trash; what can, a prize
Begotten from the moment as it flies.   340
   But what magnetic thing compels my gaze?
This phial fascinates me, like the sight
Of soothing moon when, deep in forest ways,
Our very thoughts are silvered with the light.
   You I salute, you flask of virtue rare,
That now I hand me down with reverent care;
In you I honour human wit and art.
You very spirit of the opiate flowers,
You distillation of the deadly powers,
Show to your master now your gracious heart: 350
To see you, touch you, soothes my strife and pain.
I hear a call towards the open main,
My tide of soul is ebbing more and more,
Lies at my feet the shining, glassy plain,
A new day beckons to another shore.

As if on wings, a chariot of fire
Draws near me. I am ready to be free.
Piercing the ether, new-born, I aspire
To rise to spheres of pure activity.
This soaring life, this bliss of godlike birth,   360
How shall we earn it, who from worms must rise?
Yet true the call: I spurn the sun of earth,
Leave, resolute, its loveliness. My eyes
I lift in daring to fling wide the gate
Whose threshold men have ever flinching trod.
The hour is come, as master of my fate
To prove in man the stature of a god,
Nor blench before the cavern black and fell,
Imagination's torment evermore,
But dare the narrow flaming pass of hell   370
And stride in strength towards the dreaded door.
This step I take in cheerful resolution,
Risk more than death, yea, dare my dissolution.

Pure crystal bowl, I take you from your case,
Come down, to help me, from your waiting-place.
Long have I owned your worth with unconcern,
You who could charm, upon high holidays,
My father's guests, and shining win their praise,
As each received the loving-cup in turn.
The pride of art, the legends in the frieze,   380
The drinker's pledge, to tell them all in rhyme,
Then lift the cup and drain it to the lees—
All brings me back the nights of youthful prime.
I shall not hand you now to any friend,
No witty praise of art do I intend,
For here's a cordial quick to drown the sense,
A chalice with dark opiate to dispense:
I choose, clear-eyed, the draught of my preparing
And drink my last, with all my spirit daring
To pledge the morrow's awful imminence. . . .   390

JANE AUSTEN

Selections from *Pride and Prejudice*

Jane Austen (1775–1817), England's first great woman novelist, published her first work, *Sense and Sensibility,* in 1811. A comic novel about middle-class, provincial life, this work staked out a part of the literary world that she soon made her own. She knew this terrain intimately, for she spent her life in small towns far from London. When *Sense and Sensibility* found an admiring public, there followed five more novels: *Pride and Prejudice* (1813); *Mansfield Park* (1814); *Emma* (1816); *Northanger Abbey* and *Persuasion,* issued jointly (1818). Of these, *Pride and Prejudice* is the most well known.

Pride and Prejudice was written during the Napoleonic Era (1799–1815), when England was nearly always fighting France. The novel, however, contains no hint of these wars, except that a soldier like Mr. Wickham appears as an eligible bachelor. Nor is there mention of the Industrial Revolution, which was changing England for the worse. The novel's world is rustic towns and unspoiled countryside with well-kept estates and tidy farms. Austen focused on a vanishing society whose smallest unit was the family and whose major problems involved shifting social relationships.

Pride and Prejudice has a simple plot: The Bennets—a shabby, genteel family of the middle class—look for suitable husbands for their five daughters. Austen turns this plot into an intriguing story through clear writing, subtle irony, and most notably, precise dissection of the manners and rituals of middle-class life: the balls, the letters and gossip, the visits back and forth, and the unexpected calamities, such as a social snub, an elopement, a betrayed secret, or a broken engagement. She was especially aware of society's constraints on women, as in the depiction of the dilemma of Charlotte Lucas, who weighs her future husband's ugly character against the social position he offers.

Austen composed *Pride and Prejudice* in the Neoclassical style, which had dominated English writing in the 1700s (see Fielding's *Tom Jones*). This style's stress on decorum and orthodox morals suited Austen's purposes very well. In effect, she treated society as a dance, with her characters going through the paces with grace, good cheer, and determination. Neither romantic nor sentimental but with great insight, she showed people of varied temperaments dealing with social conventions.

Reading the Selections

Pride and Prejudice's first three chapters show Austen's skillful handling of the characters and her good ear for dialogue. Chapter I deftly lays out the dynamics in the Bennet family: Mrs. Bennet is a social climber, eager to provide rich husbands for her daughters; she is vulgar in comparison to Mr. Bennet, who is beleaguered by his wife's prattling yet does not stop her scheming. Mr. Bennet is partial to daughter Lizzy—Elizabeth—the highspirited heroine, as it turns out, of this delightful novel.

In Chapter II, Mr. Bennet reveals his social call on Mr. Bingley, a potential suitor for his daughters. Four daughters are introduced, and they begin to assert their individual natures.

Chapter III presents the last Bennet daughter, Jane; the wealthy Mr. Bingley; and the haughty Mr. Darcy. Thereafter Darcy and Elizabeth give the novel its focus: Proud Darcy and equally proud Elizabeth must endure mutual slights and disagreements before love can dissolve their prejudices against one another.

Chapter I

It is a truth universally acknowledged, that a single man in possession of a good fortune, must be in want of a wife.

However little known the feelings or views of such a man may be on his first entering a neighbourhood, this truth is so well fixed in the minds of the surrounding families, that he is considered as the rightful property of some one or other of their daughters.

'My dear Mr Bennet,' said his lady to him one day, 'have you heard that Netherfield Park is let at last?'

Mr Bennet replied that he had not.

'But it is,' returned she; 'for Mrs Long has just been here, and she told me all about it.'

Mr Bennet made no answer.

'Do not you want to know who has taken it?' cried his wife impatiently.

'*You* want to tell me, and I have no objection to hearing it.'

This was invitation enough.

'Why, my dear, you must know, Mrs Long says that Netherfield is taken by a young man of large fortune from the north of England; that he came down on Monday in a chaise and four to see the place, and was so much delighted with it that he agreed with Mr Morris immediately; that he is to take possession before Michaelmas, and some of his servants are to be in the house by the end of next week.'

'What is his name?'

'Bingley.'

'Is he married or single?'

'Oh! single my dear, to be sure! A single man of large fortune; four or five thousand a year. What a fine thing for our girls!'

'How so? how can it affect them?'

'My dear Mr Bennet,' replied his wife, 'how can you be so tiresome! You must know that I am thinking of his marrying one of them.'

'Is that his design in settling here?'

'Design! nonsense, how can you talk so! But it is very likely that he *may* fall in love with one of them, and therefore you must visit him as soon as he comes.'

'I see no occasion for that. You and the girls may go, or you may send them by themselves, which perhaps will be still better, for as you are as handsome as any of them, Mr Bingley might like you the best of the party.'

'My dear, you flatter me. I certainly *have* had my share of beauty, but I do not pretend to be any thing extraordinary now. When a woman has five grown up daughters, she ought to give over thinking of her own beauty.'

'In such cases, a woman has not often much beauty to think of.'

'But, my dear, you must indeed go and see Mr Bingley when he comes into the neighbourhood.'

'It is more than I engage for, I assure you.'

'But consider your daughters. Only think what an establishment it would be for one of them. Sir William and Lady Lucus are determined to go, merely on that account, for in general you know they visit no new comers. Indeed you must go, for it will be impossible for *us* to visit him, if you do not.'

'You are over scrupulous surely. I dare say Mr Bingley will be very glad to see you; and I will send a few lines by you to assure him of my hearty consent to his marrying which ever he chuses of the girls; though I must throw in a good word for my little Lizzy.'

'I desire you will do no such thing. Lizzy is not a bit better than the others; and I am sure she is not half so handsome as Jane, nor half so good humored as Lydia. But you are always giving *her* the preference.'

'They have none of them much to recommend them,' replied he; 'they are all silly and ignorant like other girls; but Lizzy has something more of quickness than her sisters.'

'Mr Bennet, how can you abuse your own children in such a way? You take delight in vexing me. You have no compassion on my poor nerves.'

'You mistake me, my dear. I have a high respect for your nerves. They are my old friends. I have heard you mention them with consideration these twenty years at least.'

'Ah! you do not know what I suffer.'

'But I hope you will get over it, and live to see many young men of four thousand a year come into the neighbourhood.'

'It will be no use to us, if twenty such should come since you will not visit them.'

'Depend upon it, my dear, that when there are twenty, I will visit them all.'

Mr Bennet was so odd a mixture of quick parts, sarcastic humour, reserve, and caprice, that the experience of three and twenty years had been sufficient to make his wife understand his character. *Her* mind was less difficult to develop. She was a woman of mean understanding, little information, and uncertain temper. When she was discontented she fancied herself nervous. The business of her life was to get her daughters married; its solace was visiting and news.

Chapter II

Mr Bennet was among the earliest of those who waited on Mr Bingley. He had always intended to visit him, though to the last always assuring his wife that he should not go; and till the evening after the visit was paid, she had no knowledge of it. It was then disclosed in the following manner. Observing his second daughter employed in trimming a hat, he suddenly addressed her with,

'I hope Mr Bingley will like it, Lizzy.'

'We are not in a way to know *what* Mr Bingley likes,' said her mother resentfully, 'since we are not to visit.'

'But you forget, mama,' said Elizabeth, 'that we shall meet him at the assemblies, and that Mrs Long has promised to introduce him.'

'I do not believe Mrs Long will do any such thing. She has two nieces of her own. She is a selfish, hypocritical woman, and I have no opinion of her.'

'No more have I,' said Mr Bennet; 'and I am glad to find that you do not depend on her serving you.'

Mrs Bennet deigned not to make any reply; but unable to contain herself, began scolding one of her daughters.

'Don't keep coughing so, Kitty, for heaven's sake! Have a little compassion on my nerves. You tear them to pieces.'

'Kitty has no discretion in her coughs,' said her father; 'she times them ill.'

'I do not cough for my own amusement,' replied Kitty fretfully.

'When is your next ball to be, Lizzy?'

'To-morrow fortnight.'

'Aye, so it is,' cried her mother,' and Mrs Long does not come back till the day before; so, it will be impossible for her to introduce him, for she will not know him herself.'

'Then, my dear, you may have the advantage of your friend, and introduce Mr Bingley to *her*.'

'Impossible, Mr Bennet, impossible, when I am not acquainted with him myself; how can you be so teazing?'

'I honour your circumspection. A fortnight's acquaintance is certainly very little. One cannot know what a man really is by the end of a fortnight. But if *we* do not venture, somebody else will; and after all, Mrs Long and her nieces must stand their chance; and therefore, as she will think it an act of kindness, if you decline the office, I will take it on myself.'

The girls stared at their father. Mrs Bennet said only, 'Nonsense, nonsense!'

'What can be the meaning of that emphatic exclamation?' he cried. 'Do you consider the forms of introduction, and the stress that is laid on them, as nonsense? I cannot quite agree with you *there*. What say you, Mary? for you are a young lady of deep reflection I know, and read great books, and make extracts.'

Mary wished to say something very sensible, but knew not how.

'While Mary is adjusting her ideas,' he continued, 'let us return to Mr Bingley.'

'I am sick of Mr Bingley,' cried his wife.

'I am sorry to hear *that*; but why did you not tell me so before? If I had known as much this morning, I certainly would not have called on him. It is very unlucky; but as I have actually paid the visit, we cannot escape the acquaintance now.'

The astonishment of the ladies was just what he wished; that of Mrs Bennet perhaps surpassing the rest; though when the first tumult of joy was over, she began to declare that it was what she had expected all the while.

'How good it was in you, my dear Mr Bennet! But I knew I should persuade you at last. I was sure you loved your girls too well to neglect such an acquaintance. Well, how pleased I am! and it is such a good joke, too, that you should have gone this morning, and never said a word about it till now.'

'Now, Kitty, you may cough as much as you chuse,' said Mr Bennet; and, as he spoke, he left the room, fatigued with the raptures of his wife.

'What an excellent father you have, girls,' said she, when the door was shut. 'I do not know how you will ever make him amends for his kindness; or me either, for that matter. At our time of life, it is not so pleasant I can tell you, to be making new acquaintance every day; but for your sakes, we would do any thing. Lydia, my love, though you *are* the youngest, I dare say Mr Bingley will dance with you at the next ball.'

'Oh!' said Lydia stoutly, 'I am not afraid; for though I *am* the youngest, I'm the tallest.'

The rest of the evening was spent in conjecturing how soon he would return Mr Bennet's visit, and determining when they should ask him to dinner.

Chapter III

Not all that Mrs Bennet, however, with the assistance of her five daughters, could ask on the subject was sufficient to draw from her husband any satisfactory description of Mr Bingley. They attacked him in various ways; with barefaced questions, ingenious suppositions, and distant surmises; but he eluded the skill of them all; and they were at last obliged to accept the second-hand intelligence of their neighbour Lady Lucas. Her report was highly favourable. Sir William had been delighted with him. He was quite young, wonderfully handsome, extremely agreeable, and to crown the whole, he meant to be at the next assembly with a large party. Nothing could be more delightful! To be fond of dancing was a certain step towards falling in love; and very lively hopes of Mr Bingley's heart were entertained.

'If I can but see one of my daughters happily settled at Netherfield,' said Mrs Bennet to her husband, 'and all the others equally well married, I shall have nothing to wish for.'

In a few days Mr Bingley returned Mr Bennet's visit, and sat about ten minutes with him in his library. He had entertained hopes of being admitted to a sight of the young ladies, of whose beauty he had heard much; but he saw only the father. The ladies were somewhat more fortunate, for they had the advantage of ascertaining from an upper window, that he wore a blue coat and rode a black horse.

An invitation to dinner was soon afterwards dispatched; and already had Mrs Bennet planned the courses that were to do credit to her housekeeping, when an answer arrived which deferred it all. Mr Bingley was obliged to be in town the following day, and consequently unable to accept the honour of their invitation, &c. Mrs Bennet was quite disconcerted. She could not imagine what business he could have in town so soon after his arrival in Hertfordshire; and she began to fear that he might be always flying about from one place to another, and never settled at Netherfield as he ought to be. Lady Lucas quieted her fears a little by starting the idea of his being gone to London only to get a large party for the ball; and a report soon followed that Mr Bingley was to bring twelve ladies and seven gentlemen with him to the assembly. The girls grieved over such a number of ladies; but were comforted the day before the ball by hearing, that instead of twelve, he had brought only six with him from London, his five sisters and a cousin. And when the party entered the assembly room, it consisted of only five altogether; Mr Bingley, his two sisters, the husband of the eldest, and another young man.

Mr Bingley was good looking and gentlemanlike; he had a pleasant countenance, and easy, unaffected manners. His sisters were fine women, with an air of decided fashion. His brother-in-law, Mr Hurst, merely looked the gentleman; but his friend Mr Darcy soon drew the attention of the room by his fine, tall person, handsome features, noble mien; and the report which was in general circulation within five minutes after his entrance, of his having ten thousand a year. The gentlemen pronounced him to be a fine figure of a man, the ladies declared he was much handsomer than Mr Bingley, and he was looked at with great admiration for about half the evening, till his manners gave a disgust which turned the tide of his popularity; for he was discovered to be proud, to be above his company, and above being pleased; and not all his large estate in Derbyshire could then save him from having a most forbidding, disagreeable countenance, and being unworthy to be compared with his friend.

Mr Bingley had soon made himself acquainted with all the principal people in the room; he was lively and unreserved, danced every dance, was angry that the ball closed so early, and talked of giving one himself at Netherfield. Such amiable qualities must speak for themselves. What a contrast between him and his friend! Mr Darcy danced only once with Mrs Hurst and once with Miss Bingley, declined being introduced to any other lady, and spent the rest of the evening in walking about the room, speaking occasionally to one of his own party. His character was decided. He was the proudest, most disagreeable man in the world, and every body hoped that he would never come there again. Amongst the most violent against him was Mrs Bennet, whose dislike of his general behaviour, was sharpened into particular resentment, by his having slighted one of her daughters.

Elizabeth Bennet had been obliged, by the scarcity of gentlemen, to sit down for two dances; and during part of that time, Mr Darcy had been standing near enough for her to overhear a conversation between him and Mr Bingley, who came from the dance for a few minutes, to press his friend to join it.

'Come, Darcy,' said he, 'I must have you dance. I hate to see you standing about by yourself in this stupid manner. You had much better dance.'

'I certainly shall not. You know how I detest it, unless I am particularly acquainted with my partner. At such an assembly as this, it would be insupportable. Your sisters are engaged, and there is not another woman in the room, whom it would not be a punishment to me to stand up with.'

'I would not be so fastidious as you are,' cried Bingley, 'for a kingdom! Upon my honour, I never met with so many pleasant girls in my life, as I have this evening; and there are several of them you see uncommonly pretty.'

'*You* are dancing with the only handsome girl in the room,' said Mr Darcy, looking at the eldest Miss Bennet.

'Oh! She is the most beautiful creature I ever beheld! But there is one of her sisters sitting down just behind you, who is very pretty, and I dare say, very agreeable. Do let me ask my partner to introduce you.'

'Which do you mean?' and turning round, he looked for a moment at Elizabeth, till catching her eye, he withdrew his own and coldly said, 'She is tolerable; but not handsome enough to tempt *me*; and I am in no humour at present to give consequence to young ladies who are slighted by other men. You had better return to your partner and enjoy her smiles, for you are wasting your time with me.'

Mr Bingley followed his advice. Mr Darcy walked off; and Elizabeth remained with no very cordial feelings towards him. She told the story however with great spirit among her friends; for she had a lively, playful disposition, which delighted in any thing ridiculous.

The evening altogether passed off pleasantly to the whole family. Mrs Bennet had seen her eldest daughter much admired by the Netherfield party. Mr Bingley had danced with her twice, and she had been distinguished by his sisters. Jane was as much gratified by this, as her mother could be, though in a quieter way. Elizabeth felt Jane's pleasure. Mary had heard herself mentioned to Miss Bingley as the most accomplished girl in the neighbourhood; and Catherine and Lydia had been fortunate enough to be never without partners, which was all that they had yet learnt to care for at a ball. They returned therefore in good spirits to Longbourn, the village where they lived, and of which they were the principal inhabitants. They found Mr Bennet still up. With a book he was regardless of time; and on the present occasion he had a good deal of curiosity as to the event of an evening which had raised such splendid expectations. He had rather hoped that all his wife's views on the stranger would be disappointed; but he soon found that he had a very different story to hear.

'Oh! my dear Mr Bennet,' as she entered the room, 'we have had a most delightful evening, a most excellent ball. I wish you had been there. Jane was so admired, nothing could be like it. Every body said how well she looked; and Mr Bingley thought her quite beautiful, and danced with

her twice. Only think of *that* my dear; he actually danced with her twice; and she was the only creature in the room that he asked a second time. First of all, he asked Miss Lucus. I was so vexed to see him stand up with her; but, however, he did not admire her at all: indeed, nobody can, you know; and he seemed quite struck with Jane as she was going down the dance. So, he enquired who she was, and got introduced, and asked her for the two next. Then, the two third he danced with Miss King, and the two fourth with Maria Lucas, and the two fifth with Jane again, and the two sixth with Lizzy, and the Boulanger—'

'If he had had any compassion for *me*,' cried her husband impatiently, 'he would not have danced half so much! For God's sake, say no more of his partners. Oh! that he had sprained his ankle in the first dance!'

'Oh! my dear,' continued Mrs Bennet, 'I am quite delighted with him. He is so excessively handsome! and his sisters are charming women. I never in my life saw any thing more elegant than their dresses. I dare say the lace upon Mrs Hurst's gown—'

Here she was interrupted again. Mr Bennet protested against any description of finery. She was therefore obliged to seek another branch of the subject, and related, with much bitterness of spirit and some exaggeration, the shocking rudeness of Mr Darcy.

'But I can assure you,' she added, 'that Lizzy does not lose much by not suiting *his* fancy; for he is a most disagreeable, horrid man, not at all worth pleasing. So high and so conceited that there was no enduring him! He walked here, and he walked there, fancying himself so very great! Not handsome enough to dance with! I wish you had been there, my dear, to have given him one of your set downs. I quite detest the man.'

MARY SHELLEY

Selections from *Frankenstein*

Shelley's *Frankenstein* (1818) is a neglected classic, for fewer people have read the novel than know the story. This neglect began soon after publication, when the novel became the basis of a popular drama. The story's appeal grew in this century, inspiring countless movies, television films, cartoons, and even a musical. Success transformed the basic story, in the Nuclear Age, into a myth of humanity's foolish attempts to unlock the secrets of nature.

Shelley's original work deserves to be read, for it is both richer and more complex than the popular tale. It belongs to the genre of epistolary novel, or novel in the form of letters and diary entries—a popular eighteenth-century form. At the core of her novel is the story of Victor Frankenstein, a Swiss scientist who discovers the secret of life and creates a being from raw materials salvaged from graves, butcher shops, and dissecting rooms.

This creature with no name—thus adding to his inhuman traits—is of such loathsome appearance that all who see him are filled with horror and disgust. Innately kind, the creature is transformed by personal loneliness and encounters with fearful humans into a monster whose rage is directed toward Frankenstein and his family. Pursuit becomes the novel's theme as the monster chases his creator across pitiless, ice-filled seas to a grim conclusion.

Frankenstein's tale is framed within a second story that concerns Robert Walton, an English sailor who seeks fame by making "a voyage of discovery towards the north pole." It is during this voyage that Walton meets Frankenstein, takes him on board ship, and hears his strange story. Walton's letters report his own exploits and those of Frankenstein and the monster, each in his own words.

Shelley intended *Frankenstein* to be a morality fable about unbridled ambition, as indicated by the subtitle, *The Modern Prometheus*. In Greek myth, Prometheus was a Titan who created the first man and woman and brought them mixed gifts, fire and sorrows. The novel's Prometheus is both Frankenstein and Walton. Together they symbolize knowledge pursued regardless of cost. This moral reflected Europe's reactionary mood in post-Napoleonic times, a period marked by economic depression and political repression.

Mary Wollstonecraft Shelley (1797–1851) had excellent literary ties, and this may have inspired her to become a writer. The daughter of the novelist William Godwin and the feminist Mary Wollstonecraft, she eloped with the poet Percy Bysshe Shelley, causing a scandal. She began *Frankenstein* in Switzerland in the summer of 1817 while recovering from the birth of her second child. The novel was sparked by an evening of ghost stories told by the poets Shelley and Lord Byron. Mary Shelley was then only twenty years old.

Reading the Selections

The selections from Chapters IV and V of *Frankenstein* give Frankenstein's story—as recorded by Walton—of the "birth" of the monster. In telling his story, the doctor knows it is too late for himself—he accepts his ultimate death at the hands of the monster—but he wants Walton to avoid a similar fate by adopting a new moral code: Stifle ambition if it weakens natural feelings. If ambition were to be controlled, he reasoned, then "America would have been discovered more gradually, and the empires of Mexico and Peru had not been destroyed." Frankenstein—and Shelley—thus make a plea for a global family united by mutual ties of affection.

Chapter IV

. . .

One of the phaenomena which had peculiarly attracted my attention was the structure of the human frame, and, indeed, any animal endued with life. Whence, I often asked myself, did the principle of life proceed? It was a bold question, and one which has ever been considered as a mystery: yet with how many things are we upon the brink of becoming acquainted, if cowardice or carelessness did not restrain our enquiries. I revolved these circumstances in my mind and determined thenceforth to apply myself more particularly to those branches of natural philosophy which relate to physiology. Unless I had been animated by an almost supernatural enthusiasm, my application to this study would have been irksome and almost intolerable. To examine the causes of life, we must first have recourse to death. I became acquainted with the science of anatomy, but this was not sufficient; I must also observe the natural decay and corruption of the human body. In my education my father had taken the greatest precautions that my mind should be impressed with no supernatural horrors. I do not ever remember to have trembled at a tale of superstition or to have feared the apparition of a spirit. Darkness had no effect upon my fancy, and a churchyard was to me merely the receptacle of bodies deprived of life, which, from being the seat of beauty and strength, had become food for the worm. Now I was led to examine the cause and progress of this decay and forced to spend days and nights in vaults and charnel-houses. My attention was fixed upon every object the most insupportable to the delicacy of the human feelings. I saw how the fine form of man was degraded and wasted; I beheld the corruption of death succeed to the blooming cheek of life; I saw how the worm inherited the wonders of the eye and brain. I paused, examining and analysing all the minutiae of causation, as exemplified in the change from life to death, and death to life, until from the midst of this darkness a sudden light broke in upon me—a light so brilliant and wondrous, yet so simple, that while I became dizzy with the immensity of the prospect which it illustrated, I was surprized that among so many men of genius who had directed their enquiries towards the same science, that I alone should be reserved to discover so astonishing a secret.

Remember, I am not recording the vision of a madman. The sun does not more certainly shine in the heavens than that which I now affirm is true. Some miracle might have produced it, yet the stages of the discovery were distinct and probable. After days and nights of incredible labour and fatigue, I succeeded in discovering the cause of generation and life; nay, more, I became myself capable of bestowing animation upon lifeless matter.

The astonishment which I had at first experienced on this discovery soon gave place to delight and rapture. After so much time spent in painful labour, to arrive at once at the summit of my desires was the most gratifying consummation of my toils. But this discovery was so great and overwhelming that all the steps by which I had been progressively led to it were obliterated, and I beheld only the result. What had been the study and desire of the wisest men since the creation of the world was now within my grasp. Not that, like a magic scene, it all opened upon me at once: the information I had obtained was of a nature rather to direct my endeavours so soon as I should point them towards the object of my search than to exhibit that object already accomplished. I was like the Arabian who had been buried with the dead and found a passage to life, aided only by one glimmering and seemingly ineffectual light.

I see by your eagerness and the wonder and hope which your eyes express, my friend, that you expect to be informed of the secret with which I am acquainted; that cannot be; listen patiently until the end of my story, and you will easily perceive why I am reserved upon that subject. I will not lead you on, unguarded and ardent as I then was, to your destruction and infallible misery. Learn from me, if not by my precepts, at least by my example, how dangerous is the acquirement of knowledge and how much happier that man is who believes his native town to be the world, than he who aspires to become greater than his nature will allow.

When I found so astonishing a power placed within my hands, I hesitated a long time concerning the manner in which I should employ it. Although I possessed the capacity of bestowing animation, yet to prepare a frame for the reception of it, with all its intricacies of fibres, muscles, and veins, still remained a work of inconceivable difficulty and labour. I doubted at first whether I should attempt the creation of a being like myself, or one of simpler organization; but my imagination was too much exalted by my first success to permit me to doubt of my ability to give life to an animal as complex and wonderful as man. The materials at present within my command hardly appeared adequate to so arduous an undertaking, but I doubted not that I should ultimately succeed. I prepared myself for a multitude of reverses; my operations might be incessantly baffled, and at last my work be imperfect; yet when I considered the improvement which every day takes place in science and mechanics, I was encouraged to hope my present attempts would at least lay the foundations of future success. Nor could I consider the magnitude and complexity of my plan as any argument of its impracticability. It was with these feelings that I began the creation of a human being. As the minuteness of the parts formed a great hindrance to my speed, I resolved, contrary to my first intention, to make the being of a gigantic stature; that is to say, about eight feet in height, and proportionately large. After having formed this determination and having spent some months in successfully collecting and arranging my materials, I began.

No one can conceive the variety of feelings which bore me onwards, like a hurricane, in the first enthusiasm of success. Life and death appeared to me ideal bounds, which I should first break through, and pour a torrent of light into our dark world. A new species would bless me as its creator and source; many happy and excellent natures would owe their being to me. No father could claim the gratitude of his child so completely as I should deserve theirs. Pursuing these reflections, I thought that if I could bestow animation upon lifeless matter, I might in process of time (although I now found it impossible) renew life where death had apparently devoted the body to corruption.

These thoughts supported my spirits, while I pursued my undertaking with unremitting ardour. My cheek had grown pale with study, and my person had become emaciated with confinement. Sometimes, on the very brink of certainty, I failed; yet still I clung to the hope which the next day or the next hour might realize. One secret which I alone possessed was the hope to which I had dedicated myself; and the moon gazed on my midnight labours, while, with unrelaxed and breathless eagerness, I pursued nature to her hiding-places. Who shall conceive the horrors of my secret toil as I dabbled among the unhallowed damps of the grave or tortured the living animal to animate the lifeless clay? My limbs now tremble, and my eyes swim with the remembrance; but then a resistless and almost frantic impulse urged me forward; I seemed to have lost all soul or sensation but for this one pursuit. It was indeed but a passing trance, that only made me feel with renewed acuteness so soon as, the unnatural stimulus ceasing to operate, I had returned to my old habits. I collected bones from charnel-houses and disturbed, with profane fingers, the tremendous secrets of the human frame. In a solitary chamber, or rather cell, at the top of the house, and separated from all the other apartments by a gallery and staircase, I kept my workshop of filthy creation: my eyeballs were starting from their sockets in attending to the details of my employment. The dissecting room and the slaughterhouse furnished many of my materials; and often did my human nature turn with loathing from my occupation, whilst, still urged on by an eagerness which perpetually increased, I brought my work near to a conclusion.

The summer months passed while I was thus engaged, heart and soul, in one pursuit. It was a most beautiful season; never did the fields bestow a more plentiful harvest or the vines yield a more luxuriant vintage: but my eyes were insensible to the charms of nature. And the same feelings which made me neglect the scenes around me caused me also to forget those friends who were so many miles absent, and whom I had not seen for so long a time. I knew my silence disquieted them, and I well remembered the words of my father: 'I know that while you are pleased with yourself you will think of us with affection, and we shall hear regularly from you. You must pardon me if I regard any interruption in your correspondence as a proof that your other duties are equally neglected.'

I knew well therefore what would be my father's feelings, but I could not tear my thoughts from my employment, loathsome in itself, but which had taken an irresistible hold of my imagination. I wished, as it were, to procrastinate all that related to my feelings of affection until the great object, which swallowed up every habit of my nature, should be completed.

I then thought that my father would be unjust if he as- cribed my neglect to vice or faultiness on my part, but I am now convinced that he was justified in conceiving that I should not be altogether free from blame. A human being in perfection ought always to preserve a calm and peace- ful mind and never to allow passion or a transitory desire to disturb his tranquillity. I do not think that the pursuit of knowledge is an exception to this rule. If the study to which you apply yourself has a tendency to weaken your affections and to destroy your taste for those simple plea- sures in which no alloy can possibly mix, then that study is certainly unlawful, that is to say, not befitting the human mind. If this rule were always observed; if no man allowed any pursuit whatsoever to interfere with the tranquillity of his domestic affections, Greece had not been enslaved, Caesar would have spared his country, America would have been discovered more gradually, and the empires of Mexico and Peru had not been destroyed.

But I forget that I am moralizing in the most interest- ing part of my tale, and your looks remind me to proceed.

My father made no reproach in his letters and only took notice of my silence by enquiring into my occupa- tions more particularly than before. Winter, spring, and summer passed away during my labours; but I did not watch the blossom or the expanding leaves—sights which before always yielded me supreme delight—so deeply was I engrossed in my occupation. The leaves of that year had withered before my work drew near to a close, and now every day showed me more plainly how well I had succeeded. But my enthusiasm was checked by my anxi- ety, and I appeared rather like one doomed by slavery to toil in the mines, or any other unwholesome trade than an artist occupied by his favourite employment. Every night I was oppressed by a slow fever, and I became nervous to a most painful degree; the fall of a leaf startled me, and I shunned my fellow creatures as if I had been guilty of a crime. Sometimes I grew alarmed at the wreck I perceived that I had become; the energy of my purpose alone sus- tained me: my labours would soon end, and I believed that exercise and amusement would then drive away in- cipient disease; and I promised myself both of these when my creation should be complete.

Chapter V

It was on a dreary night of November that I beheld the ac- complishment of my toils. With an anxiety that almost amounted to agony, I collected the instruments of life around me, that I might infuse a spark of being into the lifeless thing that lay at my feet. It was already one in the morning; the rain pattered dismally against the panes, and my candle was nearly burnt out, when, by the glimmer of the half-extinguished light, I saw the dull yellow eye of the creature open; it breathed hard, and a convulsive motion agitated its limbs.

How can I describe my emotions at this catastrophe, or how delineate the wretch whom with such infinite pains and care I had endeavoured to form? His limbs were in proportion, and I had selected his features as beautiful. Beautiful! Great God! His yellow skin scarcely covered the work of muscles and arteries beneath; his hair was of a lustrous black, and flowing; his teeth of pearly whiteness; but these luxuriances only formed a more horrid contrast with his watery eyes, that seemed almost of the same colour as the dun-white sockets in which they were set, his shrivelled complexion and straight black lips.

The different accidents of life are not so changeable as the feelings of human nature. I had worked hard for nearly two years, for the sole purpose of infusing life into an inanimate body. For this I had deprived myself of rest and health. I had desired it with an ardour that far ex- ceeded moderation; but now that I had finished, the beauty of the dream vanished, and breathless horror and disgust filled my heart. Unable to endure the aspect of the being I had created, I rushed out of the room and contin- ued a long time traversing my bedchamber, unable to compose my mind to sleep. At length lassitude succeeded to the tumult I had before endured, and I threw myself on the bed in my clothes, endeavouring to seek a few mo- ments of forgetfulness. But it was in vain; I slept, indeed, but I was disturbed by the wildest dreams. I thought I saw Elizabeth, in the bloom of health, walking in the streets of Ingolstadt. Delighted and surprised, I embraced her, but as I imprinted the first kiss on her lips, they became livid with the hue of death; her features appeared to change, and I thought that I held the corpse of my dead mother in my arms; a shroud enveloped her form, and I saw the grave-worms crawling in the folds of the flannel. I started from my sleep with horror; a cold dew covered my fore- head, my teeth chattered, and every limb became con- vulsed; when, by the dim and yellow light of the moon, as it forced its way through the window shutters, I beheld the wretch—the miserable monster whom I had created. He held up the curtain of the bed; and his eyes, if eyes they may be called, were fixed on me. His jaws opened, and he muttered some inarticulate sounds, while a grin wrinkled his cheeks. He might have spoken, but I did not hear; one hand was stretched out, seemingly to detain me, but I es- caped and rushed downstairs. I took refuge in the court- yard belonging to the house which I inhabited, where I remained during the rest of the night, walking up and down in the greatest agitation, listening attentively, catch- ing and fearing each sound as if it were to announce the approach of the daemoniacal corpse to which I had so mis- erably given life.

Oh! No mortal could support the horror of that coun- tenance. A mummy again endued with animation could not be so hideous as that wretch. I had gazed on him while unfinished; he was ugly then, but when those muscles and joints were rendered capable of motion, it became a thing such as even Dante could not have conceived.

I passed the night wretchedly. Sometimes my pulse beat so quickly and hardly that I felt the palpitation of every artery; at others, I nearly sank to the ground through languor and extreme weakness. Mingled with this horror, I felt the bitterness of disappointment; dreams that had been my food and pleasant rest for so long a space were now become a hell to me; and the change was so rapid, the overthrow so complete! . . .

GEORGE GORDON, LORD BYRON

Selection from *Don Juan*

George Gordon, Lord Byron (1788–1824), was a titanic figure who was regarded by his generation as the spirit of Romanticism. Although his popularity has waned today, he remains an influential writer of the Romantic period. Unlike Wordsworth (see "Tintern Abbey"), who extolled the unity of the human and natural realms and avoided direct references to politics, Byron was a European poet who was actively engaged with the major people and issues of his time. Through his poems, he sought to identify patterns linking the present to the recent and distant past.

What made these poems memorable was that Byron made himself their center, speaking in either his own voice or through a heroic surrogate. From his first to his last works, he thought of himself as both a man and a poet with a mission, even if dimly understood. Thus he represented himself in his poems as a figure of destiny on whom both the broad sweep of history and the entire Western poetic tradition converged. Byron's pose as a world-historical figure ruled by his "star" became an enduring image of the Romantic era and influenced later artists and writers, most notably Nietzsche (see *The Gay Science*, etc.).

The crucial dates in Byron's life are 1812, when he soared to fame with *Childe Harold's Pilgrimage*, a poem about his travels on the continent; 1816, when his marriage failed amid scandal involving charges of incest (probably true) with his half-sister, causing him to flee England, never to return; and 1824, when he died in Greece, in pursuit of republican ideals and fighting for Greek independence.

Reading the Selection

Byron's greatest poem, *Don Juan* (Cantos I and II, 1819; Cantos III–V, 1821; and Cantos VI–XXVI, 1823–1824), dates from his years of exile, when he declared himself "born for opposition." Reflecting despair over the future, the poem condemned the political reaction set in motion by England and its allies after Napoleon's defeat. It also reflected Byron's rejection of his earlier Romanticism as well as the entire Romantic movement, especially the Lake Poets (see "Tintern Abbey"). *Don Juan,* with its colloquial voice, republicanism, and celebration of life outside existing moral and social codes, was meant to be an antidote to conservative Lake poetry.

This poem is ostensibly about the notorious Spanish seducer Don Juan, whom Byron transforms into a virtuous hero. Like Byron, the Don is a culturally and socially alienated aristocrat, an ideal alter ego for the poet's plan to expose English hypocrisy. In the poem, Don Juan's story forms only the first level, extending from 1789 until the Don's death on the guillotine in 1793. A second level ranges over the period 1789 to 1823, showing how Europe betrayed its best political ideals; and a third level covers Byron's meteoric years from *Childe Harold* until his disgrace. Using these levels to comment upon one another, Byron conveys both a sense of distance and immediacy, as if time were frozen and everything were known.

This selection constitutes 56 of the 222 verses in Canto I. The verse form is *ottava rima* (Italian, "eighth rhyme"), an eight-line stanza rhyming abababcc. (A word of advice: the pronunciation of Don Juan is English; that is, the second syllable rhymes with "new one" and "true one.") *Ottava rima* had earlier been used by English poets such as Behn (see "The Willing Mistress"), but Byron followed Italian writers who employed it for serio-comic effect. In *Don Juan,* this form gave him the artistic freedom that the wide-ranging subject matter demanded.

—⁓—

Canto I

1

I want a hero: an uncommon want,
    When every year and month sends forth a new one,
Till, after cloying the gazettes with cant,
    The age discovers he is not the true one;
Of such as these I should not care to vaunt,
    I'll therefore take our ancient friend Don Juan—
We all have seen him, in the pantomime,
Sent to the Devil somewhat ere his time.

. . . .

6

Most epic poets plunge *"in media res"*
    (Horace makes this the heroic turnpike road),
And then your hero tells, when'er you please,
    What went before—by way of episode,
While seated after dinner at his ease,
    Beside his mistress in some soft abode,
Palace, or garden, paradise, or cavern,
Which serves the happy couple for a tavern.   10

7

That is the usual method, but not mine—
    My way is to begin with the beginning;
The regularity of my design
    Forbids all wandering as the worst of sinning,   20
And therefore I shall open with a line
    (Although it cost me half an hour in spinning),
Narrating somewhat of Don Juan's father,
And also of his mother, if you'd rather.

8

In Seville was he born, a pleasant city,
    Famous for oranges and women—he
Who has not seen it will be much to pity,
    So says the proverb—and I quite agree;
Of all the Spanish towns is none more pretty,
    Cadiz perhaps—but that you soon may see;   30
Don Juan's parents lived beside the river,
A noble stream, and called the Guadalquivir.

9

His father's name was José—*Don,* of course—
    A true Hidalgo, free from every stain
Of Moor or Hebrew blood, he traced his source
    Through the most Gothic gentlemen of Spain;

A better cavalier ne'er mounted horse,
    Or, being mounted, e'er got down again,
Than José, who begot our hero, who
Begot—but that's to come—Well, to renew: 40

10

His mother was a learnéd lady, famed
    For every branch of every science known—
In every Christian language ever named,
    With virtues equaled by her wit alone:
She made the cleverest people quite ashamed,
    And even the good with inward envy groan,
Finding themselves so very much exceeded,
In their own way, by all the things that she did.

11

Her memory was a mine: she knew by heart
    All Calderon and greater part of Lopé,   50
So, that if any actor missed his part,
    She could have served him for the prompter's copy;
For her Feinagle's were an useless art,
    And he himself obliged to shut up shop—he
Could never make a memory so fine as
That which adorned the brain of Donna Inez.

12

Her favorite science was the mathematical,
    Her noblest virtue was her magnanimity,
Her wit (she sometimes tried at wit) was Attic all,
    Her serious sayings darkened to sublimity;   60
In short, in all things she was fairly what I call
    A prodigy—her morning dress was dimity,
Her evening silk, or, in the summer, muslin,
And other stuffs, with which I won't stay puzzling.

13

She knew the Latin—that is, "the Lord's prayer,"
    And Greek—the alphabet—I'm nearly sure;
She read some French romances here and there,
    Although her mode of speaking was not pure;
For native Spanish she had no great care,
    At least her conversation was obscure;   70
Her thoughts were theorems, her words a problem,
As if she deemed that mystery would ennoble 'em.

. . . .

17

Oh! she was perfect past all parallel—
  Of any modern female saint's comparison;
So far above the cunning powers of Hell,
  Her Guardian Angel had given up his garrison;
Even her minutest motions went as well
  As those of the best time-piece made by Harrison;
In virtues nothing earthly could surpass her,
Save thine "incomparable oil," Macassar!   80

. . . .

23

Don José and his lady quarrelled—*why*,
  Not any of the many could divine,
Though several thousand people chose to try,
  'Twas surely no concern of theirs nor mine;
I loath that low vice—curiosity;
  But if there's anything in which I shine,
'Tis in arranging all my friends' affairs,
Not having, of my own, domestic cares.

24

And so I interfered, and with the best
  Intentions, but their treatment was not kind; 90
I think the foolish people were possessed,
  For neither of them could I ever find,
Although their porter afterwards confessed—
  But that's no matter, and the worst's behind,
For little Juan o'er me threw, down stairs,
A pail of housemaid's water unawares.

25

A little curly-headed, good-for-nothing,
  And mischief-making monkey from his birth;
His parents ne'er agreed except in doting
  Upon the most unquiet imp on earth; 100
Instead of quarrelling, had they been but both in
  Their senses, they'd have sent young master forth
To school, or had him soundly whipped at home,
To teach him manners for the time to come.

26

Don José and the Donna Inez led
  For some time an unhappy sort of life,
Wishing each other, not divorced, but dead;
  They lived respectably as man and wife,
Their conduct was exceedingly well-bred,
  And gave no outward signs of inward strife, 110
Until at length the smothered fire broke out,
And put the business past all kind of doubt.

27

For Inez called some druggists and physicians,
  And tried to prove her loving lord was *mad*,
But as he had some lucid intermissions,
  She next decided he was only *bad*;
Yet when they asked her for her depositions,
  No sort of explanation could be had,
Save that her duty both to man and God
Required this conduct—which seemed very odd. 120

28

She kept a journal, where his faults were noted,
  And opened certain trunks of books and letters,
All which might, if occasion served, be quoted;
  And then she had all Seville for abettors,
Besides her good old grandmother (who doted);
  The hearers of her case became repeaters,
Then advocates, inquisitors, and judges,
Some for amusement, others for old grudges.

29

And then this best and meekest woman bore
  With such serenity her husband's woes, 130
Just as the Spartan ladies did of yore,
  Who saw their spouses killed, and nobly chose
Never to say a word about them more—
  Calmly she heard each calumny that rose,
And saw *his* agonies with such sublimity,
That all the world exclaimed, "What magnanimity!"

. . . .

32

Their friends had tried at reconciliation,
  Then their relations, who made matters worse.
('Twere hard to tell upon a like occasion
  To whom it may be best to have recourse— 140
I can't say much for friend or yet relation):
  The lawyers did their utmost for divorce,
But scarce a fee was paid on either side
Before, unluckily, Don José died.

. . . .

38

Sagest of women, even of widows, she
  Resolved that Juan should be quite a paragon,
And worthy of the noblest pedigree,
  (His Sire was of Castile, his Dam from Aragon):
Then, for accomplishments of chivalry,
  In case our Lord the King should go to war again, 150
He learned the arts of riding, fencing, gunnery,
And how to scale a fortress—or a nunnery.

39

But that which Donna Inez most desired,
   And saw into herself each day before all
The learnéd tutors whom for him she hired,
   Was, that his breeding should be strictly moral:
Much into all his studies she inquired,
   And so they were submitted first to her, all,
Arts, sciences—no branch was made a mystery
To Juan's eyes, excepting natural history.   160

40

The languages, especially the dead,
   The sciences, and most of all the abstruse,
The arts, at least all such as could be said
   To be the most remote from common use,
In all these he was much and deeply read:
   But not a page of anything that's loose,
Or hints continuation of the species,
Was ever suffered, lest he should grow vicious.

41

His classic studies made a little puzzle,
   Because of filthy loves of gods and goddesses,   170
Who in the earlier ages raised a bustle,
   But never put on pantaloons or bodices;
His reverend tutors had at times a tussle,
   And for their Aeneids, Iliads, and Odysseys,
Were forced to make an odd sort of apology,
For Donna Inez dreaded the Mythology.

42

Ovid's a rake, as half his verses show him,
   Anacreon's morals are a still worse sample,
Catullus scarcely has a decent poem,
   I don't think Sappho's Ode a good example,   180
Although Longinus tells us there is no hymn
   Where the Sublime soars forth on wings more ample;
But Virgil's songs are pure, except that horrid one
Beginning with *"Formosum Pastor Corydon."*

43

Lucretius' irreligion is too strong
   For early stomachs, to prove wholesome food;
I can't help thinking Juvenal was wrong,
   Although no doubt his real intent was good,
For speaking out so plainly in his song,
   So much indeed as to be downright rude;   190
And then what proper person can be partial
To all those nauseous epigrams of Martial?

. . . .

44

Juan was taught from out the best edition,
   Expurgated by learnéd men, who place,
Judiciously, from out the schoolboy's vision,
   The grosser parts; but, fearful to deface
Too much their modest bard by this omission,
   And pitying sore his mutilated case,
They only add them all in an appendix,
Which saves, in fact, the trouble of an index.   200

. . . .

47

Sermons he read, and lectures he endured,
   And homilies, and lives of all the saints;
To Jerome and to Chrysostom inured,
   He did not take such studies for restraints;
But how Faith is acquired, and then insured,
   So well not one of the aforesaid paints
As Saint Augustine in his fine Confessions,
Which make the reader envy his transgressions.

. . . .

54

Young Juan now was sixteen years of age,
   Tall, handsome, slender, but well knit: he seemed   210
Active, though not so sprightly, as a page;
   And everybody but his mother deemed
Him almost man; but she flew in a rage
   And bit her lips (for else she might have screamed)
If any said so—for to be precocious
Was in her eyes a thing the most atrocious.

55

Amongst her numerous acquaintance, all
   Selected for discretion and devotion,
There was the Donna Julia, whom to call
   Pretty were but to give a feeble notion   220
Of many charms in her as natural
   As sweetness to the flower, or salt to Ocean,
Her zone to Venus, or his bow to Cupid,
(But this last simile is trite and stupid.)

. . . .

60

Her eye (I'm very fond of handsome eyes)
   Was large and dark, suppressing half its fire
Until she spoke, then through its soft disguise
   Flashed an expression more of pride than ire,
And love than either; and there would arise
   A something in them which was not desire,   230
But would have been, perhaps, but for the soul
Which struggled through and chastened down the whole.

61

Her glossy hair was clustered o'er a brow
   Bright with intelligence, and fair, and smooth;
Her eyebrow's shape was like the aërial bow,
   Her cheek all purple with the beam of youth,
Mounting, at times, to a transparent glow,
   As if her veins ran lightning; she, in sooth,
Possessed an air and grace by no means common:
Her stature tall—I hate a dumpy woman.   240

62

Wedded she was some years, and to a man
   Of fifty, and such husbands are in plenty;
And yet, I think, instead of such a ONE
   'Twere better to have TWO of five-and-twenty,
Especially in countries near the sun:
   And now I think on't, *"mi vien in mente,"*
Ladies even of the most uneasy virtue
Prefer a spouse whose age is short of thirty.

. . . .

69

Juan she saw, and, as a pretty child,
   Caressed him often—such a thing might be   250
Quite innocently done, and harmless styled,
   When she had twenty years, and thirteen he;
But I am not so sure I should have smiled
   When he was sixteen, Julia twenty-three;
These few short years make wondrous alterations,
Particularly amongst sun-burnt nations.

70

Whate'er the cause might be, they had become
   Changed; for the dame grew distant, the youth shy,
Their looks cast down, their greetings almost dumb,
   And much embarrassment in either eye;   260
There surely will be little doubt with some
   That Donna Julia knew the reason why,
But as for Juan, he had no more notion
Than he who never saw the sea of Ocean.

71

Yet Julia's very coldness still was kind,
   And tremulously gentle her small hand
Withdrew itself from his, but left behind
   A little pressure, thrilling, and so bland
And slight, so very slight, that to the mind
   'Twas but a doubt; but ne'er magician's wand   270
Wrought change with all Armida's fairy art
Like what this light touch left on Juan's heart.

72

And if she met him, though she smiled no more,
   She looked a sadness sweeter than her smile,
As if her heart had deeper thoughts in store
   She must not own, but cherished more the while
For that compression in its burning core;
   Even Innocence itself has many a wile,
And will not dare to trust itself with truth,
And Love is taught hypocrisy from youth.   280

. . . .

75

Poor Julia's heart was in an awkward state;
   She felt it going, and resolved to make
The noblest efforts for herself and mate,
   For Honor's, Pride's, Religion's, Virtue's sake:
Her resolutions were most truly great,
   And almost might have made a Tarquin quake:
She prayed the Virgin Mary for her grace,
As being the best judge of a lady's case.

76

She vowed she never would see Juan more,
   And next day paid a visit to his mother,   290
And looked extremely at the opening door,
   Which, by the Virgin's grace, let in another;
Grateful she was, and yet a little sore—
   Again it opens, it can be no other,
'Tis surely Juan now—No! I'm afraid
That night the Virgin was no further prayed.

77

She now determined that a virtuous woman
   Should rather face and overcome temptation,
That flight was base and dastardly, and no man
   Should ever give her heart the least sensation,   300
That is to say, a thought beyond the common
   Preference, that we must feel, upon occasion,
For people who are pleasanter than others,
But then they only seem so many brothers.

78

And even if by chance—and who can tell?
   The Devil's so very sly—she should discover
That all within was not so very well,
   And, if still free, that such or such a lover
Might please perhaps, a virtuous wife can quell
   Such thoughts, and be the better when they're over;   310
And if the man should ask, 'tis but denial:
I recommend young ladies to make trial.

79

And, then, there are such things as Love divine,
   Bright and immaculate, unmixed and pure,
Such as the angels think so very fine,
   And matrons, who would be no less secure,
Platonic, perfect, "just such love as mine";
   Thus Julia said—and thought so, to be sure;
And so I'd have her think, were *I* the man
On whom her reveries celestial ran.   320

. . . .

90

Young Juan wandered by the glassy brooks,
   Thinking unutterable things; he threw
Himself at length within the leafy nooks
   Where the wild branch of the cork forest grew;
There poets find materials for their books,
   And every now and then we read them through,
So that their plan and prosody are eligible,
Unless, like Wordsworth, they prove unintelligible.

91

He, Juan (and not Wordsworth), so pursued   330
   His self-communion with his own high soul,
Until his mighty heart, in its great mood,
   Had mitigated part, though not the whole
Of its disease; he did the best he could
   With things not very subject to control,
And turned, without perceiving his condition,
Like Coleridge, into a metaphysician.

92

He thought about himself, and the whole earth,
   Of man the wonderful, and of the stars,
And how the deuce they ever could have birth;
   And then he thought of earthquakes, and of wars,   340
How many miles the moon might have in girth,
   Of air-balloons, and of the many bars
To perfect knowledge of the boundless skies;—
And then he thought of Donna Julia's eyes.

93

In thoughts like these true Wisdom may discern
   Longings sublime, and aspirations high,
Which some are born with, but the most part learn
   To plague themselves withal, they know not why:
'Twas strange that one so young should thus concern
   His brain about the action of the sky;   350
If *you* think 'twas Philosophy that this did,
I can't help thinking puberty assisted.

94

He pored upon the leaves, and on the flowers,
   And heard a voice in all the winds; and then
He thought of wood-nymphs and immortal bowers,
   And how the goddesses came down to men:
He missed the pathway, he forgot the hours,
   And when he looked upon his watch again,
He found how much old Time had been a winner—
He also found that he had lost his dinner.   360

. . . .

104

'Twas on the sixth of June, about the hour
   Of half-past six—perhaps still nearer seven—
When Julia sate within as pretty a bower
   As e'er held houri in that heathenish heaven
Described by Mahomet, and Anacreon Moore,
   To whom the lyre and laurels have been given,
With all the trophies of triumphant song—
He won them well, and may he wear them long!

105

She sate, but not alone; I know not well   370
   How this same interview had taken place,
And even if I knew, I should not tell—
   People should hold their tongues in any case;
No matter how or why the thing befell,
   But there were she and Juan, face to face—
When two such faces are so, 'twould be wise,
But very difficult, to shut their eyes.

106

How beautiful she looked! her conscious heart
   Glowed in her cheek, and yet she felt no wrong:
Oh Love! how perfect is thy mystic art,
   Strengthening the weak, and trampling on the strong!   380
How self-deceitful is the sagest part
   Of mortals whom thy lure hath led along!
The precipice she stood on was immense,
So was her creed in her own innocence.

107

She thought of her own strength, and Juan's youth,
   And of the folly of all prudish fears,
Victorious Virtue, and domestic Truth,
   And then of Don Alfonso's fifty years:
I wish these last had not occurred, in sooth,
   Because that number rarely much endears,   390
And through all climes, the snowy and the sunny,
Sounds ill in love, whate'er it may in money.

. . . .

111

The hand which still held Juan's, by degrees
   Gently, but palpably confirmed its grasp,
As if it said, "Detain me, if you please";
   Yet there's no doubt she only meant to clasp
His fingers with a pure Platonic squeeze;
   She would have shrunk as from a toad, or asp,
Had she imagined such a thing could rouse
A feeling dangerous to a prudent spouse.   400

112

I cannot know what Juan thought of this,
   But what he did, is much what you would do;
His young lip thanked it with a grateful kiss,
   And then, abashed at its own joy, withdrew
In deep despair, lest he had done amiss—
   Love is so very timid when 'tis new:
She blushed, and frowned not, but she strove to speak,
And held her tongue, her voice was grown so weak.

113

The sun set, and up rose the yellow moon:
   The Devil's in the moon for mischief; they   410
Who called her CHASTE, methinks, began too soon
   Their nomenclature; there is not a day,
The longest, not the twenty-first of June,
   Sees half the business in a wicked way,
On which three single hours of moonshine smile—
And then she looks so modest all the while!

114

There is a dangerous silence in that hour,
   A stillness, which leaves room for the full soul
To open all itself, without the power
   Of calling wholly back its self-control;   420

The silver light which, hallowing tree and tower,
   Sheds beauty and deep softness o'er the whole,
Breathes also to the heart, and o'er it throws
A loving languor, which is not repose.

115

And Julia sate with Juan, half embraced
   And half retiring from the glowing arm,
Which trembled like the bosom where 'twas placed;
   Yet still she must have thought there was no harm,
Or else 'twere easy to withdraw her waist;
   But then the situation had its charm,   430
And then—God knows what next—I can't go on;
I'm almost sorry that I e'er begun.

116

Oh Plato! Plato! you have paved the way,
   With your confounded fantasies, to more
Immoral conduct by the fancied sway
   Your system feigns o'er the controlless core
Of human hearts, than all the long array
   Of poets and romancers:—You're a bore,
A charlatan, a coxcomb—and have been,
At best, no better than a go-between.   440

117

And Julia's voice was lost, except in sighs,
   Until too late for useful conversation;
The tears were gushing from her gentle eyes,
   I wish, indeed, they had not had occasion;
But who, alas! can love, and then be wise?
   Not that Remorse did not oppose Temptation;
A little still she strove, and much repented,
And whispering "I will ne'er consent"—consented.

. . . .

PERCY BYSSHE SHELLEY
Poems

Today, Percy Bysshe Shelley (1792–1822) is regarded as a great Romantic poet; in his own day, however, his works were not widely known. Of about 450 poems, only 70 or so were in print when he died. Poems issued during his life, such as *Queen Mab* (1813), gave him a reputation for atheism and radicalism. Moreover, his scandalous life cast a shadow over his poetry and obscured its true meaning.

When Shelley fled England in 1818, he left behind a legend of bohemianism and rebellion dating from early youth. As a student at Oxford, he was expelled for refusing to disown an atheistical pamphlet he had written. This expulsion led to a break with his wealthy father, who later disinherited him. After university, he offended middle-class norms by sharing households with like-minded friends, including unattached women. Both of his marriages began as elopements. The second elopement hastened the suicide of his first wife; her family then obtained a court order denying him access to his children. The second marriage, to Mary Wollstonecraft Godwin, was more stable; still, the Shelleys fled England for the continent both because of debts and for the not unreasonable fear that their children might also be taken away.

Shelley's last four years, wandering in Italy, brought maturity and some of his best poems, including *Prometheus Unbound* (1820), the story of the Titan persecuted by divine forces for his efforts to help humanity—a work whose subtext was Shelley's own trials. Back home, the legend of "Shelley-the-Monster" grew so that few mourned Shelley's drowning in Italy a month before his thirtieth birthday.

This century's critics have discovered a Shelley much different from the one of legend. He is a Platonist who advocated (a) the doctrine of Platonic love, which holds that physical beauty is secondary to intellectual beauty, and (b) the idea that the poet is an inspired person ("the unacknowledged legislator of the world"). He is also considered a reformer today and less of a revolutionary, because he was repelled by violence of all kinds; and his causes, such as nonviolence, democracy, free speech, and vegetarianism, have entered the mainstream.

Reading the Selections

"Ozymandias" (1817) and "England in 1819" (1819) are Shelley's most splendid sonnets. "Ozymandias" grew out of Romantic Hellenism, which made Greece into an imaginary world where hearts troubled by the present sought nourishment from the glorious past. Shelley's inspiration was a Greek writer's record of an inscription honoring Ozymandias, another name for Egypt's Ramses II. Shelley used the inscription (lines 10–11) to underscore the Platonic theme that human achievement is illusory. In "England in 1819," written during this exile, he described his country in the grip of post-Napoleonic reaction, though he ended with the prediction of a new day.

"Ode to the West Wind" (1820) is one of Shelley's most famous poems. It marked a personal crisis, following the loss of a second child in Italy, and savage reviews of new poems in England. In form, it comprises five sonnets, each built of three *terza rima* verses in the style of Dante (see *The Divine Comedy*) plus an end-couplet. The ode builds in emotional power as it moves along. The images of the first three sonnets—the leaf, the cloud, and the wave—are folded into the fourth sonnet with the words "If I were. . . ." In the fifth sonnet, the poem changes to become a prayer. Typically, the poem ends on a hopeful note: "If Winter comes, can Spring be far behind?"

—※—

"Ozymandias"

I met a traveler from an antique land 1
Who said: Two vast and trunkless legs of stone
Stand in the desert . . . Near them, on the sand,
Half sunk, a shattered visage lies, whose frown,
And wrinkled lip, and sneer of cold command,
Tell that its sculptor well those passions read
Which yet survive, stamped on these lifeless things,

The hand that mocked them, and the heart that fed:
And on the pedestal these words appear: 10
"My name is Ozymandias, king of kings:
Look on my works, ye Mighty, and despair!"
Nothing beside remains. Round the decay
Of that colossal wreck, boundless and bare
The lone and level sands stretch far away.

—※—

"England in 1819"

An old, mad, blind, despised, and dying King; 1
Princes, the dregs of their dull race, who flow
Through public scorn,—mud from a muddy spring;
Rulers who neither see nor feel nor know,
But leechlike to their fainting country cling
Till they drop, blind in blood, without a blow.
A people starved and stabbed in th' untilled field;

An army, whom liberticide and prey
Makes as a two-edged sword to all who wield;
Golden and sanguine laws which tempt and slay; 10
Religion Christless, Godless—a book sealed;
A senate, Time's worst statute, unrepealed—
Are graves from which a glorious Phantom may
Burst, to illumine our tempestuous day.

—※—

"Ode to the West Wind"

I

O wild West Wind, thou breath of Autumn's being, 1
Thou, from whose unseen presence the leaves dead
Are driven, like ghosts from an enchanter fleeing,

Yellow, and black, and pale, and hectic red,
Pestilence-stricken multitudes: O thou,
Who chariotest to their dark wintry bed

The wingéd seeds, where they lie cold and low,
Each like a corpse within its grave, until
Thine azure sister of the Spring shall blow

Her clarion o'er the dreaming earth, and fill 10
(Driving sweet buds like flocks to feed in air)
With living hues and odors plain and hill:

Wild Spirit, which art moving everywhere;
Destroyer and preserver; hear, oh, hear!

II

Thou on whose stream, mid the steep sky's commotion,
Loose clouds like earth's decaying leaves are shed,
Shook from the tangled boughs of Heaven and Ocean,

Angels of rain and lightning: there are spread
On the blue surface of thine aery surge,
Like the bright hair uplifted from the head 20

Of some fierce Maenad, even from the dim verge
Of the horizon to the zenith's height,
The locks of the approaching storm. Thou dirge

Of the dying year, to which this closing night
Will be the dome of a vast sepulcher,
Vaulted with all thy congregated might

Of vapors, from whose solid atmosphere
Black rain, and fire, and hail will burst: oh, hear!

III

Thou who didst waken from his summer dreams
The blue Mediterranean, where he lay,   30
Lulled by the coil of his crystálline streams,

Beside a pumice isle in Baiae's bay
And saw in sleep old palaces and towers
Quivering within the wave's intenser day,

All overgrown with azure moss and flowers
So sweet, the sense faints picturing them! Thou
For whose path the Atlantic's level powers

Cleave themselves into chasms, while far below
The sea-blooms and the oozy woods which wear
The sapless foliage of the ocean, know   40

Thy voice, and suddenly grow gray with fear,
And tremble and despoil themselves; oh, hear!

IV

If I were a dead leaf thou mightest bear;
If I were a swift cloud to fly with thee;
A wave to pant beneath thy power, and share

The impulse of thy strength, only less free
Than thou, O uncontrollable! If even
I were as in my boyhood, and could be

The comrade of thy wanderings over Heaven,
As then, when to outstrip thy skyey speed   50
Scarce seemed a vision; I would ne'er have striven

As thus with thee in prayer in my sore need.
Oh, lift me as a wave, a leaf, a cloud!
I fall upon the thorns of life! I bleed!

A heavy weight of hours has chained and bowed
One too like thee: tameless, and swift, and proud.

V

Make me thy lyre, even as the forest is:
What if my leaves are falling like its own!
The tumult of thy mighty harmonies

Will take from both a deep, autumnal tone,   60
Sweet though in sadness. Be thou, Spirit fierce,
My spirit! Be thou me, impetuous one!

Drive my dead thoughts over the universe
Like withered leaves to quicken a new birth!
And, by the incantation of this verse,

Scatter, as from an unextinguished hearth
Ashes and sparks, my words among mankind!
Be through my lips to unawakened earth

The trumpet of a prophecy! O Wind,
If Winter comes, can Spring be far behind?   70

JOHN KEATS

Poems

Keats was the third of the triumvirate of Romantic poets whose meteoric careers brightened the literary skies of Regency England. A dark period of political reaction and economic downturn, it lasted from 1812 to 1820, when the future George IV was regent for his mad father, King George III. All three poets' talents were abruptly extinguished by early deaths, thereby giving rise to the mystique that has surrounded this poetic trio ever since. Lord Byron was thirty-six when he died of fever in Greece in 1824; Shelley was twenty-nine when he drowned in the sea off northern Italy in 1822; and saddest of all, Keats was twenty-five when he died of tuberculosis in Rome, where he had gone to escape the harsh English winter in 1820. For the romantic imagination, the untimely deaths, in a sense, guaranteed the genius of the three poets.

John Keats (1795–1820), who was little known to his generation, rocketed to fame after his death. The three books of poems issued during his life (comprising about one-third of the 150 poems

GEORG WILHELM FRIEDRICH HEGEL

Selection from *Reason in History*

Hegelianism, the philosophy of the German Georg Wilhelm Friedrich Hegel (1770–1831), dominated Western thought from his time until World War I. Nationalists and conservatives on the right and so-cialists and communists (see Marx and Engels, *The Communist Manifesto*) on the left all claimed him as their own. Hegel's appeal sprang from many sources. He was a genius at borrowing from others, in-cluding Plato and the German philosopher Immanuel Kant (1724–1804), to forge a compelling system meant to supersede older philosophies. He also garnered support because he harmonized the era's main currents of thought, the rationalism of the Enlightenment and the emotionalism of Romanti-cism. Most important, his philosophical arguments offered an option to Judeo-Christian beliefs that were under siege from science and biblical criticism.

The rationalist Hegel approached philosophy in the spirit of medieval mysticism. Obsessed with uncovering the final nature and meaning of the universe and human history, he constructed an all-encompassing metaphysical system that has become fabled for complexity and obscurity. The guiding force of his system is the World Spirit, also known as Reason, Logic, Idea, and Absolute. In his system, philosophy and history are virtually indistinguishable, so that each is the expression of the other though in different guises. Thus history is created by the World Spirit, and at the same time the World Spirit reaches self-awareness through the unfolding of historical events.

Hegel was not the first to employ dialectical reasoning—the belief that growth occurs through the clash of opposites. That honor belongs to the ancient Greek thinker Heraclitus (fl. 500 B.C.). But Hegel's version of the dialectic is the one best known in modern times. In his philosophy, Hegel uses the dialectic to explain how the World Spirit operates. However, the World Spirit, unable to act inde-pendently, enters and guides the masses to its own ends without their awareness, thereby making them part of the dialectical process. On the philosophic level, the dialectic manifests itself as a clash between an idea (thesis) and its adversary (antithesis); in some cases, a resolution (synthesis) may emerge that preserves the best of the opposing forces and thus represents a new and higher stage of life. In contrast, on the history level, the dialectic constitutes a "slaughter bench" on which mortal armies, incarnating opposing ideas of the World Spirit, fight to the death. Because struggle embodies the World Spirit, Hegel praised warfare for its benefits to society.

Reading the Selection

This selection from Hegel's *Reason in History*, also called *Lectures on the Philosophy of History*, was pub-lished posthumously in 1837. The text represents Hegel's lecture notes delivered at the University of Berlin, where he became professor in 1818. The lectures have been supplemented and clarified by students' notes. As a professor, Hegel was so revered by state officials that enemies viewed him as the mouthpiece of Prussia's reactionary monarchy. In fairness, however, he was a moderate lib-eral, supporting constitutional government but preferring monarchy to democracy and opposing individualism.

Several key Hegelian ideas appear here:

1. Reason considered as Idea, Nature, and Spirit
2. Three main phases of world history: Asiatic, rule by absolute monarch; Greco-Roman, with freedom for the few; and Germanic-European, typified by nation-states devoted to freedom for all under the law
3. Freedom, or obedience to law, as the goal of history
4. The passions in history—a Romantic idea
5. The State as the realization of the divine Idea

—⁓—

III. The Idea of History and Its Realization

The question of how Reason is determined in itself and what its relation is to the world coincides with the question, *What is the ultimate purpose of the world?* This question implies that the purpose is to be actualized and realized. Two things, then, must be considered: first, the content of this ultimate purpose, the determination as such, and, secondly, its realization.

To begin with, we must note that world history goes on within the realm of Spirit. The term "world" includes both physical and psychical nature. Physical nature does play a part in world history, and from the very beginning we shall draw attention to the fundamental natural relations thus involved. But Spirit, and the course of its development, in the substance of history. We must not contemplate nature as a rational system in itself, in its own particular domain, but only in its relation to Spirit.

[*After the creation of nature appears Man. He constitutes the antithesis to the natural world; he is the being that lifts itself up to the second world. We have in our universal consciousness two realms, the realm of Nature and the realm of Spirit. The realm of Spirit consists in what is produced by man. One may have all sorts of ideas about the Kingdom of God; but it is always a realm of Spirit to be realized and brought about in man.*

The realm of Spirit is all-comprehensive; it includes everything that ever has interested or ever will interest man. Man is active in it; whatever he does, he is the creature within which the Spirit works. Hence it is of interest, in the course of history, to learn to know spiritual nature in its existence, that is, the point where Spirit and Nature unite, namely, human nature. In speaking of human nature we mean something permanent. The concept of human nature must fit all men and all ages, past and present. This universal concept may suffer infinite modifications; but actually the universal is one and the same essence in its most various modifications. Thinking reflection disregards the variations and adheres to the universal, which under all circumstances is active in the same manner and shows itself in the same interest. The universal type appears even in what seems to deviate from it most strongly; in the most distorted figure we can still discern the human. . . .

This kind of reflection abstracts from the content, the purpose of human activity. . . . But the cultured human mind cannot help making distinctions between inclinations and desires as they manifest themselves in small circumstances and as they appear in the struggle of world-wide historical interests. Here appears an objective interest, which impresses us in two aspects, that of the universal aim and that of the individual who represents this aim. It is this which makes history so fascinating. These are the aims and individuals whose loss and decline we mourn. When we have before us the struggle of the Greeks against the Persians or Alexander's mighty dominion, we know very well what interests us. We want to see the Greeks saved from barbarism, we want the Athenian state preserved, and we are interested in the ruler under whose leadership the Greeks subjugated Asia. If it were only a matter of human passion, we would not feel any loss in imagining that Alexander would have

failed in his enterprise. We could very well content ourselves in seeing here a mere play of passions, but we would not feel satisfied. We have here a substantial, an objective interest. . . .

In contemplating world history we must thus consider its ultimate purpose. This ultimate purpose is what is willed in the world itself. We know of God that He is the most perfect; He can will only Himself and what is like Him. God and the nature of His will are one and the same; these we call philosophically, the Idea. Hence, it is the Idea in general, in its manifestation as human spirit, which we have to contemplate. More precisely it is the idea of human freedom. The purest form in which the Idea manifests itself is Thought itself. In this aspect the Idea is treated in Logic. Another form is that of physical Nature.[1] The third form, finally is that of Spirit in general.] Spirit, on the stage on which we observe it, that of world history, is in its most concrete reality. But nevertheless—or rather in order to understand also the general idea of this concrete existence of Spirit—we must set forth, first, some general definition of the *nature of Spirit.* But this can only be done here as a mere assertion; this is not the place to develop the idea of Spirit through philosophical speculation. As was mentioned above, what can be said in an introduction can be taken only historically—as an assumption to be explained and proved elsewhere or to be verified by the science of history itself.

We have therefore to indicate here:

1. The abstract characteristics of the nature of Spirit.
2. The means Spirit uses in order to realize its Idea.
3. The form which the complete realization of Spirit assumes in existence—the State.

1. The Idea of Freedom

The nature of Spirit may be understood by a glance at its direct opposite—Matter. The essence of matter is gravity, the essence of Spirit—its substance—is Freedom. It is immediately plausible to everyone that, among other properties, Spirit also possesses Freedom. But philosophy teaches us that *all* the properties of Spirit exist only through Freedom. All are but means of attaining Freedom; all seek and produce this and this alone. It is an insight of speculative philosophy that Freedom is the sole truth of Spirit. Matter possesses gravity by virtue of its tendency toward a central point; it is essentially composite, consisting of parts that exclude each other. It seeks its unity and thereby its own abolition; it seeks its opposite. If it would attain this it would be matter no longer, but would have perished. It strives toward ideality, for in unity it exists ideally. Spirit, on the contrary, is that which has its center in itself. It does not have unity outside of itself but has found it: it is in itself and with itself. Matter has its substance outside of itself; Spirit is Being-within-itself (self-contained existence).

---

[1] In this aspect the Idea is treated in the Philosophy of Nature.

But this, precisely, is Freedom. For when I am dependent, I refer myself to something else which I am not; I cannot exist independently of something external. I am free when I am within myself. This self-contained existence of Spirit is self-consciousness, consciousness of self.

Two things must be distinguished in consciousness, first, *that* I know and, secondly, *what* I know. In self-consciousness the two coincide, for Spirit knows itself. It is the judgment of its own nature and, at the same time, the operation of coming to itself, to produce itself, to make itself (actually) into that which it is in itself (potentially). Following this abstract definition it may be said that world history is the exhibition of spirit striving to attain knowledge of its own nature. As the germ bears in itself the whole nature of the tree, the taste and shape of its fruit, so also the first traces of Spirit virtually contain the whole of history. Orientals do not yet know that Spirit—Man as such—is free. And because they do not know it, they are not free. They only know that *one* is free; but for this very reason such freedom is mere caprice, ferocity, dullness of passion, or, perhaps, softness and tameness of desire—which again is nothing but an accident of nature and thus, again, caprice. This *one* is therefore only a despot, not a free man. The consciousness of freedom first arose among the Greeks, and therefore they were free. But they, and the Romans likewise, only knew that some are free—not man as such. This not even Plato and Aristotle knew. For this reason the Greeks not only had slavery, upon which was based their whole life and the maintenance of their splendid liberty, but their freedom itself was partly an accidental, transient, and limited flowering and partly a severe thralldom of human nature. Only the Germanic peoples came, through Christianity, to realize that man as man is free and that freedom of Spirit is the very essence of man's nature. This realization first arose in religion, in the innermost region of spirit; but to introduce it in the secular world was a further task which could only be solved and fulfilled by a long and severe effort of civilization. Thus slavery did not cease immediately with the acceptance of the Christian religion. Liberty did not suddenly predominate in states nor reason in governments and constitutions. The application of the principle to secular conditions, the thorough molding and interpenetration of the secular world by it, is precisely the long process of history. I have already drawn attention to this distinction between a principle as such and its application, its introduction and execution in the actuality of life and spirit. This is a fundamental fact in our science and must be kept constantly in mind. Just as we noted it in the Christian principle of self-consciousness and freedom, so it shows itself in the principle of freedom in general. World history is the progress of the consciousness and freedom—a progress whose necessity we have to investigate.

The preliminary statement given above of the various grades in the consciousness of freedom—that the Orientals knew only that *one* is free, the Greeks and Romans that *some* are free, while we know that *all* men absolutely, that is, as men, are free—is at the same time the natural division of world history and the manner in which we shall

treat it. But this is only mentioned in passing; first, we must explain some other concepts.

· · ·

2. The Means of Realization

(A) The Idea and the Individual

The question of the *means* whereby Freedom develops itself into a world leads us directly to the phenomenon of history. Although Freedom as such is primarily an internal idea, the means it uses are the external phenomena which in history present themselves directly before our eyes. The first glance at history convinces us that the actions of men spring from their needs, their passions, their interests, their characters, and their talents. Indeed, it appears as if in this drama of activities these needs, passions, and interests are the sole springs of action and the main efficient cause. It is true that this drama involves also universal purposes, benevolence, or noble patriotism. But such virtues and aims are insignificant on the broad canvas of history. We may, perhaps, see the ideal of Reason actualized in those who adopt such aims and in the spheres of their influence; but their number is small in proportion to the mass of the human race and their influence accordingly limited. Passions, private aims, and the satisfaction of selfish desires are, on the contrary, tremendous springs of action. Their power lies in the fact that they respect none of the limitations which law and morality would impose on them; and that these natural impulses are closer to the core of human nature than the artificial and troublesome discipline that tends toward order, self-restraint, law, and morality.

When we contemplate this display of passions and the consequences of their violence, the unreason which is associated not only with them, but even—rather we might say *especially*—with *good* designs and righteous aims; when we see arising therefrom the evil, the vice, the ruin that has befallen the most flourishing kingdoms which the mind of man ever created, we can hardly avoid being filled with sorrow at this universal taint of corruption. And since this decay is not the work of mere nature, but of human will, our reflections may well lead us to a moral sadness, a revolt of the good will (spirit)—if indeed it has a place within us. Without rhetorical exaggeration, a simple, truthful account of the miseries that have overwhelmed the noblest of nations and polities and the finest exemplars of private virtue forms a most fearful picture and excites emotions of the profoundest and most hopeless sadness, counter-balanced by no consoling result. We can endure it and strengthen ourselves against it only by thinking that this is the way it had to be—it is fate; nothing can be done. And at last, out of the boredom with which this sorrowful reflection threatens us, we draw back into the vitality of the present, into our aims and interests of the moment; we retreat, in short, into the selfishness that stands on the quiet shore and thence enjoys in safety the distant spectacle of wreckage and confusion.

· · ·

3. The State

(A) THE STATE AS REALIZATION OF THE IDEA

The third point, then, concerns the end to be attained by these means, that is, the form it assumes in the realm of the actual. We have spoken of means; but the carrying out of a subjective, limited aim also requires a *material* element, either already present or to be procured or to serve this actualization. Thus the question would arise: What is the material in which the final end of Reason is to be realized? It is first of all the subjective agent itself, human desires, subjectivity in general. In human knowledge and volition, as its material basis, the rational attains existence. We have considered subjective volition with its purpose, namely, the truth of reality, insofar as moved by a great world-historical passion. As a subjective will in limited passions it is dependent; it can gratify its particular desires only within this dependence. But the subjective will has also a substantial life, a reality where it moves in the region of essential being and has the essential itself as the object of its existence. This essential being is the union of the subjective with the rational will; it is the moral whole, the *State*. It is that actuality in which the individual has and enjoys his freedom, but only as knowing, believing, and willing the universal. This must not be understood as if the subjective will of the individual attained its gratification and enjoyment through the common will and the latter were a means for it—as if the individual limited his freedom among the other individuals, so that this common limitation, the mutual constraint of all, might secure a small space of liberty for each. (This would only be negative freedom.) Rather, law, morality, the State, and they alone, are the positive reality and satisfaction of freedom. The caprice of the individual is not freedom. It is this caprice which is being limited, the license of particular desires.

The subjective will, passion, is the force which actualizes and realizes. The Idea is the interior; the State is the externally existing, genuinely moral life. It is the union of the universal and essential with the subjective will, and as such it is *Morality*. The individual who lives in this unity has a moral life, a value which consists in this substantiality alone. Sophocles' Antigone says: "The divine commands are not of yesterday nor of today; no, they have an infinite existence, and no one can say whence they came."

The laws of ethics are not accidental, but are rationality itself. It is the end of the State to make the substantial prevail and maintain itself in the actual doings of men and in their convictions. It is the absolute interest of Reason that this moral whole exist; and herein lies the justification and merit of heroes who have founded states, no matter how crude.

. . .

[The state] is the realization of Freedom, of the absolute, final purpose, and exists for its own sake. All the value man has, all the spiritual reality, he has only through the state. For his spiritual reality is the knowing presence to him of his own essence, of rationality, of its objective, immediate actuality present in and for him. Only thus is he truly a consciousness, only thus does he partake in morality, in the legal and moral life of the state. For the True is the unity of the universal and particular will. And the universal in the state is in its laws, its universal and rational provisions. The state is the divine Idea as it exists on earth. 15

Thus the State is the definite object of world history proper. In it freedom achieves its objectivity and lives in the enjoyment of this objectivity. For law is the objectivity of Spirit; it is will in its true form. Only the will that obeys the law is free, for it obeys itself and, being in itself, is free. In so far as the state, our country, constitutes a community of existence, and as the subjective will of man subjects itself to the laws, the antithesis of freedom and necessity disappears. The rational, like the substantial, is necessary. We are free when we recognize it as law and follow it as the substance of our own being. The objective and the subjective will are then reconciled and form one and the same harmonious whole. For the ethos of the state is not of the moral, the reflective kind in which one's own conviction rules supreme. This latter is rather the peculiarity of the modern world. The true and antique morality is rooted in the principle that everybody stands in his place of duty. An Athenian citizen did what was required of him, as it were from instinct. But if I reflect on the object of my activity, I must have the consciousness that my will counts. Morality, however, is the duty, the substantial law, the second nature, as it has been rightly called; for the first nature of man is his immediate, animalic existence.

THE TRIUMPH OF THE BOURGEOISIE
1830–1871

Selection from *Narrative of the Life of Frederick Douglass*

Frederick Douglass's autobiography reflects the maturity of the trend toward globalization of the world's culture, which began in about 1500. From then on, Europe exported peoples, technology, religions, and ideas to colonies in Asia, Africa, and the Americas; in return, Europe received slaves and servants, foodstuffs, raw materials, religions, and ideas. Central to this process in the New World was the uprooting and transportation of Africans to work as slaves. The faint contours of a global literary culture were first visible in the 1600s, when European writers began to draw on colonial life. Spanish and English America now gave birth to colonial literatures, though at first heavily indebted to Europe. Hence the appearance in 1845 of *Narrative of the Life of Frederick Douglass, an American Slave* was a literary milestone. It introduced a unique literary genre, the slave narrative, thus loosening America's dependency on European models. Also, it was one of the first great books in the West since the fall of Rome to be written by a person of color; thus, it pointed toward a unified world literature freed from the racial segregation that had so far characterized the varied literatures of the world since the Middle Ages. Douglass's later life also furthered globalization, as he was America's first ambassador (1889–1895) to Haiti, the Western Hemisphere's first black-ruled state.

Douglass's slave narrative is only the most famous and the most superbly crafted of the thousands of representative examples of the slave experiences of African Americans that were published between the founding of the United States of America and the outbreak of its Civil War. These works, many of which sold by the thousands and some of which were translated into Dutch, German, and Celtic, made converts for Abolitionism, the anti-slavery movement that began in the late eighteenth century. Abolitionism was concentrated in New England and helped prepare the moral ground for the Civil War. By focusing on the psychic wounds of slavery, the writers of slave narrative forced readers, then and now, to recognize that attempts to forge an American national identity would have to come to grips with the country's slave past.

Reading the Selection

Frederick Douglass (about 1818–1895) was born on a Maryland plantation, the son of a slave woman and a white man, perhaps his master. Caught in his first bid for freedom, he finally slipped slavery's chains in 1838 when he rode the train (the "upperground" railroad [his term]) from Baltimore to New York. He married Anna Murray, a Baltimore freewoman who had helped him escape, and they moved to Massachusetts, living as respected members of the black community. Becoming an advocate of Abolitionism, he wrote his life story in 1845, partly to satisfy a creative need and partly to silence critics who thought him too eloquent to have ever been a slave.

This selection covers Douglass's youth in the Baltimore household of his then master, Hugh Auld. Douglass describes his efforts to learn to read and write and the sense of empowerment conveyed by being literate. It is a heroic story in which he moves from "mental darkness" to the light of knowledge, overcoming private and social obstacles erected by white society to keep slaves ignorant of their rights. Possessing literacy placed Douglass within the context of this period's reformers who made education the universal panacea—a legacy of the Age of Reason.

I lived in Master Hugh's family about seven years. During this time, I succeeded in learning to read and write. In accomplishing this, I was compelled to resort to various stratagems. I had no regular teacher. My mistress, who had kindly commenced to instruct me, had, in compliance with the advice and direction of her husband, not only ceased to instruct, but had set her face against my being instructed by any one else. It is due, however, to my mistress to say of her, that she did not adopt this course of treatment immediately. She at first lacked the depravity indispensable to shutting me up in mental darkness. It was at least necessary for her to have some training in the exercise of irresponsible power, to make her equal to the task of treating me as though I were a brute.

My mistress was, as I have said, a kind and tender-hearted woman; and in the simplicity of her soul she commenced, when I first went to live with her, to treat me as she supposed one human being ought to treat another. In entering upon the duties of a slaveholder, she did not seem to perceive that I sustained to her the relation of a mere chattel, and that for her to treat me as a human being was not only wrong, but dangerously so. Slavery proved as injurious to her as it did to me. When I went there, she was a pious, warm, and tender-hearted woman. There was no sorrow or suffering for which she had not a tear. She had bread for the hungry, clothes for the naked, and comfort for every mourner that came within her reach. Slavery soon proved its ability to divest her of these heavenly qualities. Under its influence, the tender heart became stone, and the lamblike disposition gave way to one of tiger-like fierceness. The first step in her downward course was in her ceasing to instruct me. She now commenced to practise her husband's precepts. She finally became even more violent in her opposition than her husband himself. She was not satisfied with simply doing as well as he had commanded; she seemed anxious to do better. Nothing seemed to make her more angry than to see me with a newspaper. She seemed to think that here lay the danger. I have had her rush at me with a face made all up of fury, and snatch from me a newspaper, in a manner that fully revealed her apprehension. She was an apt woman; and a little experience soon demonstrated, to her satisfaction, that education and slavery were incompatible with each other.

From this time I was most narrowly watched. If I was in a separate room any considerable length of time, I was sure to be suspected of having a book, and was at once called to give an account of myself. All this, however, was too late. The first step had been taken. Mistress, in teaching me the alphabet, had given me the *inch*, and no precaution could prevent me from taking the *ell*.

The plan which I adopted, and the one by which I was most successful, was that of making friends of all the little white boys whom I met in the street. As many of these as I could, I converted into teachers. With their kindly aid, obtained at different times and in different places, I finally succeeded in learning to read. When I was sent on errands, I always took my book with me, and by doing one part of my errand quickly, I found time to get a lesson before my return. I used also to carry bread with me, enough of which was always in the house, and to which I was always welcome; for I was much better off in this regard than many of the poor white children in our neighborhood. This bread I used to bestow upon the hungry little urchins, who, in return, would give me that more valuable bread of knowledge. I am strongly tempted to give the names of two or three of those little boys, as a testimonial of the gratitude and affection I bear them; but prudence forbids;—not that it would injure me, but it might embarrass them; for it is almost an unpardonable offence to teach slaves to read in this Christian country. It is enough to say of the dear little fellows, that they lived on Philpot Street, very near Durgin and Bailey's ship-yard. I used to talk this matter of slavery over with them. I would sometimes say to them, I wished I could be as free as they would be when they got to be men. "You will be free as soon as you are twenty-one, *but I am a slave for life!* Have not I as good a right to be free as you have?" These words used to trouble them; they would express for me the liveliest sympathy, and console me with the hope that something would occur by which I might be free.

I was now about twelve years old, and the thought of being *a slave for life* began to bear heavily upon my heart. Just about this time, I got hold of a book entitled "The Columbian Orator." Every opportunity I got, I used to read this book. Among much of other interesting matter, I found in it a dialogue between a master and his slave. The slave was represented as having run away from his master three times. The dialogue represented the conversation which took place between them, when the slave was re-taken the third time. In this dialogue, the whole argument in behalf of slavery was brought forward by the master, all of which was disposed of by the slave. The slave was made to say some very smart as well as impressive things in reply to his master—things which had the desired though unexpected effect; for the conversation resulted in the voluntary emancipation of the slave on the part of the master.

In the same book, I met with one of Sheridan's mighty speeches on and in behalf of Catholic emancipation. These were choice documents to me. I read them over and over again with unabated interest. They gave tongue to interesting thoughts of my own soul, which had frequently flashed through my mind, and died away for want of utterance. The moral which I gained from the dialogue was the power of truth over the conscience of even a slave-holder. What I got from Sheridan was a bold denunciation of slavery, and a powerful vindication of human rights. The reading of these documents enabled me to utter my thoughts, and to meet the arguments brought forward to sustain slavery; but while they relieved me of one difficulty, they brought on another even more painful than the one of which I was relieved. The more I read, the more I was led to abhor and detest my enslavers. I could regard them in no other light than a band of successful robbers, who had left their homes, and gone to Africa, and stolen us from our homes, and in a strange land reduced us to slavery. I loathed them as being the meanest as well as the most wicked of men. As I read and contemplated the subject, behold! that very discontentment which Master Hugh had predicted would follow my learning to read had already come, to torment and sting my soul to unutterable anguish. As I writhed under it, I would at times feel that learning to read had been a curse rather than a blessing. It had given me a view of my wretched condition, without the remedy. It opened my eyes to the horrible pit, but to no ladder upon which to get out. In moments of agony, I envied my fellow-slaves for their stupidity. I have often wished myself a beast. I preferred the condition of the meanest reptile to my own. Any thing, no matter what, to get rid of thinking! It was this everlasting thinking of my condition that tormented me. There was no getting rid of it. It was pressed upon me by every object within sight or hearing, animate or inanimate. The silver trump of freedom had roused my soul to eternal wakefulness. Freedom now appeared, to disappear no more forever. It was heard in every sound, and seen in every thing. It was ever present to torment me with a sense of my wretched condition. I saw nothing without seeing it, I heard nothing without hearing it, and felt nothing without feeling it. It looked from every star, it smiled in every calm, breathed in every wind, and moved in every storm.

I often found myself regretting my own existence, and wishing myself dead; and but for the hope of being free, I have no doubt but that I should have killed myself, or done something for which I should have been killed. While in this state of mind, I was eager to hear any one speak of slavery. I was a ready listener. Every little while, I could hear something about the abolitionists. It was some time before I found what the word meant. It was always used in such connections as to make it an interesting word to me. If a slave ran away and succeeded in getting clear, or if a slave killed his master, set fire to a barn, or did any thing very wrong in the mind of a slaveholder, it was spoken of as the fruit of *abolition.* Hearing the word in this connection very often, I set about learning what it meant. The dictionary afforded me little or no help. I found it was "the act of abolishing"; but then I did not know what was to be abolished. Here I was perplexed. I did not dare to ask any one about its meaning, for I was satisfied that it was something they wanted me to know very little about. After a patient waiting, I got one of our city papers, containing an account of the number of petitions from the north, praying for the abolition of slavery in the District of Columbia, and of the slave trade between the States. From this time I understood the words *abolition* and *abolitionist,* and always drew near when that word was spoken, expecting to hear something of importance to myself and fellow-slaves. The light broke in upon me by degrees. I went one day down on the wharf of Mr. Waters; and seeing two Irishmen unloading a scow of stone, I went, unasked, and helped them. When we had finished, one of them came to me and asked me if I were a slave. I told him I was. He asked, "Are ye a slave for life?" I told him that I was. The good Irishman seemed to be deeply affected by the statement. He said to the other that it was a pity so fine a little fellow as myself should be a slave for life. He said it was a shame to hold me. They both advised me to run away to the north; that I should find friends there, and that I should be free. I pretended not to be interested in what they said, and treated them as if I did not understand them; for I feared they might be treacherous. White men have been known to encourage slaves to escape, and then, to get the reward, catch them and return them to their masters. I was afraid that these seemingly good men might use me so; but I nevertheless remembered their advice, and from that time I resolved to run away. I looked forward to a time at which it would be safe for me to escape. I was too young to think of doing so immediately; besides, I wished to learn how to write, as I might have occasion to write my own pass. I consoled myself with the hope that I should one day find a good chance. Meanwhile, I would learn to write.

The idea as to how I might learn to write was suggested to me by being in Durgin and Bailey's ship-yard, and frequently seeing the ship carpenters, after hewing, and getting a piece of timber ready to use, write on the timber the name of that part of the ship for which it was intended. When a piece of timber was intended for the larboard side, it would be marked thus—"L." When a piece was for the starboard side, it would be marked thus—"S." A piece for the larboard side forward, would be marked thus—"L. F." When a piece was for starboard side forward, it would be marked thus— "S. F." For larboard aft, it would be marked thus—"L. A." For starboard aft, it would be marked thus—"S. A." I soon learned the names of these letters, and for what they were intended when placed upon a piece of timber in the ship-yard. I immediately commenced copying them, and in a short time was able to make the four letters named. After that, when I met with any boy who I knew could write, I would tell him I could write as well as he. The next word would be, "I don't believe you. Let me see you try it." I would then make the letters which I had been so fortunate as to learn, and ask him to beat that. In this way I got a good many lessons in writing, which it is quite possible I should never have gotten in any other way. During this time, my copy-book was the board fence, brick wall, and pavement; my pen and ink was a lump of chalk. With these, I learned mainly how to write. I then commenced and continued copying the Italics in Webster's Spelling Book, until I could make them all without looking on the book. By this time, my little Master Thomas had gone to school, and learned how to write, and had written over a number of copy-books. These had been brought home, and shown to some of our near neighbors, and then laid aside. My mistress used to go to class meeting at the Wilk Street meetinghouse every Monday afternoon, and leave me to take care of the house. When left thus, I used to spend time in writing in the spaces left in Master Thomas's copy-book, copying what he had written. I continued to do this until I could write a hand very similar to that of Master Thomas. Thus, after a long, tedious effort for years, I finally succeeded in learning how to write.

CHARLOTTE BRONTË

Selection from *Jane Eyre*

Charlotte Brontë (1816–1855) was the oldest member of perhaps the West's most famous literary family, which also included her two younger sisters, Emily (1818–1848) and Anne (1820–1849). The offspring of an Anglican priest, the Brontë daughters spent most of their youth at Haworth, a parsonage deep in rural Yorkshire in northern England. Haworth was a gloomy dwelling—all that the poor parish could provide—and was next to the churchyard, which early claimed the Brontë mother. Isolated thus from urban culture, the Brontë children were educated mainly at home but with some months at shabby boarding schools. As a result, the children turned to each other and fashioned fantasy kingdoms; these became the subject of their first juvenile works, including tales, poems, journals, serial stories, and a monthly magazine—some of which survive. Without fully realizing it, the Brontës spent their youth preparing for literary careers.

The Brontë sisters left an indelible mark on Western letters. They wrote novels in the Gothic style, with varied degrees of success. In order to be taken seriously by Victorian critics who often treated women writers with disdain, they published their works under masculine names. The youngest sister, Anne, writing as "Acton Bell," won modest acclaim with *The Tenant of Wildfell Hall* (1848), a novel still in print today. The middle sister, Emily, writing as "Ellis Bell," achieved undying fame with *Wuthering Heights* (1847), one of the most popular novels ever written, though not at the time. And the eldest sister, Charlotte, writing as "Currer Bell," was the most successful of the group with *Jane Eyre* (1847), *Shirley* (1849), and *Villette* (1852). Today, Charlotte's reputation remains high, mainly due to the popularity of *Jane Eyre*, in both its original form and as the source for movies, TV dramas, and most recently, a novel, *Wide Sargasso Sea*, by Jean Rhys.

Reading the Selection

Jane Eyre is the story of the sufferings of a young woman without wealth and social connections, as she struggles to find a place for herself in the world. The novel traces Jane's life from an unloved childhood at Gateshead, to her schooling at Lowood, to her adolescence at Thornfield Hall, where she was a governess. Finally, we read of her fulfillment, as she marries her employer at Ferndean. *Jane Eyre* is a pioneering novel in its frank portrayal of a heroine who refuses to accept her appointed place in society.

Jane Eyre reflected Charlotte's reading and her experiences. Inspired by Romantic poets such as Byron (see *Don Juan*), she wanted to capture the sense of "felt" life, "what throbs fast and full, though hidden, what the blood rushes through, what is the unseen seat of life and the sentient target of death." In part autobiographical, this novel drew on her inner life and aspirations. Charlotte also made *Jane Eyre* "as plain and as small as" herself, for she wanted to show that "a heroine could be interesting without being beautiful."

Chapter XXIII of *Jane Eyre* concerns Jane's life at Thornfield, where she is governess to Adèle, the daughter of Mr. Rochester. Thoroughly Romantic in style, this chapter juxtaposes stormy nature with Jane's wild emotions. It ends with Jane planning marriage to her employer, Mr. Rochester, who later will be revealed as already married. The problems resulting from Jane's engagement to Mr. Rochester take up much of the rest of the novel.

—m—

Chapter XXIII

A splendid Midsummer shone over England: skies so pure, suns so radiant as were then seen in long succession, seldom favour, even singly, our wave-girt land. It was as if a band of Italian days had come from the South, like a flock of glorious passenger birds, and lighted to rest them on the cliffs of Albion. The hay was all got in; the fields round Thornfield were green and shorn; the roads white and baked; the trees were in their dark prime; hedge and wood, full-leaved and deeply tinted, contrasted well with the sunny hue of the cleared meadows between.

On Midsummer-eve, Adèle, weary with gathering wild strawberries in Hay Lane half the day, had gone to bed with the sun. I watched her drop asleep, and when I left her, I sought the garden.

It was now the sweetest hour of the twenty-four: 'day its fervid fires had wasted', and dew fell cool on panting plain and scorched summit. Where the sun had gone down in simple state—pure of the pomp of clouds—spread a solemn purple, burning with the light of red jewel and furnace flame at one point, on one hill-peak, and extending high and wide, soft and still softer, over half heaven. The east had its own charm of fine, deep blue, and its own modest gem, a rising and solitary star: soon it would boast the moon; but she was yet beneath the horizon.

I walked a while on the pavement; but a subtle, well-known scent—that of a cigar—stole from some window; I saw the library casement open a hand-breadth; I knew I might be watched thence; so I went apart into the orchard. No nook in the grounds more sheltered and more Eden-like; a very high wall shut it out from the court on one side; on the other a beech avenue screened it from the lawn. At the bottom was a sunk fence, its sole separation from lonely fields: a winding walk, bordered with laurels and terminating in a giant horse-chestnut, circled at the base by a seat, led down to the fence. Here one could wander unseen. While such honeydew fell, such silence reigned, such gloaming gathered, I felt as if I could haunt such shade for ever; but in treading the flower and fruit parterres at the upper part of the enclosure, enticed there by the light the now rising moon cast on this more open quarter, my step is stayed—not by sound, not by sight, but once more by a warning fragrance.

Sweet-brier and southernwood, jasmine, pink, and rose have long been yielding their evening sacrifice of in-

cense: this new scent is neither of shrub nor flower; it is—I know it well—it is Mr Rochester's cigar. I look round and listen. I see trees laden with ripening fruit. I hear a nightingale warbling in a wood half a mile off: no moving form is visible, no coming step audible; but that perfume increases: I must flee. I make for the wicket leading to the shrubbery, and I see Mr Rochester entering. I step aside into the ivy recess; he will not stay long: he will soon return whence he came, and if I sit still he will never see me.

But no—eventide is as pleasant to him as to me, and this antique garden as attractive; and he strolls on, now lifting the gooseberry-tree branches to look at the fruit, large as plums, with which they are laden; now taking a ripe cherry from the wall; now stooping towards a knot of flowers, either to inhale their fragrance or to admire the dew-beads on their petals. A great moth goes humming by me; it alights on a plant at Mr Rochester's foot: he sees it, and bends to examine it.

'Now he has his back towards me,' thought I, 'and he is occupied too; perhaps, if I walk softly, I can slip away unnoticed.'

I trod on an edging of turf that the crackle of the pebbly gravel might not betray me: he was standing among the beds at a yard or two distant from where I had to pass; the moth apparently engaged him. 'I shall get by very well,' I meditated. As I crossed his shadow, thrown long over the garden by the moon, not yet risen high, he said quietly, without turning—

'Jane, come and look at this fellow.'

I had made no noise: he had not eyes behind— could his shadow feel? I started at first, and then I approached him.

'Look at his wings,' said he; 'he reminds me rather of a West Indian insect; one does not often see so large and gay a night-rover in England; there! he is flown.'

The moth roamed away. I was sheepishly retreating also; but Mr Rochester followed me, and when we reached the wicket he said—

'Turn back: on so lovely a night it is a shame to sit in the house; and surely no one can wish to go to bed while sunset is thus at meeting with moonrise.'

It is one of my faults, that though my tongue is sometimes prompt enough at answer, there are times when it sadly fails me in framing an excuse; and always the lapse occurs at some crisis, when a facile word or plausible pretext is specially wanted to get me out of painful embarrassment. I did not like to walk at this hour alone with Mr Rochester in the shadowy orchard; but I could not find a reason to allege for leaving him. I followed with lagging step, and thoughts busily bent on discovering a means of extrication; but he himself looked so composed and so grave also, I became ashamed of feeling any confusion: the evil—if evil existent or prospective there was—seemed to lie with me only; his mind was unconscious and quiet.

'Jane,' he recommenced, as we entered the laurel walk and slowly strayed down in the direction of the sunk fence and the horse-chestnut, 'Thornfield is a pleasant place in summer, is it not?' 15

'Yes, sir.'

'You must have become in some degree attached to the house—you who have an eye for natural beauties, and a good deal of the organ of Adhesiveness?'

'I am attached to it, indeed.'

'And though I don't comprehend how it is, I perceive you have acquired a degree of regard for that foolish little child Adèle, too; and even for simple Dame Fairfax?'

'Yes, sir; in different ways, I have an affection for both.' 20

'And would be sorry to part with them?'

'Yes.'

'Pity!' he said, and sighed and paused.

'It is always the way of events in this life,' he continued presently: 'no sooner have you got settled in a pleasant resting-place, than a voice calls out to you to rise and move on, for the hour of repose is expired.'

'Must I move on, sir?' I asked. 'Must I leave Thornfield?' 25

'I believe you must, Jane. I am sorry, Jane, but I believe indeed you must.'

This was a blow: but I did not let it prostrate me.

'Well, sir, I shall be ready when the order to march comes.'

'It is come now—I must give it to-night.'

'Then you *are* going to be married, sir?' 30

'Ex-act-ly—pre-cise-ly: with your usual acuteness, you have hit the nail straight on the head.'

'Soon, sir?'

'Very soon, my—that is, Miss Eyre: and you'll remember, Jane, the first time I, or Rumour, plainly intimated to you that it was my intention to put my old bachelor's neck into the sacred noose, to enter into the holy state of matrimony—to take Miss Ingram to my bosom, in short (she's an extensive armful: but that's not to the point—one can't have too much of such a very excellent thing as my beautiful Blanche): well, as I was saying—listen to me, Jane! You're not turning your head to look after more moths, are you? That was only a lady-clock, child, "flying away home". I wish to remind you that it was you who first said to me, with that discretion I respect in you—with that foresight, prudence, and humility which befit your responsible and dependent position—that in case I married Miss Ingram, both you and little Adèle had better trot forthwith. I pass over the sort of slur conveyed in this suggestion on the character of my beloved; indeed, when you are far away, Jane, I'll try to forget it: I shall notice only its wisdom; which is such that I have made it my law of action. Adèle must go to school; and you, Miss Eyre, must get a new situation.'

'Yes, sir, I will advertise immediately: and meantime, I suppose—' I was going to say, 'I suppose I may stay here, till I find another shelter to betake myself to': but I stopped, feeling it would not do to risk a long sentence, for my voice was not quite under command.

'In about a month I hope to be a bridegroom,' continued Mr Rochester; 'and in the interim, I shall myself look out for employment and an asylum for you.' 35

'Thank you, sir; I am sorry to give—'

'Oh, no need to apologize! I consider that when a dependent does her duty as well as you have done yours, she has a sort of claim upon her employer for any little assistance he can conveniently render her; indeed, I have already, through my future mother-in-law, heard of a place that I think will suit: it is to undertake the education of the five daughters of Mrs Dionysius O'Gall of Bitternutt Lodge, Connaught, Ireland. You'll like Ireland, I think: they're such warm-hearted people there, they say.'

'It is a long way off, sir.'

'No matter—a girl of your sense will not object to the voyage or the distance.'

'Not the voyage but the distance: and then the sea is a barrier—' 40

'From what, Jane?'

'From England and from Thornfield; and—'

'Well?'

'From *you*, sir.'

I said this almost involuntarily, and with as little sanction of free will, my tears gushed out. I did not cry so as to be heard, however; I avoided sobbing. The thought of Mrs O'Gall and Bitternutt Lodge struck cold to my heart; and colder the thought of all the brine and foam destined, as it seemed, to rush between me and the master at whose side I now walked; and coldest the remembrance of the wider ocean—wealth, caste, custom—intervened between me and what I naturally and inevitably loved. 45

'It is a long way,' I again said.

'It is, to be sure; and when you get to Bitternutt Lodge, Connaught, Ireland, I shall never see you again, Jane: that's morally certain. I never go over to Ireland, not having myself much of a fancy for the country. We have been good friends, Jane; have we not?'

'Yes, sir.'

'And when friends are on the eve of separation, they like to spend the little time that remains to them close to each other. Come! we'll talk over the voyage and the parting quietly, half an hour or so, while the stars enter into their shining life up in heaven yonder: here is the chestnut-tree: here is the bench at its old roots. Come, we will sit there in peace to-night, though we should never more be destined to sit there together.'

He seated me and himself.

'It is a long way to Ireland, Jane, and I am sorry to send my little friend on such weary travels: but if I can't do better, how is it to be helped? Are you anything akin to me, do you think, Jane?' 50

Reading the Selection

In this selection from "Civil Disobedience," Thoreau ignores his personal situation and addresses broader issues raised by his refusal to pay taxes: the growing power of government, the wrongful power exercised by the majority over the minority, the manipulation of voters by political leaders, and the acquiescence of citizens to their government's actions, whether legitimate or not. His basic argument is that there is a higher law—a Transcendental concept—that supersedes the laws made by human devising. Thus, laws should be obeyed only when they are just—that is, in accord with the higher law. Unjust laws, such as those in support of slavery, have no validity and should be resisted by the citizenry. He also asserts that governments have no power over individuals or their property, except what is conceded by each person. In effect, the individual is a "higher and independent power," superior to the state. He predicts that a free and enlightened government will never exist so long as the state dominates its citizens.

Unjust laws exist: shall we be content to obey them, or shall we endeavor to amend them, and obey them until we have succeeded, or shall we transgress them at once? Men generally, under such a government as this, think that they ought to wait until they have persuaded the majority to alter them. They think that, if they should resist, the remedy would be worse than the evil. But it is the fault of the government itself that the remedy *is* worse than the evil. *It* makes it worse. Why is it not more apt to anticipate and provide for reform? Why does it not cherish its wise minority? Why does it cry and resist before it is hurt? Why does it not encourage its citizens to be on the alert to point out its faults, and *do* better than it would have them? Why does it always crucify Christ, and excommunicate Copernicus and Luther, and pronounce Washington and Franklin rebels?

One would think, that a deliberate and practical denial of its authority was the only offence never contemplated by government; else, why has it not assigned its definite, its suitable and proportionate penalty? If a man who has no property refuses but once to earn nine shillings for the State, he is put in prison for a period unlimited by any law that I know, and determined only by the discretion of those who placed him there: but if he should steal ninety times nine shillings from the State, he is soon permitted to go at large again.

If the injustice is part of the necessary friction of the machine of government, let it go, let it go: perchance it will wear smooth,—certainly the machine will wear out. If the injustice has a spring, or a pulley, or a rope, or a crank, exclusively for itself, then perhaps you may consider whether the remedy will not be worse than the evil; but if it is of such a nature that it requires you to be the agent of injustice to another, then, I say, break the law. Let your life be a counter friction to stop the machine. What I have to do is to see, at any rate, that I do not lend myself to the wrong which I condemn.

As for adopting the ways which the State has provided for remedying the evil, I know not of such ways. They take too much time, and a man's life will be gone. I have other affairs to attend to. I came into this world, not chiefly to make this a good place to live in, but to live in it, be it good or bad. A man has not every thing to do, but something; and because he cannot do *every thing*, it is not necessary that he should do *something* wrong. It is not my business to be petitioning the governor or the legislature any more than it is theirs to petition me; and, if they should not hear my petition, what should I do then? But in this case the State has provided no way: its very Constitution is the evil. This may seem to be harsh and stubborn and unconciliatory; but it is to treat with the utmost kindness and consideration the only spirit that can appreciate or deserves it. So is all change for the better, like birth and death which convulse the body.

I do not hesitate to say, that those who call themselves abolitionists should at once effectually withdraw their support, both in person and property, from the government of Massachusetts, and not wait till they constitute a majority of one, before they suffer the right to prevail through them. I think that it is enough if they have God on their side, without waiting for that other one. Moreover, any man more right than his neighbors, constitutes a majority of one already. . . .

They who know of no purer sources of truth, who have traced up its stream no higher, stand, and wisely stand, by the Bible and the Constitution, and drink at it there with reverence and humility; but they who behold where it comes trickling into this lake or that pool, gird up their loins once more, and continue their pilgrimage toward its fountain-head.

No man with a genius for legislation has appeared in America. They are rare in the history of the world. There are orators, politicians, and eloquent men, by the thousand; but the speaker has not yet opened his mouth to speak, who is capable of settling the much-vexed questions of the day. We love eloquence for its own sake, and not for any truth which it may utter, or any heroism it may inspire. Our legislators have not yet learned the comparative value of free-trade and of freedom, of union, and of rectitude, to a nation. They have no genius or talent for comparatively humble questions of taxation and finance, commerce and manufactures and agriculture. If we were left solely to the wordy wit of legislators in Congress for our guidance, uncorrected by the seasonable experience and the effectual complaints of the people, America would not long retain her rank among the nations. For eighteen hundred years, though perchance I have no right to say it, the New Testament has been written; yet where is the legislator who has wisdom and practical talent enough to avail himself of the light which it sheds on the science of legislation?

The authority of government, even such as I am willing to submit to,—for I will cheerfully obey those who know and can do better than I, and in many things even those who neither know nor can do so well,—is still an impure one: to be strictly just, it must have the sanction and consent of the governed. It can have no pure right over my person and property but what I concede to it. The progress from an absolute to a limited monarchy, from a limited monarchy to a democracy, is a progress toward a true respect for the individual. Is a democracy, such as we know it, the last improvement possible in government? Is it not possible to take a step further towards recognizing and organizing the rights of man? There will never be a really free and enlightened State, until the State comes to recognize the individual as a higher and independent power, from which all its own power and authority are derived, and treats him accordingly. I please myself with imagining a State at last which can afford to be just to all men, and to treat the individual with respect as a neighbor; which even would not think it inconsistent with its own repose, if a few were to live aloof from it, not meddling with it, nor embraced by it, who fulfilled all the duties of neighbors and fellow-men. A State which bore this kind of fruit, and suffered it to drop off as fast as it ripened, would prepare the way for a still more perfect and glorious State, which also I have imagined, but not yet anywhere seen.

CHARLES DICKENS

Selection from *Hard Times*

Charles Dickens's (1812–1870) prolific and frenetic career made him the most popular and most successful author of the Victorian Age, perhaps second only to Shakespeare in popularity in the whole of English letters. Discovering his literary gift, Dickens rose from poverty (his father and family were in debtors' prison at one time): He became, first, a court transcriber; next, a reporter in Parliament; and then a recorder of the human comedy, with his *Sketches by Boz* serialized in popular magazines. His reputation grew with the *Pickwick Papers*, which he followed with a stream of novels and a lecture tour of America, where he was lionized as the greatest author of the age. In the 1850s he founded his own magazine and embraced many social causes that became themes in his writings. By the mid-1860s, having written fourteen novels, published a magazine, and acted in amateur plays, his strenuous life began to undermine his health. When he died in 1870, he received national honors and was buried in Westminster Abbey.

Dickens combined a keen eye and ear for detail and dialect with his personal experiences to produce novels that rank as some of the masterpieces of nineteenth-century Realism. He was England's leading exponent of Realism, which had risen in part as a reaction against both Classicism and Romanticism. Rejecting the elegant writing ideal of Classicism and the sentimentality of Romanticism, the Realists believed that literature should serve a purpose and not be judged alone on its aesthetic merits. They were concerned with the world around them, not only with daily events but also with political and social issues, and they believed that life should be portrayed as it was, neither idealized nor romanticized. Realism came to be defined as a bold and honest treatment of the human condition with specific details.

Reading the Selection

Dickens published *Hard Times* between 1851 and 1854, at the height of his social and political crusades that he waged in his magazine and novels. In *Bleak House* he attacked the corrupt legal system, and in *Little Dorrit* he criticized the government's conduct of the Crimean War. In *Hard Times* he addressed three current topics: class struggle, education, and Utilitarianism (the doctrine set forth in the social theory of Jeremy Bentham that the goal of society is "the greatest good for the greatest number").

Through the characters representing management (Gradgrind) and labor (Sissy's father) in Coketown (probably based on the factory town of Preston), Dickens publicized the class struggle that was being called in the 1840s the "Condition of England question." In Chapter V, "The Key-note," the central idea is caught in the vivid picture of Coketown, its ugly buildings, polluted river, and ill-dressed inhabitants; the middle class's contempt for workers is seen in Gradgrind and Bounderby's hasty opinions. Gradgrind and Bounderby's prejudices flare up in the exchange with the working-class youths, Bitzer and Sissy, who are judged disrespectful; Sissy's father, the object of Gradgrind and Bounderby's excursion into this run-down section of Coketown, is assumed to be a lazy drunk.

Prior to Chapter V, Dickens satirized the Utilitarian approach to schooling with its unrelenting emphasis on "facts, facts, facts." In this selection, the reference to M'Choakumchild's school further registers his contempt for the period's style of education, with its emphasis on corporal punishment as a necessary aid to learning.

—*···*—

Chapter V: The Key-note

Coketown, to which Messrs Bounderby and Gradgrind now walked, was a triumph of fact; it had no greater taint of fancy in it than Mrs Gradgrind herself. Let us strike the key-note, Coketown, before pursuing our tune.

It was a town of red brick, or of brick that would have been red if the smoke and ashes had allowed it; but, as matters stood it was a town of unnatural red and black like the painted face of a savage. It was a town of machinery and tall chimneys, out of which interminable serpents of smoke trailed themselves for ever and ever, and never got uncoiled. It had a black canal in it, and a river that ran purple with ill-smelling dye, and vast piles of building full of windows where there was a rattling and a trembling all day long, and where the piston of the steam-engine worked monotonously up and own, like the head of an elephant in a state of melancholy madness. It contained several large streets all very like one another, and many small streets still more like one another, inhabited by people equally like one another, who all went in and out at the same hours, with the same sound upon the same pavements, to do the same work, and to whom every day was the same as yesterday and tomorrow, and every year the counterpart of the last and the next.

These attributes of Coketown were in the main inseparable from the work by which it was sustained; against them were to be set off, comforts of life which found their way all over the world, and elegancies of life which made, we will not ask how much of the fine lady, who could scarcely bear to hear the place mentioned. The rest of its features were voluntary, and they were these.

You saw nothing in Coketown but what was severely workful. If the members of a religious persuasion built a chapel there—as the members of eighteen religious persuasions had done—they made it a pious warehouse of red brick, with sometimes (but this only in highly ornamented examples) a bell in a bird-cage on the top of it. The solitary exception was the New Church; a stuccoed edifice with a square steeple over the door, terminating in four short pinnacles like florid wooden legs. All the public inscriptions in the town were painted alike, in severe characters of black and white. The jail might have been the infirmary, the infirmary might have been the jail, the town-hall might have been either, or both, or anything else, for anything that appeared to the contrary in the graces of their construction. Fact, fact, fact, everywhere in the material aspect of the town; fact, fact, fact, everywhere in the immaterial. The M'Choakumchild school was all fact, and the school of design was all fact, and the relations between master and man were all fact, and everything was fact between the lying-in hospital and the cemetery, and what you couldn't state in figures, or show to be purchaseable in the cheapest market and saleable in the dearest, was not, and never should be, world without end, Amen.

A town so sacred to fact, and so triumphant in its assertion, of course got on well? Why no, not quite well. No? Dear me!

No. Coketown did not come out of its own furnaces, in all respects like gold that had stood the fire. First, the perplexing mystery of the place was, Who belonged to the eighteen denominations? Because, whoever did, the labouring people did not. It was very strange to walk through the streets on a Sunday morning, and note how few of *them* the barbarous jangling of bells that was driving the sick and nervous mad, called away from their own quarter, from their own close rooms, from the corners of their own streets, where they lounged listlessly, gazing at all the church and chapel going, as at a thing with which they had no manner of concern. Nor was it merely the stranger who noticed this, because there was a native organization in Coketown itself, whose members were to be heard of in the House of Commons every session, indignantly petitioning for acts of parliament that should make these people religious by main force. Then, came the Tee-total Society, who complained that these same people *would* get drunk, and showed in tabular statements that they did get drunk, and proved at tea parties that no inducement, human or Divine (except a medal), would induce them to forego their custom of getting drunk. Then, came the chemist and druggist, with other tabular statements, showing that when they didn't get drunk, they took opium. Then, came the experienced chaplain of the jail, with more tabular statements, outdoing all the previous tabular statements, and showing that the same people *would* resort to low haunts, hidden from the public eye, where they heard low singing and saw low dancing, and mayhap joined in it; and where A. B., aged twenty-four next birthday, and committed for eighteen months' solitary, had himself said (not that he had ever shown himself particularly worthy of belief) his ruin began, as he was perfectly sure and confident that otherwise he would have been a tip-top moral specimen. Then, came Mr Gradgrind and Mr Bounderby, the two gentlemen at this present moment walking through Coketown, and both eminently practical, who could, on occasion, furnish more tabular statements derived from their own personal experience, and illustrated by cases they had known and seen, from which it clearly appeared—in short it was the only clear thing in the case—that these same people were a bad lot altogether, gentlemen; that do what you would for them they were never thankful for it, gentlemen; that they were restless, gentlemen; that they never knew what they wanted; that they lived upon the best, and bought fresh butter, and insisted on Mocha coffee, and rejected all but prime parts of meat, and yet were eternally dissatisfied and unmanageable. In short it was the moral of the old nursery fable:

> *There was an old woman, and what do you think?*
> *She lived upon nothing but victuals and drink;*
> *Victuals and drink were the whole of her diet,*
> *And yet this old woman would* NEVER *be quiet.*

Is it possible, I wonder, that there was any analogy between the case of the Coketown population and the case of the little Gradgrinds? Surely, none of us in our sober senses and acquainted with figures, are to be told at this time of day, that one of the foremost elements in the existence of the Coketown working people had been for scores of years, deliberately set at nought? That there was any Fancy in them demanding to be brought into healthy existence instead of struggling on in convulsions? That exactly in the ratio as they worked long and monotonously, the craving grew within them for some physical relief— some relaxation, encouraging good humour and good spirits, and giving them a vent—some recognized holiday, though it were but for an honest dance to a stirring band of music—some occasional light pie in which even M'Choakumchild had no finger—which craving must and would be satisfied aright, or must and would inevitably go wrong, until the laws of the Creation were repealed?

'This man lives at Pod's End, and I don't quite know Pod's End,' said Mr Gradgrind. 'Which is it, Bounderby?'

Mr Bounderby knew it was somewhere down town, but knew no more respecting it. So they stopped for a moment, looking about.

Almost as they did so, there came running round the 10 corner of the street at a quick pace and with a frightened look, a girl whom Mr Gradgrind recognized. 'Halloa!' said he. 'Stop! Where are you going? Stop!' Girl number twenty stopped then, palpitating, and made him a curtsey.

'Why are you tearing about the streets,' said Mr Gradgrind, 'in this improper manner?'

'I was—I was run after, sir,' the girl panted, 'and I wanted to get away.'

'Run after?' repeated Mr Gradgrind. 'Who would run after *you?*'

The question was unexpectedly and suddenly answered for her, by the colourless boy, Bitzer, who came round the corner with such blind speed and so little anticipating a stoppage on the pavement, that he brought himself up against Mr Gradgrind's waistcoat, and rebounded into the road.

'What do you mean, boy?' said Mr Gradgrind. 'What 15 are you doing? How dare you dash against—everybody— in this manner?'

Bitzer picked up his cap, which the concussion had knocked off; and backing, and knuckling his forehead, pleaded that it was an accident.

'Was this boy running after you, Jupe?' asked Mr Gradgrind.

'Yes, sir,' said the girl reluctantly.

'No, I wasn't, sir!' cried Bitzer. 'Not till she run away from me. But the horse-riders never mind what they say, sir; they're famous for it. You know the horse-riders are famous for never minding what they say,' addressing Sissy. 'It's as well known in the town as—please, sir, as the multiplication table isn't known to the horse-riders.' Bitzer tried Mr Bounderby with this.

'He frightened me so,' said the girl, 'with his cruel 20 faces!'

'Oh!' cried Bitzer. 'Oh! An't you one of the rest! An't you a horse-rider! I never looked at her, sir. I asked her if she would know how to define a horse tomorrow, and offered to tell her again, and she ran away, and I ran after her, sir, that she might know how to answer when she was asked. You wouldn't have thought of saying such mischief if you hadn't been a horse-rider!'

'Her calling seems to be pretty well known among 'em,' observed Mr Bounderby. 'You'd have had the whole school peeping in a row, in a week.'

'Truly, I think so,' returned his friend. 'Bitzer, turn you about and take yourself home. Jupe, stay here a moment. Let me hear of your running in this manner any more, boy, and you will hear of me through the master of the school. You understand what I mean. Go along.'

The boy stopped in his rapid blinking, knuckled his forehead again, glanced at Sissy, turned about, and retreated.

'Now, girl,' said Mr Gradgrind, 'take this gentleman 25 and me to your father's; we are going there. What have you got in that bottle you are carrying?'

'Gin,' said Mr Bounderby.

'Dear, no sir! It's the nine oils.'

'The what?' cried Mr Bounderby.

'The nine oils, sir. To rub father with.' Then, said Mr Bounderby, with a loud, short laugh, 'What the devil do you rub your father with nine oils for?'

'It's what our people always use, sir, when they get ³⁰ any hurts in the ring,' replied the girl, looking over her shoulder, to assure herself that her pursuer was gone. 'They bruise themselves very bad sometimes.'

'Serve 'em right,' said Mr Bounderby, 'for being idle.' She glanced up at his face, with mingled astonishment and dread.

'By George!' said Mr Bounderby, 'when I was four or five years younger than you, I had worse bruises upon me than ten oils, twenty oils, forty oils, would have rubbed off. I didn't get 'em by posture-making, but by being banged about. There was no rope-dancing for me; I danced on the bare ground and was larruped with the rope.'

Mr Gradgrind, though hard enough, was by no means so rough a man as Mr Bounderby. His character was not unkind, all things considered; it might have been a very kind one indeed, if he had only made some round mistake in the arithmetic that balanced it, years ago. He said, in what he meant for a reassuring tone, as they turned down a narrow road, 'And this is Pod's End; is it, Jupe?'

'This is it, sir, and—if you wouldn't mind, sir—this is the house.'

She stopped, at twilight, at the door of a mean little ³⁵ public house, with dim red lights in it. As haggard and as shabby, as if, for want of custom, it had itself taken to drinking, and had gone the way all drunkards go, and was very near the end of it.

'It's only crossing the bar, sir, and up the stairs, if you wouldn't mind, and waiting there for a moment till I get a candle. If you should hear a dog, sir, it's only Merrylegs, and he only barks.'

'Merrylegs and nine oils, eh!' said Mr Bounderby, entering last with his metallic laugh. 'Pretty well this, for a self-made man!'

KARL MARX AND FRIEDRICH ENGELS

Selection from *The Communist Manifesto*

Not all of Marxist ideology is to be found in *The Communist Manifesto*, but this short pamphlet of barely fifty pages, with its striking phrases and call to revolution, is the best introduction available to the ideas of Karl Marx (1818–1883) and Friedrich Engels (1820–1895), his close friend and collaborator. This work shows how Marxism interprets the unfolding of history, provides a practical plan to change the existing social system, and predicts the future. Labeled by the first communists as their "confession of faith," the *Manifesto* constitutes the most inspiring, yet precise and practical, document for the followers of the "religion" of Marxism. A secular gospel, this document offers true believers a materialistic, scientific analysis of the past, complete with unquestioned dogmas and a call to arms for a new heaven on earth—a communist society free of class conflict and with justice for all.

Marx and Engels coauthored the *Manifesto*, but Engels was always modest in his own claims, accepting without protest that the world called their philosophy Marxism, not Engelism. Thus Marx is usually the focus of discussions of Marxism. Nonetheless, Engels's contribution was significant, and it should be noted that the two authors had much in common. Both were born middle-class but with a difference: Their families were assimilated German Jews, a source of prejudice toward them because of lingering anti-Semitism. As youths, both spent time among left-wing Hegelians (see *Reason in History*) who were atheistic and communistic (Marx as a university student in Bonn, Berlin, and Jena, and Engels as a visitor). Both came to identify with the proletariat, or working class, as the revolutionary hope for the future, substantiated by Marx's contacts with the downtrodden in Paris and by Engels's experience with factory workers in industrially advanced England.

These founders of communism first met in the early 1840s, when Marx was writer and then editor of the *Rheinische Zeitung* (*Rhineland Times*) and Engels was the self-educated son of a wealthy Rhineland industrialist. Marx, having completed a doctorate in philosophy, was in journalism only because his radical politics had effectively blocked him from a post at one of the German universities. Politics inevitably cost Marx the job at the newspaper, and he moved to Paris, then alive with intellectual ferment, especially by socialists intent on remodeling the world. In Paris in 1844 he cemented his friendship with Engels, and in what was to become a lifelong pattern, Engels gave Marx financial aid. After managing his father's textile factory in Manchester, England, Engels had just written his first major work, *The Condition of the Working Class in England in 1844* (1845), a damning indictment of industrialism.

For the rest of Marx's life, he and Engels were a team, with Engels, who never married, providing financial, intellectual, and emotional sustenance to Marx. When French authorities, prodded by the Prussians, invited Marx to move to Belgium in 1845, Engels joined him there and they collaborated on three books, including *The Communist Manifesto* (1848). Marx and his family settled permanently in England in 1849, and Engels was there to provide him with support upon the deaths of two children and the birth of an illegitimate one. Recent research has uncovered the fact that Engels wrote about one-fourth of the articles supposedly written by Marx and collaborated in several others that were published in the New York *Tribune* between 1851 and 1862. Engels, by means of financial gifts, also eased the Marx family's poverty, especially in the early London years.

The Communist Manifesto was written in Belgium at the request of a group of exiled German workers called the Communist League. Marx's major contribution to this work, according to Engels, was the "truly original idea" that culture is an outgrowth of prevailing economic conditions—in other words, economic determinism. Engels's primary role was to supply firsthand knowledge of the workers, showing how the factory system had turned them into wage slaves and stripped them of their dignity and humanity. Together, Marx and Engels devised a dialectical approach to history, based on a marriage of economic determinism with the Hegelian dialectic. In the Marxist dialectic, the driving force is class struggle, in which the haves (thesis) and have nots (antithesis) battle endlessly, with the occasional emergence of a new and dominant class (synthesis) when economic conditions permit. Marx and Engels envisioned an end to class struggle only with the destruction of the bourgeoisie and the capitalist system by their enemies, the proletariat, who will then set up a classless society under a communist economy.

Reading the Selection

The opening paragraphs of *The Communist Manifesto* have been repeated so often that they have become a cliché, but when read by fresh minds, they still raise hope for those who see themselves as victims of economic and social repression. After discussing the causes for the rise of the bourgeoisie, Marx and Engels detail the ways this class controls the modes of production and society. They then explain the relationship between the communists and the proletariat, noting that the former will join the latter in its struggle for freedom and justice. At the end of this section, the authors catalogue the measures needed to ensure the establishment of proletariat rule, in which "the free development of each is the condition for the free development of all"— a classic expression of the humanitarian thinking of these writers. The concluding call to arms—"Workingmen of all countries, unite!"—opposes the ages's nationalism and represents the belief (which turned out to be false) that a country's workers have more in common with foreign workers than they do with their middle-class oppressors at home.

—m—

A specter is haunting Europe—the specter of communism. All the powers of old Europe have entered into a holy alliance to exorcise this specter: Pope and Czar, Meternich and Guizot, French Radicals and German police spies.

Where is the party in opposition that has not been decried as communistic by its opponents in power? Where the Opposition that has not hurled back the branding reproach of communism, against the more advanced opposition parties, as well as against its reactionary adversaries?

Two things result from this fact:

I. Communism is already acknowledged by all European powers to be itself a power.

II. It is high time that Communists should openly, in the face of the whole world, publish their views, their aims, their tendencies, and meet this nursery tale of the specter of communism with a manifesto of the party itself.

To this end, Communists of various nationalities have assembled in London, and sketched the following manifesto, to be published in the English, French, German, Italian, Flemish, and Danish languages. . . .

The bourgeoisie has played a most revolutionary role in history.

The bourgeoisie, wherever it has got the upper hand, has put an end to all feudal, patriarchal, idyllic relations. It has pitilessly torn asunder the motley feudal ties that bound man to his "natural superiors," and has left no other bond between man and man than naked self-interest, than callous "cash payment." It has drowned the most heavenly ecstasies of religious fervor, of chivalrous enthusiasm, of philistine sentimentalism, in the icy water of egotistical calculation. It has resolved personal worth into exchange value, and in place of the numberless indefeasible chartered freedoms, has set up that single, unconscionable freedom—Free Trade. In one word, for exploitation, veiled by religious and political illusions, it has substituted naked, shameless, direct, brutal exploitation.

The bourgeoisie has stripped of its halo every occupation hitherto honored and looked up to with reverent awe. It has converted the physician, the lawyer, the priest, the poet, the man of science, into its paid wage-laborers.

The bourgeoisie has torn away from the family its sentimental veil, and has reduced the family relation to a mere money relation.

The bourgeoisie has disclosed how it came to pass that the brutal display of vigor in the Middle Ages, which reactionaries so much admire, found its fitting complement in the most slothful indolence. It has been the first to show what man's activity can bring about. It has accomplished wonders far surpassing Egyptian pyramids, Roman aqueducts, and Gothic cathedrals; it has conducted expeditions that put in the shade all former migrations of nations and crusades.

The bourgeoisie cannot exist without constantly revolutionizing the instruments of production, and thereby the relations of production, and with them the whole relations of society. Conservation of the old modes of production in unaltered form was, on the contrary, the first condition of existence for all earlier industrial classes. Constant revolutionizing of production, uninterrupted disturbance of all social conditions, everlasting uncertainty and agitation distinguish the bourgeois epoch from all earlier ones. All fixed, fast-frozen relations, with their train of ancient and venerable prejudices and opinions, are swept away, all new-formed ones become antiquated before they can ossify. All that is solid melts into air, all that is holy is profaned, and man is at last compelled to face with sober senses his real conditions of life and his relations with his kind.

The need of a constantly expanding market for its products chases the bourgeoisie over the whole surface of the globe. It must nestle everywhere, settle everywhere, establish connections everywhere.

The bourgeoisie has through its exploitation of the world market given a cosmopolitan character to production and consumption in every country. To the great chagrin of reactionaries, it has drawn from under the feet of industry the national ground on which it stood. All old-established national industries have been destroyed or are daily being destroyed. They are dislodged by new industries, whose introduction becomes a life and death question for all civilized nations, by industries that no longer work up indigenous raw material, but raw material drawn from the remotest zones; industries whose products are consumed, not only at home, but in every quarter of the globe. In place of the old wants, satisfied by the production of the country, we find new wants, requiring for their satisfaction the products of distant lands and climes. In place of the old local and national seclusion and self-sufficiency, we have intercourse in every direction, universal interdependence of nations. And as in material, so also in intellectual production. The intellectual creations of individual nations become common property. National one-sidedness and narrow-mindedness become more and

more impossible, and from the numerous national and local literatures there arises a world literature. . . .

We have seen above, that the first step in the revolution by the working class, is to raise the proletariat to the position of ruling class, to establish democracy.

The proletariat will use its political supremacy to wrest, by degrees, all capital from the bourgeoisie, to centralize all instruments of production in the hands of the state, *i.e.*, of the proletariat organized as the ruling class; and to increase the total of productive forces as rapidly as possible.

Of course, in the beginning, this cannot be effected except by means of despotic inroads on the rights of property, and on the conditions of bourgeois production; by means of measures, therefore, which appear economically insufficient and untenable, but which, in the course of the movement, outstrip themselves, necessitate further inroads upon the old social order, and are unavoidable as a means of entirely revolutionizing the mode of production.

These measures will of course be different in different countries.

Nevertheless in the most advanced countries, the following will be pretty generally applicable.

1. Abolition of property in land and application of all rents of land to public purposes.

2. A heavy progressive or graduated income tax.

3. Abolition of all right of inheritance.

4. Confiscation of the property of all emigrants and rebels.

5. Centralization of credit in the hands of the state, by means of a national bank with state capital and an exclusive monopoly.

6. Centralization of the means of communication and transport in the hands of the state.

7. Extension of factories and instruments of production owned by the state; the bringing into cultivation of waste lands, and the improvement of the soil generally in accordance with a common plan.

8. Equal obligation of all to work. Establishment of industrial armies, especially for agriculture.

9. Combination of agriculture with manufacturing industries; gradual abolition of the distinction between town and country, by a more equable distribution of the population over the country.

10. Free education for all children in public schools. Abolition of child factory labor in its present form. Combination of education with industrial production, etc.

When, in the course of development, class distinctions have disappeared, and all production has been concentrated in the hands of a vast association of the whole nation, the public power will lose its political character. Political power, properly so called, is merely the organized power of one class for oppressing another. If the proletariat during its contest with the bourgeoisie is compelled, by the force of circumstances, to organize itself as a class; if, by means of a revolution, it makes itself the ruling class, and, as such sweeps away by force the old conditions of production, then it will, along with these conditions, have swept away the conditions for the existence of class antagonisms, and of classes generally, and will thereby have abolished its own supremacy as a class.

In place of the old bourgeois society, with its classes and class antagonisms, we shall have an association, in which the free development of each is the condition for the free development of all. . . .

The Communists fight for the attainment of the immediate aims, for the enforcement of the momentary interests of the working class; but in the movement of the present, they also represent and take care of the future of that movement. In France the Communists ally themselves with the Social-Democrats, against the conservative and radical bourgeoisie, reserving, however, the right to take up a critical position in regard to phrases and illusions traditionally handed down from the great Revolution.

In Switzerland they support the Radicals, without losing sight of the fact that this party consists of antagonistic elements, partly of Democratic Socialists, in the French sense, partly of radical bourgeois.

In Poland they support the party that insists on an agrarian revolution as the prime condition for national emancipation, that party which fomented the insurrection of Cracow in 1846. 35

In Germany they fight with the bourgeoisie whenever it acts in a revolutionary way, against the absolute monarchy, the feudal squirearchy, and the petty bourgeoisie.

But they never cease, for a single instant, to instill into the working class the clearest possible recognition of the hostile antagonism between bourgeoisie and proletariat, in order that the German workers may straightway use, as so many weapons against the bourgeoisie, the social and political conditions that the bourgeoisie must necessarily introduce along with its supremacy, and in order that, after the fall of the reactionary classes in Germany, the fight against the bourgeoisie itself may immediately begin.

The Communists turn their attention chiefly to Germany, because that country is on the eve of a bourgeois revolution that is bound to be carried out under more advanced conditions of European civilization and with a much more developed proletariat than what existed in England in the 17th and in France in the 18th century, and because the bourgeois revolution in Germany will be but the prelude to an immediately following proletarian revolution.

In short, the Communists everywhere support every revolutionary movement against the existing social and political order of things.

In all these movements they bring to the front, as the leading question in each case, the property question, no matter what its degree of development at the time. 40

Finally, they labor everywhere for the union and agreement of the democratic parties of all countries.

The Communists disdain to conceal their views and aims. They openly declare that their ends can be attained only by the forcible overthrow of all existing social conditions. Let the ruling classes tremble at a Communist revolution. The proletarians have nothing to lose but their chains. They have a world to win.

Workingmen of all countries, unite!

GUSTAVE FLAUBERT

Selection from *Madame Bovary*

Flaubert's *Madame Bovary* (1857) is considered the greatest novel in the French language. Its heroine, Emma Bovary, is the first of a line of unhappy middle-class wives, such as the Russian writer Tolstoy's Anna Karenina, who appear in modern fiction. Flaubert's story of Emma's revolt against marriage led officials to prosecute him (unsuccessfully) for "immorality." Such a charge is ludicrous today, partly because morals are more relaxed, and partly because studies of sexuality (see Freud's *Civilization;* Beauvoir's *The Second Sex*) have made Emma's adultery more understandable. Hence Flaubert's novel is a pioneering work in the literature of female consciousness.

Although published in 1857, when France was undergoing rapid change fueled by the rise of the railroad, telegraph, and newspaper, *Madame Bovary* was set in a slightly earlier, more stable period, before new technologies destroyed old ways of life. The novel's general subject is provincial culture (the subtitle was *Moeurs de province,* "provincial life"), which Flaubert despised with a vehemence akin to Marx's. Unlike Marx, he remained a loyal member of the middle class, but he used this novel to portray the narrowness, mediocrity, and hypocrisy of small-town culture. This culture he expressed in the imaginary towns of Tostes and Yonville, in cultural artifacts (a keepsake album, a medical journal, and a shop ledger), speech patterns (everyone speaks in clichés), and social events (a local ball and an opera performance).

The novel's specific subject is Emma Bovary, whose personal tragedy is inevitable, given Flaubert's dark vision of provincial life. Convent educated, innately sensual, and addicted to Romantic novels, Emma is also a stupid, vulgar, and cruel woman. She marries Charles Bovary, a physician, who is good-hearted but insensitive, and within weeks she says: "Oh, why, dear God, did I marry him?" Bored with her husband, she allows herself to be seduced by Rodolphe Boulanger, a wealthy landowner and sexual libertine. She plunges into a downward spiral of pleasure-seeking, all of which ends in further disappointment. Beset by debt and despair, she takes arsenic and dies. Charles, now penniless, dies soon after.

Gustave Flaubert (1821–1880) practically invented the Realistic-style novel with this work. Its setting and characters were true to his world near Rouen, where he, the son of a doctor, lived on a private income (he left Rouen for three years to study law in Paris and for eighteen months to tour the Near East). Its meticulously prosaic language reflected the banal speech that he heard in Rouen (he kept a *Dictionary of Received Ideas* to collect choice examples of overheard clichés). Emma Bovary, he claimed, was patterned after himself: "Madame Bovary, c'est moi!" (I am Madame Bovary!)

Reading the Selection

This selection from Chapter VIII of *Madame Bovary* takes place on the day of Yonville's agricultural show. Flaubert's account is cinematic, shifting back and forth between fragments of Rodolphe's seduction of Emma, which takes place upstairs in the Town Hall, and fragments of the town official Lieuvain's speech, which occurs out-of-doors. Emma sits mesmerized by Rodolphe's smooth whisperings ("You know that I am yours!"), just as Yonville's citizens listen transfixed by Lieuvain's oratory ("Keep steadily ahead!"). Hence, in Flaubert's vision, there is no escape from this provincial world, either through love or material progress: Both are illusions.

Chapter VIII

. . .

'Madame Bovary!' exclaimed Homais. 'I must run and pay her my respects. She might like to have a seat in the enclosure, under the peristyle.' 1

And turning a deaf ear to the rest of the Widow Lefrançois' story, the chemist hurried off, with a smile on his lips, a jaunty stride, and any number of bowings in all directions, taking up a great deal of space with the long tails of his dress-coat flapping in the breeze behind him.

Rodolphe had noticed him from a distance and quickened his pace, but as Madame Bovary got out of breath, he slowed up again, smiling at her as he explained brusquely:

'That was to escape from the heavy fellow—you know, the chemist.'

She gave him a nudge. 5

'What's the meaning of that?' he asked himself, and as he walked along he surveyed her out of the corner of his eye.

Her calm profile gave no hint. It showed clear in the light, framed in the oval of her bonnet, which was tied with pale reed-like ribbons. She was looking straight in front of her, beneath her long curving lashes, and though her eyes were fully open they appeared slightly narrowed because of the blood that pulsated gently beneath the fine skin that covered her cheek-bones. Where her nostrils met was a pale pink glow. Her head leaned a little to one side, and between her parted lips you saw the pearly tips of her white teeth.

'Is she laughing at me?' Rodolphe wondered.

Emma's nudge had been simply a warning, however. Monsieur Lheureux was walking along beside them. Every now and then he made some conversational remark, such as 'What a glorious day!' 'Everybody's out of doors!' 'The wind's in the east!'

Madame Bovary took as little notice of his advances 10 as did Rodolphe, though the draper came sidling up to them at their least movement, touching his hat and saying, 'Beg pardon?'

Outside the blacksmith's, instead of keeping on up to the gate along the roadway, Rodolphe turned abruptly down a side-path, drawing Madame Bovary with him.

'Farewell, Monsieur Lheureux!' he called out. ''Till we meet again!'

'How you got rid of him!' she said with a laugh.

'Why let people hang on to one?' he answered. 'And today, when I'm fortunate enough to be with you . . .'

Emma blushed. He left the sentence unfinished, and 15 started talking about the lovely weather, and the delight of walking on the grass.

Some daisies were growing there.

'What pretty daisies!' he said. 'Oracles in plenty for all the local girls in love! . . . Suppose I pick one,' he added. 'What do you say?'

'Are *you* in love?' she asked, with a little cough.

'Eh! eh! who knows?' answered Rodolphe.

The show-ground was beginning to fill up, and the women helpers kept bumping into you with their big umbrellas, their baskets and their babies. You had frequently to be getting out of the way of a long row of peasant-girls, maidservants in blue stockings and flat shoes, with silver rings on their fingers, who smelt of milk when you came close to them. They spread out hand in hand all across the field, from the row of aspens up to the marquee. By now the judging was due to start, and one after another the farmers were filing into a kind of arena marked off by a long rope hung on stakes.

Inside were the animals, their muzzles towards the rope, their rumps jostling together in a rough line. Somnolent pigs sank their snouts in the ground, calves lowed, sheep bleated, cows sprawled their bellies out on the grass, with one leg bent beneath them, and chewed with deliberation, blinking their heavy eyelids as the midges buzzed round them. Shirt-sleeved wagoners were holding the restive stallions, which kept neighing vociferously in the direction of the mares. These stood quite quiet, stretching out their necks, their manes drooping, while their foals rested in their shadows, or came up from time to time to suck. Above the undulating line of massed beasts, you saw a white mane ruffling up like a wave in the breeze, a pair of sharp horns jutting out, or the heads of some men running. Outside the arena, a hundred yards farther on, a big black bull stood apart, muzzled, with an iron ring through its nostrils, moving no more than an animal of bronze. A ragged child held it by a rope.

Sundry gentlemen were now advancing with heavy tread between the two rows of animals, examining each in turn and then conferring together in low tones. One, who looked more important than the rest, made jottings in a notebook as he went. This was the chairman of the judges, Monsieur Derozerays de la Panville. The minute he recognized Rodolphe he stepped briskly towards him.

'What's this, Monsieur Boulanger?' he said, with a pleasant smile. 'Are you deserting us?'

Rodolphe assured him he was coming directly. But when the chairman was once more out of earshot he said, 'I think not! When I can be with you!'

While ridiculing the Show, Rodolphe nevertheless produced his blue ticket, so that they could move about wherever they pleased, and he even halted occasionally in front of one of the fine 'exhibits'. Noticing, however, that Madame Bovary was unimpressed by these, he started making fun of the Yonville ladies and the way they were turned out. He apologized for being so carelessly dressed himself. His clothes were an incongruous mixture of the workaday and the elegant, such as is taken by the vulgar to denote an eccentric way of life, an emotional disturbance, or a subservience to aesthetics, combined always with a certain contempt for convention, by which they are either fascinated or exasperated. Frilly at the cuffs, his cambric shirt

fluttered out in front between the revers of his grey drill waistcoat wherever the breeze took it. His broad-striped trousers terminated at the ankle above a pair of nankeen boots vamped with patent leather. These were so highly polished that you could see the grass in them; and in them he went trampling over the horse-dung, with one hand in his jacket pocket, his straw hat tilted to the side of his head.

'But then, when you live in the country . . .' he added.

'. . . There's no point in bothering,' said Emma.

'Exactly!' Rodolphe replied. 'Just fancy, there's not one of all these good people who's capable of understanding so much as the cut of a coat.'

They spoke of the dullness of the country, the lives that were smothered by it, the illusions that perished there.

'That's why,' said Rodolphe, 'I'm sinking into such a state of gloom. . . .'

'You!' she exclaimed in surprise. 'Why, I thought you were a very cheerful person.'

'Oh, on the surface, yes. I wear my jester's mask in public. But how often I've looked at a graveyard in the moonlight and wondered whether I wouldn't be better off lying there asleep with the rest of them!'

'Oh! But what about your friends?' she said. 'Don't you think of them?'

'My friends? What friends? Have I got any? Is there anyone who cares about me?'—and he accompanied these last words with a little hissing sound.

However, they had to step aside for a man coming up behind them with an immense scaffolding of chairs. He was so loaded that you could see nothing of him but the toes of his sabots and the tips of his outstretched arms. It was Lestiboudois the sexton, carting round the church chairs among the crowd. Full of ideas where his own interests were concerned, he had hit upon this method of turning the Show to account; and his enterprise was rewarded, for he had more customers than he could cope with. The villagers, feeling the warmth, had actually started squabbling over those straw seats that reeked of incense; and against their stout backs, covered with blobs of candle-grease, they were leaning with a certain awe.

Madame Bovary took Rodolphe's arm again.

'Yes,' he went on as though to himself, 'I've missed a lot, always being alone. If only I'd had some aim in life. If I'd met with affection. If I'd found someone . . . Oh, I'd have used all the energy I possessed—conquered everything, smashed down every obstacle.'

'It doesn't seem to me you've got much to grumble about,' said Emma.

'You think not?'

'After all, you're free'—she hesitated—'and rich.'

'You're laughing at me!' he exclaimed.

She assured him she was not. As she spoke, they heard the boom of a cannon. Everybody at once started rushing back to the village.

It was a false alarm; there was no sign of the Prefect. The judges were in a quandary: should they wait, or open the proceedings?

At last, from the far end of the square, appeared a large hired landau drawn by a pair of skinny horses, which were being roundly lashed by a coachman in a white hat. Binet just had time to shout 'Fall in!' and the Colonel to follow suit. There was a dive for the piled rifles. In the commotion, some of the men forgot to fasten their collars. The official equipage seemed to divine their discomfiture, however, for the pair of hacks slowed up, tugging at their chain, and ambled to a halt outside the Town Hall, just as the militia and the fire-brigade were deploying to the beat of the drums.

'Mark time!' shouted Binet.   45

'Halt!' shouted the Colonel. 'Into line—left—turn!'

After a 'Present arms', in which the smacking of the bands came rattling out like a copper kettle rolling downstairs, all the rifles were lowered again.

Thereupon a gentleman in a short silver-trimmed jacket was seen to step out of the carriage. He was bald in front and tufted behind, sallow-complexioned, and with an appearance of the utmost benignity. He narrowed his large heavy-lidded eyes to scan the crowd, lifted his pointed nose in the air and set a smile on his sunken mouth. Recognizing the mayor by his sash, he explained that the Prefect had been prevented from coming. He himself was an official on the Prefect's staff. He added a few words of apology. Tuvache responded in complimentary terms. The visitor declared himself overwhelmed. So they stood there face to face, their foreheads almost touching, surrounded by the judges, the councillors, the important personages, the militia, and the crowd at large. Holding his little black three-cornered hat against his chest, the great man reiterated his greetings, while Tuvache, bent like a bow, smiled back at him, stuttering and stammering and making protestation of his loyalty to the throne and his appreciation of the honour that was being done to Yonville.

Hippolyte, the groom from the inn, came limping up on his club-foot to take the reins from the coachman, and led the horses off beneath the archway of the Golden Lion, where a crowd of peasants gathered round to inspect the carriage. There was a tattoo on the drums, the howitzer thundered, and the gentlemen filed up and took their places on the platform, in the easy-chairs of red Utrecht velvet lent by Madame Tuvache.

A homogeneous group they were, with their soft, fair,   50
slightly tanned faces, the colour of new cider, and their bushy whiskers sticking out above tall stiff collars supported by white cravats tied in a floppy bow. Every one of the waistcoats had velvet revers, every watch carried an oval cornelian seal at the end of a long band. Hands all rested on thighs, carefully lifting the creases of their trousers, which were of unsponged cloth and shone more brilliantly than their stout leather boots.

The ladies of the party kept at the back, between the pillars in the vestibule, while the body of the crowd faced them, standing up, or seated on Lestiboudois' chairs. For he had brought a load along with him from the meadow, and was all the while running off to get more from the church, causing such congestion with his trade that one had great difficulty in reaching the platform steps.

'I think myself,' said Monsieur Lheureux to the chemist, as the latter passed along to take his seat, 'that

they ought to have put up a couple of Venetian masts, with something rich and a bit severe in the way of draping. It would have made a fine sight.'

'Certainly it would,' answered Homais. 'But there, what can you expect? The mayor *would* do the whole thing on his own. Poor old Tuvache, he hasn't got much taste; in fact, he's completely lacking in any sort of artistic sense.'

Meanwhile Rodolphe and Madame Bovary had gone up to the Council Chamber on the first floor of the Town Hall. It was empty, and so he declared that they would be able to enjoy the spectacle in comfort up there. Fetching three stools from the oval table under the bust of the King, he placed them by one of the windows, and they sat down side by side.

There was a great commotion on the platform, much   55
whispering and parleying, and at last the Prefect's deputy rose. His name, now known to be Lieuvain, was being passed round among the crowd. After collecting his papers together and holding them close up to his eyes to see them better, he began:

'Gentlemen,

'Let me first be permitted, before addressing you on the object of our gathering here today—and this sentiment will, I am sure, be shared by all of you—let me be permitted, I say, to pay a fitting tribute to the Authorities, to the Government and, gentlemen, to our beloved Monarch and Sovereign Lord the King, to whom no branch of public or private prosperity is indifferent, and who steers the chariot of state with a hand at once so firm and so wise, amid the ceaseless perils of a stormy sea—who knows, moreover, how to gain respect for peace no less than for war—for Trade and for Industry, for Agriculture and for the Arts.'

'I ought to get a bit farther back,' said Rodolphe.

'Why?' said Emma.

But at that moment the official's voice rose to a re-   60
markable pitch as he declaimed:

'Those days are past, gentlemen, when civil discord stained our public places with blood, when landowner, merchant, and working-man alike, as they courted peaceful slumbers, would tremble lest they be awakened by the clang of the tocsin; when the most subversive slogans were aimed in all audacity at the very foundations—'

'They might see me from down there,' Rodolphe explained, 'and then I'd have to spend a fortnight apologizing. And with my bad reputation . . .'

'What a thing to say about yourself!'

'No, no, it's abominable, I assure you.'

'However, gentlemen,' the speaker proceeded, 'if, driv-   65
ing those sombre pictures from my mind, I turn my gaze now to the present state of our fair land, what do I see? Everywhere, trade and the arts flourish. Everywhere new paths of communication, new arteries within the body politic, are opening up new contacts. Our great manufacturing centres thrive once more. Religion finds new strength and smiles in every heart. Our ports are full. Confidence returns. At last France breathes again!'

'Though I dare say I deserve it by ordinary standards,' Rodolphe added.

'How is that?' she asked.

'Why, do you not know that there are souls for ever in turmoil? Souls that must have dream and action turn and turn about—a passion of utter purity, and an orgy of self-indulgence? It leads one into all kinds of adventures and escapades.'

She gazed at him then as one might gaze at a traveller who has journeyed through strange lands.

'We poor women haven't even that diversion,' she remarked. 70

'Sorry diversion, for it never brings happiness.'

'Does anything?'

'Yes,' he answered, 'it comes along one day.'

'And this,' the distinguished visitor was saying, 'this you have realized, you who cultivate the land and labour in the fields, peaceable pioneers in a true task of civilization! Progressive and high-minded men! You have realized, I say, that the storms of political strife are, in very truth, more devastating than the riot of the elements!'

'It comes along one day,' Rodolphe repeated, 'all of a 75 sudden, just when you are despairing of it. Then, new vistas open. It's as if a voice cried out "Behold!" You feel you must reveal yourself, give everything, sacrifice everything, to that person. Nothing need be said. You know! You have seen each other in your dreams'—and his eyes rested on hers. 'There before you, shining, sparkling, is the treasure you have sought so long. Still you doubt. You dare not believe. You stand dazed as if you had stepped out of darkness into light.'

Here Rodolphe helped out his words with motions, passing his hand over his face like a man in a trance. Then he let it fall on Emma's. She withdrew hers. The official read on:

'And who can wonder at it, gentlemen? Only he who remains so blind, so immersed, so deeply immersed, I do not fear to say, in the prejudices of a past age, as still to misconceive the spirit of our agricultural communities. Where, indeed, can one find more patriotism than in the country, more devotion to the common weal, in a word, more intelligence? I do not mean, gentlemen, a superficial intelligence—that vain embellishment of idle minds—but a profound and balanced intelligence that applies itself first and foremost to the pursuit of useful ends, contributing thus to the good of each, to the general advancement, and to the upholding of the State—the fruit of respect for law and fulfillment of duty!'

'Duty again!' said Rodolphe. 'Always on about duty. I'm sick to death of the word. What a lot of flannel-waistcoated old fogeys they are, pious old women with beads and bedsocks, for ever twittering in our ears about "Duty, duty!" To feel nobly and to love what is beautiful—that's our duty. Not to accept all the conventions of society and the humiliations society imposes on us.'

'Still . . . all the same . . .' Madame Bovary demurred.

'No! Why inveigh against the passions? Are they not 80 the one beautiful thing there is on earth; the source of all heroism and enthusiasm, poetry, music, art, everything?'

'All the same,' said Emma, 'we must take some notice of what the world thinks, and conform to its morality.'

'But you see, there are two moralities,' he replied. 'One is the petty, conventional morality of men, clamorous, ever-changing, that flounders about on the ground, of the earth earthy, like that mob of nincompoops down there. The other, the eternal morality, is all about and above us, like the countryside that surrounds us and the blue heavens that give us light.'

Monsieur Lieuvain had just wiped his mouth with his handkerchief. He resumed:

'Now what should I be doing here, gentlemen, demonstrating the usefulness of farming to *you*? Who supplies our wants, who provides us with the means of life, but the farmer? The farmer, gentlemen, who, sowing with laborious hand the fertile furrows of our countryside, brings forth the corn which, crushed and ground by ingenious machinery, issues thence in the guise of flour, to be conveyed to our cities and speedily delivered to the baker, who makes it into a food for rich and poor alike. Is it not the farmer, again, who fattens his rich flocks to give us clothes? How should we clothe, or feed, ourselves were it not for the farmer? Nay, gentlemen, need we go even so far afield for our examples? Who has not frequently pondered on the great importance to us of that homely animal, the adornment of our poultry-yards, that provides us with soft pillows to sleep on, succulent flesh for our tables, and eggs?—But I could go on for ever enumerating, one by one, the various products that the well-tended earth lavishes like a bountiful mother upon her children. Here the vine, there the cider apple, elsewhere colza, cheese, or flax—gentlemen, let us not forget flax!—which has made such strides in recent years, and to which I would more especially draw your attention.'

He had no need to draw it, for the multitude sat open- 85 mouthed to drink in his words. Tuvache, next to him, listened with staring eyes. Monsieur Derozerays gently closed his now and then. Farther along, the chemist, with his son Napoléon between his knees, had his hand cupped behind his ear so as not to lose a single syllable. The rest of the judges nodded their chins slowly up and down in their waistcoats to signify assent. The fire-brigade leaned on their bayonet-scabbards at the foot of the platform, and Binet stood motionless, his elbow stuck out, the point of his sabre in the air. He may have heard, but he could not have seen anything for the visor of his helmet, which came right down over his nose. His lieutenant, Monsieur Tuvache's youngest son, had his visor at a still more exaggerated angle. He was wearing an enormous helmet that wobbled on top of his head and allowed one end of his calico handkerchief to slip down behind. He smiled beneath it with a perfectly child-like sweetness, and his little white face, running with sweat, wore an expression of enjoyment, exhaustion and somnolence.

The crowd stretched right across to the houses on the far side of the square. There were people leaning out of every window, standing in every doorway. Justin, outside the chemist's shop, seemed quite transfixed by the sight that met his eyes. In spite of the silence, Monsieur Lieuvain's voice failed to carry in the air, and reached you only in fragmentary phrases, drowned here and there by the scraping of chairs among the crowd. Then all of a sudden you heard the long lowing of a bullock behind you, or lambs bleating to each other at the corners of the streets. They had been driven down by the shepherds and cowherds, and gave voice from time to time as their tongues snatched at a morsel of foliage hanging above their muzzles.

Rodolphe had drawn closer to Emma and was talking rapidly in a low voice.

'Doesn't this conspiracy of society revolt you? Is there a single feeling it does not condemn? The noblest instincts, the purest sympathies, are reviled and persecuted, and if ever two poor souls do meet, then everything is organized to prevent their union. They'll attempt it all the same, they'll flap their wings and call to one another. And no matter what happens, sooner or later, in six months or ten years, they'll meet again and love—because Fate ordains it, because they were born for one another.'

He sat with his arms folded on his knees. Raising his eyes to Emma's, he gazed at her closely, fixedly. She saw little gleams of gold playing about his dark pupils. She was near enough to him to smell the cream on his glossy hair. She felt limp, she remembered the Viscount who had waltzed with her at La Vaubyessard: his beard had exhaled that same perfume of lemon and vanilla. Mechanically her eyelids narrowed as she breathed in the scent. She straightened up in her chair, and as she did so she caught a glimpse, right away on the farthest horizon, of the ancient *Hirondelle* slowly descending Leux Hill, trailing a long plume of dust behind it. It was in that yellow coach that Léon had so often come back to her; and along that road that he had gone from her for ever. She had a vision of him at his window across the way. Then everything blurred, the sky clouded over, and it seemed to her that she was still circling in the waltz, in the glare of the chandeliers, on the Viscount's arm, and Léon was not far away, he was just coming. . . . But all the while she was conscious of Rodolphe's face beside her. Her old desires became imbued with the sweetness of the present sensation, and, on this subtle breath of perfume that was being shed upon her soul, they were tossed about like grains of sand in a gust of wind. Her nostrils dilated rapidly, vigorously, breathing in the freshness of the ivy round the tops of the columns. She took off her gloves, wiped her hands, fanned her face with her handkerchief, while through the throbbing at her temples she could hear the hum of the crowd below and the speaker still droning out his singsong.

'Keep steadily ahead!' he was saying. 'Listen neither to the voice of hidebound habit nor to the impulsive counsels of rash experiment! Work above all at the improvement of the soil, at producing rich fertilizers, at breeding fine horses and cattle, fine sheep and pigs! Let this Agricultural Show be a peaceful arena where victor extends the hand of brotherhood to vanquished and wishes him success next time! . . . And now, to all those venerable retainers, lowly servants whose laborious toils have never before been recognized by any Government, I say: Come forward and receive the meed of your silent virtues! Rest assured that from this day forth the State will never lose

sight of you, that it will encourage and protect you, will satisfy your just demands, and lighten, so far as in it lies, the painful burden of your sacrifice!'

And Monsieur Lieuvain sat down.

Monsieur Derozerays rose and began his speech. This was far less ornate than the official's, and recommended itself by a more positive flavour—a matter of more specialized knowledge and more exalted reflections. Eulogistic reference to the Government had less place in it, farming and religion had more. The bond that existed between the two was made clear—they had always worked together for civilization . . . While Rodolphe was talking to Madame Bovary about dreams, presentiments and magnetic attraction, the speaker went back to the infancy of society, to those savage times when men lived on acorns in the heart of great forests; from which he passed on to the period at which they had given up animals' skins for a covering of cloth, had ploughed the land and planted the vine. Now was this an improvement? Were there not perhaps more disadvantages than advantages in these discoveries? Monsieur Derozerays asked himself the question. Rodolphe had led on gradually from magnetism to affinities; and while the Chairman alluded to Cincinnatus at his plough, to Diocletian among his cabbages, to the Chinese emperors ushering in the new year with the sowing of seed, the young man was explaining to the young woman that the cause of these irresistible attractions lay in some previous existence.

'We, now, why did we meet? What turn of fate decreed it? Was it not that, like two rivers gradually converging across the intervening distance, our own natures propelled us towards one another?'

He took her hand, and she did not withdraw it.

'General Prize!' cried the Chairman.

'Just now, for instance, when I came to call on you . . .'

'Monsieur Bizet of Quincampoix.'

'. . . how could I know that I should escort you here?'

'Seventy francs!'

'And I've stayed with you, because I couldn't tear myself away, though I've tried a hundred times.'

'Manure!'

'And so I'd stay tonight and tomorrow and every day for all the rest of my life.'

'To Monsieur Caron of Argueil, a Gold Medal!'

'For I have never been so utterly charmed with anyone before.'

'To Monsieur Bain of Givry St Martin.'

'And so I shall cherish the memory of you.'

'For a merino ram . . .'

'But you'll forget me. I shall have passed like a shadow . . .'

'To Monsieur Belot of Notre-Dame . . .'

'No, say I shan't! Tell me I shall count for something in your thoughts, in your life?'

'Pigs: Prize divided! Monsieur Lehérissé and Monsieur Cullembourg, sixty francs each!'

Rodolphe squeezed her hand. He felt it warm and vibrant in his, like a captive turtle-dove trying to take wing. Whether she was trying to withdraw it, or responding to his pressure, her fingers made a movement.

'Oh, thank you, you do not repulse me!' he said. 'How sweet you are! You know that I am yours! Only let me look at you, let me gaze upon you!'

A breeze from the window ruffled the cloth on the table, and down in the square the peasant women's big bonnets lifted up, fluttering like white butterflies' wings.

'Oil-cake,' the Chairman continued. He began to go faster; 'Flemish fertilizer—Flax—Drainage—Long Leases— Domestic Service.'

Rodolphe had stopped speaking. They looked at one another, and their dry lips quivered in a supreme desire. Gently, effortlessly, their fingers intertwined. . . .

¹¹⁵

FYODOR DOSTOEVSKY

Selection from *Notes from Underground*

The Russian novelist Fyodor Dostoevsky (1821–1881), a master of nineteenth-century Realism, is acclaimed today as both a giant of world literature and a prophet of this century's culture.

Much of Dostoevsky's fame stems from his uncanny insight into the motives of his tormented heroes—like Raskalnikov in *Crime and Punishment* (1864) and Ivan and Dmitri in *The Brothers Karamazov* (1879–1880); he lays bare the latent violence in their souls, thus anticipating the findings of depth psychology. He is equally known for his political wisdom, for he predicted the ultimate failure of liberalism and socialism, the rival theories that claimed to hold the key to the West's future. In contrast to these godless theories, which saw humanity as good and rational, Dostoevsky believed that mankind was depraved, irrational, and rebellious—thus incapable of self-rule. He concluded that the whole point of life is to seek salvation through suffering and love, a belief based on his mystical Orthodox faith.

Dostoevsky did not always have such a gloomy outlook. When he began to write in 1844, after giving up a military career, he was a "Westernizer," a term for Russians who thought that their country should model itself on France and England, then Europe's leading progressive states. As a Westernizer, he believed that socialism would help alleviate the suffering of Russia's masses. His novels, such as *Poor Folk* (1846), reflected this hope and were written in the sentimental Romantic style then popular in the West. Events in 1848–1849 changed his point of view forever. He was arrested by the police on a charge of subversion (he belonged to a young socialist cell). Jailed and taken out to be shot, he was reprieved at the last minute, as part of a carefully orchestrated plan, and was sentenced to prison in Siberia. In prison he had his eyes opened to cruelty by the behavior of both jailers and inmates. When he returned from Siberia in 1859, he was a Slavophile—a Russian who thought that his country should keep true to its Slavic roots—and claimed that Russians were God's chosen people. His writings thereafter expressed his hatred of Europe and were written in a Realistic style, which dwelt on suffering, with no hope of redemption except in heaven, if then.

Reading the Selection

The first three episodes of Part One of *Notes from Underground* (1862) (there are only two parts) introduce the "Mousehole Man," the unnamed social "dropout" who narrates the novel. In form, the novel is the Mousehole Man's monologue protesting his age's advanced ideas—liberalism, democracy, socialism, and science—each of which saw enlightened self-interest as the key to human happiness. His protest springs from his conviction that human whims and wishes are bound to clash with what is socially useful—an idea Freud later made popular (see *Civilization and Its Discontents*). The narrator calls himself an "anti-hero," the first mention of this concept so central to this century's literature (see Kafka's *Metamorphosis*). Bitter, self-mocking, and ironic, he speaks with Dostoevsky's own "nasty" voice, a fact confirmed by those who knew the author. A mountain of hate, he cannot decide which to loathe more: the West's dream of a well-fed, happy society, symbolized by the Crystal Palace (the 1851 London exhibition, the first world's fair), or his fellow Russians' enthusiasm for French socialists like Charles Fourier (1772–1837), whose ideas Dostoevsky once shared and who now seemed foolish and shallow.

—///—

Part I

Underground

I

I am a sick man . . . I am a spiteful man. I am an unpleasant man. I think my liver is diseased. However, I don't know beans about my disease, and I am not sure what is bothering me. I don't treat it and never have, though I respect medicine and doctors. Besides, I am extremely superstitious, let's say sufficiently so to respect medicine. (I am educated enough not to be superstitious, but I am.) No, I refuse to treat it out of spite. You probably will not understand that. Well, but *I* understand it. Of course, I can't explain to you just whom I am annoying in this case by my spite. I am perfectly well aware that I cannot "get even" with the doctors by not consulting them. I know better than anyone that I thereby injure only myself and no one else. But still, if I don't treat it, it is out of spite. My liver is bad, well then—let it get even worse!

I have been living like that for a long time now—twenty years. I am forty now. I used to be in the civil service, but no longer am. I was a spiteful official. I was rude and took pleasure in being so. After all, I did not accept bribes, so I was bound to find a compensation in that, at least. (A bad joke but I will not cross it out. I wrote it thinking it would sound very witty; but now that I see myself that I only wanted to show off in a despicable way, I will purposely not cross it out!) When petitioners would come to my desk for information I would gnash my teeth at them, and feel intense enjoyment when I succeeded in distressing some one. I was almost always successful. For the most part they were all timid people—of course, they were petitioners. But among the fops there was one officer in particular I could not endure. He simply would not be humble, and clanked his sword in a disgusting way. I carried on a war with him for eighteen months over that sword. At last I got the better of him. He left off clanking it. However, that happened when I was still young. But do you know, gentlemen, what the real point of my spite was? Why, the whole trick, the real vileness of it lay in the fact that continually, even in moments of the worst spleen, I was inwardly conscious with shame that I was not only not spiteful but not even an embittered man, that I was simply frightening sparrows at random and amusing myself by it. I might foam at the mouth, but bring me some kind of toy, give me a cup of tea with sugar, and I would be appeased. My heart might even be touched, though probably I would gnash my teeth at myself afterward and lie awake at night with shame for months after. That is the way I am.

I was lying when I said just now that I was a spiteful official. I was lying out of spite. I was simply indulging myself with the petitioners and with the officer, but I could never really become spiteful. Every moment I was conscious in myself of many, very many elements completely opposite to that. I felt them positively teeming in me, these opposite elements. I knew that they had been teeming in me all my life, begging to be let out, but I would not let them, would not let them, purposely would not let them out. They tormented me till I was ashamed; they drove me to convulsions, and finally, they bored me, how they bored me! Well, are you not imagining, gentlemen, that I am repenting for something now, that I am asking your forgiveness for something? I am sure you are imagining that. However, I assure you it does not matter to me if you are.

Not only could I not become spiteful, I could not even become anything: neither spiteful nor kind, neither a rascal nor an honest man, neither a hero nor an insect. Now, I am living out my life in my corner, taunting myself with the spiteful and useless consolation that an intelligent man cannot seriously become anything and that only a fool can become something. Yes, an intelligent man in the nineteenth century must and morally ought to be pre-eminently a characterless creature; a man of character, an active man, is pre-eminently a limited creature. That is the conviction of my forty years. I am forty years old now, and forty years, after all, is a whole lifetime; after all, that is extreme old age. To live longer than forty years is bad manners; it is vulgar, immoral. Who does live beyond forty? Answer that, sincerely and honestly. I will tell you who do: fools and worthless people do. I tell all old men that to their face, all those respectable old men, all those silver-haired and reverend old men! I tell the whole world that to its face. I have a right to say so, for I'll go on living to sixty myself. I'll live till seventy! Till eighty! Wait, let me catch my breath.

No doubt you think, gentlemen, that I want to amuse you. You are mistaken in that, too. I am not at all such a merry person as you imagine, or as you may imagine; however, if irritated by all this babble (and I can feel that you are irritated) you decide to ask me just who I am—then my answer is, I am a certain low-ranked civil servant. I was in the service in order to have something to eat (but only for that reason), and when last year a distant relation left me six thousand roubles in his will I immediately retired from the service and settled down in my corner. I used to live in this corner before, but now I have settled down in it. My room is a wretched, horrid one on the outskirts of town. My servant is an old country-woman, spiteful out of stupidity, and, moreover, she always smells bad. I am told that the Petersburg climate is bad for me, and that with my paltry means it is very expensive to live in Petersburg. I know all that better than all these sage and experienced counsellors and monitors. But I am going to stay in Petersburg. I will not leave Petersburg! I will not leave because . . . Bah, after all it does not matter in the least whether I leave or stay.

But incidentally, what can a decent man speak about with the greatest pleasure?

Answer: About himself.

Well, then, I will talk about myself.

II

Now I want to tell you, gentlemen, whether you care to hear it or not, why I could not even become an insect. I tell you solemnly that I wanted to become an insect many times. But I was not even worthy of that. I swear to you, gentlemen, that to be hyperconscious is a disease, a real positive disease. Ordinary human consciousness would be too much for man's everyday needs, that is, half or a quarter of the amount which falls to the lot of a cultivated man of our unfortunate nineteenth century, especially one who has the particular misfortune to inhabit Petersburg, the most abstract and intentional city in the whole world. (There are intentional and unintentional cities.) It would have been quite enough, for instance, to have the consciousness by which all so-called straightforward persons and men of action live. I'll bet you think I am writing all this to show off, to be witty at the expense of men of action; and what is more, that out of ill-bred showing-off, I am clanking a sword, like my officer. But, gentlemen, whoever can pride himself on his diseases and even show off with them?

However, what am I talking about? Everyone does that. They do pride themselves on their diseases, and I, perhaps, more than any one. There is no doubt about it: my objection was absurd. Yet just the same, I am firmly convinced not only that a great deal of consciousness, but that any consciousness is a disease. I insist on it. Let us drop that, too, for a minute. Tell me this: why did it happen that at the very, yes, at the very moment when I was most capable of recognizing every refinement of "all the sublime and beautiful," as we used to say at one time, I would, as though purposely, not only feel but do such hideous things, such that—well, in short, such as everyone probably does but which, as though purposely, occurred to me at the very time when I was most conscious that they ought not to be done. The more conscious I was of goodness, and of all that "sublime and beautiful," the more deeply I sank into my mire and the more capable I became of sinking into it completely. But the main thing was that all this did not seem to occur in me accidentally, but as though it had to be so. As though it were my most normal condition, and not in the least disease or depravity, so that finally I even lost the desire to struggle against this depravity. It ended by my almost believing (perhaps actually believing) that probably this was really my normal condition. But at first, in the beginning, that is, what agonies I suffered in that struggle! I did not believe that others went through the same things, and therefore I hid this fact about myself as a secret all my life. I was ashamed (perhaps I am even ashamed now). I reached the point of feeling a sort of secret abnormal, despicable enjoyment in returning home to my corner on some disgusting Petersburg night, and being acutely conscious that that day I had again done something loathsome, that what was done could never be undone, and secretly, inwardly gnaw, gnaw at myself for it, nagging and consuming myself till at last the bitterness turned into a sort of shameful accursed sweetness, and finally into real positive enjoyment!

Yes, into enjoyment, into enjoyment! I insist upon that. And that is why I have started to speak, because I keep wanting to know for a fact whether other people feel such an enjoyment. Let me explain: the enjoyment here consisted precisely in the hyperconsciousness of one's own degradation; it was from feeling oneself that one had reached the last barrier, that it was nasty, but that it could not be otherwise; that you no longer had an escape; that you could never become a different person; that even if there remained enough time and faith for you to change into something else you probably would not want to change; or if you did want to, even then you would do nothing; because perhaps in reality there was nothing for you to change into. And the worst of it, and the root of it all, was that it all proceeded according to the normal and fundamental laws of hyperconsciousness, and with the inertia that was the direct result of those laws, and that consequently one could not only not change but one could do absolutely nothing. Thus it would follow, as the result of hyperconsciousness, that one is not to blame for being a scoundrel, as though that were any consolation to the scoundrel once he himself has come to realize that he actually is a scoundrel. But enough. Bah, I have talked a lot of nonsense, but what have I explained? Can this enjoyment be explained? But I will explain it! I will get to the bottom of it! That is why I have taken up my pen.

To take an instance, I am terribly vain. I am as suspicious and touchy as a hunchback or a dwarf. But to tell the truth, there have been moments when if someone had happened to slap my face I would, perhaps, have even been glad of that. I say, very seriously, that I would probably have been able to discover a peculiar sort of enjoyment even in that—the enjoyment, of course, of despair; but in despair occur the most intense enjoyments, especially when one is very acutely conscious of one's hopeless position. As for the slap in the face—why then the consciousness of being beaten to a pulp would positively overwhelm one. The worst of it is, no matter how I tried, it still turned out that I was always the most to blame in everything, and what is most humiliating of all, to blame for no fault of my own but, so to say, through the laws of nature. In the first place, to blame because I am cleverer than any of the people surrounding me. (I have always considered myself cleverer than any of the people surrounding me, and sometimes, would you believe it, I have even been ashamed of that. At any rate, all my life, I have, as it were, looked away and I could never look people straight in the eye.) To blame, finally, because even if I were magnanimous, I would only have suffered more from the consciousness of all its uselessness. After all, I would probably never have been able to do anything with my magnanimity—neither to forgive, for my assailant may have slapped me because of the laws of nature, and one cannot forgive the laws of nature; nor to forget, for even if it were the laws of nature, it is insulting all the same. Finally, even if I had wanted to be anything but magnanimous, had desired on the contrary to revenge myself on the man who insulted me, I could not have revenged myself on anyone nor anything because I would certainly never have made up my mind to do anything, even if I had been able to. Why would I not have made up my mind? I want to say a few words about that in particular.

III

After all, people who know how to revenge themselves and to take care of themselves in general, how do they do it? After all, when they are possessed, let us suppose, by the feeling of revenge, then for the time there is nothing else but that feeling left in their whole being. Such a man simply rushes straight toward his object like an infuriated bull with its horns down, and nothing but a wall will stop him. (By the way: facing the wall, such people—that is, the straightforward persons and men of action—are genuinely nonplussed. For them a wall is not an evasion, as for example for us people who think and consequently do nothing; it is not an excuse for turning aside, an excuse for which our kind is always very glad, though we scarcely believe in it ourselves, usually. No, they are nonplussed in all sincerity. The wall has for them something tranquilizing, morally soothing, final—maybe even something mysterious . . . but of the wall later.) Well, such a direct person I regard as the real normal man, as his tender mother nature wished to see him when she graciously brought him into being on the earth. I envy such a man till I am green in the face. He is stupid. I am not disputing that, but perhaps the normal man should be stupid, how do you know? Perhaps it is very beautiful, in fact. And I am all the more convinced of that suspicion, if one can call it so, by the fact that if, for instance, you take the antithesis of the normal man, that is, the hyperconscious man, who has come, of course, not out of the lap of nature but out of a retort (this is almost mysticism, gentlemen, but I suspect this, too), this retort-made man is sometimes so nonplussed in the presence of his antithesis that with all his hyperconsciousness he genuinely thinks of himself as a mouse and not a man. It may be a hyperconscious mouse, yet it is a mouse, while the other is a man, and therefore, etc. And the worst is, he himself, his very own self, looks upon himself as a mouse. No one asks him to do so. And that is an important point. Now let us look at this mouse in action. Let us suppose, for instance, that it feels insulted, too (and it almost always does feel insulted), and wants to revenge itself too. There may even be a greater accumulation of spite in it than in *l'homme de la nature et de la vérité*. The base, nasty desire to repay with spite whoever has offended it, rankles perhaps even more nastily in it than in *l'homme de la nature et de la vérité*, because *l'homme de la nature et de la vérité* through his innate stupidity looks upon his revenge as justice pure and simple; while in consequence of his hyperconsciousness the mouse does not believe in the justice of it. To come at last to the deed itself, to the very act of revenge. Apart from the one fundamental nastiness the unfortunate mouse succeeds in creating around it so many other nastinesses in the form of doubts and questions, adds to the one question so many unsettled questions, that there inevitably works up around it a sort of fatal brew, a stinking mess, made up of its doubts, agitations and lastly of the contempt spat upon it by the straightforward men of action who stand solemnly about it as judges and arbitrators, laughing at it till their healthy sides ache. Of course the only thing left for it is to dismiss all that with a wave of its paw, and, with a smile of assumed contempt in which it does not even believe itself, creep ignominiously into its mouse-hole. There, in its nasty, stinking, underground home our insulted, crushed and ridiculed mouse promptly becomes absorbed in cold, malignant and, above all, everlasting spite. For forty years together it will remember its injury down to the smallest, most shameful detail, and every time will add, of itself, details still more shameful, spitefully teasing and irritating itself with its own imagination. It will be ashamed of its own fancies, but yet it will recall everything, it will go over it again and again, it will invent lies against itself pretending that those things might have happened, and will forgive nothing. Maybe it will begin to revenge itself, too, but, as it were, piecemeal, in trivial ways, from behind the stove, incognito, without believing either in its own right to vengeance, or in the success of its revenge, knowing beforehand that from all its efforts at revenge it will suffer a hundred times more than he on whom it revenges itself, while he, probably will not even feel it. On its deathbed it will recall it all over again, with interest accumulated over all the years. But it is just in that cold, abominable half-despair, half-belief, in that conscious burying oneself alive for grief in the underworld for forty years, in that hyperconsciousness and yet to some extent doubtful hopelessness of one's position, in that hell of unsatisfied desires turned inward, in that fever of oscillations, of resolutions taken for ever and regretted again a minute later—that the savor of that strange enjoyment of which I have spoken lies. It is so subtle, sometimes so difficult to analyze consciously, that somewhat limited people, or simply people with strong nerves, will not understand anything at all in it. "Possibly," you will add on your own account with a grin, "people who have never received a slap in the face will not understand it either," and in that way you will politely hint to me that I, too, perhaps, have been slapped in the face in my life, and so I speak as an expert. I'll bet that you are thinking that. But set your minds at rest, gentlemen, I have not received a slap in the face, though it doesn't matter to me at all what you may think about it. Possibly, I even myself regret that I have given so few slaps in the face during my life. But enough, not another word on the subject of such extreme interest to you.

I will continue calmly about people with strong nerves who do not understand a certain refinement of enjoyment. Though in certain circumstances these gentlemen bellow their loudest like bulls, though this, let us suppose, does them the greatest honor, yet, as I have already said, confronted with the impossible they at once resign themselves. Does the impossible mean the stone wall? What stone wall? Why, of course, the laws of nature, the conclusions of natural science, of mathematics. As soon as they prove to you, for instance, that you are descended from a monkey, then it is no use scowling, accept it as a fact. When they prove to you that in reality one drop of your own fat must be dearer to you than a hundred thousand of your fellow creatures, and that this conclusion is the final solution of all so-called virtues and duties and all such ravings and prejudices, then you might as well accept it, you can't do anything about it, because two times two is a law of mathematics. Just try refuting it.

"But really," they will shout at you, "there is no use protesting; it is a case of two times two makes four! Nature does not ask your permission, your wishes, and whether you like or dislike her laws does not concern her. You are bound to accept her as she is, and consequently also all her conclusions. A wall, you see, is a wall—etc. etc." Good God! but what do I care about the laws of nature and arithmetic, when, for some reason, I dislike those laws and the fact that two times two makes four? Of course I cannot break through a wall by battering my head against it if I really do not have the strength to break through it, but I am not going to resign myself to it simply because it is a stone wall and I am not strong enough.

As though such a stone wall really were a consolation, 15 and really did contain some word of conciliation, if only because it is as true as two times two makes four. Oh, absurdity of absurdities! How much better it is to understand it all, to be conscious of it all, all the impossibilities and the stone walls, not to resign yourself to a single one of those impossibilities and stone walls if it disgusts you to resign yourself; to reach, through the most inevitable, logical combinations, the most revolting conclusions on the everlasting theme that you are yourself somehow to blame even for the stone wall, though again it is as clear as day you are not to blame in the least, and therefore grinding your teeth in silent impotence sensuously to sink into inertia, brooding on the fact that it turns out that there is even no one for you to feel vindictive against, that you have not, and perhaps never will have, an object for your spite, that it is a sleight-of-hand, a bit of juggling, a card-sharper's trick, that it is simply a mess, no knowing what and no knowing who, but in spite of all these uncertainties, and jugglings, still there is an ache in you, and the more you do not know, the worse the ache.

WALT WHITMAN

"When Lilacs Last in the Dooryard Bloom'd"

Walt Whitman (1819–1892), America's first world-class poet, was also America's most American poet. Unlike any poet before or after, he made his own country the subject of his lifelong project. The poem group entitled *Leaves of Grass* (first edition, 1855; ninth or Deathbed edition, 1891–1892) is a hymn celebrating the whole life of the nation, with the poet identifying himself with male and female, young and old, white and black, slave and free, healthy and handicapped—and animals, too. Speaking in a mystical, biblical voice, he sang of the body and the soul, of night, earth, and sea, of vice and virtue. *Leaves of Grass* was a living work that evolved in structure over thirty-seven years, with almost constant revision, reordering, additions, and subtractions, starting with 12 and expanding to 383 poems in the Deathbed edition. It was meant to represent the growth of his country, to give voice to "a composite, electric, democratic personality," to embody America's Soul—the mystical Reality of national consciousness. "When Lilacs Last in the Dooryard Bloom'd" is one of the collection's most famous poems.

Leaves of Grass, innovative in form, style, and subject, helped free American poetry from European tradition. At the same time, it opened up European writing to fresh voices in the ever-widening global culture. Whitman's work attracted admirers among England's writers, who charged that Americans did not fully appreciate him. Though Whitman was not neglected at home (Emerson, then dean of American letters, welcomed *Leaves of Grass* with these words: "I greet you at the beginning of a great career. . . ."), it is true that Whitman had to deal with the criticism that *Leaves of Grass* was an immoral book because of sexual overtones in certain poems. Indeed, because of this work, he was fired from a government clerkship after serving less than six months.

Whitman's reputation has grown since the late 1950s, when he was rediscovered by America's Beat Generation—a group of writers who were repulsed by society's materialism and militarism. The leading Beat poet, Allen Ginsberg (see "A Supermarket in California"), found a brother spirit in Whitman; they shared not only a contempt for elegant writing, but also homosexual feelings, a beard, and an unkempt appearance. Both, too, shared a decided preference for society's rejects, called "beats" by Ginsberg but "roughs" by Whitman (a poem in *Leaves of Grass* introduced "Walt Whitman, an American, one of the roughs, a kosmos"). The bohemian Whitman was only one phase of his life, the time prior to the Civil War. After working during the war as a nurse to Northern and Southern soldiers in army hospitals in Washington, D.C., he settled down into a new persona that he kept to the end: the "good gray poet," living quietly and receiving visitors.

Reading the Selection

"When Lilacs Last in the Dooryard Bloom'd" commemorates the assassination of President Lincoln (never mentioned by name) on April 15, 1865. Deeply moved by Lincoln, whom he thought the proto-typical democratic man, the living symbol of his own message to America, Whitman wanted to convey both his own grief and the universal meaning of this death. In form, the poem interweaves three symbols reflective of the springtime, the season of the president's death—the lilacs (the poet's love), the fallen western star (Lincoln), and the hermit thrush (the chant of death). This poem, along with three others, was added to *Leaves of Grass* in the 1871 edition.

—⁜—

1

When lilacs last in the dooryard bloom'd,   1
And the great star early droop'd in the western sky in the
    night,
I mourn'd, and yet shall mourn with ever-returning spring.

Ever-returning spring, trinity sure to me you bring,
Lilac blooming perennial and drooping star in the west,
And thought of him I love.

2

O powerful western fallen star!
O shades of night—O moody, tearful night!
O great star disappear'd—O the black murk that hides the
    star!
O cruel hands that hold me powerless—O helpless soul
    of me!   10
O harsh surrounding cloud that will not free my soul.

3

In the dooryard fronting an old farm-house near the
    whitewash'd palings,
Stands the lilac-bush tall-growing with heart-shaped
    leaves of rich green,
With many a pointed blossom rising delicate, with the
    perfume strong I love,
With every leaf a miracle—and from this bush in the
    dooryard,
With delicate-color'd blossoms and heart-shaped leaves of
    rich green,
A sprig with its flower I break.

4

In the swamp in secluded recesses,
A shy and hidden bird is warbling a song.

Solitary the thrush,   20
The hermit withdrawn to himself, avoiding the
    settlements,
Sings by himself a song.

Song of the bleeding throat,
Death's outlet song of life, (for well dear brother I know,
If though wast not granted to sing thou would'st
    surely die.)

5

Over the breast of the spring, the land, amid cities,
Amid lanes and through old woods, where lately the vio-
    lets peep'd from the ground, spotting the gray debris,
Amid the grass in the fields each side of the lanes, passing
    the endless grass,
Passing the yellow-spear'd wheat, every grain from its
    shroud in the dark-brown fields uprisen,
Passing the apple-tree blows of white and pink in the
    orchards,   30
Carrying a corpse to where it shall rest in the grave,
Night and day journeys a coffin.

6

Coffin that passes through lanes and streets,
Through day and night with the great cloud darkening the
    land,
With the pomp of the inloop'd flags with the cities draped
    in black,
With the show of the States themselves as of crape-veil'd
    women standing,
With processions long and winding and the flambeaus of
    the night,
With the countless torches lit, with the silent sea of faces
    and the unbared heads,
With the waiting depot, the arriving coffin, and the
    sombre faces,

With dirges through the night, with the thousand voices
    rising strong and solemn,   40
With all the mournful voices of the dirges pour'd around
    the coffin,
The dim-lit churches and the shuddering organs—where
    amid these you journey,
With the tolling tolling bells' perpetual clang,
Here, coffin that slowly passes,
I give you my sprig of lilac.

7

(Nor for you, for one alone,
Blossoms and branches green to coffins all I bring,
For fresh as the morning, thus would I chant a song for
    you O sane and sacred death.

All over bouquets of roses,
O death, I cover you over with roses and early lilies,   50
But mostly and now the lilac that blooms the first,
Copious I break, I break the sprigs from the bushes,
With loaded arms I come, pouring for you,
For you and the coffins all of you O death.)

8

O western orb sailing the heaven,
Now I know what you must have meant as a month since
    I walk'd,
As I walk'd in silence the transparent shadowy night,
As I saw you had something to tell as you bent to me
    night after night,
As you droop'd from the sky low down as if to my side,
    (while the other stars all look'd on,)
As we wander'd together the solemn night, (for
    something I know not what kept me from sleep,)   60
As the night advanced, and I saw on the rim of the west
    how full you were of woe,
As I stood on the rising ground in the breeze in the cool
    transparent night,
As I watch'd where you pass'd and was lost in the
    netherward black of the night,
As my soul in its trouble dissatisfied sank, as where you
    sad orb,
Concluded, dropt in the night, and was gone.

9

Sing on there in the swamp,
O singer bashful and tender, I hear your notes, I hear
    your call,
I hear, I come presently, I understand you,
But a moment I linger, for the lustrous star has
    detain'd me,
The star my departing comrade holds and detains me.   70

10

O how shall I warble myself for the dead one there I loved?
And how shall I deck my song for the large sweet soul
    that has gone?
And what shall my perfume be for the grave of him I love?
Sea-winds blown from east and west,
Blown from the Eastern sea and blown from the Western
    sea, till there on the prairies meeting,
These and with these and the breath of my chant,
I'll perfume the grave of him I love.

11

O what shall I hang on the chamber walls?
And what shall the pictures be that I hang on the walls,
To adorn the burial-house of him I love?   80

Pictures of growing spring and farms and homes,
With the Fourth-month eve at sundown, and the gray
    smoke lucid and bright,
With floods of the yellow gold of the gorgeous, indolent,
    sinking sun, burning, expanding the air,
With the fresh sweet herbage under foot, and the pale
    green leaves of the trees prolific,
In the distance the flowing glaze, the breast of the river,
    with a wind-dapple here and there,
With ranging hills on the banks, with many a line against
    the sky, and shadows,
And the city at hand with dwellings so dense, and stacks
    of chimneys,
And all the scenes of life and the workshops, and the
    workmen homeward returning.

12

Lo, body and soul—this land,
My own Manhattan with spires, and the sparkling and
    hurrying tides, and the ships,   90
The varied and ample land, the South and the North in the
    light, Ohio's shores and flashing Missouri,
And ever the far-spreading prairies cover'd with grass
    and corn.

Lo, the most excellent sun so calm and haughty,
The violet and purple morn with just-felt breezes,
The gentle soft-born measureless light,
The miracle spreading bathing all, the fulfill'd noon,
The coming eve delicious, the welcome night and the
    stars,
Over my cities shining all, enveloping man and land.

13

Sing on, sing on you gray-brown bird,
Sing from the swamps, the recesses, pour your chant from
    the bushes,
Limitless out of the dusk, out of the cedars and pines.   100

Sing on dearest brother, warble your reedy song,
Loud human song, with voice of uttermost woe.

O liquid and free and tender!
O wild and loose to my soul—O wondrous singer!

You only I hear—yet the star holds me, (but will soon
    depart,)
Yet the lilac with mastering odor holds me.

14

Now while I sat in the day and look'd forth,
In the close of the day with its light and the fields of
    spring, and the farmers preparing their crops,
In the large unconscious scenery of my land with its lakes
    and forests,   110
In the heavenly aerial beauty, (after the perturb'd winds
    and the storms,)
Under the arching heavens of the afternoon swift passing,
    and the voices of children and women,
The many-moving sea-tides, and I saw the ships how they
    sail'd,
And the summer approaching with richness, and the
    fields all busy with labor,
And the infinite separate houses, how they all went on,
    each with its meals and minutia of daily usages,
And the streets how their throbbings throbb'd, and the
    cities pent—lo, then and there,
Falling upon them all and among them all, enveloping me
    with the rest,
Appear'd the cloud, appear'd the long black trail,
And I knew death, its thought, and the sacred knowledge
    of death.

Then with the knowledge of death as walking one side
    of me,
And the thought of death close-walking the other side   120
    of me,
And I in the middle as with companions, and as holding
    the hands of companions,
I fled forth to the hiding receiving night that talks not,
Down to the shores of the water, the path by the swamp in
    the dimness,
To the solemn shadowy cedars and ghostly pines so still.

And the singer so shy to the rest receiv'd me,
The gray-brown bird I know receiv'd us comrades three,
And he sang the carol of death, and a verse for him I love.

From deep secluded recesses,
From the fragrant cedars and the ghostly pines so still,   130
Came the carol of the bird.

And the charm of the carol rapt me,
As I held as if by their hands my comrades in the night,
And the voice of my spirit tallied the song of the bird.

Come lovely and soothing death,
Undulate round the world, serenely arriving, arriving,
In the day, in the night, to all, to each,
Sooner or later delicate death.

Prais'd be the fathomless universe,
For life and joy, and for objects and knowledge curious,   140
And for love, sweet love—but praise! praise! praise!
For the sure-enwinding arms of cool-enfolding death.

Dark mother always gliding near with soft feet,
Have none chanted for thee a chant of fullest welcome?
Then I chant it for thee, I glorify thee above all,
I bring thee a song that when thou must indeed come, come
    unfalteringly.

Approach strong deliveress,
When it is so, when thou hast taken them I joyously sing the
    dead,
Lost in the loving floating ocean of thee,
Laved in the flood of thy bliss O death.   150

From me to thee glad serenades,
Dances for thee I propose saluting thee, adornments and feast-
    ings for thee,
And the sights of the open landscape and the high-spread sky are
    fitting,
And life and the fields, and the huge and thoughtful night.
The night in silence under many a star,
The ocean shore and the husky whispering wave whose voice I
    know,
And the soul turning to thee O vast and well-veil'd death,
And the body gratefully nestling close to thee.

Over the tree-tops I float thee a song,
Over the rising and sinking waves, over the myriad fields and
    the prairies wide,
Over the dense-pack'd cities all and the teeming wharves and 160
    ways,
I float this carol with joy, with joy to thee O death.

15

To the tally of my soul,
Loud and strong kept up the gray-brown bird,
With pure deliberate notes spreading filling the night.

Loud in the pines and cedars dim,
Clear in the freshness moist and the swamp-perfume,
And I with my comrades there in the night.

While my sight that was bound in my eyes unclosed,
As to long panoramas of visions.   170

And I saw askant the armies,
I saw as in noiseless dreams hundreds of battle-flags,
Borne through the smoke of the battles and pierc'd with
    missiles I saw them,

And carried hither and yon through the smoke, and torn
    and bloody,
And at last but a few shreds left on the staffs, (and all in
    silence,)
And the staffs all splinter'd and broken.

I saw battle-corpses, myriads of them,
And the white skeletons of young men, I saw them,
I saw the debris and debris of all the slain soldiers of
    the war,
But I saw they were not as was thought,   180
They themselves were fully at rest, they suffer'd not,
The living remain'd and suffer'd, the mother suffer'd,
And the wife and the child and the musing comrade
    suffer'd,
And the armies that remain'd suffer'd.

16

Passing the visions, passing the night,
Passing, unloosing the hold of my comrades' hands,
Passing the song of the hermit bird and the tallying song
    of my soul,
Victorious song, death's outlet song, yet varying
    ever-altering song,
As low and wailing, yet clear the notes, rising and falling,
    flooding the night,

Sadly sinking and fainting, as warning and warning, and
    yet again bursting with joy,   190
Covering the earth and filling the spread of the heaven,
As that powerful psalm in the night I heard from recesses,
Passing, I leave thee lilac with heart-shaped leaves,
I leave thee there in the door-yard, blooming, returning
    with spring.

I cease from my song for thee,
From my gaze on thee in the west, fronting the west,
    communing with thee,
O comrade lustrous with silver face in the night.

Yet each to keep and all, retrievements out of the night,
The song, the wondrous chant of the gray-brown bird,
And the tallying chant, the echo arous'd in my soul,   200
With the lustrous and drooping star with the countenance
    full of woe,
With the holders holding my hand nearing the call of the
    bird,
Comrades mine and I in the midst, and their memory ever
    to keep, for the dead I loved so well,
For the sweetest, wisest soul of all my days and lands—
    and this for his dear sake,
Lilac and star and bird twined with the chant of my soul,
There in the fragrant pines and the cedars dusk and dim.

CHARLES DARWIN

Selection from *The Descent of Man*

Darwin's *The Descent of Man* (1871) is one of the West's most explosive books. In two volumes, the first limited to man and the second given to the role of sexual selection in evolution, it is written in matter-of-fact prose and backed by masses of scientific data. Darwin argues that evolution—the idea that all life began with a common ancestor, an amoeba-like being—is not a hypothesis, as had been claimed when this notion first appeared in Greek thought; rather, it is a principle of biology operating throughout nature. In other words, viewed over the course of millennia, the plant, animal, and human worlds constitute a vast cousinhood. Thus Darwin's book destroyed the biblical view of human genesis, or creationism—Adam and Eve were the first parents, having been created by God after he had made the plant and animal kingdoms—an idea that had dominated Western thought since Christianity became the religion of Rome in about A.D. 400. Darwin replaced it with the principle of evolution. The full meaning of evolution, that humans are creatures without souls and that life is without purpose, is still being worked out today.

    The Descent of Man, while controversial, did not raise the firestorm of criticism that had greeted his earlier work, *The Origin of Species* (1859). It was in the 1859 work that he first advanced the principle of evolution, but he had not included the human species in his discussion of animal species, though he hinted at it. *The Origin of Species* had sold out on the first day of publication, but it also made him and his ideas notorious, a distressing turn of events for one of the most staid men in the Victorian Age—a period obsessed with respectability. (Darwin even became seriously ill when confronted with unpleasant ideas.) At the same time he was the quintessential expression of the period's realism, a pure scientist, totally disinterested in theory and devoted solely to facts. It was only after amassing incontrovertible data, collected between 1831 and 1836 on his voyage to South America with the British ship *Beagle*, and in the 1850s in his investigation of orchids, that he was prepared to publish his research. By 1871 the principle of evolution, proven by Darwin's documentation, had won over his fellow scientists, so that when *The Descent of Man* appeared, despite the explosive theme, it was soon adopted into the worldview of most educated people.

The blind force "guiding" Darwinian evolution is natural selection, the notion that favorable variations within a species tend to be preserved, while unfavorable variations are destroyed; the result is the formation of new species. The variations occur randomly, without design on the part of a divine creator or desire on the part of the organism. Darwin claimed that the idea of natural selection was inspired by his reading of Thomas Malthus's essay *On Population* (1797). The idea, however, was also explicitly stated in Herbert Spencer's *Population* (1852), where it was called "survival of the fittest." It was Spencer's term that Darwin appropriated and made his own.

Reading the Selection

This passage is taken from the last chapter of *The Descent of Man*. Darwin praises man's intellectual ("godlike intellect") and moral faculties ("sympathy . . . for the most debased," and "benevolence . . . to other men [and] living creature[s]"), claiming them to be the result of natural selection instead of divine origin.

—ⁱⁱⁱ—

The main conclusion arrived at in this work, and now held by many naturalists who are well competent to form a sound judgment, is that man is descended from some less highly organized form. The grounds upon which this conclusion rests will never be shaken, for the close similarity between man and the lower animals in embryonic development, as well as in innumerable points of structure and constitution, both of high and of the most trifling importance—the rudiments which he retains, and the abnormal reversions to which he is occasionally liable—are facts which cannot be disputed. They have long been known, but until recently they told us nothing with respect to the origin of man. Now when viewed by the light of our knowledge of the whole organic world, their meaning is unmistakable. The great principle of evolution stands up clear and firm, when these groups of facts are considered in connection with others, such as the mutual affinities of the members of the same group, their geographical distribution in past and present times, and their geological succession. It is incredible that all these facts should speak falsely. He who is not content to look, like a savage, at the phenomena of nature as disconnected cannot any longer believe that man is the work of a separate act of creation. He will be forced to admit that the close resemblance of the embryo of man to that, for instance, of a dog—the construction of his skull, limbs, and whole frame, independently of the uses to which the parts may be put, on the same plan with that of other mammals—the occasional reappearance of various structures, for instance of several distinct muscles, which man does not normally possess, but which are common to the Quadrumana—and a crowd

1

of analogous facts—all point in the plainest manner to the conclusion that man is the codescendant with other mammals of a common progenitor.

. . .

The main conclusion arrived at in this work, namely that man is descended from some lowly-organized form, will, I regret to think, be highly distasteful to many persons. But there can hardly be a doubt that we are descended from barbarians. The astonishment which I felt on first seeing a party of Fuegians on a wild and broken shore will never be forgotten by me, for the reflection at once rushed into my mind—such were our ancestors. These men were absolutely naked and bedaubed with paint, their long hair was tangled, their mouths frothed with excitement, and their expression was wild, startled, and distrustful. They possessed hardly any arts, and like wild animals lived on what they could catch; they had no government, and were merciless to everyone not of their own small tribe. He who has seen a savage in his native land will not feel much shame, if forced to acknowledge that the blood of some more humble creature flows in his veins. For my own part I would as soon be descended from that heroic little monkey, who braved his dreaded enemy in order to save the life of his keeper; or from that old baboon, who, descending from the mountains, carried away in triumph his young comrade from a crowd of astonished dogs—as from a savage who delights to torture his enemies, offers up bloody sacrifices, practices infanticide without remorse, treats his wives like slaves, knows no decency, and is haunted by the grossest superstitions.

Man may be excused for feeling some pride at having risen, though not through his own exertions, to the very summit of the organic scale; and the fact of his having thus risen, instead of having been aboriginally placed there, may give him hopes for a still higher destiny in the distant future. But we are not here concerned with hopes or fears, only with the truth as far as our reason allows us to discover it. I have given the evidence to the best of my ability; and we must acknowledge, as it seems to me, that man with all his noble qualities, with sympathy which feels for the most debased, with benevolence which extends not only to other men but to the humblest living creature, with his godlike intellect which has penetrated into the movements and constitution of the solar system—with all these exalted powers—Man still bears in his bodily frame the indelible stamp of his lowly origin.

EMILY DICKINSON

Poems

Emily Dickinson (1830–1886) was America's first great woman poet, but she was virtually unknown when she died. She published only three poems while living, and their original style doomed her to obscurity. Her world was New England, and though Puritan values were in decline, a literary career for a woman then was hard to manage. She nonetheless pioneered the way for other female writers.

For the most part, Dickinson lived in Amherst, Massachusetts, where her father, Edward Dickinson, was treasurer of Amherst College for forty years. She is known to have made only two forays from Amherst—the first in 1847–1848 when she was a student at Mount Holyoke Female Seminary, and the second in 1854 when she visited her father in Washington, D.C., where he was a congressman. After 1862, she became a recluse in her father's house, devoting her time to writing a "letter to the world"—the 1,775 poems that constitute her legacy. These poems, which she asked to be destroyed at her death, were saved for posterity by her sister Lavinia. Aided by Thomas Wentworth Higginson, a minor literary figure who had been Dickinson's sole tie with the wider literary world, and Mabel Todd Loomis, the gifted wife of an Amherst professor, Lavinia produced the first selection of Emily's poems in 1891. It was not until the 1920s, with the appearance of a rebellious generation, that Dickinson's works found a welcoming audience. Since World War II, especially with the rise of feminism, her reputation has grown exponentially. Today this literary star is deemed of the magnitude of Thoreau and Whitman, who, with Dickinson, helped to create a unique American style of writing. In recent years her name has been kept before the public by the success of the stage production *Belle of Amherst*, based on her life and works.

Dickinson's poems were characterized by discordant metaphors drawn from flowers, village life, the Bible, the law, and the mechanical and domestic arts. Compressed and elusive, her works prefigure Modernism, the ruling style from 1870 to 1970, which used rich metaphors; yet, at the same time, they reflect Late Romanticism (see Brontë's *Jane Eyre*), with their claustrophobic images and sexual disturbance.

Reading the Selections

As life passed her by, Dickinson became ever more eccentric. Dressed in white, she became a village legend; some thought her half-demented. Death became a near obsession, as reflected in four poems printed here. "There's a certain Slant of light" (about 1861) shows her thoughts wandering to death, inspired surprisingly by the normally optimistic images of sunlight and church hymns. "I felt a Funeral, in my Brain" (about 1861) presents the unusual metaphor of a parade of persons trampling up and down her brain as corresponding to her state of disillusion; the poem is unfinished, a typical feature. "I heard a Fly buzz—when I died—" (about 1862) calls up a disturbed sexual image of the poet seated, the air moved only by the buzz of a fly—perhaps a metaphor of Dickinson's fate of life in death. "Because I could not stop for Death—" (about 1863) speaks to her feeling that death too soon ends life's little pleasures, such as "the School, where Children strove at Recess."

The remaining poem, "Much Madness is divinest Sense—," reveals Dickinson as a rebel, as she joins the "mad" against the sensible majority; the word "Chain" evokes a sense of being imprisoned.

—⚏—

"There's a certain Slant of light"

There's a certain Slant of light,   1
Winter Afternoons—
That oppresses, like the Heft
Of Cathedral Tunes—

Heavenly Hurt, it gives us—
We can find no scar,
But internal difference,
Where the Meanings, are—

None may teach it—Any—
'Tis the Seal Despair—   10
An imperial affliction
Sent us of the Air—

When it comes, the Landscape lister
Shadows—hold their breath—
When it goes, 'tis like the Distance
On the look of Death—

—⚏—

"I felt a Funeral, in my Brain"

I felt a Funeral, in my Brain,   1
And Mourners to and fro
Kept treading—treading—till it seemed
That Sense was breaking through—

And when they all were seated,
A Service, like a Drum—
Kept beating—beating—till I thought
My Mind was going numb—

And then I heard them lift a Box
And creak across my Soul   10

With those same Boots of Lead, again,
Then Space—began to toll,

As all the Heavens were a Bell,
And Being, but an Ear,
And I, and Silence, some strange Race
Wrecked, solitary, here—

And then a Plank in Reason, broke,
And I dropped down, and down—
And hit a World, at every plunge,
And Finished knowing—then—   20

—⚏—

"Much Madness is divinest Sense—"

Much Madness is divinest Sense—   1
To a discerning Eye—
Much Sense—the starkest Madness—
'Tis the Majority

In this, as All, prevail—
Assent—and you are sane—
Demur—you're straightway dangerous—
And handled with a Chain—

"I heard a Fly buzz—when I died—"

I heard a Fly buzz—when I died—   1
The Stillness in the Room
Was like the Stillness in the Air—
Between the Heaves of Storm—

The Eyes around—had wrung them dry—
And Breaths were gathering firm
For that last Onset—when the King
Be witnessed—in the Room—

I willed my Keepsakes—Signed away
What portion of me be   10
Assignable—and then it was
There interposed a Fly—

With Blue—uncertain stumbling Buzz—
Between the light—and me—
And then the Windows failed—and then
I could not see to see—

"Because I could not stop for Death—"

Because I could not stop for Death—   1
He kindly stopped for me—
The Carriage held but just Ourselves—
And Immortality.

We slowly drove—He knew no haste
And I had put away
My labor and my leisure too,
For His Civility—

We passed the School, where Children strove
At Recess—in the Ring—   10
We passed the Fields of Gazing Grain—
We passed the Setting Sun—

Or rather—He passed Us—
The Dews drew quivering and chill—
For only Gossamer, my Gown—
My Tippet—only Tulle—

We paused before a House that seemed
A Swelling of the Ground—
The Roof was scarcely visible—
The Cornice—in the Ground—   20

Since then—'tis Centuries—and yet
Feels shorter than the Day
I first surmised the Horses' Heads
Were toward Eternity—

$$19$$

THE AGE OF EARLY MODERNISM

1871–1914

FRIEDRICH NIETZSCHE

Selections from *The Gay Science* and *Thus Spake Zarathustra*

The German thinker Friedrich Nietzsche (1844–1900) is a key, though paradoxical, figure in Western thought. Supremely influential on the diverse minds of his own day and those of succeeding generations (see Freud, Sartre, and Beauvoir), he nonetheless felt an extreme psychological isolation from European culture. He eventually slipped into a paralyzing madness (perhaps the result of syphilis) for the last eleven years of his life. Even so, in his writings he registered his poignantly ambivalent vision of the emerging nihilism—belief in nothing—which has characterized the West since 1900. He was both a prophet of Modernism, the century-long movement (1870 to 1970) that sought to wipe the cultural slate clean of both the Judeo-Christian and Greco-Roman traditions, as well as a prophet of Post-Modernism, Modernism's successor starting around 1970. Post-Modernism aims at an open-ended, indeterminate set of attitudes democratically embracing the contributions, tastes, and ideas of many groups of people of all races and all countries, past and present.

Nietzsche is also one of the most passionate and misunderstood writers in the West, in part because German Nazis in the 1930s made him their favorite philosopher and linked him to their campaign against the Jews and in favor of Aryan superiority. He is also misunderstood through his own doing, for Nietzsche's thought is clouded by an excess of adolescent emotion and his writing style is filled with aphorisms, or pithy sayings, that are easily misinterpreted when quoted out of context. Today Nietzsche's linkage to Nazism has been exposed as false, since his writings repeatedly ridicule anti-Semites and German nationalists. Nietzsche's linkage to Nazism is now viewed as a joint fabrication by Nazis who twisted his ideas to support their cause and by his sister, a Nazi sympathizer and his literary executor, who edited his works to make this connection. As to interpretive problems arising from his style, that remains a central concern for all readers of this challenging writer.

Reading the Selections

These selections from *The Gay Science* (1882) and *Thus Spake Zarathustra* (1883) offer examples of Nietzsche's striking, biblical-sounding prose. Two themes dominate here: uncompromising hostility to religion and emphatic support of the idea of the Will to Power. He was the first major Western thinker to

200

break completely with religion ("God is dead") and deny the truth of all transcendent belief. Much of his thought, such as radical perspectivism and rejection of universal values, was simply an attempt to come to terms with the full meaning of a godless world.

Nietzsche's second central theme was that inorganic and organic nature is ruled by the Will to Power, the blind force that courses through all things—an idea derived from Darwin (see *The Descent of Man*). Nietzsche thought societies healthy in which the Will to Power dominated; there, a natural hierarchy emerged where the strong ("masters") ruled the weak ("slaves"). In contrast, he thought societies doomed that suppressed the Will to Power. He particularly objected to Christianity and its secular cousin socialism, classifying them as faiths of "little people" who paraded weaknesses as moral principles. His intent was to prepare the way for the *Ubermensch*, or Overman, a new human type who with his robber instincts would be able to manipulate the masses and who was a law unto himself.

The Gay Science

4

What preserves the species. The strongest and most evil spirits have so far advanced humanity the most: they have always rekindled the drowsing passions—all ordered society puts the passions to sleep; they have always reawakened the sense of comparison, of contradiction, of joy in the new, the daring, and the untried; they force men to meet opinion with opinion, model with model. For the most part by arms, by the overthrow of boundary stones, and by offense to the pieties, but also by new religions and moralities. The same "malice" is to be found in every teacher and preacher of the new. . . (The new is always *the evil*, as that which wants to conquer, to overthrow the old boundary stones and the old pieties; and only the old is the good.) The good men of every age are those who dig the old ideas deep down and bear fruit with them, the husbandmen of the spirit. But all land is finally exhausted, and the plow of evil must always return.

There is a fundamentally erroneous doctrine in contemporary morality, celebrated particularly in England: according to this, the judgments "good" and "evil" are condensations of the experiences concerning "expedient" and "inexpedient"; what is called good preserves the species, while what is called evil is harmful to the species. In truth, however, the evil urges are expedient and indispensable and preserve the species to as high a degree as the good ones—only their function is different.

. . .

125

The Madman. Have you not heard of that madman who lit a lantern in the bright morning hours, ran to the market place, and cried incessantly, "I seek God! I seek God!" As many of those do not believe in God were standing around just then, he provoked much laughter. Why, did he get lost? said one. Did he lose his way like a child? said another. Or is he hiding? Is he afraid of us? Has he gone on a

voyage? or emigrated? Thus they yelled and laughed. The madman jumped into their midst and pierced them with his glances.

"Whither is God?" he cried. "I shall tell you. *We have killed him*—you and I. All of us are his murderers. But how have we done this? How were we able to drink up the sea? Who gave us the sponge to wipe away the entire horizon? What did we do when we unchained this earth from its sun? Whither is it moving now? Whither are we moving now? Away from all suns? Are we not plunging continually? Backward, sideward, forward, in all directions? Is there any up or down left? Are we not straying as through an infinite nothing? Do we not feel the breath of empty space? Has it not become colder? Is not night and more night coming on all the while? Must not lanterns be lit in the morning? Do we not hear anything yet of the noise of the gravediggers who are burying God? Do we not smell anything yet of God's decomposition? Gods too decompose. God is dead. God remains dead. And we have killed him. How shall we, the murderers of all murderers, comfort ourselves? What was holiest and most powerful of all that the world has yet owned has bled to death under our knives. Who will wipe this blood off us? What water is there for us to clean ourselves? What festivals of atonement, what sacred games shall we have to invent? Is not the greatness of this deed too great for us? Must not we ourselves become gods simply to seem worthy of it? There has never been a greater deed; and whoever will be born after us—for the sake of this deed he will be part of a higher history than all history hitherto."

Here the madman fell silent and looked again at his listeners; and they too were silent and stared at him in astonishment. At last he threw his lantern on the ground, and it broke and went out. "I come too early," he said then; "my time has not come yet. This tremendous event is still on its way, still wandering—it has not yet reached the ears of man. Lightning and thunder require time, the light of the stars requires time, deeds require time even after they are done, before they can be seen and heard. This deed is still more distant from them than the most distant stars—*and yet they have done it themselves.*"

It has been related further that on that same day the madman entered divers churches and there sang his *requiem aeternam deo*. Led out and called to account, he is said to have replied each time, "What are these churches now if they are not the tombs and sepulchers of God?"

. . .

341

The greatest stress. How, if some day or night a demon were to sneak after you into your loneliest loneliness and say to you, "This life as you now live it and have lived it, you will have to live once more and innumerable times more; and there will be nothing new in it, but every pain and every joy and every thought and sigh and everything immeasurably small or great in your life must return to you—all in the same succession and sequence—even this spider and this moonlight between the trees, and even this moment and I myself. The eternal hourglass of existence is turned over and over, and you with it, a dust grain of dust." Would you not throw yourself down and gnash your teeth and curse the demon who spoke thus? Or did you once experience a tremendous moment when you would have answered him, "You are a god, and never have I heard anything more godly." If this thought were to gain possession of you, it would change you, as you are, or perhaps crush you. The question in each and every thing, "Do you want this once more and innumerable times more?" would weigh upon your actions as the greatest stress. Or how well disposed would you have to become to yourself and to life to *crave nothing more fervently* than this ultimate eternal confirmation and seal?

Thus Spake Zarathustra
Part I

3

When Zarathustra came into the next town, which lies on the edge of the forest, he found many people gathered together in the market place; for it had been promised that there would be a tightrope walker. And Zarathustra spoke thus to the people:

"*I teach you the overman.* Man is something that shall be overcome. What have you done to overcome him?

"All beings so far have created something beyond themselves; and do you want to be the ebb of this great flood and even go back to the beasts rather than overcome man? What is the ape to man? A laughingstock or a painful embarrassment. And man shall be just that for the overman: a laughingstock or a painful embarrassment. You have made your way from worm to man, and much in you is still worm. Once you were apes, and even now, too, man is more ape than any ape.

"Whoever is the wisest among you is also a mere conflict and cross between plant and ghost. But do I bid you become ghosts or plants?

"Behold, I teach you the overman. The overman is the meaning of the earth. Let your will say: the overman *shall be* the meaning of the earth! I beseech you, my brothers, *remain faithful to the earth,* and do not believe those who speak to you of otherworldly hopes! Poison-mixers are they, whether they know it or not. Despisers of life are they, decaying and poisoned themselves, of whom the earth is weary: so let them go.

"Once the sin against God was the greatest sin; but God died, and these sinners died with him. To sin against the earth is now the most dreadful thing, and to esteem the entrails of the unknowable higher than the meaning of the earth.

"Once the soul looked contemptuously upon the body, and then this contempt was the highest: she wanted the body meager, ghastly, and starved. Thus she hoped to escape it and the earth. Oh, this soul herself was still meager, ghastly, and starved: and cruelty was the lust of this soul. But you, too, my brothers, tell me: what does your body proclaim of your soul? Is not your soul poverty and filth and wretched contentment?

"Verily, a polluted stream is man. One must be a sea to be able to receive a polluted stream without becoming unclean. Behold, I teach you the overman: he is this sea; in him your great contempt can go under.

"What is the greatest experience you can have? It is the hour of the great contempt. The hour in which your happiness, too, arouses your disgust, and even your reason and your virtue.

"The hour when you say, 'What matters my happiness? It is poverty and filth and wretched contentment. But my happiness ought to justify existence itself.'

"The hour when you say, 'What matters my reason? Does it crave knowledge as the lion his food? It is poverty and filth and wretched contentment.'

"The hour when you say, 'What matters my virtue? As yet it has not made me rage. How weary I am of my good and my evil! All that is poverty and filth and wretched contentment.'

"The hour when you say, 'What matters my justice? I do not see that I am flames and fuel. But the just are flames and fuel.'

"The hour when you say, 'What matters my pity? Is not pity the cross on which he is nailed who loves man? But my pity is no crucifixion.'

"Have you yet spoken thus? Have you yet cried thus? 15 Oh, that I might have heard you cry thus!

"Not your sin but your thrift cries to heaven; your meanness even in your sin cries to heaven.

"Where is the lightning to lick you with its tongue? Where is the frenzy with which you should be inoculated?

"Behold, I teach you the overman: he is this lightning, he is this frenzy."

When Zarathustra had spoken thus, one of the people cried: "Now we have heard enough about the tightrope walker; now let us see him too!" And all the people laughed at Zarathustra. But the tightrope walker, believing that the word concerned him, began his performance.

. . .

5

When Zarathustra had spoken these words he beheld the 1 people again and was silent. "There they stand," he said to his heart; "there they laugh. They do not understand me; I am not the mouth for these ears. Must one smash their ears before they learn to listen with their eyes? Must one clatter like kettledrums and preachers of repentance? Or do they believe only the stammerer?

"They have something of which they are proud. What do they call that which makes them proud? Education they call it; it distinguishes them from goatherds. That is why they do not like to hear the word 'contempt' applied to them. Let me then address their pride. Let me speak to them of what is most contemptible: but that is the *last man*."

And thus spoke Zarathustra to the people: "The time has come for man to set himself a goal. The time has come for man to plant the seed of his highest hope. His soil is still rich enough. But one day this soil will be poor and domesticated, and no tall tree will be able to grow in it. Alas, the time is coming when man will no longer shoot the arrow of his longing beyond man, and the string of his bow will have forgotten how to whir!

"I say unto you: one must still have chaos in oneself to be able to give birth to a dancing star. I say unto you: you still have chaos in yourselves.

"Alas, the time is coming when man will no longer 5

give birth to a star. Alas, the time of the most despicable man is coming, he that is no longer able to despise himself. Behold, I show you the *last man*.

"'What is love? What is creation? What is longing? What is a star?' thus asks the last man, and he blinks.

"The earth has become small, and on it hops the last man, who makes everything small. His race is as ineradicable as the flea-beetle; the last man lives longest.

"'We have invented happiness,' say the last men, and they blink. They have left the regions where it was hard to live, for one needs warmth. One still loves one's neighbor and rubs against him, for one needs warmth.

"Becoming sick and harboring suspicion are sinful to them: one proceeds carefully. A fool, whoever still stumbles over stones or human beings! A little poison now and then: that makes for agreeable dreams. And much poison in the end, for an agreeable death.

"One still works, for work is a form of entertainment. 10 But one is careful lest the entertainment be too harrowing. One no longer becomes poor or rich: both require too much exertion. Who still wants to rule? Who obey? Both require too much exertion.

"No shepherd and one herd! Everybody wants the same, everybody is the same: whoever feels different goes voluntarily into a madhouse.

"'Formerly, all the world was mad,' say the most refined, and they blink.

"One is clever and knows everything that has ever happened: so there is no end of derision. One still quarrels, but one is soon reconciled—else it might spoil the digestion.

"One has one's little pleasure for the day and one's little pleasure for the night: but one has a regard for health.

"'We have invented happiness,' say the last men, and 15 they blink."

And here ended Zarathustra's first speech, which is also called "the Prologue"; for at this point he was interrupted by the clamor and delight of the crowd. "Give us this last man, O Zarathustra," they shouted. "Turn us into these last men! Then we shall make you a gift of the overman!" And all the people jubilated and clucked with their tongues.

But Zarathustra became sad and said to his heart: "They do not understand me: I am not the mouth for these ears. I seem to have lived too long in the mountains; I listened too much to brooks and trees: now I talk to them as to goatherds. My soul is unmoved and bright as the mountains in the morning. But they think I am cold and I jeer and make dreadful jests. And now they look at me and laugh: and as they laugh they even hate me. There is ice in their laughter."

JORIS-KARL HUYSMANS

Selections from *Against Nature*

Joris-Karl Huysmans (1848–1907) was the spiritual guide of the Decadents, the French literary group who advocated artificiality as a panacea for the disgust inspired by modern life and, most especially, the growing Americanization of manners. Flourishing between 1850 and 1900 and inspired by the Symbolist poetry of Charles Baudelaire (1821–1867), the Decadents expressed a love of artificiality through exotic images, such as extravagant illusions, unnatural loves, and perverse pleasures. This cultivation of the artificial contrasted with the era's reigning Naturalism, the literary style pioneered by the French novelist Émile Zola (1840–1902). Whereas Naturalist fiction was democratic in its focus on working-class life, the Decadents were unabashedly elitist in their concern for the superior outsider, such as a bohemian artist or an eccentric aristocrat. Despite this emphasis on outsiders, the Decadents failed to stem the West's rush to democratize all phases of life—symbolized by the rise of mass culture. From today's perspective, though, the Decadents left a strong legacy to later Modernist writers: the belief that literature should address an elite of knowledgeable readers (see Eliot, Joyce, Woolf, and Stein).

Huysmans began his literary career in 1874 as a member of the Naturalist school. For a decade he wrote working-class novels, documenting each with the scientific detail prized by Zola's followers. That changed, however, with the publication of *ÀRebours* (*Against Nature*) (1884), Huysmans's masterpiece. This novel created a sensation and became, in the words of a contemporary, "the Bible" of the Decadents. Des Esseintes, its eccentric hero, is the prototype of the Decadent outsider disgusted by middle-class respectability and mediocrity. To escape from spiritual malaise, he dedicates himself to bizarre sensations, a quest that leads him to replace the natural with the unnatural and artificial.

The two most likely models for Des Esseintes were Robert Comte de Montesquieu-Fezensac and Huysmans himself. The Comte de Montesquieu, heir to one of France's oldest families, was a fabled dandy in Huysmans's day. Of greater import, however, Des Esseintes embodies the author's own neurotic sensibility: love of solitude, hatred of mediocrity, and passion for novelty.

Ironically, Huysmans was neither an aristocrat nor, ultimately, a frivolous seeker of the sensual. For thirty-two years he toiled as a clerk for the state, writing governmental reports by day and composing fiction at night. In his later years he returned to the Catholic faith he had abandoned as a youth—finding in religion the solution to his own disillusionment with the world.

Reading the Selections

Against Nature is an encyclopedic work in which the neurotic Des Esseintes, physically and emotionally ill, lives in shiplike surroundings, attended by unseen servants. He experiments to satisfy his delight in the perverse and artificial; for example, his infatuation with flowers that appear diseased in some way and his design of a "mouth organ" made from casks of aromatic liqueurs.

In the first selection, taken from Chapter X, Des Esseintes remembers counterfeit flowers with odors supplied by nearby perfume factories; this remembrance in turn evokes his hatred for this "unwholesome world." The second selection, from Chapter XVI, concludes the novel and is a diatribe against American culture.

Chapter X

[O]ne memory in particular haunted him, stirring up a forgotten world of old thoughts and ancient perfumes—the memory of an afternoon he had spent with this woman at Pantin, partly for want of anything better to do and partly out of curiosity, at the house of one of her sisters. While the two women were chattering away and showing each other their frocks, he had gone to the window and, through the dusty panes, had seen the muddy street stretching into the distance and heard it echo with the incessant beat of galoshes tramping through the puddles.

This scene, though it belonged to a remote past, suddenly presented itself to him in astonishing detail. Pantin was there before him, bustling and alive in the dead green water of the moon-rimmed mirror into which his unthinking gaze was directed. An hallucination carried him away far from Fontenay; the looking-glass conjured up for him not only the Pantin street but also the thoughts that street had once evoked; and lost in a dream, he said over to himself the ingenious, melancholy, yet consoling anthem he had composed that day on getting back to Paris:

'Yes, the season of the great rains is upon us; hearken to the song of the gutter-pipes retching under the pavements; behold the horse-dung floating in the bowls of coffee hollowed out of the macadam; everywhere the foot-baths of the poor are overflowing.

'Under the lowering sky, in the humid atmosphere, the houses ooze black sweat and their ventilators breathe foul odours; the horror of life becomes more apparent and the grip of spleen more oppressive; the seeds of iniquity that lie in every man's heart begin to germinate; a craving for filthy pleasures takes hold of the puritanical, and the minds of respected citizens are visited by criminal desires.

'And yet, here I am, warming myself in front of a blazing fire, while a basket of full-blown flowers on the table fills the room with the scent of benzoin, geranium, and vetiver. In mid-November it is still springtime at Pantin in the Rue de Paris, and I can enjoy a quiet laugh at the expense of those timorous families who, in order to avoid the approach of winter, scuttle away at full speed to Antibes or to Cannes.

'Inclement Nature has nothing to do with this extraordinary phenomenon; let it be said at once that it is to industry, and industry alone, that Pantin owes this factitious spring.

'The truth is that these flowers are made of taffeta and mounted on binding wire, while this vernal fragrance has come filtering in through cracks in the window-frame from the neighbouring factories where the Pinaud and St James perfumes are made.

'For the artisan worn out by the hard labour of the workshops, for the little clerk blessed with too many offspring, the illusion of enjoying a little fresh air is a practical possibility—thanks to these manufacturers.

'Indeed, out of this fabulous counterfeit of the countryside a sensible form of medical treatment could be developed. At present, gay dogs suffering from consumption who are carted away to the south generally die down there, finished off by the change in their habits, by their nostalgic longing for the Parisian pleasures that have laid them low. Here, in an artificial climate maintained by open stoves, their lecherous memories would come back to them in a mild and harmless form, as they breathed in the languid feminine emanations given off by the scent factories. By means of this innocent deception, the physician could supply his patient platonically with the atmosphere of the boudoirs and brothels of Paris, in place of the deadly boredom of provincial life. More often than not, all that would be needed to complete the cure would be for the sick man to show a little imagination.

'Seeing that nowadays there is nothing wholesome left in this world of ours; seeing that the wine we drink and the freedom we enjoy are equally adulterate and derisory; and finally, seeing that it takes a considerable degree of goodwill to believe that the governing classes are worthy of respect and that the lower classes are worthy of help or pity, it seems to me,' concluded Des Esseintes, 'no more absurd or insane to ask of my fellow men a sum total of illusion barely equivalent to that which they expend every day on idiotic objects, to persuade themselves that the town of Pantin is an artificial Nice, a factitious Menton.'

. . .

'All that,' he muttered, interrupted in his reflections by a sudden feeling of faintness, 'doesn't alter the fact that I shall have to beware of these delicious, atrocious experiments, which are just wearing me out.'

He heaved a sigh.

'Ah, well, that means more pleasures to cut down on, more precautions to take!'—and he shut himself up in his study, hoping that there he would find it easier to escape from the obsessive influence of all these perfumes.

He threw the window wide open, delighted to take a bath of fresh air; but suddenly it struck him that the breeze was bringing with it a whiff of bergamot oil, mingled with a smell of jasmine, cassia and rose-water. He gave a gasp of horror, and began to wonder whether he might not be in the grip of one of those evil spirits they used to exorcize in the Middle Ages. Meanwhile the odour, though just as persistent, underwent a change. A vague scent of tincture of Tolu, Peruvian balsam, and saffron, blended with a few drops of musk and amber, now floated up from the sleeping village at the foot of the hill; then all at once the metamorphosis took place, these scattered whiffs of perfume came together, and the familiar scent of frangipane, the elements of which his sense of smell had detected and recognized, spread from the valley of Fontenay all the way to the Fort, assailing his jaded nostrils, shaking anew his shattered nerves, and throwing him into such a state of prostration that he fell fainting, almost dying, across the window-sill.

—ᴡᴡ—

Chapter XVI

. . .

In painting, the result was a deluge of lifeless inanities; in literature, a torrent of hackneyed phrases and conventional ideas—honesty to flatter the shady speculator, integrity to please the swindler who hunted for a dowry for his son while refusing to pay his daughter's, and chastity to satisfy the anti-clerical who accused the clergy of rape and lechery when he himself was forever haunting the local brothel, a stupid hypocrite without even the excuse of deliberate depravity, sniffing at the greasy water in the wash-basins and the hot, spicy smell of dirty petticoats.

This was the vast bagnio of America transported to the continent of Europe; this was the limitless, unfathomable, immeasurable scurviness of the financier and the self-made man, beaming down like a shameful sun on the idolatrous city, which grovelled on its belly, chanting vile songs of praise before the impious tabernacle of the Bank.

'Well, crumble then, society! perish, old world!' cried Des Esseintes, roused to indignation by the ignominious spectacle he had conjured up—and the sound of his voice broke the oppressive spell the nightmare had laid on him.

'Ah!' he groaned, 'To think that all this isn't just a bad dream! To think that I'm about to rejoin the base and servile riff-raff of the age!'

To soothe his wounded spirit he called upon the consoling maxims of Schopenhauer, and repeated to himself Pascal's sorrowful maxim: 'The soul sees nothing that does not distress it on reflection'; but the words echoed in his mind like meaningless noises, his weariness of spirit breaking them up, stripping them of all significance, all sedative virtue, all effective and soothing force.

He realized at last that the arguments of pessimism were powerless to comfort him, that only the impossible belief in a future life could bring him peace of mind.

A fit of rage swept away like a hurricane all his would-be resignation, all his attempted indifference. He could no longer shut his eyes to the fact that there was nothing to be done, nothing whatever, that it was all over; the bourgeois were guzzling like picnickers from paper bags among the imposing ruins of the Church—ruins which had become a place of assignation, a pile of debris defiled by unspeakable jokes and scandalous jests. Could it be that the terrible God of Genesis and the pale martyr of Golgotha would not prove their existence once for all by renewing the cataclysms of old, by rekindling the rain of fire that once consumed those accursed towns, the cities of the plain? Could it be that this slime would go on spreading until it covered with its pestilential filth this old world where now only seeds of iniquity sprang up and only harvests of shame were gathered?

The door suddenly flew open. In the distance, framed in the opening, some men in cocked hats appeared with clean-shaven cheeks and tufts of hair on their chins, trundling packing-cases along and moving furniture; then the door closed again behind the manservant, who disappeared carrying a bundle of books.

Des Esseintes collapsed into a chair.

'In two days' time I shall be in Paris,' he told himself. 'Well, it is all over now. Like a tide-race, the waves of human mediocrity are rising to the heavens and will engulf this refuge, for I am opening the flood-gates myself, against my will. Ah! but my courage fails me, and my heart is sick within me!—Lord, take pity on the Christian who doubts, on the unbeliever who would fain believe, on the galley-slave of life who puts out to sea alone, in the night, beneath a firmament no longer lit by the consoling beacon-fires of the ancient hope!'

—ᴡᴡ—

KATE CHOPIN

"The Story of an Hour"

Kate Chopin (born Catherine O'Flaherty, 1851–1904) was an important American writer around 1900, but she was neglected for most of this century. Famed as a local colorist, she wrote about Creole and Cajun life in Louisiana (in two collections of stories, *Bayou Folk* [1894] and *A Night in Acadie* [1897], and in a novel, *At Fault* [1890]). It was a world she knew well from her twelve-year marriage to a Creole planter and merchant. Ultimately, she set in motion events that abruptly ended her literary career when she published *The Awakening* (1899), her masterpiece. A tale of adulterous passion about a woman who awakens to find the man she loves is not her husband (inevitably called the American equivalent of Flaubert's *Madame Bovary*), this novel unleashed a firestorm of public criticism when it first appeared. Libraries across the nation banned it, and in her home town of St. Louis, the Fine Arts

Club denied her membership, despite her obvious distinction. Sensitive to the cry raised against the novel, Chopin was stunned into silence and never wrote again. When she died, her name and works passed from memory until rediscovered in the sixties, prompted by the burgeoning feminist movement. Today her reputation has been restored to the literary pantheon, and she is regarded as a pioneer of Post-Modernism, with her keen interest in marginal people and feminist themes.

Reading the Selection

Chopin's "The Story of an Hour" is actually little more than an anecdote. In the Middle Ages it would have been a moral fable that delivered a religious message. In Chopin's hands, however, it became a story meant to surprise with its ironic twist at the end—a type of tale pioneered by the then popular writer O. Henry (1862–1910), the pen name of William Sydney Porter. Chopin's story recounts the ironic fate of Louise Mallard, who secretly welcomes the news of her husband Brently's unexpected death in a railroad disaster; then she discovers that he is still very much alive, having "been far from the scene of the accident," at which point she falls down dead, the victim of "heart disease."

Chopin manages to make several points with this sad little tale. She has Louise condemn the institution of marriage because it allows "men and women [to] believe that they have a right to impose a private will upon a fellow-creature." Indeed, Louise's initial joy on hearing of Brently's death is that she is finally free of him: "Free! Body and soul free!" Chopin also is a keen student of the world, for she has an exquisite grasp of the poignant disjuncture that the death of a loved one creates for a survivor—as in the way that Louise's grief is engulfed by the sounds of life ("a peddler was crying his wares . . . some one was singing . . . sparrows were twittering"). Chopin also understands the human heart, as in her description of Louise's kaleidoscopic emotions: from weeping, to locking herself in her room, to listening to life in the square, to stifling a sob, and ultimately, to accepting her true feelings.

What makes the story especially intriguing is that it has an autobiographical aspect, though to what degree is not clear. Chopin heard the news of her husband's unexpected death just as Louise did here; however, whereas Louise is "killed by joy," Chopin was left at age thirty-two with six children to support. One wonders if, given such a great material burden, Chopin's husband's death allowed her to "live for herself," Louise's wish.

—⁓—

Knowing that Mrs. Mallard was afflicted with a heart trouble, great care was taken to break to her as gently as possible the news of her husband's death.

It was her sister Josephine who told her, in broken sentences; veiled hints that revealed in half concealing. Her husband's friend Richards was there, too, near her. It was he who had been in the newspaper office when intelligence of the railroad disaster was received, with Brently Mallard's name leading the list of "killed." He had only taken the time to assure himself of its truth by a second telegram, and had hastened to forestall any less careful, less tender friend in bearing the sad message.

She did not hear the story as many women have heard the same, with a paralyzed inability to accept its significance. She wept at once, with sudden, wild abandonment, in her sister's arms. When the storm of grief had spent itself she went away to her room alone. She would have no one follow her.

There stood, facing the open window, a comfortable, roomy armchair. Into this she sank, pressed down by a physical exhaustion that haunted her body and seemed to reach into her soul.

She could see in the open square before her house the tops of trees that were all aquiver with the new spring life. The delicious breath of rain was in the air. In the street below a peddler was crying his wares. The notes of a distant song which some one was singing reached her faintly, and countless sparrows were twittering in the eaves.

There were patches of blue sky showing here and there through the clouds that had met and piled one above the other in the west facing her window.

She sat with her head thrown back upon the cushion of the chair, quite motionless, except when a sob came up into her throat and shook her, as a child who has cried itself to sleep continues to sob in its dreams.

She was young, with a fair, calm face, whose lines bespoke repression and even a certain strength. But now there was a dull stare in her eyes, whose gaze was fixed away off yonder on one of those patches of blue sky. It was not a glance of reflection, but rather indicated a suspension of intelligent thought.

There was something coming to her and she was waiting for it, fearfully. What was it? She did not know; it was too subtle and elusive to name. But she felt it, creeping out of the sky, reaching toward her through the sounds, the scents, the color that filled the air.

Now her bosom rose and fell tumultuously. She was beginning to recognize this thing that was approaching to possess her, and she was striving to beat it back with her will—as powerless as her two white slender hands would have been.

When she abandoned herself a little whispered word escaped her slightly parted lips. She said it over and over under her breath: "free, free, free!" The vacant stare and the look of terror that had followed it went from her eyes. They stayed keen and bright. Her pulses beat fast, and the coursing blood warmed and relaxed every inch of her body.

She did not stop to ask if it were or were not a monstrous joy that held her. A clear and exalted perception enabled her to dismiss the suggestion as trivial.

She knew that she would weep again when she saw the kind, tender hands folded in death; the face that had never looked save with love upon her, fixed and gray and dead. But she saw beyond that bitter moment a long procession of years to come that would belong to her absolutely. And she opened and spread her arms out to them in welcome.

There would be no one to live for her during those coming years; she would live for herself. There would be no powerful will bending hers in that blind persistence with which men and women believe they have a right to impose a private will upon a fellow-creature. A kind intention or a cruel intention made the act seem no less a crime as she looked upon it in that brief moment of illumination.

And yet she had loved him—sometimes. Often she had not. What did it matter! What could love, the un-

solved mystery, count for in face of this possession of self-assertion which she suddenly recognized as the strongest impulse of her being!

"Free! Body and soul free!" she kept whispering.

Josephine was kneeling before the closed door with her lips to the keyhole, imploring for admission. "Louise, open the door! I beg; open the door—you will make yourself ill. What are you doing, Louise? For heaven's sake open the door."

"Go away. I am not making myself ill." No; she was drinking in a very elixir of life through that open window.

Her fancy was running riot along those days ahead of her. Spring days, and summer days, and all sorts of days that would be her own. She breathed a quick prayer that life might be long. It was only yesterday she had thought with a shudder that life might be long.

She arose at length and opened the door to her sister's importunities. There was a feverish triumph in her eyes, and she carried herself unwittingly like a goddess of Victory. She clasped her sister's waist, and together they descended the stairs. Richards stood waiting for them at the bottom.

Some one was opening the front door with a latchkey. It was Brently Mallard who entered, a little travel-stained, composedly carrying his gripsack and umbrella. He had been far from the scene of accident, and did not even know there had been one. He stood amazed at Josephine's piercing cry; at Richards' quick motion to screen him from the view of his wife.

But Richards was too late.

When the doctors came they said she had died of heart disease—of joy that kills.

FRANZ KAFKA

Selection from *Metamorphosis*

The Austrian Franz Kafka (1883–1924) is generally described as one of the founders of Modernist fiction, but scholars are divided over the meaning of his life for twentieth-century culture.

One school of thought labels Kafka a prophet of modern life and emphasizes his triple alienation: a German-speaking Jew from the Czech-speaking and Protestant section of largely Roman Catholic Austria. This school further claims that Kafka, a deeply self-aware writer, used his own plight to create literary heroes—each a modern Everyman often named "K."—who were victims of forces beyond their control. Thus, in this view, Kafka's works may be interpreted variously as existentialist parables about meaning in a godless age, or as religious allegories about the retreat of the divine in modern times, or as satires on modern bureaucracy and its oppression of the individual (Kafka was a lifelong civil servant).

Downplaying Kafka as a prophet, another school of thought stresses the autobiographical in his works. Impressed by the soul-searching revealed in his *Diaries* (2 vols., 1948–1949), this school claims that Kafka was tormented by conflict with his father: Kafka, the frail, sensitive, and intellectual son, was dominated by his physically fit, no-nonsense, businessman father. Indeed, Kafka once asserted that all his works were about his father. Thus, in this view, Kafka was always writing about his own condition.

As usual, the true meaning of Kafka probably lies between the two rival views, part visionary, part anguished son. Whatever the view, his works inspired the term "Kafkaesque," a self-absorbed style marked by feelings of guilt and paranoid helplessness.

Despite present fame, Kafka in his own day doubted the worth of his literary efforts. When *Metamorphosis and Other Stories* (1915) and *The Penal Colony* (1919) met with little critical acclaim, he planned to have the rest of his work destroyed at his death. His literary executor frustrated this wish and (happily) arranged for these remaining works to be published: *The Trial* (1925), *The Castle* (1926), and *Amerika* (1927)—all classics of Modernist literature.

Reading the Selection

"When Gregor Samsa woke up one morning from unsettling dreams, he found himself changed in his bed into a monstrous vermin [cockroach]." Kafka's opening line from *Metamorphosis* helped change Modernist literature, opening it to the theme of transformation, as in Philip Roth's *The Breast* (the hero is changed into a human breast); and in general, Kafka enabled fiction to go beyond Realism and Naturalism. Probably inspired by Ovid's *Metamorphoses,* Kafka's story was unlike anything in Ovid's work. While Ovid concentrated on external effects, Kafka wrote from the inside, detailing the hero's feelings and reactions as he adapted to his changed form.

Interpretation of the symbolic story of Gregor Samsa, who is clearly Kafka's alter ego, leads to two different directions. On the one hand, Samsa's change into a cockroach is a sign of Kafka's inferiority toward his oppressive father. It is seen clearly by Samsa's father's forcing his cockroach-son back into the closed room—a concrete sign of struggle with the paternal as set forth by Freud, whose ideas were still new when Kafka wrote. On the other hand, Samsa's alienation—feeling cut off from human society—corresponds with the then current theory of Max Weber regarding the dehumanizing impact of bureaucratization on society.

When Gregor Samsa woke up one morning from unsettling dreams, he found himself changed in his bed into a monstrous vermin. He was lying on his back as hard as armor plate, and when he lifted his head a little, he saw his vaulted brown belly, sectioned by arch-shaped ribs, to whose dome the cover, about to slide off completely, could barely cling. His many legs, pitifully thin compared with the size of the rest of him, were waving helplessly before his eyes.

"What's happened to me?" he thought. It was no dream. His room, a regular human room, only a little on the small side lay quiet between the four familiar walls. Over the table, on which an unpacked line of fabric samples was all spread out—Samsa was a traveling salesman—hung the picture which he had recently cut out of a glossy magazine and lodged in a pretty gilt frame. It showed a lady done up in a fur hat and a fur boa, sitting upright and raising up against the viewer a heavy fur muff in which her whole forearm had disappeared.

Gregor's eyes then turned to the window, and the overcast weather—he could hear raindrops hitting against the metal window ledge—completely depressed him. "How about going back to sleep for a few minutes and forgetting all this nonsense," he thought, but that was completely impracticable, since he was used to sleeping on his

right side and in his present state could not get into that position. No matter how hard he threw himself onto his right side, he always rocked onto his back again. He must have tried it a hundred times, closing his eyes so as not to have to see his squirming legs, and stopped only when he began to feel a slight, dull pain in his side, which he had never felt before.

"Oh God," he thought, "what a grueling job I've picked! Day in, day out—on the road. The upset of doing business is much worse than the actual business in the home office, and, besides, I've got the torture of traveling, worrying about changing trains, eating miserable food at all hours, constantly seeing new faces, no relationships that last or get more intimate. To the devil with it all!" He felt a slight itching up on top of his belly; shoved himself slowly on his back closer to the bedpost, so as to be able to lift his head better; found the itchy spot, studded with small white dots which he had no idea what to make of; and wanted to touch the spot with one of his legs but immediately pulled it back, for the contact sent a cold shiver through him.

He slid back again into his original position. "This getting up so early," he thought, "makes anyone a complete idiot. Human beings have to have their sleep. Other traveling salesmen live like harem women. For instance, when I go back to the hotel before lunch to write up the business I've done, these gentlemen are just having breakfast. That's all I'd have to try with my boss; I'd be fired on the spot. Anyway, who knows if that wouldn't be a very good thing for me. If I didn't hold back for my parents' sake, I would have quit long ago, I would have marched up to the boss and spoken my piece from the bottom of my heart. He would have fallen off the desk! It is funny, too, the way he sits on the desk and talks down from the heights to the employees, especially when they have to come right up close on account of the boss's being hard of hearing. Well, I haven't given up hope completely; once I've gotten the money together to pay off my parents' debt to him—that will probably take another five or six years—I'm going to do it without fail. Then I'm going to make the big break. But for the time being I'd better get up, since my train leaves at five."

And he looked over at the alarm clock, which was ticking on the chest of drawers. "God Almighty!" he thought. It was six-thirty, the hands were quietly moving forward, it was actually past the half-hour, it was already nearly a quarter to. Could it be that the alarm hadn't gone off? You could see from the bed that it was set correctly for four o'clock; it certainly had gone off, too. Yes, but was it possible to sleep quietly through a ringing that made the furniture shake? Well, he certainly hadn't slept quietly, but probably all the more soundly for that. But what should he do now? The next train left at seven o'clock; to make it, he would have to hurry like a madman, and the line of samples wasn't packed yet, and he himself didn't feel especially fresh and ready to march around. And even if he did make the train, he could not avoid getting it from the boss, because the messenger boy had been waiting at the five-o'clock train and would have long ago reported his not showing up. He was a tool of the boss, without brains or backbone. What if he were to say he was sick? But that would be extremely embarrassing and suspicious because during his five years with the firm Gregor had not been sick even once. The boss would be sure to come with the health-insurance doctor, blame his parents for their lazy son, and cut off all excuses by quoting the health-insurance doctor, for whom the world consisted of people who were completely healthy but afraid to work. And, besides, in this case would he be so very wrong? In fact, Gregor felt fine, with the exception of his drowsiness, which was really unnecessary after sleeping so late, and he even had a ravenous appetite.

Just as he was thinking all this over at top speed, without being able to decide to get out of bed—the alarm clock had just struck a quarter to seven—he heard a cautious knocking at the door next to the head of his bed. "Gregor," someone called—it was his mother—"it's a quarter to seven. Didn't you want to catch the train?" What a soft voice! Gregor was shocked to hear his own voice answering, unmistakably his own voice, true, but in which, as if from below, an insistent distressed chirping intruded, which left the clarity of his words intact only for a moment really, before so badly garbling them as they carried that no one could be sure if he had heard right. Gregor had wanted to answer in detail and to explain everything, but, given the circumstances, confined himself to saying, "Yes, yes, thanks, Mother, I'm just getting up." The wooden door must have prevented the change in Gregor's voice from being noticed outside, because his mother was satisfied with this explanation and shuffled off. But their little exchange had made the rest of the family aware that, contrary to expectations, Gregor was still in the house, and already his father was knocking on one of the side doors, feebly but with his fist. "Gregor, Gregor," he called, "what's going on?" And after a little while he called again in a deeper, warning voice, "Gregor! Gregor!" At the other side door, however, his sister moaned gently, "Gregor? Is something the matter with you? Do you want anything?" Toward both sides Gregor answered: "I'm all ready," and made an effort, by meticulous pronunciation and by inserting long pauses between individual words, to eliminate everything from his voice that might betray him. His father went back to his breakfast, but his sister whispered, "Gregor, open up, I'm pleading with you." But Gregor had absolutely no intention of opening the door and complimented himself instead on the precaution he had adopted from his business trips, of locking all the doors during the night even at home.

First of all he wanted to get up quietly, without any excitement; get dressed; and, the main thing, have breakfast, and only then think about what to do next, for he saw clearly that in bed he would never think things through to a rational conclusion. He remembered how even in the past he had often felt some kind of slight pain, possibly caused by lying in an uncomfortable position, which, when he got up, turned out to be purely imaginary, and he was eager to see how today's fantasy would gradually fade away. That the change in his voice was nothing more than the first sign of a bad cold, an occupational ailment of the traveling salesman, he had no doubt in the least.

It was very easy to throw off the cover; all he had to do was puff himself up a little, and it fell off by itself. But after this, things got difficult, especially since he was so unusually broad. He would have needed hands and arms to lift himself up, but instead of that he had only his numerous little legs, which were in every different kind of perpetual motion and which, besides, he could not control. If he wanted to bend one, the first thing that happened was that it stretched itself out; and if he finally succeeded in getting this leg to do what he wanted, all the others in the meantime, as if set free, began to work in the most intensely painful agitation. "Just don't stay in bed being useless," Gregor said to himself.

First he tried to get out of bed with the lower part of his body, but this lower part—which by the way he had not seen yet and which he could not form a clear picture of—proved too difficult to budge; it was taking so long; and when finally, almost out of his mind, he lunged forward with all his force, without caring, he had picked the wrong direction and slammed himself violently against the lower bedpost, and the searing pain he felt taught him that exactly the lower part of his body was, for the moment anyway, the most sensitive.

He therefore tried to get the upper part of his body out of bed first and warily turned his head toward the edge of the bed. This worked easily, and in spite of its width and weight, the mass of his body finally followed, slowly, the movement of his head. But when at last he stuck his head over the edge of the bed into the air, he got too scared to continue any further, since if he finally let himself fall in this position, it would be a miracle if he didn't injure his head. And just now he had better not for the life of him lose consciousness; he would rather stay in bed.

But when, once again, after the same exertion, he lay in his original position, sighing, and again watched his little legs struggling, if possible more fiercely, with each other and saw no way of bringing peace and order into this mindless motion, he again told himself that it was impossible for him to stay in bed and that the most rational thing was to make any sacrifice for even the smallest hope of freeing himself from the bed. But at the same time he did not forget to remind himself occasionally that thinking things over calmly—indeed, as calmly as possible—was much better than jumping to desperate decisions. At such moments he fixed his eyes as sharply as possible on the window, but unfortunately there was little confidence and cheer to be gotten from the view of the morning fog, which shrouded even the other side of the narrow street. "Seven o'clock already," he said to himself as the alarm clock struck again, "seven o'clock already and still such a fog." And for a little while he lay quietly, breathing shallowly, as if expecting, perhaps, from the complete silence the return of things to the way they really and naturally were.

But then he said to himself, "Before it strikes a quarter past seven, I must be completely out of bed without fail. Anyway, by that time someone from the firm will be here to find out where I am, since the office opens before seven." And now he started rocking the complete length of his body out of the bed with a smooth rhythm. If he let himself topple out of bed in this way, his head, which on falling he planned to lift up sharply, would presumably remain unharmed. His back seemed to be hard; nothing was likely to happen to it when it fell onto the carpet. His biggest misgiving came from his concern about the loud crash that was bound to occur and would probably create, if not terror, at least anxiety behind all the doors. But that would have to be risked.

When Gregor's body already projected halfway out of bed—the new method was more of a game than a struggle, he only had to keep on rocking and jerking himself along—he thought how simple everything would be if he could get some help. Two strong persons—he thought of his father and the maid—would have been completely sufficient; they would have had to shove their arms under his arched back, in this way scoop him off the bed, bend down with their burden, and then just be careful and patient while he managed to swing himself down onto the floor, where his little legs would hopefully acquire some purpose. Well, leaving out the fact that the doors were locked, should he really call for help? In spite of all his miseries, he could not repress a smile at this thought.

He was already so far along that when he rocked more strongly he could hardly keep his balance, and very soon he would have to commit himself, because in five minutes it would be a quarter past seven—when the doorbell rang. 15

"It's someone from the firm," he said to himself and almost froze, while his little legs only danced more quickly. For a moment everything remained quiet. "They're not going to answer," Gregor said to himself, captivated by some senseless hope. But then, of course, the maid went to the door as usual with her firm stride and opened up. Gregor only had to hear the visitor's first word of greeting to know who it was—the office manager himself. Why was only Gregor condemned to work for a firm where at the slightest omission they immediately suspected the worst? Were all employees louts without exception, wasn't there a single loyal, dedicated worker among them who, when he had not fully utilized a few hours of the morning for the firm, was driven half-mad by pangs of conscience and was actually unable to get out of bed? Really, wouldn't it have been enough to send one of the apprentices to find out—if this prying were absolutely necessary—did the manager himself have to come, and did the whole innocent family have to be shown in this way that the investigation of this suspicious affair could be entrusted only to the intellect of the manager? And more as a result of the excitement produced in Gregor by these thoughts than as a result of any real decision, he swung himself out of bed with all his might. There was a loud thump, but it was not a real crash. The fall was broken a little by the carpet, and Gregor's back was more elastic than he had thought, which explained the not very noticeable muffled sound. Only he had not held his head carefully enough and hit it; he turned it and rubbed it on the carpet in anger and pain.

"Something fell in there," said the manager in the room on the left. Gregor tried to imagine whether something like what had happened to him today could one day happen even to the manager; you really had to grant the possibility. But, as if in rude reply to this question, the manager took a few decisive steps in the next room and made his patent leather boots creak. From the room on the right his sister whispered, to inform Gregor, "Gregor, the manager is here." "I know," Gregor said to himself; but he did not dare raise his voice enough for his sister to hear.

"Gregor," his father now said from the room on the left, "the manager has come and wants to be informed why you didn't catch the early train. We don't know what we should say to him. Besides, he wants to speak to you personally. So please open the door. He will certainly be so kind as to excuse the disorder of the room." "Good morning, Mr. Samsa," the manager called in a friendly voice. "There's something the matter with him," his mother said to the manager while his father was still at the door, talking. "Believe me, sir, there's something the matter with him. Otherwise how would Gregor have missed a train? That boy has nothing on his mind but the business. It's almost begun to rile me that he never goes out nights. He's been back in the city for eight days now, but every night he's been home. He sits there with us at the table, quietly reading the paper or studying timetables. It's already a distraction for him when he's busy working with his fretsaw. For instance, in the span of two or three evenings he carved a little frame. You'll be amazed how pretty it is; it's hanging inside his room. You'll see it right away when Gregor opens the door. You know, I'm glad that you've come, sir.

We would never have gotten Gregor to open the door by ourselves; he's so stubborn. And there's certainly something wrong with him, even though he said this morning there wasn't." "I'm coming right away," said Gregor slowly and deliberately, not moving in order not to miss a word of the conversation. "I haven't any other explanation myself," said the manager. "I hope it's nothing serious. On the other hand, I must say that we businessmen—fortunately or unfortunately, whichever you prefer—very often simply have to overcome a slight indisposition for business reasons." "So can the manager come in now?" asked his father, impatient, and knocked on the door again. "No," said Gregor. In the room on the left there was an embarrassing silence; in the room on the right his sister began to sob.

Why didn't his sister go in to the others? She had probably just got out of bed and not even started to get dressed. Then what was she crying about? Because he didn't get up and didn't let the manager in, because he was in danger of losing his job, and because then the boss would start hounding his parents about the old debts? For the time being, certainly, her worries were unnecessary. Gregor was still here and hadn't the slightest intention of letting the family down. True, at the moment he was lying on the carpet, and no one knowing his condition could seriously have expected him to let the manager in. But just because of this slight discourtesy, for which an appropriate excuse would easily be found later on, Gregor could not simply be dismissed. And to Gregor it seemed much more sensible to leave him alone now than to bother him with crying and persuasion. But it was just the uncertainty that was tormenting the others and excused their behavior.

"Mr. Samsa," the manager now called, raising his voice, "what's the matter? You barricade yourself in your room, answer only 'yes' and 'no,' cause your parents serious, unnecessary worry, and you neglect—I mention this only in passing—your duties to the firm in a really shocking manner. I am speaking here in the name of your parents and of your employer and ask you in all seriousness for an immediate, clear explanation. I'm amazed, amazed. I thought I knew you to be a quiet, reasonable person, and now you suddenly seem to want to start strutting about, flaunting strange whims. The head of the firm did suggest to me this morning a possible explanation for your tardiness—it concerned the cash payments recently entrusted to you—but really, I practically gave my word of honor that this explanation could not be right. But now, seeing your incomprehensible obstinacy, I am about to lose even the slightest desire to stick up for you in any way at all. And your job is not the most secure. Originally I intended to tell you all this in private, but since you make me waste my time here for nothing, I don't see why your parents shouldn't hear too. Your performance of late has been very unsatisfactory; I know it is not the best season for doing business, we all recognize that; but a season for not doing any business, there is no such thing, Mr. Samsa, such a thing cannot be tolerated."

"But, sir," cried Gregor, beside himself, in his excitement forgetting everything else, "I'm just opening up, in a minute. A slight indisposition, a dizzy spell, prevented me from getting up. I'm still in bed. But I already feel fine

again. I'm just getting out of bed. Just be patient for a minute! I'm not as well as I thought yet. But really I'm fine. How something like this could just take a person by surprise! Only last night I was fine, my parents can tell you, or wait, last night I already had a slight premonition. They must have been able to tell by looking at me. Why didn't I report it to the office! But you always think that you'll get over a sickness without staying home. Sir! Spare my parents! There's no basis for any of the accusations that you're making against me now; no one has ever said a word to me about them. Perhaps you haven't seen the last orders I sent in. Anyway, I'm still going on the road with the eight o'clock train; these few hours of rest have done me good. Don't let me keep you, sir. I'll be at the office myself right away, and be so kind as to tell them this, and give my respects to the head of the firm."

And while Gregor hastily blurted all this out, hardly knowing what he was saying, he had easily approached the chest of drawers, probably as a result of the practice he had already gotten in bed, and now he tried to raise himself up against it. He actually intended to open the door, actually present himself and speak to the manager; he was eager to find out what the others, who were now so anxious to see him, would say at the sight of him. If they were shocked, then Gregor had no further responsibility and could be calm. But if they took everything calmly, then he, too, had no reason to get excited and could, if he hurried, actually be at the station by eight o'clock. At first he slid off the polished chest of drawers a few times, but at last, giving himself a final push, he stood upright; he no longer paid any attention to the pains in his abdomen, no matter how much they were burning. Now he let himself fall against the back of a nearby chair, clinging to its slats with his little legs. But by doing this he had gotten control of himself and fell silent, since he could now listen to what the manager was saying.

"Did you understand a word?" the manager was asking his parents. "He isn't trying to make fools of us, is he?" "My God," cried his mother, already in tears, "maybe he's seriously ill, and here we are, torturing him. Grete! Grete!" she then cried. "Mother?" called his sister from the other side. They communicated by way of Gregor's room. "Go to the doctor's immediately. Gregor is sick. Hurry, get the doctor. Did you just hear Gregor talking?' "That was the voice of an animal," said the manager, in a tone conspicuously soft compared with the mother's yelling. "Anna!" "Anna!" the father called through the foyer into the kitchen, clapping his hands, "get a locksmith right away!" And already the two girls were running with rustling skirts through the foyer—how could his sister have gotten dressed so quickly?—and tearing open the door to the apartment. The door could not be heard slamming; they had probably left it open, as is the custom in homes where a great misfortune has occurred.

But Gregor had become much calmer. It was true that they no longer understood his words, though they had seemed clear enough to him, clearer than before, probably because his ear had grown accustomed to them. But still, the others now believed that there was something the matter with him and were ready to help him. The assurance and confidence with which the first measures had been taken did him good. He felt integrated into human society once again and hoped for marvelous, amazing feats from both the doctor and the locksmith, without really distinguishing sharply between them. In order to make his voice as clear as possible for the crucial discussions that were approaching, he cleared his throat a little—taking pains, of course, to do so in a very muffled manner, since this noise, too, might sound different from human coughing, a thing he no longer trusted himself to decide. In the next room, meanwhile, everything had become completely still. Perhaps his parents were sitting at the table with the manager, whispering; perhaps they were all leaning against the door and listening.

Gregor slowly lugged himself toward the door, pushing the chair in front of him, then let go of it, threw himself against the door, held himself upright against it—the pads on the bottom of his little legs exuded a little sticky substance—and for a moment rested there from the exertion. But then he got started turning the key in the lock with his mouth. Unfortunately it seemed that he had no real teeth—what was he supposed to grip the key with?—but in compensation his jaws, of course, were very strong; with their help he actually got the key moving and paid no attention to the fact that he was undoubtedly hurting himself in some way, for a brown liquid came out of his mouth, flowed over the key, and dripped onto the floor. "Listen," said the manager in the next room, "he's turning the key." This was great encouragement to Gregor; but everyone should have cheered him on, his father and mother too. "Go, Gregor," they should have called, "keep going, at that lock, harder, harder!" And in the delusion that they were all following his efforts with suspense, he clamped his jaws madly on the key with all the strength he could muster. Depending on the progress of the key, he danced around the lock; holding himself upright only by his mouth, he clung to the key, as the situation demanded, or pressed it down again with the whole weight of his body. The clearer click of the lock as it finally snapped back literally woke Gregor up. With a sigh of relief he said to himself, "So I didn't need the locksmith after all," and laid his head down on the handle in order to open wide [one wing of the double doors.]

Since he had to use this method of opening the door, it was really opened very wide while he himself was still invisible. He first had to edge slowly around the one wing of the door, and do so very carefully if he was not to fall flat on his back just before entering. He was still busy with this difficult maneuver and had no time to pay attention to anything else when he heard the manager burst out with a loud "Oh!"—it sounded like a rush of wind—and now he could see him, standing closest to the door, his hand pressed over his open mouth, slowly backing away, as if repulsed by an invisible, unrelenting force. His mother—in spite of the manager's presence she stood with her hair still unbraided from the night, sticking out in all directions—first looked at his father with her hands clasped, then took two steps toward Gregor, and sank down in the midst of her skirts spreading out around her, her face completely hidden on her breast. With a hostile expression his father clenched his fist, as if to drive Gregor back into his room, then looked uncertainly around the living room, shielded his eyes with his hands, and sobbed with heaves of his powerful chest.

Now Gregor did not enter the room after all but leaned against the inside of the firmly bolted wing of the door, so that only half his body was visible and his head above it, cocked to one side and peeping out at the others. In the meantime it had grown much lighter; across the street one could see clearly a section of the endless, grayish-black building opposite—it was a hospital—with its regular windows starkly piercing the façade; the rain was still coming down, but only in large, separately visible drops that were also pelting the ground literally one at a time. The breakfast dishes were laid out lavishly on the table, since for his father breakfast was the most important meal of the day, which he would prolong for hours while reading various newspapers. On the wall directly opposite hung a photograph of Gregor from his army days, in a lieutenant's uniform, his hand on his sword, a carefree smile on his lips, demanding respect for his bearing and his rank. The door to the foyer was open, and since the front door was open too, it was possible to see out onto the landing and the top of the stairs going down.

"Well," said Gregor—and he was thoroughly aware of being the only one who had kept calm—"I'll get dressed right away, pack up my samples, and go. Will you, will you please let me go? Now, sir, you see, I'm not stubborn and I'm willing to work; traveling is a hardship, but without it I couldn't live. Where are you going, sir? To the office? Yes? Will you give an honest report of everything? A man might find for a moment that he was unable to work, but that's exactly the right time to remember his past accomplishments and to consider that later on, when the obstacle has been removed, he's bound to work all the harder and more efficiently. I'm under so many obligations to the head of the firm, as you know very well. Besides, I also have my parents and my sister to worry about. I'm in a tight spot, but I'll also work my way out again. Don't make things harder for me than they already are. Stick up for me in the office, please. Traveling salesmen aren't well liked there, I know. People think they make a fortune leading the gay life. No one has any particular reason to rectify this prejudice. But you, sir, you have a better perspective on things than the rest of the office, an even better perspective, just between the two of us, than the head of the firm himself, who in his capacity as owner easily lets his judgment be swayed against an employee. And you also know very well that the traveling salesman, who is out of the office practically the whole year round, can so easily become the victim of gossip, coincidences, and unfounded accusations, against which he's completely unable to defend himself, since in most cases he knows nothing at all about them except when he returns exhausted from a trip, and back home gets to suffer on his own person the grim consequences, which can no longer be traced back to their causes. Sir, don't go away without a word to tell me you think I'm at least partly right!"

But at Gregor's first words the manager had already turned away and with curled lips looked back at Gregor only over his twitching shoulder. And during Gregor's speech he did not stand still for a minute but, without letting Gregor out of his sight, backed toward the door, yet very gradually, as if there were some secret prohibition against leaving the room. He was already in the foyer, and from the sudden movement with which he took his last step from the living room, one might have thought he had just burned the sole of his foot. In the foyer, however, he stretched his right hand far out toward the staircase, as if nothing less than an unearthly deliverance were awaiting him there.

Gregor realized that he must on no account let the manager go away in this mood if his position in the firm were not to be jeopardized in the extreme. His parents did not understand this too well; in the course of the years they had formed the conviction that Gregor was set for life in this firm; and furthermore, they were so preoccupied with their immediate troubles that they had lost all consideration for the future. But Gregor had this forethought. The manager must be detained, calmed down, convinced, and finally won over; Gregor's and the family's future depended on it! If only his sister had been there! She was perceptive; she had already begun to cry when Gregor was still lying calmly on his back. And certainly the manager, this ladies' man, would have listened to her; she would have shut the front door and in the foyer talked him out of his scare. But his sister was not there, Gregor had to handle the situation himself. And without stopping to realize that he had no idea what his new faculties of movement were, and without stopping to realize either that his speech had possibly—indeed, probably—not been understood again, he let go of the wing of the door; he shoved himself through the opening, intending to go to the manager, who was already on the landing, ridiculously holding onto the banisters with both hands; but groping for support, Gregor immediately fell down with a little cry onto his numerous little legs. This had hardly happened when for the first time that morning he had a feeling of physical well-being; his little legs were on firm ground; they obeyed him completely, as he noted to his joy; they even strained to carry him away wherever he wanted to go; and he already believed that final recovery from all his sufferings was imminent. But at that very moment, as he lay on the floor rocking with repressed motion, not far from his mother and just opposite her, she, who had seemed so completely self-absorbed, all at once jumped up, her arms stretched wide, her fingers spread, and cried, "Help, for God's sake, help!" held her head bent as if to see Gregor better, but inconsistently darted madly backward instead; had forgotten that the table laden with the breakfast dishes stood behind her; sat down on it hastily, as if her thoughts were elsewhere, when she reached it; and did not seem to notice at all that near her the big coffeepot had been knocked over and coffee was pouring in a steady stream onto the rug.

"Mother, Mother," said Gregor softly and looked up at her. For a minute the manager had completely slipped his mind; on the other hand at the sight of the spilling coffee he could not resist snapping his jaws several times in the air. At this his mother screamed once more, fled from

the table, and fell into the arms of his father, who came rushing up to her. But Gregory had no time now for his parents; the manager was already on the stairs; with his chin on the banister, he was taking a last look back. Gregor was off to a running start, to be as sure as possible of catching up with him; the manager must have suspected something like this, for he leaped down several steps and disappeared; but still he shouted "Agh," and the sound carried through the whole staircase. Unfortunately the manager's flight now seemed to confuse his father completely, who had been relatively calm until now, for instead of running after the manager himself, or at least not hindering Gregor in his pursuit, he seized in his right hand the manager's cane, which had been left behind on a chair with his hat and overcoat, picked up in his left hand a heavy newspaper from the table, and stamping his feet, started brandishing the cane and the newspaper to drive Gregor back into his room. No plea of Gregor's helped, no plea was even understood; however humbly he might turn his head, his father merely stamped his feet more forcefully. Across the room his mother had thrown open a window in spite of the cool weather, and leaning out, she buried her face, far outside the window, in her hands. Between the alley and the staircase a strong draft was created, the window curtains blew in, the newspapers on the table rustled, single sheets fluttered across the floor. Pitilessly his father came on, hissing like a wild man. Now Gregor had not had any practice at all walking in reverse, it was really very slow going. If Gregor had only been allowed to turn around, he could have gotten into his room right away, but he was afraid to make his father impatient by this time-consuming gyration, and at any minute the cane in his father's hand threatened to come down on his back or his head with a deadly blow. Finally, however, Gregor had no choice, for he noticed with horror that in reverse he could not keep going in one direction; and so, incessantly throwing uneasy side-glances at his father, he began to turn around as quickly as possible, in reality turning only very slowly. Perhaps his father realized his good intentions, for he did not interfere with him; instead, he even now and then directed the maneuver from afar with the tip of his cane. If only his father did not keep making this intolerable hissing sound! It made Gregor lose his head completely. He had almost finished the turn when—his mind continually on this hissing—he made a mistake and even started turning back around to his original position. But when he had at last successfully managed to get his head in front of the opened door, it turned out that his body was too broad to get through as it was. Of course in his father's present state of mind it did not even remotely occur to him to open the other wing of the door in order to give Gregor enough room to pass through. He had only the fixed idea that Gregor must return to his room as quickly as possible. He would never have allowed the complicated preliminaries Gregor needed to go through in order to stand up on one end and perhaps in this way fit through the door. Instead he drove Gregor on, as if there were no obstacle, with exceptional loudness; the voice behind Gregor did not sound like that of only a single father; now this was really no joke any

30

more, and Gregor forced himself—come what may—into the doorway. One side of his body rose up, he lay lopsided in the opening, one of his flanks was scraped raw, ugly blotches marred the white door, soon he got stuck and could not have budged any more by himself, his little legs on one side dangled tremblingly in midair, those on the other were painfully crushed against the floor—when from behind his father gave him a hard shove, which was truly his salvation, and bleeding profusely, he flew far into his room. The door was slammed shut with the cane, then at last everything was quiet.

———⁓———

SIGMUND FREUD

Selection from *Civilization and Its Discontents*

The Austrian physician and psychologist Sigmund Freud (1856–1939), like the English biologist Darwin, was a pioneer of twentieth-century thinking. Indeed, it may be said that Freud began where Darwin (see *The Descent of Man*) left off. Darwin claimed that life was not the result of a divine plan set up at the dawn of time by a benevolent God; rather, it was the outcome of millennia of purposeless and random changes in an endless competition of survival of the fittest, so that the one thing that remains true for the human enterprise is the constancy of struggle. From this starting point, Freud argued that endless struggle, both within each individual and between the individual and society, is the basic nature of the human condition.

The founder of psychoanalysis—that is, the probing of the mind through the "free association" of ideas buried in it—Freud was one of the first to map out the subconscious, as he sought to prove that each person's self is a battle zone. The results of this probing into depth psychology led him to conclude that below the surface of human consciousness (ego) lurks a set of innate drives (id). The id is mainly sexual and aggressive, engaged in a continual war with the individual's socially acquired standards of right and wrong, called conscience (superego). Whether the ego can successfully negotiate the continual conflict between the id and the superego has dramatic meaning, resulting in either happiness or self-destructive behavior. With this reasoning, Freud insisted on the primacy of the unconscious mind in helping to shape the self and thereby laid to rest the psychology of Locke, which had claimed that human consciousness is molded exclusively by the environment.

Near the end of his life as he was suffering from cancer of the mouth, Freud wrote *Civilization and Its Discontents* (1929), in which he applied his new insights to the field of history. Written in the shadow of the rise of totalitarian states of both the right and the left across Europe, and perhaps tinged with a sense of his own impending death, this book offers a gloomy philosophy of history. Freud argues that humanity collectively is locked in a never-ending conflict between the aggressive drives of the collective id (Thanatos, the death instinct) and the sexual drives (Eros, the pleasure principle)—a macrocosmic version of the private war inside each person. The book ends with a question added in 1931 when the menace of the Nazi leader Hitler was becoming apparent, and it is expressive of Freud's ambiguous hopes— "Who can foresee [the] result?"

Reading the Selection

Chapter V, one of the eight short chapters in this monograph, focuses on the conflict between private sexual drives and the demands of civilization for cooperation. For Freud, this conflict is unresolvable, partly because love-relationships at their height exclude all interest in other people, and partly because civilization is relentless in demanding that all members of society bond together in strong ties of friendship. Aggravating the conflict between sexuality and civilization is the aggressive drive, a force that civilization must hold in check in order to survive.

Freud next discusses one of the powerful ideologies of the time, communism, whose basic premise—that human nature is wholly good until corrupted by private property—contradicts his ruling idea that humans are innately aggressive. To him, communism is an "untenable illusion" because it teaches that the abolition of private property will eliminate ill-will and bring forth a golden age. Instead, he asserts that aggressiveness is endemic in history, as demonstrated by several examples. At the end of the day, Freud sides with civilization, in imposing controls on aggressiveness and sexuality. This solution inevitably makes people unhappy, but of greater worth, it provides security for communal life.

In the last paragraph, Freud casts his gaze critically on American society, thinking it perhaps too successful in forging a collective identity—an allusion to "the masses," a key political theme when he wrote. The danger in the American experience, he notes, is that its leaders fail to lead, as they become mouthpieces of an ignorant group. Having raised the topic, he quickly drops it, thinking it sufficient to point out this potential problem.

Chapter V

Psycho-analytic work has shown us that it is precisely these frustrations of sexual life which people known as neurotics cannot tolerate. The neurotic creates substitutive satisfactions for himself in his symptoms, and these either cause him suffering in themselves or become sources of suffering for him by raising difficulties in his relations with his environment and the society he belongs to. The latter fact is easy to understand; the former presents us with a new problem. But civilization demands other sacrifices besides that of sexual satisfaction.

We have treated the difficulty of cultural development as a general difficulty of development by tracing it to the inertia of the libido, to its disinclination to give up an old position for a new one. We are saying much the same thing when we derive the antithesis between civilization and sexuality from the circumstance that sexual love is a relationship between two individuals in which a third can only be superfluous or disturbing, whereas civilization depends on relationships between a considerable number of individuals. When a love-relationship is at its height there is no room left for any interest in the environment; a pair of lovers are sufficient to themselves, and do not even need the child they have in common to make them happy. In no other case does Eros so clearly betray the core of his being, his purpose of making one out of more than one; but when he has achieved this in the proverbial way through the love of two human beings, he refuses to go further.

So far, we can quite well imagine a cultural community consisting of double individuals like this, who, libidinally satisfied in themselves, are connected with one another through the bonds of common work and common interests. If this were so, civilization would not have to withdraw any energy from sexuality. But this desirable state of things does not, and never did, exist. Reality shows us that civilization is not content with the ties we have so far allowed it. It aims at binding the members of the community together in a libidinal way as well and employs every means to that end. It favours every path by which strong identifications can be established between the members of the community, and it summons up aim-inhibited libido on the largest scale so as to strengthen the communal bond by relations of friendship. In order for these aims to be fulfilled, a restriction upon sexual life is unavoidable. But we are unable to understand what the necessity is which forces civilization along this path and which causes its antagonism to sexuality. There must be some disturbing factor which we have not yet discovered.

The clue may be supplied by one of the ideal demands, as we have called them, of civilized society. It runs: 'Thou shalt love thy neighbour as thyself.' It is known throughout the world and is undoubtedly older than Christianity, which puts it forward as its proudest claim. Yet it is certainly not very old; even in historical times it was still strange to mankind. Let us adopt a naïve attitude towards it, as though we were hearing it for the first time; we shall be unable then to suppress a feeling of surprise and bewilderment. Why should we do it? What good will it do us? But, above all, how shall we achieve it? How can it be possible? My love is something valuable to me which I ought not to throw away without reflection. It imposes duties on me for whose fulfilment I must be ready to make sacrifices. If I love someone, he must deserve it in some way. (I leave out of account the use he may be to me, and also his possible significance for me as a sexual object, for neither of these two kinds of relationship comes into question where the precept to love my neighbour is concerned.) He deserves it if he is so like me in important ways that I can love myself in him; and he deserves it if he is so much more perfect than myself that I can love my ideal of my own self in him. Again, I have to love him if he is my friend's son, since the pain my friend would feel if any harm came to him would be my pain too—I should have to share it. But if he is a stranger to me and if he cannot attract me by any worth of his own or any significance that he may already have acquired for my emotional life, it will be hard for me to love him. Indeed, I should be wrong to do so, for my love is valued by all my own people as a sign of my preferring them, and it is an injustice to them if I put a stranger on a par with them. But if I am to love him (with this universal love) merely because he, too, is an inhabitant of this earth, like an insect, an earth-worm or a grass-snake, then I fear that only a small modicum of my love will fall to his share—not by any possibility as much as, by the judgement of my reason, I am entitled to retain for myself. What is the point of a precept enunciated with so much solemnity if its fulfilment cannot be recommended as reasonable?

On closer inspection, I find still further difficulties. Not merely is this stranger in general unworthy of my love; I must honestly confess that he has more claim to my hostility and even my hatred. He seems not to have the least trace of love for me and shows me not the slightest consideration. If it will do him any good he has no hesitation in injuring me, nor does he ask himself whether the amount of advantage he gains bears any proportion to the extent of the harm he does to me. Indeed, he need not even obtain an advantage; if he can satisfy any sort of desire by it, he thinks nothing of jeering at me, insulting me, slandering me and showing his superior power; and the more secure he feels and the more helpless I am, the more certainly I can expect him to behave like this to me. If he behaves differently, if he shows me consideration and forbearance as a stranger, I am ready to treat him in the same way, in any case and quite apart from any precept. Indeed, if this grandiose commandment had run 'Love thy neighbour as they neighbor loves thee', I should not take exception to it. And there is a second commandment, which seems to me even more incomprehensible and arouses still stronger opposition in me. It is 'Love thine enemies'. If I think it over, however, I see that I am wrong in treating it as a greater imposition. At bottom it is the same thing. . . .

The existence of this inclination to aggression, which we can detect in ourselves and justly assume to be present in others, is the factor which disturbs our relations with our neighbour and which forces civilization into such a high expenditure [of energy]. In consequence of this primary mutual hostility of human beings, civilized society is perpetually threatened with disintegration. The interest of work in common would not hold it together; instinctual passions are stronger than reasonable interests. Civilization has to use its utmost efforts in order to set limits to man's aggressive instincts and to hold the manifestations of them in check by psychical reaction-formations. Hence, therefore, the use of methods intended to incite people into identifications and aim-inhibited relationships of love, hence the restriction upon sexual life, and hence too the ideal's commandment to love one's neighbour as oneself—a commandment which is really justified by the fact that nothing else runs so strongly counter to the original nature of man. In spite of every effort, these endeavours of civilization have not so far achieved very much. It hopes to prevent the crudest excesses of brutal violence by itself assuming the right to use violence against criminals, but the law is not able to lay hold of the more cautious and refined manifestations of human aggressiveness. The time comes when each one of us has to give up as illusions the expectations which, in his youth, he pinned upon his fellow-men, and when he may learn how much difficulty and pain has been added to his life by their ill-will. At the same time, it would be unfair to reproach civilization with trying to eliminate strife and competition from human activity. These things are undoubtedly indispensable. But

opposition is not necessarily enmity; it is merely misused and made an *occasion* for enmity.

The communists believe that they have found the path to deliverance from our evils. According to them, man is wholly good and is well-disposed to his neighbour; but the institution of private property has corrupted his nature. The ownership of private wealth gives the individual power, and with it the temptation to ill-treat his neighbour; while the man who is excluded from possession is bound to rebel in hostility against his oppressor. If private property were abolished, all wealth held in common, and everyone allowed to share in the enjoyment of it, ill-will and hostility would disappear among men. Since everyone's needs would be satisfied, no one would have any reason to regard another as his enemy; all would willingly undertake the work that was necessary. I have no concern with any economic criticisms of the communist system; I cannot enquire into whether the abolition of private property is expedient or advantageous. But I am able to recognize that the psychological premises on which the system is based are an untenable illusion. In abolishing private property we deprive the human love of aggression of one of its instruments, certainly a strong one, though certainly not the strongest; but we have in no way altered the differences in power and influence which are misused by aggressiveness, nor have we altered anything in its nature. Aggressiveness was not created by property. It reigned almost without limit in primitive times, when property was still very scanty, and it already shows itself in the nursery almost before property has given up its primal, anal form; it forms the basis of every relation of affection and love among people (with the single exception, perhaps, of the mother's relation to her male child). If we do away with personal rights over material wealth, there still remains prerogative in the field of sexual relationships, which is bound to become the source of the strongest dislike and the most violent hostility among men who in other respects are on an equal footing. If we were to remove this factor, too, by allowing complete freedom of sexual life and thus abolishing the family, the germ-cell of civilization, we cannot, it is true, easily foresee what new paths the development of civilization could take; but one thing we can expect, and that is that this indestructible feature of human nature will follow it there.

It is clearly not easy for men to give up the satisfaction of this inclination to aggression. They do not feel comfortable without it. The advantage which a comparatively small cultural group offers of allowing this instinct an outlet in the form of hostility against intruders is not to be despised. It is always possible to bind together a considerable number of people in love, so long as there are other people left over to receive the manifestations of their aggressiveness. I once discussed the phenomenon that it is precisely communities with adjoining territories, and related to each other in other ways as well, who are engaged in constant feuds and in ridiculing each other—like the Spaniards and Portuguese, for instance, the North Germans and South Germans, the English and Scotch, and so on. I gave this phenomenon the name of 'the narcissism of minor differences', a name which does not do much to explain it. We can now see that it is a convenient and relatively harmless satisfaction of the inclination to aggression, by means of which cohesion between the members of the community is made easier. In this respect the Jewish people, scattered everywhere, have rendered most useful services to the civilizations of the countries that have been their hosts; but unfortunately all the massacres of the Jews in the Middle Ages did not suffice to make that period more peaceful and secure for their Christian fellows. When once the Apostle Paul had posited universal love between men as the foundation of his Christian community, extreme intolerance on the part of Christendom towards those who remained outside it became the inevitable consequence. To the Romans, who had not founded their communal life as a State upon love, religious intolerance was something foreign, although with them religion was a concern of the State and the State was permeated by religion. Neither was it an unaccountable chance that the dream of a Germanic worlddominion called for anti-semitism as its complement; and it is intelligible that the attempt to establish a new, communist civilization in Russia should find its psychological support in the persecution of the bourgeois. One only wonders, with concern, what the Soviets will do after they have wiped out their bourgeois.

If civilization imposes such great sacrifices not only on man's sexuality but on his aggressivity, we can understand better why it is hard for him to be happy in that civilization. In fact, primitive man was better off in knowing no restrictions of instinct. To counterbalance this, his prospects of enjoying this happiness for any length of time were very slender. Civilized man has exchanged a portion of his possibilities of happiness for a portion of security. We must not forget, however, that in the primal family only the head of it enjoyed this instinctual freedom; the rest lived in slavish suppression. In that primal period of civilization, the contrast between a minority who enjoyed the advantages of civilization and a majority who were robbed of those advantages was, therefore, carried to extremes. As regards the primitive peoples who exist to-day, careful researches have shown that their instinctual life is by no means to be envied for its freedom. It is subject to restrictions of a different kind but perhaps of greater severity than those attaching to modern civilized man.

When we justly find fault with the present state of our civilization for so inadequately fulfilling our demands for a plan of life that shall make us happy, and for allowing the existence of so much suffering which could probably be avoided—when, with unsparing criticism, we try to uncover the roots of its imperfection, we are undoubtedly exercising a proper right and are not showing ourselves enemies of civilization. We may expect gradually to carry through such alterations in our civilization as will better satisfy our needs and will escape our criticisms. But perhaps we may also familiarize ourselves with the idea that there are difficulties attaching to the nature of civilization which will not yield to any attempt at reform. Over and above the tasks of restricting the instincts, which we are prepared for, there forces itself on our notice the danger of a state of things which might be termed 'the psychological poverty of groups'. This danger is most threatening where the bonds of a society are chiefly constituted by the identification of its members with one another, while individuals of the leader type do not acquire the importance that should fall to them in the formation of a group. The present cultural state of America would give us a good opportunity for studying the damage to civilization which is thus to be feared. But I shall avoid the temptation of entering upon a critique of American civilization; I do not wish to give an impression of wanting myself to employ American methods.

20

THE AGE OF THE MASSES AND THE ZENITH OF MODERNISM

1914–1945

T. S. ELIOT

"The Love Song of J. Alfred Prufrock"

Eliot's "The Love Song of J. Alfred Prufrock" (1915) is one of the first great works of Modernist poetry, which flourished from about 1904 until about 1939. Modernist poetry continued to be written after 1939, but its zenith was reached in the earlier time. Its aim is typical of Modernism in general, to make a radical break with the nineteenth century and establish a new style more in keeping with the kaleidoscopic changes taking place today.

Modernist poetry, first of all, is not Victorian, for it is opposed to the sentimentality of Romanticism, the fine writing of Neoclassicism, and the illustration of Realism—the leading styles of the Victorian Age. Modernist poetry also offers neither a moral lesson nor a popular message; instead, it is deliberately difficult. Its difficulty springs from its dense writing, its rich allusiveness (quotations from other literary works), and its high intellectual tone. Though antitraditional, it is the heir of the Hellenistic (see Theocritus's *Idylls*) and the Metaphysical poets, both of whom specialized in difficult and learned works. Modernist poetry is often composed in free verse, which has no regular meter or line length and relies on natural speech and the variation of stressed and unstressed syllables, a type of poetry perfected by Whitman (see "When Lilacs Last in the Dooryard Bloom'd").

The Anglo-American T. S. Eliot (born Thomas Stearns Eliot), the pioneer of Modernist poetry, grew up in a middle-class St. Louis family, studied at Harvard, and earned a Ph.D. in philosophy. He migrated to England on the eve of World War I, marrying a genteel English woman who later became psychotic and whom he divorced and put in an insane asylum. Although he never held an academic post, choosing to support himself first as a banker and later as a publisher—particularly of Modernist works—he became the dominant poet of his day and a powerbroker of Modernist literature. He was also one of this period's leading critics, helping to develop what came to be called the New Criticism, which was ideally suited to interpreting Modernist poetry. It advocated "close reading" and detailed textual analysis of the work rather than an interest in the mind and personality of the poet, sources, the history of ideas, and political and social implications.

Reading the Selection

To read "The Love Song of J. Alfred Prufrock" in terms of New Criticism is not to read it as the work of T. S. Eliot, but to study it as the expression of J. Alfred Prufrock, whoever he may be. He indeed may be Eliot's alter ego, but that is irrelevant. The reader has, in effect, been given an intellectual puzzle—to figure out Prufrock and his loves. The epigraph, the opening quotation from Dante's *Inferno*, establishes that Prufrock is shy about revealing himself, just as is the character in Dante. Drawing the reader into the text, "Let us go then, you and I," Prufrock takes the reader on a walk through a seedy neighborhood where the image of yellow fog and smoke engulfs everything. Shyly, Prufrock reveals himself, his lack of self-confidence, his hesitancy to do anything, his sad confession that his life is measured with coffee spoons. He lacks the courage to make an overture to a woman whose bare arms and perfume haunt his memory. Confused, he fears failure and the onset of age ("I grow old") and wonders what he will be like as an old man. At the end, the imagery shifts to seductive mermaids who lure him ever onward into another world, or perhaps to his destruction.

—⚏—

S'io credesse che mia risposta fosse
A persona che mai tornasse al mondo,
Questa fiamma staria senza più scosse.
Ma per ciò che giammai di questo fondo
Non tornò vivo alcun, s'i'odo il vero,
Senza tema d'infamia ti rispondo.[1]

Let us go then, you and I,   1
When the evening is spread out against the sky
Like a patient etherized upon a table;
Let us go, through certain half-deserted streets,
The muttering retreats
Of restless nights in one-night cheap hotels
And sawdust restaurants with oyster-shells:
Streets that follow like a tedious argument
Of insidious intent
To lead you to an overwhelming question . . .   10
Oh, do not ask, "What is it?"
Let us go and make our visit.

In the room the women come and go
Talking of Michelangelo.

The yellow fog that rubs its back upon the window-panes
The yellow smoke that rubs its muzzle on the window-panes
Licked its tongue into the corners of the evening,
Lingered upon the pools that stand in drains,
Let fall upon its back the soot that falls from chimneys,
Slipped by the terrace, made a sudden leap,   20
And seeing that it was a soft October night,
Curled once about the house, and fell asleep.

And indeed there will be time
For the yellow smoke that slides along the street,
Rubbing its back upon the window-panes;
There will be time, there will be time
To prepare a face to meet the faces that you meet;
There will be time to murder and create,
And time for all the works and days of hands
That lift and drop a question on your plate;   30
Time for you and time for me,
And time yet for a hundred indecisions,
And for a hundred visions and revisions,
Before the taking of a toast and tea.

In the room the women come and go
Talking of Michelangelo.

And indeed there will be time
To wonder, "Do I dare?" and, "Do I dare?"
Time to turn back and descend the stair,
With a bald spot in the middle of my hair—   40
[They will say: "How his hair is growing thin!"]
My morning coat, my collar mounting firmly to the chin,
My necktie rich and modest, but asserted by a simple pin—
[They will say: "But how his arms and legs are thin!"]
Do I dare
Disturb the universe?
In a minute there is time
For decisions and revisions which a minute will reverse.

For I have known them all already, known them all:
Have known the evenings, mornings, afternoons,   50

[1]Epigraph from Dante's *Inferno*, Canto XXVII, 61–66: "If I thought my answer were given to anyone who could ever return to the world, this flame would shake no more; but since none ever did return above from this depth, if what I hear is true, without fear of infamy, I answer thee." This response is given by Guido da Montefeltro when he is asked who he is.

I have measured out my life with coffee spoons;
I know the voices dying with a dying fall
Beneath the music from a farther room.
   So how should I presume?

And I have known the eyes already, known them all—
The eyes that fix you in a formulated phrase,
And when I am formulated, sprawling on a pin,
When I am pinned and wriggling on the wall,
Then how should I begin
To spit out all the butt-ends of my days and ways?   60
   And how should I presume?

And I have known the arms already, known them all—
Arms that are braceleted and white and bare
[But in the lamplight, downed with light brown hair!]
Is it perfume from a dress
That makes me so digress?
Arms that lie along a table, or wrap about a shawl.
   And should I then presume?
   And how should I begin?

. . . .

Shall I say, I have gone at dusk through narrow streets   70
And watched the smoke that rises from the pipes
Of lonely men in shirt-sleeves, leaning out of windows? . . .

I should have been a pair of ragged claws
Scuttling across the floors of silent seas.

. . . .

And the afternoon, the evening, sleeps so peacefully!
Smoothed by long fingers,
Asleep . . . tired . . . or it malingers,
Stretched on the floor, here beside you and me.
Should I, after tea and cakes and ices,
Have the strength to force the moment to its crisis?   80
But though I have wept and fasted, wept and prayed,
Though I have seen my head [grown slightly bald]
   brought in upon a platter,
I am no prophet—and here's no great matter;
I have seen the moment of my greatness flicker,
And I have seen the eternal Footman hold my coat, and
   snicker,
And in short, I was afraid.

And would it have been worth it, after all,
After the cups, the marmalade, the tea,
Among the porcelain, among some talk of you and me,
Would it have been worth while,   90
To have bitten off the matter with a smile,

To have squeezed the universe into a ball
To roll it toward some overwhelming question,
To say: "I am Lazarus, come from the dead,
Come back to tell you all, I shall tell you all"—
If one, settling a pillow by her head,
   Should say: "That is not what I meant at all.
   That is not it, at all."

And would it have been worth it, after all,
Would it have been worth while,   100
After the sunsets and the dooryards and the sprinkled
   streets,
After the novels, after the teacups, after the skirts that trail
   along the floor—
And this, and so much more?—
It is impossible to say just what I mean!
But as if a magic lantern threw the nerves in patterns on a
   screen:
Would it have been worth while
If one, settling a pillow or throwing off a shawl,
And turning toward the window, should say:
   "That is not it at all,
   That is not what I meant, at all."   110

. . . .

No! I am not Prince Hamlet, nor was meant to be;
Am an attendant lord, one that will do
To swell a progress, start a scene or two,
Advise the prince; no doubt, an easy tool,
Deferential, glad to be of use,
Politic, cautious, and meticulous;
Full of high sentence, but a bit obtuse;
At times, indeed, almost ridiculous—
Almost, at times, the Fool.

I grow old . . . I grow old . . .   120
I shall wear the bottoms of my trousers rolled.

Shall I part my hair behind? Do I dare to eat a peach?
I shall wear white flannel trousers, and walk upon the
   beach.
I have heard the mermaids singing, each to each.

I do not think that they will sing to me.

I have seen them riding seaward on the waves
Combing the white hair of the waves blown back
When the wind blows the water white and black.

We have lingered in the chambers of the sea
By sea-girls wreathed with seaweed red and brown   130
Till human voices wake us, and we drown.

JAMES JOYCE
Selection from *Ulysses*

Joyce's *Ulysses* is now recognized as perhaps the greatest Modernist novel, though it met stiff resistance, except in avant-garde circles, when it was published in Paris in 1922. Part of the resistance stemmed from the novelty of the Modernist novel's form itself, which, despite the best efforts of Woolf (see *To the Lighthouse*) and Stein (see *The Autobiography of Alice B. Toklas*), had not yet been fully accepted by middle-class readers. *Ulysses* was typical of Modernist innovation in that the telling of the story became secondary to the project of describing a "sensibility" (a term popularized by Eliot, meaning "creative faculty of a writer"). Above all, the narrative voice was not omniscient but was fragmented among several characters who spoke their thoughts in a stream-of-consciousness way. Part of the resistance to *Ulysses* was also its difficulty, for it was a nearly-one-thousand-page modern version of Homer's *Odyssey*, contrasting the ancient author's twenty-four books of heroic deeds with an ordinary day in the lives of three middle-class Dubliners—Stephen Dedalus and Leopold and Molly Bloom. Most of all, *Ulysses* met resistance because of its explicit sexual language, which offended middle-class morals. The novel, which did not appear in America or England until the 1930s, became the age's test case for artistic freedom.

The Irish author James Joyce (1882–1941) came from a large Catholic family in Dublin, studied there at University College (the Catholic counterpart to Protestant Trinity College), and spent time in medical school. Unlike most of his fellow students, he was not attracted to the Irish Renaissance, which was then flourishing; indeed, he heaped scorn upon it and its leaders, notably Yeats. From the beginning, Joyce aligned himself with the world of European letters. He soon settled on the Continent, living the rest of his life in Paris, Zurich, and Trieste. In Paris he fell under the influence of Edouard Dujardin, a French Symbolist poet who introduced him to "stream of consciousness" technique.

Reading the Selection

This selection from Chapter Three, "Proteus," of *Ulysses* recounts, in a stream-of-consciousness style, the actions and thoughts of Stephen Dedalus, Joyce's alter ego and whose last name is taken from the Greek hero famed for his creativity. As Stephen walks along Sandymount Strand in Dublin, he thinks about his family, his rejected Catholic upbringing, his disappointments as a writer, Irish politics and literature, and the meaning of his life.

This passage shows the rich allusiveness (quotations from other works) of Joyce's style, weaving together Classical themes (Plato's "Demiurgos"), Christian theology ("wombed in sin"), especially with references to ancient heresies ("Arius"), foreign words and phrases (five different tongues), music (*aria de sortita*), various quotations, and memories of Stephen's (Joyce's) family and friends.

The stream-of-consciousness method may be seen clearly here: A reference is made to abortion, midwives or *Frauenzimmer*, which leads to thoughts of "navelcords," which in turn symbolize connections among humans. This line of thought results in speculation about Eve's smooth stomach since she had no navel, being born from Adam's rib.

Puns and plays on words abound, the hallmark of Joyce's mature style. The passage concludes with Stephen mocking his literary ambition, as he refers to the ancient library at Alexandria and to the Renaissance scholar Pico della Mirandola (see *On the Dignity of Man*).

Proteus

Ineluctable modality of the visible: at least that if no more, thought through my eyes. Signatures of all things I am here to read, seaspawn and seawrack, the nearing tide, that rusty boot. Snotgreen, bluesilver, rust: coloured signs. Limits of the diaphane. But he adds: in bodies. Then he was aware of them bodies before of them coloured. How? By knocking his sconce against them, sure. Go easy. Bald he was and a millionaire, *maestro di color che sanno.* Limit of the diaphane in. Why in? Diaphane, adiaphane. If you can put your five fingers through it, it is a gate, if not a door. Shut your eyes and see.

Stephen closed his eyes to hear his boots crush crackling wrack and shells. You are walking through it howsomever. I am, a stride at a time. A very short space of time through very short times of space. Five, six: the *nacheinander.* Exactly: and that is the ineluctable modality of the audible. Open your eyes. No. Jesus! If I fell over a cliff that beetles o'er his base, fell through the *nebeneinander* ineluctably. I am getting on nicely in the dark. My ash sword hangs at my side. Tap with it: they do. My two feet in his boots are at the end of his legs, *nebeneinander.* Sounds solid: made by the mallet of *Los Demiurgos.* Am I walking into eternity along Sandymount strand? Crush, crack, crick, crick. Wild sea money. Dominie Deasy kens them a'.

> *Won't you come to Sandymount,*
> *Madeline the mare?*

Rhythm begins, you see. I hear. A catalectic tetrameter of iambs marching. No, agallop: *deline the mare.*

Open your eyes now. I will. One moment. Has all vanished since? If I open and am for ever in the black adiaphane. *Basta!* I will see if I can see.

See now. There all the time without you: and ever [5] shall be, world without end.

They came down the steps from Leahy's terrace prudently, *Frauenzimmer:* and down the shelving shore flabbily their splayed feet sinking in the silted sand. Like me, like Algy, coming down to our mighty mother. Number one swung lourdily her midwife's bag, the other's gamp poked in the beach. From the liberties, out for the day. Mrs Florence MacCabe, relict of the late Patk MacCabe, deeply lamented, of Bride Street. One of her sisterhood lugged me squealing into life. Creation from nothing. What has she in the bag? A misbirth with a trailing navelcord, hushed in ruddy wool. The cords of all link back, strandentwining cable of all flesh. That is why mystic monks. Will you be as gods? Gaze in your omphalos. Hello. Kinch here. Put me on to Edenville. Aleph, alpha: nought, nought, one.

Spouse and helpmate of Adam Kadmon: Heva, naked Eve. She had no navel. Gaze. Belly without blemish, bulging big, a buckler of taut vellum, no; whiteheaped corn, orient and immortal, standing from everlasting to everlasting. Womb of sin.

Wombed in sin darkness I was too, made not begotten. By them, the man with my voice and my eyes and a ghost-woman with ashes on her breath. They clasped and sundered, did the coupler's will. From before the ages He willed me and now may not will me away or ever. A *lex eterna* stays about him. Is that then the divine substance wherein Father and Son are consubstantial? Where is poor dear Arius to try conclusions? Warring his life long on the contransmagnificandjewbangtantiality. Illstarred heresiarch. In a Greek watercloset he breathed his last: euthanasia. With beaded mitre and with crozier, stalled upon his throne, widower of a widowed see, with upstiffed omophorion, with clotted hinderparts.

Airs romped around him, nipping and eager airs. They are coming, waves. The whitemaned seahorses, champing, brightwindbridled, the steeds of Mananaan.

I mustn't forget his letter for the press. And after? The [10] Ship, half twelve. By the way go easy with that money like a good young imbecile. Yes, I must.

His pace slackened. Here. Am I going to Aunt Sara's or not? My consubstantial father's voice. Did you see anything of your artist brother Stephen lately? No? Sure he's not down in Strasburg terrace with his aunt Sally? Couldn't he fly a bit higher than that, eh? And and and and tell us Stephen, how is uncle Si? O weeping God, the things I married into. De boys up in de hayloft. The drunken little costdrawer and his brother, the cornet player. Highly respectable gondoliers. And skeweyed Walter sirring his father, no less. Sir. Yes, sir. No, sir. Jesus wept: and no wonder, by Christ.

I pull the wheezy bell of their shuttered cottage: and wait. They take me for a dun, peer out from a coign of vantage.

—It's Stephen, sir.

—Let him in. Let Stephen in.

A bolt drawn back and Walter welcomes me. [15]

—We thought you were someone else.

In his broad bed nuncle Richie, pillowed and blanketed, extends over the hillock of his knees a sturdy forearm. Cleanchested. He has washed the upper moiety.

—Morrow, nephew.

He lays aside the lapboard whereon he drafts his bills of costs for the eyes of Master Goff and Master Shapland Tandy, filing consents and common searches and a writ of *Duces Tecum.* A bogoak frame over his bald head: Wilde's *Requiescat.* The drone of his misleading whistle brings Walter back.

—Yes, sir? [20]

—Malt for Richie and Stephen, tell mother. Where is she?

—Bathing Crissie, sir.

Papa's little bedpal. Lump of love.

—No, uncle Richie . . .

—Call me Richie. Damn your lithia water. It lowers. [25] Whusky!

—Uncle Richie, really . . .

—Sit down or by the law Harry I'll knock you down. Walter squints vainly for a chair.

—He has nothing to sit down on, sir.

—He has nowhere to put it, you mug. Bring in our Chippendale chair. Would you like a bite of something? None of your damned lawdeedaw air here; the rich of a rasher fried with a herring? Sure? So much the better. We have nothing in the house but backache pills. ⁣30

All'erta!

He drones bars of Ferrando's *aria de sortita*. The grandest number, Stephen, in the whole opera. Listen.

His tuneful whistle sounds again, finely shaded, with rushes of the air, his fists bigdrumming on his padded knees.

This wind is sweeter.

Houses of decay, mine, his and all. You told the Clongowes gentry you had an uncle a judge and an uncle a general in the army. Come out of them, Stephen. Beauty is not there. Nor in the stagnant bay of Marsh's library where you read the fading prophecies of Joachim Abbas. For whom? The hundred-headed rabble of the cathedral close. A hater of his kind ran from them to the wood of madness, his mane foaming in the moon, his eyeballs stars. Houyhnhnm, horse-nostrilled. The oval equine faces. Temple, Buck Mulligan, Foxy Campbell. Lantern jaws. Abbas father, furious dean, what offence laid fire to their brains? Paff! *Descende, calve, ut ne nimium decalveris.* A garland of grey hair on his comminated head see him me clambering down to the footpace (*descende*), clutching a monstrance, basiliskeyed. Get down, bald poll! A choir gives back menace and echo, assisting about the altar's horns, the snorted Latin of jackpriests moving burly in their albs, tonsured and oiled and gelded, fat with the fat of kidneys of wheat. ⁣35

And at the same instant perhaps a priest round the corner is elevating it. Dringdring! And two streets off another locking it into a pyx. Dringadring! And in a ladychapel another taking housel all to his own cheek. Dringdring! Down, up, forward, back. Dan Occam thought of that, invincible doctor. A misty English morning the imp hypostasis tickled his brain. Bringing his host down and kneeling he heard twine with his second bell the first bell in the transept (he is lifting his) and, rising, heard (now I am lifting) their two bells (he is kneeling) twang in diphthong.

Cousin Stephen, you will never be a saint. Isle of saints. You were awfully holy, weren't you? You prayed to the Blessed Virgin that you might not have a red nose. You prayed to the devil in Serpentine avenue that the fubsy widow in front might lift her clothes still more from the wet street. *O si, certo!* Sell your soul for that, do, dyed rag pinned round a squaw. More tell me, more still! On the top of the Howth tram alone crying to the rain: *naked women!* What about that, eh?

What about what? What else were they invented for?

Reading two pages apiece of seven books every night, eh? I was young. You bowed to yourself in the mirror, stepping forward to applause earnestly, striking face. Hurray for the God-damned idiot! Hray! No-one saw: tell noone. Books you were going to write with letters for titles. Have you read his F? O yes, but I prefer Q. Yes, but W is wonderful. O yes, W. Remember your epiphanies on green oval leaves, deeply deep, copies to be sent if you died to all the great libraries of the world, including Alexandria? Someone was to read them there after a few thousand years, a mahamanvantara. Pico della Mirandola like. Ay, very like a whale. When one reads these strange pages of one long gone one feels that one is at one with one who once . . .

The grainy sand had gone from under his feet. His boots trod again a damp crackling mast, razorshells, squeaking pebbles, that on the unnumbered pebbles beats, wood sieved by the shipworm, lost Armada. Unwholesome sandflats waited to suck his treading soles, breathing upward sewage breath. He coasted them, walking warily. A porter-bottle stood up, stogged to its waist, in the cakey sand dough. A sentinel: isle of dreadful thirst. Broken hoops on the shore; at the land a maze of dark cunning nets; farther away chalkscrawled backdoors and on the higher beach a drying-line with two crucified shirts. Ringsend: wigwams of brown steersmen and master mariners. Human shells. . . . ⁣40

LANGSTON HUGHES

Poems

Langston Hughes (1902–1967) is one of the first great African American poets and the most published black writer of his era. Altogether he wrote sixteen books of poetry, two novels, seven books of short stories, two autobiographies, five works of nonfiction, and nine books for children. He also edited nine anthologies, translated several Haitian and Spanish writers, and wrote about thirty plays. Reviewed widely in mainstream journals by mainstream writers and acquainted with leading artists and writers at home and abroad, Hughes was sometimes described during his lifetime as the "poet laureate of the American Negro" or as "Shakespeare in Harlem."

Hughes was a web of paradoxes that largely reflected his anguish as a black man in a white world. The son of a black middle-class family in Joplin, Missouri (his father was a businessman and his mother was a schoolteacher), he came to speak for America's poor black masses. Passionate about writing, yet distant and difficult to know, Hughes was apparently a very lonely man who never seemed to have any deep or longstanding love affairs. Familiar with standard English, having studied at Columbia University in New York (1921–1922) and graduated from Lincoln University in Pennsylvania (1929), he made his literary task the creation of a body of works based on vernacular speech of the black working and rural classes. This innovation succeeded, since subsequent black writers (see Walker's "Everyday Use") followed his lead. A citizen of the world, fluent in French and Spanish and widely traveled in Europe, Asia, Africa, and Mexico, he never wavered in his commitment to black vernacular culture.

Hughes, mainly through his poetry, soared to fame in the Harlem Renaissance, the 1920s cultural revival centered in the black area of New York City called Harlem. Jazz, blues, and folk ballads went mainstream, and Hughes was one of the first black writers to recognize the genius of this music and incorporate it into his works. He appropriated the cadences of jazz and the moods and themes of blues and folk ballads to create a soulful poetry.

Resisting the temptation encouraged by the period's growing and mobile black middle class to write in a Europeanized style, Hughes wrote primarily about blackness. His poems often concerned the struggle of black artists to be true to their race, and, at the same time, to be Americans. In 1927 he wrote: "American standardization [requires us] to be as little Negro and as much American as possible." He gradually came to see poetry as a kind of salvation, for it allowed him to speak in his African American voice and yet identify with America's heritage; for example, he claimed kinship with the reclusive poet Emily Dickinson.

Reading the Selections

"The Negro Speaks of Rivers" (1921) is Hughes's best-known poem, written when he was nineteen and a student at Columbia. This poem was inspired by a quarrel with his father, who apparently hated his own race, but it is surprisingly free of rancor on Hughes's part. The poem celebrates black history, linking it to storied rivers—the Euphrates, the Congo, the Nile, and the Mississippi.

"Theme for English B" (1951) and "Harlem" (1951) continue Hughes's project of integrating the black experience into American letters. It should be noted that the latter poem contains the phrase "a raisin in the sun," made even more memorable later when it became the title of a Pulitzer Prize play written by Lorraine Hansberry.

—m—

"The Negro Speaks of Rivers"

I've known rivers:
I've known rivers ancient as the world and older than the
    flow of human blood in human veins.

My soul has grown deep like the rivers.

I bathed in the Euphrates when dawns were young.
I built my hut near the Congo and it lulled me to sleep.
I looked upon the Nile and raised the pyramids above it.

1

I heard the singing of the Mississippi when Abe Lincoln
    went down to New Orleans, and I've seen its muddy
    bosom turn all golden in the sunset.

I've known rivers:
Ancient, dusky rivers.

My soul has grown deep like the rivers.

10

—⚏—

"Theme for English B"

The instructor said,

   Go home and write
  a page tonight.

   And let that page come out of you—
   Then, it will be true.

I wonder if it's that simple?

I am twenty-two, colored, born in Winston-Salem.
I went to school there, then Durham, then here
to this college on the hill above Harlem.
I am the only colored student in my class.
The steps from the hill lead down to Harlem,
through a park, then I cross St. Nicholas,
Eighth Avenue, Seventh, and I come to the Y,
the Harlem Branch Y, where I take the elevator
up to my room, sit down, and write this page:

It's not easy to know what is true for you or me
at twenty-two, my age. But I guess I'm what
I feel and see and hear. Harlem, I hear you:
hear you, hear me—we two—you, me talk on this page.

(I hear New York, too.) Me—who?
Well, I like to eat, sleep, drink, and be in love.
I like to work, read, learn, and understand life.
I like a pipe for a Christmas present,
or records—Bessie, bop, or Bach.

I guess being colored doesn't make me not like
the same things other folks like who are other races.
So will my page be colored that I write?
Being me, it will not be white.
But it will be
a part of you, instructor.
You are white—
yet a part of me, as I am a part of you.
That's American.
Sometimes perhaps you don't want to be a part of me.
Nor do I often want to be a part of you.
But we are, that's true!
As I learn from you,
I guess you learn from me—
although you're older—and white—
and somewhat more free.

This is my page for English B.

—⚏—

"Harlem"

What happens to a dream deferred?

   Does it dry up
   like a raisin in the sun?
   Or fester like a sore—
   And then run?
   Does it stink like rotten meat?

   Or crust and sugar over—
   like a syrupy sweet?

   Maybe it just sags
   like a heavy load.

   Or does it explode?

VIRGINIA WOOLF

Selection from *To the Lighthouse*

Virginia Woolf (1882–1941) was a major force in the Modernist project of dethroning the past and establishing the reign of newness everywhere. Much of her power as a catalyst sprang from her role in the Bloomsbury group, the coterie of writers who lived between the wars in the Bloomsbury area of London and had a strong impact on letters, art, and philosophy. A founder of the Hogarth Press, she influenced what people of this period read, publishing writers such as Eliot (see "The Love Song of J. Alfred Prufrock"), who shared her Modernist outlook. Through her essays, she assisted in the triumph of new art, as, for example, in her 1910 piece welcoming the first London exhibit of the Post-Impressionist school. When feminism slowed down after British women won the right to vote in 1918, she renewed the feminist cause with her essay *A Room of One's Own* (1929), in which she advocated cultural freedom for women. A toughminded critic (*The Common Reader*, 2 vols., 1925, 1932), she interpreted and made popular the era's new writings. Beyond all this, she was a novelist trying new narrative methods, and it was in this area that she made her greatest contribution.

Woolf's novels reflected distaste for Realism, the style favored by late-nineteenth-century writers who focused on the surface of life while ignoring the mind's intersection with the external world. Woolf thought such intersections crucial, for it was there that readers achieved insight by understanding not only facts but their symbolic import. To this end, she adopted the stream-of-consciousness method, pioneered by Joyce (see *Ulysses*), to explore how different characters in her novels reacted and felt about each other and their environment. For example, in *Mrs Dalloway* (1925) she skillfully showed her upper-class heroine's complexity beneath a conventional exterior by presenting in a single day all the lives that touched hers, near or far, even unseen. Partly modeled on herself (Woolf was the daughter of Leslie Stephen, a famous man of letters in nineteenth-century London), Mrs. Dalloway was the society woman Woolf might have become had she not pursued a literary career.

Reading the Selection

To the Lighthouse (1927) is concerned with the nature of reality as filtered through memory. It is set in the out-of-the-way Hebrides Islands off Scotland, with a lighthouse nearby, in the Ramsays' summer house crammed with family and guests. Nothing much happens except that life unfolds, revealing petty tensions and old wounds among the assembled household. In form, the novel is divided into three sections resembling successive waves on the shore, each wave transcending its predecessor. Part I, "The Window," is filled with idle summer chatter, and a trip to the lighthouse is canceled when the weather turns foul. Part II, "Time Passes" (the selection here), describes the summer house over several years (Mrs. Ramsay is now dead) through an anonymous voice that moves freely backward and forward in time, describing a world of objects bereft of human meaning. Part III, "The Lighthouse," presents the much delayed sailing trip to the lighthouse, portraying it as a quietly healing event for those who make it—ancient hurts are set aside and new ties are forged among the Ramsay family. The section closes with the vision, partly moral, partly aesthetic, of the houseguest Lily Briscoe, who was in love with the Ramsay family. Woolf's work, growing out of childhood summers with the Stephen family, transforms a personal memory into a universal story of love and forgiveness.

—⁓—

Time Passes

I

"Well, we must wait for the future to show," said Mr.   1
Bankes, coming in from the terrace.

"It's almost too dark to see," said Andrew, coming up
from the beach.

"One can hardly tell which is the sea and which is the
land," said Prue.

"Do we leave that light burning?" said Lily as they
took their coats off indoors.

"No," said Prue, "not if every one's in."   5

"Andrew," she called back, "just put out the light in
the hall."

One by one the lamps were all extinguished, except
that Mr. Carmichael, who liked to lie awake a little reading
Virgil, kept his candle burning rather longer than the rest.

II

So with the lamps all put out, the moon sunk, and a thin
rain drumming on the roof a downpouring of immense
darkness began. Nothing, it seemed, could survive the
flood, the profusion of darkness which, creeping in at key-
holes and crevices, stole round window blinds, came into
bedrooms, swallowed up here a jug and basin, there a
bowl of red and yellow dahlias, there the sharp edges and
firm bulk of a chest of drawers. Not only was furniture
confounded; there was scarcely anything left of body or
mind by which one could say, "This is he" or "This is she."
Sometimes a hand was raised as if to clutch something or
ward off something, or somebody groaned, or somebody
laughed aloud as if sharing a joke with nothingness.

Nothing stirred in the drawing-room or in the dining-
room or on the staircase. Only through the rusty hinges
and swollen sea-moistened woodwork certain airs, detached from the body of the wind (the house was ram-
shackle after all) crept round corners and ventured
indoors. Almost one might imagine them, as they entered
the drawing-room questioning and wondering, toying
with the flap of hanging wall-paper, asking, would it hang
much longer, when would it fall? Then smoothly brushing
the walls, they passed on musingly as if asking the red and
yellow roses on the wall-paper whether they would fade,
and questioning (gently, for there was time at their disposal) the torn letters in the waste-paper basket, the flowers, the books, all of which were now open to them and
asking, Were they allies? Were they enemies? How long
would they endure?

So some random light directing them with its pale   10
footfall upon stair and mat, from some uncovered star, or
wandering ship, or the Lighthouse even, the little airs
mounted the staircase and nosed round bedroom doors.
But here surely, they must cease. Whatever else may perish and disappear, what lies here is steadfast. Here one
might say to those sliding lights, those fumbling airs that
breathe and bend over the bed itself, here you can neither
touch nor destroy. Upon which, wearily, ghostily, as if they
had feather-light fingers and the light persistency of feathers, they would look, once, on the shut eyes, and the
loosely clasping fingers, and fold their garments wearily
and disappear. And so, nosing, rubbing, they went to the
window on the staircase, to the servants' bedrooms, to the
boxes in the attics; descending, blanched the apples on the
dining-room table, fumbled the petals of roses, tried the
picture on the easel, brushed the mat and blew a little sand
along the floor. At length, desisting, all ceased together,
gathered together, all sighed together; all together gave off
an aimless gust of lamentation to which some door in the
kitchen replied; swung wide; admitted nothing; and
slammed to.

[Here Mr. Carmichael, who was reading Virgil, blew
out his candle. It was midnight.]

III

But what after all is one night? A short space, especially
when the darkness dims so soon, and so soon a bird sings,
a cock crows, or a faint green quickens, like a turning leaf,
in the hollow of the wave. Night, however, succeeds to
night. The winter holds a pack of them in store and deals
them equally, evenly, with indefatigable fingers. They
lengthen; they darken. Some of them hold aloft clear planets, plates of brightness. The autumn trees, ravaged as
they are, take on the flash of tattered flags kindling in the
gloom of cool cathedral caves where gold letters on marble pages describe death in battle and how bones bleach
and burn far away in Indian sands. The autumn trees
gleam in the yellow moonlight, in the light of harvest
moons, the light which mellows the energy of labour, and
smooths the stubble, and brings the wave lapping blue to
the shore.

It seemed now as if, touched by human penitence and
all its toil, divine goodness had parted the curtain and displayed behind it, single, distinct, the hare erect; the wave
falling; the boat rocking, which, did we deserve them,
should be ours always. But alas, divine goodness, twitching the cord, draws the curtain; it does not please him; he
covers his treasures in a drench of hail, and so breaks
them, so confuses them that it seems impossible that their
calm should ever return or that we should ever compose
from their fragments a perfect whole or read in the littered
pieces the clear words of truth. For our penitence deserves
a glimpse only; our toil respite only.

The nights now are full of wind and destruction; the
trees plunge and bend and their leaves fly helter skelter
until the lawn is plastered with them and they lie packed
in gutters and choke rain-pipes and scatter damp paths.
Also the sea tosses itself and breaks itself, and should any
sleeper fancying that he might find on the beach an answer to his doubts, a sharer of his solitude, throw off his

bedclothes and go down by himself to walk on the sand, no image with semblance of serving and divine promptitude comes readily to hand bringing the night to order and making the world reflect the compass of the soul. The hand dwindles in his hand; the voice bellows in his ear. Almost it would appear that it is useless in such confusion to ask the night those questions as to what, and why, and wherefore, which tempt the sleeper from his bed to seek an answer.

[Mr. Ramsay, stumbling along a passage one dark morning, stretched his arms out, but Mrs. Ramsay having died rather suddenly the night before, his arms, though stretched out, remained empty.]

IV

So with the house empty and the doors locked and the mattresses rolled round, those stray airs, advance guards of great armies, blustered in, brushed bare boards, nibbled and fanned, met nothing in bedroom or drawing-room that wholly resisted them but only hangings that flapped, wood that creaked, the bare legs of tables, saucepans and china already furred, tarnished, cracked. What people had shed and left—a pair of shoes, a shooting cap, some faded skirts and coats in wardrobes—those alone kept the human shape and in the emptiness indicated how once they were filled and animated; how once hands were busy with hooks and buttons; how once the looking-glass had held a face; had held a world hollowed out in which a figure turned, a hand flashed, the door opened, in came children rushing and tumbling; and went out again. Now, day after day, light turned, like a flower reflected in water, its sharp image on the wall opposite. Only the shadows of the trees, flourishing in the wind, made obeisance on the wall, and for a moment darkened the pool in which light reflected itself; or birds, flying, made a soft spot flutter slowly across the bedroom floor.

So loveliness reigned and stillness, and together made the shape of loveliness itself, a form from which life had parted; solitary like a pool at evening, far distant, seen from a train window, vanishing so quickly that the pool, pale in the evening, is scarcely robbed of its solitude, though once seen. Loveliness and stillness clasped hands in the bedroom, and among the shrouded jugs and sheeted chairs even the prying of the wind, and the soft nose of the clammy sea airs, rubbing, snuffling, iterating, and reiterating their questions—"Will you fade? Will you perish?"—scarcely disturbed the peace, the indifference, the air of pure integrity, as if the question they asked scarcely needed that they should answer: we remain.

Nothing it seemed could break that image, corrupt that innocence, or disturb the swaying mantle of silence which, week after week, in the empty room, wove into itself the falling cries of birds, ships hooting, the drone and hum of the fields, a dog's bark, a man's shout, and folded them round the house in silence. Once only a board sprang on the landing; once in the middle of the night with a roar, with a rupture, as after centuries of quiescence, a rock rends itself from the mountain and hurtles crashing into

the valley, one fold of the shawl loosened and swung to and fro. Then again peace descended; and the shadow wavered; light bent to its own image in adoration on the bedroom wall; and Mrs. McNab, tearing the veil of silence with hands that had stood in the wash-tub, grinding it with boots that had crunched the shingle, came as directed to open all windows, and dust the bedrooms.

V

As she lurched (for she rolled like a ship at sea) and leered (for her eyes fell on nothing directly, but with a sidelong glance that deprecated the scorn and anger of the world— she was witless, she knew it), as she clutched the banisters and hauled herself upstairs and rolled from room to room, she sang. Rubbing the glass of the long looking-glass and leering sideways at her swinging figure a sound issued from her lips—something that had been gay twenty years before on the stage perhaps, had been hummed and danced to, but now, coming from the toothless, bonneted, care-taking woman, was robbed of meaning, was like the voice of witlessness, humour, persistency itself, trodden down but springing up again, so that as she lurched, dusting, wiping, she seemed to say how it was one long sorrow and trouble, how it was getting up and going to bed again, and bringing things out and putting them away again. It was not easy or snug this world she had known for close on seventy years. Bowed down she was with weariness. How long, she asked, creaking and groaning on her knees under the bed, dusting the boards, how long shall it endure? but hobbled to her feet again, pulled herself up, and again with her sidelong leer which slipped and turned aside even from her own face, and her own sorrows, stood and gaped in the glass, aimlessly smiling, and began again the old amble and hobble, taking up mats, putting down china, looking sideways in the glass, as if, after all, she had her consolations, as if indeed there twined about her dirge some incorrigible hope. Visions of joy there must have been at the wash-tub, say with her children (yet two had been base-born and one had deserted her), at the public-house, drinking; turning over scraps in her drawers. Some cleavage of the dark there must have been, some channel in the depths of obscurity through which light enough issued to twist her face grinning in the glass and make her, turning to her job again, mumble out the old music hall song. The mystic, the visionary, walking the beach on a fine night, stirring a puddle, looking at a stone, asking themselves "What am I?," "What is this?" had suddenly an answer vouchsafed them: (they could not say what it was) so that they were warm in the frost and had comfort in the desert. But Mrs. McNab continued to drink and gossip as before.

VI

The spring without a leaf to toss, bare and bright like a virgin fierce in her chastity, scornful in her purity, was laid out on fields wide-eyed and watchful and entirely careless of what was done or thought by the beholders. [Prue Ramsay, leaning on her father's arm, was given in marriage. What, people said, could have been more fitting? And, they added, how beautiful she looked!]

As summer neared, as the evenings lengthened, there came to the wakeful, the hopeful, walking the beach, stirring the pool, imaginations of the strangest kind—of flesh turned to atoms which drove before the wind, of stars flashing in their hearts, of cliff, sea, cloud, and sky brought purposely together to assemble outwardly the scattered parts of the vision within. In those mirrors, the minds of men, in those pools of uneasy water, in which clouds for ever turn and shadows form, dreams persisted, and it was impossible to resist the strange intimation which every gull, flower, tree, man and woman, and the white earth itself seemed to declare (but if questioned at once to withdraw) that good triumphs, happiness prevails, order rules; or to resist the extraordinary stimulus to range hither and thither in search of some absolute good, some crystal of intensity, remote from the known pleasures and familiar virtues, something alien to the processes of domestic life, single, hard, bright, like a diamond in the sand, which would render the possessor secure. Moreover, softened and acquiescent, the spring with her bees humming and gnats dancing threw her cloak about her, veiled her eyes, averted her head, and among passing shadows and flights of small rain seemed to have taken upon her a knowledge of the sorrows of mankind.

[Prue Ramsay died that summer in some illness connected with childbirth, which was indeed a tragedy, people said, everything, they said, had promised so well.]

And now in the heat of summer the wind sent its spies about the house again. Flies wove a web in the sunny rooms; weeds that had grown close to the glass in the night tapped methodically at the window-pane. When darkness fell, the stroke of the Lighthouse, which had laid itself with such authority upon the carpet in the darkness, tracing its pattern, came now in the softer light of spring mixed with moonlight gliding gently as if it laid its caress and lingered stealthily and looked and came lovingly again. But in the very lull of this loving caress, as the long stroke leant upon the bed, the rock was rent asunder; another fold of the shawl loosened; there it hung, and swayed. Through the short summer nights and the long summer days, when the empty rooms seemed to murmur with the echoes of the fields and the hum of flies, the long streamer waved gently, swayed aimlessly; while the sun so striped and barred the rooms and filled them with yellow haze that Mrs. McNab, when she broke in and lurched about, dusting, sweeping, looked like a tropical fish oaring its way through sun-lanced waters.

But slumber and sleep though it might there came later in the summer ominous sounds like the measured blows of hammers dulled on felt, which, with their repeated shocks still further loosened the shawl and cracked the tea-cups. Now and again some glass tinkled in the cupboard as if a giant voice had shrieked so loud in its agony that tumblers stood inside a cupboard vibrated too. Then again silence fell; and then, night after night, and sometimes in plain mid-day when the roses were bright and light turned on the wall its shape clearly there seemed to drop into this silence, this indifference, this integrity, the thud of something falling.

[A shell exploded. Twenty or thirty young men were blown up in France, among them Andrew Ramsay, whose death, mercifully, was instantaneous.]

At that season those who had gone down to pace the beach and ask of the sea and sky what message they reported or what vision they affirmed had to consider among the usual tokens of divine bounty—the sunset on the sea, the pallor of dawn, the moon rising, fishing-boats against the moon, and children making mud pies or pelting each other with handfuls of grass, something out of harmony with this jocundity and this serenity. There was the silent apparition of an ashen-coloured ship for instance, come, gone; there was a purplish stain upon the bland surface of the sea as if something had boiled and bled, invisibly, beneath. This intrusion into a scene calculated to stir the most sublime reflections and lead to the most comfortable conclusions stayed their pacing. It was difficult blandly to overlook them; to abolish their significance in the landscape; to continue, as one walked by the sea, to marvel how beauty outside mirrored beauty within.

Did Nature supplement what man advanced? Did she complete what he began? With equal complacence she saw his misery, his meanness, and his torture. That dream, of sharing, completing, of finding in solitude on the beach an answer, was then but a reflection in a mirror, and the mirror itself was but the surface glassiness which forms in quiescence when the nobler powers sleep beneath? Impatient, despairing yet loth to go (for beauty offers her lures, has her consolations), to pace the beach was impossible; contemplation was unendurable; the mirror was broken.

[Mr. Carmichael brought out a volume of poems that spring, which had an unexpected success. The war, people said, had revived their interest in poetry.]

VII

Night after night, summer and winter, the torment of storms, the arrow-like stillness of fine weather, held their court without interference. Listening (had there been any one to listen) from the upper rooms of the empty house only gigantic chaos streaked with lightning could have been heard tumbling and tossing, as the winds and waves disported themselves like the amorphous bulks of leviathans whose brows are pierced by no light of reason, and mounted one on top of another, and lunged and plunged in the darkness or the daylight (for night and day, month and year ran shapelessly together) in idiot games, until it seemed as if the universe were battling and tumbling, in brute confusion and wanton lust aimlessly by itself.

In spring the garden urns, casually filled with windblown plants, were gay as ever. Violets came and daffodils. But the stillness and the brightness of the day were as strange as the chaos and tumult of night, with the trees standing there, and the flowers standing there, looking before them, looking up, yet beholding nothing, eyeless, and so terrible.

VIII

Thinking no harm, for the family would not come, never again, some said, and the house would be sold at Michaelmas perhaps, Mrs. McNab stooped and picked a bunch of flowers to take home with her. She laid them on the table while she dusted. She was fond of flowers. It was a pity to let them waste. Suppose the house were sold (she stood arms akimbo in front of the looking-glass) it would want seeing to—it would. There it had stood all these years without a soul in it. The books and things were mouldy, for, what with the war and help being hard to get, the house had not been cleaned as she could have wished. It was beyond one person's strength to get it straight now. She was too old. Her legs pained her. All those books needed to be laid out on the grass in the sun; there was plaster fallen in the hall; the rainpipe had blocked over the study window and let the water in; the carpet was ruined quite. But people should come themselves; they should have sent somebody down to see. For there were clothes in the cupboards; they had left clothes in all the bedrooms. What was she to do with them? They had the moth in them—Mrs. Ramsay's things. Poor lady! She would never want *them* again. She was dead, they said; years ago, in London. There was the old grey cloak she wore gardening (Mrs. McNab fingered it). She could see her, as she came up the drive with the washing, stooping over her flowers (the garden was a pitiful sight now, all run to riot, and rabbits scuttling at you out of the beds)—she could see her with one of the children by her in the grey cloak. There were boots and shoes; and a brush and comb left on the dressing-table, for all the world as if she expected to come back tomorrow. (She had died very sudden at the end, they said.) And once they had been coming, but had put off coming, what with the war, and travel being so difficult these days; they had never come all these years; just sent her money; but never wrote, never came, and expected to find things as they had left them, ah, dear! Why the dressing-table drawers were full of things (she pulled them open), handkerchiefs, bits of ribbon. Yes, she could see Mrs. Ramsay as she came up the drive with the washing.

"Good-evening, Mrs. McNab," she would say.

She had a pleasant way with her. The girls all liked her. But, dear, many things had changed since then (she shut the drawer); many families had lost their dearest. So she was dead; and Mr. Andrew killed; and Miss Prue dead too, they said, with her first baby; but every one had lost some one these years. Prices had gone up shamefully, and didn't come down again neither. She could well remember her in her grey cloak.

"Good-evening, Mrs. McNab," she said, and told cook to keep a plate of milk soup for her—quite thought she wanted it, carrying that heavy basket all the way up from town. She could see her now, stooping over her flowers; and faint and flickering, like a yellow beam or the circle at the end of a telescope, a lady in a grey cloak,

stooping over her flowers, went wandering over the bedroom wall, up the dressing-table, across the wash-stand, as Mrs. McNab hobbled and ambled, dusting, straightening. And cook's name now? Mildred? Marian?—some name like that. Ah, she had forgotten—she did forget things. Fiery, like all red-haired women. Many a laugh they had had. She was always welcome in the kitchen. She made them laugh, she did. Things were better then than now.

She sighed; there was too much work for one woman. She wagged her head this side and that. This had been the nursery. Why, it was all damp in here; the plaster was falling. Whatever did they want to hang a beast's skull there? gone mouldy too. And rats in all the attics. The rain came in. But they never sent; never came. Some of the locks had gone, so the doors banged. She didn't like to be up here at dusk alone neither. It was too much for one woman, too much, too much. She creaked, she moaned. She banged the door. She turned the key in the lock, and left the house alone, shut up, locked.

IX

The house was left; the house was deserted. It was left like a shell on a sandhill to fill with dry salt grains now that life had left it. The long night seemed to have set in; the trifling airs, nibbling, the clammy breaths, fumbling, seemed to have triumphed. The saucepan had rusted and the mat decayed. Toads had nosed their way in. Idly, aimlessly, the swaying shawl swung to and fro. A thistle thrust itself between the tiles in the larder. The swallows nested in the drawing-room; the floor was strewn with straw; the plaster fell in shovelfuls; rafters were laid bare; rats carried off this and that to gnaw behind the wainscots. Tortoise-shell butterflies burst from the chrysalis and pattered their life out on the windowpane. Poppies sowed themselves among the dahlias; the lawn waved with long grass; giant artichokes towered among roses; a fringed carnation flowered among the cabbages; while the gentle tapping of a weed at the window had become, on winters' nights, a drumming from sturdy trees and thorned briars which made the whole room green in summer.

What power could now prevent the fertility, the insensibility of nature? Mrs. McNab's dream of a lady, of a child, of a plate of milk soup? It had wavered over the walls like a spot of sunlight and vanished. She had locked the door; she had gone. It was beyond the strength of one woman, she said. They never sent. They never wrote. There were things up there rotting in the drawers—it was a shame to leave them so, she said. The place was gone to rack and ruin. Only the Lighthouse beam entered the rooms for a moment, sent its sudden stare over bed and wall in the darkness of winter, looked with equanimity at the thistle and the swallow, the rat and the straw. Nothing now withstood them; nothing said no to them. Let the wind blow; let the poppy seed itself and the carnation mate with the cabbage. Let the swallow build in the drawing-room, and the thistle thrust aside the tiles, and the butterfly sun itself on the faded chintz of the arm-chairs.

Let the broken glass and the china lie out on the lawn and be tangled over with grass and wild berries.

For now had come that moment, that hesitation when dawn trembles and night pauses, when if a feather alight in the scale it will be weighed down. One feather, and the house, sinking, falling, would have turned and pitched downwards to the depths of darkness. In the ruined room, picnickers would have lit their kettles; lovers sought shelter there, lying on the bare boards; and the shepherd stored his dinner on the bricks, and the tramp slept with his coat round him to ward off the cold. Then the roof would have fallen; briars and hemlocks would have blotted out path, step, and window; would have grown, unequally but lustily over the mound, until some trespasser, losing his way, could have told only by a red-hot poker among the nettles, or a scrap of china in the hemlock that here once some one had lived; there had been a house.

If the feather had fallen, if it had tipped the scale downwards, the whole house would have plunged to the depths to lie upon the sands of oblivion. But there was a force working; something not highly conscious; something that leered, something that lurched; something not inspired to go about its work with dignified ritual or solemn chanting. Mrs. McNab groaned; Mrs. Bast creaked. They were old; they were stiff; their legs ached. They came with their brooms and pails at last; they got to work. All of a sudden, would Mrs. McNab see that the house was ready, one of the young ladies wrote: would she get this done; would she get that done; all in a hurry. They might be coming for the summer; had left everything to the last; expected to find things as they had left them. Slowly and painfully, with broom and pail, mopping, scouring, Mrs. McNab, Mrs. Bast, stayed the corruption and the rot; rescued from the pool of Time that was fast closing over them now a basin, now a cupboard; fetched up from oblivion all the Waverley novels and a tea-set one morning; in the afternoon restored to sun and air a brass fender and a set of steel fire-irons. George, Mrs. Bast's son, caught the rats, and cut the grass. They had the builders. Attended with the creaking of hinges and the screeching of bolts, the slamming and banging of damp-swollen woodwork some rusty laborious birth seemed to be taking place, as the women, stooping, rising, groaning, singing, slapped and slammed, upstairs now, now down in the cellars. Oh, they said, the work!

They drank their tea in the bedroom sometimes, or in the study; breaking off work at mid-day with the smudge on their faces, and their old hands clasped and cramped with the broom handles. Flopped on chairs, they contemplated now the magnificent conquest over taps and bath; now the more arduous, more partial triumph over long rows of books, black as ravens once, now white-stained, breeding pale mushrooms and secreting furtive spiders. Once more, as she felt the tea warm in her, the telescope fitted itself to Mrs. McNab's eyes, and in a ring of light she saw the old gentleman, lean as a rake, wagging his head, as she came up with the washing, talking to himself, she supposed, on the lawn. He never noticed her. Some said he was dead; some said she was dead. Which was it? Mrs. Bast didn't know for certain either. The young gentleman

40

was dead. That she was sure. She had read his name in the papers.

There was the cook now, Mildred, Marian, some such name as that—a red-headed woman, quick-tempered like all her sort, but kind, too, if you knew the way with her. Many a laugh they had had together. She saved a plate of soup for Maggie; a bite of ham, sometimes; whatever was over. They lived well in those days. They had everything they wanted (glibly, jovially, with the tea hot in her, she unwound her ball of memories, sitting in the wicker armchair by the nursery fender). There was always plenty doing, people in the house, twenty staying sometimes, and washing up till long past midnight.

Mrs. Bast (she had never known them; had lived in Glasgow at that time) wondered, putting her cup down, whatever they hung that beast's skull there for? Shot in foreign parts no doubt.

It might well be, said Mrs. McNab, wantoning on with her memories; they had friends in eastern countries; gentlemen staying there, ladies in evening dress; she had seen them once through the dining-room door all sitting at dinner. Twenty she dared say all in their jewellery, and she asked to stay help wash up, might be till after midnight.

Ah, said Mrs. Bast, they'd find it changed. She leant out of the window. She watched her son George scything the grass. They might well ask, what had been done to it? seeing how old Kennedy was supposed to have charge of it, and then his leg got so bad after he fell from the cart; and perhaps then no one for a year, or the better part of one; and then Davie Macdonald, and seeds might be sent, but who should say if they were ever planted? They'd find it changed.

She watched her son scything. He was a great one for work—one of those quiet ones. Well they must be getting along with the cupboards, she supposed. They hauled themselves up. 45

At last, after days of labour within, of cutting and digging without, dusters were flicked from the windows, the windows were shut to, keys were turned all over the house; the front door was banged; it was finished.

And now as if the cleaning and the scrubbing and the scything and the mowing had drowned it there rose that half-heard melody, that intermittent music which the ear half catches but lets fall; a bark, a bleat; irregular, intermittent, yet somehow related; the hum of an insect, the tremor of cut grass, dissevered yet somehow belonging; the jar of a dorbeetle, the squeak of a wheel, loud, low, but mysteriously related; which the ear strains to bring together and is always on the verge of harmonising, but they are never quite heard, never fully harmonised, and at last, in the evening, one after another the sounds die out, and the harmony falters, and silence falls. With the sunset sharpness was lost, and like mist rising, quiet rose, quiet spread, the wind settled; loosely the world shook itself down to sleep, darkly here without a light to it, save what came green suffused through leaves, or pale on the white flowers in the bed by the window.

(Lily Briscoe had her bag carried up to the house late one evening in September.)

X

Then indeed peace had come. Messages of peace breathed from the sea to the shore. Never to break its sleep any more, to lull it rather more deeply to rest, and whatever the dreamers dreamt holily, dreamt wisely, to confirm—what else was it murmuring—as Lily Briscoe laid her head on the pillow in the clean still room and heard the sea. Through the open window the voice of the beauty of the world came murmuring, too softly to hear exactly what it said—but what mattered if the meaning were plain? entreating the sleepers (the house was full again; Mrs. Beckwith was staying there, also Mr. Carmichael), if they would not actually come down to the beach itself at least to lift the blind and look out. They would see then night flowing down in purple; his head crowned; his sceptre jewelled; and how in his eyes a child might look. And if they still faltered (Lily was tired out with travelling and slept almost at once; but Mr. Carmichael read a book by candlelight), if they still said no, that it was vapour, this splendour of his, and the dew had more power than he,

and they preferred sleeping; gently then without complaint, or argument, the voice would sing its song. Gently the waves would break (Lily heard them in her sleep); tenderly the light fell (it seemed to come through her eyelids). And it all looked, Mr. Carmichael thought, shutting his book, falling asleep, much as it used to look.

Indeed the voice might resume, as the curtains of dark wrapped themselves over the house, over Mrs. Beckwith, Mr. Carmichael, and Lily Briscoe so that they lay with several folds of blackness on their eyes, why not accept this, be content with this, acquiesce and resign? The sigh of all the seas breaking in measure round the isles soothed them; the night wrapped them; nothing broke their sleep, until, the birds beginning and the dawn weaving their thin voices in to its whiteness, a cart grinding, a dog somewhere barking, the sun lifted the curtains, broke the veil on their eyes, and Lily Briscoe stirring in her sleep. She clutched at her blankets as a faller clutches at the turf on the edge of a cliff. Her eyes opened wide. Here she was again, she thought, sitting bolt upright in bed. Awake.

ZORA NEALE HURSTON

"How It Feels to Be Colored Me"

The African American writer Zora Neale Hurston (1891–1960) is probably the most widely read black woman writer in schools and colleges today, but her literary reputation, like her life, has been a rollercoaster. She once exulted: "I have been in Sorrow's kitchen and licked out all the pots. Then I have stood on the peaky mountain wrapped in rainbows, with a harp and a sword in my hands."

Born in Florida, poor and subjected to racism, Hurston moved north where she shone as one of the most original voices of the Harlem Renaissance. From 1925 to 1945, she was a widely acclaimed writer, author of three novels (*Jonah's Gourd Vine*, 1934; *Their Eyes Were Watching God*, 1937; and *Moses, Man of the Mountain*, 1939); two books of folklore (*Mules and Men*, 1935, and *Tell My Horse*, 1938); an autobiography (*Dust Tracks on a Road*, 1942); and many short stories, essays, and plays. After 1945, she continued to write, publishing a fourth novel (*Seraph on the Suwanee*, 1948) and a few stories and essays, but her audience lost interest and she fell into oblivion. In 1950 she worked as a maid, and when she died in a welfare home, she had all but been forgotten. That changed when growing interest in black culture led scholars to rediscover her works and restore her to a preeminent place in American letters.

Hurston's literary task resembled that of Hughes (see "The Negro Speaks of Rivers," etc.), her contemporary, in that both wrote about being black in a white-dominated world, expressed themselves in black vernacular speech, and drew on jazz, blues, and folk tales. Also like Hughes, Hurston was educated; she studied at Howard University in Washington, D.C. (1921–1924) and graduated from Barnard College, New York City, in 1928. She then spent some years in Columbia University's graduate program in anthropology (her books on folklore are based on research in the American South, Jamaica, Haiti, and Bermuda). Still, when compared to Hughes, Hurston was doubly disadvantaged, for as a black and a woman writer, she had to contend with both racism and sexism. In the 1930s most black male writers dismissed her on the grounds that her writing sounded like a minstrel show. Even Hughes, while admiring her works, found her personally too ingratiating to whites: "In her youth she was always getting scholarships and things from wealthy white people, some of whom simply paid her to sit around and represent the Negro race for them, she did it in such a racy fashion." "Representing the Negro race for whites" was of course the project of the Harlem Renaissance, and Hurston's genius was that in her writings, she did it better than anyone else.

Reading the Selection

Hurston's essay "How It Feels to Be Colored Me" (1928) registers—as if in answer to an unspoken question—her complex feelings about being born black in white America. Reviewing her life (she was thirty-seven at the time), she offers a set of conflicting and ironic stereotypes to describe herself, "the 'happy Negro' who performed for white folks," "the exotic primitive," "the eternal feminine," "a brown bag in company with other bags, white, red, and yellow," only to dismiss all of them in the essay's last words: "Who knows?" Hurston's response affirms that identity, rather than being fixed, is shape-shifting—a matter of situation and strategy.

Hurston's essay is written in mainstream English, though it is barely able to contain her irrepressible spirit, which in later works was more at home in the idiom of the black oral tradition.

I am colored but I offer nothing in the way of extenuating circumstances except the fact that I am the only Negro in the United States whose grandfather on the mother's side was *not* an Indian chief.

I remember the very day that I became colored. Up to my thirteenth year I lived in the little Negro town of Eatonville, Florida. It is exclusively a colored town. The only white people I knew passed through the town going to or coming from Orlando. The native whites rode dusty horses, the Northern tourists chugged down the sandy village road in automobiles. The town knew the Southerners and never stopped cane chewing when they passed. But the Northerners were something else again. They were peered at cautiously from behind curtains by the timid. The more venturesome would come out on the porch to watch them go past and got just as much pleasure out of the tourists as the tourists got out of the village.

The front porch might seem a daring place for the rest of the town, but it was a gallery seat for me. My favorite place was atop the gate-post. Proscenium box for a born first-nighter. Not only did I enjoy the show, but I didn't mind the actors knowing that I liked it. I usually spoke to them in passing. I'd wave at them and when they returned my salute, I would say something like this: "Howdy-do-well-I-thank-you-where-you-goin'?" Usually automobile or the horse paused at this, and after a queer exchange of compliments, I would probably "go a piece of the way" with them, as we say in farthest Florida. If one of my family happened to come to the front in time to see me, of course negotiations would be rudely broken off. But even so, it is clear that I was the first "welcome-to-our-state" Floridian, and I hope the Miami Chamber of Commerce will please take notice.

During this period, white people differed from colored to me only in that they rode through town and never lived there. They liked to hear me "speak pieces" and sing and wanted to see me dance the parse-mela, and gave me generously of their small silver for doing these things, which seemed strange to me for I wanted to do them so much that I needed bribing to stop. Only they didn't know it. The colored people gave no dimes. They deplored any joyful tendencies in me, but I was their Zora nevertheless. I belonged to them, to the nearby hotels, to the county—everybody's Zora.

But changes came in the family when I was thirteen, and I was sent to school in Jacksonville. I left Eatonville, the town of the oleanders, as Zora. When I disembarked from the riverboat at Jacksonville, she was no more. It seemed that I had suffered a sea change. I was not Zora of Orange County any more, I was now a little colored girl. I found it out in certain ways. In my heart as well as in the mirror, I became a fast brown—warranted not to rub nor run.

But I am not tragically colored. There is no great sorrow dammed up in my soul, nor lurking behind my eyes. I do not mind at all. I do not belong to the sobbing school of Negrohood who hold that nature somehow has given them a lowdown dirty deal and whose feelings are all hurt about it. Even in the helter-skelter skirmish that is my life, I have seen that the world is to the strong regardless of a little pigmentation more or less. No, I do not weep at the world—I am too busy sharpening my oyster knife.

Someone is always at my elbow reminding me that I am the granddaughter of slaves. It fails to register depression with me. Slavery is sixty years in the past. The operation was successful and the patient is doing well, thank you. The terrible struggle that made me an American out of a potential slave said "On the line!" The Reconstruction said "Get set!"; and the generation before said "Go!" I am off to a flying start and I must not halt in the stretch to look behind and weep. Slavery is the price I paid for civilization, and the choice was not with me. It is a bully adventure and worth all that I have paid through my ancestors for it. No one on earth ever had a greater chance for glory. The world to be won and nothing to be lost. It is thrilling to think—to know that for any act of mine, I shall get twice as much praise or twice as much blame. It is quite exciting to hold the center of the national stage, with the spectators not knowing whether to laugh or to weep.

The position of my white neighbor is much more difficult. No brown specter pulls up a chair beside me when I sit down to eat. No dark ghost thrusts its leg against mine in bed. The game of keeping what one has is never so exciting as the game of getting.

I do not always feel colored. Even now I often achieve the unconscious Zora of Eatonville before the Hegira. I feel most colored when I am thrown against a sharp white background.

For instance at Barnard. "Beside the waters of the Hudson" I feel my race. Among the thousand white persons, I am a dark rock surged upon, and overswept, but through it all, I remain myself. When covered by the waters, I am; and the ebb but reveals me again.

Sometimes it is the other way around. A white person is set down in our midst, but the contrast is just as sharp for me. For instance, when I sit in the drafty basement that is The New World Cabaret with a white person, my color comes. We enter chatting about any little nothing that we have in common and are seated by the jazz waiters. In the abrupt way that jazz orchestras have, this one plunges into a number. It loses no time in circumlocutions, but gets right down to business. It constricts the thorax and splits the heart with its tempo and narcotic harmonies. This orchestra grows rambunctious, rears on its hind legs and attacks the tonal veil with primitive fury, rending it, clawing it until it breaks through to the jungle beyond. I follow those heathen—follow them exultingly. I dance wildly inside myself; I yell within, I whoop; I shake my assegai above my head, I hurl it true to the mark *yeeeeooww!* I am in the jungle and living in the jungle way. My face is painted red and yellow and my body is painted blue. My pulse is throbbing like a war drum. I want to slaughter something—give pain, give death to what, I do not know. But the piece ends. The men of the orchestra wipe their lips and rest their fingers. I creep back slowly to the veneer we call civilization with the last tone and find the white friend sitting motionless in his seat, smoking calmly.

"Good music they have here," he remarks, drumming the table with his fingertips.

Music. The great blobs of purple and red emotion have not touched him. He has only heard what I felt. He is far away and I see him but dimly across the ocean and the continent that have fallen between us. He is so pale with his whiteness then and I am *so* colored.

At certain times I have no race, I am *me*. When I set my hat at a certain angle and saunter down Seventh Avenue, Harlem City, feeling as snooty as the lions in front of the Forty-Second Street Library, for instance. So far as my feelings are concerned, Peggy Hopkins Joyce on the Boule Mich with her gorgeous raiment, stately carriage, knees knocking together in a most aristocratic manner, has nothing on me. The cosmic Zora emerges. I belong to no race nor time. I am the eternal feminine with its string of beads.

I have no separate feeling about being an American citizen and colored. I am merely a fragment of the Great Soul that surges within the boundaries. My country, right or wrong.

Sometimes, I feel discriminated against, but it does not make me angry. It merely astonishes me. How *can* any deny themselves the pleasure of my company? It's beyond me.

But in the main, I feel like a brown bag of miscellany propped against a wall. Against a wall in company with other bags, white, red and yellow. Pour out the contents, and there is discovered a jumble of small things priceless and worthless. A first-water diamond, an empty spool, bits of broken glass, lengths of string, a key to a door long since crumbled away, a rusty knife-blade, old shoes saved for a road that never was and never will be, a nail bent under the weight of things too heavy for any nail, a dried flower or two still a little fragrant. In your hand is the brown bag. On the ground before you is the jumble it held—so much like the jumble in the bags, could they be emptied, that all might be dumped in a single heap and the bags refilled without altering the content of any greatly. A bit of colored glass more or less would not matter. Perhaps that is how the Great Stuffer of Bags filled them in the first place—who knows?

WILLIAM FAULKNER

Selection from *The Sound and the Fury*

The Sound and the Fury (1929), a novel about the American South, is one of the classics of Modernism. With its stream-of-consciousness narrative, adopted from Joyce (see *Ulysses*) and Woolf (see *To the Lighthouse*), this novel introduced European-style experimentation into American letters and made William Faulkner (1897–1962) a force in world literature. By 1939, for example, translations of *The Sound and the Fury* and five other novels by Faulkner were available to French writers, such as Camus, who imitated their "interior monologue" technique. Largely neglected in the 1940s, Faulkner re-emerged onto the international stage in 1950 when he received the Nobel Prize for literature, a recognition of his heroic achievement.

Faulkner belonged to that species of writer who finds the world in a grain of sand, metaphorically speaking. His "grain of sand" was Yoknapatawpha, the fictional Mississippi county—based on Faulkner's own Lafayette County—whose history he wrote in the series of sixteen novels beginning with *Sartoris* (1929) and ending with *The Reivers* (1962). These novels deal with the period mainly between the end of the Civil War and the time Faulkner was writing. An old social order characterized by a gentleman's code of behavior was passing away, defeated from within, and a new social pattern expressed in a code of "everyone looking out for number one" was being born. In some novels this changing order is represented through, respectively, the Sartoris family, who are gentry in decline, and the money-grubbing Snopes clan, who are "poor whites" on the make. White society is usually the foreground, but black life, providing an element of stability, is always present, represented by black servants who hold white families together. Racism is sometimes a theme (*Light in August,* 1932), and when it is, Faulkner portrays black victims with sympathy. Yoknapatawpha functions as a symbol of the entire South, but it also stands for any place where there is a decline in old ways.

Reading the Selection

This passage—the first few pages of *The Sound and the Fury*—shows Faulkner blending "local color" with experimental method. Tough going for a first-time Faulkner reader, the passage begins to make sense only with great difficulty. The speaker is Benjamin, the thirty-three-year-old idiot son of the Compsons, the Yoknapatawpha family gone to seed, whose history is the focus of the novel. This opening gambit, as well as the novel's title, is derived from Shakespeare's famous line in *Macbeth,* Act V, Scene V: "Life's . . . a tale / Told by an idiot, full of sound and fury, / Signifying nothing." Benjamin's untrustworthy monologue runs for almost one hundred pages.

The novel is about the dissolution of the Compson family, but this theme is clouded initially because Benjamin is the narrator, and in his disordered mind, reality and memory are merged. The full tragedy of the Compsons comes into view only later in the novel when other family members tell their stories. When the novel opens, Benjamin is watching a golf game while being looked after by Luster, the fourteen-year-old son of Dilsey, the black cook. At the same time, the past asserts itself in Benjamin's memories of Caddy, or Candace, his sister and protector when he was a child. Only gradually is it learned that the family has banished the adult Candace for reasons of sexual promiscuity, and her daughter, Quentin, who lives with the Compsons, may be a child of incest.

—⁓—

April Seventh, 1928.

Through the fence, between the curling flower spaces, I could see them hitting. They were coming toward where the flag was and I went along the fence. Luster was hunting in the grass by the flower tree. They took the flag out, and they were hitting. Then they put the flag back and they went to the table, and he hit and the other hit. Then they went on, and I went along the fence. Luster came away from the flower tree and we went along the fence and they stopped and we stopped and I looked through the fence while Luster was hunting in the grass.

"Here, caddie." He hit. They went away across the pasture. I held to the fence and watched them going away.

"Listen at you, now." Luster said. "Aint you something, thirty three years old, going on that way. After I done went all the way to town to buy you that cake. Hush up that moaning. Aint you going to help me find that quarter so I can go to the show tonight."

They were hitting little, across the pasture. I went back along the fence to where the flag was. It flapped on the bright grass and the trees.

"Come on." Luster said. "We done looked there. They aint no more coming right now. Les go down to the branch and find that quarter before them niggers finds it."

It was red, flapping on the pasture. Then there was a bird slanting and tilting on it. Luster threw. The flag flapped on the bright grass and the trees. I held to the fence.

"Shut up that moaning." Luster said. "I cant make them come if they aint coming, can I. If you dont hush up, mammy aint going to have no birthday for you. If you dont hush, you know what I going to do. I going to eat that cake all up. Eat them candles, too. Eat all them thirty three candles. Come on, les go down to the branch. I got to find my quarter. Maybe we can find one of they balls. Here.

Here they is. Way over yonder. See." He came to the fence and pointed his arm. "See them. They aint coming back here no more. Come on."

We went along the fence and came to the garden fence, where our shadows were. My shadow was higher than Luster's on the fence. We came to the broken place and went through it.

"Wait a minute." Luster said. "You snagged on that nail again. Cant you never crawl through here without snagging on that nail."

Caddy uncaught me and we crawled through. Uncle 10
Maury said to not let anybody see us, so we better stoop over,
Caddy said. Stoop over, Benjy. Like this, see. We stooped over
and crossed the garden, where the flowers rasped and rattled
against us. The ground was hard. We climbed the fence, where
the pigs were grunting and snuffing. I expect they're sorry be-
cause one of them got killed today, Caddy said. The ground was
hard, churned and knotted.

Keep your hands in your pockets, Caddy said. Or they'll get
froze. You dont want your hands froze on Christmas, do you.

"It's too cold out there." Versh said. "You dont want to go out doors."

"What is it now." Mother said.

"He want to go out doors." Versh said.

"Let him go." Uncle Maury said. 15

"It's too cold." Mother said. "He'd better stay in. Benjamin. Stop that, now."

"It wont hurt him." Uncle Maury said.

"You, Benjamin." Mother said. "If you dont be good, you'll have to go to the kitchen."

"Mammy say keep him out the kitchen today." Versh said. "She say she got all that cooking to get done."

"Let him go, Caroline." Uncle Maury said. "You'll 20 worry yourself sick over him."

"I know it." Mother said. "It's a judgment on me. I sometimes wonder."

"I know, I know." Uncle Maury said. "You must keep your strength up. I'll make you a toddy."

"It just upsets me that much more." Mother said. "Dont you know it does."

"You'll feel better." Uncle Maury said. "Wrap him up good, boy, and take him out for a while."

Uncle Maury went away. Versh went away. 25

"Please hush." Mother said. "We're trying to get you out as fast as we can. I dont want you to get sick."

Versh put my overshoes and overcoat on and we took my cap and went out. Uncle Maury was putting the bottle away in the sideboard in the diningroom.

"Keep him out about half an hour, boy." Uncle Maury said. "Keep him in the yard, now."

"Yes, sir." Versh said. "We dont never let him get off the place."

We went out doors. The sun was cold and bright. 30

"Where you heading for." Versh said. "You dont think you going to town, does you." We went through the rattling leaves. The gate was cold. "You better keep them hands in your pockets." Versh said. "You get them froze onto that gate, then what you do. Whyn't you wait for them in the house." He put my hands into my pockets. I

could hear him rattling in the leaves. I could smell the cold. The gate was cold.

"Here some hickeynuts. Whooey. Git up that tree. Look here at this squirl, Benjy."

I couldn't feel the gate at all, but I could smell the bright cold.

"You better put them hands back in your pockets."

Caddy was walking. Then she was running, her book- 35
satchel swinging and jouncing behind her.

"Hello, Benjy." Caddy said. She opened the gate and came in and stooped down. Caddy smelled like leaves. "Did you come to meet me." she said. "Did you come to meet Caddy. What did you let him get his hands so cold for, Versh."

"I told him to keep them in his pockets." Versh said. "Holding on to that ahun gate."

"Did you come to meet Caddy." she said, rubbing my hands. "What is it. What are you trying to tell Caddy." Caddy smelled like trees and like when she says we were asleep.

What are you moaning about, Luster said. You can watch
them again when we get to the branch. Here. Here's you a jimson
weed. He gave me the flower. We went through the fence, into
the lot.

"What is it." Caddy said. "What are you trying to tell 40
Caddy. Did they send him out, Versh."

"Couldn't keep him in." Versh said. "He kept on until they let him go and he come right straight down here, looking through the gate."

"What is it." Caddy said. "Did you think it would be Christmas when I came home from school. Is that what you thought. Christmas is the day after tomorrow. Santy Claus, Benjy. Santy Claus. Come on, let's run to the house and get warm." She took my hand and we ran through the bright rustling leaves. We ran up the steps and out of the bright cold, into the dark cold. Uncle Maury was putting the bottle back in the sideboard. He called Caddy. Caddy said,

"Take him in to the fire, Versh. Go with Versh." she said. "I'll come in a minute."

We went to the fire. Mother said,

"Is he cold, Versh." 45

"Nome." Versh said.

"Take his overcoat and overshoes off." Mother said. "How many times do I have to tell you not to bring him into the house with his overshoes on."

"Yessum." Versh said. "Hold still, now." He took my overshoes off and unbuttoned my coat. Caddy said,

"Wait, Versh. Cant he go out again, Mother. I want him to go with me."

"You'd better leave him here." Uncle Maury said. 50 "He's been out enough today."

"I think you'd both better stay in." Mother said. "It's getting colder, Dilsey says."

"Oh, Mother." Caddy said.

"Nonsense." Uncle Maury said. "She's been in school all day. She needs the fresh air. Run along, Candace."

"Let him go, Mother." Caddy said. "Please. You know he'll cry."

"Then why did you mention it before him." Mother said. "Why did you come in here. To give him some excuse to worry me again. You've been out enough today. I think you'd better sit down here and play with him."

"Let them go, Caroline." Uncle Maury said. "A little cold wont hurt them. Remember, you've got to keep your strength up."

"I know." Mother said. "Nobody knows how I dread Christmas. Nobody knows. I am not one of these women who can stand things. I wish for Jason's and the children's sakes I was stronger."

"You must do the best you can and not let them worry you." Uncle Maury said. "Run along, you two. But dont stay out long, now. Your mother will worry."

"Yes, sir." Caddy said. "Come on, Benjy. We're going out doors again." She buttoned my coat and we went toward the door.

"Are you going to take that baby out without his overshoes." Mother said. "Do you want to make him sick, with the house full of company."

"I forgot." Caddy said. "I thought he had them on."

We went back. "You must think." Mother said. *Hold still now* Versh said. He put my overshoes on. "Someday I'll be gone, and you'll have to think for him." *Now stomp* Versh said. "Come here and kiss Mother, Benjamin."

Caddy took me to Mother's chair and Mother took my face in her hands and then she held me against her.

"My poor baby." she said. She let me go. "You and Versh take good care of him, honey."

"Yessum." Caddy said. We went out. Caddy said,

"You needn't go, Versh. I'll keep him for a while."

"All right." Versh said. "I aint going out in that cold for no fun." He went on and we stopped in the hall and Caddy knelt and put her arms around me and her cold bright face against mine. She smelled like trees.

"You're not a poor baby. Are you. Are you. You've got your Caddy. Haven't you got your Caddy."

Cant you shut up that moaning and slobbering, Luster said. Aint you shamed of yourself, making all this racket. We passed the carriage house, where the carriage was. It had a new wheel.

"Git in, now, and set still until your maw come." Dilsey said. She shoved me into the carriage. T. P. held the reins. "Clare I dont see how come Jason wont get a new surrey." Dilsey said. "This thing going to fall to pieces under you all some day. Look at them wheels."

Mother came out, pulling her veil down. She had some flowers.

"Where's Roskus." she said.

"Roskus cant lift his arms, today." Dilsey said. "T. P. can drive all right."

"I'm afraid to." Mother said. "It seems to me you all could furnish me with a driver for the carriage once a week. It's little enough I ask, Lord knows."

"You know just as well as me that Roskus got the rheumatism too bad to do more than he have to, Miss Cahline." Dilsey said. "You come on and get in, now. T. P. can drive you just as good as Roskus."

"I'm afraid to." Mother said. "With the baby."

Dilsey went up the steps. "You calling that thing a baby." she said. She took Mother's arm. "A man big as T. P. Come on, now, if you going."

"I'm afraid to." Mother said. They came down the steps and Dilsey helped Mother in. "Perhaps it'll be the best thing, for all of us." Mother said.

"Aint you shamed, talking that way." Dilsey said. "Dont you know it'll take more than a eighteen year old nigger to make Queenie run away. She older than him and Benjy put together. And dont you start no projecking with Queenie, you hear me. T. P. If you dont drive to suit Miss Cahline, I going to put Roskus on you. He aint too tied up to do that."

"Yessum." T. P. said.

"I just know something will happen." Mother said. "Stop, Benjamin."

"Give him a flower to hold." Dilsey said. "That what he wanting." She reached her hand in.

"No, no." Mother said. "You'll have them all scattered."

"You hold them." Dilsey said. "I'll get him one out." She gave me a flower and her hand went away.

"Go on now, fore Quentin see you and have to go too." Dilsey said.

"Where is she." Mother said.

"She down to the house playing with Luster." Dilsey said. "Go on, T. P. Drive that surrey like Roskus told you, now."

"Yessum." T. P. said. "Hum up, Queenie."

"Quentin." Mother said. "Dont let   "

"Course I is." Dilsey said.

The carriage jolted and crunched on the drive. "I'm afraid to go and leave Quentin." Mother said. "I'd better not go. T. P." We went through the gate, where it didn't jolt anymore. T. P. hit Queenie with the whip.

"You, T. P." Mother said.

"Got to get her going." T. P. said. "Keep her wake up till we get back to the barn."

"Turn around." Mother said. "I'm afraid to go and leave Quentin."

"Cant turn here." T. P. said. Then it was broader.

"Cant you turn here." Mother said.

"All right." T. P. said. We began to turn.

"You, T. P." Mother said, clutching me.

"I got to turn around some how." T. P. said. "Whoa, Queenie." We stopped.

"You'll turn us over." Mother said.

"What you want to do, then." T. P. said.

"I'm afraid for you to try to turn around." Mother said.

"Get up, Queenie." T. P. said. We went on.

"I just know Dilsey will let something happen to Quentin while I'm gone." Mother said. "We must hurry back."

"Hum up, there." T. P. said. He hit Queenie with the whip.

"You, T. P." Mother said, clutching me. I could hear Queenie's feet and the bright shapes went smooth and steady on both sides, the shadows of them flowing across Queenie's back. They went on like the bright tops of wheels. Then those on one side stopped at the tall white post where the soldier was. But on the other side they went on smooth and steady, but a little slower.

"What do you want." Jason said. He had his hands in his pockets and a pencil behind his ear.

"We're going to the cemetery." Mother said.

"All right." Jason said. "I dont aim to stop you, do I. Was that all you wanted with me, just to tell me that."

"I know you wont come." Mother said. "I'd feel safer if you would." ¹¹⁰

"Safe from what." Jason said. "Father and Quentin cant hurt you."

Mother put her handkerchief under her veil. "Stop it, Mother." Jason said. "Do you want to get that damn looney to bawling in the middle of the square. Drive on, T. P."

"Hum up, Queenie." T. P. said.

"It's a judgment on me." Mother said. "But I'll be gone too, soon."

"Here." Jason said. ¹¹⁵

"Whoa." T. P. said. Jason said,

"Uncle Maury's drawing on you for fifty. What do you want to do about it."

"Why ask me." Mother said. "I dont have any say so. I try not to worry you and Dilsey. I'll be gone soon, and then you."

"Go on, T. P." Jason said.

"Hum up, Queenie." T. P. said. The shapes flowed on. ¹²⁰ The ones on the other side began again, bright and fast and smooth, like when Caddy says we are going to sleep.

Cry baby, Luster said. Aint you shamed. We went through the barn. The stalls were all open. You aint got no spotted pony to ride now, Luster said. The floor was dry and dusty. The roof was falling. The slanting holes were full of spinning yellow. What do you want to go that way, for. You want to get your head knocked off with one of them balls.

"Keep your hands in your pockets." Caddy said. "Or they'll be froze. You dont want your hands froze on Christmas, do you."

We went around the barn. The big cow and the little one were standing in the door, and we could hear Prince and Queenie and Fancy stomping inside the barn. "If it wasn't so cold, we'd ride Fancy." Caddy said. "But it's too cold to hold on today." Then we could see the branch, where the smoke was blowing. "That's where they are killing the pig." Caddy said. "We can come back by there and see them." We went down the hill.

"You want to carry the letter." Caddy said. "You can carry it." She took the letter out of her pocket and put it in mine. "It's a Christmas present." Caddy said. "Uncle Maury is going to surprise Mrs Patterson with it. We got to give it to her without letting anybody see it. Keep your hands in your pockets good, now." We came to the branch.

"It's froze." Caddy said. "Look." She broke the top of ¹²⁵ the water and held a piece of it against my face. "Ice. That means how cold it is." She helped me across and we went up the hill. "We cant even tell Mother and Father. You know what I think it is. I think it's a surprise for Mother and Father and Mr Patterson both, because Mr Patterson sent you some candy. Do you remember when Mr Patterson sent you some candy last summer."

There was a fence. The vine was dry, and the wind rattled in it.

"Only I dont see why Uncle Maury didn't send Versh." Caddy said. "Versh wont tell." Mrs Patterson was looking out the window. "You wait here." Caddy said. "Wait right here, now. I'll be back in a minute. Give me the letter." She took the letter out of my pocket. "Keep your hands in your pockets." She climbed the fence with the letter in her hand and went through the brown, rattling flowers. Mrs Patterson came to the door and opened it and stood there.

Mr Patterson was chopping in the green flowers. He stopped chopping and looked at me. Mrs Patterson came across the garden, running. When I saw her eyes I began to cry. You idiot, Mrs Patterson said, I told him never to send you alone again. Give it to me. Quick. Mr Patterson came fast, with the hoe. Mrs Patterson leaned across the fence, reaching her hand. She was trying to climb the fence. Give it to me, she said. Give it to me. Mr Patterson climbed the fence. I saw her eyes again and I ran down the hill.

"They aint nothing over yonder but houses." Luster said. "We going down to the branch."

They were washing down at the branch. One of them ¹³⁰ was singing. I could smell the clothes flapping, and the smoke blowing across the branch. . . .

GERTRUDE STEIN

Selection from *The Autobiography of Alice B. Toklas*

The American expatriate Gertrude Stein (1874–1946) was a maddeningly original genius. Her apartment in Paris was for more than forty years a meeting place for the avant-garde, and her experimental writings helped define Modernism. Misunderstood in her own day because of the impenetrability of her prose, she earned the title of America's best-known unread author. What was known about her was sufficient to make her a legendary character, part fraud, part genius. Stein fueled this image with her enigmatic sayings, as in this comment about America, "there is no there there," and in her most famous remark, "a rose is a rose is a rose is a rose." Now, fifty years after her death, she is a classic, and her works, back in print, are studied in college classrooms.

A rarity in her time, Stein was an independent woman who lived her life as she pleased. Born to a wealthy Jewish family in San Francisco and trained at The Johns Hopkins University in medicine, she passed up a medical career and instead moved to Paris in 1902. There she set up house in 1910 with Alice B. Toklas (1877–1967), a fellow San Franciscan who became her lifelong companion. Their personalities balanced one another, so that when they entertained, the male "geniuses" sat with Stein and the "wives" were relegated to the side with Toklas. Stein, avid for life, pursued cultural lions (Picasso and Hemingway) and anyone else who amused her; she dreamed of becoming a cultural lion herself ("think of the bible and Homer, think of Shakespeare and think of me"). In contrast, Toklas ran the domestic sphere (there is an *Alice B. Toklas Cookbook, 1954*) and seemed delighted to bask in Stein's reflected glory. During their lives, the Stein-Toklas household was the focus for the American love affair with France.

Stein's literary experiments bore little resemblance to Joyce's (see *Ulysses*) "interior monologues." Her literary project was to be abstract, as in Cubism. Wanting to break with all literary tradition, she slowly got rid of narrative, punctuation, logic, forms or genres, even meanings in any normal sense. She achieved a fully abstract style in *Tender Buttons* (1914), a work divided into three sections called "Objects," "Food," and "Room," marked by repetition and obscurity ("chicken"; "Alas a dirty word, alas a dirty third alas a dirty third, alas a dirty bird"). Earlier, in *Three Lives* (1909), about servant women in 1900 Baltimore, Stein was still a Realist, though experimenting with Modernist effects—especially repetition and unfocused narrative structure.

Reading the Selection

Who would have thought of writing the life of a cherished companion and passing it off as an autobiography? Yet, this is just what Stein did, perhaps as a stunt to make money, perhaps as just another eccentric gesture to call attention to herself. Setting aside for the moment her own abstract style, Stein wrote in a deliberate imitation of Tolkas's deadpan, slightly sour speech pattern. The popular and critical success of the book was so unexpected that Stein was unable to write for a year.

The following passage from *The Autobiography of Alice B. Toklas* (1933) is typical of the work, in the name-dropping, the provocative portraits of the famous, the highly opinionated judgments ("And so cubism is spanish"), and above all, the centrality of Stein. In most ways, this book is a double autobiography of this eccentric couple.

—⁊⁊—

But to return to the beginning of my life in Paris. It was based upon the rue de Fleurus and the Saturday evenings and it was like a kaleidoscope slowly turning.

What happened in those early years. A great deal happened.

As I said when I became an habitual visitor at the rue de Fleurus the Picassos were once more together, Pablo and Fernande. That summer they went again to Spain and he came back with some spanish landscapes and one may say that these landscapes, two of them still at the rue de Fleurus and the other one in Moscow in the collection that Stchoukine founded and that is now national property, were the beginning of cubism. In these there was no african sculpture influence. There was very evidently a strong Cézanne influence, particularly the influence of the late Cézanne water colours, the cutting up the sky not in cubes but in spaces.

But the essential thing, the treatment of the houses was essentially spanish and therefore essentially Picasso. In these pictures he first emphasised the way of building in spanish villages, the line of the houses not following the landscape but cutting across and into the landscape, becoming undistinguishable in the landscape by cutting across the landscape. It was the principle of the camouflage of the guns and the ships in the war. The first year of the war, Picasso and Eve, with whom he was living then, Gertrude Stein and myself, were walking down the boulevard Raspail a cold winter evening. There is nothing in the world colder than the Raspail on a cold winter evening, we used to call it the retreat from Moscow. All of a sudden down the street came some big cannon, the first any of us had seen painted, that is camouflaged. Pablo stopped, he was spell-bound. C'est nous qui avons fit ça, he said, it is we that have created that, he said. And he was right, he had. From Cézanne through him they had come to that. His foresight was justified.

But to go back to the three landscapes. When they were first put up on the wall naturally everybody objected. As it happened he and Fernande had taken some photographs of the villages which he had painted and he had given copies of these photographs to Gertrude Stein. When people said that the few cubes in the landscapes looked like nothing but cubes, Gertrude Stein would laugh and say, if you had objected to these landscapes as being too realistic there would be some point in your objection. And she would show them the photographs and really the pictures as she rightly said might be declared to be too photographic a copy of nature. Years after Elliot Paul at Gertrude Stein's suggestion had a photograph of the painting by Picasso and the photographs of the village reproduced on the same page in transition and it was extraordinarily interesting. This then was really the beginning of cubism. The colour too was characteristically spanish, the pale silver yellow with the faintest suggestion of green, the colour afterwards so well known in Picasso's cubist pictures, as well as in those of his followers.

Gertrude Stein always says that cubism is a purely spanish conception and only spaniards can be cubists and that the only real cubism is that of Picasso and Juan Gris. Picasso created it and Juan Gris permeated it with his clarity and his exaltation. To understand this one has only to read the life and death of Juan Gris by Gertrude Stein, written upon the death of one of her two dearest friends, Picasso and Juan Gris, both spaniards.

She always says that americans can understand spaniards. That they are the only two western nations that can realise abstraction. That in americans it expresses itself by disembodiedness, in literature and machinery, in Spain by ritual so abstract that it does not connect itself with anything but ritual.

I always remember Picasso saying disgustedly apropos of some germans who said they liked bull-fights, they would, he said angrily, they like bloodshed. To a spaniard it is not bloodshed, it is ritual.

Americans, so Gertrude Stein says, are like spaniards, they are abstract and cruel. They are not brutal they are cruel. They have no close contact with the earth such as most europeans have. Their materialism is not the materialism of existence, of possession, it is the materialism of action and abstraction. And so cubism is spanish.

We were very much struck, the first time Gertrude Stein and I went to Spain, which was a year or so after the beginning of cubism, to see how naturally cubism was made in Spain. In the shops in Barcelona instead of post cards they had square little frames and inside it was placed a cigar, a real one, a pipe, a bit of handkerchief etcetera, all absolutely the arrangement of many a cubist picture and helped out by cut paper representing other objects. That is the modern note that in Spain had been done for centuries.

Picasso in his early cubist pictures used printed letters as did Juan Gris to force the painted surface to measure up to something rigid, and the rigid thing was the printed letter. Gradually instead of using the printed thing they painted the letters and all was lost, it was only Juan Gris who could paint with such intensity a printed letter that it still made the rigid contrast. And so cubism came little by little but it came.

It was in these days that the intimacy between Braque and Picasso grew. It was in these days that Juan Gris, a raw rather effusive youth came from Madrid to Paris and began to call Picasso cher maître to Picasso's great annoyance. It was apropos of this that Picasso used to address Braque as cher maître, passing on the joke, and I am sorry to say that some foolish people have taken this joke to mean that Picasso looked up to Braque as a master.

But I am once more running far ahead of those early Paris days when I first knew Fernande and Pablo.

In those days then only the three landscapes had been painted and he was beginning to paint some heads that seemed cut out in planes, also long loaves of bread.

At this time Matisse, the school still going on, was really beginning to be fairly well known, so much so that to everybody's great excitement Bernheim jeune, a very middle class firm indeed, was offering him a contract to take all his work at a very good price. It was an exciting moment.

This was happening because of the influence of a man named Fénéon. Il est très fin, said Matisse, much impressed by Fénéon. Fénéon was a journalist, a french journalist who had invented the thing called a feuilleton en deux lignes, that is to say he was the first one to hit off the news of the day in two lines. He looked like a caricature of Uncle Sam made french and he had been painted standing in front of a curtain in a circus picture by Toulouse-Lautrec.

And now the Bernheims, how or wherefor I do not know, taking Fénéon into their employ, were going to connect themselves with the new generation of painters.

Something happened, at any rate this contract did not last long, but for all that it changed the fortunes of Matisse. He now had an established position. He bought a house and some land in Clamart and he started to move out there. Let me describe the house as I saw it.

This home in Clamart was very comfortable, to be sure the bath-room, which the family much appreciated from long contact with americans, although it must be said that the Matisses had always been and always were scrupulously neat and clean, was on the ground floor adjoining the dining room. But that was alright, and is and was a french custom, in french houses. It gave more privacy to a bath-room to have it on the ground floor. Not so long ago in going over the new house Braque was building the bath-room was again below, this time underneath the dining room. When we said, but why, they said because being nearer the furnace it would be warmer.

The grounds at Clamart were large and the garden was what Matisse between pride and chagrin called un petit Luxembourg. There was also a glass forcing house for flowers. Later they had begonias in them that grew smaller and smaller. Beyond were lilacs and still beyond a big demountable studio. They liked it enormously. Madame Matisse with simple recklessness went out every day to look at it and pick flowers, keeping a cab waiting for her. In those days only millionaires kept cabs waiting and then only very occasionally.

They moved out and were very comfortable and soon the enormous studio was filled with enormous statues and enormous pictures. It was that period of Matisse. Equally soon he found Clamart so beautiful that he could not go home to it, that is when he came into Paris to his hour of sketching from the nude, a thing he had done every afternoon of his life ever since the beginning of things, and he came in every afternoon. His school no longer existed, the government had taken over the old convent to make a Lycée of it and the school had come to an end.

These were the beginning of very prosperous days for the Matisses. They went to Algeria and they went to Tangiers and their devoted german pupils gave them Rhine wines and a very fine black police dog, the first of the breed that any of us had seen.

And then Matisse had a great show of his pictures in Berlin. I remember so well one spring day, it was a lovely day and we were to lunch at Clamart with the Matisses. When we got there they were all standing around an enormous packing case with its top off. We went up and joined them and there in the packing case was the largest laurel wreath that had ever been made, tied with a beautiful red ribbon. Matisse showed Gertrude Stein a card that had been in it. It said on it, To Henri Matisse, Triumphant on the Battlefield of Berlin, and was signed Thomas Whittemore. Thomas Whittemore was a bostonian archeologist and professor at Tufts College, a great admirer of Matisse and this was his tribute. Said Matisse, still more rueful, but I am not dead yet. Madame Matisse, the shock once over said, but Henri look, and leaning down she plucked a leaf and tasted it, it is real laurel, think how good it will be in soup. And, said she still further brightening, the ribbon will do wonderfully for a long time as a hair ribbon for Margot.

The Matisses stayed in Clamart more or less until the war. During this period they and Gertrude Stein were seeing less and less of each other. Then after the war broke out they came to the house a good deal. They were lonesome and troubled, Matisse's family in Saint-Quentin, in the north, were within the german lines and his brother was a hostage. It was Madame Matisse who taught me how to knit woollen gloves. She made them wonderfully neatly and rapidly and I learned to do so too. Then Matisse went to live in Nice and in one way and another, although remaining perfectly good friends, Gertrude Stein and the Matisses never see each other. . . .

21

THE AGE OF ANXIETY AND BEYOND
1945–

JEAN-PAUL SARTRE
Selection from *The Humanism of Existentialism*

France's Jean-Paul Sartre (1905–1980) was his era's greatest popularizer of existentialism, the individ-
ualistic philosophy that dominated Western thought for much of this century. Introduced to existentialism in the 1920s while studying with the German thinker Martin Heidegger (1889–1976), Sartre
later developed his own ideas—freedom, choice, commitment, self-definition, and authenticity, centered around the principle of personal responsibility—all derived from Heidegger. Sartre's theoretical
works make difficult reading for the layperson, but his novels, plays, and short stories, which are inseparable from his philosophy, are quite accessible and provide insight into existentialism in practice.
In addition to direct influence, he also indirectly affected his age through other writers who adopted
his ideas, as in the feminist theory of Simone de Beauvoir (see *The Second Sex*), his lifelong companion,
and in the revolutionary thought of Frantz Fanon, a black disciple from Martinique.

The term "existentialism" derives from *existence,* one half of the pair of terms (the other is *essence*) coined by Aristotle. *Essence* means unchanging human nature, while *existence* denotes human
aspects that are impermanent. Western thought from Plato to Nietzsche is essentialist, emphasizing
the *essence* shared by humanity. Nietzsche begins existentialist thought, which denies human nature
and stresses the human ability to change at will.

The twentieth century embraced existentialism, partly to fill the void left by the collapse of
traditional religion but mainly as a response to the period's unfolding horrors. Helplessly watching
the killing inflicted during two world wars, the evil made manifest in the Holocaust, the unyielding
threat of nuclear disaster, and the cruel social problems seemingly impervious to capitalistic or social-
istic solutions, many Westerners came to believe, like Nietzsche, that God was dead. Many, including
Sartre, embraced existentialism as a sort of self-help panacea. For them, existentialism was a way to
remain sane, by keeping a private moral sense in a world gone mad.

Reading the Selection

The Humanism of Existentialism was given first as a lecture by Sartre in 1945, as the West was trying to
recover from history's most destructive war. Spoken amid the ruins and proclaiming a message of

personal responsibility, Sartre's words were seen as a sign that Europe would rise again from the ashes. Issued as an essay, these words became an instant classic and made Sartre's name formidable around the world.

In this essay Sartre explores the full meaning of atheism, starting with the idea that there is no such thing as human nature (*essence*) "since there is no God to conceive it." He then develops the Heideggerian notion that human beings are "thrust into the world" ("appear on the scene"). Thus human beings do not choose to be born, but having been born, they "choose" (take responsibility for) their individual existence, including sex, skin color, age, economic condition, health, disposition, and personality. In what is the shakiest part of Sartre's thought, he reasons that when human beings choose themselves, "we mean that every one of us chooses all men. . . ." This "existential condition" of "legislating" for all humankind leads to "anguish," "forlornness," and "despair"—key Sartrean concepts. Nevertheless, Sartre remains optimistic, since in the final analysis, "man's destiny is within himself."

. . .

Atheistic existentialism, which I represent, is more coherent. It states that if God does not exist, there is at least one being in whom existence precedes essence, a being who exists before he can be defined by any concept, and that this being is man, or, as Heidegger says, human reality. What is meant here by saying that existence precedes essence? It means that, first of all, man exists, turns up, appears on the scene, and, only afterwards, defines himself. If man, as the existentialist conceives him, is indefinable, it is because at first he is nothing. Only afterwards will he be something, and he himself will have made what he will be. Thus, there is no human nature, since there is no God to conceive it. Not only is man what he conceives himself to be, but he is also only what he wills himself to be after this thrust toward existence.

Man is nothing else but what he makes of himself. Such is the first principle of existentialism. It is also what is called subjectivity, the name we are labeled with when charges are brought against us. But what do we mean by this, if not that man has a greater dignity than a stone or table? For we mean that man first exists, that is, that man first of all is the being who hurls himself toward a future and who is conscious of imagining himself as being in the future. Man is at the start a plan which is aware of itself, rather than a patch of moss, a piece of garbage, or a cauliflower; nothing exists prior to this plan; there is nothing in heaven; man will be what he will have planned to be. Not what he will want to be. Because by the word "will" we generally mean a conscious decision, which is subsequent to what we have already made of ourselves. I may want to belong to a political party, write a book, get married; but all that is only a manifestation of an earlier, more spontaneous choice that is called "will." But if existence really does precede essence, man is responsible for what he is. Thus, existentialism's first move is to make every man aware of what he is and to make the full responsibility of his existence rest on him. And when we say that a man is responsible for himself, we do not only mean that he is responsible for his own individuality, but that he is responsible for all men.

The word subjectivism has two meanings, and our opponents play on the two. Subjectivism means, on the one hand, that an individual chooses and makes himself; and, on the other, that it is impossible for man to transcend human subjectivity. The second of these is the essential meaning of existentialism. When we say that man chooses his own self, we mean that every one of us does likewise; but we also mean by that that in making this choice he also chooses all men. In fact, in creating the man that we want to be, there is not a single one of our acts which does not at the same time create an image of man as we think he ought to be. To choose to be this or that is to affirm at the same time the value of what we choose, because we can never choose evil. We always choose the good, and nothing can be good for us without being good for all.

If, on the other hand, existence precedes essence, and if we grant that we exist and fashion our image at one and the same time, the image is valid for everybody and for our whole age. Thus, our responsibility is much greater than we might have supposed, because it involves all mankind. If I am a workingman and choose to join a Christian trade-union rather than be a communist, and if by being a member I want to show that the best thing for man is resignation, that the kingdom of man is not of this world, I am not only involving my own case—I want to be resigned for everyone. As a result, my action has involved all humanity. To take a more individual matter, if I want to marry, to have children; even if this marriage depends solely on my own circumstances or passion or wish, I am involving all humanity in monogamy and not merely myself. Therefore, I am responsible for myself and for everyone else. I am creating a certain image of man of my own choosing. In choosing myself, I choose man.

This helps us understand what the actual content is of such rather grandiloquent words as anguish, forlornness, despair. As you will see, it's all quite simple.

First, what is meant by anguish? The existentialists say at once that man is anguish. What that means is this: the man who involves himself and who realizes that he is not only the person he chooses to be, but also a lawmaker who is, at the same time, choosing all mankind as well as himself, can not help escape the feeling of his total and deep responsibility. Of course, there are many people who are not anxious; but we claim that they are hiding their anxiety, that they are fleeing from it. Certainly, many people believe that when they do something, they themselves are the only ones involved, and when someone says to them, "What if everyone acted that way?" they shrug their shoulders and answer, "Everyone doesn't act that way." But really, one should always ask himself, "What would happen if everybody looked at things that way?" There is no escaping this disturbing thought except by a kind of double-dealing. A man who lies and makes excuses for himself by saying "Not everybody does that," is someone with an uneasy conscience, because the act of lying implies that a universal value is conferred upon the lie.

Anguish is evident even when it conceals itself. This is the anguish that Kierkegaard called the anguish of Abraham. You know the story: an angel has ordered Abraham to sacrifice his son; if it really were an angel who has come and said, "You are Abraham, you shall sacrifice your son," everything would be all right. But everyone might first wonder, "Is it really an angel, and am I really Abraham? What proof do I have?"

There was a madwoman who had hallucinations; someone used to speak to her on the telephone and give her orders. Her doctor asked her, "Who is it who talks to you?" She answered, "He says it's God." What proof did she really have that it was God? If an angel comes to me, what proof is there that it's an angel? And if I hear voices, what proof is there that they come from heaven and not from hell, or from the subconscious, or a pathological condition? What proves that they are addressed to me? What proof is there that I have been appointed to impose my choice and my conception of man on humanity? I'll never find any proof or sign to convince me of that. If a voice addresses me, it is always for me to decide that this is the angel's voice; if I consider that such an act is a good one, it is I who will choose to say that it is good rather than bad.

Now, I'm not being singled out as an Abraham, and yet at every moment I'm obliged to perform exemplary acts. For every man, everything happens as if all mankind had its eyes fixed on him and were guiding itself by what he does. And every man ought to say to himself, "Am I really the kind of man who has the right to act in such a way that humanity might guide itself by my actions?" And if he does not say that to himself, he is masking his anguish.

There is no question here of the kind of anguish which would lead to quietism, to inaction. It is a matter of a simple sort of anguish that anybody who has had responsibilities is familiar with. For example, when a military officer takes the responsibility for an attack and sends a certain number of men to death, he chooses to do so, and in the main he alone makes the choice. Doubtless, orders come from above, but they are too broad; he interprets them, and on this interpretation depend the lives of ten or fourteen or twenty men. In making a decision he can not help having a certain anguish. All leaders know this anguish. That doesn't keep them from acting; on the contrary, it is the very condition of their action. For it implies

that they envisage a number of possibilities, and when they choose one, they realize that it has value only because it is chosen. We shall see that this kind of anguish, which is the kind that existentialism describes, is explained, in addition, by a direct responsibility to the other men whom it involves. It is not a curtain separating us from action, but is part of action itself.

When we speak of forlornness, a term Heidegger was fond of, we mean only that God does not exist and that we have to face all the consequences of this. The existentialist is strongly opposed to a certain kind of secular ethics which would like to abolish God with the least possible expense. About 1880, some French teachers tried to set up a secular ethics which went something like this: God is a useless and costly hypothesis; we are discarding it; but, meanwhile, in order for there to be an ethics, a society, a civilization, it is essential that certain values be taken seriously and that they be considered as having an *a priori* existence. It must be obligatory, *a priori,* to be honest, not to lie, not to beat your wife, to have children, etc., etc. So we're going to try a little device which will make it possible to show that values exist all the same, inscribed in a heaven of ideas, though otherwise God does not exist. In other words—and this, I believe, is the tendency of everything called reformism in France—nothing will be changed if God does not exist. We shall find ourselves with the same norms of honesty, progress, and humanism, and we shall have made of God an outdated hypothesis which will peacefully die off by itself.

The existentialist, on the contrary, thinks it very distressing that God does not exist, because all possibility of finding values in a heaven of ideas disappears along with Him; there can no longer be an *a priori* Good, since there is no infinite and perfect consciousness to think it. Nowhere is it written that the Good exists, that we must be honest, that we must not lie; because the fact is we are on a plane where there are only men. Dostoievsky said, "If God didn't exist, everything would be possible." That is the very starting point of existentialism. Indeed, everything is permissible if God does not exist, and as a result man is forlorn, because neither within him nor without does he find anything to cling to. He can't start making excuses for himself.

If existence really does precede essence, there is no explaining things away by reference to a fixed and given human nature. In other words, there is no determinism, man is free, man is freedom. On the other hand, if God does not exist, we find no values or commands to turn to which legitimize our conduct. So, in the bright realm of values, we have no excuse behind us, nor justification before us. We are alone, with no excuses.

That is the idea I shall try to convey when I say that man is condemned to be free. Condemned, because he did not create himself, yet, in other respects is free; because, once thrown into the world, he is responsible for everything he does. . . .

As for despair, the term has a very simple meaning. It means that we shall confine ourselves to reckoning only with what depends upon our will, or on the ensemble of probabilities which make our action possible. When we want something, we always have to reckon with probabilities.

I may be counting on the arrival of a friend. The friend is coming by rail or street-car; this supposes that the train will arrive on schedule, or that the street-car will not jump the track. I am left in the realm of possibility; but possibilities are to be reckoned with only to the point where my action comports with the ensemble of these possibilities, and no further. The moment the possibilities I am considering are not rigorously involved by my action, I ought to disengage myself from them, because no God, no scheme, can adapt the world and its possibilities to my will. When Descartes said, "Conquer yourself rather than the world," he meant essentially the same thing. . . .

When all is said and done, what we are accused of, at bottom, is not our pessimism, but an optimistic toughness. If people throw up to us our works of fiction in which we write about people who are soft, weak, cowardly, and sometimes even downright bad, it's not because these people are soft, weak, cowardly, or bad; because if we were to say, as Zola did, that they are that way because of heredity, the workings of environment, society, because of biological or psychological determinism, people would be reassured. They would say, "Well, that's what we're like, no one can do anything about it." But when the existentialist writes about a coward, he says that this coward is responsible for his cowardice. . . .

What the existentialist says is that the coward makes himself cowardly, that the hero makes himself heroic. There's always a possibility for the coward not to be cowardly any more and for the hero to stop being heroic. What counts is total involvement; some one particular action or set of circumstances is not total involvement.

Thus, I think we have answered a number of the charges concerning existentialism. You see that it can not be taken for a philosophy of quietism, since it defines man in terms of action; nor for a pessimistic description of man—there is no doctrine more optimistic, since man's destiny is within himself; nor for an attempt to discourage man from acting, since it tells him that the only hope is in his acting and that action is the only thing that enables a man to live. Consequently, we are dealing here with an ethics of action and involvement. . . .

The third objection is the following: "You take something from one pocket and put it into the other. That is, fundamentally, values aren't serious, since you choose them." My answer to this is that I'm quite vexed that that's the way it is; but if I've discarded God the Father, there has to be someone to invent values. You've got to take things as they are. Moreover, to say that we invent values means nothing else but this: life has no meaning *a priori*. Before you come alive, life is nothing; it's up to you to give it a meaning, and value is nothing else but the meaning that you choose. In that way, you see, there is a possibility of creating a human community. . . .

But it can not be granted that a man may make a judgment about man. Existentialism spares him from any such judgment. The existentialist will never consider man as an end because he is always in the making. Nor should we believe that there is a mankind to which we might set up a cult in the manner of Auguste Comte. The cult of mankind ends in the self-enclosed humanism of Comte, and, let it be said, of fascism. This kind of humanism we can do without.

But there is another meaning of humanism. Fundamentally it is this: man is constantly outside of himself; in projecting himself, in losing himself outside of himself, he makes for man's existing; and, on the other hand, it is by pursuing transcendent goals that he is able to exist; man, being this state of passing-beyond, and seizing upon things only as they bear upon this passing-beyond, is at the heart, at the center of this passing-beyond. There is no universe other than a human universe, the universe of human subjectivity. This connection between transcendency, as a constituent element of man—not in the sense that God is transcendent, but in the sense of passing beyond—and subjectivity, in the sense that man is not closed in on himself but is always present in a human universe, is what we call existentialist humanism. Humanism, because we remind man that there is no lawmaker other than himself, and that in his forlornness he will decide by himself; because we point out that man will fulfill himself as man, not in turning toward himself, but in seeking outside of himself a goal which is just this liberation, just this particular fulfillment.

—m—

SIMONE DE BEAUVOIR

Selection from *The Second Sex*

Beauvoir's *The Second Sex* (1949), a treatise on female sexuality and a classic text of feminism, appeared at a time when the push for women's rights had temporarily lost forward motion. Women in most countries of the West now had voting rights (starting in Britain in 1918), thereby achieving the goal of the first phase of feminism; and no other issue drew women together as did the suffrage cause. Beauvoir's treatise did not so much offer a specific issue for women to rally around, as it constituted a more general call to action—for women to rethink the way that the sexes functioned and interacted. The burden of her message may be summed up in her bold line "One is not born, but rather becomes a woman." She rejected innate sexual differences and proclaimed that femaleness is learned and thus subject to revision. Her message launched a second wave of feminism, revolutionizing millions of readers who have dramatically revised the way they think and act.

Simone de Beauvoir (1908–1986), this apostle of latter-day feminism, was herself a contradictory figure. France's outstanding woman of letters from 1945 onward, she wrote, besides *The Second Sex*, well-received novels (*She Came to Stay,* 1943; *The Mandarins,* 1954) and books of autobiography (*Memoirs of a Dutiful Daughter,* 1958; *The Prime of Life,* 1960). Yet she was content to take second place to Sartre, her lifelong mentor and the lover with whom she was involved in an unlicensed, open "marriage." At all stages of her life with Sartre, she readily set aside her own plans to edit, sharpen, and deliver detailed responses to his writing, duties she considered an honor. Beauvoir condemned female subservience in *The Second Sex*, but in her own life she created a myth of Sartre's genius, apparently thinking her own fame dependent on his.

Reading the Selection

This selection, taken from the "Introduction" to *The Second Sex*, summarizes Beauvoir's argument for sexual equality. Two of her prime analytical tools are the concepts of "the Self" and "the Other," borrowed from the German thinker Georg Wilhelm Friedrich Hegel (1770–1831). With these terms, she shows that in society as currently arranged, Man is the "Self," the essential being, the necessary sex; as such, Man defines Woman as "the Other," the inessential being, "the second sex." The category of "Otherness"—which, according to Beauvoir, Woman shares with the American Negro, the Jew, and the proletariat—is a primordial way of thinking in which privileged groups distinguish themselves from those they consider inferior, mysterious, and thus in need of control.

Even more than Hegel, the spirit of Sartre hovers over this work. Following Sartre, Beauvoir rejects preexisting social and moral categories, so that a woman is not "a feminine creature" but is instead what she wills herself to be. Beauvoir does not claim that a woman should become a masculinized female. Indeed, she recognizes that a woman has "ovaries, a uterus [and] these . . . circumscribe her within the limits of her own nature." But a woman, just as a man, must "choose" (take responsibility for) her situation, including her sex. In Beauvoir's new social order, women will live side by side with men, economically and intellectually separate, each engaged in the project of transcendence; that is, both will work to leave behind a permanent record—such as states, art, literature, architecture, and philosophies.

Introduction

A man would never get the notion of writing a book on the peculiar situation of the human male. But if I wish to define myself, I must first of all say: "I am a woman"; on this truth must be based all further discussion. A man never begins by presenting himself as an individual of a certain sex; it goes without saying that he is a man. The terms *masculine* and *feminine* are used symmetrically only as a matter of form, as on legal papers. In actuality the relation of the two sexes is not quite like that of two electrical poles, for man represents both the positive and the neutral, as is indicated by the common use of *man* to designate human beings in general; whereas woman represents only the negative, defined by limiting criteria, without reciprocity. In the midst of an abstract discussion it is vexing to hear a man say: "You think thus and so because you are a woman"; but I know that my only defense is to reply: "I think thus and so because it is true," thereby removing my subjective self from the argument. It would be out of the question to reply: "And you think the contrary because you are a man," for it is understood that the fact of being a man is no peculiarity. A man is in the right in being a man; it is the woman who is in the wrong. It amounts to this: just as for the ancients there was an absolute vertical with reference to which the oblique was defined, so there is an absolute human type, the masculine. Woman has ovaries, a uterus; these peculiarities imprison her in her subjectivity, circumscribe her within the limits of her own nature. It is often said that she thinks with her glands. Man superbly ignores the fact that his anatomy also includes glands, such as the testicles, and that they secrete hormones. He thinks of his body as a direct and normal connection with the world, which he believes he apprehends objectively, whereas he regards the body of woman as a hindrance, a prison, weighed down by everything peculiar to it. "The female is a female by virtue of a certain *lack* of qualities," said Aristotle; "we should regard the female nature as afflicted with a natural defectiveness." And St. Thomas for his part pronounced woman to be an "imperfect man," an "incidental" being. This is symbolized in Genesis where Eve is depicted as made from what Bossuet called "a supernumerary bone" of Adam.

Thus humanity is male and man defines woman not in herself but as relative to him; she is not regarded as an autonomous being. Michelet writes: "Woman, the relative being. . . ." And Benda is most positive in his *Rapport d'Uriel:* "The body of man makes sense in itself quite apart from that of woman, whereas the latter seems wanting in significance by itself. . . . Man can think of himself without woman. She cannot think of herself without man." And she is simply what man decrees; thus she is called "the sex," by which is meant that she appears essentially to the male as a sexual being. For him she is sex—absolute sex, no less. She is defined and differentiated with reference to man and not he with reference to her; she is the incidental, the inessential as opposed to the essential. He is the Subject, he is the Absolute—she is the Other.

The category of the *Other* is as primordial as consciousness itself. In the most primitive societies, in the most ancient mythologies, one finds the expression of a duality—that of the Self and the Other. This duality was not originally attached to the division of the sexes; it was not dependent upon any empirical facts. It is revealed in such works as that of Granet on Chinese thought and those of Dumézil on the East Indies and Rome. The feminine element was at first no more involved in such pairs as Varuna-Mitra, Uranus-Zeus, Sun-Moon, and Day-Night than it was in the contrasts between Good and Evil, lucky and unlucky auspices, right and left, God and Lucifer. Otherness is a fundamental category of human thought.

Thus it is that no group ever sets itself up as the One without at once setting up the Other over against itself. If three travelers chance to occupy the same compartment, that is enough to make vaguely hostile "others" out of all the rest of the passengers on the train. In small-town eyes all persons not belonging to the village are "strangers" and suspect; to the native of a country all who inhabit other countries are "foreigners"; Jews are "different" for the anti-Semite, Negroes are "inferior" for American racists, aborigines are "natives" for colonists, proletarians are the "lower class" for the privileged.

Lévi-Strauss, at the end of a profound work on the various forms of primitive societies, reaches the following conclusion: "Passage from the state of Nature to the state of Culture is marked by man's ability to view biological relations as a series of contrasts; duality, alternation, opposition, and symmetry, whether under definite or vague forms, constitute not so much phenomena to be explained as fundamental and immediately given data of social reality." These phenomena would be incomprehensible if in fact human society were simply a *Mitsein* or fellowship based on solidarity and friendliness. Things become clear, on the contrary, if, following Hegel, we find in consciousness itself a fundamental hostility toward every other consciousness; the subject can be posed only in being op-

posed—he sets himself up as the essential, as opposed to the other, the inessential, the object.

But the other consciousness, the other ego, sets up a reciprocal claim. The native traveling abroad is shocked to find himself in turn regarded as a "stranger" by the natives of neighboring countries. As a matter of fact, wars, festivals, trading, treaties, and contests among tribes, nations, and classes tend to deprive the concept *Other* of its absolute sense and to make manifest its relativity; willy-nilly, individuals and groups are forced to realize the reciprocity of their relations. How is it, then, that this reciprocity has not been recognized between the sexes, that one of the contrasting terms is set up as the sole essential, denying any relativity in regard to its correlative and defining the latter as pure otherness? Why is it that women do not dispute male sovereignty? No subject will readily volunteer to become the object, the inessential; it is not the Other who, in defining himself as the Other, establishes the One. The Other is posed as such by the One in defining himself as the One. But if the Other is not to regain the status of being the One, he must be submissive enough to accept this alien point of view. Whence comes this submission in the case of woman?

There are, to be sure, other cases in which a certain category has been able to dominate another completely for a time. Very often this privilege depends upon inequality of numbers—the majority imposes its rule upon the minority or persecutes it. But women are not a minority, like the American Negroes or the Jews; there are as many women as men on earth. Again, the two groups concerned have often been originally independent; they may have been formerly unaware of each other's existence, or perhaps they recognized each other's autonomy. But a historical event has resulted in the subjugation of the weaker by the stronger. The scattering of the Jews, the introduction of slavery into America, the conquests of imperialism are examples in point. In these cases the oppressed retained at least the memory of former days; they possessed in common a past, a tradition, sometimes a religion or a culture.

The parallel drawn by Bebel between women and the proletariat is valid in that neither ever formed a minority or a separate collective unit of mankind. And instead of a single historical event it is in both cases a historical development that explains their status as a class and accounts for the membership of *particular individuals* in that class. But proletarians have not always existed, whereas there have always been women. They are women in virtue of their anatomy and physiology. Throughout history they have always been subordinated to men, and hence their dependency is not the result of a historical event or a social change—it was not something that *occurred*. The reason why otherness in this case seems to be an absolute is in part that it lacks the contingent or incidental nature of historical facts. A condition brought about at a certain time can be abolished at some other time, as the Negroes of Haiti and others have proved; but it might seem that a natural condition is beyond the possibility of change. In truth, however, the nature of things is no more immutably given, once for all, than is historical reality. If woman seems to be the inessential which never becomes the essential, it is because she herself fails to bring about this change. Proletarians say "We"; Negroes also. Regarding themselves as subjects, they transform the bourgeois, the whites, into "others." But women do not say "We," except at some congress of feminists or similar formal demonstration; men say "women," and women use the same word in referring to themselves. They do not authentically assume a subjective attitude. The proletarians have accomplished the revolution in Russia, the Negroes in Haiti, the Indo-Chinese are battling for it in Indo-China; but the women's effort has never been anything more than a symbolic agitation. They have gained only what men have been willing to grant; they have taken nothing, they have only received.

The reason for this is that women lack concrete means for organizing themselves into a unit which can stand face to face with the correlative unit. They have no past, no history, no religion of their own; and they have no such solidarity of work and interest as that of the proletariat. They are not even promiscuously herded together in the way that creates community feeling among the American Negroes, the ghetto Jews, the workers of Saint-Denis, or the factory hands of Renault. They live dispersed among the males, attached through residence, housework, economic condition, and social standing to certain men—fathers or husbands—more firmly than they are to other women. If they belong to the bourgeoisie, they feel solidarity with men of that class, not with proletarian women; if they are white, their allegiance is to white men, not to Negro women. The proletariat can propose to massacre the ruling class, and a sufficiently fanatical Jew or Negro might dream of getting sole possession of the atomic bomb and making humanity wholly Jewish or black; but woman cannot even dream of exterminating the males. The bond that unites her to her oppressors is not comparable to any other. The division of the sexes is a biological fact, not an event in human history. Male and female stand opposed within a primordial *Mitsein*, and woman has not broken it. The couple is a fundamental unity with its two halves riveted together, and the cleavage of society along the line of sex is impossible. Here is to be found the basic trait of woman: she is the Other in a totality of which the two components are necessary to one another.

One could suppose that this reciprocity might have facilitated the liberation of woman. When Hercules sat at the feet of Omphale and helped with her spinning, his desire for her held him captive; but why did she fail to gain a lasting power? To revenge herself on Jason, Medea killed their children; and this grim legend would seem to suggest that she might have obtained a formidable influence over him through his love for his offspring. In *Lysistrata* Aristophanes gaily depicts a band of women who joined forces to gain social ends through the sexual needs of their men; but this is only a play. In the legend of the Sabine women, the latter soon abandoned their plan of remaining sterile to punish their ravishers. In truth woman has not been socially emancipated through man's need—sexual desire and the desire for offspring—which makes the male dependent for satisfaction upon the female.

Master and slave, also, are united by a reciprocal need, in this case economic, which does not liberate the slave. In the relation of master to slave the master does not make a point of the need that he has for the other; he has in his grasp the power of satisfying this need through his own action; whereas the slave, in his dependent condition, his hope and fear, is quite conscious of the need he has for his master. Even if the need is at bottom equally urgent for both, it always works in favor of the oppressor and against the oppressed. That is why the liberation of the working class, for example, has been slow.

Now, woman has always been man's dependent, if not his slave; the two sexes have never shared the world in equality. And even today woman is heavily handicapped, though her situation is beginning to change. Almost nowhere is her legal status the same as man's, and frequently it is much to her disadvantage. Even when her rights are legally recognized in the abstract, long-standing custom prevents their full expression in the mores. In the economic sphere men and women can almost be said to make up two castes; other things being equal, the former hold the better jobs, get higher wages, and have more opportunity for success than their new competitors. In industry and politics men have a great many more positions and they monopolize the most important posts. In addition to all this, they enjoy a traditional prestige that the education of children tends in every way to support, for the present enshrines the past—and in the past all history has been made by men. At the present time, when women are beginning to take part in the affairs of the world, it is still a world that belongs to men—they have no doubt of it at all and women have scarcely any. To decline to be the Other, to refuse to be a party to the deal—this would be for women to renounce all the advantages conferred upon them by their alliance with the superior caste. Man-the-sovereign will provide woman-the-liege with material protection and will undertake the moral justification of her existence; thus she can evade at once both economic risk and the metaphysical risk of a liberty in which ends and aims must be contrived without assistance. Indeed, along with the ethical urge of each individual to affirm his subjective existence, there is also the temptation to forgo liberty and become a thing. This is an inauspicious road, for he who takes it—passive, lost, ruined—becomes henceforth the creature of another's will, frustrated in his transcendence and deprived of every value. But it is an easy road; on it one avoids the strain involved in undertaking an authentic existence. When man makes of woman the *Other*, he may, then, expect her to manifest deep-seated tendencies toward complicity. Thus, woman may fail to lay claim to the status of subject because she lacks definite resources, because she feels the necessary bond that ties her to man regardless of reciprocity, and because she is often very well pleased with her role as the *Other*.

But it will be asked at once: how did all this begin? It is easy to see that the duality of the sexes, like any duality, gives rise to conflict. And doubtless the winner will assume the status of absolute. But why should man have won from the start? It seems possible that women could have won the victory; or that the outcome of the conflict might never have been decided. How is it that this world has always belonged to the men and that things have

10

begun to change only recently? Is this change a good thing? Will it bring about an equal sharing of the world between men and women?

These questions are not new, and they have often been answered. But the very fact that woman *is the Other* tends to cast suspicion upon all the justifications that men have ever been able to provide for it. These have all too evidently been dictated by men's interest. A little-known feminist of the seventeenth century, Poulain de la Barre, put it this way: "All that has been written about women by men should be suspect, for the men are at once judge and party to the lawsuit." Everywhere, at all times, the males have displayed their satisfaction in feeling that they are the lords of creation. "Blessed be God . . . that He did not make me a woman," say the Jews in their morning prayers, while their wives pray on a note of resignation: "Blessed be the Lord, who created me according to His will." The first among the blessings for which Plato thanked the gods was that he had been created free, not enslaved; the second, a man, not a woman. But the males could not enjoy this privilege fully unless they believed it to be founded on the absolute and the eternal; they sought to make the fact of their supremacy into a right. "Being men, those who have made and compiled the laws have favored their own sex, and jurists have elevated these laws into principles," to quote Poulain de la Barre once more.

Legislators, priests, philosophers, writers, and scientists have striven to show that the subordinate position of woman is willed in heaven and advantageous on earth. The religions invented by men reflect this wish for domination. In the legends of Eve and Pandora men have taken up arms against women. They have made use of philosophy and theology, as the quotations from Aristotle and St. Thomas have shown. Since ancient times satirists and moralists have delighted in showing up the weaknesses of women. We are familiar with the savage indictments hurled against women throughout French literature. Montherlant, for example, follows the tradition of Jean de Meung, though with less gusto. This hostility may at times be well founded, often it is gratuitous; but in truth it more or less successfully conceals a desire for self-justification. As Montaigne says, "It is easier to accuse one sex than to excuse the other." Sometimes what is going on is clear enough. For instance, the Roman law limiting the rights of woman cited "the imbecility, the instability of the sex" just when the weakening of family ties seemed to threaten the interests of male heirs. And in the effort to keep the married woman under guardianship, appeal was made in the sixteenth century to the authority of St. Augustine, who

declared that "woman is a creature neither decisive nor constant," at a time when the single woman was thought capable of managing her property. Montaigne understood clearly how arbitrary and unjust was woman's appointed lot: "Women are not in the wrong when they decline to accept the rules laid down for them, since the men make these rules without consulting them. No wonder intrigue and strife abound." But he did not go so far as to champion their cause.

It was only later, in the eighteenth century, that genuinely democratic men began to view the matter objectively. Diderot, among others, strove to show that woman is, like man, a human being. Later John Stuart Mill came fervently to her defense. But these philosophers displayed unusual impartiality. In the nineteenth century the feminist quarrel became again a quarrel of partisans. One of the consequences of the industrial revolution was the entrance of women into productive labor, and it was just here that the claims of the feminists emerged from the realm of theory and acquired an economic basis, while their opponents became the more aggressive. Although landed property lost power to some extent, the bourgeoisie clung to the old morality that found the guarantee of private property in the solidity of the family. Woman was ordered back into the home the more harshly as her emancipation became a real menace. Even within the working class the men endeavored to restrain woman's liberation, because they began to see the women as dangerous competitors—the more so because they were accustomed to work for lower wages. . . .

So it is that many men will affirm as if in good faith that women *are* the equals of man and that they have nothing to clamor for, while *at the same time* they will say that women can never be the equals of man and that their demands are in vain. It is, in point of fact, a difficult matter for man to realize the extreme importance of social discriminations which seem outwardly insignificant but which produce in women moral and intellectual effects so profound that they appear to spring from her original nature. The most sympathetic of men never fully comprehend woman's concrete situation. And there is no reason to put much trust in the men when they rush to the defense of privileges whose full extent they can hardly measure. We shall not, then, permit ourselves to be intimidated by the number and violence of the attacks launched against women, nor to be entrapped by the self-seeking eulogies bestowed on the "true woman," nor to profit by the enthusiasm for woman's destiny manifested by men who would not for the world have any part of it. . . .

DORIS LESSING
Selection from *Martha Quest*

Doris Lessing (b. 1919), writing from the vantage point of a marginal observer, has created an outstanding body of works—novels, short stories, poetry, dramas, and autobiography—to become one of the world's most important living writers. Her marginal status began at birth in Persia (now Iran) to British expatriates who later migrated to the British colony of Rhodesia (now Zimbabwe). Growing up on a farm far removed from Rhodesia's capital city, she experienced freedom from traditional female constraints. Unusual for the time and place, her father taught her to use a rifle and permitted her to wander the nearby veldt, or open grazing area, stalking game for the family table. This early freedom instilled in her a love of independence, which nevertheless has not prevented her from being involved with the main political and social issues of the modern world and with ideologies ranging from Marxism (see Marx and Engels's *The Communist Manifesto*) to Sufism, an Islamic mystical sect. Throughout her career, however, she has kept her marginal status, refusing to be coopted by any group or ideology for long.

Lessing's marginal status, manifested in an antiestablishment point of view, was evident from the start. In her first novel, *The Grass Is Singing* (1950), she gave a withering analysis of colonial Rhodesia, portraying the clash of value systems between white settlers and native blacks, rich and poor, and men and women. Later novels took up other adversarial themes, such as communism, the relations of women to men and each other, and the future in space. Ironically, Lessing supports women's rights, but she refuses to endorse the women's movement because she thinks women's issues should be addressed only as part of the liberation of all groups. The boldest instance of her freethinking was the announcement in 1984 that she had fooled the literary establishment by issuing two novels under the name of Jane Somers—*The Diary of a Good Neighbor* (1983) and *If the Old Could . . .* (1984).

Reading the Selection

Martha Quest (1952) is the first of Lessing's *Children of Violence* series, a quintet of novels written in the Realist style. The other volumes are *A Proper Marriage* (1954), *A Ripple from the Storm* (1958), *Landlocked* (1965), and *The Four-Gated City* (1969). According to Lessing, this series constitutes a *Bildungsroman*, a type of novel that narrates the education of the protagonist. This definition indeed does apply, for the novels focus on the evolving consciousness of Martha Quest from her adolescence in Zambesia (a fictional Rhodesia) through failed marriages, mental breakdown, and nuclear disaster, to a serene death on a Scottish island.

In this selection, comprising the opening pages of *Martha Quest*, the fifteen-year-old heroine is introduced along with other major characters and images. Half-dreamy, half-rebellious, Martha is daily tormented while she ponders her future. She is repulsed by marriage and motherhood, symbolized by her mother and her mother's friend. She is attracted to, but ultimately confused by, the far-off world of culture and England, symbolized by the Cohen brothers. On a deeper level, she experiences a vision of the future (last paragraph): the four-gated city of the veldt with its gardens and fountains—a dynamic symbol of the balance between civilization and nature, races, and generations, the individual and the whole. This four-gated city represents Lessing's own hope for the future.

Chapter I

Two elderly women sat knitting on that part of the verandah which was screened from the sun by a golden shower creeper; the tough stems were so thick with flower it was as if the glaring afternoon was dammed against them in a surf of its own light made visible in the dripping, orange-coloured clusters. Inside this coloured barrier was a darkened recess, rough mud walls (the outer walls of the house itself) forming two sides, the third consisting of a bench

Mrs. Van Rensberg hesitated, and then said firmly (the firmness was directed against her own hesitation), "A girl must make men respect her." She was startled at the hatred and contempt in Martha's suddenly raised eyes, and looked for support towards Mrs. Quest.

"That's right," said Mrs. Quest, rather uncertainly. "A man will never marry a girl he does not respect."

Martha slowly sat up, closing her book as if it were of no more use to her, and stared composedly at them. She was now quite white with the effort of controlling that hatred. She got up, and said in a low tight voice, "You are loathsome, bargaining and calculating and . . ." She was unable to continue. "You are *disgusting*," she ended lamely, with trembling lips. Then she marched off down the garden, and ran into the bush.

The two ladies watched her in silence. Mrs. Quest was upset, for she did not know why her daughter thought her disgusting, while Mrs. Van Rensberg was trying to find a sympathetic remark likely to be acceptable to her friend.

"She's so difficult," murmured Mrs. Quest apologetically; and Mrs. Van Rensberg said, "It's the age, my Marnie's just as bad." She did not know she had failed to find the right remark: Mrs. Quest did not consider her daughter to be on a level with Marnie, whom she found in altogether bad taste, wearing grown-up clothes and lipstick at fifteen, and talking about "boys." Mrs. Van Rensberg was quite unconscious of the force of her friend's feeling. She dismissed her strictness with Martha as one of those English foibles; and besides, she knew Marnie to be potentially a sensible woman, a good wife and mother. She continued to talk about Marnie, while Mrs. Quest listened with the embarrassment due to a social *gaffe*, saying "Quite" or "Exactly," thinking that her daughter's difficulty was caused by having to associate with the wrong type of child, meaning Marnie herself. But the Dutchwoman was unsnubbable, since her national pride was as deep as the Englishwoman's snobbishness, and soon their conversation drifted back to servants and cooking. That evening, each would complain to her husband—one, with the English inarticulateness over matters of class, that Mrs. Van Rensberg was "really so trying," while the other, quite frankly, said that these rooineks got her down, they were all the same, they thought they owned the earth they walked on. Then, from unacknowledged guilt, they would ring each other up on the district telephone, and talk for half an hour or so about cooking and servants. Everything would continue as usual, in fact.

In the meantime, Martha, in an agony of adolescent misery, was lying among the long grass under a tree, repeating to herself that her mother was hateful, all these old women hateful, every one of these relationships, with their lies, evasions, compromises, wholly disgusting. For she was suffering that misery peculiar to the young, that they are going to be cheated by circumstances out of the full life every nerve and instinct is clamouring for.

After a short time, she grew more composed. A self-preserving nerve had tightened in her brain, and with it her limbs and even the muscles of her face became set and hardened. It was with a bleak and puzzled look that she stared at a sunlit and glittering bush which stood at her feet; for she did not see it, she was seeing herself, and in the only way she was equipped to do this—through literature. For if one reads novels from earlier times, and if novels accurately reflect, as we hope and trust they do, the life of their era, then one is forced to conclude that being young was much easier then than it is now. Did X and Y and Z, those blithe heroes and heroines, loathe school, despise their parents and teachers who never understood them, spend years of their lives fighting to free themselves from an environment they considered altogether beneath them? No, they did not; while in a hundred years' time people will read the novels of this century and conclude that everyone (no less) suffered adolescence like a disease, for they will hardly be able to lay hands on a novel which does not describe the condition. What then? For Martha was tormented, and there was no escaping it.

Perhaps, she thought (retreating into the sour humour that was her refuge at such moments), one should simply take the years from, let us say, fourteen to twenty as read, until those happier times arrive when adolescents may, and with a perfectly clear conscience, again enjoy themselves? How lucky, she thought, those coming novelists, who would be able to write cheerfully, and without the feeling that they were evading a problem: "Martha went to school in the usual way, liked the teachers, was amiable with her parents, and looked forward with confidence to a happy and well-spent life"! But then (and here she suffered a twisting spasm of spite against those cold-minded mentors who so persistently analyzed her state, and in so many volumes), what would they have to write about?

That defensive spite released her, and it was almost with confidence that she again lay back, and began to consider herself. For if she was often resentfully conscious that she was expected to carry a burden that young people of earlier times knew nothing about, then she was no less conscious that she was developing a weapon which would enable her to carry it. She was not only miserable, she could focus a dispassionate eye on that misery. This detached observer, felt perhaps as a clear-lit space situated just behind the forehead, was the gift of the Cohen boys at the station, who had been lending her books for the last two years. Joss Cohen tended towards economics and sociology, which she read without feeling personally implicated. Solly Cohen was in love (there is no other word for it) with psychology; he passionately defended everything to do with it, even when his heroes contradicted each other. And from these books Martha had gained a clear picture of herself, from the outside. She was adolescent, and therefore bound to be unhappy; British, and therefore uneasy and defensive; in the fourth decade of the twentieth century, and therefore inescapably beset with problems of race and class; female, and obliged to repudiate the shackled women of the past. She was tormented with guilt and responsibility and self-consciousness; and she did not regret the torment, though there were moments when she saw quite clearly that in making her see herself thus the Cohen boys took a malicious delight which was only too natural. There were moments, in fact, when she hated them.

But what they perhaps had not foreseen was that this sternly objective picture of herself merely made her think, no doubt unreasonably, Well, if all this has been said, why do I have to go through with it? If we *know* it, why do we have to go through the painful business of living it? She felt, though dimly, that now it was time to move on to something new, the act of giving names to things should be enough.

Besides, the experts themselves seemed to be in doubt as to how she should see herself. There was the group which stated that her life was already determined when she still crouched sightless in the womb of Mrs. Quest. She grew through phases of fish and lizard and monkey, rocked in the waters of ancient seas, her ears lulled by the rhythm of the tides. But these tides, the pulsing blood of Mrs. Quest, sang no uncertain messages to Martha, but songs of anger, or love, or fear or resentment, which sank into the passive brain of the infant, like a doom.

Then there were those who said it was the birth itself which set Martha on a fated road. It was during the long night of terror, the night of the difficult birth, when the womb of Mrs. Quest convulsed and fought to expel its burden through the unwilling gates of bone (for Mrs. Quest was rather old to bear a first child), it was during that birth, from which Martha emerged shocked and weary, her face temporarily scarred purple from the forceps, that her character and therefore her life were determined for her.

And what of the numerous sects who agreed on only one thing, that it was the first five years of life which laid an unalterable basis for everything that followed? During those years (though she could not remember them), events had occurred which had marked her fatally forever. For the feeling of fate, of doom, was the one message they all had in common. Martha, in violent opposition to her parents, was continually being informed that their influence on her was unalterable, and that it was much too late to change herself. She had reached the point where she could not read one of these books without feeling as exhausted as if she had just concluded one of her arguments with her mother. When a native bearer came hastening over the veld with yet another parcel of books from the Cohen boys, she felt angry at the mere sight of them, and had to fight against a tired reluctance before she could bring herself to read them. There were, at this very moment, half a dozen books lying neglected in her bedroom, for she knew quite well that if she read them she would only be in possession of yet more information about herself, and with even less idea of how to use it.

But if to read their books made her unhappy, those occasions when she could visit them at the store were the happiest of her life. Talking to them exhilarated her, everything seemed easy. She walked over to the kaffir store when her parents made the trip into the station; sometimes she got a lift from a passing car. Sometimes, though secretly, since this was forbidden, she rode in on her bicycle. But there was always an uneasiness about this friendship, because of Mrs. Quest; only last week, she had challenged Martha. Being what she was, she could not say outright, "I don't want you to know Jewish shopkeepers." She launched into a tirade about how Jews and Greeks ex-

30

ploited the natives worse than anyone, and ended by saying that she did not know what to do with Martha, who seemed bent on behaving so as to make her mother as unhappy as possible. And for the first time that Martha could remember, she wept; and though her words were dishonest, her emotion was not. Martha had been deeply disturbed by those tears.

Yesterday, Martha had been on the point of getting out her bicycle in order to ride in to the station, so badly did she need to see the Cohen boys, when the thought of another scene with her mother checked her. Guiltily, she left the bicycle where it was. And now, although she wanted more than anything else to tell them about her silly and exaggerated behaviour in front of Mrs. Van Rensberg, so that they might laugh good-naturedly at it, and restore it to proportion, she could not make the effort to rise from under the big tree, let alone get out the bicycle and go secretly into the station, hoping she would not be missed. And so she remained under the tree, whose roots were hard under her back, like a second spine, and looked up through the leaves to the sky, which shone in a bronze clamour of light. She ripped the fleshy leaves between her fingers, and thought again of her mother and Mrs. Van Rensberg. She would *not* be like Mrs. Van Rensberg, a fat and earthy housekeeping woman; she would *not* be bitter and nagging and dissatisfied, like her mother. But then, who was she to be like? Her mind turned towards the heroines she had been offered, and discarded them. There seemed to be a gap between herself and the past, and so her thoughts swam in a mazed and unfed way through her mind, and she sat up, rubbing her stiffened back, and looked down the aisles of stunted trees, over a wash of pink feathery grass, to the red clods of a field which was invisible from the house.

There moved a team of oxen, a plough, a native driver with his long whip, and at the head of the team a small black child, naked except for a loincloth, tugging at the strings which passed through the nostrils of the leaders of the team. The driver she did not like—he was a harsh and violent man who used that whip with too much zest; but the pity she refused herself flooded out and surrounded the black child like a protective blanket. And again her mind swam and shook, like clearing water, and now, instead of one black child, she saw a multitude, and so lapsed easily into her familiar daydream. She looked away over the ploughed land, across the veld to the Dumfries Hills, and refashioned that unused country to the scale of her imagination. There arose, glimmering whitely over the harsh scrub and the stunted trees, a noble city, set foursquare and colonnaded along its falling, flower-bordered terraces. There were splashing fountains, and the sound of flutes; and its citizens moved, grave and beautiful, black and white and brown together; and these groups of elders paused, and smiled with pleasure at the sight of the children—the blue-eyed, fair-skinned children of the North playing hand in hand with the bronze-skinned, dark-eyed children of the South. Yes, they smiled and approved these many-fathered children, running and playing among the flowers and the terraces, through the white pillars and tall trees of this fabulous and ancient city . . .

ALLEN GINSBERG

"A Supermarket in California"

The American Allen Ginsberg (b. 1926–1997) was the best-known poet writing in English to appear after 1945. He was the voice of the Beat Generation, the group of writers and artists who dropped out of the "rat-race" during Truman's and Eisenhower's presidencies (1945–1961). The "beats" sought alternative styles of living through drugs, drink, casual sex, Buddhism, jazz, long car trips, and identification with society's "beaten-down" fringes. Bursting on the world like a bombshell, Ginsberg's poem *Howl* (1956) glorified and at the same time lamented the "destruction by madness" of his fellow "beats" at the hands of capitalist America. *Howl* became the subject of an obscenity trial, though found not to be obscene. The furor caused it to become a bestseller and made Ginsberg a celebrity. In the 1960s he cemented his place in the counterculture when he wrote poems protesting the Vietnam War ("Pentagon Exorcism," 1967) and the arms race ("War Profit Litany," 1967).

Critics tend to read Ginsberg's poetry as sections of an ongoing autobiography. Thus two key events in the Ginsberg saga are the death of his mother, Naomi (1894–1956), in a mental ward, and his mystical visions of the poet William Blake (1757–1827), which he experienced in 1948–1949. His mother's death led him to write *Kaddish* (1958–1960), based on the Jewish prayer for the dead but cleansed of its religious affirmations; it is, except for *Howl,* his most successful work. The Blakean visions caused him to organize his poetry around them for about fifteen years. Also influencing Ginsberg's poetry was Whitman (see "When Lilacs Last in the Dooryard Bloom'd"), whose democratic spirit and bohemianism seemed to anticipate the Beat Generation.

Reading the Selection

The theme of "A Supermarket in California" (1955) is the contrast between Whitman's nineteenth-century and Ginsberg's twentieth-century America. As if in a dream, Ginsberg moves through a supermarket ("Aisles full of husbands! Wives in the avocados, babies in the tomatoes!") checking out the produce and fantasizing about Whitman shopping too: "I saw you . . . childless, lonely old grubber, poking among the meats in the refrigerator and eyeing the grocery boys." Ginsberg, homosexual and lonely, shares Whitman's marginal social status. He also stresses the poet's disquieting role in society, when he imagines that he and Whitman are followed by the store detective. The poem ends with a question (paraphrased here): What America did you leave behind when you died, Walt Whitman?

Typical of Ginsberg's works, this poem seems to express his artistic freedom and love of whimsy, relying, he says, on his own "neural" (nerve) and writing impulses rather than trying to fill in the pattern of a preexisting plan. Despite its spontaneous feel, however, this poem is carefully worked out and is firmly rooted in literary tradition. It does not unfold logically or tell a story but depends for its effect on the accumulation of parallel words and sounds, in the repetition of "what" and "I" and in the refrain of words beginning with "w." This constitutes a blending of the devices of accumulation and parallelism, used by Whitman, developed in Hebrew poetry (see *The Holy Scripture*), and rooted in Egyptian models. Whitman is also the inspiration for the poem's basic unit, the unaccented line; there are twelve lines altogether, each line constituting a single thought.

"García Lorca" refers to the Spanish poet of the same name, 1898–1936, one of whose poems about Whitman was translated by Ginsberg.

——— ⁂ ———

What thoughts I have of you tonight, Walt Whitman, for I walked down the sidestreets under the trees with a headache self-conscious looking at the full moon.

In my hungry fatigue, and shopping for images, I went into the neon fruit supermarket, dreaming of your enumerations!

1

What peaches and what penumbras! Whole families shopping at night! Aisles full of husbands! Wives in the avocados, babies in the tomatoes—and you García Lorca, what were you doing down by the watermelons?

I saw you, Walt Whitman, childless, lonely old grubber, poking among the meats in the refrigerator and eyeing the grocery boys.

I heard you asking questions of each: Who killed the pork chops? What price bananas? Are you my Angel?

I wandered in and out of the brilliant stacks of cans following you, and followed in my imagination by the store detective.

We strode down the open corridors together in our solitary fancy tasting artichokes, possessing every frozen delicacy, and never passing the cashier.

Where are we going Walt Whitman? The doors close in an hour. Which way does your beard point tonight?

(I touch your book and dream of our odyssey in the supermarket and feel absurd.)

Will we walk all night through solitary streets? The trees add shade to shade, lights out in the houses, we'll both be lonely.

Will we stroll dreaming of the lost America of love past blue automobiles in driveways, home to our silent cottage?

Ah, dear father, graybeard, lonely old courage-teacher, what America did you have when Charon quit poling his ferry and you got out on a smoking bank and stood watching the boat disappear on the black waters of Lethe?

10

ELIE WIESEL

Selection from *Night*

Of all the moral dilemmas raised by World War II, including America's dropping of atomic bombs on nonstrategic cities and both Allied and Axis air attacks on civilian populations, the dominant issue in the postwar world has been the Holocaust—Nazi Germany's master plan. Termed by its leaders the Final Solution, it was intended to eliminate the Jewish people, which involved the murder of six million Jews out of a population of nine million, along with perhaps six million other people deemed undesirable, including gypsies, the handicapped and disabled, and homosexuals. In a sense it was the German people who provided the terrifying vision of the Holocaust. Race paranoia, especially anti-Semitism, or hatred of Jews, was deeply embedded in German culture, fostered by generations of nationalist-minded intellectuals since the dawn of the Romantic era in about 1800. It was only during World War II, as part of a national response to war, that the Nazis provided the means to carry out this colossal crime.

Since World War II, in an effort to come to terms with these senseless killings, a vast Holocaust literature has emerged. Novels, short stories, plays, essays, memoirs, histories, anthropological studies, sociological analyses, and theological treatises, as well as countless films and TV productions, deal in part or in whole with this theme. The Hungarian writer Elie Wiesel (b. 1928), a survivor of a Nazi death camp, has been in the forefront of Holocaust literature. As a writer of international stature, Wiesel has adopted the literary task of keeping the world's attention focused unflinchingly on the Holocaust, lest it be forgotten and history repeat itself.

Wiesel was first interned by the Nazis in 1944 at Auschwitz, Poland, where his mother and youngest sister were killed in gas chambers; his two older sisters were taken elsewhere and killed. He and his father were then moved to the camp in Buchenwald, Germany, where his father died from hunger and disease. Wiesel survived to be freed by American troops during the war's final days. After the war, he became part of the homeless refugee population called displaced persons, or "D.P.'s," roaming over Europe, until he settled in Paris to study philosophy and literature. From Paris he traveled to Asia, where he shifted his interest to comparative mysticism, a subject that led him to make the Holocaust his lifelong literary project. He became a U.S. citizen in 1963 and was awarded the Nobel Peace Prize in 1986.

Reading the Selection

Wiesel's novel *Night* (1960) belongs to Holocaust literature, the genre whose central concern is the question of how a beneficent God could have allowed the Final Solution. One of the first and in many ways the most powerful of the Holocaust's accounts, it not only chronicles the atrocities inflicted on the Jews but raises the question of God's apparent indifference to human suffering.

In *Night*, prior to this selection: The time is near the end of World War II, when Russian invaders appeared to have the Germans on the run; the scholarly narrator, living in an isolated village, tells of the disruption of his biblical study. A fellow Jew, fleeing from the Nazis, warns him and the rest of the village about mass killings. The villagers fail to heed this warning, only to fall victim to a last-ditch Nazi effort that results in shipping the entire village to a death camp. In the following selection, the Holocaust's horror is personalized in scenes of humiliation, deprivation, and murder. In the end, the narrator's spirit is crushed, as he questions God's existence.

—※—

The cherished objects we had brought with us thus far were left behind in the train, and with them, at last, our illusions. [1]

Every two yards or so an SS man held his tommy gun trained on us. Hand in hand we followed the crowd.

An SS noncommissioned officer came to meet us, a truncheon in his hand. He gave the order:

"Men to the left! Women to the right!"

Eight words spoken quietly, indifferently, without emotion. Eight short, simple words. Yet that was the moment when I parted from my mother. I had not had time to think, but already I felt the pressure of my father's hand: we were alone. For a part of a second I glimpsed my mother and my sisters moving away to the right. Tzipora held Mother's hand. I saw them disappear into the distance; my mother was stroking my sister's fair hair, as though to protect her, while I walked on with my father and the other men. And I did not know that in that place, at that moment, I was parting from my mother and Tzipora forever. I went on walking. My father held onto my hand. [5]

Behind me, an old man fell to the ground. Near him was an SS man, putting his revolver back in its holster.

My hand shifted on my father's arm. I had one thought not to lose him. Not to be left alone.

The SS officers gave the order:

"Form fives!"

Commotion. At all costs we must keep together. [10]

"Here, kid, how old are you?"

It was one of the prisoners who asked me this. I could not see his face, but his voice was tense and weary.

"I'm not quite fifteen yet."

"No. Eighteen."

"But I'm not," I said. "Fifteen." [15]

"Fool. Listen to what *I* say."

Then he questioned my father, who replied:

"Fifty."

The other grew more furious than ever.

"No, not fifty. Forty. Do you understand? Eighteen and forty." [20]

He disappeared into the night shadows. A second man came up, spitting oaths at us.

"What have you come here for, you sons of bitches? What are you doing here, eh?"

Someone dared to answer him.

"What do you think? Do you suppose we've come here for our own pleasure? Do you think we asked to come?"

A little more, and the man would have killed him. [25]

"You shut your trap, you filthy swine, or I'll squash you right now! You'd have done better to have hanged yourselves where you were than come here. Didn't you know what was in store for you at Auschwitz? Haven't you heard about it? In 1944?"

No, we had not heard. No one had told us. He could not believe his ears. His tone of voice became increasingly brutal.

"Do you see that chimney over there? See it? Do you see those flames? (Yes, we did see the flames.) Over there—that's where you're going to be taken. That's your grave, over there. Haven't you realized it yet? You dumb bastards, don't you understand anything? You're going to be burned. Frizzled away. Turned into ashes."

He was growing hysterical in his fury. We stayed motionless, petrified. Surely it was all a nightmare? An unimaginable nightmare?

I heard murmurs around me. [30]

"We've got to do something. We can't let ourselves be killed. We can't go like beasts to the slaughter. We've got to revolt."

There were a few sturdy young fellows among us. They had knives on them, and they tried to incite the others to throw themselves on the armed guards.

One of the young men cried:

"Let the world learn of the existence of Auschwitz. Let everybody hear about it, while they can still escape...."

But the older ones begged their children not to do anything foolish: [35]

"You must never lose faith, even when the sword hangs over your head. That's the teaching of our sages...."

The wind of revolt died down. We continued our march toward the square. In the middle stood the notorious Dr. Mengele (a typical SS officer: a cruel face, but not devoid of intelligence, and wearing a monocle); a conductor's baton in his hand, he was standing among the other officers. The baton moved unremittingly, sometimes to the right, sometimes to the left.

I was already in front of him:

"How old are you?" he asked, in an attempt at a paternal tone of voice.

"Eighteen." My voice was shaking.

"Are you in good health?"

"Yes."

"What's your occupation?"

Should I say that I was a student?

"Farmer," I heard myself say.

This conversation cannot have lasted more than a few seconds. It had seemed like an eternity to me.

The baton moved to the left. I took half a step forward. I wanted to see first where they were sending my father. If he went to the right, I would go after him.

The baton once again pointed to the left for him too. A weight was lifted from my heart.

We did not yet know which was the better side, right or left; which road led to prison and which to the crematory. But for the moment I was happy; I was near my father. Our procession continued to move slowly forward.

Another prisoner came up to us:

"Satisfied?"

"Yes," someone replied.

"Poor devils, you're going to the crematory."

He seemed to be telling the truth. Not far from us, flames were leaping up from a ditch, gigantic flames. They were burning something. A lorry drew up at the pit and delivered its load—little children. Babies! Yes, I saw it—saw it with my own eyes . . . those children in the flames. (Is it surprising that I could not sleep after that? Sleep had fled from my eyes.)

So this was where we were going. A little farther on was another and larger ditch for adults.

I pinched my face. Was I still alive? Was I awake? I could not believe it. How could it be possible for them to burn people, children, and for the world to keep silent? No, none of this could be true. It was a nightmare. . . . Soon I should wake with a start, my heart pounding, and find myself back in the bedroom of my childhood, among my books. . . .

My father's voice drew me from my thoughts:

"It's a shame . . . a shame that you couldn't have gone with your mother. . . . I saw several boys of your age going with their mothers. . . ."

His voice was terribly sad. I realized that he did not want to see what they were going to do to me. He did not want to see the burning of his only son.

My forehead was bathed in cold sweat. But I told him that I did not believe that they could burn people in our age, that humanity would never tolerate it. . . .

"Humanity? Humanity is not concerned with us. Today anything is allowed. Anything is possible, even these crematories. . . ."

His voice was choking.

"Father," I said, "if that is so, I don't want to wait here. I'm going to run to the electric wire. That would be better than slow agony in the flames."

He did not answer. He was weeping. His body was shaken convulsively. Around us, everyone was weeping. Someone began to recite the Kaddish, the prayer for the dead. I do not know if it has ever happened before, in the long history of the Jews, that people have ever recited the prayer for the dead for themselves.

"*Yitgadal veyitkadach shmé raba.* . . . May His name be blessed and magnified. . . ." whispered my father.

For the first time, I felt revolt rise up in me. Why should I bless His name? The Eternal, Lord of the Universe, the All-Powerful and Terrible, was silent. What had I to thank Him for?

We continued our march. We were gradually drawing closer to the ditch, from which an infernal heat was rising. Still twenty steps to go. If I wanted to bring about my own death, this was the moment. Our line had now only fifteen paces to cover. I bit my lips so that my father would not hear my teeth chattering. Ten steps still. Eight. Seven. We marched slowly on, as though following a hearse at our own funeral. Four steps more. Three steps. There it was now, right in front of us, the pit and its flames. I gathered all that was left of my strength, so that I could break from the ranks and throw myself upon the barbed wire. In the depths of my heart, I bade farewell to my father, to the whole universe; and, in spite of myself, the words formed themselves and issued in a whisper from my lips: *Yitgadal veyitkadach shmé raba.* . . . May His name be blessed and magnified. . . . My heart was bursting. The moment had come. I was face to face with the Angel of Death. . . .

No. Two steps from the pit we were ordered to turn to the left and made to go into a barracks.

I pressed my father's hand. He said:

"Do you remember Madame Schächter, in the train?"

Never shall I forget that night, the first night in camp, which has turned my life into one long night, seven times cursed and seven times sealed. Never shall I forget that smoke. Never shall I forget the little faces of the children, whose bodies I saw turned into wreaths of smoke beneath a silent blue sky.

Never shall I forget those flames which consumed my faith forever.

Never shall I forget that nocturnal silence which deprived me, for all eternity, of the desire to live. Never shall I forget those moments which murdered my God and my soul and turned my dreams to dust. Never shall I forget these things, even if I am condemned to live as long as God Himself. Never.

The barracks we had been made to go into was very long. In the roof were some blue-tinged skylights. The antechamber of Hell must look like this. So many crazed men, so many cries, so much bestial brutality!

There were dozens of prisoners to receive us, truncheons in their hands, striking out anywhere, at anyone, without reasons. Orders:

"Strip! Fast! *Los!* Keep only your belts and shoes in your hands. . . ."

We had to throw our clothes at one end of the barracks. There was already a great heap there. New suits and old, torn coats, rags. For us, this was the true equality, nakedness. Shivering with the cold.

Some SS officers moved about in the room, looking for strong men. If they were so keen on strength, perhaps one should try and pass oneself off as sturdy? My father thought the reverse. It was better not to draw attention to oneself. Our fate would then be the same as the others. (Later, we were to learn that he was right. Those who were selected that day were enlisted in the *Sonder-Kommando*, the unit which worked in the crematories. Bela Katz—son of a big tradesman from our town—had arrived at Birkenau with the first transport, a week before us. When he heard of our arrival, he managed to get word to us that, having been chosen for his strength, he had himself put his father's body into the crematory oven.)

Blows continued to rain down.

"To the barber!"   80

Belt and shoes in hand, I let myself be dragged off to the barbers. They took our hair off with clippers, and shaved off all the hair on our bodies. The same thought buzzed all the time in my head—not to be separated from my father.

Freed from the hands of the barbers, we began to wander in the crowd, meeting friends and acquaintances. These meetings filled us with joy—yes, joy—"Thank God! You're still alive!"

But others were crying. They used all their remaining strength in weeping. Why had they let themselves be brought here? Why couldn't they have died in their beds? Sobs choked their voices.

Suddenly, someone threw his arms round my neck in an embrace: Yechiel, brother of the rabbi of Sighet. He was sobbing bitterly. I thought he was weeping with joy at still being alive.

"Don't cry, Yechiel," I said. "Don't waste your tears. . . ."   85

"Not cry? We're on the threshold of death. . . . Soon we shall have crossed over. . . . Don't you understand? How could I not cry?"

Through the blue-tinged skylights I could see the darkness gradually fading. I had ceased to feel fear. And then I was overcome by an inhuman weariness.

Those absent no longer touched even the surface of our memories. We still spoke of them—"Who knows what may have become of them?"—but we had little concern for their fate. We were incapable of thinking of anything at all. Our senses were blunted; everything was blurred as in a fog. It was no longer possible to grasp anything. The instincts of self-preservation, of self-defense, of pride, had all deserted us. In one ultimate moment of lucidity it seemed to me that we were damned souls wandering in the half-world, souls condemned to wander through space till the generations of man came to an end, seeking their redemption, seeking oblivion—without hope of finding it.

Toward five o'clock in the morning, we were driven out of the barracks. The Kapos beat us once more, but I had ceased to feel any pain from their blows. An icy wind enveloped us. We were naked, our shoes and belts in our hands. The command: "Run!" And we ran. After a few minutes of racing, a new barracks.

A barrel of petrol at the entrance. Disinfection. Every-   90 one was soaked in it. Then a hot shower. At high speed. As we came out from the water, we were driven outside. More running. Another barracks, the store. Very long tables. Mountains of prison clothes. On we ran. As we passed, trousers, tunic, shirt, and socks were thrown to us.

Within a few seconds, we had ceased to be men. If the situation had not been tragic, we should have roared with laughter. Such outfits! Meir Katz, a giant, had a child's trousers, and Stern, a thin little chap, a tunic which completely swamped him. We immediately began the necessary exchanges.

I glanced at my father. How he had changed! His eyes had grown dim. I would have liked to speak to him, but I did not know what to say.

The night was gone. The morning star was shining in the sky. I too had become a completely different person. The student of the Talmud, the child that I was, had been consumed in the flames. There remained only a shape that looked like me. A dark flame had entered into my soul and devoured it.

So much had happened within such a few hours that I had lost all sense of time. When had we left our houses? And the ghetto? And the train? Was it only a week? One night—*one single night?*

How long had we been standing like this in the icy   95 wind? An hour? Simply an hour? Sixty minutes?

Surely it was a dream.

Not far from us there were some prisoners at work. Some were digging holes, others carrying sand. None of them so much as glanced at us. We were so many dried-up trees in the heart of a desert. Behind me, some people were talking. I had not the slightest desire to listen to what they were saying, to know who was talking or what they were talking about. No one dared to raise his voice, though there was no supervisor near us. People whispered. Perhaps it was because of the thick smoke which poisoned the air and took one by the throat. . . .

We were made to go into a new barracks, in the "gypsies' camp." In ranks of five.

"And now stay where you are!"

There was no floor. A roof and four walls. Our feet   100 sank into the mud.

Another spell of waiting began. I went to sleep standing up. I dreamed of a bed, of my mother's caress. And I woke up: I was standing, my feet in the mud. Some people collapsed and lay where they were. Others cried:

"Are you mad? We've been told to stay standing. Do you want to bring trouble on us all?"

As if all the trouble in the world had not descended already upon our heads! Gradually, we all sat down in the mud. But we had to jump up constantly, every time a Kapo came in to see if anybody had a pair of new shoes. If so, they had to be given up to him. It was no use opposing this: blows rained down and in the final reckoning you had lost your shoes anyway.

I had new shoes myself. But as they were coated with a thick layer of mud, no one had noticed them. I thanked God, in an improvised prayer, for having created mud in His infinite and wonderful universe.

Suddenly the silence grew oppressive. An SS officer   105 had come in and, with him, the odor of the Angel of Death. We stared fixedly at his fleshy lips. From the middle of the barracks, he harangued us:

"You're in a concentration camp. At Auschwitz. . . ."

A pause. He observed the effect his words had produced. His face has stayed in my memory to this day. A tall man, about thirty, with crime inscribed upon his brow and in the pupils of his eyes. He looked us over as if we were a pack of leprous dogs hanging onto our lives.

"Remember this," he went on. "Remember it forever. Engrave it into your minds. You are at Auschwitz. And Auschwitz is not a convalescent home. It's a concentration camp. Here, you have got to work. If not, you will go straight to the furnace. To the crematory. Work or the crematory—the choice is in your hands."

We had already lived through so much that night, we thought nothing could frighten us any more. But his clipped words made us tremble. Here the word "furnace" was not a word empty of meaning: it floated on the air, mingling with the smoke. It was perhaps the only word which did have any real meaning here. He left the barracks. Kapos appeared, crying:

"All skilled workers—locksmiths, electricians, watchmakers—one step forward!" 110

The rest of us were made to go to another barracks, a stone one this time. With permission to sit down. A gypsy deportee was in charge of us.

My father was suddenly seized with colic. He got up and went toward the gypsy, asking politely, in German:

"Excuse me, can you tell me where the lavatories are?"

The gypsy looked him up and down slowly, from head to foot. As if he wanted to convince himself that this man addressing him was really a creature of flesh and bone, a living being with a body and a belly. Then, as if he had suddenly woken up from a heavy doze, he dealt my father such a clout that he fell to the ground, crawling back to his place on all fours.

I did not move. What had happened to me? My father 115 had just been struck, before my very eyes, and I had not flickered an eyelid. I had looked on and said nothing. Yesterday, I should have sunk my nails into the criminal's flesh. Had I changed so much, then? So quickly? Now remorse began to gnaw at me. I thought only: I shall never forgive them for that. My father must have guessed my feelings. He whispered in my ear, "It doesn't hurt." His cheek still bore the red mark of the man's hand.

"Everyone outside!"

Ten gypsies had come and joined our supervisor. Whips and truncheons cracked round me. My feet were running without my being aware of it. I tried to hide from the blows behind the others. The spring sunshine.

"Form fives!"

The prisoners whom I had noticed in the morning were working at the side. There was no guard near them, only the shadow of the chimney. . . . Dazed by the sunshine and by my reverie, I felt someone tugging at my sleeve. It was my father. "Come on, my boy."

We marched on. Doors opened and closed again. On 120 we went between the electric wires. At each step, a white placard with a death's head on it stared us in the face. A caption: "Warning. Danger of death." Mockery: was there a single place here where you were not in danger of death?

The gypsies stopped near another barracks. They were replaced by SS, who surrounded us. Revolvers, machine guns, police dogs.

The march had lasted half an hour. Looking around me, I noticed that the barbed wires were behind us. We had left the camp.

It was a beautiful April day. The fragrance of spring was in the air. The sun was setting in the west.

But we had been marching for only a few moments when we saw the barbed wire of another camp. An iron door with this inscription over it:

"Work is liberty!" 125
Auschwitz.

. . .

ALEXANDER SOLZHENITSYN

Selections from *One Day in the Life of Ivan Denisovich*

In 1962, when the Soviet government began to publicize Joseph Stalin's widespread crimes, the writer Alexander Solzhenitsyn (b. 1918) joined those denouncing the late dictator's oppressive regime. But in 1974 he was abruptly deported because his novels were critical of life under communism. A stateless exile, he moved to the United States and continued to write novels; however, in interviews and public lectures he now alternated complaints against the USSR with stinging rebukes of his host country's rampant consumerism, lack of moral courage in blocking the spread of communism, and abdication of its responsibility to be the world's advocate of human rights and personal freedom. Having lost faith in the two most powerful nations on earth, he condemned both as morally decadent and spiritually bankrupt. With the collapse of the communist system, Solzhenitsyn regained faith in Russia, now stripped of its empire, and returned to his beloved homeland in 1994. What role he may have envisioned for himself in a post-communist society seems to have disappeared in a rapidly changing country uncertain about its commitment to democracy and a market economy.

Solzhenitsyn grew up in Rostov-on-Don, a large provincial city in European Russia near the Black Sea. Reared in poverty by his widowed mother, he excelled in school and graduated in mathematics and physics from the local university. At the same time, he finished correspondence courses in Russian and Western history and literature—his lifelong passions. When World War II came, he distinguished himself in battle and rose quickly through the ranks, becoming an artillery officer. Disaster struck just before the war ended: He was arrested and charged with crimes against the state because he had criticized Stalin in letters to a friend. He was sent to a labor camp as a political prisoner. From 1945 to 1953 Solzhenitsyn served time in a number of camps and prisons before being released and exiled to Asiatic Russia, where he taught in a secondary school. In the late 1950s the authorities allowed him to return to European Russia, and he continued to teach.

In 1962, during Premier Nikita Khrushchev's de-Stalinization campaign, when many political prisoners were freed and rehabilitated into Soviet life, Solzhenitsyn's first novel, *One Day in the Life of Ivan Denisovich*, was published with the premier's blessings. This book was perhaps the most influential book to circulate freely in the USSR since the 1917 revolution. Solzhenitsyn quickly followed it with several short stories and two novels—*The Cancer Ward*, based on his experiences as a cancer patient, and *The First Circle*, drawn from his years as a victim of Soviet prisons and state bureaucracy. The latter title, taken from Dante's *Divine Comedy*, reveals Solzhenitsyn's continuing interest in European literature.

With the fall of Khrushchev in 1964 and the rise of the more conservative Leonid Brezhnev, Solzhenitsyn came increasingly under fire from Soviet officials. His works were rejected for publication, and the all-powerful Writers' Union expelled him from membership—a blow that ended his literary career in Russia. Meanwhile, his novels were smuggled out of the USSR and published to great acclaim in the West. In 1970 he received the Nobel Prize for literature. This award infuriated the Soviet establishment, and pressures against him continued to mount until he was forced into exile in 1974.

In terms of style, Solzhenitsyn works in the Realist mode with a strong moral dimension. Considering himself an oppositional force to the existing government, he has made it his task to expose, through literature, the lies and evils of the Soviet system. His novels, plays, and essays tend to reflect his own experiences, such as military service, imprisonment, state-funded research, hospital stays, and classroom teaching. These experiences are then reworked around three central themes: indignation at the exploitation of the weak by the strong; conviction that spiritual values outshine worldly concerns; and faith in human survival against all odds. The moral core of his being springs from his deep Orthodox Christian faith, a quality he shares with the great Dostoevsky (see *Notes from Underground*), the writer whom he most resembles.

Reading the Selections

One Day describes in meticulous detail a twenty-four-hour period in the life of Ivan Denisovich Shukhov, a Russian John Doe who is a political prisoner in a Siberian labor camp. The novel's time frame may be Classical, based as it is on Aristotle's unity of time (see *Poetics*), but the petty horrors of camp life are unmistakable signs of totalitarian regimes in the twentieth century. Solzhenitsyn details with such vividness the most ordinary events that mark the average prisoner's day—for example, getting dressed or competing for small and tasteless morsels of food—that the reader is pulled into the camp setting and quickly identifies with Ivan Denisovich and the rest of the inmates. The novel's theme is a kind of bleak humanism in which the prisoners conspire to stay alive under intolerable conditions. Solzhenitsyn shows them working in teams to complete impossible tasks and outwitting the guards to get an extra morsel of bread or a better pair of shoes.

The first selection describes the start of the day. The prisoners line up before marching to the work site, while the guards, ever mindful that their superiors want to extract the maximum labor with the least threat of an uprising, constantly keep their charges in a state of fear. The second selection depicts life in the barracks after an exhausting day in the freezing cold. For a few precious minutes, the prisoners relax, assert their individuality by breaking a few rules, and speak words of comfort to one another. In the conclusion (not included here), Ivan Denisovich falls asleep, remembering fondly the day's events and counting the days remaining in his sentence.

While the men tramped wordlessly one after another into the corridor, then through the entryway out onto the porch, and the foreman of No. 20, taking his cue from Tyurin, called "All out" in turn, Shukhov had managed to pull his boots over the two layers of foot rags, put his overcoat on over his jerkin, and tie a length of rope tightly around his waist. (If you arrived in a special camp with a leather belt, it was taken away from you—not allowed.)

So he was ready on time, and caught up with the last of his gang as their numbered backs were passing through the door onto the porch. In single file, making no effort to keep up with each other, every man looking bulky because he was muffled up in every piece of clothing he possessed, they trudged across to the midway with not a sound except for the crunch of snow underfoot.

It was still dark, although a greenish light was brightening in the east. A thin, treacherous breeze was creeping in from the same direction.

There is no worse moment than when you turn out for work parade in the morning. In the dark, in the freezing cold, with a hungry belly, and the whole day ahead of you. You lose the power of speech. You haven't the slightest desire to talk to each other.

The junior work assigner was restlessly pacing the midway. "Come on, Tyurin, how long have we got to wait for you? Dragging your feet again, eh?"

Somebody like Shukhov might be afraid of the junior work assigner, but Tyurin wasn't. Wouldn't waste breath on him in that frost. Just tramped ahead without a word. And the whole gang tramped after him: stomp, stomp, crunch, crunch.

Tyurin must have handed over the kilo of fatback, though—because, looking at the other teams, you could see that 104 was in its old position. Some other lot, poorer and more stupid, would be shunted off to Sotsgorodok. It would be murder out there—twenty-seven below, with a mean wind blowing, no shelter, and no hope of a warm!

The foreman needed plenty of fatback—for the PPS, and to keep his own belly purring. He might not get parcels himself, but he never went short. Every man in the gang who did get a parcel gave him a present right away.

It was that or perish.

The senior work assigner was ticking off names on his board.

"One sick, Tyurin, twenty-three on parade?"

The foreman nodded. "Twenty-three."

Who was missing? Panteleyev. Who said he was sick, though?

A whisper went around the gang. Panteleyev, that son of a bitch, had stayed behind in camp again. He wasn't sick at all, the security officer had kept him back. He'd be squealing on somebody again.

Nothing to stop them sending for him later in the day and keeping him for three hours if necessary. Nobody would be there to see or hear.

They could pretend he was in sick bay.

The whole midway was black with prison jackets as the gangs slowly jostled each other toward the checkpoint. Shukhov remembered that he'd meant to freshen up the number on his jerkin, and squeezed through the crowd to the other side of the road. Two or three zeks were lining up for the artist already. Shukhov stood behind them. Those numbers were the plague of a zek's life. A warder could spot him a long way off. One of the guards might make a note of it: And if you didn't get it touched up in time, you were in the hole for not looking after it!

There were three artists in the camp. They painted pictures for the bosses, free, and also took turns painting numbers on work parade. This time it was the old man with the little gray beard. The way his brush moved as he painted a number on a cap made you think of a priest anointing a man's forehead with holy oil. He would paint for a bit and then stop to breathe into his glove. It was a thin knitted glove, and his hand would get too numb to trace the figures.

The artist renewed the Shcha-854 on Shukhov's jerkin. He wasn't far from the search point, so he didn't bother to fasten his jacket but overtook the rest of the gang with his rope belt in his hand. He suddenly spotted a chance of scrounging a butt: one of the gang, Tsezar, was smoking a cigarette instead of his usual pipe. Shukhov didn't ask straight out, though. Just took his stand near Tsezar, half facing him and looking past him.

He was gazing at something in the distance, trying to look uninterested, but seeing the cigarette grow shorter and the red tip creep closer to the holder every time Tsezar took an absentminded drag.

That scavenger Fetyukov was there too, leeching onto Tsezar, standing right in front of him and staring hot-eyed at his mouth.

Shukhov had not a shred of tobacco left, and couldn't see himself getting hold of any before evening. He was on tenterhooks. Right then he seemed to yearn for that butt more than for freedom itself, but he wouldn't lower himself like Fetyukov, wouldn't look at Tsezar's mouth.

Tsezar was a mixture of all nationalities. No knowing whether he was Greek, Jew, or gypsy. He was still young. Used to make films, but they'd put him inside before he finished his first picture. He had a heavy black walrus mustache. They'd have shaved it off, only he was wearing it when they photographed him for the record.

Fetyukov couldn't stand it any longer. "Tsezar Markovich," he drooled. "Save me just one little drag."

His face was twitching with greed.

. . . Tsezar raised his half-closed eyelids and turned his dark eyes on Fetyukov. He'd taken to smoking a pipe to avoid this sort of thing—people barging in, begging for the last drag. He didn't grudge them the tobacco, but he didn't like being interrupted when he was thinking. He smoked to set his mind racing in pursuit of some idea. But the moment he lit a cigarette he saw "Leave a puff for me!" in several pairs of eyes.

. . . He turned to Shukhov and said, "Here you are, Ivan Denisovich."

His thumb eased the glowing butt out of the short amber holder.

That was all Shukhov had been waiting for. He sprang into action and gratefully caught hold of the butt, keeping the other hand underneath for safety. He wasn't offended that Tsezar was too fussy to let him finish the cigarette in the holder. Some mouths are clean, others are dirty, and anyway his horny fingers could hold the glowing tip without getting burned. The great thing was that he'd cut the scavenger Fetyukov out and was now inhaling smoke, with the hot ash beginning to burn his lips. Ah, lovely. The smoke seemed to reach every part of his hungry body, he felt it in his feet as well as in his head.

But no sooner had this blissful feeling pervaded his body than Ivan Denisovich heard a rumble of protest: "They're taking our undershirts off us."

A zek's life was always the same. Shukhov was used to it: relax for a minute and somebody was at your throat.

What was this about undershirts? The camp commandant had issued them himself. No, it couldn't be right.

There were only two gangs ahead waiting to be searched, so everybody in 104 got a good view: the disciplinary officer, Lieutenant Volkovoy, walked over from HQ hut and barked at the warders. They had been frisking the men halfheartedly before Volkovoy appeared, but now they went mad, setting upon the prisoners like wild beasts, with the head warder yelling, "Unbutton your shirts!"

Volkovoy was dreaded not just by the zeks and the warders but, so it was said, by the camp commandant himself. God had marked the scoundrel with a name to suit his wolfish looks. He was lanky, dark, beetle-browed, quick on his feet: he would pop up when you least expected him, shouting, "Why are you all hanging around here?" There was no hiding from him. At one time he'd carried a lash, a plaited leather thing as long as your forearm. They said he thrashed people with it in the camp jail. Or else, when zeks were huddled outside the door during the evening hut search, he would creep up and slash you across the neck with it: "Why aren't you lined up properly, you scum?" The crowd would reel back like an ebbing wave. The whipped man would clutch his burning neck, wipe the blood away, and say nothing: he didn't want a spell in the hole as well.

Just lately he'd stopped carrying his lash for some reason.

In frosty weather, body searches were usually less strict in the morning than in the evening; the prisoner simply undid his jacket and held its skirts away from his body. Prisoners advanced five at a time, and five warders stood ready for them. They slapped the sides of each zek's belted jerkin, and tapped the one permitted pocket on his right knee. They would be wearing gloves themselves, and if they felt something strange they didn't immediately pull it out but lazily asked what it was.

What would you expect to find on a zek in the morning? A knife? They don't carry knives out, they bring them in. Just make sure he hasn't got three kilograms of food on him, to run away with—that's all that matters in the morning. At one time they got so worried about the two hundred grams every zek took with him for dinner that each gang was ordered to make a wooden chest to hold the lot. Why the bastards thought that would do any good was a mystery. They were probably just out to make life more miserable, give the men something extra to worry about. You took a bite and looked hard at your bread before you put it in the chest. But the pieces were still all alike, still just bread, so you couldn't help fretting all the way to work in case somebody switched rations. Men argued with each other and sometimes came to blows. Then one day three men helped themselves to a chest full of bread and escaped from a work site in a truck. The brass came to their senses, had the chests chopped up in the guardhouse, and let everybody carry his own ration again.

Another thing the searchers looked for in the morning: men wearing civilian dress under prison clothes. Never mind that everybody had been stripped of his civilian belongings long ago, and told that he'd get them back the day his sentence ended (a day nobody in that camp had yet seen).

And one other thing—prisoners carrying letters for free workers to smuggle out. Only, if you searched everybody for letters, you'd be messing about till dinnertime.

But Volkovoy only had to bawl out an order and the warders peeled off their gloves, made the prisoners unbelt the jerkins under which they were all hugging the warmth of the hut and unbutton their shirts, and set about feeling for anything hidden underneath contrary to regulations. A zek was allowed two shirts—shirt and undershirt; everything else must come off. That was the order from Volkovoy relayed from rank to rank. The teams that had gone past earlier were the lucky ones. Some of them were already through the gates, but for those left behind, it was "Open up!" All those with too much on underneath must take it off right there in the cold.

. . .

By now he'd pulled his boots off, climbed up on his bunk, taken the fragment of steel out of his mitten, examined it, and made up his mind to look for a good stone next day and hone himself a cobbler's knife—work at it a bit morning and evening and in four days he'd have a great little knife with a sharp, curved blade.

For the time being, the steel had to be hidden, even at night. He could wedge it between his bedboards and one of the crossbars. While the captain wasn't there for the dust to fall in his face, Shukhov turned back his heavy mattress (stuffed with sawdust, not shavings) at the pillow end, and set about hiding the blade.

His neighbors up top—Alyoshka the Baptist and the two Estonian brothers on the next bunk across the gangway—could see him, but Shukhov knew he was safe with them.

Fetyukov passed down the hut, sobbing. He was bent double. His lips were smeared with blood. He must have been beaten up again for licking out bowls. He walked past the whole team without looking at anybody, not trying to hide his tears, climbed onto his bunk, and buried his face in his mattress.

You felt sorry for him, really. He wouldn't see his time out. He didn't know how to look after himself. 45

At that point the captain appeared, looking happy, carrying specially brewed tea in a mess tin. There were two buckets of tea in the hut, if you could call it tea. Warm and tea-colored, all right, but like dishwater. And the bucket made it smell of moldy wood pulp. Tea for the common working man, that was. Buynovsky must have gotten a handful of real tea from Tsezar, popped it in the mess tin, and fetched hot water from the boiler. He settled down at his nightstand, mighty pleased with himself.

"Nearly scalded my fingers under the tap," he said, showing off.

Down below there, Tsezar unfolded a sheet of paper and laid things out on it. Shukhov put his mattress back in place, so he wouldn't see and get upset. But yet again they couldn't manage without him. Tsezar rose to his full height in the gangway, so that his eyes were on a level with Shukhov's, and winked: "Denisovich! Lend us your ten-day gadget."

The little folding knife, he meant. Shukhov had one hidden in his bed. Smaller than your finger crooked at the middle knuckle, but the devil would cut fatback five fingers thick. Shukhov had made a beautiful job of that knife and kept it well honed.

He felt for the knife, drew it out, and handed it over. 50 Tsezar gave him a nod and vanished again.

The knife was another earner. Because you could land in the hole (ten days!) for keeping it. Only somebody with no conscience at all would say lend us your knife so we can cut our sausage, and don't think you're getting any.

Tsezar had put himself in debt to Shukhov again.

Now that he'd dealt with the bread and the knives, Shukhov fished out his pouch. He took from it a pinch exactly as big as that he had borrowed and held it out across the gangway to the Estonian, with a thank-you.

The Estonian's lips straightened into a smile of sorts, he muttered something to his brother, and they rolled a separate cigarette to sample Shukhov's tobacco.

Go ahead and try it, it's no worse than yours! 55 Shukhov would have tried it himself, but the clock in his guts said it was very close to roll call. Just the time for the warders to come prowling round the huts. If he wanted a smoke he'd have to go out in the corridor quick, and he fancied it was a bit warmer up on his top bunk. It wasn't at all warm in the hut, and the ceiling was still patterned with hoarfrost. You'd get pretty chilly at night, but for the time being, it was just about bearable.

All his little jobs done, Shukhov began breaking bits from his two hundred grams. He couldn't help listening to the captain and Tsezar drinking tea and talking down below.

"Help yourself, Captain, don't be shy! Have some of this smoked fish. Have some sausage."

"Thank you, I will."

"Butter yourself a piece of this loaf! It's a real Moscow baton!"

"Dear-oh-dear-oh-dear, I just can't believe that some- 60 where or other batons are still being baked. This sudden abundance reminds me of something that once happened

to me. It was at Sevastopol, before the Yalta Conference. The town was absolutely starving and we had to show an American admiral around. So they set up a shop specially, chockful of foodstuff, but it wasn't to be opened until they saw us half a block away, so that the locals wouldn't have time to crowd the place out. Even so, the shop was half full one minute after it opened. And you couldn't ask for the wrong thing. 'Look, butter!' people were shouting, 'Real butter! And white bread!'"

Two hundred harsh voices were raising a din in their half of the hut, but Shukhov still thought he could make out the clanging on the rail. Nobody else heard, though. Shukhov also noticed that the warder they called Snub Nose—a short, red-faced young man—had appeared in the hut. He was holding a piece of paper, and this and his whole manner showed that he hadn't come to catch people smoking or drive them outside for roll call, but was looking for somebody in particular.

Snub Nose consulted his piece of paper and asked: "Where's 104?"

"Here," they answered. The Estonians concealed their cigarettes and waved the smoke away.

"Where's the foreman?"

"What do you want?" Tyurin spoke from his bed, 65 swinging his legs over the edge so that his feet barely touched the floor.

"Have the men who were told to submit written explanations got them ready?"

"They're doing it," Tyurin said confidently.

"They should have been in by now."

"Some of my men are more or less illiterate, it's hard work for them." (Tsezar and the captain, he was talking about. He was sharp, Tyurin. Never stuck for an answer.) "We've got no pens, or ink."

"Well, you should have."

"They keep confiscating it." 70

"Watch it, foreman, just mind what you're saying, or I'll have you in the cell block," Snub Nose promised, mildly. "The explanatory notes will be in the warders' barracks before work parade in the morning! And you will report that all prohibited articles have been handed in to the personal-property store. Understood?"

"Understood."

("The captain's in the clear!" Shukhov thought. The captain himself was purring over his sausage and didn't hear a thing.)

"Now, then," said the warder. "Shcha-301—is he in 75 your gang?"

"I'll have to look at the list," the foreman said, pretending ignorance. "How can anybody be expected to remember these blasted numbers?" (If he could drag it out till roll call, he might save Buynovsky at least for the night.)

"Buynovsky—is he here?"

"Eh? That's me!" the captain piped up from his hiding place under Shukhov's top bunk.

The quick louse is always first on the comb.

"You, is it? Right then, Shcha-301. Get ready." 80

"To go where?"

"You know where."

The captain only sighed and groaned. Taking a squadron of torpedo boats out into a stormy sea in the pitch dark must have been easier for him than leaving his friends' company for the icy cell block.

"How many days?" he asked in a faint voice.

"Ten. Come along now, hurry it up!"   85

Just then the orderlies began yelling, "Roll call! Everybody out for roll call!"

The warder sent to call the roll must be in the hut already.

The captain looked back, wondering whether to take his overcoat. If he did, though, they'd whip it off him and leave him just his jerkin. So better go as he was. The cap-

tain had hoped for a while that Volkovoy would forget—but Volkovoy never forgot or forgave—and had made no preparations, hadn't even hidden himself a bit of tobacco in his jerkin. No good holding it in his hand—they'd take it off him the moment they frisked him.

All the same, Tsezar slipped him a couple of cigarettes while he was putting his cap on.

"Well, so long, chums," the captain said with a miser-   90
able look, nodding to his teammates, and followed the warder out of the hut.

Several voices called after him, "Keep smiling," "Don't let them get you down"—but there was nothing much you could say.

JAMES BALDWIN

"Stranger in the Village"

The writer James Baldwin (1926–1987) aspired to be the voice of his generation of African Americans, the ones who came of age in 1954 when the U.S. Supreme Court made intergation the law of the land. To this end, he produced a body of works including five novels (*Another Country*, 1962), two plays (*Blues for Mr. Charlie*, 1964), and five books of essays (*Nobody Knows My Name*, 1961). These made him a major figure in world letters and brought him prizes, honorary degrees, and France's Legion of Honor—a rare honor for a non-Frenchman. But his dream of becoming a leading advocate of his race eluded him because religious groups within the black community were offended by his homosexuality, which he did not bother to conceal (his 1956 novel, *Giovanni's Room*, is a pioneering study of gay life). Baldwin's reception in black America can be illustrated by two contrasting events in 1963: He was among the black leaders who met with Robert Kennedy, the federal attorney general, on May 24, to discuss racial matters; and he was excluded from the roster of black speakers who addressed the March on Washington, D.C., in August. Throughout his career, Baldwin was forced to labor under the double burden of being black *and* homosexual.

Born in Harlem, the illegitimate son of a cleaning woman, James Baldwin knew what it was like to be black and poor. Times were not easy, living with his stepfather, David Baldwin, a laborer and storefront preacher; movies and secular music were strictly forbidden, and education was suspect as a delusion devised by whites to confuse black men. After high school, James Baldwin's life turned more sour as he encountered racism in menial jobs, sparking a "rage in the blood," a fever that he thought finally infected all black people. At the same time, he was struggling with his sexual identity. He began to think of himself as a writer, publishing a few reviews and essays; but feeling alienated from America, he exiled himself to Paris (1948–1958), the traditional haven for American expatriates, black and white, straight and gay. In Paris, Baldwin flourished, learning to accept his homosexuality and launching his writing career with the novel *Go Tell It on the Mountain* (1953) and the essay collection *Notes of a Native Son* (1955)—books that united autobiographical material with social issues.

Reading the Selection

Although Baldwin found freedom in Paris as an expatriate, he still struggled with private demons: depression, poverty, racial identity, and most telling, the manuscript of his unfinished novel *Go Tell It on the Mountain*. Thus, partly for a change of scenery and partly for reasons of economy, Baldwin spent the winter of 1951–1952 in the Swiss village of Loèche-les-Bains, staying at a friend's family chalet. "Stranger in the Village" reflects Baldwin's evolving consciousness in this idyllic setting, as he confronted his past and pondered his future.

In this essay, Loèche-les-Bains, with its unintentionally racist inhabitants ("the children shout *Neger! Neger!* as I walk along the streets"), becomes a complex metaphor for Europe, and Baldwin symbolizes the black race. His sense of alienation in this setting makes him long for home in America. He concludes with the thought—which became a guiding ideal in his later years—that America is different from Europe because white and black contact at home has changed both races forever. "No road whatever will lead Americans back to the simplicity of this European village where white men still have the luxury of looking on me as a stranger." For Baldwin, "this world is white no longer, and it will never be white again."

"Stranger in the Village" was first published by *Harper's Magazine* in October 1953, and in 1962 Baldwin assisted and appeared in a Swiss television movie based on this essay.

—⁓—

From all available evidence no black man had ever set foot in this tiny Swiss village before I came. I was told before arriving that I would probably be a "sight" for the village; I took this to mean that people of my complexion were rarely seen in Switzerland, and also that city people are always something of a "sight" outside of the city. It did not occur to me—possibly because I am an American—that there could be people anywhere who had never seen a Negro.

It is a fact that cannot be explained on the basis of the inaccessibility of the village. The village is very high, but it is only four hours from Milan and three hours from Lausanne. It is true that it is virtually unknown. Few people making plans for a holiday would elect to come here. On the other hand, the villagers are able, presumably, to come and go as they please—which they do: to another town at the foot of the mountain, with a population of approximately five thousand, the nearest place to see a movie or go to the bank. In the village there is no movie house, no bank, no library, no theater; very few radios, one jeep, one station wagon; and, at the moment, one typewriter, mine, an invention which the woman next door to me here had never seen. There are about six hundred people living here, all Catholic—I conclude this from the fact that the Catholic church is open all year round, whereas the Protestant chapel, set off on a hill a little removed from the village, is open only in the summertime when the tourists arrive. There are four or five hotels, all closed now, and four or five *bistros*, of which, however, only two do any business during the winter. These two do not do a great deal, for life in the village seems to end around nine or ten o'clock. There are a few stores, butcher, baker, *épicerie*, a hardware store, and a moneychanger—who cannot change travelers' checks, but must send them down to the bank, an operation which takes two or three days. There is something called the *Ballet Haus*, closed in the winter and used for God knows what, certainly not ballet, during the summer. There seems to be only one schoolhouse in the village, and this for the quite young children; I suppose this to mean that their older brothers and sisters at some point descend from these mountains in order to complete their education—possibly, again, to the town just below. The landscape is absolutely forbidding, mountains towering on all four sides, ice and snow as far as the eye can

reach. In this white wilderness, men and women and children move all day, carrying washing, wood, buckets of milk or water, sometimes skiing on Sunday afternoons. All week long boys and young men are to be seen shoveling snow off the rooftops, or dragging wood down from the forest in sleds.

The village's only real attraction, which explains the tourist season, is the hot spring water. A disquietingly high proportion of these tourists are cripples, or semi-cripples, who come year after year—from other parts of Switzerland, usually—to take the waters. This lends the village, at the height of the season, a rather terrifying air of sanctity, as though it were a lesser Lourdes. There is often something beautiful, there is always something awful, in the spectacle of a person who has lost one of his faculties, a faculty he never questioned until it was gone, and who struggles to recover it. Yet people remain people, on crutches or indeed on deathbeds; and wherever I passed, the first summer I was here, among the native villagers or among the lame, a wind passed with me—of astonishment, curiosity, amusement, and outrage. That first summer I stayed two weeks and never intended to return. But I did return in the winter, to work; the village offers, obviously, no distractions whatever and has the further advantage of being extremely cheap. Now it is winter again, a year later, and I am here again. Everyone in the village knows my name, though they scarcely ever use it, knows that I come from America—though, this, apparently, they will never really believe: black men come from Africa—and everyone knows that I am the friend of the son of a woman who was born here, and that I am staying in their chalet. But I remain as much a stranger today as I was the first day I arrived, and the children shout *Neger! Neger!* as I walk along the streets.

It must be admitted that in the beginning I was far too shocked to have any real reaction. In so far as I reacted at all, I reacted by trying to be pleasant—it being a great part of the American Negro's education (long before he goes to school) that he must make people "like" him. This smile-and-the-world-smiles-with-you routine worked about as well in this situation as it had in the situation for which it was designed, which is to say that it did not work at all. No one, after all, can be liked whose human weight and complexity cannot be, or has not been, admitted. My smile was simply another unheard-of phenomenon which allowed them to see my teeth—they did not, really, see my smile and I began to think that, should I take to snarling, no one would notice any difference. All of the physical characteristics of the Negro which had caused me, in America, a very different and almost forgotten pain were nothing less than miraculous—or infernal—in the eyes of the village people. Some thought my hair was the color of tar, that it had the texture of wire, or the texture of cotton. It was jocularly suggested that I might let it all grow long and make myself a winter coat. If I sat in the sun for more than five minutes some daring creature was certain to come along and gingerly put his fingers on my hair, as though he were afraid of an electric shock, or put out his hand on my hand, astonished that the color did not rub off. In all of this, in which it must be conceded there was the charm of genuine wonder and in which there was certainly no element of intentional unkindness, there was yet no suggestion that I was human: I was simply a living wonder.

I knew that they did not mean to be unkind, and I know it now; it is necessary, nevertheless, for me to repeat this to myself each time that I walk out of the chalet. The children who shout *Neger!* have no way of knowing the echoes this sound raises in me. They are brimming with good humor and the more daring swell with pride when I stop to speak with them. Just the same, there are days when I cannot pause and smile, when I have no heart to play with then; when, indeed, I mutter sourly to myself, exactly as I muttered on the streets of a city these children have never seen, when I was no bigger than these children are now: *Your mother was a nigger.* Joyce is right about history being a nightmare—but it may be the nightmare from which no one can awaken. People are trapped in history and history is trapped in them.

There is a custom in the village—I am told it is repeated in many villages—of "buying" African natives for the purpose of converting them to Christianity. There stands in the church all year round a small box with a slot for money, decorated with a black figurine, and into this box the villagers drop their francs. During the *carnaval* which precedes Lent, two village children have their faces blackened—out of which bloodless darkness their blue eyes shine like ice—and fantastic horsehair wigs are placed on their blond heads; thus disguised, they solicit among the villagers for money for the missionaries in Africa. Between the box in the church and the blackened children, the village "bought" last year six or eight African natives. This was reported to me with pride by the wife of one of the *bistro* owners and I was careful to express astonishment and pleasure at the solicitude shown by the village for the souls of black folk. The *bistro* owner's wife beamed with pleasure far more genuine than my own and seemed to feel that I might now breathe more easily concerning the souls of at least six of my kinsmen.

I tried not to think of these so lately baptized kinsmen, of the price paid for them, or the peculiar price they themselves would pay, and said nothing about my father, who having taken his own conversion too literally never, at bottom, forgave the white world (which he described as

heathen) for having saddled him with a Christ in whom, to judge at least from their treatment of him, they themselves no longer believed. I thought of white men arriving for the first time in an African village, strangers there, as I am a stranger here, and tried to imagine the astounded populace touching their hair and marveling at the color of their skin. But there is a great difference between being the first white man to be seen by Africans and being the first black man to be seen by whites. The white man takes the astonishment as tribute, for he arrives to conquer and to convert the natives, whose inferiority in relation to himself is not even to be questioned; whereas I, without a thought of conquest, find myself among a people whose culture controls me, has even, in a sense, created me, people who have cost me more in anguish and rage than they will ever know, who yet do not even know of my existence. The astonishment with which I might have greeted them, should they have stumbled into my African village a few hundred years ago, might have rejoiced their hearts. But the astonishment with which they greet me today can only poison mine.

And this is so despite everything I may do to feel differently, despite my friendly conversations with the *bistro* owner's wife, despite their three-year-old son who has at last become my friend, despite the *saluts* and *bonsoirs* which I exchange with people as I walk, despite the fact that I know that no individual can be taken to task for what history is doing, or has done. I say that the culture of these people controls me—but they can scarcely be held responsible for European culture. America comes out of Europe, but these people have never seen America, nor have most of them seen more of Europe than the hamlet at the foot of their mountain. Yet they move with an authority which I shall never have; and they regard me, quite rightly, not as a stranger in their village but as a suspect latecomer, bearing no credentials, to everything they have—however unconsciously—inherited.

For this village, even were it incomparably more remote and incredibly more primitive, is the West, the West onto which I have been so strangely grafted. These people cannot be, from the point of view of power, strangers anywhere in the world; they have made the modern world, in effect, even if they do not know it. The most illiterate among them is related, in a way that I am not, to Dante, Shakespeare, Michelangelo, Aeschylus, Da Vinci, Rembrandt, and Racine; the cathedral at Chartres says something to them which it cannot say to me, as indeed would New York's Empire State Building, should anyone here ever see it; out of their hymns and dances come Beethoven and Bach. Go back a few centuries and they are in their full glory—but I am in Africa, watching the conquerors arrive.

The rage of the disesteemed is personally fruitless, but it is also absolutely inevitable; this rage, so generally discounted, so little understood even among the people whose daily bread it is, is one of the things that makes history. Rage can only with difficulty, and never entirely, be brought under the domination of the intelligence and is therefore not susceptible to any arguments whatever. This is a fact which ordinary representatives of the Herrenvolk, having never felt this rage and being unable to imagine it, quite fail to understand. Also, rage cannot be hidden, it can only be dissembled. This dissembling deludes the thoughtless, and strengthens rage and adds, to rage, contempt. There are, no doubt, as may ways of coping with the resulting complex of tensions as there are black men in the world, but no black man can hope ever to be entirely liberated from this internal warfare—rage, dissembling, and contempt having inevitably accompanied his first realization of the power of white men. What is crucial here is that, since white men represent in the black man's world so heavy a weight, white men have for black men a reality which is far from being reciprocal; and hence all black men have toward all white men an attitude which is designed, really, either to rob the white man of the jewel of his naivete, or else to make it cost him dear.

The black man insists, by whatever means he finds at his disposal, that the white man cease to regard him as an exotic rarity and recognize him as a human being. This is a very charged and difficult moment, for there is a great deal of will power involved in the white man's naivete. Most people are not naturally reflective any more than they are naturally malicious, and the white man prefers to keep the black man at a certain human remove because it is easier for him thus to preserve his simplicity and avoid being called to account for crimes committed by his forefathers, or his neighbors. He is inescapably aware, nevertheless, that he is in a better position in the world than black men are, nor can he quite put to death the suspicion that he is hated by black men therefore. He does not wish to be hated, neither does he wish to change places, and at this point in his uneasiness he can scarcely avoid having recourse to those legends which white men have created about black men, the most usual effect of which is that the white man finds himself enmeshed, so to speak, in his own language which describes hell, as well as the attributes which lead one to hell, as being as black as night.

Every legend, moreover, contains its residuum of truth, and the root function of language is to control the universe by describing it. It is of quite considerable significance that black men remain, in the imagination, and in overwhelming numbers in fact, beyond the disciplines of salvation; and this despite the fact that the West has been "buying" African natives for centuries. There is, I should hazard, an instantaneous necessity to be divorced from this so visibly unsaved stranger, in whose heart, moreover, one cannot guess what dreams of vengeance are being nourished; and, at the same time, there are few things on earth more attractive than the idea of the unspeakable liberty which is allowed the unredeemed. When, beneath the black mask, a human being begins to make himself felt one cannot escape a certain awful wonder as to what kind of human being it is. What one's imagination makes of other people is dictated, of course, by the laws of one's own personality and it is one of the ironies of black-white relations that, by means of what the white man imagines the black man to be, the black man is enabled to know who the white man is.

I have said, for example, that I am as much a stranger in this village today as I was the first summer I arrived, but this is not quite true. The villagers wonder less about the texture of my hair than they did then, and wonder rather more about me. And the fact that their wonder now exists on another level is reflected in their attitudes and in their eyes. There are the children who make those delightful, hilarious, sometimes astonishingly grave overtures of friendship in the unpredictable fashion of children; other children, having been taught that the devil is a black man, scream in genuine anguish as I approach. Some of the older women never pass without a friendly greeting, never pass, indeed, if it seems that they will be able to engage me in conversation; other women look down or look away or rather contemptuously smirk. Some of the men drink with me and suggest that I learn how to ski—partly, I gather, because they cannot imagine what I would look like on skis—and want to know if I am married, and ask questions about my *metier*. But some of the men have accused *le sale negre*—behind my back—of stealing wood and there is already in the eyes of some of them that peculiar, intent, paranoiac malevolence which one sometimes surprises in the eyes of American white men when, out walking with their Sunday girl, they see a Negro male approach.

There is a dreadful abyss between the streets of this village and the streets of the city in which I was born, between the children who shout *Neger* today and those who shouted *Nigger* yesterday—the abyss is experience, the American experience. The syllable hurled behind me today expresses, above all, wonder: I am a stranger here. But I am not a stranger in America and the same syllable riding on the American air expresses the war my presence has occasioned in the American soul.

For this village brings home to me this fact: that there was a day, and not really a very distant day, when Americans were scarcely Americans at all but discontented Europeans, facing a great unconquered continent and strolling, say, into a marketplace and seeing black men for the first time. The shock this spectacle afforded is suggested, surely, by the promptness with which they decided that these black men were not really men but cattle. It is true that the necessity on the part of the settlers of the New World of reconciling their moral assumptions with the fact—and the necessity—of slavery enhanced immensely the charm of this idea, and it is also true that the idea expresses, with a truly American bluntness, the attitude which to varying extents all masters have had toward all slaves.

But between all former slaves and slave-owners and the drama which begins for Americans over three hundred years ago at Jamestown, there are at least two differences to be observed. The American Negro slave could not suppose, for one thing, as slaves in past epochs had supposed and often done, that he would ever be able to wrest the power from his master's hands. This was a supposition which the modern era, which was to bring about such vast changes in the aims and dimensions of power, put to death; it only begins, in unprecedented fashion, and with dreadful implications, to be resurrected today. But even had this supposition persisted with undiminished force, the American Negro slave could not have used it to lend his condition dignity, for the reason that this supposition rests on another: that the slave in exile yet remains related

15

to his past, has some means—if only in memory—of revering and sustaining the forms of his former life, is able, in short, to maintain his identity.

This was not the case with the American Negro slave. He is unique among the black men of the world in that his past was taken from him, almost literally, at one blow. One wonders what on earth the first slave found to say to the first dark child he bore. I am told that there are Haitians able to trace their ancestry back to African kings, but any American Negro wishing to go back so far will find his journey through time abruptly arrested by the signature on the bill of sale which served as the entrance paper for his ancestor. At the time—to say nothing of the circumstances—of the enslavement of the captive black man who was to become the American Negro, there was not the remotest possibility that he would ever take power from his master's hands. There was no reason to suppose that his situation would ever change, nor was there, shortly, anything to indicate that his situation had ever been different. It was his necessity, in the words of E. Franklin Frazier, to find a "motive for living under American culture or die." The identity of the American Negro comes out of this extreme situation, and the evolution of this identity was a source of the most intolerable anxiety in the minds and lives of his masters.

For the history of the American Negro is unique also in this: that the question of his humanity, and of his rights therefore as a human being, became a burning one for several generations of Americans, so burning a question that it ultimately became one of those used to divide the nation. It is out of this argument that the venom of the epithet *Nigger!* is derived. It is an argument which Europe has never had, and hence Europe quite sincerely fails to understand how or why the argument arose in the first place, why its effects are so frequently disastrous and always so unpredictable, why it refuses until today to be entirely settled. Europe's black possessions remained—and do remain—in Europe's colonies, at which remove they represented no threat whatever to European identity. If they posed any problem at all for the European conscience, it was a problem which remained comfortingly abstract: in effect, the black man, *as a man*, did not exist for Europe. But in America, even as a slave, he was an inescapable part of the general social fabric and no American could escape having an attitude toward him. Americans attempt until today to make an abstraction of the Negro, but the very nature of these abstractions reveals the tremendous effects the presence of the Negro has had on the American character.

When one considers the history of the Negro in America it is of the greatest importance to recognize that the moral beliefs of a person, or a people, are never really as tenuous as life—which is not moral—very often causes them to appear; these create for them a frame of reference and a necessary hope, the hope being that when life has done its worst they will be enabled to rise above themselves and to triumph over life. Life would scarcely be bearable if this hope did not exist. Again, even when the worst has been said, to betray a belief is not by any means to have put oneself beyond its power; the betrayal of a be-

lief is not the same thing as ceasing to believe. If this were not so there would be no moral standards in the world at all. Yet one must also recognize that morality is based on ideas and that all ideas are dangerous—dangerous because ideas can only lead to action and where the action leads no man can say. And dangerous in this respect: that confronted with the impossibility of remaining faithful to one's beliefs, and the equal impossibility of becoming free of them, one can be driven to the most inhuman excesses. The ideas on which American beliefs are based are not, though Americans often seem to think so, ideas which originated in America. They came out of Europe. And the establishment of democracy on the American continent was scarcely as radical a break with the past as was the necessity, which Americans faced, of broadening this concept to include black men.

This was, literally, a hard necessity. It was impossible, [20] for one thing, for Americans to abandon their beliefs, not only because these beliefs alone seemed able to justify the sacrifices they had endured and the blood that they had spilled, but also because these beliefs afforded them their only bulwark against a moral chaos as absolute as the physical chaos of the continent it was their destiny to conquer. But in the situation in which Americans found themselves, these beliefs threatened an idea which, whether or not one likes to think so, is the very warp and woof of the heritage of the West, the idea of white supremacy.

Americans have made themselves notorious by the shrillness and the brutality with which they have insisted on this idea, but they did not invent it; and it has escaped the world's notice that those very excesses of which Americans have been guilty imply a certain, unprecedented uneasiness over the idea's life and power, if not, indeed, the idea's validity. The idea of white supremacy rests simply on the fact that white men are the creators of civilization (the present civilization, which is the only one that matters; all previous civilizations are simply "contributions" to our own) and are therefore civilization's guardians and defenders. Thus it was impossible for Americans to accept the black man as one of themselves, for to do so was to jeopardize their status as white men. But not so to accept him was to deny his human reality, his human weight and complexity, and the strain of denying the overwhelmingly undeniable forced Americans into rationalizations so fantastic that they approached the pathological.

At the root of the American Negro problem is the necessity of the American white man to find a way of living with the Negro in order to be able to live with himself. And the history of this problem can be reduced to the means used by Americans—lynch law and law, segregation and legal acceptance, terrorization and concession—either to come to terms with this necessity, or to find a way around it, or (most usually) to find a way of doing both these things at once. The resulting spectacle, at once foolish and dreadful, led someone to make the quite accurate observation that "the Negro-in-America is a form of insanity which overtakes white man."

In this long battle, a battle by no means finished, the unforeseeable effects of which will be felt by many future generations, the white man's motive was the protection of his identity; the black man was motivated by the need to establish an identity. And despite the terrorization which the Negro in America endured and endures sporadically until today, despite the cruel and totally inescapable ambivalence of his status in his country, the battle for his identity has long ago been won. He is not a visitor to the West, but a citizen there, an American; as American as the Americans who despise him, the Americans who fear him, the Americans who love him—the Americans who became less than themselves, or rose to be greater than themselves by virtue of the fact that the challenge he represented was inescapable. He is perhaps the only black man in the world whose relationship to white men is more terrible, more subtle, and more meaningful than the relationship of bitter possessed to uncertain possessor. His survival depended, and his development depends, on his ability to turn his peculiar status in the Western world to his own advantage and, it may be, to the very great advantage of that world. It remains for him to fashion out of his experience that which will give him sustenance, and a voice.

The cathedral at Chartres, I have said, says something to the people of this village which it cannot say to me; but it is important to understand that this cathedral says something to me which it cannot say to them. Perhaps they are struck by the power of the spires, the glory of the windows; but they have known God, after all, longer than I have known him, and in a different way, and I am terrified by the slippery bottomless well to be found in the crypt, down which heretics were hurled to death, and by the obscene, inescapable gargoyles jutting out of the stone and seeming to say that God and the devil can never be divorced. I doubt that the villagers think of the devil when they face a cathedral because they have never been identified with the devil. But I must accept the status which myth, if nothing else, gives me in the West before I can hope to change the myth.

Yet, if the American Negro has arrived at his identity by virtue of the absoluteness of his estrangement from his past, American white men still nourish the illusion that there is some means of recovering the European innocence, of returning to a state in which black men do not

exist. This is one of the greatest errors Americans can make. The identity they fought so hard to protect has, by virtue of that battle, undergone a change: Americans are as unlike any other white people in the world as it is possible to be. I do not think, for example, that it is too much to suggest that the American vision of the world—which allows so little reality, generally speaking, for any of the darker forces in human life, which tends until today to paint moral issues in glaring black and white—owes a great deal to the battle waged by Americans to maintain between themselves and black men a human separation which could not be bridged. It is only now beginning to be borne in on us—very faintly, it must be admitted, very slowly, and very much against our will—that this vision of the world is dangerously inaccurate, and perfectly useless. For it protects our moral high-mindedness at the terrible expense of weakening our grasp of reality. People who shut their eyes to reality simply invite their own destruction, and anyone who insists on remaining in a state of innocence long after that innocence is dead turns himself into a monster.

The time has come to realize that the interracial drama acted out on the American continent has not only created a new black man, it has created a new white man, too. No road whatever will lead Americans back to the simplicity of this European village where white men still have the luxury of looking on me as a stranger. I am not, really, a stranger any longer for any American alive. One of the things that distinguishes Americans from other people is that no other people has ever been so deeply involved in the lives of black men, and vice versa. This fact faced, with all its implications, it can be seen that the history of the American Negro problem is not merely shameful, it is also something of an achievement. For even when the worst has been said, it must also be added that the perpetual challenge posed by this problem was always, somehow, perpetually met. It is precisely this black-white experience which may prove of indispensable value to us in the world we face today. This world is white no longer, and it will never be white again.

MARTIN LUTHER KING, JR.
Selection from "Letter from a Birmingham Jail"

From 1862 when President Abraham Lincoln issued the Emancipation Proclamation ending slavery to the historic 1963 March on Washington, D.C., which culminated nearly a decade of civil rights struggle, African Americans have suffered from legal and informal segregation. Barred from the mainstream of American society, they were exploited economically by capitalist forces and denied nearly all of the basic civil rights guaranteed by law and tradition to other groups, such as the waves of immigrants who came to the United States during the nineteenth and early twentieth centuries. Emerging after World War II as the leader of the so-called Free World, the United States entered a business boom (lasting to the early 1970s) that provided many opportunities for its citizens. But until the early 1960s, African Americans remained on the margins, unable to take advantage of the growing economy and shut out of the political process. In 1954 the Supreme Court in *Brown versus Board of Education* overturned the legal policy of "separate but equal" schools for the races and in effect made integration the national policy. Thereafter, African Americans, led by black leaders and often joined by many white supporters, began a series of marches, legal challenges, and political maneuverings that aimed to eliminate racial discrimination and integrate blacks into America's political, social, and economic institutions. The civil rights movement was born. By the early 1960s civil rights for African Americans had become probably the central domestic issue in the United States.

In the mid-1950s the Protestant pastor Martin Luther King, Jr. (1929–1968), stepped forward to become the civil rights movement's most forceful and eloquent voice. The son of a prominent Atlanta preacher, King attended college, seminary, and graduate school before becoming pastor of a church in Montgomery, Alabama. In 1956 he led a successful boycott against the local bus company's segregated seating policy. Within three years the charismatic King, with the backing of southern black churches, was a national figure. During the Kennedy-Johnson era, he emerged as the most powerful African American leader in the nation, indeed in American history. After 1967, he headed a coalition linking the cause of poverty, the Vietnam War, and civil rights. While trying to unite his followers on these issues, he was assassinated in Memphis, Tennessee.

Reading the Selection

King's leadership was rooted in the Judeo-Christian tradition of personal salvation and social justice. Gifted with sound political instincts and a masterful command of the English language, he inspired those around him to hold to the policy of passive resistance as an agent of change, rather than resort to violence. King's tactic proved quite effective, for it won the sympathy of most Americans, white and black, as well as peoples around the world. He based his passive resistance approach on the actions of two men whom he admired—Henry David Thoreau (see *Civil Disobedience*), who defied his state government over what he deemed an immoral law, and Gandhi, the Indian leader who used nonviolent civil disobedience in his drive to free India from British rule.

Jailed in Birmingham for civil disobedience in April 1963, King wrote a letter addressing his critics, in both races, who felt that he either had not suffered enough for his law-breaking or was moving too fast in his efforts to overthrow America's segregated society. To answer the second charge, he compared the "horse and buggy pace" of the civil rights movement with the "jetlike speed" of the nations of Asia and Africa who were racing to free themselves from their imperialist oppressors. He accentuated the reason for his haste in ending segregation by listing many painful examples of racial injustice suffered by African Americans every day.

As to the charge of breaking the law when one opposes segregation, King answered his critics by appealing to the distinction between just and unjust laws. He reasoned that because segregation cannot be squared with the moral law or the law of God, it is an unjust law and thus possesses no power to coerce obedience. This argument was based on the writings of some of the best minds in Judeo-Christian thought, including the Christian thinkers Augustine (see *The City of God*), Thomas Aquinas (see *Summa theologica*), the modern Protestant theologian Paul Tillich, and the modern Jewish theologian Martin Buber.

Later in this "letter," King, rejecting the label of extremist, claims to occupy the middle ground in the black community, between the forces of complacency and the forces of bitterness. He asserts the reasonableness of his position in articulating the long-overdue demands for justice for America's black citizens. He cautions that if these just demands are not met, then the forces of bitterness, represented by black nationalist groups, may be unleashed and lead the country to a "frightening racial nightmare."

—w—

MY DEAR FELLOW CLERGYMEN,

While confined here in the Birmingham city jail, I came across your recent statement calling our present activities "unwise and untimely." Seldom, if ever, do I pause to answer criticism of my work and ideas. If I sought to answer all of the criticisms that cross my desk, my secretaries would be engaged in little else in the course of the day, and I would have no time for constructive work. But since I feel that you are men of genuine good will and your criticisms are sincerely set forth, I would like to answer your statement in what I hope will be patient and reasonable terms.

I think I should give the reason for my being in Birmingham, since you have been influenced by the argument of "outsiders coming in." I have the honor of serving as president of the Southern Christian Leadership Conference, an organization operating in every southern state, with headquarters in Atlanta, Georgia. We have some eighty-five affiliate organizations all across the South— one being the Alabama Christian Movement for Human Rights. Whenever necessary and possible we share staff, educational and financial resources with our affiliates. Several months ago our local affiliate here in Birmingham invited us to be on call to engage in a nonviolent direct-action program if such were deemed necessary. We readily consented and when the hour came we lived up to our promises. So I am here, along with several members of my staff, because we were invited here. I am here because I have basic organizational ties here.

Beyond this, I am in Birmingham because injustice is here. Just as the eighth-century prophets left their little villages and carried their "thus saith the Lord" far beyond the boundaries of their hometowns; and just as the Apostle Paul left his little village of Tarsus and carried the gospel of Jesus Christ to practically every hamlet and city of the Graeco-Roman world, I too am compelled to carry the gospel of freedom beyond my particular hometown. Like Paul, I must constantly respond to the Macedonian call for aid.

Moreover, I am cognizant of the interrelatedness of all communities and states. I cannot sit idly by in Atlanta and not be concerned about what happens in Birmingham. Injustice anywhere is a threat to justice everywhere. We are caught in an inescapable network of mutuality, tied in a single garment of destiny. Whatever affects one directly affects all indirectly. Never again can we afford to live with the narrow, provincial "outside agitator" idea. Anyone who lives in the United States can never be considered an outsider anywhere in this country.

You deplore the demonstrations that are presently taking place in Birmingham. But I am sorry that your statement did not express a similar concern for the conditions that brought the demonstrations into being. I am sure that each of you would want to go beyond the superficial social analyst who looks merely at effects, and does not grapple with underlying causes. I would not hesitate to say that it is unfortunate that so-called demonstrations are taking place in Birmingham at this time, but I would say in more emphatic terms that it is even more unfortunate that the white power structure of this city left the Negro community with no other alternative.

In any nonviolent campaign there are four basic steps: (1) collection of the facts to determine whether injustices are alive, (2) negotiation, (3) self-purification, and (4) direct action. We have gone through all of these steps in Birmingham. There can be no gainsaying of the fact that racial injustice engulfs this community. . . .

You express a great deal of anxiety over our willingness to break laws. This is certainly a legitimate concern. Since we so diligently urge people to obey the Supreme Court's decision of 1954 outlawing segregation in public schools, it is rather strange and paradoxical to find us consciously breaking laws. One may well ask, "How can you advocate breaking some laws and obeying others?" The answer is found in the fact that there are two types of laws: there are *just* and there are *unjust* laws. I would agree with Saint Augustine that "An unjust law is no law at all."

Now what is the difference between the two? How does one determine when a law is just or unjust? A just law is a man-made code that squares with the moral law or the law of God. An unjust law is a code that is out of harmony with the moral law. To put it in the terms of Saint Thomas Aquinas, an unjust law is a human law that is not rooted in eternal and natural law. Any law that uplifts human personality is just. Any law that degrades human personality is unjust. All segregation statutes are unjust because segregation distorts the soul and damages the personality. It gives the segregator a false sense of superiority, and the segregated a false sense of inferiority. To use the words of Martin Buber, the great Jewish philosopher, segregation substitutes an "I-it" relationship for the "I-thou" relationship, and ends up relegating persons to the status of things. So segregation is not only politically, economically and sociologically unsound, but it is morally wrong and sinful. Paul Tillich has said that sin is separation. Isn't segregation an existential expression of man's tragic separation, an expression of his awful estrangement, his terrible sinfulness? So I can urge men to disobey segregation ordinances because they are morally wrong. . . .

Let me give another explanation. An unjust law is a code inflicted upon a minority which that minority had no part in enacting or creating because they did not have the unhampered right to vote. Who can say that the legislature of Alabama which set up the segregation laws was democratically elected? Throughout the state of Alabama all types of conniving methods are used to prevent Negroes from becoming registered voters and there are some counties without a single Negro registered to vote despite the fact that the Negro constitutes a majority of the population. Can any law set up in such a state be considered democratically structured?

These are just a few examples of unjust and just laws. There are some instances when a law is just on its face and unjust in its application. For instance, I was arrested Friday on a charge of parading without a permit. Now there is nothing wrong with an ordinance which requires a permit for a parade, but when the ordinance is used to preserve segregation and to deny citizens the First Amendment privilege of peaceful assembly and peaceful protest, then it becomes unjust.

I hope you can see the distinction I am trying to point out. In no sense do I advocate evading or defying the law as the rabid segregationist would do. This would lead to anarchy. One who breaks an unjust law must do it *openly*, *lovingly* (not hatefully as the white mothers did in New Orleans when they were seen on television screaming, "nigger, nigger, nigger"), and with a willingness to accept the penalty. I submit that an individual who breaks a law that conscience tells him is unjust, and willingly accepts the penalty by staying in jail to arouse the conscience of the community over its injustice, is in reality expressing the very highest respect for law.

Of course, there is nothing new about this kind of civil disobedience. It was seen sublimely in the refusal of Shadrach, Meshach and Abednego to obey the laws of Nebuchadnezzar because a higher moral law was involved. It was practiced superbly by the early Christians who were willing to face hungry lions and the excruciating pain of chopping blocks, before submitting to certain unjust laws of the Roman Empire. To a degree academic freedom is a reality today because Socrates practiced civil disobedience.

We can never forget that everything Hitler did in Germany was "legal" and everything the Hungarian freedom fighters did in Hungary was "illegal." It was "illegal" to aid and comfort a Jew in Hitler's Germany. But I am sure that if I had lived in Germany during that time I would have aided and comforted my Jewish brothers even though it was illegal. If I lived in a Communist country today where certain principles dear to the Christian faith are suppressed, I believe I would openly advocate disobeying these anti-religious laws. I must make two honest confessions to you, my Christian and Jewish brothers. First, I must confess that over the last few years I have been gravely disappointed with the white moderate. I have almost reached the regrettable conclusion that the Negro's great stumbling block in the stride toward freedom is not the White Citizens Counciler or the Ku Klux Klanner, but the white moderate who is more devoted to "order" than to justice; who prefers a negative peace which is the absence of tension to a positive peace which is the presence of justice; who constantly says, "I agree with you in the goal you seek, but I can't agree with your methods of direct action"; who paternalistically feels that he can set the timetable for another man's freedom; who lives by the myth of time and who constantly advised the Negro to wait until a "more convenient season." Shallow understanding from people of good will is more frustrating than absolute misunderstanding from people of ill will. Lukewarm acceptance is much more bewildering than outright rejection. . . .

Oppressed people cannot remain oppressed forever. The urge for freedom will eventually come. This is what happened to the American Negro. Something within has reminded him of his birthright of freedom; something without has reminded him that he can gain it. Consciously and unconsciously, he has been swept in by what the Germans call the *Zeitgeist*, and with his black brothers of Africa, and his brown and yellow brothers of Asia, South America and the Caribbean, he is moving with a sense of cosmic urgency toward the promised land of racial justice. Recognizing this vital urge that has engulfed the Negro community, one should readily understand public demonstrations. The Negro has many pent-up resentments and latent frustrations. He has to get them out. So let him march sometime; let him have his prayer pilgrimages to the city hall; understand why he must have sit-ins and freedom rides. If his repressed emotions do not come out in these nonviolent ways, they will come out in ominous expressions of violence. This is not a threat; it is a fact of history. So I have not said to my people "get rid of your discontent." But I have tried to say that this normal and healthy discontent can be channelized through the creative outlet of nonviolent direct action. Now this approach is being dismissed as extremist. I must admit that I was initially disappointed in being so categorized.

But as I continued to think about the matter I gradually gained a bit of satisfaction from being considered an extremist. Was not Jesus an extremist in love—"Love your enemies, bless them that curse you, pray for them that despitefully use you." Was not Amos an extremist for justice—"Let justice roll down like waters and righteousness like a mighty stream." Was not Paul an extremist for the gospel of Jesus Christ—"I bear in my body the marks of the Lord Jesus." Was not Martin Luther an extremist—"Here I stand; I can do none other so help me God." Was not John Bunyan an extremist—"I will stay in jail to the end of my days before I make a butchery of my conscience." Was not Abraham Lincoln an extremist—"This nation cannot survive half slave and half free." Was not Thomas Jefferson an extremist—"We hold these truths to be self-evident, that all men are created equal." So the question is not whether we will be extremist but what kind of extremist will we be. Will we be extremists for hate or will we be extremists for love? Will we be extremists for the preservation of injustice—or will we be extremists for the cause of justice? In that dramatic scene on Calvary's hill, three men were crucified. We must not forget that all three were crucified for the same crime—the crime of extremism. Two were extremists for immorality, and thusly fell below their environment. The other, Jesus Christ, was an extremist for love, truth and goodness, and thereby rose above his environment. So, after all, maybe the South, the nation and the world are in dire need of creative extremists.

MALCOLM X AND ALEX HALEY
Selection from *The Autobiography of Malcolm X*

In the 1950s most African American leaders, rallying around King, adopted the political agenda of racial integration into the American mainstream. However, more militant leaders also began to emerge—leaders who saw the future of their race as separate from white culture and society. Believing whites to be basically against full integration, they argued that blacks should strive to become independent from white control; to this end, they advocated the use of violence if conditions called for it. The militant agenda of these leaders appealed to the minority of blacks on the margin of black society, particularly those who had run afoul of the white justice system or who believed, for whatever reason, that black separatism was necessary.

Malcolm X (born Malcolm Little, 1925–1965) was the most charismatic of these militant black leaders of the 1950s. His ideas are enjoying a renaissance today among a large group of African Americans, his life having become the subject of a major film. Malcolm X came from a poor midwestern family who suffered at the hands of white racists, their home being burned and the father brutally murdered. Malcolm's mentally unstable mother, unable to care for eight children, allowed them to be assigned to relatives' homes and state institutions. The teenage Malcolm wound up first in Boston and then in New York, where he became a hustler and petty thief. Prison became his school. There, he learned about the Black Muslims, an American version of the Islamic religion, which gave him a new purpose in life. His name change, from Little to X, reflected the new direction he intended to take. Released from prison in the 1950s, he became a leader of the Black Muslims, calling on African Americans, in striking and bold language, to separate themselves completely from white society. His militancy alarmed most whites and upset many black leaders at the time. However, his pleas for self-respect attracted young blacks in the 1960s. After a trip to Mecca, Malcolm X worked for closer cooperation with whites, but before he could launch his new program, he was assassinated.

Reading the Selection

The record of Malcolm X's struggle for both his own identity and that of his fellow African Americans was made possible by the patience and writing skills of Alex Haley (1921–1992). Haley was a black writer who later achieved fame with his book *Roots*, which was a search for Haley's African and slave forebears. During the writing of *The Autobiography*, Haley interviewed Malcolm X at length and accompanied him on speaking engagements where he could observe Malcolm's personality, oratorical skills, and the reactions of admirers and detractors.

This selection from Chapter XI, "Saved," of *The Autobiography of Malcolm X* recounts Malcolm X's prison days as he began to educate himself, learning to read and studying books in the prison library. Earlier chapters detailed his criminal past, and later chapters laid out his triumphs as a black leader. Chapter XI represents the turning point of his life. In prison he studied the teachings of Elijah Muhammad, the founder of the Black Muslims and learned from him that white writers leave "the black man" out of history books. This fact reinforced Malcolm's growing conviction that whites could not be trusted and that blacks must recover their own history as a first step to gaining self-respect.

Chapter XI
Saved

. . .

I became increasingly frustrated at not being able to express what I wanted to convey in letters that I wrote, especially those to Mr. Elijah Muhammad. In the street, I had been the most articulate hustler out there—I had commanded attention when I said something. But now, trying to write simple English, I not only wasn't articulate, I wasn't even functional. How would I sound writing in slang, the way I would *say* it, something such as "Look, daddy, let me pull your coat about a cat, Elijah Muhammad—"

Many who today hear me somewhere in person, or on television, or those who read something I've said, will think I went to school far beyond the eighth grade. This impression is due entirely to my prison studies.

It had really begun back in the Charlestown Prison, when Bimbi first made me feel envy of his stock of knowledge. Bimbi had always taken charge of any conversation he was in, and I had tried to emulate him. But every book I picked up had few sentences which didn't contain anywhere from one to nearly all of the words that might as well have been in Chinese. When I just skipped those words, of course, I really ended up with little idea of what the book said. So I had come to the Norfolk Prison Colony still going through only book-reading motions. Pretty soon, I would have quit even these motions, unless I had received the motivation that I did.

I saw that the best thing I could do was get hold of a dictionary—to study, to learn some words. I was lucky enough to reason also that I should try to improve my penmanship. It was sad. I couldn't even write in a straight line. It was both ideas together that moved me to request a dictionary along with some tablets and pencils from the Norfolk Prison Colony school.

I spent two days just riffling uncertainly through the dictionary's pages. I'd never realized so many words existed! I didn't know *which* words I needed to learn. Finally, just to start some kind of action, I began copying.

In my slow, painstaking, ragged handwriting, I copied into my tablet everything printed on that first page, down to the punctuation marks.

I believe it took me a day. Then, aloud, I read back, to myself, everything I'd written on the tablet. Over and over, aloud, to myself, I read my own handwriting.

I woke up the next morning, thinking about those words—immensely proud to realize that not only had I written so much at one time, but I'd written words that I never knew were in the world. Moreover, with a little effort, I also could remember what many of these words meant. I reviewed the words whose meanings I didn't remember. Funny thing, from the dictionary first page right now, that "aardvark" springs to my mind. The dictionary had a picture of it, a long-tailed, long-eared, burrowing African mammal, which lives off termites caught by sticking out its tongue as an anteater does for ants.

I was so fascinated that I went on—I copied the dictionary's next page. And the same experience came when I studied that. With every succeeding page, I also learned of people and places and events from history. Actually the dictionary is like a miniature encyclopedia. Finally the dictionary's A section had filled a whole tablet—and I went on into the B's. That was the way I started copying what eventually became the entire dictionary. It went a lot faster after so much practice helped me to pick up handwriting speed. Between what I wrote in my tablet, and writing letters, during the rest of my time in prison I would guess I wrote a million words.

I suppose it was inevitable that as my word-base broadened, I could for the first time pick up a book and read and now begin to understand what the book was saying. Anyone who has read a great deal can imagine the new world that opened. Let me tell you something: from then until I left that prison, in every free moment I had, if I was not reading in the library, I was reading on my bunk. You couldn't have gotten me out of books with a wedge. Between Mr. Muhammad's teachings, my correspondence, my visitors—usually Ella and Reginald—and my reading of books, months passed without my even thinking about being imprisoned. In fact, up to then, I never had been so truly free in my life.

The Norfolk Prison Colony's library was in the school building. A variety of classes was taught there by instructors who came from such places as Harvard and Boston universities. The weekly debates between inmate teams were also held in the school building. You would be astonished to know how worked up convict debaters and audiences would get over subjects like "Should Babies Be Fed Milk?"

Available on the prison library's shelves were books on just about every general subject. Much of the big private collection that Parkhurst had willed to the prison was still in crates and boxes in the back of the library—thousands of old books. Some of them looked ancient: covers faded, old-time parchment-looking binding. Parkhurst, I've mentioned, seemed to have been principally interested in history and religion. He had the money and the special interest to have a lot of books that you wouldn't have in general circulation. Any college library would have been lucky to get that collection.

As you can imagine, especially in a prison where there was heavy emphasis on rehabilitation, an inmate was smiled upon if he demonstrated an unusually intense interest in books. There was a sizable number of well-read inmates, especially the popular debaters. Some were said by many to be practically walking encyclopedias. They were almost celebrities. No university would ask any student to devour literature as I did when this new world opened to me, of being able to read and *understand*.

I read more in my room than in the library itself. An inmate who was known to read a lot could check out more than the permitted maximum number of books. I preferred reading in the total isolation of my own room.

When I had progressed to really serious reading, every night at about ten P.M. I would be outraged with the "lights out." It always seemed to catch me right in the middle of something engrossing.

Fortunately, right outside my door was a corridor light that cast a glow into my room. The glow was enough to read by, once my eyes adjusted to it. So when "lights out" came, I would sit on the floor where I could continue reading in that glow.

At one-hour intervals the night guards paced past every room. Each time I heard the approaching footsteps, I jumped into bed and feigned sleep. And as soon as the guard passed, I got back out of bed onto the floor area of that light-glow, where I would read for another fifty-eight minutes—until the guard approached again. That went on until three or four every morning. Three or four hours of sleep a night was enough for me. Often in the years in the streets I had slept less than that.

The teachings of Mr. Muhammad stressed how history had been "whitened"—when white men had written history books, the black man simply had been left out. Mr. Muhammad couldn't have said anything that would have struck me much harder. I had never forgotten how when my class, me and all of those whites, had studied seventh-grade United States history back in Mason, the history of the Negro had been covered in one paragraph, and the teacher had gotten a big laugh with his joke, "Negroes' feet are so big that when they walk, they leave a hole in the ground."

This is one reason why Mr. Muhammad's teachings spread so swiftly all over the United States, among *all* Negroes, whether or not they became followers of Mr. Muhammad. The teachings ring true—to every Negro. You can hardly show me a black adult in America—or a white one, for that matter—who knows from the history books anything like the truth about the black man's role. In my own case, once I heard of the "glorious history of the black man," I took special pains to hunt in the library for books that would inform me on details about black history.

I can remember accurately the very first set of books that really impressed me. I have since bought that set of books and have it at home for my children to read as they grow up. It's called *Wonders of the World*. It's full of pictures of archeological finds, statues that depict, usually, non-European people.

I found books like Will Durant's *Story of Civilization*. I read H. G. Wells' *Outline of History*. *Souls Of Black Folk* by W. E. B. Du Bois gave me a glimpse into the black people's history before they came to this country. Carter G. Woodson's *Negro History* opened my eyes about black empires before the black slave was brought to the United States, and the early Negro struggles for freedom.

J. A. Rogers' three volumes of *Sex and Race* told about race-mixing before Christ's time; about Aesop being a black man who told fables; about Egypt's Pharaohs; about the great Coptic Christian Empires; about Ethiopia, the earth's oldest continuous black civilization, as China is the oldest continuous civilization.

Mr. Muhammad's teachings about how the white man had been created led me to *Findings In Genetics* by Gregor Mendel. (The dictionary's G section was where I had learned what "genetics" meant.) I really studied this book by the Austrian monk. Reading it over and over, especially certain sections, helped me to understand that if you started with a black man, a white man could be produced; but starting with a white man, you never could produce a black man—because the white gene is recessive. And since no one disputes that there was but one Original Man, the conclusion is clear.

During the last year or so, in the *New York Times*, Arnold Toynbee used the word "bleached" in describing the white man. (His words were: "White (i.e. bleached) human beings of North European origin. . . .") Toynbee also referred to the European geographic area as only a peninsula of Asia. He said there is no such thing as Europe. And if you look at the globe, you will see for yourself that America is only an extension of Asia. (But at the same time Toynbee is among those who have helped to bleach history. He has written that Africa was the only continent that produced no history. He won't write that again. Every day now, the truth is coming to light.)

I never will forget how shocked I was when I began reading about slavery's total horror. It made such an impact upon me that it later became one of my favorite subjects when I became a minister of Mr. Muhammad's. The world's most monstrous crime, the sin and the blood on the white man's hands, are almost impossible to believe. Books like the one by Frederick Olmstead opened my eyes to the horrors suffered when the slave was landed in the United States. The European woman, Fannie Kimball, who had married a Southern white slaveowner, described how human beings were degraded. Of course I read *Uncle Tom's Cabin*. In fact, I believe that's the only novel I have ever read since I started serious reading.

Parkhurst's collection also contained some bound pamphlets of the Abolitionist Anti-Slavery Society of New England. I read descriptions of atrocities, saw those illustrations of black slave women tied up and flogged with whips; of black mothers watching their babies being dragged off, never to be seen by their mothers again; of dogs after slaves, and of the fugitive slave catchers, evil white men with whips and clubs and chains and guns. I read about the slave preacher Nat Turner, who put the fear of God into the white slavemaster. Nat Turner wasn't going around preaching pie-in-the-sky and "non-violent" freedom for the black man. There in Virginia one night in 1831, Nat and seven other slaves started out at his master's home and through the night they went from one plantation "big house" to the next, killing, until by the next morning 57 white people were dead and Nat had about 70 slaves following him. White people, terrified for their lives, fled from their homes, locked themselves up in public buildings, hid in the woods, and some even left the state. A small army of soldiers took two months to catch and hang Nat Turner. Somewhere I have read where Nat Turner's example is said to have inspired John Brown to invade Virginia and attack Harper's Ferry nearly thirty years later, with thirteen white men and five Negroes.

I read Herodotus, "the father of History," or, rather, I read about him. And I read the histories of various nations, which opened my eyes gradually, then wider and wider, to how the whole world's white men had indeed acted like devils, pillaging and raping and bleeding and draining the whole world's non-white people. I remember, for instance, books such as Will Durant's story of Oriental civilization, and Mahatma Gandhi's accounts of the struggle to drive the British out of India.

Book after book showed me how the white man had brought upon the world's black, brown, red, and yellow peoples every variety of the sufferings of exploitation. I saw how since the sixteenth century, the so-called "Christian trader" white man began to ply the seas in his lust for Asian and African empires, and plunder, and power. I read, I saw, how the white man never has gone among the non-white peoples bearing the Cross in the true manner and spirit of Christ's teachings—meek, humble, and Christ-like.

I perceived, as I read, how the collective white man had been actually nothing but a piratical opportunist who used Faustian machinations to make his own Christianity his initial wedge in criminal conquests. First, always "religiously," he branded "heathen" and "pagan" labels upon ancient non-white cultures and civilizations. The stage thus set, he then turned upon his non-white victims his weapons of war.

I read how, entering India—half a *billion* deeply religious brown people—the British white man, by 1759, through promises, trickery and manipulations, controlled much of India through Great Britain's East India Company. The parasitical British administration kept tentacling out to half of the subcontinent. In 1857, some of the desperate people of India finally mutinied—and, excepting the African slave trade, nowhere has history recorded any more unnecessary bestial and ruthless human carnage than the British suppression of the non-white Indian people.

Over 115 million African blacks—close to the 1930's population of the United States—were murdered or enslaved during the slave trade. And I read how when the slave market was glutted, the cannibalistic white powers of Europe next carved up, as their colonies, the richest areas of the black continent. And Europe's chancelleries for the next century played a chess game of naked exploitation and power from Cape Horn to Cairo.

Ten guards and the warden couldn't have torn me out of those books. Not even Elijah Muhammad could have been more eloquent than those books were in providing indisputable proof that the collective white man had acted like a devil in virtually every contact he had with the world's collective non-white man. I listen today to the radio, and watch television, and read the headlines about the collective white man's fear and tension concerning China. When the white man professes ignorance about why the Chinese hate him so, my mind can't help flashing back to what I read, there in prison, about how the blood forebears of this same white man raped China at a time when China was trusting and helpless. Those original white

"Christian traders" sent into China millions of pounds of opium. By 1839, so many of the Chinese were addicts that China's desperate government destroyed twenty thousand chests of opium. The first Opium War was promptly declared by the white man. Imagine! Declaring *war* upon someone who objects to being narcotized! The Chinese were severely beaten, with Chinese-invented gunpowder.

The Treaty of Nanking made China pay the British white man for the destroyed opium; forced open China's major ports to British trade; forced China to abandon Hong Kong; fixed China's import tariffs so low that cheap British articles soon flooded in, maiming China's industrial development.

After a second Opium War, the Tientsin Treaties legalized the ravaging opium trade, legalized a British-French-American control of China's customs. China tried delaying that Treaty's ratification; Peking was looted and burned.

"Kill the foreign white devils!" was the 1901 Chinese war cry in the Boxer Rebellion. Losing again, this time the Chinese were driven from Peking's choicest areas. The vicious, arrogant white man put up the famous signs, "Chinese and dogs not allowed."

Red China after World War II closed its doors to the Western white world. Massive Chinese agricultural, scientific, and industrial efforts are described in a book that *Life* magazine recently published. Some observers inside Red China have reported that the world never has known such a hate-white campaign as is now going on in this non-white country where, present birth-rates continuing, in fifty more years Chinese will be half the earth's population. And it seems that some Chinese chickens will soon come home to roost, with China's recent successful nuclear tests.

Let us face reality. We can see in the United Nations a new world order being shaped, along color lines—an alliance among the non-white nations. America's U.N. Ambassador Adlai Stevenson complained not long ago that in the United Nations "a skin game" was being played. He was right. He was facing reality. A "skin game" *is* being played. But Ambassador Stevenson sounded like Jesse James accusing the marshal of carrying a gun. Because who in the world's history ever has played a worse "skin game" than the white man?

Mr. Muhammad, to whom I was writing daily, had no idea of what a new world had opened up to me through my efforts to document his teachings in books.

When I discovered philosophy, I tried to touch all the landmarks of philosophical development. Gradually, I read most of the old philosophers, Occidental and Oriental. The Oriental philosophers were the ones I came to prefer; finally, my impression was that most Occidental philosophy had largely been borrowed from the Oriental thinkers. Socrates, for instance, traveled in Egypt. Some sources even say that Socrates was initiated into some of the Egyptian mysteries. Obviously Socrates got some of this wisdom among the East's wise men.

I have often reflected upon the new vistas that reading opened to me. I knew right there in prison that reading had changed forever the course of my life. As I see it today, the ability to read awoke inside me some long dormant craving to be mentally alive. I certainly wasn't seeking any degree, the way a college confers a status symbol upon its students. My homemade education gave me, with every additional book that I read, a little bit more sensitivity to the deafness, dumbness, and blindness that was afflicting the black race in America. Not long ago, an English writer telephoned me from London, asking questions. One was, "What's your alma mater?" I told him, "Books." You will never catch me with a free fifteen minutes in which I'm not studying something I feel might be able to help the black man.

Yesterday I spoke in London, and both ways on the plane across the Atlantic I was studying a document about how the United Nations proposes to insure the human rights of the oppressed minorities of the world. The American black man is the world's most shameful case of minority oppression. What makes the black man think of himself as only an internal United States issue is just a catch-phrase, two words, "civil rights." How is the black man going to get "civil rights" before first he wins his *human* rights? If the American black man will start thinking about his *human* rights, and then start thinking of him-self as part of one of the world's great peoples, he will see he has a case for the United Nations.

I can't think of a better case! Four hundred years of black blood and sweat invested here in America, and the white man still has the black man begging for what every immigrant fresh off the ship can take for granted the minute he walks down the gangplank.

But I'm digressing. I told the Englishman that my alma mater was books, a good library. Every time I catch a plane, I have with me a book that I want to read—and that's a lot of books these days. If I weren't out here every day battling the white man, I could spend the rest of my life reading, just satisfying my curiosity—because you can hardly mention anything I'm not curious about. I don't think anybody ever got more out of going to prison than I did. In fact, prison enabled me to study far more intensively than I would have if my life had gone differently and I had attended some college. I imagine that one of the biggest troubles with colleges is there are too many distractions, too much panty-raiding, fraternities, and boola-boola and all of that. Where else but in a prison could I have attacked my ignorance by being able to study intensely sometimes as much as fifteen hours a day? . . .

KENZABURO OË

Selections from *A Personal Matter*

Kenzaburo Oë's (b. 1935) command of language, sensitivity to the human condition, and appeal to a worldwide audience have made him one of the most famous writers working today. Although Oë is recognized as a Post-Modernist, his earliest experiences are firmly rooted in the era of late Modernism. He was ten years old when the Japanese surrendered to the Allies at the end of World War II in 1945. He later remembered this date as the most important event of his life, for it was then that he first heard Emperor Hirohito, speaking over the radio, announcing Japan's defeat. Unaccustomed to the sound of the emperor's voice because rulers were revered as gods, distant from and never speaking with mortals, Oë was devastated to discover that Hirohito was only human, no different from other men. This discovery caused Oë to question what he had learned in school about the emperor cult, that the emperor demands unquestioning loyalty and subjects must be prepared to sacrifice their lives for the heaven-sent ruler. After this experience, Oë's attitude toward the old Japanese ways would never be the same.

The demystification of Hirohito symbolized the beginning of the destruction of Oë's Japan as he understood it as a child. Living in American-occupied Japan, he had to confront the dramatic changes underway in his country, his generation, and himself. At Tokyo University, Japan's premier institution of higher learning, he studied Western literature and thought, in particular the works of the French thinker Jean-Paul Sartre (see *The Humanism of Existentialism*) and the novels of the Americans Herman Melville, William Faulkner (see *The Sound and the Fury*), and Norman Mailer.

As Oë's literary career unfolded, he passed under a number of influences, most of them from the West, as reflected in the content of his works. His first novels feature young Japanese heroes engaged in existential quests for meaning in a society from which they feel alienated. Freud's ideas also affected Oë, as may be seen in his characters who, lacking any moral sense, are driven to sexual promiscuity and violence. In addition, Oë wrote essays on political subjects, espousing democratic ideas initially, but in the 1960s coming under the sway of Mao Zedong and Chinese communism.

Oë's writing also owed much to Western models and styles, particularly Realist fiction with a strong moral dimension. The most memorable of his early works is the partly autobiographical novel *A Personal Matter* (1964), whose compelling plot revolves around a brain-damaged child (Oë's first son was born with this condition). In the novel, Bird, the young father, tries to escape the reality of his son's condition, first by throwing himself into an orgy of sex and alcohol, and next by plotting the baby's murder. Eventually Bird faces up to his responsibility, and a brighter world opens for him. In the West, critics admired Oë's skills as a writer, but they found fault with Oë's relatively quick and painless resolution of Bird's mistakes and change of heart. In Japan, however, critics were more understanding, finding Bird's struggle both heroic and completely realistic. Oë's later works have won literary awards in Japan, as he has attracted readers around the world. His global reputation was sealed in 1994, when he received the Nobel Prize for literature; the Nobel committee praised him, in part, for "creating an imagined world where life and myth condense to form a disconcerting picture of the human predicament."

Reading the Selections

In Chapter III, modern technology, unfeeling hospital personnel, and unsympathetic relatives add to Bird's traumatic shock as he confronts the harsh truth of his new son's condition. The doctor is so concerned over a foul-up in the hospital's bureaucracy that he never expresses any sympathy to Bird. The ambulance driver and the anesthetist raise Bird's emotional temperature as they engage in idle chit-chat, oblivious to the pain he is suffering. Bird's mother-in-law, eager to keep bad news from the birth mother, her daughter, wants to have the baby quietly disposed of and urges the distraught Bird to stay out of reach. Driven almost to distraction, Bird finds solace in a humdrum event: He decides to get a shave.

In Chapter XIII, the last, Bird gains a measure of wisdom. The chapter begins with Bird and his mistress, Himiko, stumbling into a gay bar run by an old acquaintance. Still undecided what to do with the brain-damaged baby, they have left it with Himiko's friend, an abortionist. On leaving the bar, Bird and Himiko quarrel, and Bird, ignoring her pleas, decides to take the baby to the hospital for an operation. The operation saves the baby's life, and Bird's wayward behavior is forgiven by his family. In the end, Bird learns to take responsibility for those less fortunate than himself.

—⁓—

Chapter III

Bird was sitting on the stairs in front of the intensive care ward, gripping his thighs with grimy hands in a battle with the fatigue that had been hounding him since his tears had dried, when the one-eyed doctor emerged from the ward looking thwarted. Bird stood up and the doctor said: "This hospital is so goddamned bureaucratic, not even the nurses will listen to a word you say." A startling change had come over the man since their ride together in the ambulance: his voice was troubled. "I have a letter of introduction from our Director to a professor of medicine here—they're distant relatives!—and I can't even find out where he is!"

Now Bird understood the doctor's sudden dejection. Here in this ward everyone was treated like an infant: the young man with the glass eye had begun to doubt his own dignity.

"And the baby?" Bird said, surprised at the commiseration in his voice.

"The baby? Oh yes, we'll know just where we stand when the brain surgeon has finished his examination. If the infant lasts that long. If he doesn't last, the autopsy will tell the full story. I doubt that the infant can hold out for more than a day—you might drop in here around three tomorrow afternoon. But let me warn you: this hospital is really bureaucratic—even the nurses!"

As though he were determined to accept no more questions from Bird, the doctor rolled both his eyes toward the ceiling, good and glass alike, and walked away. Bird followed him like a washerwoman, holding the baby's empty basket against his side. At the passageway that led to the main wing, they were joined by the ambulance driver and the anesthetist. These firemen seemed to notice right away that the doctor's earlier joviality had deserted him. Not that they retained any dazzle themselves: while they had been racing their ambulance through the heart of the city as though it were a truck careening across an open field, shrilling the siren pretentiously and jumping traffic lights that bound the law-abiding citizen, a certain dignity had swelled their stoic uniforms. But now even that was gone. From the back, Bird noticed, the two firemen were alike as identical twins. No longer young, there were of medium height and build and both were balding in the same way.

"You need oxygen on the first job of the day, you need it all day long," one said with feeling.

"Yes, you've always said that," the other as feelingly replied.

This little exchange the one-eyed doctor ignored. Bird, though not much moved, understood that the men were nourishing each other's gloom, but when he turned to the fireman in charge of oxygen and nodded sympathetically, the man stiffened as though he had been asked a question, and with a nervous, grunted "huh?" forced Bird to speak. Disconcerted, Bird said: "I was wondering about the ambulance—can you use your siren to run traffic lights on the way back, too?"

"*On the way back?*" Like the fire department's most talented singing twins, the firemen repeated the question in unison, exchanged a look, their faces flushing drunkenly, and snorted a laugh which dilated the wings of their noses. Bird was both angry at the silliness of his question and at the firemen's response. And his anger was connected by a slender pipe to a tank of huge, dark rage compressed inside him. A rage he had no way of releasing had been building inside him under increasing pressure since dawn.

But the firemen seemed to wither now, as if they regretted having laughed imprudently at an unfortunate young father; their obvious distress closed a valve in the tapline to Bird's fury. He even felt a twinge of remorse. Who had asked that silly, anticlimactic question in the first place? And hadn't the question seeped from a fault which had opened in his own brain, pickled in the vinegar of his grief and lack of sleep? [10]

Bird looked into the baby's hamper under his arm. Now it was like an empty hole which had been dug unnecessarily. Only a folded blanket remained in the hamper, and some absorbent cotton and a roll of gauze. The blood on the cotton and the gauze, though still a vivid red, already failed to evoke an image of the baby lying there with its head in bandages, inhaling oxygen a little at a time from the rubber tubes inside its nose. Bird couldn't even recall accurately the grotesqueness of the baby's head, or the shimmering membrane of fat that gloved its fiery skin. Even now, the baby was receding from him at full speed. Bird felt a mixture of guilty relief and bottomless fear. He thought: Soon I'll forget all about the baby, a life that appeared out of infinite darkness, hovered for nine months in a fetal state, tasted a few hours of cruel discomfort, and descended once again into darkness, final and infinite. I wouldn't be surprised if I forgot about the baby right away. And when it's time for me to die I may remember, and, remembering, if the agony and fear of death increase for me, I will have fulfilled a small part of my obligation as a father.

Bird and the others reached the front entrance of the main wing. The firemen ran for the parking lot. Since theirs was a profession that involved them in emergencies all the time, running around breathlessly must have represented the normal attitude toward life. Off they dashed across the glistening concrete square, arms flailing, as if a hungry devil were snapping at their behinds. Meanwhile, the one-eyed doctor telephoned his hospital from a phone booth and asked for the Director. He explained the situation in a very few words: almost no new developments to report. Bird's mother-in-law came to the phone: "It's your wife's mother," said the doctor, turning. "Do you want to speak?"

Hell no! Bird wanted to shout. Since those frequent telephone conversations the night before, the sound of his mother-in-law's voice reaching him over the telephone line, like the helpless droning of a mosquito, had hounded Bird like an obsession. Bird set the baby's basket on the concrete floor and took the receiver glumly.

"The brain specialist hasn't made his examination yet. I have to come back tomorrow afternoon."

"But what's the point of it all; I mean, what can you [15] hope to accomplish?" Bird's mother-in-law cross-examined him in the tone of voice he had hoped most to be spared, as if she held him directly responsible.

"The *point* is that the baby happens to be alive at the moment," Bird said, and waited with a premonition of disgust for the woman to speak again. But she was silent; from the other end of the line came only a faint sound of troubled breathing.

"I'll be right over and explain," Bird said, and he started to hang up.

"*Hello?* Please don't come back here," his mother-in-law added hurriedly. "That child thinks you've taken the baby to a heart clinic. If you come now she'll be suspicious. It would be more natural if you came in a day or so, when she's calmer, and said that the baby had died of a weak heart. You can always get in touch with me by telephone."

Bird agreed. "I'll go right over to the college and explain what's happened," he was saying, when he heard the hard click of the connection being broken arbitrarily at the other end of the line. So his own voice had filled the listener with disgust, too. Bird put the receiver back and picked up the baby's basket. The one-eyed doctor was already in the ambulance. Bird, instead of climbing in after him, set the basket on the canvas stretcher.

"Thanks for everything. I think I'll go alone."

"You're going home alone?" the doctor said. [20]

"Yes," Bird replied, meaning "I'm going *out* alone." He had to report the circumstances of the birth to his father-in-law, but after that he would have some free time. And a visit to the professor, compared to returning to his wife and mother-in-law, held a promise of pure therapy.

The doctor closed the door from the inside and the ambulance moved away silently, observing the speed limit, like a *former* monster now powerless an deprived of voice. Through the same window from which, an hour earlier, weeping, he had gazed at pedestrians in the street, Bird saw the doctor and one of the firemen lurch forward toward the driver. He knew they were going to gossip about him and his baby, and it didn't bother him. From the telephone conversation with the old woman had come an unexpected furlough, time to himself to be spent alone and as he liked—the thought pumped strong, fresh blood into his head.

Bird started across the hospital square, wide and long as a soccer field. Halfway, he turned around and looked up at the building where he had just abandoned his first child, a baby on the brink of death. A gigantic building, with an overbearing presence, like a fort. Glistening in the sunlight of early summer, it made the baby who was faintly screaming in one of its obscure corners seem meaner than a grain of sand.

What if I *do* come back tomorrow, I might get lost in the labyrinth of this modern fort and wander in bewilderment; I might never find my dying or maybe already dead baby. The notion carried Bird one step away from his misfortune. He strode through the front gate and hurried down the street. . . . 25

—⚬—

Chapter XIII

Leaving the sports car at a garage, they set out in a cab for the gay bar Himiko knew. They were exhausted, anguished with a need to sleep, but their mouths were dry with an occult excitement that made them uneasy about returning all by themselves to that gloomy house. 1

They stopped the cab in front of a clumsy imitation of a gas lantern with word KIKUHIKO in blue paint written on the glass globe. Bird pushed open a door held together tenuously with a few boards of unequal length and stepped into a room as crude and narrow as a shed for livestock; there was only a short counter and, against the opposite wall, two sets of outlandishly high-backed chairs. The bar was empty except for the smallish man standing in a far corner behind the counter who now confronted the two intruders. He was of a curious rotundity, with lips like a young girl's and misted sheep-eyes which were warily inspecting but by no means rejecting them. Bird stood where he was, just inside the door, and returned his gaze. Gradually, a memento of his young friend Kikuhiko permeated the membrane of the ambiguous smile on the man's face.

"Would you believe, it's Himi, and looking a sight!" The man spoke through pursed lips, his eyes still on Bird. "I know this one; it's been ages now, but didn't they used to call him Bird?"

"We might as well sit down," Himiko said. She appeared to be discovering only an atmosphere of anticlimax in the drama of this reunion. Not that Kikuhiko was exciting any very poignant emotion in Bird. He was fatigued utterly, he was sleepy: he felt certain nothing in the world remained that could interest him vitally. Bird found himself sitting down a little apart from Himiko.

"What do they call this one now, Himi?" 5

"Bird."

"You can't mean it. Still? It's been seven years." Kikuhiko moved over to Bird. "What are you drinking, Bird?"

"Whisky, please. Straight."

"And Himi?"

"The same for me." 10

"You both have that tired look and it's still so early in the night!"

"Well, it has nothing to do with sex—we spent half the day driving around in circles."

Bird reached for the glass of whisky that had been poured for him and, feeling something tighten in his chest, hesitated. Kikuhiko—he can't be more than twenty-two yet he looks like a more formidable adult than I; on the other hand, he seems to have retained a lot of what he was at fifteen—Kikuhiko, like an amphibian at home in two ages.

Kikuhiko was drinking straight whisky, too. He poured himself another drink, and one for Himiko, who had emptied her first glass in a swallow. Bird found himself watching Kikuhiko and Kikuhiko glanced repeatedly at Bird, the nerves of his body arching like the back of a threatened cat. At last he turned directly to Bird and said: "Bird, do you remember me?"

"Of course," said Bird. Strange, he was more conscious of talking to the proprietor of a gay bar (this was his first time) than to a sometime friend whom he hadn't seen in years. 15

"It's been ages, hasn't it, Bird. Ever since that day we went over to the next town and saw a G.I. looking out of a train window with the bottom half of his face shot off."

"What's all this about a G.I.?" Himiko said. Kikuhiko told her, his eyes impudently roaming Bird.

"It was during the Korean war and these gorgeous soldier boys who'd been all wounded in the field were being shipped back to bases in Japan. Whole trainloads of them and we saw one of those trains one day. Bird, do you suppose they were passing through our district all the time?"

"Not all the time, no."

"You used to hear stories about slave dealers catching Japanese high-school boys and selling them as soldiers, there were even rumors that the government was going to ship us off to Korea—I was terrified in those days." 20

Of course! Kikuhiko had been horribly afraid. The night they had quarreled and separated, he had shouted "Bird, I was afraid!" Bird thought about his baby and decided it was still incapable of fear. He felt relieved, a suspect, brittle relief. "Those rumors were certainly meaningless," he said, trying to veer his consciousness from the baby.

"You say, but I did all kinds of nasty things on account of rumors like that. Which reminds me, Bird. Did you have any trouble catching that madman we were chasing?"

"He was dead when I found him, he'd hung himself on Castle Hill—I knocked myself out for nothing." The taste of an old regret returned sourly to the tip of Bird's tongue. "We found him at dawn, the dogs and I. Talk about something being meaningless!"

"I wouldn't say that. You kept up the chase until dawn and I dropped out and ran in the middle of the night and our lives have been completely different ever since. You stopped mixing with me and my kind and went to a college in Tokyo, didn't you? But I've been like falling steadily ever since that night and look at me now—tucked away nice and comfy in this nelly little bar. Bird, if you hadn't . . . gone on alone that night, I might be in a very different groove now."

"If Bird hadn't abandoned you that night, you wouldn't have become a homosexual?" Himiko audaciously asked.

Rattled, Bird had to look away.

"A homosexual is someone who has chosen to let himself love a person of the same sex: and I made that decision myself. So the responsibility is all my own." Kikuhiko's voice was quiet.

"I can see you've read the existentialists," Himiko said.

"When you run a bar for faggots, you have to know where all kinds of things are at!" As though it were part of the song of his profession, Kikuhiko sang the line. Then he turned to Bird and said, in his normal voice, "I'm sure you've been on the rise all the time I've been falling. What are you doing now, Bird?"

"I've been teaching at a cram-school, but it turns out that I'm fired as of the summer vacation—'on the rise' isn't quite how I'd put it," Bird said. "And that isn't all; it's been one weird hassle after another."

"Now that you mention it, the Bird I knew at twenty was never this droopy-woopy. It's as if something has got you awfully scared and you're trying to run away from it—" This was a shrewd and observant Kikuhiko, no longer the simple fairy Bird had known: his friend's life of apostasy and descent could not have been easy or uninvolved.

"You're right," Bird admitted. "I'm all used up. I'm afraid. I'm trying to run away."

"When he was twenty this one was immune to fear, I never saw him frightened of anything," Kikuhiko said to Himiko. Then he turned back to Bird, and, provokingly: "But tonight you seem extra sensitive to fear; it's like you're so afraid you don't have the foggiest notion where your head is at!"

"I'm not twenty anymore," Bird said.

Kikuhiko's face froze over with icy indifference. "The old gray mare just ain't what she used to be," he said, and moved abruptly to Himiko's side.

A minute later two of them began a game of dice and Bird was given his freedom. Relieved, he lifted his glass of whisky. After a blank of seven years it had taken him and his friend just seven minutes of conversation to eliminate everything worthy of their mutual curiosity. I'm not twenty anymore! And of all my possessions at the age of

twenty, the only thing I've managed not to lose is my childish nickname—Bird gulped down his first whisky of what had been a long day. Seconds later, something substantial and giant stirred sluggishly inside him. The whisky he had just poured into his stomach Bird effortlessly puked. Kikuhiko swiftly wiped the counter clean and set up a glass of water; Bird only stared dumbly into space. What was he trying to protect from that monster of a baby that he must run so hard and so shamelessly? What was it in himself he was so frantic to defend? The answer was horrifying—nothing! Zero!

Bird eased out of the bucket chair and slowly lowered his feet to the floor. To Himiko, questioning him with eyes slackened by fatigue and sudden drunkenness, he said: "I've decided to take the baby back to the university hospital and let them operate. I've stopped rushing at every exit door."

"What are you talking about?" Himiko said suspiciously. "Bird! What's happened to you! What kind of time is this to start talking about an operation!"

"Ever since the morning my baby was born I've been running away," Bird said with certainty.

"But you're having that baby murdered right this minute, dirtying your hands and mine. How can you call that running away? Besides, we're leaving for Africa together!"

"I left the baby with that abortionist and then I ran away, I fled here," Bird said obstinately. "I've been running the whole time, running and running, and I pictured Africa as the land at the end of all flight, the final spot, the terminal—you know, you're running away, too. You're just another cabaret girl running off with an embezzler."

"I'm participating, Bird, dirtying my own hands along with yours. *Don't you say I'm running away!*" Himiko's shout echoed in the caves of her hysteria.

"Have you forgotten that you drove the car into a pothole today rather than run over a dead sparrow? Is that what a person does just before he cuts a baby's throat?"

Himiko's large face flushed, swelling, then darkened with fury and a presentiment of despair. She glared at Bird, shuddering in vexation: she was trying to fault him and couldn't find her voice.

"If I want to confront this monster honestly instead of running away from it, I have only two alternatives: I can strangle the baby to death with my own hands or I can accept him and bring him up. I've understood that from the beginning but I haven't had the courage to ac-cept it—"

"But Bird," Himiko interrupted, waving her fingers threateningly, "that baby is coming down with pneumonia! If you tried to take him back to the hospital he'd die in the car on the way. Then where would you be? They'd arrest you, that's where!"

"If that happened, it would mean that I'd killed the baby with my own two hands. And I'd deserve whatever I got. I guess I'd be able to take the responsibility."

Bird spoke calmly. He felt that he was now evading deception's final trap, and he was restoring his faith in himself.

Himiko glowered at Bird with tears collecting in her eyes; she appeared to be groping frantically for a new psychological attack, and when at last a strategy occurred, she leaped at it: "Let's say you let them operate and saved the baby's life, what would you have then, Bird? You told me yourself that your son would never be more than a vegetable! Don't you see, it's not only that you'd be creating misery for yourself, you'd be nurturing a life that meant absolutely nothing to this world! Do you suppose that would be for the baby's good? Do you, Bird?"

"It's for my own good. It's so I can stop being a man who's always running away," Bird said.

But Himiko still refused to understand. She stared distrustfully at Bird, challenging him still, and then she labored to smile despite the tears welling in her eyes and mockingly said: "So you're going to manhandle a baby with the faculties of a vegetable into staying alive—Bird! is that part of your new *humanism?*"

"All I want is to stop being a man who continually runs away from responsibility."

"But . . . Bird . . ." Himiko sobbed, ". . . what about our promise to go to Africa together? *What about our promise?*"

"For God's sake Himi, get ahold of yourself! Once Bird here begins worrying about himself, he won't hear you no matter how loud you cry."

Bird saw something akin to raw hatred glitter in Kikuhiko's clouded eyes. But his former friend's command to Himiko was the cue she had been waiting for: once again she became the Himiko who had welcomed Bird several days before when he had arrived so forlornly at her door with his bottle of Johnnie Walker, a girl no longer young, infinitely generous: tender, placid Himiko.

"That's all right, Bird. You don't have to come. I'll sell the house and property and go to Africa anyway. I'll take that boy who stole the tire along for company. Now that I think about it, I've been pretty horrid to him." The tearfulness remained, but there was no mistaking that Himiko had ridden the storm of her hysteria.

"Miss Himi will be all right now," Kikuhiko prompted.

"Thank you," Bird said simply, meaning it, no more to one than to the other.

"Bird, you are going to have to endure all kinds of pain," Himiko said. It was meant as encouragement. "So long, Bird. Take care of yourself!"

Bird nodded, and left the bar.

The taxi raced down the wet streets at horrendous speed. If I die in an accident now before I save the baby, my whole twenty-seven years of life will have meant exactly nothing. Bird was stricken with a sense of fear more profound than any he had ever known.

It was the end of autumn. When Bird came downstairs after saying good-by to the surgeon, his parents-in-law greeted him with a smile in front of the intensive care ward; his wife stood between them with the baby in her arms.

"Congratulations, Bird," his father-in-law called. "He looks like you, you know."

"In a way," Bird said with reserve. A week after the operation the baby had looked almost human; the following week it had begun to resemble Bird. "That fault in the baby's skull was only a few millimeters across and it seems to be closing now. I can show you when we get home, I bor-

rowed the X rays. It turns out the brain wasn't protruding from the skull; so it wasn't a brain hernia after all, just a benign tumor. There were apparently two hard kernels as white as ping-pong balls in that lump they cut away."

"This is one family that has a lot to be grateful for." The professor had been waiting for a lull in the rush of Bird's talk.

"Bird gave so much of his own blood for all those transfusions during the operation, he came out looking as pale as a princess after a date with Dracula." A rare attempt at humor from Bird's exuberant mother-in-law. "Seriously, Bird, you were as courageous and untiring as a young lion."

Frightened by the sudden change in environment, the baby lay in shriveled and unmoving silence, observing the adults out of eyes which must still have been nearly sightless. Since the women stopped repeatedly to cluck and coo over the baby, Bird and the professor gradually drew ahead as they talked. "This time you really met your problem head on," the professor said.

"As a matter of fact, I kept trying to run away. And I almost did. But it seems that reality compels you to live properly when you live in the real world. I mean, even if you intend to get yourself caught in a trap of deception, you find somewhere along the line that your only choice is to avoid it." Bird was surprised at the muted resentment in his voice. "That's what I've found, anyway."

"But it is possible to live in the real world in quite a different way, Bird. There are people who leap-frog from one deception to another until the day they die."

Through half-closed eyes Bird saw again the freighter bound for Zanzibar that had sailed a few days before with Himiko on board. He pictured himself, having killed the baby, standing at her side in place of that boyish man—a sufficiently enticing prospect of Hell. And perhaps just such a reality was being played out in one of Himiko's universes. Bird opened his eyes, turning back to the problems in the universe in which he had chosen to remain. "There is a possibility that the baby's development will be normal," he said, "but there's an equal danger that he'll grow up with an extremely low I.Q. That means I'm going to have to put away as much as I can for his future as well as our own. Naturally, I'm not going to ask you to help me find another job, not after the mess I made of the one I had. I've decided to forget about a career in college teaching—I'm thinking of becoming a guide for foreign tourists. A dream of mine has always been to go to Africa and hire a native guide, so I'll just be reversing the fantasy: I'll be the native guide, for the foreigners who come to Japan."

The professor started to say something in reply when they both had to step aside for a youth with his arm in an exaggerated sling who was being hurried down the corridor by a gang of his friends. The boys swept by, ignoring Bird and his father-in-law. They all wore soiled, shabby jackets which already looked too light for the chilliness of the season. Bird saw the dragons emblazoned on their backs and realized that this was the gang he had battled that night in early summer when his baby was being born.

"I know those boys, but for some reason they didn't pay any attention to me," he said.

"In a few weeks' time you've become almost another person; that probably explains it."

"Do you suppose?"

"You've changed." The professor's voice was warm [75] with a relative's affection. "A childish nickname like Bird doesn't suit you anymore."

Bird waited for the women to catch up and peered down at his son in the cradle of his wife's arms. He wanted to try reflecting his face in the baby's pupils. The mirror of the baby's eyes was a deep, lucid gray and it did begin to reflect an image, but one so excessively fine that Bird couldn't confirm his new face. As soon as he got home he would take a look in the mirror. Then he would try the Balkan dictionary that Mr. Delchef had presented him before his legation had shipped him home. On the inside cover, Mr. Delchef had written the word for *hope*. Bird intended to look up *forbearance*.

GABRIEL GARCÍA MÁRQUEZ
Selection from *One Hundred Years of Solitude*

The Colombian author García Márquez's *One Hundred Years of Solitude* is arguably the most important novel to appear since 1945. When published in Buenos Aires in 1967, it provoked a literary earthquake across the Hispanic world. Critics hailed it as a masterpiece and the public quickly agreed, buying up copies so fast that, at one point, new editions were appearing weekly. Its spectacular success made García Márquez into a celebrity on the order of a great soccer player or a pop music star. Similar critical and public acclaim resulted when the novel was translated into other languages around the world, winning literary prizes in many countries and rocketing to the top of bestseller lists, where it stayed for months. In 1982 García Márquez was awarded the Nobel Prize for literature, the first Latin American novelist to be so honored.

García Márquez's book was responsible for putting the Spanish-American novel on the international map. Since 1945, a literary explosion—called "El Boom"—had been underway in Latin America, with the result that the region's writers turned away from the realist tradition that had dominated their literature since about 1870. Instead, they adopted Modernist methods, learned from reading Woolf (see *To the Lighthouse*) and others. The defining feature of this new type of fiction in Spanish America was its insistence on the right of invention, resulting in what has been called "magic realism," a genre that mixes realistic and supernatural elements. García Márquez's novel, rather than pioneering "magic realism," simply brought this already successful Spanish-American genre to the world's notice.

Gabriel García Márquez (b. 1929) gives credit to Faulkner for his becoming a writer, and this influence is felt in *One Hundred Years of Solitude*. Inspired by Faulkner's fictional county of Yoknapatawpha, Mississippi, García Márquez invented the town of Macondo to serve as a symbol of his Colombian birthplace, Aracataca. In this small town near the Caribbean coast, he spent the first eight years of his life with his grandparents, the rest of his family living elsewhere. The grandparents are the source of the fantastic events that unfold in the novel; for in García Márquez's years with them, both grandparents, who were superstitious and impressionable, delighted in evenings of storytelling about local history and legends and unexplained mysteries—nothing was too strange for them. García Márquez has written many other novels, including the well-received *The Autumn of the Patriarch* (1976)—but none has the compelling fascination of this work.

Reading the Selection

This selection contains the opening pages of *One Hundred Years of Solitude*, in which the intertwined histories of the Buendía family and the town of Macondo are introduced. A hallucinatory mood is created in the first sentence. The reader is plunged into the middle of the story, and future ("many years later"), present, and past ("that distant afternoon") are co-mingled and then left obscure, at least for the moment. Adding to the sense of fantasy is this description of Macondo's early years: "the world was so recent that many things lacked names," thus suggesting a biblical paradise. Holding this sprawling work together is the narrative voice—an attitude of naturalness and indifference toward absolutely everything—a Modernist device but one that was also inspired by the voice of García Márquez's grandmother in Aracataca.

—∭—

Chapter I

Many years later, as he faced the firing squad, Colonel Aureliano Buendía was to remember that distant afternoon when his father took him to discover ice. At that time Macondo was a village of twenty adobe houses, built on the bank of a river of clear water that ran along a bed of polished stones, which were white and enormous, like prehistoric eggs. The world was so recent that many things lacked names, and in order to indicate them it was necessary to point. Every year during the month of March a family of ragged gypsies would set up their tents near the village, and with a great uproar of pipes and kettledrums they would display new inventions. First they brought the magnet. A heavy gypsy with an untamed beard and sparrow hands, who introduced himself as Melquíades, put on a bold public demonstration of what he himself called the eighth wonder of the learned alchemists of Macedonia. He went from house to house dragging two metal ingots and everybody was amazed to see pots, pans, tongs, and braziers tumble down from their places and beams creak from the desperation of nails and screws trying to emerge, and even objects that had been lost for a long time appeared from where they had been searched for most and went dragging along in turbulent confusion behind Melquíades' magical irons. "Things have a life of their own," the gypsy proclaimed with a harsh accent. "It's simply a matter of waking up their souls." José Arcadio Buendía, whose unbridled imagination always went beyond the genius of nature and even beyond miracles and magic, thought that it would be possible to make use of that useless invention to extract gold from the bowels of the earth. Melquíades, who was an honest man, warned him: "It won't work for that." But José Arcadio Buendía at that time did not believe in the honesty of gypsies, so he traded his mule and a pair of goats for the two magnetized ingots. Úrsula Iguarán, his wife, who relied on those animals to increase their poor domestic holdings, was unable to dissuade him. "Very soon we'll have gold enough and more to pave the floors of the house," her husband replied. For several months he worked hard to demonstrate the truth of his idea. He explored every inch of the region, even the riverbed, dragging the two iron ingots along and reciting Melquíades' incantation aloud. The only thing he succeeded in doing was to unearth a suit of fifteenth-century armor which had all of its pieces soldered together with rust and inside of which there was the hollow resonance of an enormous stone-filled gourd. When José Arcadio Buendía and the four men of his expedition managed to take the armor apart, they found inside a calcified skeleton with a copper locket containing a woman's hair around its neck.

In March the gypsies returned. This time they brought a telescope and a magnifying glass the size of a drum, which they exhibited as the latest discovery of the Jews of Amsterdam. They placed a gypsy woman at one end of the village and set up the telescope at the entrance to the

tent. For the price of five reales, people could look into the telescope and see the gypsy woman an arm's length away. "Science has eliminated distance," Melquíades proclaimed. "In a short time, man will be able to see what is happening in any place in the world without leaving his own house." A burning noonday sun brought out a startling demonstration with the gigantic magnifying glass: they put a pile of dry hay in the middle of the street and set it on fire by concentrating the sun's rays. José Arcadio Buendía, who had still not been consoled for the failure of his magnets, conceived the idea of using that invention as a weapon of war. Again Melquíades tried to dissuade him, but he finally accepted the two magnetized ingots and three colonial coins in exchange for the magnifying glass. Úrsula wept in consternation. That money was from a chest of gold coins that her father had put together over an entire life of privation and that she had buried underneath her bed in hopes of a proper occasion to make use of it. José Arcadio Buendía made no attempt to console her, completely absorbed in his tactical experiments with the abnegation of a scientist and even at the risk of his own life. In an attempt to show the effects of the glass on enemy troops, he exposed himself to the concentration of the sun's rays and suffered burns which turned into sores that took a long time to heal. Over the protests of his wife, who was alarmed at such a dangerous invention, at one point he was ready to set the house on fire. He would spend hours on end in his room, calculating the strategic possibilities of his novel weapon until he succeeded in putting together a manual of startling instructional clarity and an irresistible power of conviction. He sent it to the government, accompanied by numerous descriptions of his experiments and several pages of explanatory sketches, by a messenger who crossed the mountains, got lost in measureless swamps, forded stormy rivers, and was on the point of perishing under the lash of despair, plague, and wild beasts until he found a route that joined the one used by the mules that carried the mail. In spite of the fact that a trip to the capital was little less than impossible at that time, José Arcadio Buendía promised to undertake it as soon as the government ordered him to so that he could put on some practical demonstrations of his invention for the military authorities and could train them himself in the complicated art of solar war. For several years he waited for an answer. Finally, tired of waiting, he bemoaned to Melquíades the failure of his project and the gypsy then gave him a convincing proof of his honesty: he gave him back the doubloons in exchange for the magnifying glass, and he left him in addition some Portuguese maps and several instruments of navigation. In his own handwriting he set down a concise synthesis of the studies by Monk Hermann, which he left José Arcadio so that he would be able to make use of the astrolabe, the compass, and the sextant. José Arcadio Buendía spent the long months of the rainy season shut up in a small room that he had built in the rear of the house so that no one would disturb his experiments. Having completely abandoned his domestic obligations, he spent entire nights in the courtyard watching the course of the stars and he almost contracted sunstroke from trying to establish an exact method to ascertain noon. When he became an expert in the use and manipulation of his instruments, he conceived a notion of space that allowed him to navigate across unknown seas, to visit uninhabited territories, and to establish relations with splendid beings without having to leave his study. That was the period in which he acquired the habit of talking to himself, of walking through the house without paying attention to anyone, as Úrsula and the children broke their backs in the garden, growing banana and caladium, cassava and yams, ahuyama roots and eggplants. Suddenly, without warning, his feverish activity was interrupted and was replaced by a kind of fascination. He spent several days as if he were bewitched, softly repeating to himself a string of fearful conjectures without giving credit to his own understanding. Finally, one Tuesday in December, at lunchtime, all at once he released the whole weight of his torment. The children would remember for the rest of their lives the august solemnity with which their father, devastated by his prolonged vigil and by the wrath of his imagination, revealed his discovery to them:

"The earth is round, like an orange."

Úrsula lost her patience. "If you have to go crazy, please go crazy all by yourself!" she shouted. "But don't try to put your gypsy ideas into the heads of the children." José Arcadio Buendía, impassive, did not let himself be frightened by the desperation of his wife, who, in a seizure of rage, smashed the astrolabe against the floor. He built another one, he gathered the men of the village in his little room, and he demonstrated to them, with theories that none of them could understand, the possibility of returning to where one had set out by consistently sailing east. The whole village was convinced that José Arcadio Buendía had lost his reason, when Melquíades returned to set things straight. He gave public praise to the intelligence of a man who from pure astronomical speculation had evolved a theory that had already been proved in practice, although unknown in Macondo until then, and as a proof of his admiration he made him a gift that was to have a profound influence on the future of the village: the laboratory of an alchemist.

By then Melquíades had aged with surprising rapidity. On his first trips he seemed to be the same age as José Arcadio Buendía. But while the latter had preserved his extraordinary strength, which permitted him to pull down a horse by grabbing its ears, the gypsy seemed to have been worn down by some tenacious illness. It was, in reality, the result of multiple and rare diseases contracted on his innumerable trips around the world. According to what he himself said as he spoke to José Arcadio Buendía while helping him set up the laboratory, death followed him everywhere, sniffing at the cuffs of his pants, but never deciding to give him the final clutch of its claws. He was a fugitive from all the plagues and catastrophes that had ever lashed mankind. He had survived pellagra in

Persia, scurvy in the Malayan archipelago, leprosy in Alexandria, beriberi in Japan, bubonic plague in Madagascar, an earthquake in Sicily, and a disastrous shipwreck in the Strait of Magellan. That prodigious creature, said to possess the keys of Nostradamus, was a gloomy man, enveloped in a sad aura, with an Asiatic look that seemed to know what there was on the other side of things. He wore a large black hat that looked like a raven with widespread wings, and a velvet vest across which the patina of the centuries had skated. But in spite of his immense wisdom and his mysterious breadth, he had a human burden, an earthly condition that kept him involved in the small problems of daily life. He would complain of the ailments of old age, he suffered from the most insignificant economic difficulties, and he had stopped laughing a long time back because scurvy had made his teeth drop out. On that suffocating noontime when the gypsy revealed his secrets, José Arcadio Buendía had the certainty that it was the beginning of a great friendship. The children were startled by his fantastic stories. Aureliano, who could not have been more than five at the time, would remember him for the rest of his life as he saw him that afternoon, sitting against the metallic and quivering light from the window, lighting up with his deep organ voice the darkest reaches of the imagination, while down over his temples there flowed the grease that was being melted by the heat. José Arcadio, his older brother, would pass on that wonderful image as a hereditary memory to all of his descendants. Úrsula, on the other hand, held a bad memory of that visit, for she had entered the room just as Melquíades had carelessly broken a flask of bichloride of mercury.

"It's the smell of the devil," she said.

"Not at all," Melquíades corrected her. "It has been proven that the devil has sulphuric properties and this is just a little corrosive sublimate."

Always didactic, he went into a learned exposition of the diabolical properties of cinnabar, but Úrsula paid no attention to him, although she took the children off to pray. That biting odor would stay forever in her mind linked to the memory of Melquíades.

The rudimentary laboratory—in addition to a profusion of pots, funnels, retorts, filters, and sieves—was made up of a primitive water pipe, a glass beaker with a long, thin neck, a reproduction of the philosopher's egg, and a still the gypsies themselves had built in accordance with modern descriptions of the three-armed alembic of Mary the Jew. Along with those items, Melquíades left samples of the seven metals that corresponded to the seven planets, the formulas of Moses and Zosimus for doubling the quantity of gold, and a set of notes and sketches concerning the processes of the Great Teaching that would permit those who could interpret them to undertake the manufacture of the philosopher's stone. Seduced by the simplicity of the formulas to double the quantity of gold, José Arcadio Buendía paid court to Úrsula for several weeks so that she would let him dig up her colonial coins and increase them by as many times as it was possible to subdivide mercury. Úrsula gave in, as always, to her husband's unyielding obstinacy. Then José Arcadio Buendía threw three doubloons into a pan and fused them with copper filings, orpiment, brimstone, and lead. He put it all to boil in a pot of castor oil until he got a thick and pestilential syrup which was more like common caramel than valuable gold. In risky and desperate processes of distillation, melted with the seven planetary metals, mixed with hermetic mercury and vitriol of Cyprus, and put back to cook in hog fat for lack of any radish oil, Úrsula's precious inheritance was reduced to a large piece of burnt hog cracklings that was firmly stuck to the bottom of the pot.

When the gypsies came back, Úrsula had turned the whole population of the village against them. But curiosity was greater than fear, for that time the gypsies went about the town making a deafening noise with all manner of musical instruments while a hawker announced the exhibition of the most fabulous discovery of the Naciancenes. So that everyone went to the tent and by paying one cent they saw a youthful Melquíades, recovered, unwrinkled, with a new and flashing set of teeth. Those who remembered his gums that had been destroyed by scurvy, his flaccid cheeks, and his withered lips trembled with fear at the final proof of the gypsy's supernatural power. The fear

10

turned into panic when Melquíades took out his teeth, intact, encased in their gums, and showed them to the audience for an instant—a fleeting instant in which he went back to being the same decrepit man of years past—and put them back again and smiled once more with the full control of his restored youth. Even José Arcadio Buendía himself considered that Melquíades' knowledge had reached unbearable extremes, but he felt a healthy excitement when the gypsy explained to him alone the workings of his false teeth. It seemed so simple and so prodigious at the same time that overnight he lost all interest in his experiments in alchemy. He underwent a new crisis of bad humor. He did not go back to eating regularly, and he would spend the day walking through the house. "Incredible things are happening in the world," he said to Úrsula. "Right there across the river there are all kinds of magical instruments while we keep on living like donkeys." Those who had known him since the foundation of Macondo were startled at how much he had changed under Melquíades' influence. . . .

ALICE WALKER
"Everyday Use"

Alice Walker (b.1944) is one of the most honored and widely read African American writer of her generation, the one that grew to maturity after 1954 when the Supreme Court handed down its ruling outlawing separate but equal schools. A prolific author who writes in varied genres, she has produced five books of poetry, two books of essays, two collections of short stories, and five novels. A measure of the quality of her work is that her books appeal to mainstream audiences while remaining true to the black experience. Her most celebrated novel, *The Color Purple* (1982), won both the Pulitzer Prize for fiction and the National Book Award in 1983, a rarity in the annals of publishing. When made into a film, it became one of the most popular movies of the 1980s—a record unmatched by any other black author at work today.

Among black writers, Walker is distinctive because of her brand of feminism. She has made her literary project the reclaiming of the matrilineal (tracing ancestry through the mothers) dimension in African American life. To this end, she has researched the female goddesses of Africa and interwoven them and their history into the texture of her novels, the genre for which she is best known. In her novels, such as *The Temple of My Familiar* (1989), she explores the black women's collective subconscious using dreams, imaginings, rituals, and legends. She also furthered black feminism by editing an anthology of works by Zora Neale Hurston (see "How It Feels to Be Colored Me"), thus restoring this neglected author to a central place in black women's writing.

Walker came of age in the social upheavals of the 1950s. Born in Georgia, the eighth child in a family of sharecroppers, she grew up, in her words, "poor [and] dusty." She received a privileged education, however, at predominantly black Spelman College in Atlanta and mainly white Sarah Lawrence College in Massachusetts. Radicalized by the civil rights movement, she registered black voters in Georgia, assisted with the Head Start program in Mississippi, and worked for the department of welfare in New York City. In her writings, Walker draws on her experience in this movement, but she refuses to deal in simple propaganda. She does portray the sufferings of blacks at the hands of whites, but she is equally interested in showing hypocrisy and cruelty within black life, disguised as militancy in support of a worthy cause.

Reading the Selection

Walker's "Everyday Use," set within today's black community, is a short story with the theme of culture clash, old versus new. In the story, two sisters with little in common are reunited after many years, only to discover that they do not like one another. In the style of a parable, the sisters represent two aspects of black culture: Sister Dee is educated, wealthy, and into trendy "blackness," as evidenced by her African name, Wangero; sister Maggie is scarred, mentally slow, poor, and untouched by civil rights advances. For a moment, a battle looms between the sisters over ownership of quilts— made by a grandmother and thus symbolic of black heritage. Dee wants the quilts for wall hangings; Maggie needs them for everyday use. Rather than fight, though, Maggie nobly agrees to give them up, at which point the mother (the narrator) "snatche[s] the quilts out of Miss Wangero's hands and dump[s] them into Maggie's lap." Thus, in this culture clash, the mother sides with Maggie and the ancestral tradition.

— ⚬ —

For Your Grandmama

1 I will wait for her in the yard that Maggie and I made so clean and wavy yesterday afternoon. A yard like this is more comfortable than most people know. It is not just a yard. It is like an extended living room. When the hard clay is swept clean as a floor and the fine sand around the edges lined with tiny, irregular grooves anyone can come and sit and look up into the elm tree and wait for the breezes that never come inside the house.

Maggie will be nervous until after her sister goes: she will stand hopelessly in corners homely and ashamed of the burn scars down her arms and legs, eyeing her sister with a mixture of envy and awe. She thinks her sister has held life always in the palm of one hand, that "no" is a word the world never learned to say to her.

You've no doubt seen those TV shows where the child who has "made it" is confronted, as a surprise, by her own mother and father, tottering in weakly from backstage. (A pleasant surprise, of course: What would they do if parent and child came on the show only to curse out and insult each other?) On TV mother and child embrace and smile into each other's faces. Sometimes the mother and father weep, the child wraps them in her arms and leans across the table to tell how she would not have made it without their help. I have seen these programs.

Sometimes I dream a dream in which Dee and I are suddenly brought together on a TV program of this sort. Out of a dark and soft-seated limousine I am ushered into a bright room filled with many people. There I meet a smiling, gray, sporty man like Johnny Carson who shakes my hand and tells me what a fine girl I have. Then we are on the stage and Dee is embracing me with tears in her eyes. She pins on my dress a large orchid, even though she has told me once that she thinks orchids are tacky flowers.

5 In real life I am a large, big-boned woman with rough, man-working hands. In the winter I wear flannel nightgowns to bed and overalls during the day. I can kill and clean a hog as mercilessly as a man. My fat keeps me hot in zero weather. I can work outside all day, breaking ice to get water for washing; I can eat pork liver cooked over the open fire minutes after it comes steaming from the hog. One winter I knocked a bull calf straight in the brain between the eyes with a sledge hammer and had the meat hung up to chill before nightfall. But of course all this does not show on television. I am the way my daughter would want me to be: a hundred pounds lighter, my skin like an uncooked barley pancake. My hair glistens in the hot bright lights. Johnny Carson has much to do to keep up with my quick and witty tongue.

But that is a mistake. I know even before I wake up. Who ever knew a Johnson with a quick tongue? Who can even imagine me looking a strange white man in the eye? It seems to me I have talked to them always with one foot raised in flight, with my head turned in whichever way is farthest from them. Dee, though. She would always look anyone in the eye. Hesitation was no part of her nature.

"How do I look, Mama?" Maggie says, showing just enough of her thin body enveloped in pink skirt and red blouse for me to know she's there, almost hidden by the door.

"Come out into the yard," I say.

Have you ever seen a lame animal, perhaps a dog run over by some careless person rich enough to own a car, sidle up to someone who is ignorant enough to be kind to him? That is the way my Maggie walks. She has been like this, chin on chest, eyes on ground, feet in shuffle, ever since the fire that burned the other house to the ground.

10 Dee is lighter than Maggie, with nicer hair and a fuller figure. She's a woman now, though sometimes I forget. How long ago was it that the other house burned? Ten, twelve years? Sometimes I can hear the flames and feel Maggie's arms sticking to me, her hair smoking and her dress falling off her in little black papery flakes. Her eyes seemed stretched open, blazed open by the flames reflected in them. And Dee. I see her standing off under the sweet gum tree she used to dig gum out of; a look of concentration on her face as she watched the last dingy gray board of the house fall in toward the red-hot brick

chimney. Why don't you do a dance around the ashes? I'd wanted to ask her. She had hated the house that much.

I used to think she hated Maggie, too. But that was before we raised the money, the church and me, to send her to Augusta to school. She used to read to us without pity; forcing words, lies, other folks' habits, whole lives upon us two, sitting trapped and ignorant underneath her voice. She washed us in a river of make-believe, burned us with a lot of knowledge we didn't necessarily need to know. Pressed us to her with the serious way she read, to shove us away at just the moment, like dimwits, we seemed about to understand.

Dee wanted nice things. A yellow organdy dress to wear to her graduation from high school; black pumps to match a green suit she'd made from an old suit somebody gave me. She was determined to stare down any disaster in her efforts. Her eyelids would not flicker for minutes at a time. Often I fought off the temptation to shake her. At sixteen she had a style of her own: and knew what style was.

I never had an education myself. After second grade the school was closed down. Don't ask me why: in 1927 colored asked fewer questions than they do now. Sometimes Maggie reads to me. She stumbles along good-naturedly but can't see well. She knows she is not bright. Like good looks and money, quickness passed her by. She will marry John Thomas (who has mossy teeth in an earnest face) and then I'll be free to sit here and I guess just sing church songs to myself. Although I never was a good singer. Never could carry a tune. I was always better at a man's job. I used to love to milk till I was hooked in the side in '49. Cows are soothing and slow and don't bother you, unless you try to milk them the wrong way.

I have deliberately turned my back on the house. It is three rooms, just like the one that burned, except the roof is tin; they don't make shingle roofs any more. There are no real windows, just some holes cut in the sides, like the portholes in a ship, but not round and not square, with rawhide holding the shutters up on the outside. This house is in a pasture, too, like the other one. No doubt when Dee sees it she will want to tear it down. She wrote me once that no matter where we "choose" to live, she will manage to come see us. But she will never bring her friends. Maggie and I thought about this and Maggie asked me, "Mama, when did Dee ever *have* any friends?"

She had a few. Furtive boys in pink shirts hanging about on washday after school. Nervous girls who never laughed. Impressed with her they worshiped the well-turned phrase, the cute shape, the scalding humor that erupted like bubbles in lye. She read to them.

When she was courting Jimmy T she didn't have much time to pay to us, but turned all her faultfinding power on him. He *flew* to marry a cheap gal from a family of ignorant flashy people. She hardly had time to recompose herself.

When she comes I will meet—but there they are!

Maggie attempts to make a dash for the house, in her shuffling way, but I stay her with my hand. "Come back here," I say. And she stops and tries to dig a well in the sand with her toe.

It is hard to see them clearly through the strong sun. But even the first glimpse of leg out of the car tells me it is Dee. Her feet were always neat-looking, as if God himself had shaped them with a certain style. From the other side of the car comes a short, stocky man. Hair is all over his head a foot long and hanging from his chin like a kinky mule tail. I hear Maggie suck in her breath. "Uhnnnh," is what it sounds like. Like when you see the wriggling end of a snake just in front of your foot on the road. "Uhnnnh."

Dee next. A dress down to the ground, in this hot weather. A dress so loud it hurts my eyes. There are yellows and oranges enough to throw back the light of the sun. I feel my whole face warming from the heat waves it throws out. Earrings gold, too, and hanging down to her shoulders. Bracelets dangling and making noises when she moves her arm up to shake the folds of the dress out of her armpits. The dress is loose and flows, and as she walks closer, I like it. I hear Maggie go "Uhnnnh" again. It is her sister's hair. It stands straight up like the wool on a sheep. It is black as night and around the edges are two long pigtails that rope about like small lizards disappearing behind her ears.

"Wa-su-zo-Tean-o!" she says, coming on in that gliding way the dress makes her move. The short stocky fellow with the hair to his navel is all grinning and he follows up with "Asalamalakim, my mother and sister!" He moves to hug Maggie but she falls back, right up against the back of my chair. I feel her trembling there and when I look up I see the perspiration falling off her chin.

"Don't get up," says Dee. Since I am stout it takes something of a push. You can see me trying to move a second or two before I make it. She turns, showing white heels through her sandals, and goes back to the car. Out she peeks next with a Polaroid. She stoops down quickly and lines up picture after picture of me sitting there in front of the house with Maggie cowering behind me. She never takes a shot without making sure the house is included. When a cow comes nibbling around the edge of the yard she snaps it and me and Maggie *and* the house. Then she puts the Polaroid in the back seat of the car, and comes up and kisses me on the forehead.

Meanwhile Asalamalakim is going through the motions with Maggie's hand. Maggie's hand is as limp as a fish, and probably as cold, despite the sweat, and she keeps trying to pull it back. It looks like Asalamalakim wants to shake hands but wants to do it fancy. Or maybe he don't know how people shake hands. Anyhow, he soon gives up on Maggie.

"Well," I say. "Dee."

"No, Mama," she says. "Not 'Dee,' Wangero Leewanika Kemanjo!"

"What happened to 'Dee'?" I wanted to know.

"She's dead," Wangero said. "I couldn't bear it any longer being named after the people who oppress me."

"You know as well as me you was named after your aunt Dicie," I said. Dicie is my sister. She named Dee. We called her "Big Dee" after Dee was born.

"But who was *she* named after?" asked Wangero.

"I guess after Grandma Dee," I said.

"And who was she named after?" asked Wangero.

"Her mother," I said, and saw Wangero was getting tired. "That's about as far back as I can trace it," I said. Though, in fact, I probably could have carried it back beyond the Civil War through the branches.

"Well," said Asalamalakim, "there you are."

"Uhnnnh," I heard Maggie say.

"There I was not," I said, "before 'Dicie' cropped up in our family, so why should I try to trace it that far back?" 35

He just stood there grinning, looking down on me like somebody inspecting a Model A car. Every once in a while he and Wangero sent eye signals over my head.

"How do you pronounce this name?" I asked.

"You don't have to call me by it if you don't want to," said Wangero.

"Why shouldn't I?" I asked. "If that's what you want us to call you, we'll call you."

"I know it might sound awkward at first," said Wangero. 40

"I'll get used to it," I said. "Ream it out again."

Well, soon we got the name out of the way. Asalamalakim had a name twice as long and three times as hard. After I tripped over it two or three times he told me to just call him Hakim-a-barber. I wanted to ask him was he a barber, but I didn't really think he was, so I didn't ask.

"You must belong to those beef-cattle peoples down the road," I said. They said "Asalamalakim" when they met you, too, but they didn't shake hands. Always too busy: feeding the cattle, fixing the fences, putting up salt-lick shelters, throwing down hay. When the white folks poisoned some of the herd the men stayed up all night with rifles in their hands. I walked a mile and a half just to see the sight.

Hakim-a-barber said, "I accept some of their doctrines, but farming and raising cattle is not my style." (They didn't tell me, and I didn't ask, whether Wangero [Dee] had really gone and married him.)

We sat down to eat and right away he said he didn't 45 eat collards and pork was unclean. Wangero, though, went on through the chitlins and corn bread, the greens and everything else. She talked a blue streak over the sweet potatoes. Everything delighted her. Even the fact that we still used the benches her daddy made for the table when we couldn't afford to buy chairs.

"Oh, Mama!" she cried. Then turned to Hakim-a-barber. "I never knew how lovely these benches are. You can feel the rump prints," she said, running her hands underneath her and along the bench. Then she gave a sigh and her hand closed over Grandma Dee's butter dish. "That's it!" she said. "I knew there was something I wanted to ask you if I could have." She jumped up from the table and went over in the corner where the churn stood, the milk in it clabber by now. She looked at the churn and looked at it.

"This churn top is what I need," she said. "Didn't Uncle Buddy whittle it out of a tree you all used to have?"

"Yes," I said.

"Uh huh," she said happily. "And I want the dasher, too."

"Uncle Buddy whittle that, too?" asked the barber. 50

Dee (Wangero) looked up at me.

"Aunt Dee's first husband whittled the dash," said Maggie so low you almost couldn't hear her. "His name was Henry, but they called him Stash."

"Maggie's brain is like an elephant's," Wangero said, laughing. "I can use the churn top as a centerpiece for the alcove table," she said, sliding a plate over the churn, "and I'll think of something artistic to do with the dasher."

When she finished wrapping the dasher the handle stuck out. I took it for a moment in my hands. You didn't even have to look close to see where hands pushing the dasher up and down to make butter had left a kind of sink in the wood. In fact, there were a lot of small sinks; you could see where thumbs and fingers had sunk into the wood. It was beautiful light yellow wood, from a tree that grew in the yard where Big Dee and Stash had lived.

After dinner Dee (Wangero) went to the trunk at the 55 foot of my bed and started rifling through it. Maggie hung back in the kitchen over the dishpan. Out came Wangero with two quilts. They had been pieced by Grandma Dee and then Big Dee and me had hung them on the quilt frames on the front porch and quilted them. One was in the Lone Star pattern. The other was Walk Around the Mountain. In both of them were scraps of dresses Grandma Dee had worn fifty and more years ago. Bits and pieces of Grandpa Jarrell's paisley shirts. And one teeny faded blue piece, about the size of a penny matchbox, that was from Great Grandpa Ezra's uniform that he wore in the Civil War.

"Mama," Wangero said sweet as a bird. "Can I have these old quilts?"

I heard something fall in the kitchen, and a minute later the kitchen door slammed.

"Why don't you take one or two of the others?" I asked. "These old things was just done by me and Big Dee from some tops your grandma pieced before she died."

"No," said Wangero. "I don't want those. They are stitched around the borders by machine."

"That'll make them last better," I said.

"That's not the point," said Wangero. "These are all 60 pieces of dresses Grandma used to wear. She did all this stitching by hand. Imagine!" She held the quilts securely in her arms, stroking them.

"Some of the pieces, like those lavender ones, come from old clothes her mother handed down to her," I said, moving up to touch the quilts. Dee (Wangero) moved back just enough so that I couldn't reach the quilts. They already belonged to her.

"Imagine!" she breathed again, clutching them closely to her bosom.

"The truth is," I said, "I promised to give them quilts to Maggie, for when she marries John Thomas."

She gasped like a bee had stung her. 65

"Maggie can't appreciate these quilts!" she said. "She'd probably be backward enough to put them to everyday use."

"I reckon she would," I said. "God knows I been saving 'em for long enough with nobody using 'em. I hope she will!" I didn't want to bring up how I had offered Dee (Wangero) a quilt when she went away to college. Then she had told me they were old-fashioned, out of style.

"But they're *priceless!*" she was saying now, furiously; for she has a temper. "Maggie would put them on the bed and in five years they'd be in rags. Less than that!"

"She can always make some more," I said. "Maggie knows how to quilt."

Dee (Wangero) looked at me with hatred. "You just will not understand. The point is these quilts, *these* quilts!" 70

"Well," I said, stumped. "What would *you* do with them?"

"Hang them," she said. As if that was the only thing you *could* do with quilts.

Maggie by now was standing in the door. I could almost hear the sound her feet made as they scraped over each other.

"She can have them, Mama," she said, like somebody used to never winning anything, or having anything reserved for her. "I can 'member Grandma Dee without the quilts."

I looked at her hard. She had filled her bottom lip 75 with checkerberry snuff and it gave her face a kind of dopey, hangdog look. It was Grandma Dee and Big Dee who taught her how to quilt herself. She stood there with her scarred hands hidden in the folds of her skirt. She looked at her sister with something like fear but she wasn't mad at her. This was Maggie's portion. This was the way she knew God to work.

When I looked at her like that something hit me in the top of my head and ran down to the soles of my feet. Just like when I'm in church and the spirit of God touches me and I get happy and shout. I did something I never had done before: hugged Maggie to me, then dragged her on into the room, snatched the quilts out of Miss Wangero's hands and dumped them into Maggie's lap. Maggie just sat there on my bed with her mouth open.

"Take one or two of the others," I said to Dee.

But she turned without a word and went out to Hakim-a-barber.

"You just don't understand," she said, as Maggie and I came out to the car.

"What don't I understand?" I wanted to know. 80

"Your heritage," she said. And then she turned to Maggie, kissed her, and said, "You ought to try to make something of yourself, too, Maggie. It's really a new day for us. But from the way you and Mama still live you'd never know it."

She put on some sunglasses that hid everything above the tip of her nose and her chin.

Maggie smiled; maybe at the sunglasses. But a real smile, not scared. After we watched the car dust settle I asked Maggie to bring me a dip of snuff. And then the two of us sat there just enjoying, until it was time to go in the house and go to bed.

MAXINE HONG KINGSTON

Selection from *The Woman Warrior*

Maxine Hong Kingston (b. 1940) is one of the most talented and original Chinese-American writers in this nation's history. Through her critically acclaimed and popular writings, she has put the Chinese-American experience into American literature. Her literary project is to "claim America," meaning to show that the Chinese have the right to belong through their labor in building the country and supporting themselves. In staking out this claim, she has been influenced by the poet William Carlos Williams (1883–1963), who envisioned an American culture distinct from Europe and built from indigenous materials and forms. On another level, she wants to combat Sinophobia, fear of the "yellow race," which has been a marked feature of American life since the first wave of Chinese immigrants in the late nineteenth century. Thus, Kingston not only celebrates Chinese achievement but she also avenges past wrongs—by calling exploitation, racism, and ignorance by their true names.

As the first-generation daughter of immigrants, Kingston uses her own life as a paradigm of Chinese-American culture. A graduate of an American university and a high-school teacher from 1965 to 1977, Kingston nevertheless feels a need to explore her ancestral roots. In China, both her parents were engaged in promising careers, the father as a schoolteacher and the mother as a midwife; both left their jobs to seek their fortunes in "Gold Mountain," an overly optimistic name for California. Once in Stockton's Chinatown, they could only find work in a laundry. The parents' fall in the world plunged her father into black moods during much of Maxine's childhood. In contrast, her mother kept her good humor by telling stories in the peasant talk-story Cantonese tradition that is the heritage of most Chinese-Americans.

Talk-stories are moral tales of ancient heroes and family secrets. It is these stories, reworked from those Kingston's mother told, written in an artful combination of Chinese rhythms and American slang, which provide the narrative structure of Kingston's best-known works: *The Woman Warrior:*

Memoirs of a Girlhood Among Ghosts (1976), dealing with matriarchal influence, and *China Men* (1980), telling of the patriarchal side. Partly written to come to terms with her family, both books have the broader aim of describing the Chinese-American predicament—being caught in a double bind between two proud, often mutually antagonistic cultures.

Reading the Selection

"No Name Woman," the first episode in *The Woman Warrior*, is the talk-story of Kingston's paternal aunt, a "ghost" who haunts the author's past. The aunt's name is unmentionable because she disgraced the family in China by becoming pregnant—perhaps by rape—while her husband was in America. When her illegitimate baby was born, villagers destroyed the family compound. In despair, "No Name" aunt drowned herself and her child in the family well.

   The talk-story of "No Name" sets the tone for *The Woman Warrior*, establishing that traditional Chinese culture has a low opinion of women. It is this oppression against which the heroic deeds of the idealized female warriors, treated in later chapters, can be judged. The "No Name" episode also reflects Kingston's self-identification as a woman warrior. Her sympathetic portrait of the aunt whom the family deliberately forgot is an act of rebellion against tradition and a vindication of the wronged relative.

—⁓—

No Name Woman

"You must not tell anyone," my mother said, "what I am about to tell you. In China your father had a sister who killed herself. She jumped into the family well. We say that your father has all brothers because it is as if she had never been born.

   "In 1924 just a few days after our village celebrated seventeen hurry-up weddings—to make sure that every young man who went 'out on the road' would responsibly come home—your father and his brothers and your grandfather and his brothers and your aunt's new husband sailed for America, the Gold Mountain. It was your grandfather's last trip. Those lucky enough to get contracts waved goodbye from the decks. They fed and guarded the stowaways and helped them off in Cuba, New York, Bali, Hawaii. 'We'll meet in California next year,' they said. All of them sent money home.

   "I remember looking at your aunt one day when she and I were dressing; I had not noticed before that she had such a protruding melon of a stomach. But I did not think, 'She's pregnant,' until she began to look like other pregnant women, her shirt pulling and the white tops of her black pants showing. She could not have been pregnant, you see, because her husband had been gone for years. No one said anything. We did not discuss it. In early summer she was ready to have the child, long after the time when it could have been possible.

   "The village had also been counting. On the night the baby was to be born the villagers raided our house. Some were crying. Like a great saw, teeth strung with lights, files of people walked zigzag across our land, tearing the rice. Their lanterns doubled in the disturbed black water, which drained away through the broken bunds. As the villagers closed in, we could see that some of them, probably men and women we knew well, wore white masks. The people with long hair hung it over their faces. Women with short

hair made it stand up on end. Some had tied white bands around their foreheads, arms, and legs.

   "At first they threw mud and rocks at the house. Then they threw eggs and began slaughtering our stock. We could hear the animals scream their deaths—the roosters, the pigs, a last great roar from the ox. Familiar wild heads flared in our night windows; the villagers encircled us. Some of the faces stopped to peer at us, their eyes rushing like search-lights. The hands flattened against the panes, framed heads, and left red prints.

   "The villagers broke in the front and the back doors at the same time, even though we had not locked the doors against them. Their knives dripped with the blood of our animals. They smeared blood on the doors and walls. One woman swung a chicken, whose throat she had slit, splattering blood in red arcs about her. We stood together in the middle of our house, in the family hall with the pictures and tables of the ancestors around us, and looked straight ahead.

   "At that time the house had only two wings. When the men came back, we would build two more to enclose our courtyard and a third one to begin a second courtyard. The villagers pushed through both wings, even your grandparents' rooms, to find your aunt's, which was also mine until the men returned. From this room a new wing for one of the younger families would grow. They ripped up her clothes and shoes and broke her combs, grinding them underfoot. They tore her work from the loom. They scattered the cooking fire and rolled the new weaving in it. We could hear them in the kitchen breaking our bowls and banging the pots. They overturned the great waist-high earthenware jugs; duck eggs, pickled fruits, vegetables burst out and mixed in acrid torrents. The old woman from the next field swept a broom through the air and loosed the spirits-of-the-broom over our heads. 'Pig.'

'Ghost.' 'Pig,' they sobbed and scolded while they ruined our house.

"When they left, they took sugar and oranges to bless themselves. They cut pieces from the dead animals. Some of them took bowls that were not broken and clothes that were not torn. Afterward we swept up the rice and sewed it back up into sacks. But the smells from the spilled preserves lasted. Your aunt gave birth in the pigsty that night. The next morning when I went for the water, I found her and the baby plugging up the family well.

"Don't let your father know that I told you. He denies her. Now that you have started to menstruate, what happened to her could happen to you. Don't humiliate us. You wouldn't like to be forgotten as if you had never been born. The villagers are watchful."

Whenever she had to warn us about life, my mother [10] told stories that ran like this one, a story to grow up on. She tested our strength to establish realities. Those in the emigrant generations who could not reassert brute survival died young and far from home. Those of us in the first American generations have had to figure out how the invisible world the emigrants built around our childhoods fits in solid America.

The emigrants confused the gods by diverting their curses, misleading them with crooked streets and false names. They must try to confuse their offspring as well, who, I suppose, threaten them in similar ways—always trying to get things straight, always trying to name the unspeakable. The Chinese I know hide their names; sojourners take new names when their lives change and guard their real names with silence.

Chinese-Americans, when you try to understand what things in you are Chinese, how do you separate what is peculiar to childhood, to poverty, insanities, one family, your mother who marked your growing with stories, from what is Chinese? What is Chinese tradition and what is the movies?

If I want to learn what clothes my aunt wore, whether flashy or ordinary, I would have to begin, "Remember Father's drowned-in-the-well sister?" I cannot ask that. My mother has told me once and for all the useful parts. She will add nothing unless powered by Necessity, a riverbank that guides her life. She plants vegetable gardens rather than lawns; she carries the odd-shaped tomatoes home from the fields and eats food left for the gods.

Whenever we did frivolous things, we used up energy; we flew high kites. We children came up off the ground over the melting cones our parents brought home from work and the American movie on New Year's Day— *Oh, You Beautiful Doll* with Betty Grable one year, and *She Wore a Yellow Ribbon* with John Wayne another year. After the one carnival ride each, we paid in guilt; our tired father counted his change on the dark walk home.

Adultery is extravagance. Could people who hatch [15] their own chicks and eat the embryos and the heads for delicacies and boil the feet in vinegar for party food, leaving only the gravel, eating even the gizzard lining—could such people engender a prodigal aunt? To be a woman, to have a daughter in starvation time was a waste enough. My aunt could not have been the lone romantic who gave

up everything for sex. Women in the old China did not choose. Some man had commanded her to lie with him and be his secret evil. I wonder whether he masked himself when he joined the raid on her family.

Perhaps she had encountered him in the fields or on the mountain where the daughters-in-law collected fuel. Or perhaps he first noticed her in the marketplace. He was not a stranger because the village housed no strangers. She had to have dealings with him other than sex. Perhaps he worked an adjoining field, or he sold her the cloth for the dress she sewed and wore. His demand must have surprised, then terrified her. She obeyed him; she always did as she was told.

When the family found a young man in the next village to be her husband, she had stood tractably beside the best rooster, his proxy, and promised before they met that she would be his forever. She was lucky that he was her age and she would be the first wife, an advantage secure now. The night she first saw him, he had sex with her. Then he left for America. She had almost forgotten what he looked like. When she tried to envision him, she only saw the black and white face in the group photograph the men had had taken before leaving.

The other man was not, after all, much different from her husband. They both gave orders: she followed. "If you tell your family, I'll beat you. I'll kill you. Be here again next week." No one talked sex, ever. And she might have separated the rapes from the rest of living if only she did not have to buy her oil from him or gather wood in the same forest. I want her fear to have lasted just as long as rape lasted so that the fear could have been contained. No drawn-out fear. But women at sex hazarded birth and hence lifetimes. The fear did not stop but permeated everywhere. She told the man, "I think I'm pregnant." He organized the raid against her.

On nights when my mother and father talked about their life back home, sometimes they mentioned an "outcast table" whose business they still seemed to be settling, their voices tight. In a commensal tradition, where food is precious, the powerful older people made wrongdoers eat alone. Instead of letting them start separate new lives like the Japanese, who could become samurais and geishas, the Chinese family, faces averted but eyes glowering sideways, hung on to the offenders and fed them leftovers. My aunt must have lived in the same house as my parents and eaten at an outcast table. My mother spoke about the raid as if she had seen it, when she and my aunt, a daughter-in-law to a different household, should not have been living together at all. Daughters-in-law lived with their husbands' parents, not their own; a synonym for marriage in Chinese is "taking a daughter-in-law." Her husband's parents could have sold her, mortgaged her, stoned her. But they had sent her back to her own mother and father, a mysterious act hinting at disgraces not told me. Perhaps they had thrown her out to deflect the avengers.

She was the only daughter; her four brothers went [20] with her father, husband, and uncles "out on the road" and for some years became western men. When the goods were divided among the family, three of the brothers took land, and the youngest, my father, chose an education.

After my grandparents gave their daughter away to her husband's family, they had dispensed all the adventure and all the property. They expected her alone to keep the traditional ways, which her brothers, now among the barbarians, could fumble without detection. The heavy, deep-rooted women were to maintain the past against the flood, safe for returning. But the rare urge west had fixed upon our family, and so my aunt crossed boundaries not delineated in space.

The work of preservation demands that the feelings playing about in one's guts not be turned into action. Just watch their passing like cherry blossoms. But perhaps my aunt, my forerunner, caught in a slow life, let dreams grow and fade and after some months or years went toward what persisted. Fear at the enormities of the forbidden kept her desires delicate, wire and bone. She looked at a man because she liked the way the hair was tucked behind his ears, or she liked the question-mark line of a long torso curving at the shoulder and straight at the hip. For warm eyes or a soft voice or a slow walk—that's all—a few hairs, a line, a brightness, a sound, a pace, she gave up family. She offered us up for a charm that vanished with tiredness, a pigtail that didn't toss when the wind died. Why, the wrong lighting could erase the dearest thing about him.

It could very well have been, however, that my aunt did not take subtle enjoyment of her friend, but, a wild woman, kept rollicking company. Imagining her free with sex doesn't fit, though. I don't know any women like that, or men either. Unless I see her life branching into mine, she gives me no ancestral help.

To sustain her being in love, she often worked at herself in the mirror, guessing at the colors and shapes that would interest him, changing them frequently in order to hit on the right combination. She wanted him to look back.

On a farm near the sea, a woman who tended her appearance reaped a reputation for eccentricity. All the married women blunt-cut their hair in flaps about their ears or pulled it back in tight buns. No nonsense. Neither style blew easily into heart-catching tangles. And at their weddings they displayed themselves in their long hair for the last time. "It brushed the backs of my knees," my mother tells me. "It was braided, and even so, it brushed the backs of my knees."

At the mirror my aunt combed individuality into her bob. A bun could have been contrived to escape into black streamers blowing in the wind or in quiet wisps about her face, but only the older women in our picture album wear buns. She brushed her hair back from her forehead, tucking the flaps behind her ears. She looped a piece of thread, knotted into a circle between her index fingers and thumbs, and ran the double strand across her forehead. When she closed her fingers as if she were making a pair of shadow geese bite, the string twisted together catching the little hairs. Then she pulled the thread away from her skin, ripping the hairs out neatly, her eyes watering from the needles of pain. Opening her fingers, she cleaned the thread, then rolled it along her hairline and the tops of her eyebrows. My mother did the same to me and my sisters and herself. I used to believe that the expression "caught by the short hairs" meant a captive held with a depilatory

string. It especially hurt at the temples, but my mother said we were lucky we didn't have to have our feet bound when we were seven. Sisters used to sit on their beds and cry together, she said, as their mothers or their slaves removed the bandages for a few minutes each night and let the blood gush back into their veins. I hope that the man my aunt loved appreciated a smooth brow, that he wasn't just a tits-and-ass man.

Once my aunt found a freckle on her chin, at a spot that the almanac said predestined her for unhappiness. She dug it out with a hot needle and washed the wound with peroxide.

More attention to her looks than these pullings of hairs and pickings at spots would have caused gossip among the villagers. They owned work clothes and good clothes, and they wore good clothes for feasting the new seasons. But since a woman combing her hair hexes beginnings, my aunt rarely found an occasion to look her best. Women looked like great sea snails—the corded wood, babies, and laundry they carried were the whorls on their backs. The Chinese did not admire a bent back; goddesses and warriors stood straight. Still there must have been a marvelous freeing of beauty when a worker laid down her burden and stretched and arched.

Such commonplace loveliness, however, was not enough for my aunt. She dreamed of a lover for the fifteen days of New Year's, the time for families to exchange visits, money, and food. She plied her secret comb. And sure enough she cursed the year, the family, the village, and herself.

Even as her hair lured her imminent lover, many other men looked at her. Uncles, cousins, nephews, brothers would have looked, too, had they been home between journeys. Perhaps they had already been restraining their curiosity, and they left, fearful that their glances, like a field of nesting birds, might be startled and caught. Poverty hurt, and that was their first reason for leaving. But another, final reason for leaving the crowded house was the never-said.

She may have been unusually beloved, the precious only daughter, spoiled and mirror gazing because of the affection the family lavished on her. When her husband left, they welcomed the chance to take her back from the in-laws; she could live like the little daughter for just a while longer. There are stories that my grandfather was different from other people, "crazy ever since the little Jap bayoneted him in the head." He used to put his naked penis on the dinner table, laughing. And one day he brought home a baby girl, wrapped up inside his brown western-style greatcoat. He had traded one of his sons, probably my father, the youngest, for her. My grandmother made him trade back. When he finally got a daughter of his own, he doted on her. They must have all loved her, except perhaps my father, the only brother who never went back to China, having once been traded for a girl.

Brothers and sisters, newly men and women, had to efface their sexual color and present plain miens. Disturbing hair and eyes, a smile like no other, threatened the ideal of five generations living under one roof. To focus blurs, people shouted face to face and yelled from room to room. The immigrants I know have loud voices, unmodulated to American tones even after years away from the village where they called their friendships out across the fields. I have not been able to stop my mother's screams in public libraries or over telephones. Walking erect (knees straight, toes pointed forward, not pigeon-toed, which is Chinese-feminine) and speaking in an inaudible voice, I have tried to turn myself American-feminine. Chinese communication was loud, public. Only sick people had to whisper. But at the dinner table, where the family members came nearest one another, no one could talk, not the outcasts nor any eaters. Every word that falls from the mouth is a coin lost. Silently they gave and accepted food with both hands. A preoccupied child who took his bowl with one hand got a sideways glare. A complete moment of total attention is due everyone alike. Children and lovers have no singularity here, but my aunt used a secret voice, a separate attentiveness.

She kept the man's name to herself throughout her labor and dying; she did not accuse him that he be punished with her. To save her inseminator's name she gave silent birth.

He may have been somebody in her own household, but intercourse with a man outside the family would have been no less abhorrent. All the village were kinsmen, and the titles shouted in loud country voices never let kinship be forgotten. Any man within visiting distance would have been neutralized as a lover—"brother," "younger brother," "older brother"—one hundred and fifteen relationship titles. Parents researched birth charts probably not so much to assure good fortune as to circumvent incest in a population that has but one hundred surnames. Everybody has eight million relatives. How useless then sexual mannerisms, how dangerous.

As if it came from an atavism deeper than fear, I used to add "brother" silently to boys' names. It hexed the boys, who would or would not ask me to dance, and made them less scary and as familiar and deserving of benevolence as girls.

But, of course, I hexed myself also—no dates. I should 35 have stood up, both arms waving, and shouted out across libraries, "Hey, you! Love me back." I had no idea, though, how to make attraction selective, how to control its direction and magnitude. If I made myself American-pretty so that the five or six Chinese boys in the class fell in love with me, everyone else—the Caucasian, Negro, and Japanese boys—would too. Sisterliness, dignified and honorable, made much more sense.

Attraction eludes control so stubbornly that whole societies designed to organize relationships among people cannot keep order, not even when they bind people to one another from childhood and raise them together. Among the very poor and the wealthy, brothers married their adopted sisters, like doves. Our family allowed some romance, paying adult brides' prices and providing dowries so that their sons and daughters could marry strangers. Marriage promises to turn strangers into friendly relatives—a nation of siblings.

In the village structure, spirits shimmered among the live creatures, balanced and held in equilibrium by time

and land. But one human being flaring up into violence could open up a black hole, a maelstrom that pulled in the sky. The frightened villagers, who depended on one another to maintain the real, went to my aunt to show her a personal, physical representation of the break she had made in the "roundness." Misallying couples snapped off the future, which was to be embodied in true offspring. The villagers punished her for acting as if she could have a private life, secret and apart from them.

If my aunt had betrayed the family at a time of large grain yields and peace, when many boys were born, and wings were being built on many houses, perhaps she might have escaped such severe punishment. But the men—hungry, greedy, tired of planting in dry soil—had been forced to leave the village in order to send food-money home. There were ghost plagues, bandit plagues, wars with the Japanese, floods. My Chinese brother and sister had died of an unknown sickness. Adultery, perhaps only a mistake during good times, became a crime when the village needed food.

The round moon cakes and round doorways, the round tables of graduated sizes that fit one roundness inside another, round windows and rice bowls—these talismans had lost their power to warn this family of the law: a family must be whole, faithfully keeping the descent line by having sons to feed the old and the dead, who in turn look after the family. The villagers came to show my aunt and her lover-in-hiding a broken house. The villagers were speeding up the circling of events because she was too shortsighted to see that her infidelity had already harmed the village, that waves of consequences would return unpredictably, sometimes in disguise, as now, to hurt her. This roundness had to be made coin-sized so that she would see its circumference: punish her at the birth of her baby. Awaken her to the inexorable. People who refused fatalism because they could invent small resources insisted on culpability. Deny accidents and wrest fault from the stars.

After the villagers left, their lanterns now scattering 40 in various directions toward home, the family broke their silence and cursed her. "Aiaa, we're going to die. Death is coming. Death is coming. Look what you've done. You've killed us. Ghost! Dead ghost! Ghost! You've never been born." She ran out into the fields, far enough from the house so that she could no longer hear their voices, and pressed herself against the earth, her own land no more. When she felt the birth coming, she thought that she had been hurt. Her body seized together. "They've hurt me too much," she thought. "This is gall, and it will kill me." With forehead and knees against the earth, her body convulsed and then relaxed. She turned on her back, lay on the ground. The black well of sky and stars went out and out and out forever; her body and her complexity seemed to disappear. She was one of the stars, a bright dot in blackness, without home, without a companion, in eternal cold and silence. An agoraphobia rose in her, speeding higher and higher, bigger and bigger; she would not be able to contain it; there would be no end to fear.

Flayed, unprotected against space, she felt pain return, focusing her body. This pain chilled her—a cold, steady kind of surface pain. Inside, spasmodically, the other pain, the pain of the child, heated her. For hours she lay on the ground, alternately body and space. Sometimes a vision of normal comfort obliterated reality: she saw the family in the evening gambling at the dinner table, the young people massaging their elders' backs. She saw them congratulating one another, high joy on the mornings the rice shoots came up. When these pictures burst, the stars drew yet further apart. Black space opened.

She got to her feet to fight better and remembered that old-fashioned women gave birth in their pigsties to fool the jealous, pain-dealing gods, who do not snatch piglets. Before the next spasms could stop her, she ran to the pigsty, each step a rushing out into emptiness. She climbed over the fence and knelt in the dirt. It was good to have a fence enclosing her, a tribal person alone.

Laboring, this woman who had carried her child as a foreign growth that sickened her every day, expelled it at last. She reached down to touch the hot, wet, moving mass, surely smaller than anything human, and could feel that it was human after all—fingers, toes, nails, nose. She pulled it up on to her belly, and it lay curled there, butt in the air, feet precisely tucked one under the other. She opened her loose shirt and buttoned the child inside. After resting, it squirmed and thrashed and she pushed it up to her breast. It turned its head this way and that until it found her nipple. There, it made little snuffling noises. She clenched her teeth at its preciousness, lovely as a young calf, a piglet, a little dog.

She may have gone to the pigsty as a last act of responsibility: she would protect this child as she had protected its father. It would look after her soul, leaving supplies on her grave. But how would this tiny child without family find her grave when there would be no marker for her anywhere, neither in the earth nor the family hall? No one would give her a family hall name. She had taken the child with her into the wastes. At its birth the two of them had felt the same raw pain of separation, a wound that only the family pressing tight could close. A child with no descent line would not soften her life but only trail after her, ghostlike, begging her to give it purpose. At dawn the villagers on their way to the fields would stand around the fence and look.

Full of milk, the little ghost slept. When it awoke, she hardened her breasts against the milk that crying loosens. Toward morning she picked up the baby and walked to the well.

Carrying the baby to the well shows loving. Otherwise abandon it. Turn its face into the mud. Mothers who love their children take them along. It was probably a girl; there is some hope of forgiveness for boys.

"Don't tell anyone you had an aunt. Your father does not want to hear her name. She has never been born." I have believed that sex was unspeakable and words so strong and fathers so frail that "aunt" would do my father mysterious harm. I have thought that my family, having settled among immigrants who had also been their neighbors in the ancestral land, needed to clean their name, and a wrong word would incite the kinspeople even here. But there is more to this silence: they want me to participate in her punishment. And I have.

In the twenty years since I heard this story I have not asked for details nor said my aunt's name; I do not know it. People who can comfort the dead can also chase after them to hurt them further—a reverse ancestor worship. The real punishment was not the raid swiftly inflicted by the villagers, but the family's deliberately forgetting her. Her betrayal so maddened them, they saw to it that she would suffer forever, even after death. Always hungry, always needing, she would have to beg food from other ghosts, snatch and steal it from those whose living descendants give them gifts. She would have to fight the ghosts massed at crossroads for the buns a few thoughtful citizens leave to decoy her away from village and home so that the ancestral spirits could feast unharassed. At peace, they could act like gods, not ghosts, their descent lines providing them with paper suits and dresses, spirit money, paper houses, paper automobiles, chicken, meat, and rice into eternity—essences delivered up in smoke and flames, steam and incense rising from each rice bowl. In an attempt to make the Chinese care for people outside the family, Chairman Mao encourages us now to give our paper replicas to the spirits of outstanding soldiers and workers, no matter whose ancestors they may be. My aunt remains forever hungry. Goods are not distributed evenly among the dead.

My aunt haunts me—her ghost drawn to me because now, after fifty years of neglect, I alone devote pages of paper to her, though not origamied into houses and clothes. I do not think she always means me well. I am telling on her, and she was a spite suicide, drowning herself in the drinking water. The Chinese are always very frightened of the drowned one, whose weeping ghost, wet hair hanging and skin bloated, waits silently by the water to pull down a substitute.

—ⱱ—

MICHEL FOUCAULT

Selection from *Discipline and Punish: The Birth of the Prison*

The ideas of Michel Foucault (1926–1984), one of the most influential and controversial thinkers in the Post-Modern world, have been either fervently embraced or scornfully rejected. On the one hand, he can be placed in that distinguished line of French skeptics who have helped to shape Western thought for nearly four hundred years: Descartes (see *Discourse on Method*), Diderot (see *Encyclopédie*), and Sartre (see *The Humanism of Existentialism*). On the other hand, angry critics claim that his writings have challenged, if not undermined, some fundamental epistemological (the study of what can and cannot be known) and philosophical assumptions of the West. His books and essays provide an intellectual foundation for scholars who call for new approaches to knowledge, for social critics who analyze the ways people in power treat others, and for political activists who want to reform Western society. Thus Foucault's writings, like those of most radical thinkers, have been taken up by many who have not fully grasped the profundity of his thought.

Foucault was born in Poitiers to bougeois parents, his father being a surgeon and professor in the local medical school. He received a traditional education, attending preparatory schools before qualifying for the prestigious École Normale Supérieure and, later, for the University of Paris. Interest in history and philosophy directed him toward those subjects, and by 1950 he held degrees in philosophy and psychology. In the 1950s and 1960s, he taught at several French universities and lectured in a few European schools. His brilliant study *Mental Illness and Psychology* (1962) established his reputation as a thinker, and in 1970 he was appointed to a professorship at the Collège de France, a post he held until his death. At the Collège de France, he continued to write books and essays. With his quick mind, multiple interests, abrasive personality, and homosexual lifestyle, he became an international academic celebrity, lecturing and teaching at some of the leading universities in Europe and the United States.

Three themes emerge from Foucault's voluminous and varied writings. In his early years, Foucault was concerned with how people communicate and identify reality; to this end, he examined how humans create their understanding of things and how language helps them determine how they perceive what is actual or real. In his middle years, he focused on the issue of relationships between knowledge and power; he concluded that people with power tend to use professional knowledge to control others, such as by denying access to information, whether critical or not. In his later years, he examined the topic of personal identity, showing that it is determined by personal experiences and interaction with others; he approached this topic through a history of sexuality—an ambitious project on which he was working when he died.

These themes grew from his research on such diverse topics as the origins of asylums, hospitals, clinics, and prisons and the roles and actions of those responsible for operating these institutions. He explained the rationale for founding these institutions stemmed from the ways that educated people thought about the treatment and incarceration of the abnormal, the deviate, and the criminal in society. He asserted that these institutions, born in the eighteenth and nineteenth centuries, have evolved in this century into huge bureaucracies with internal political systems that control how people caught in their web communicate, behave, and think. However, he rejects the commonly held view that these institutions are the end result of orderly trends. Instead, his research shows that institutions grow out of discontinuity, evolving in unpredictable and unexpected ways. Thus today's massive organizations cannot be explained by a single, synthesizing idea, such as rationality or economic determinism, or progress but are instead products of discontinuous developments.

Reading the Selection

In *Discipline and Punish: The Birth of the Prison*, Foucault's theme is power and knowledge. On the surface this work is a conventional history, as Foucault traces the origins of the prison as a social institution. But as a subtext, he claims to be writing about the present. In effect, the discipline and punishment used by jailers in the first prisons to regulate the lives of the convicts is a paradigm of how society's agents in today's institutions use similar social codes to deprive other powerless persons of control of their bodies. Since 1977, when this book was published, interest groups such as women's and civil rights' groups, who perceive themselves as exploited, have used Foucault's argument to support protests against their exploiters, who, through varied forms of disciplining and punishing, keep the weak from being empowered.

In the first excerpt, Foucault explicitly spells out his dual mission of writing both a history of penal reform and an analysis of the modern soul, to the extent that it is the subject of power and control at the hands of others. He then lays down four rules that have guided this study. The second excerpt begins with a description of the *Panopticon*, the model prison envisioned by Jeremy Bentham, the nineteenth-century founder of Utilitarianism, the hedonistic philosophy based on the principle of "the greatest good for the greatest number." Foucault demonstrates that Bentham's proposed prison, rather than being the enlightened and humane facility it was claimed to be, was actually another device for those in power to exercise their knowledge and control over the bodies and the souls of the poor, the powerless, and the ignorant.

This book is intended as a correlative history of the modern soul and of a new power to judge; a genealogy of the present scientifico-legal complex from which the power to punish derives its bases, justifications and rules, from which it extends its effects and by which it masks its exorbitant singularity.

But from what point can such a history of the modern soul on trial be written? If one confined oneself to the evolution of legislation or of penal procedures, one would run the risk of allowing a change in the collective sensibility, an increase in humanization or the development of the human sciences to emerge as a massive, external, inert and primary fact. By studying only the general social forms, as Durkheim did (cf. Bibliography), one runs the risk of positing as the principle of greater leniency in punishment processes of individualization that are rather one of the effects of the new tactics of power, among which are to be included the new penal mechanisms. This study obeys four general rules:

1. Do not concentrate the study of the punitive mechanisms on their 'repressive' effects alone, on their 'punishment' aspects alone, but situate them in a whole series of their possible positive effects, even if these seem marginal at first sight. As a consequence, regard punishment as a complex social function.

2. Analyse punitive methods not simply as consequences of legislation or as indicators of social structures, but as techniques possessing their own specificity in the more general field of other ways of exercising power. Regard punishment as a political tactic.

3. Instead of treating the history of penal law and the history of the human sciences as two separate series whose overlapping appears to have had on one or the other, or perhaps on both, a disturbing or useful effect, according to one's point of view, see whether there is not some common matrix or whether they do not both derive from a single process of 'epistemologico-juridical' formation; in short, make the technology of power the very principle both of the humanization of the penal system and of the knowledge of man.

4. Try to discover whether this entry of the soul on to the scene of penal justice, and with it the insertion in legal practice of a whole corpus of 'scientific' knowledge, is not the effect of a transformation of the way in which the body itself is invested by power relations.

In short, try to study the metamorphosis of punitive methods on the basis of a political technology of the body in which might be read a common history of power relations and object relations. Thus, by an analysis of penal leniency as a technique of power, one might understand both how man, the soul, the normal or abnormal individual have come to duplicate crime as objects of penal intervention; and in what way a specific mode of subjection was able to give birth to man as an object of knowledge for a discourse with a 'scientific' status. . . .

Bentham's *Panopticon* is the architectural figure of this composition. We know the principle on which it was based: at the periphery, an annular building; at the centre, a tower; this tower is pierced with wide windows that open onto the inner side of the ring; the peripheric building is divided into cells, each of which extends the whole width of the building; they have two windows, one on the inside, corresponding to the windows of the tower; the other, on the outside, allows the light to cross the cell from one end to the other. All that is needed, then, is to place a supervisor in a central tower and to shut up in each cell a madman, a patient, a condemned man, a worker or a schoolboy. By the effect of backlighting, one can observe from the tower, standing out precisely against the light, the small captive shadows in the cells of the periphery. They are like so many cages, so many small theatres, in which each actor is alone, perfectly individualized and constantly visible. The panoptic mechanism arranges spatial unities that make it possible to see constantly and to recognize immediately. In short, it reverses the principle of the dungeon; or rather of its three functions—to enclose, to deprive of light and to hide—it preserves only the first and eliminates the other two. Full lighting and the eye of a supervisor capture better than darkness, which ultimately protected. Visibility is a trap.

To begin with, this made it possible—as a negative effect—to avoid those compact, swarming, howling masses that were to be found in places of confinement, those painted by Goya or described by Howard. Each individual, in his place, is securely confined to a cell from which he is seen from the front by the supervisor; but the side walls prevent him from coming into contact with his companions. He is seen, but he does not see; he is the object of information, never a subject in communication. The arrangement of his room, opposite the central tower, imposes on him an axial visibility; but the divisions of the ring, those separated cells, imply a lateral invisibility. And this invisibility is a guarantee of order. If the inmates are convicts, there is no danger of a plot, an attempt at collective escape, the planning of new crimes for the future, bad reciprocal influences; if they are patients, there is no danger of contagion; if they are madmen there is no risk of their committing violence upon one another; if they are schoolchildren, there is no copying, no noise, no chatter, no waste of time; if they are workers, there are no disorders, no theft, no coalitions, none of those distractions that slow down the rate of work, make it less perfect or cause accidents. The crowd, a compact mass, a locus of multiple exchanges, individualities merging together, a collective effect, is abolished and replaced by a collection of separated individualities. From the point of view of the guardian, it is replaced by a multiplicity that can be numbered and supervised; from the point of view of the inmates, by a sequestered and observed solitude (Bentham, 60–64).

Hence the major effect of the Panopticon: to induce in the inmate a state of conscious and permanent visibility that assures the automatic functioning of power. So to arrange things that the surveillance is permanent in its effects, even if it is discontinuous in its action; that the perfection of power should tend to render its actual exercise unnecessary; that this architectural apparatus should be a machine for creating and sustaining a power relation independent of the person who exercises it; in short, that the inmates should be caught up in a power situation of which they are themselves the bearers. To achieve this, it is at once too much and too little that the prisoner should be constantly observed by an inspector: too little, for what matters is that he knows himself to be observed; too much, because he has no need in fact of being so. In view of this, Bentham laid down the principle that power should be visible and unverifiable. Visible: the inmate will constantly have before his eyes the tall outline of the central tower from which he is spied upon. Unverifiable: the inmate must never know whether he is being looked at at any one moment; but he must be sure that he may always be so. In order to make the presence or absence of the inspector unverifiable, so that the prisoners, in their cells, cannot even see a shadow, Bentham envisaged not only venetian blinds on the windows of the central observation hall, but, on the inside, partitions that intersected the hall at right angles and, in order to pass from one quarter to the other, not

doors but zig-zag openings; for the slightest noise, a gleam of light, a brightness in a half-opened door would betray the presence of the guardian. The Panopticon is a machine for dissociating the see/being seen dyad: in the peripheric ring, one is totally seen, without ever seeing; in the central tower, one sees everything without ever being seen.

It is an important mechanism, for it automatizes and disindividualizes power. Power has its principle not so much in a person as in a certain concerted distribution of bodies, surfaces, lights, gazes; in an arrangement whose internal mechanisms produce the relation in which individuals are caught up. The ceremonies, the rituals, the marks by which the sovereign's surplus power was manifested are useless. There is a machinery that assures dissymmetry, disequilibrium, difference. Consequently, it does not matter who exercises power. Any individual, taken almost at random, can operate the machine: in the absence of the director, his family, his friends, his visitors, even his servants (Bentham, 45). Similarly, it does not matter what motive animates him: the curiosity of the indiscreet, the malice of a child, the thirst for knowledge of a philosopher who wishes to visit this museum of human nature, or the perversity of those who take pleasure in spying and punishing. The more numerous those anonymous and temporary observers are, the greater the risk for the inmate being surprised and the greater his anxious awareness of being observed. The Panopticon is a marvellous machine which, whatever use one may wish to put it to, produces homogeneous effects of power.

A real subjection is born mechanically from a fictitious relation. So it is not necessary to use force to constrain the convict to good behaviour, the madman to calm, the worker to work, the schoolboy to application, the patient to the observation of the regulations. Bentham was surprised that panoptic institutions could be so light: there were no more bars, no more chains, no more heavy locks; all that was needed was that the separations should be clear and the openings well arranged. The heaviness of the old 'houses of security', with their fortress-like architecture, could be replaced by the simple, economic geometry of a 'house of certainty'. The efficiency of power, its constraining force have, in a sense, passed over to the other side—to the side of its surface of application. He who is subjected to a field of visibility, and who knows it, assumes responsibility for the constraints of power; he makes them play spontaneously upon himself; he inscribes in himself the power relation in which he simultaneously plays both roles; he becomes the principle of his own subjection. By this very fact, the external power may throw off its physical weight; it tends to the non-corporal; and, the more it approaches this limit, the more constant, profound and permanent are its effects: it is a perpetual victory that avoids any physical confrontation and which is always decided in advance.

Bentham does not say whether he was inspired, in his project, by Le Vaux's menagerie at Versailles: the first menagerie in which the different elements are not, as they traditionally were, distributed in a park (Loisel, 104–7). At the centre was an octagonal pavilion which, on the first floor, consisted of only a single room, the king's *salon*; on every side large windows looked out onto seven cages (the eighth side was reserved for the entrance), containing different species of animals. By Bentham's time, this menagerie had disappeared. But one finds in the programme of the Panopticon a similar concern with individualizing observation, with characterization and classification, with the analytical arrangement of space. The Panopticon is a royal menagerie; the animal is replaced by man, individual distribution by specific grouping and the king by the machinery of a furtive power. With this exception, the Panopticon also does the work of a naturalist. It makes it possible to draw up differences: among patients, to observe the symptoms of each individual, without the proximity of beds, the circulation of miasmas, the effects of contagion confusing the clinical tables; among schoolchildren, it makes it possible to observe performances (without there being any imitation or copying), to map aptitudes, to assess characters, to draw up rigorous classifications and, in relation to normal development, to distinguish 'laziness and stubbornness' from 'incurable imbecility'; among workers, it makes it possible to note the aptitudes of each worker, compare the time he takes to perform a task, and if they are paid by the day, to calculate their wages (Bentham, 60–64).

So much for the question of observation. But the Panopticon was also a laboratory; it could be used as a machine to carry out experiments, to alter behaviour, to train or correct individuals. To experiment with medicines and monitor their effects. To try out different punishments on prisoners, according to their crimes and character, and to seek the most effective ones. To teach different techniques simultaneously to the workers, to decide which is the best. To try out pedagogical experiments—and in particular to take up once again the well-debated problem of secluded education, by using orphans. One would see what would happen when, in their sixteenth or eighteenth year, they were presented with other boys or girls; one could verify whether, as Helvetius thought, anyone could learn any-

thing; one would follow 'the genealogy of every observable idea'; one could bring up different children according to different systems of thought, making certain children believe that two and two do not make four or that the moon is a cheese, then put them together when they are twenty or twenty-five years old; one would then have discussions that would be worth a great deal more than the sermons or lectures on which so much money is spent; one would have at least an opportunity of making discoveries in the domain of metaphysics. The Panopticon is a privileged place for experiments on men, and for analysing with complete certainty the transformations that may be obtained from them. The Panopticon may even provide an apparatus for supervising its own mechanisms. In this central tower, the director may spy on all the employees that he has under his orders: nurses, doctors, foremen, teachers, warders; he will be able to judge them continuously, alter their behaviour, impose upon them the methods he thinks best; and it will even be possible to observe the director himself. An inspector arriving unexpectedly at the centre of the Panopticon will be able to judge at a glance, without anything being concealed from him, how the entire establishment is functioning. And, in any case, enclosed as he is in the middle of this architectural mechanism, is not the director's own fate entirely bound up with it? The incompetent physician who has allowed contagion to spread, the incompetent prison governor or workshop manager will be the first victims of an epidemic or a revolt. '"By every tie I could devise", said the master of the Panopticon, "my own fate had been bound up by me with theirs"' (Bentham, 177). The Panopticon functions as a kind of laboratory of power. Thanks to its mechanisms of observation, it gains in efficiency and in the ability to penetrate into men's behaviour; knowledge follows the advances of power, discovering new objects of knowledge over all the surfaces on which power is exercised.

MILAN KUNDERA

Selections from *The Unbearable Lightness of Being*

The Czech writer Milan Kundera (b. 1929) is one of Europe's most important authors working today. Short story writer, essayist, playwright, and poet, he is best known for his novels, which embody his aesthetic theories as set forth in *The Art of the Novel* (1990), a work of literary criticism. What is most striking about Kundera's novels is their lack of obedience to the rule of unity of action; instead of traditional narrative structures, they present parallel stories on related themes. The result is a type of novel that (in his words): "searches and poses questions. I don't know which of my characters is right. I invent stories, confront one with the other, and by this means I ask questions." The roots of this type of novel are in Cervantes and Kafka; however, the disorienting methods—patterns based on musical forms and disjointed time frames—reflect Kundera's training in music and film.

In the 1960s Kundera was often grouped with the East European "dissident" writers, a coterie of writers who used their fiction to play secret games against the communist regimes then in power in Poland, Hungary, Czechoslovakia, and East Germany. Hating the term "dissident," he always rejected it as a label, for he claimed that his writings were not innately political. Still, his early works challenged the authorities with sly humor, as in *The Joke* (1967), his first novel; in it, the student hero is sent to work in the mines because he mailed a postcard bearing a joke about Lenin. When Russian troops invaded Czechoslovakia in 1968, local leaders, who previously distrusted Kundera, expelled him from the communist party and fired him from his teaching post. His works were removed from libraries and bookstores, and he was forbidden to publish in his own country. In 1976, invited to teach at a French university, he escaped to France, where he lives in permanent exile. The Czech government canceled his citizenship upon publication of the novel *The Book of Laughter and Forgetting* in 1979.

The novel that made Kundera a world literary figure was *The Unbearable Lightness of Being* (1984), whose success was partly due to the popularity of the erotic movie based on it. In theme, the novel argues that keeping a clear memory is a way to protect oneself in a world where history is daily distorted, whether for ideological reasons under socialism or out of indifference under capitalism. To explore this theme, he presented two couples—Tomas and Tereza, and Franz and Sabina—portraying their doomed affairs with ironic humor and brutal eroticism. Situated mainly in Czechoslovakia during the 1968 Russian invasion, but with scenes set in Switzerland, this novel suggests the hopelessness of life under modern conditions.

Reading the Selection

The first six episodes of *The Unbearable Lightness of Being* introduce two of the novel's main characters, Tomas and Tereza. Unlike in conventional novels, these characters seem to be an afterthought: "I have been thinking about Tomas for many years. But only in the light of these reflections did I see him clearly." They appear after a digression on the Nietzschean idea of "the eternal return"—that is, history repeats itself endlessly with no moral lessons learned. Framed within this idea, the novel seems destined to portray (as it does) the futility of trying to be moral under the hostile conditions of modern life—an existential view shared with Sartre (see *The Humanism of Existentialism*).

—⁂—

Chapter I

The idea of eternal return is a mysterious one, and Nietzsche has often perplexed other philosophers with it: to think that everything recurs as we once experienced it, and that the recurrence itself recurs ad infinitum! What does this mad myth signify?

Putting it negatively, the myth of eternal return states that a life which disappears once and for all, which does not return, is like a shadow, without weight, dead in advance, and whether it was horrible, beautiful, or sublime, its horror, sublimity, and beauty mean nothing. We need take no more note of it than of a war between two African kingdoms in the fourteenth century, a war that altered nothing in the destiny of the world, even if a hundred thousand blacks perished in excruciating torment.

Will the war between two African kingdoms in the fourteenth century itself be altered if it recurs again and again, in eternal return?

It will: it will become a solid mass, permanently protuberant, its inanity irreparable.

If the French Revolution were to recur eternally, French historians would be less proud of Robespierre. But because they deal with something that will not return, the bloody years of the Revolution have turned into mere words, theories, and discussions, have become lighter than feathers, frightening no one. There is an infinite difference between a Robespierre who occurs only once in history and a Robespierre who eternally returns, chopping off French heads.

Let us therefore agree that the idea of eternal return implies a perspective from which things appear other than as we know them: they appear without the mitigating circumstance of their transitory nature. This mitigating circumstance prevents us from coming to a verdict. For how can we condemn something that is ephemeral, in transit? In the sunset of dissolution, everything is illuminated by the aura of nostalgia, even the guillotine.

Not long ago, I caught myself experiencing a most incredible sensation. Leafing through a book on Hitler, I was touched by some of his portraits: they reminded me of my childhood. I grew up during the war; several members of my family perished in Hitler's concentration camps; but what were their deaths compared with the memories of a lost period in my life, a period that would never return?

This reconciliation with Hitler reveals the profound moral perversity of a world that rests essentially on the nonexistence of return, for in this world everything is pardoned in advance and therefore everything cynically permitted.

Chapter II

If every second of our lives recurs an infinite number of times, we are nailed to eternity as Jesus Christ was nailed to the cross. It is a terrifying prospect. In the world of eternal return the weight of unbearable responsibility lies heavy on every move we make. That is why Nietzsche called the idea of eternal return the heaviest of burdens (*das schwerste Gewicht*).

If eternal return is the heaviest of burdens, then our lives can stand out against it in all their splendid lightness.

But is heaviness truly deplorable and lightness splendid?

The heaviest of burdens crushes us, we sink beneath it, it pins us to the ground. But in the love poetry of every age, the woman longs to be weighed down by the man's body. The heaviest of burdens is therefore simultaneously an image of life's most intense fulfillment. The heavier the burden, the closer our lives come to the earth, the more real and truthful they become.

Conversely, the absolute absence of a burden causes man to be lighter than air, to soar into the heights, take leave of the earth and his earthly being, and become only half real, his movements as free as they are insignificant.

What then shall we choose? Weight or lightness?

Parmenides posed this very question in the sixth century before Christ. He saw the world divided into pairs of opposites: light/darkness, fineness/coarseness, warmth/cold, being/non-being. One half of the opposition he called positive (light, fineness, warmth, being), the other negative. We might find this division into positive and negative poles childishly simple except for one difficulty: which one is positive, weight or lightness?

Parmenides responded: lightness is positive, weight negative.

Was he correct or not? That is the question. The only certainty is: the lightness/weight opposition is the most mysterious, most ambiguous of all.

Chapter III

I have been thinking about Tomas for many years. But only in the light of these reflections did I see him clearly. I saw him standing at the window of his flat and looking across the courtyard at the opposite walls, not knowing what to do.

He had first met Tereza about three weeks earlier in a small Czech town. They had spent scarcely an hour together. She had accompanied him to the station and waited with him until he boarded the train. Ten days later she paid him a visit. They made love the day she arrived. That night she came down with a fever and stayed a whole week in his flat with the flu.

He had come to feel an inexplicable love for this all but complete stranger; she seemed a child to him, a child someone had put in a bulrush basket daubed with pitch and sent downstream for Tomas to fetch at the riverbank of his bed.

She stayed with him a week, until she was well again, then went back to her town, some hundred and twenty-five miles from Prague. And then came the time I have just spoken of and see as the key to his life: Standing by the window, he looked out over the courtyard at the walls opposite him and deliberated.

Should he call her back to Prague for good? He feared the responsibility. If he invited her to come, then come she would, and offer him up her life.

Or should he refrain from approaching her? Then she would remain a waitress in a hotel restaurant of a provincial town and he would never see her again.

Did he want her to come or did he not?

He looked out over the courtyard at the opposite walls, seeking an answer.

He kept recalling her lying on his bed; she reminded him of no one in his former life. She was neither mistress nor wife. She was a child whom he had taken from a bulrush basket that had been daubed with pitch and sent to the riverbank of his bed. She fell asleep. He knelt down next to her. Her feverous breath quickened and she gave out a weak moan. He pressed his face to hers and whispered calming words into her sleep. After a while he felt her breath return to normal and her face rise unconsciously to meet his. He smelled the delicate aroma of her fever and breathed it in, as if trying to glut himself with the intimacy of her body. And all at once he fancied she had been with him for many years and was dying. He had a sudden clear feeling that he would not survive her death. He would lie down beside her and want to die with her. He pressed his face into the pillow beside her head and kept it there for a long time.

Now he was standing at the window trying to call that moment to account. What could it have been if not love declaring itself to him?

But was it love? The feeling of wanting to die beside her was clearly exaggerated: he had seen her only once before in his life! Was it simply the hysteria of a man who, aware deep down of his inaptitude for love, felt the self-deluding need to simulate it? His unconscious was so cowardly that the best partner it could choose for its little comedy was this miserable provincial waitress with practically no chance at all to enter his life!

Looking out over the courtyard at the dirty walls, he realized he had no idea whether it was hysteria or love.

And he was distressed that in a situation where a real man would instantly have known how to act, he was vacillating and therefore depriving the most beautiful moments he had ever experienced (kneeling at her bed and thinking he would not survive her death) of their meaning.

He remained annoyed with himself until he realized that not knowing what he wanted was actually quite natural.

We can never know what to want, because, living only one life, we can neither compare it with our previous lives nor perfect it in our lives to come.

Was it better to be with Tereza or to remain alone?

There is no means of testing which decision is better, because there is no basis for comparison. We live everything as it comes, without warning, like an actor going on cold. And what can life be worth if the first rehearsal for life is life itself? That is why life is always like a sketch. No, "sketch" is not quite the word, because a sketch is an outline of something, the groundwork for a picture, whereas the sketch that is our life is a sketch for nothing, an outline with no picture.

Einmal ist keinmal, says Tomas to himself. What happens but once, says the German adage, might as well not have happened at all. If we have only one life to live, we might as well not have lived at all.

Chapter IV

But then one day at the hospital, during a break between operations, a nurse called him to the telephone. He heard Tereza's voice coming from the receiver. She had phoned him from the railway station. He was overjoyed. Unfortunately, he had something on that evening and could not invite her to his place until the next day. The moment he hung up, he reproached himself for not telling her to go straight there. He had time enough to cancel his plans, after all! He tried to imagine what Tereza would do in Prague during the thirty-six long hours before they were to meet, and had half a mind to jump into his car and drive through the streets looking for her.

She arrived the next evening, a handbag dangling from her shoulder, looking more elegant than before. She had a thick book under her arm. It was *Anna Karenina*. She seemed in a good mood, even a little boisterous, and tried to make him think she had just happened to drop in, things had just worked out that way: she was in Prague on business, perhaps (at this point she became rather vague) to find a job.

Later, as they lay naked and spent side by side on the bed, he asked her where she was staying. It was night by then, and he offered to drive her there. Embarrassed, she answered that she still had to find a hotel and had left her suitcase at the station.

Only two days ago, he had feared that if he invited her to Prague she would offer him up her life. When she told him her suitcase was at the station, he immediately realized that the suitcase contained her life and that she had left it at the station only until she could offer it up to him.

The two of them got into his car, which was parked in front of the house, and drove to the station. There he claimed the suitcase (it was large and enormously heavy) and took it and her home.

How had he come to make such a sudden decision when for nearly a fortnight he had wavered so much that he could not even bring himself to send a postcard asking her how she was?

He himself was surprised. He had acted against his principles. Ten years earlier, when he had divorced his wife, he celebrated the event the way others celebrate a marriage. He understood he was not born to live side by side with any woman and could be fully himself only as a bachelor. He tried to design his life in such a way that no woman could move in with a suitcase. That was why his flat had only the one bed. Even though it was wide enough, Tomas would tell his mistresses that he was unable to fall asleep with anyone next to him, and drive them home after midnight. And so it was not the flu that kept him from sleeping with Tereza on her first visit. The first night he had slept in his large armchair, and the rest of that week he drove each night to the hospital, where he had a cot in his office.

But this time he fell asleep by her side. When he woke up the next morning, he found Tereza, who was still asleep, holding his hand. Could they have been hand in hand all night? It was hard to believe.

And while she breathed the deep breath of sleep and held his hand (firmly: he was unable to disengage it from her grip), the enormously heavy suitcase stood by the bed.

He refrained from loosening his hand from her grip for fear of waking her, and turned carefully on his side to observe her better.

Again it occurred to him that Tereza was a child put in a pitch-daubed bulrush basket and sent downstream. He couldn't very well let a basket with a child in it float down a stormy river! If the Pharaoh's daughter hadn't snatched the basket carrying little Moses from the waves, there would have been no Old Testament, no civilization as we now know it! How many ancient myths begin with the rescue of an abandoned child! If Polybus hadn't taken in the young Oedipus, Sophocles wouldn't have written his most beautiful tragedy!

Tomas did not realize at the time that metaphors are dangerous. Metaphors are not to be trifled with. A single metaphor can give birth to love.

Chapter V

He lived a scant two years with his wife, and they had a son. At the divorce proceedings, the judge awarded the infant to its mother and ordered Tomas to pay a third of his salary for its support. He also granted him the right to visit the boy every other week.

But each time Tomas was supposed to see him, the boy's mother found an excuse to keep him away. He soon realized that bringing them expensive gifts would make things a good deal easier, that he was expected to bribe the mother for the son's love. He saw a future of quixotic attempts to inculcate his views in the boy, views opposed in every way to the mother's. The very thought of it exhausted him. When, one Sunday, the boy's mother again canceled a scheduled visit, Tomas decided on the spur of the moment never to see him again.

Why should he feel more for that child, to whom he was bound by nothing but a single improvident night, than for any other? He would be scrupulous about paying support; he just didn't want anybody making him fight for his son in the name of paternal sentiments!

Needless to say, he found no sympathizers. His own parents condemned him roundly: if Tomas refused to take an interest in his son, then they, Tomas's parents, would no longer take an interest in theirs. They made a great show of maintaining good relations with their daughter-in-law and trumpeted their exemplary stance and sense of justice.

Thus in practically no time he managed to rid himself of wife, son, mother, and father. The only thing they bequeathed to him was a fear of women. Tomas desired but feared them. Needing to create a compromise between fear and desire, he devised what he called "erotic friendship." He would tell his mistresses: the only relationship that can make both partners happy is one in which sentimentality has no place and neither partner makes any claim on the life and freedom of the other.

To ensure that erotic friendship never grew into the aggression of love, he would meet each of his long-term mistresses only at intervals. He considered this method flawless and propagated it among his friends: "The important thing is to abide by the rule of threes. Either you see a woman three times in quick succession and then never again, or you maintain relations over the years but make sure that the rendezvous are at least three weeks apart."

The rule of threes enabled Tomas to keep intact his liaisons with some women while continuing to engage in short-term affairs with many others. He was not always understood. The woman who understood him best was Sabina. She was a painter. "The reason I like you," she would say to him, "is you're the complete opposite of kitsch. In the kingdom of kitsch you would be a monster."

It was Sabina he turned to when he needed to find a job for Tereza in Prague. Following the unwritten rules of erotic friendship, Sabina promised to do everything in her power, and before long she had in fact located a place for Tereza in the darkroom of an illustrated weekly. Although her new job did not require any particular qualifications, it raised her status from waitress to member of the press. When Sabina herself introduced Tereza to everyone on the weekly, Tomas knew he had never had a better friend as a mistress than Sabina.

Chapter VI

The unwritten contract of erotic friendship stipulated that Tomas should exclude all love from his life. The moment he violated that clause of the contract, his other mistresses would assume inferior status and become ripe for insurrection.

Accordingly, he rented a room for Tereza and her heavy suitcase. He wanted to be able to watch over her, protect her, enjoy her presence, but felt no need to change his way of life. He did not want word to get out that Tereza was sleeping at his place: spending the night together was the corpus delicti of love.

He never spent the night with the others. It was easy enough if he was at their place: he could leave whenever he pleased. It was worse when they were at his and he had to explain that come midnight he would have to drive them home because he was an insomniac and found it impossible to fall asleep in close proximity to another person.

Though it was not far from the truth, he never dared tell them the whole truth: after making love he had an uncontrollable craving to be by himself; waking in the middle of the night at the side of an alien body was distasteful to him, rising in the morning with an intruder repellent; he had no desire to be overheard brushing his teeth in the bathroom, nor was he enticed by the thought of an intimate breakfast.

That is why he was so surprised to wake up and find Tereza squeezing his hand tightly. Lying there looking at her, he could not quite understand what had happened. But as he ran through the previous few hours in his mind, he began to sense an aura of hitherto unknown happiness emanating from them.

From that time on they both looked forward to sleeping together. I might even say that the goal of their lovemaking was not so much pleasure as the sleep that followed it. She especially was affected. Whenever she stayed overnight in her rented room (which quickly became only an alibi for Tomas), she was unable to fall asleep; in his arms she would fall asleep no matter how wrought up she might have been. He would whisper impromptu fairy tales about her, or gibberish, words he repeated monotonously, words soothing or comical, which turned into vague visions lulling her through the first dreams of the night. He had complete control over her sleep: she dozed off at the second he chose.

While they slept, she held him as on the first night, keeping a firm grip on wrist, finger, or ankle. If he wanted to move without waking her, he had to resort to artifice. After freeing his finger (wrist, ankle) from her clutches, a process which, since she guarded him carefully even in her sleep, never failed to rouse her partially, he would calm her by slipping an object into her hand (a rolled-up pajama top, a slipper, a book), which she then gripped as tightly as if it were a part of his body.

Once, when he had just lulled her to sleep but she had gone no farther than dream's antechamber and was therefore still responsive to him, he said to her, "Good-bye, I'm going now." "Where?" she asked in her sleep. "Away," he answered sternly. "Then I'm going with you," she said, sitting up in bed. "No, you can't. I'm going away for good," he said, going out into the hall. She stood up and followed him out, squinting. She was naked beneath her short nightdress. Her face was blank, expressionless, but she moved energetically. He walked through the hall of the flat into the hall of the building (the hall shared by all the occupants), closing the door in her face. She flung it open and continued to follow him, convinced in her sleep that he meant to leave her for good and she had to stop him. He walked down the stairs to the first landing and waited for her there. She went down after him, took him by the hand, and led him back to bed.

Tomas came to this conclusion: Making love with a woman and sleeping with a woman are two separate passions, not merely different but opposite. Love does not make itself felt in the desire for copulation (a desire that extends to an infinite number of women) but in the desire for shared sleep (a desire limited to one woman).

TIM O'BRIEN

Selection from *The Things They Carried*

War novels, usually based on the author's experiences, have been popular for more than a century in American literature, going back to Stephen Crane's *The Red Badge of Courage,* about the Civil War. Crane's realistic treatment of the common soldier's reaction to battle and his fear of dying set a pattern for the war novel genre. Books on World War I often followed this model but with more of an emphasis on the futility of conflict and the senseless loss of human life for "causes" that could not be justified in the author's opinion. The war novels coming out of World War II continued along these same lines but were much more explicit; they used a great deal of profanity and detailed the fighting and killing. Post–World War II authors also brought in Freud and stream-of-consciousness narration techniques; further, they were influenced by Kafka (see *Metamorphosis*) and Sartre (see *The Humanism of Existentialism*) about the absurdity of human existence, especially in situations in which normal values and human relationships seemed irrelevant, as in combat. Since the Vietnam War, a handful of veterans and writers have begun to emerge, taking the war novel in a somewhat different direction. They are trying to come to grips with their own experiences in America's most controversial war, one whose moral ambiguity remains a factor in American political life.

The best of the new wave of war novelists is Tim O'Brien (b. 1946), the author of six novels, all or parts of which reflect his experiences as a foot soldier in Vietnam. After graduation from college in Minnesota in the late 1960s, he was drafted to fight in a war of which he did not approve; he felt compelled to serve out of fear of family and social pressure. After his return, O'Brien went to graduate school and wrote for a newspaper before starting his career as a full-time writer, which is now his chief occupation.

Reading the Selection

This selection is taken from O'Brien's third novel, *The Things They Carried* (1990), a collection of "stories" about the war and its combatants. In a lecture he once said, "Everything I write is made up, but that doesn't mean it's not true." Thus when he begins with these words, "This is true," he is being playfully ironic. In a sense, he is trying to catch the mood of the war, which he claimed, among soldiers, was dominated by an overwhelming feeling of monotony.

O'Brien's literary style is sort of a pastiche, a patchwork of other writers' methods. This technique is often used in Post-Modernism, the post-1970 movement that seeks not to obliterate Modernism but to take it to a higher level. In O'Brien's writing, there are echoes of Hemingway, for example, in the "tough guy voice," the stripped-down prose, and the general air of midwestern muscularity. There is also something of the absurdity of Joseph Heller, author of *Catch 22;* for example, in the off-the-wall things the soldiers are willing to do in order to escape the system, either by direct action or through flights of the imagination. Last, there is a "magic realist" quality, in the manner of García Márquez (see *One Hundred Years of Solitude*); for example, when the same scene—the precise moment of Lemon's death—gets replayed in the "story." O'Brien also repeats the traditional war novel's themes of bravery, comradeship, and the transformation of young boys into men. Perhaps the major issue in O'Brien's work is, what is war really like? Although he approaches this issue from many angles, ultimately the reader must conclude that it is not possible to represent war in words.

—*᠁*—

How to Tell a True War Story

This is true.

I had a buddy in Vietnam. His name was Bob Kiley, but everybody called him Rat.

A friend of his gets killed, so about a week later Rat sits down and writes a letter to the guy's sister. Rat tells her what a great brother she had, how together the guy was, a number one pal and comrade. A real soldier's soldier, Rat says. Then he tells a few stories to make the point, how her brother would always volunteer for stuff nobody else would volunteer for in a million years, dangerous stuff, like doing recon or going out on these really badass night patrols. Stainless steel balls, Rat tells her. The guy was a little crazy, for sure, but crazy in a good way, a real daredevil, because he liked the challenge of it, he liked testing himself, just man against gook. A great, great guy, Rat says.

Anyway, it's a terrific letter, very personal and touching. Rat almost bawls writing it. He gets all teary telling about the good times they had together, how her brother made the war seem almost fun, always raising hell and lighting up villes and bringing smoke to bear every which way. A great sense of humor, too. Like the time at this river when he went fishing with a whole damn crate of hand grenades. Probably the funniest thing in world history, Rat says, all that gore, about twenty zillion dead gook fish. Her brother, he had the right attitude. He knew how to have a good time. On Halloween, this real hot spooky night, the dude paints up his body all different colors and puts on this weird mask and hikes over to a ville and goes trick-or-treating almost stark naked, just boots and balls and an M-16. A tremendous human being, Rat says. Pretty nutso sometimes, but you could trust him with your life.

And then the letter gets very sad and serious. Rat pours his heart out. He says he loved the guy. He says the guy was his best friend in the world. They were like soul mates, he says, like twins or something, they had a whole lot in common. He tells the guy's sister he'll look her up when the war's over.

So what happens?

Rat mails the letter. He waits two months. The dumb cooze never writes back.

A true war story is never moral. It does not instruct, nor encourage virtue, nor suggest models of proper human behavior, nor restrain men from doing the things men have always done. If a story seems moral, do not believe it. If at the end of a war story you feel uplifted, or if you feel that some small bit of rectitude has been salvaged from the larger waste, then you have been made the victim of a very old and terrible lie. There is no rectitude whatsoever. There is no virtue. As a first rule of thumb, therefore, you can tell a true war story by its absolute and uncompromising allegiance to obscenity and evil. Listen to Rat Kiley. Cooze, he says. He does not say bitch. He certainly does not say woman, or girl. He says cooze. Then he spits and stares. He's nineteen years old—it's too much for him—so he looks at you with those big sad gentle killer eyes and says *cooze,* because his friend is dead, and because it's so incredibly sad and true: she never wrote back.

You can tell a true war story if it embarrasses you. If you don't care for obscenity, you don't care for the truth; if you don't care for the truth, watch how you vote. Send guys to war, they come home talking dirty.

Listen to Rat: "Jesus Christ, man, I write this beautiful fuckin' letter, I slave over it, and what happens? The dumb cooze never writes back."

The dead guy's name was Curt Lemon. What happened was, we crossed a muddy river and marched west into the mountains, and on the third day we took a break along a trail junction in deep jungle. Right away, Lemon and Rat Kiley started goofing. They didn't understand about the spookiness. They were kids; they just didn't know. A nature hike, they thought, not even a war, so they went off into the shade of some giant trees—quadruple canopy, no sunlight at all—and they were giggling and calling each other yellow mother and playing a silly game they'd invented. The game involved smoke grenades, which were harmless unless you did stupid things, and what they did was pull out the pin and stand a few feet apart and play catch under the shade of those huge trees. Whoever chickened out was a yellow mother. And if nobody chickened out, the grenade would make a light popping sound and they'd be covered with smoke and they'd laugh and dance around and then do it again.

It's all exactly true.

It happened, to *me*, nearly twenty years ago, and I still remember that trail junction and those giant trees and a soft dripping sound somewhere beyond the trees. I remember the smell of moss. Up in the canopy there were tiny white blossoms, but no sunlight at all, and I remember the shadows spreading out under the trees where Curt Lemon and Rat Kiley were playing catch with smoke grenades. Mitchell Sanders sat flipping his yo-yo. Norman Bowker and Kiowa and Dave Jensen were dozing, or half dozing, and all around us were those ragged green mountains.

Except for the laughter things were quiet.

At one point, I remember, Mitchell Sanders turned and looked at me, not quite nodding, as if to warn me about something, as if he already *knew,* then after a while he rolled up his yo-yo and moved away.

It's hard to tell you what happened next.

They were just goofing. There was a noise, I suppose, which must've been the detonator, so I glanced behind me and watched Lemon step from the shade into bright sunlight. His face was suddenly brown and shining. A handsome kid, really. Sharp gray eyes, lean and narrow-waisted, and when he died it was almost beautiful, the way the sunlight came around him and lifted him up and sucked him high into a tree full of moss and vines and white blossoms.

In any war story, but especially a true one, it's difficult to separate what happened from what seemed to happen. What seems to happen becomes its own happening and has to be told that way. The angles of vision are skewed. When a booby trap explodes, you close your eyes and duck and float outside yourself. When a guy dies, like Curt Lemon, you look away and then look back for a moment and then look away again. The pictures get jumbled; you tend to miss a lot. And then afterward, when you go to tell about it, there is always that surreal seemingness, which makes the story seem untrue, but which in fact represents the hard and exact truth as it *seemed.*

. . .

In many cases a true war story cannot be believed. If you believe it, be skeptical. It's a question of credibility. Often the crazy stuff is true and the normal stuff isn't, because the normal stuff is necessary to make you believe the truly incredible craziness.

In other cases you can't even tell a true war story. Sometimes it's just beyond telling.

I heard this one, for example, from Mitchell Sanders. It was near dusk and we were sitting at my foxhole along a wide muddy river north of Quang Ngai. I remember how peaceful the twilight was. A deep pinkish red spilled out on the river, which moved without sound, and in the morning we would cross the river and march west into the mountains. The occasion was right for a good story.

"God's truth," Mitchell Sanders said. "A six-man patrol goes up into the mountains on a basic listening-post operation. The idea's to spend a week up there, just lie low and listen for enemy movement. They've got a radio along, so if they hear anything suspicious—anything—they're supposed to call in artillery or gunships, whatever it takes. Otherwise they keep strict field discipline. Absolute silence. They just listen."

Sanders glanced at me to make sure I had the scenario. He was playing with his yo-yo, dancing it with short, tight little strokes of the wrist.

His face was blank in the dusk.

"We're talking regulation, by-the-book LP. These six guys, they don't say boo for a solid week. They don't got tongues. *All* ears."

"Right," I said.

"Understand me?"

"Invisible."

Sanders nodded.

"Affirm," he said. "Invisible. So what happens is, these guys get themselves deep in the bush, all camouflaged up, and they lie down and wait and that's all they do, nothing else, they lie there for seven straight days and just listen. And man, I'll tell you—it's spooky. This is mountains. You don't *know* spooky till you been there. Jungle, sort of, except it's way up in the clouds and there's always this fog—like rain, except it's not raining—everything's all wet and swirly and tangled up and you can't see jack, you can't find your own pecker to piss with. Like you don't even have a body. Serious spooky. You just go with the vapors—the fog sort of takes you in . . . And the sounds, man. The sounds carry forever. You hear stuff nobody should *ever* hear."

Sanders was quiet for a second, just working the yo-yo, then he smiled at me.

"So after a couple days the guys start hearing this real soft, kind of wacked-out music. Weird echoes and stuff. Like a radio or something, but it's not a radio, it's this strange gook music that comes right out of the rocks. Faraway, sort of, but right up close, too. They try to ignore it. But it's a listening post, right? So they listen. And every night they keep hearing that crazyass gook concert. All kinds of chimes and xylophones. I mean, this is wilderness—no way, it can't be real—but there it *is,* like the mountains are tuned in to Radio fucking Hanoi. Naturally they get nervous. One guy sticks Juicy Fruit in his ears. Another guy almost flips. Thing is, though, they can't report music. They can't get on the horn and call back to base and say, 'Hey, listen, we need some firepower, we got to blow away this weirdo gook rock band.' They can't do that. It wouldn't go down. So they lie there in the fog and keep their mouths shut. And what makes it extra bad, see, is the poor dudes can't horse around like normal. Can't joke it away. Can't even talk to each other except maybe in whispers, all hush-hush, and that just revs up the willies. All they do is listen."

Again there was some silence as Mitchell Sanders looked out on the river. The dark was coming on hard now, and off to the west I could see the mountains rising in silhouette, all the mysteries and unknowns.

"This next part," Sanders said quietly, "you won't believe."

"Probably not," I said.

"You won't. And you know why?" He gave me a long, tired smile. "Because it happened. Because every word is absolutely dead-on true."

Sanders made a sound in his throat, like a sigh, as if to say he didn't care if I believed him or not. But he did care. He wanted me to feel the truth, to believe by the raw force of feeling. He seemed sad, in a way.

"These six guys," he said, "they're pretty fried out by now, and one night they start hearing voices. Like at a cocktail party. That's what it sounds like, this big swank gook cocktail party somewhere out there in the fog. Music and chitchat and stuff. It's crazy, I know, but they hear the champagne corks. They hear the actual martini glasses. Real hoity-toity, all very civilized, except this isn't civilization. This is Nam.

"Anyway, the guys try to be cool. They just lie there and groove, but after a while they start hearing—you won't believe this—they hear chamber music. They hear violins and cellos. They hear this terrific mama-san soprano. Then after a while they hear gook opera and a glee club and the Haiphong Boys Choir and a barbershop quartet and all kinds of weird chanting and Buddha-Buddha stuff. And the whole time, in the background, there's still that cocktail party going on. All these different voices. Not human voices, though. Because it's the mountains. Follow me? The rock—it's *talking*. And the fog, too, and the grass and the goddamn mongooses. Everything talks. The trees talk politics, the monkeys talk religion. The whole country. Vietnam. The place talks. It talks. Understand? Nam—it truly *talks.*

"The guys can't cope. They lose it. They get on the radio and report enemy movement—a whole army, they say—and they order up the firepower. They get arty and gunships. They call in air strikes. And I'll tell you, they fuckin' crash that cocktail party. All night long, they just smoke those mountains. They make jungle juice. They blow away trees and glee clubs and whatever else there is to blow away. Scorch time. They walk napalm up and down the ridges. They bring in the Cobras and F-4s, they use Willie Peter and HE and incendiaries. It's all fire. They make those mountains burn.

"Around dawn things finally get quiet. Like you never even *heard* quiet before. One of those real thick, real misty days—just clouds and fog, they're off in this special zone—and the mountains are absolutely dead-flat silent. Like Brigadoon—pure vapor, you know? Everything's all sucked up inside the fog. Not a single sound, except they still *hear* it.

"So they pack up and start humping. They head down the mountain, back to base camp, and when they get there they don't say diddly. They don't talk. Not a word, like they're deaf and dumb. Later on this fat bird colonel comes up and asks what the hell happened out there. What'd they hear? Why all the ordnance? The man's ragged out, he gets down tight on their case. I mean, they spent six trillion dollars on firepower, and this fatass colonel wants answers, he wants to know what the fuckin' story is.

"But the guys don't say zip. They just look at him for a while, sort of funny like, sort of amazed, and the whole war is right there in that stare. It says everything you can't ever say. It says, man, you got *wax* in your ears. It says, poor bastard, you'll never know—wrong frequency—you don't *even* want to hear this. Then they salute the fucker and walk away, because certain stories you don't ever tell."

You can tell a true war story by the way it never seems to end. Not then, not ever. Not when Mitchell Sanders stood up and moved off into the dark.

It all happened.

Even now, at this instant, I remember that yo-yo. In a way, I suppose, you had to be there, you had to hear it, but I could tell how desperately Sanders wanted me to believe him, his frustration at not quite getting the details right, not quite pinning down the final and definitive truth.

And I remember sitting at my foxhole that night, watching the shadows of Quang Ngai, thinking about the coming day and how we would cross the river and march west into the mountains, all the ways I might die, all the things I did not understand.

Late in the night Mitchell Sanders touched my shoulder.

"Just came to me," he whispered. "The moral, I mean. Nobody listens. Nobody hears nothin'. Like that fatass colonel. The politicians, all the civilian types. Your girlfriend. My girlfriend. Everybody's sweet little virgin girlfriend. What they need is to go out on LP. The vapors, man. Trees and rocks—you got to *listen* to your enemy."

And then again, in the morning, Sanders came up to me. The platoon was preparing to move out, checking weapons, going through all the little rituals that preceded a day's march. Already the lead squad had crossed the river and was filing off toward the west.

"I got a confession to make," Sanders said. "Last night, man, I had to make up a few things."

"I know that."

"The glee club. There wasn't any glee club."

"Right."

"No opera."

"Forget it, I understand."

"Yeah, but listen, it's still true. Those six guys, they heard wicked sound out there. They heard sound you just plain won't believe."

Sanders pulled on his rucksack, closed his eyes for a moment, then almost smiled at me. I knew what was coming.

"All right," I said, "what's the moral?"

"Forget it."

"No, go ahead."

For a long while he was quiet, looking away, and the silence kept stretching out until it was almost embarrassing. Then he shrugged and gave me a stare that lasted all day.

"Hear that quiet, man?" he said. "That quiet—just listen. There's your moral."

In a true war story, if there's a moral at all, it's like the thread that makes the cloth. You can't tease it out. You can't extract the meaning without unraveling the deeper meaning. And in the end, really, there's nothing much to say about a true war story, except maybe "Oh."

True war stories do not generalize. They do not indulge in abstraction or analysis. [65]

For example: War is hell. As a moral declaration the old truism seems perfectly true, and yet because it abstracts, because it generalizes, I can't believe it with my stomach. Nothing turns inside.

It comes down to gut instinct. A true war story, if truly told, makes the stomach believe.

.   .   .

This one does it for me. I've told it before—many times, many versions—but here's what actually happened.

We crossed that river and marched west into the mountains. On the third day, Curt Lemon stepped on a booby-trapped 105 round. He was playing catch with Rat Kiley, laughing, and then he was dead. The trees were thick; it took nearly an hour to cut an LZ for the dustoff.

Later, higher in the mountains, we came across a baby VC water buffalo. What it was doing there I don't know— no farms or paddies—but we chased it down and got a rope around it and led it along to a deserted village where we set up for the night. After supper Rat Kiley went over and stroked its nose. [70]

He opened up a can of C rations, pork and beans, but the baby buffalo wasn't interested.

Rat shrugged.

He stepped back and shot it through the right front knee. The animal did not make a sound. It went down hard, then got up again, and Rat took careful aim and shot off an ear. He shot it in the hindquarters and in the little hump at its back. He shot it twice in the flanks. It wasn't to kill; it was to hurt. He put the rifle muzzle up against the mouth and shot the mouth away. Nobody said much. The whole platoon stood there watching, feeling all kinds of things, but there wasn't a great deal of pity for the baby water buffalo. Curt Lemon was dead. Rat Kiley had lost his best friend in the world. Later in the week he would write a long personal letter to the guy's sister, who would not write back, but for now it was a question of pain. He shot off the tail. He shot away chunks of meat below the ribs. All around us there was the smell of smoke and filth and deep greenery, and the evening was humid and very hot. Rat went to automatic. He shot randomly, almost casually, quick little spurts in the belly and butt. Then he reloaded, squatted down, and shot it in the left front knee. Again the animal fell hard and tried to get up, but this time it couldn't quite make it. It wobbled and went down sideways. Rat shot it in the nose. He bent forward and whispered something, as if talking to a pet, then he shot it in the throat. All the while the baby buffalo was silent, or almost silent, just a light bubbling sound where the nose had been. It lay very still. Nothing moved except the eyes, which were enormous, the pupils shiny black and dumb.

Rat Kiley was crying. He tried to say something, but then cradled his rifle and went off by himself.

The rest of us stood in a ragged circle around the baby [75] buffalo. For a time no one spoke. We had witnessed some-

thing essential, something brand-new and profound, a piece of the world so startling there was not yet a name for it.

Somebody kicked the baby buffalo.

It was still alive, though just barely, just in the eyes.

"Amazing," Dave Jensen said. "My whole life, I never seen anything like it."

"Never?"

"Not hardly. Not once." [80]

Kiowa and Mitchell Sanders picked up the baby buffalo. They hauled it across the open square, hoisted it up, and dumped it in the village well.

Afterward, we sat waiting for Rat to get himself together.

"Amazing," Dave Jensen kept saying. "A new wrinkle. I never seen it before."

Mitchell Sanders took out his yo-yo. "Well that's Nam," he said. "Garden of Evil. Over here, man, every sin's real fresh and original."

How do you generalize? [85]

War is hell, but that's not the half of it, because war is also mystery and terror and adventure and courage and discovery and holiness and pity and despair and longing and love. War is nasty; war is fun. War is thrilling; war is drudgery. War makes you a man; war makes you dead.

The truths are contradictory. It can be argued, for instance, that war is grotesque. But in truth war is also beauty. For all its horror, you can't help but gape at the awful majesty of combat. You stare out at tracer rounds unwinding through the dark like brilliant red ribbons. You crouch in ambush as a cool, impassive moon rises over the nighttime paddies. You admire the fluid symmetries of troops on the move, the harmonies of sound and shape and proportion, the great sheets of metal-fire streaming down from a gunship, the illumination rounds, the white phosphorus, the purply orange glow of napalm, the rocket's red glare. It's not pretty, exactly. It's astonishing. It fills the eye. It commands you. You hate it, yes, but your eyes do not. Like a killer forest fire, like cancer under a microscope, any battle or bombing raid or artillery barrage has the aesthetic purity of absolute moral indifference—a powerful, implacable beauty—and a true war story will tell truth about this, though the truth is ugly.

To generalize about war is like generalizing about peace. Almost everything is true. Almost nothing is true. At its core, perhaps, war is just another name for death, and yet any soldier will tell you, if he tells the truth, that proximity to death brings with it a corresponding proximity to life. After a firefight, there is always the immense pleasure of aliveness. The trees are alive. The grass, the soil—everything. All around you things are purely living, and you among them, and the aliveness makes you tremble. You feel an intense, out-of-the-skin awareness of your living self—your truest self, the human being you want to be and then become by the force of wanting it. In the midst of evil you want to be a good man. You want decency. You want justice and courtesy and human concord, things you never knew you wanted. There is a kind of largeness to it, a kind of godliness. Though it's odd, you're never more alive than when you're almost dead. You recognize what's valuable.

Freshly, as if for the first time, you love what's best in yourself and in the world, all that might be lost. At the hour of dusk you sit at your foxhole and look out on a wide river turning pinkish red, and at the mountains beyond, and although in the morning you must cross the river and go into the mountains and do terrible things and maybe die, even so, you find yourself studying the fine colors on the river, you feel wonder and awe at the setting of the sun, and you are filled with a hard, aching love for how the world could be and always should be, but now is not.

Mitchell Sanders was right. For the common soldier, at least, war has the feel—the spiritual texture—of a great ghostly fog, thick and permanent. There is no clarity. Everything swirls. The old rules are no longer binding, the old truths no longer true. Right spills over into wrong. Order blends into chaos, love into hate, ugliness into beauty, law into anarchy, civility into savagery. The vapors suck you in. You can't tell where you are, or why you're there, and the only certainty is overwhelming ambiguity.

In war you lose your sense of the definite, hence your sense of truth itself, and therefore it's safe to say that in a true war story nothing is ever absolutely true. [90]

Often in a true war story there is not even a point, or else the point doesn't hit you until twenty years later, in your sleep, and you wake up and shake your wife and start telling the story to her, except when you get to the end you've forgotten the point again. And then for a long time you lie there watching the story happen in your head. You listen to your wife's breathing. The war's over. You close your eyes. You smile and think, Christ, what's the *point?*

This one wakes me up.

In the mountains that day, I watched Lemon turn sideways. He laughed and said something to Rat Kiley. Then he took a peculiar half step, moving from shade into bright sunlight, and the booby-trapped 105 round blew him into a tree. (The parts were just hanging there, so Dave Jensen and I were ordered to shinny up and peel him off. I remember the white bone of an arm. I remember pieces of skin and something wet and yellow that must've been the intestines. The gore was horrible, and stays with me. But what wakes me up twenty years later is Dave Jensen singing "Lemon Tree" as we threw down the parts.)

You can tell a true war story by questions you ask. Somebody tells a story, let's say, and afterward you ask, "Is it true?" and if the answer matters, you've got your answer.

For example, we've all heard this one. Four guys go [95] down a trail. A grenade sails out. One guy jumps on it and takes the blast and saves his three buddies.

Is it true?

The answer matters.

You'd feel cheated if it never happened. Without the grounding reality, it's just a trite bit of puffery, pure Hollywood, untrue in the way all such stories are untrue. Yet even if it did happen—and maybe it did, anything's possible—even then you know it can't be true, because a true war story does not depend upon that kind of truth. Absolute occurrence is irrelevant. A thing may happen and be a total lie; another thing may not happen and be truer than the truth. For example: Four guys go down a trail. A grenade sails out. One guy jumps on it and takes the blast, but it's a killer grenade and everybody dies anyway. Before they die, though, one of the dead guys says, "The fuck you do *that* for?" and the jumper says, "Story of my life, man," and the other guy starts to smile but he's dead.

That's a true story that never happened.

Twenty years later, I can still see the sunlight on Lemon's [100] face. I can see him turning, looking back at Rat Kiley, then he laughed and took that curious half step from shade into sunlight, his face suddenly brown and shining, and when his foot touched down, in that instant, he must've thought it was the sunlight that was killing him. It was not the sunlight. It was a rigged 105 round. But if I could ever get the story right, how the sun seemed to gather around him and pick him up and lift him high into a tree, if I could somehow recreate the fatal whiteness of that light, the quick glare, the obvious cause and effect, then you would believe the last thing Curt Lemon believed, which for him must've been the final truth.

Now and then, when I tell this story, someone will come up to me afterward and say she liked it. It's always a woman. Usually it's an older woman of kindly temperament and humane politics. She'll explain that as a rule she hates war stories; she can't understand why people want to wallow in all the blood and gore. But this one she liked. The poor baby buffalo, it made her sad. Sometimes, even, there are little tears. What I should do, she'll say, is put it all behind me. Find new stories to tell.

I won't say it but I'll think it.

I'll picture Rat Kiley's face, his grief, and I'll think, *You dumb cooze.*

Because she wasn't listening.

It *wasn't* a war story. It was a *love* story. [105]

But you can't say that. All you can do is tell it one more time, patiently, adding and subtracting, making up a few things to get at the real truth. No Mitchell Sanders, you tell her. No Lemon, no Rat Kiley. No trail junction. No baby buffalo. No vines or moss or white blossoms. Beginning to end, you tell her, it's all made up. Every goddamn detail—the mountains and the river and especially that poor dumb baby buffalo. None of it happened. *None* of it. And even if it did happen, it didn't happen in the mountains, it happened in this little village on the Batangan Peninsula, and it was raining like crazy, and one night a guy named Stink Harris woke up screaming with a leech on his tongue. You can tell a true war story if you just keep on telling it.

And in the end, of course, a true war story is never about war. It's about sunlight. It's about the special way that dawn spreads out on a river when you know you must cross the river and march into the mountains and do things you are afraid to do. It's about love and memory. It's about sorrow. It's about sisters who never write back and people who never listen.

—m—

FRANCIS FUKUYAMA

Selection from *The End of History and the Last Man*

The American-born, Harvard-trained Francis Fukuyama (b. 1952) is currently riding the crest of the zeitgeist with *The End of History and the Last Man*. The basic thesis of "the End of History" first saw daylight as a sixteen-page article in a foreign policy journal (*The National Interest*, summer 1989), just as communism was on the way out and he was a consultant to the U.S. State Department. Notoriety for Fukuyama followed as the article engendered much debate around the world. Inevitably, with encouragement from an interested publisher, he revised and expanded his brief work into a four-hundred-page book. Published in 1992, the book reached a huge audience (as a *New York Times* best-seller), sparked new controversy that has not yet subsided, and won literary prizes. It has now been translated into more than a dozen languages.

The first major work of political theory to emerge in the post-communist era, *The End of History and the Last Man* captures the ambivalent spirit of Post-Modernism. The first half of Fukuyama's thesis is optimistic. Taking an analytic overview of today's global politics, he argues that history moves in a positive direction and that it has evolved to its logical end—liberal democracy. This conclusion, based in part on Hegel's philosophy of history (see *Reason in History*), centers on the belief that one form of government will ultimately triumph over the rest. To Fukuyama, the reunification of Germany and the failure of Marxism are testaments to the victory of liberal democracy.

The second half of Fukuyama's thesis is somewhat pessimistic, though not completely so. Projecting a future freed from the clash of political ideologies, he predicts that people will focus on solving technological problems, but that it will be "a very sad time" because there will be the danger of turning into "last men"—a term taken from Nietzsche (see *Thus Spake Zarathustra*) and which Fukuyama equates with mindless consumers and "couch potatoes." Fukuyama leaves the door slightly open to hope as he concludes with this question: With liberal democracy's triumph around the world, and the cessation of warfare among nations, can there be meaningful lives that touch the deepest aspirations of the human spirit?

Reading the Selection

In the selection, taken from Section XXXI, the concluding part of *The End of History and the Last Man*, Fukuyama foresees trouble for liberal democracies because of individuals driven by *megalothymia*, a concept derived from Plato (see *The Republic*) but given a twist by Nietzsche. Fukuyama reasons that all human beings want to be recognized and given respect, or *thymos*—a term of Plato's. But a few individuals are greedy for glory; that is, they possess *thymos* in "an extreme and pathological form," or *megalothymia*—that's Nietzsche's "superman." According to Fukuyama, *megalothymic* people constitute constant dangers because it is questionable whether or not their insatiable appetites for glory can be satisfied by the blandness of consumerist societies.

—m—

Section XXXI
Immense Wars of the Spirit

The decline of community life suggests that in the future, we risk becoming secure and self-absorbed last men, devoid of thymotic striving for higher goals in our pursuit of private comforts. But the opposite danger exists as well, namely, that we will return to being first men engaged in bloody and pointless prestige battles, only this time with modern weapons. Indeed, the two problems are related to one another, for the absence of regular and constructive outlets for *megalothymia* may simply lead to its later resurgence in an extreme and pathological form.

It is reasonable to wonder whether all people will believe that the kinds of struggles and sacrifices possible in a self-satisfied and prosperous liberal democracy are sufficient to call forth what is highest in man. For are there not reservoirs of idealism that cannot be exhausted—indeed, that are not even touched—if one becomes a developer like Donald Trump, or a mountain climber like Reinhold Messner, or politician like George Bush? Difficult as it is, in many ways, to be these individuals, and for all the recognition they receive, their lives are not the most difficult, and the causes they serve are not the most serious or the most just. And as long as they are not, the horizon of human possibilities that they define will not be ultimately satisfying for the most thymotic natures.

In particular, the virtues and ambitions called forth by war are unlikely to find expression in liberal democracies. There will be plenty of metaphorical wars—corporate lawyers specializing in hostile takeovers who will think of themselves as sharks or gunslingers, and bond traders who imagine, as in Tom Wolfe's novel *The Bonfire of the Vanities*, that they are "masters of the universe." (They will believe this, however, only in bull markets.) But as they sink into the soft leather of their BMWs, they will know somewhere in the back of their minds that there have been real gunslingers and masters in the world, who would feel contempt for the petty virtues required to become rich or famous in modern America. How long *megalothymia* will be satisfied with metaphorical wars and symbolic victories is an open question. One suspects that some people will not be satisfied until they prove themselves by that very act that constituted their humanness at the beginning of history: they will want to risk their lives in a violent battle, and thereby prove beyond any shadow of a doubt to themselves and to their fellows that they are free. They will deliberately seek discomfort and sacrifice, because the pain will be the only way they have of proving definitively that they can *think well of themselves*, that they remain *human beings*.

Hegel . . . understood that the need to feel pride in one's humanness would not necessarily be satisfied by the "peace and prosperity" of the end of history. Men would face the constant danger of degenerating from citizens to mere *bourgeois*, and feeling contempt for themselves in the process. The ultimate crucible of citizenship therefore was and would remain the willingness to die for one's country: the state would have to require military service and continue to fight wars.

This aspect of Hegel's thought has led to the charge that he was a militarist. But he never glorified war for its own sake, or saw it as the chief end of man; war was important for its secondary effects on character and community. Hegel believed that without the possibility of war and the sacrifices demanded by it, men would grow soft and self-absorbed; society would degenerate into a morass of selfish hedonism and community would ultimately dissolve. Fear of man's "lord and master, Death" was a force like no other, capable of drawing men outside of themselves and reminding them that they were not isolated atoms, but members of communities built around shared ideals. A liberal democracy that could fight a short and decisive war every generation or so to defend its own liberty and independence would be far healthier and more satisfied than one that experienced nothing but continuous peace.

Hegel's view of war reflects a common experience of combat: for while men suffer horribly and are seldom as frightened and miserable, their experience if they survive has the tendency of putting all other things in a certain perspective. What is commonly called heroism and sacrifice in civilian life seems positively petty, friendship and valor take on new and more vivid meanings, and their lives are henceforth transformed by the memory of having participated in something much greater than themselves. As one writer noted of the end of the American Civil War—surely one of the bloodiest and most terrible conflicts of modern times—"One of Sherman's veterans, going home with all the rest, found that when the armies did melt back into the heart of the people the adjustment was a little difficult. The men had been everywhere and had seen everything, life's greatest experience had ended with most of life still to be lived, to find common purpose in the quiet days of peace would be hard . . ."

But supposing that the world has become "filled up," so to speak, with liberal democracies, such that there exist no tyranny and oppression worthy of the name against which to struggle? Experience suggests that if men cannot struggle on behalf of a just cause because that just cause was victorious in an earlier generation, then they will struggle *against* the just cause. They will struggle for the sake of struggle. They will struggle, in other words, out of a certain boredom: for they cannot imagine living in a world without struggle. And if the greater part of the world in which they live is characterized by peaceful and prosperous liberal democracy, then they will struggle *against* that peace and prosperity, and against democracy.

. . .

Modern thought raises no barriers to a future nihilistic war against liberal democracy on the part of those brought up in its bosom. Relativism—the doctrine that maintains that all values are merely relative and which attacks all "privileged perspectives"—must ultimately end up undermining democratic and tolerant values as well. Relativism is not a weapon that can be aimed selectively at the enemies one chooses. It fires indiscriminately, shooting out the legs of not only the "absolutisms," dogmas, and certainties of the Western tradition, but that tradition's emphasis on tolerance, diversity, and freedom of thought as well. If nothing can be true absolutely, if all values are culturally determined, then cherished principles like human equality have to go by the wayside as well.

There is no better example of this than the thought of Nietzsche himself. Nietzsche believed that man's awareness that nothing was true was both a threat and an opportunity. It was a threat because, as noted earlier, it undermined the possibility of life "within a horizon." But it was also an opportunity, because it permitted total human freedom from prior moral constraints. The ultimate form of human creativity for Nietzsche was not art but the creation of what was highest, new values. His project, once he liberated himself from the shackles of earlier philosophy that believed in the possibility of absolute truth or right, was to "revalue all values," beginning with those of Christianity. He deliberately sought to undermine belief in human equality, arguing that this was simply a prejudice instilled in us by Christianity. Nietzsche hoped that the principle of equality would give way one day to a morality justifying the domination of the weak by the strong, and ended up celebrating what amounted to a doctrine of cruelty. He hated societies that were diverse and tolerant, preferring instead those that were intolerant, instinctive, and without remorse—the Indian *Chandala* caste that tried to breed distinct races of men, or the "blond beasts of prey" which "unhesitatingly lay (their) terrible claws upon a populace." Nietzsche's relationship to German fascism has been debated at great length, and while he can be defended from the narrow charges of being the forefather of National Socialism's simpleminded doctrines, the relationship between his thought and nazism is not accidental. Just as in the case of his follower, Martin Heidegger, Nietzsche's relativism shot out all of the philosophical props holding up Western liberal democracy, and replaced it with a doctrine of strength and domination. Nietzsche believed the era of European nihilism, which he was helping to inaugurate, would lead to "immense wars" of the spirit, objectless wars whose only purpose was to affirm war itself.

The modern liberal project attempted to shift the basis of human societies from *thymos* to the more secure ground of desire. Liberal democracy "solved" the problem of *megalothymia* by constraining and sublimating it through a complex series of institutional arrangements—the principle of popular sovereignty, the establishment of rights, the rule of law, separation of powers, and the like. Liberalism also made possible the modern economic world by liberating desire from all constraints on acquisitiveness, and allying it to reason in the form of modern natural science. A new, dynamic, and infinitely rich field of endeavor was suddenly opened up to man. According to the Anglo-Saxon theorists of liberalism, idle masters were to be persuaded to give up their vainglory, and to make their home in this economic world instead. *Thymos* was to be subordinated to desire and reason, that is, desire guided by reason.

Hegel too understood that the fundamental transition that had occurred in modern life was the domestication of the master, and his metamorphosis into economic man. But he realized that this did not mean the abolition of *thymos* so much as its transformation into a new and, he believed, higher form. The *megalothymia* of the few would have to give way to the *isothymia* of the many. Men would not cease to have chests, but their chests would no longer inflate with such overbearing pride. Those whom the old, pre-democratic world failed to satisfy were the vast majority of mankind; those left unsatisfied in the modern world of universal recognition are many fewer in number. Hence the remarkable stability and strength of democracy in the contemporary world.

Nietzsche's life work can be seen, in a sense, as an effort to shift the balance back radically in the direction of *megalothymia*. The anger of Plato's guardians no longer had to be constrained by any concept of the common good. There was no common good: all efforts to define such a good simply reflected the strength of those doing the defining. Certainly a common good that protected the self-satisfaction of the last man was impoverished. There were no longer well- or badly-trained guardians, only ones who were more or less angry. They would henceforth be distinguished from one another primarily by the strength of their anger—that is, by their ability to impose

their "values" on others. Rather than being one of three parts, as it had been for Plato, *thymos* became the whole of man for Nietzsche.

Looking backward, we who live in the old age of mankind might come to the following conclusion. No regime—no "socioeconomic system"—is able to satisfy all men in all places. This includes liberal democracy. This is not a matter of the incompleteness of the democratic revolution, that is, because the blessings of liberty and equality have not been extended to all people. Rather, the dissatisfaction arises precisely where democracy has triumphed most completely: it is a dissatisfaction *with* liberty and equality. Thus those who remain dissatisfied will always have the potential to restart history.

Moreover, it appears to be the case that rational recognition is not self-sustaining, but must rely on pre-modern, non-universal forms of recognition to function properly. Stable democracy requires a sometimes irrational democratic culture, and a spontaneous civil society growing out of pre-liberal traditions. Capitalist prosperity is best promoted by a strong work ethic, which in turn depends on the ghosts of dead religious beliefs, if not those beliefs themselves, or else an irrational commitment to nation or race. Group rather than universal recognition can be a better support for both economic activity and community life, and even if it is ultimately irrational, that irrationality can take a very long time before it undermines the societies that practice it. Thus, not only is universal recognition not universally satisfying, but the ability of liberal democratic societies to establish and sustain themselves on a rational basis over the long term is open to some doubt.

Aristotle believed that history would be cyclical rather than secular because all regimes were imperfect in some way, and those imperfections would constantly lead people to want to change the regime they lived under into something different. For all of the reasons just enumerated, could we not say the same of modern democracy? Following Aristotle, we might postulate that a society of last men composed entirely of desire and reason would give way to one of bestial first men seeking recognition alone, and vice versa, in an unending oscillation.

And yet, the two legs of this dyad are hardly equal. The Nietzschean alternative forces us to break completely with the desiring part of the soul. This century has taught us the horrendous consequences of the effort to resurrect unbridled *megalothymia*, for in it we have, in a sense, already experienced some of the "immense wars" foretold by Nietzsche. Those pro-war crowds in August 1914 got the sacrifice and danger that they wanted, and much more besides. The subsequent course of the Great War demonstrated that whatever war's beneficial secondary effects in terms of building character or community, they were completely overwhelmed by the destructiveness of its primary consequences. By the twentieth century, the risk of life in a bloody battle had become thoroughly democratized. Rather than the mark of exceptional character, it became an experience forced on masses of men, and ultimately women and children as well. It led not to the satisfaction of recognition, but to anonymous and objectless death. Far from reinforcing virtue or creativity, contemporary war undermined popular faith in the meaning of concepts like courage and heroism, and fostered a deep sense of alienation and *anomie* among those who experienced it. If men of the future become bored with peace and prosperity, and seek new thymotic struggles and challenges, the consequences threaten to be even more horrendous. For now we have nuclear and other weapons of mass destruction, which will allow millions to be killed instantly and anonymously.

Standing as a bulwark against the revival of history and the return of the first man is the imposing Mechanism of modern natural science that we described in Part Two of this book, the Mechanism driven by unlimited desire and guided by reason. A revival of *megalothymia* in the modern world would mean a break with this powerful and dynamic economic world, and an attempt to rupture the logic of technological development. Such ruptures have proved possible at particular times and places—as when a country like Germany or Japan immolated itself for the sake of national recognition—but it is questionable whether the world as a whole can make such a rupture for any extended length of time. Germany and Japan were driven by the desire for recognition of their superiority during the wars of the first half of the twentieth century, but they also believed that they were securing their economic future as well by conquering for themselves neomercantilist *Lebensraum* or a "co-prosperity sphere." Subsequent experience demonstrated to both countries that economic security was much more easily obtained through liberal free trade than through war, and that the path of military conquest was utterly destructive of economic values.

Looking around contemporary America, it does not strike me that we face the problem of an excess of *megalothymia*. Those earnest young people trooping off to law and business school, who anxiously fill out their résumés in hopes of maintaining the lifestyles to which they believe themselves entitled, seem to be much more in danger of becoming last men, rather than reviving the passions of the first man. For them, the liberal project of filling one's life with material acquisitions and safe, sanctioned ambitions appears to have worked all too well. It is hard to detect great, unfulfilled longings or irrational passions lurking just beneath the surface of the average first-year law associate.

The same is true in other parts of the post-historical world. During the 1980s, the leaders of most West European countries did not display yearnings for great struggle or sacrifice when confronted with issues like the Cold War, abolition of hunger in the Third World, or military action against terrorism. There were fanatics among the young who joined the German Red Army faction or the Red Brigades in Italy, but they represented a small lunatic fringe kept alive with Soviet bloc aid. After the great events of the fall of 1989 in Eastern Europe, a significant number of Germans had doubts about the wisdom of unification *because it would cost too much*. These are not the hallmarks of a civilization wound tight like a spring, ready to immolate itself on the pyre of new and unforeseen fanaticisms, but rather of one quite satisfied with what it is and will be.

·   ·   ·

It is possible that if events continue to unfold as they have done over the past few decades, that the idea of a universal and directional history leading up to liberal democracy may become more plausible to people, and that the relativist impasse of modern thought will in a sense solve itself. That is, cultural relativism (a European invention) has seemed plausible to our century because for the first time Europe found itself forced to confront non-European cultures in a serious way through the experience of colonialism and de-colonization. Many of the developments of the past century—the decline of the moral self-confidence of European civilization, the rise of the Third World, and the emergence of new ideologies—tended to reinforce belief in relativism. But if, over time, more and more societies with diverse cultures and histories exhibit similar long-term patterns of development; if there is a continuing convergence in the types of institutions governing most advanced societies; and if the homogenization of mankind continues as a result of economic development, then the idea of relativism may seem much stranger than it does now. For the apparent differences between peoples' "languages of good and evil" will appear to be an artifact of their particular stage of historical development.

Rather than a thousand shoots blossoming into as many different flowering plants, mankind will come to seem like a long wagon train strung out along a road. Some wagons will be pulling into town sharply and crisply, while others will be bivouacked back in the desert, or else stuck in ruts in the final pass over the mountains. Several wagons, attacked by Indians, will have been set aflame and abandoned along the way. There will be a few wagoneers who, stunned by the battle, will have lost their sense of direction and are temporarily heading in the wrong direction, while one or two wagons will get tired of the journey and decide to set up permanent camps at particular points back along the road. Others will have found alternative routes to the main road, though they will discover that to get through the final mountain range they all must use the same pass. But the great majority of wagons will be making the slow journey into town, and most will eventually arrive there. The wagons are all similar to one another: while they are painted different colors and are constructed of varied materials, each has four wheels and is drawn by horses, while inside sits a family hoping and praying that their journey will be a safe one. The apparent differences in the situations of the wagons will not be seen as reflecting permanent and necessary differences between the people riding in the wagons, but simply a product of their different positions along the road.

·   ·   ·

It is doubtful that we are at that point now, for despite the recent worldwide liberal revolution, the evidence available to us now concerning the direction of the wagons' wanderings must remain provisionally inconclusive. Nor can we in the final analysis know, provided a majority of the wagons eventually reach the same town, whether their occupants, having looked around a bit at their new surroundings, will not find them inadequate and set their eyes on a new and more distant journey.

CREDITS

INDEX